The Blackwell Companion to Catholicism

Blackwell Companions to Religion

The Blackwell Companions to Religion series presents a collection of the most recent scholarship and knowledge about world religions. Each volume draws together newly-commissioned essays by distinguished authors in the field, and is presented in a style which is accessible to under-graduate students, as well as scholars and the interested general reader. These volumes approach the subject in a creative and forward-thinking style, providing a forum in which leading scholars in the field can make their views and research available to a wider audience.

Published

The Blackwell Companion to Judaism
Edited by Jacob Neusner and Alan J. Avery-Peck

The Blackwell Companion to Sociology of Religion
Edited by Richard K. Fenn

The Blackwell Companion to the Hebrew Bible
Edited by Leo G. Perdue

The Blackwell Companion to Postmodern Theology
Edited by Graham Ward

The Blackwell Companion to Hinduism
Edited by Gavin Flood

The Blackwell Companion to Political Theology
Edited by Peter Scott and William T. Cavanaugh

The Blackwell Companion to Protestantism
Edited by Alister E. McGrath and Darren C. Marks

The Blackwell Companion to Modern Theology
Edited by Gareth Jones

The Blackwell Companion to Christian Ethics
Edited by Stanley Hauerwas and Samuel Wells

The Blackwell Companion to Religious Ethics
Edited by William Schweiker

The Blackwell Companion to Christian Spirituality
Edited by Arthur Holder

The Blackwell Companion to the Study of Religion
Edited by Robert A. Segal

The Blackwell Companion to the Qur'ān
Edited by Andrew Rippin

The Blackwell Companion to Contemporary Islamic Thought
Edited by Ibrahim M. Abu-Rabi'

The Blackwell Companion to the Bible and Culture
Edited by John F.A. Sawyer

The Blackwell Companion to Catholicism
Edited by James J. Buckley, Frederick Christian Bauerschmidt, and Trent Pomplun

Forthcoming

The Blackwell Companion to the New Testament
Edited by David Aune

The Blackwell Companion to Eastern Christianity
Edited by Ken Parry

The Blackwell Companion to Catholicism

Edited by James J. Buckley,
Frederick Christian Bauerschmidt,
and Trent Pomplun

Blackwell
Publishing

BLACKWELL PUBLISHING
350 Main Street, Malden, MA 02148–5020, USA
9600 Garsington Road, Oxford OX4 2DQ, UK
550 Swanston Street, Carlton, Victoria 3053, Australia

First published 2007 by Blackwell Publishing Ltd

1   2007

Library of Congress Cataloging-in-Publication Data

The Blackwell Companion to Catholicism / edited by James J. Buckley, Frederick Christian
Bauerschmidt, and Trent Pomplun
       p.   cm.—(Blackwell companions to religion)
     Includes bibliographical references and index.
     ISBN-13: 978-1-4051-1224-6 (hardcover : alk. paper)
     ISBN-10: 1-4051-1224-7 (hardcover : alk. paper) 1. Catholic church. I. Buckley, James
Joseph, 1947– II. Bauerschmidt, Frederick Christian. III. Pomplun, Trent.

BX880.B53 2007
282—dc22

2006019316

A catalogue record for this title is available from the British Library.

Set in 10 on 12.5 pt Photina
by The Running Head Limited, Cambridge, www.therunninghead.com
Printed and bound in Singapore
by C.O.S. Printers Pte Ltd

For further information on
Blackwell Publishing, visit our website:
www.blackwellpublishing.com

Contents

Notes on Contributors

Fr Robert Barron is Professor of Systematic Theology at the University of St Mary of the Lake/Mundelein Seminary outside of Chicago. He received his masters degree in philosophy from the Catholic University of America in Washington, DC, in 1982 and was ordained to the priesthood for the Archdiocese of Chicago in 1986. He received his doctorate from the Institut Catholique de Paris. His recent books include *The Strangest Way: Walking the Christian Path* (Orbis Books, 2002) and *Bridging the Great Divide: Musings of a Post-Liberal, Post-Conservative, Evangelical Catholic* (Sheed and Ward, 2004). His numerous articles on theology and spirituality have appeared in a variety of journals. He also gives frequent retreats, missions, and workshops on various aspects of the spiritual life.

Frederick Christian Bauerschmidt (PhD Duke University) is Associate Professor of Theology at Loyola College in Maryland. He is the author of *Julian of Norwich and the Mystical Body Politic of Christ*, *Why the Mystics Matter Now*, and *Holy Teaching: Introducing the Summa Theologiae of St Thomas Aquinas*, as well as essays in a variety of scholarly journals. He was co-editor of *Modern Theology*, 2001–6. fbauerschmidt@loyala.edu

Fr Charles J. Borges sj has his doctorate in history from the University of Bombay, India. He has served as the director of the Xavier Centre of Historical Research in Goa and currently teaches European and Indian history, religions, and film at Loyola College in Maryland. He is an editor of *Indo-Portuguese History: Global Trends* (2005). He can be reached at cborges@loyola.edu or 4603 Millbrook Rd/Baltimore, MD 21212.

James J. Buckley is Professor of Theology and Dean of the College of Arts and Sciences at Loyola College in Maryland. He has written *Seeking the Humanity of God: Practices, Doctrines, and Catholic Theology* (Liturgical Press, 1992) and for various theological journals. He is an associate editor for *Modern Theology*, and associate director of the Center for Catholic and Evangelical Theology. He is married to Christine Krajenta Buckley, and their son David would have many interesting opinions about this volume. Jbuckley@loyola.edu

David B. Burrell CSC is currently Theodore Hesburgh Professor in Philosophy and Theology at the University of Notre Dame, and has been working since 1982 in comparative issues in philosophical theology in Judaism, Christianity, and Islam, most recently *Al-Ghazali on Faith in Divine Unity and Trust in Divine Providence* [Book 35 of his *Ihya Ulum ad-Din*] (Louisville: Fons Vitae, 2001). With Elena Malits he co-authored *Original Peace* (New York: Paulist, 1998). He is currently completing a translation of the portion of existence from Mulla Sadra's [Sadr al-Din al-Shirazi] *Asfar al-Arbain*, as well as a theological commentary on the book of Job (Brazos Press series).

Peter J. Casarella received his PhD in religious studies from Yale University. He taught theology for two years at The University of Dallas before moving in 1993 to the Catholic University of America. His most recent edited volume is: *Cusanus: The Legacy of Learned Ignorance* (The Catholic University of America Press, 2006). He lives with his wife Maria and their three daughters. He can be contacted at casarelp@cua.edu or School of Theology and Religious Studies, The Catholic University of America, Washington, DC, 20064.

Angela Russell Christman received her doctorate from the University of Virginia and is currently a member of the Theology Department at Loyola College in Maryland. She is the author of *"What Did Ezekiel See?" Christian Exegesis of Ezekiel's Vision of the Chariot from Irenaeus to Gregory the Great* and a contributor to the Isaiah volume of *The Church's Bible*. She is married and lives with her husband and two daughters in Catonsville, MD. She can be contacted at achristman@loyola.edu

John A. Coleman SJ is the Casassa Professor of Social Values at Loyola Marymount University, Los Angeles. He holds a PhD in sociology from the University of California, Berkeley, and did postgraduate work in theological ethics at the University of Chicago. Among Coleman's 18 edited or written books, his most recent is John A. Coleman and William Ryan (eds.) *Globalization and Catholic Social Thought: Present Crisis, Future Hope* (Orbis Press, 2005).

Gavin D'Costa is Head of Theology and Religious Studies at the University of Bristol. He advises the Roman Catholic Church in England and Wales and Vatican City on inter-religious dialog. Recent books include *Sexing the Trinity* (2000), *The Meeting of Religions and the Trinity* (2000), and *Theology in the Public Square* (Blackwell, 2005). He is currently researching theological social issues raised by religious pluralism in liberal democracies. Department of Theology and Religious Studies/University of Bristol. 3 Woodland Road/Bristol BS8 1TB Email: gavin.dcosta@bristol.ac.uk

Joseph Augustine DiNoia OP has his doctorate from Yale University. He taught for 20 years at the Dominican House of Studies, Washington, DC, and currently serves the undersecretary of the Congregation for the Doctrine of the Faith. He is the author of *The Diversity of Religions* (Catholic University of America Press), and has published in *The Thomist*, *Religious Studies*, *Modern Theology*, *The Journal of Religion*, *Nova et Vetera* and in other journals. He lives in Vatican City and can be contacted at the Palazzo del S. Uffizio, 00120 Vatican City State, and by email at jadop@myrealbox.com

Avery Cardinal Dulles SJ, who was made a cardinal by Pope John Paul II in 2001, is McGinley Professor of Theology at Fordham University. He has authored numerous articles and books, including *Models of the Church, The Craft of Theology* (1995), *The Priestly Office* (1997), *The Assurance of Things Hoped For* (1997), *The Splendor of Faith. The Theological Vision of Pope John Paul II* (2003), and *Newman* (2005). dullessj@fordham.edu

Carlos M.N. Eire is the Riggs Professor of History and Religious Studies at Yale University. Before joining the Yale faculty in 1996, he taught at St John's University and the University of Virginia, and resided for two years at the Institute for Advanced Study in Princeton. He is the author of *War Against the Idols* (Cambridge, 1986), *From Madrid to Purgatory* (Cambridge, 1995), and co-author of *Jews, Christians, Muslims* (Prentice Hall, 1997). His memoir of the Cuban Revolution, *Waiting for Snow in Havana* (Free Press, 2003), won the National Book Award in nonfiction for 2003.

Michael Heller is Professor at the Faculty of Philosophy of the Pontifical Academy of Theology, Krakow, Poland, and an adjoined member of the Vatican Observatory. Specializing in general relativity and cosmology, he has published over 300 articles and 30 books on science, philosophy, and religion.

Kelly Johnson holds a doctorate from Duke University and currently teaches theological ethics at the University of Dayton. Her book, *The Fear of Beggars: Stewardship and Poverty in Christian Ethics*, will be published by Eerdmans in 2007.

Luke Timothy Johnson received his PhD from Yale University, and has taught at Yale Divinity School and Indiana University. He is presently the Robert W. Woodruff Distinguished Professor of New Testament and Christian Origins at the Candler School of Theology, Emory University. He has written over 25 books and over 300 articles and reviews, and has contributed frequently to the Catholic journals, *Commonweal* and *Priests and People*. Formerly a Benedictine monk and priest, he is now a lay member of Sacred Heart Parish in Atlanta, Georgia.

Emmanuel Katongole holds degrees from Makerere University, the Pontifical University in Rome and the Catholic University in Louvain, Belgium. He is Associate Research Professor of Theology and World Christianity at Duke Divinity School and the co-director of the Center of Reconciliation at the Divinity School. His published works include: *Beyond Universal Reason, African Theology Today* (2002), and more recently, *A Future for Africa* (2005). A priest in the Roman Catholic Church, Fr Katongole has served parishes in Uganda, Belgium, New York, Pennsylvania, Indiana, and currently in Cary, North Carolina. He can be contacted at ekatongole@div.duke.edu

Fergus Kerr OP entered the Order of Preachers in 1956. His books include *Theology after Wittgenstein* (1986, 2nd edition 1997), *Immortal Longings: Versions of Transcending Humanity* (1997), and *After Aquinas: Versions of Thomism* (2002). He is a past president of the Catholic Theological Association and an elected fellow of the Royal Society of Edinburgh.

David Matzko McCarthy (PhD Duke University) teaches at Mount St Mary's University where is the Fr James M. Forker Professor of Catholic Social Teaching. He has written *Sex and Love in the Home: A Theology of the Household* (SCM Press 2004) and *The Good Life* (Brazos 2004), and is the co-editor of *Gathered for the Journey: Moral Theology in Catholic Perspective* (SCM Press/Eerdmans 2007). He lives in Maryland with his wife and five children.

Claire Mathews McGinnis is Associate Professor of Theology at Loyola College in Maryland and director of the College's Center for the Humanities. She received her PhD in Hebrew Bible/Old Testament from Yale University's Department of Religious Studies. She is the author of *Defending Zion* (BZAW, Walter DeGruyter) and co-editor of *As Those Who Are Taught: The Interpretation of Isaiah from the LXX to the SBL* (SBL Symposium Series, Scholars Press). She has published a handful of essays in edited collections, and is currently writing a book on the theological interpretation of Exodus. She lives in Baltimore with her husband, Colin P. McGinnis, and their two children, Killian and Patrick. She may be reached at the Department of Theology, Loyola College, 4501 N. Charles Street, Baltimore, MD, 21210, or by email at CMathews@loyola.edu (note the one 't').

Angel F. Méndez Montoya OP is a native of Mexico. He is a Dominican Friar in the Southern Province (US). He holds an MA in theology and an MDiv. He is currently a PhD candidate in philosophical theology at the University of Virginia, writing a thesis entitled "Food Matters; Prolegomena to Eucharistic Discourse," whose main goal is an analysis of the dilemma of talking about God in contemporary discourse. It suggests using food/alimentation as the analog par excellence to describe God's suberabundant generosity and to challenge theology to recover the discourse of charity. He has been a scholar-in-residence at Cambridge University and currently teaches philosophy and theology at Blackfriars, Oxford.

Sandra Yocum Mize has her doctorate from Marquette University. She has taught at Loyola College of Maryland and Saint Mary's College, South Bend, Indiana, and currently teaches historical theology at the University of Dayton. She edited with William Portier, *American Catholic Traditions: Resources for Renewal*. College Theology Society, Annual Volume No. 42 and has published in *Theological Studies*, *Horizons*, *Church History*, and *U.S. Catholic Historian*. She is married and lives with her husband, Bryan J. Mize. They have two sons, Matthew and Christopher. She can be contacted at mizes@notes. udayton.edu/Religious Studies Department, University of Dayton, 300 College Park Ave, Dayton, OH 45469–1530.

Edward T. Oakes SJ currently teaches theology at University of St Mary of the Lake/ Mundelein Seminary, the Catholic seminary for the Archdiocese of Chicago. He earned his PhD in systematic theology from Union Theological Seminary in New York City in 1987. He is the author of *Pattern of Redemption: The Theology of Hans Urs von Balthasar* (New York: Continuum, 2nd edition 1997), the editor of *German Essays on Religion* (Continuum, 1994) and the co-editor, with David Moss, of the *Cambridge Companion to*

Hans Urs von Balthasar as well as translator of many of Balthasar's works into English. He can be contacted through the Mundelein website: www.usml.edu

Mary Aquin O'Neill RSM holds the doctorate from Vanderbilt University. She left the University of Notre Dame to co-found and direct the Mount Saint Agnes Theological Center for Women in Baltimore, Maryland. Her articles have appeared in anthologies and journals, including *Theological Studies*. Some have been translated into Spanish and Polish. The MSA website, www.mountsaintagnes.org, gives all contact information.

Emmanuel Perrier OP, born in 1969, is currently head of the Dominican Theological Studium of Toulouse (France). He is Professor of Dogmatic Theology at the Studium and is invited Professor of Philosophy of Law at the Catholic University of Toulouse. He has published articles in the *Revue Thomiste*, *Liberté Politique*, *Nova et Vetera* (French and English edition), and *Modern Theology*. He is the author of a study in the Trinitarian theology of Saint Thomas Aquinas: *La Fécondite en Dieu* (Paris, 2007). He can be reached at emmanuel.perrier@dominicains.com

Peter C. Phan holds three earned doctorates, one from the Universitas Pontificia Salesiana, Rome, and the other two from the University of London, and an honorary doctorate from Catholic Theological Union, Chicago. He was the Warren-Blanding Professor of Religion and Culture at the Catholic University of America prior to becoming the inaugural holder of the Ignacio Ellacuria Chair of Catholic Social Thought at Georgetown University. His most recent publications include a trilogy on Asian theology: *Christianity with an Asian Face*, *In Our Own Tongues*, and *Being Religious Interreligiously*.

Trent Pomplun is an Assistant Professor of Theology at Loyola College in Maryland. A frequent contributor to *Pro Ecclesia*, *Nova et Vetera*, and *Modern Theology*, he writes about late medieval and early modern Catholicism, with special interests in scholasticism, positive theology, and inter-religious dialog.

Michael Root is Dean and Professor of Systematic Theology at Lutheran Theological Southern Seminary, Columbia, SC, and Director of the Center for Catholic and Evangelical Theology. He served earlier as Research Professor and Director of the Institute for Ecumenical Research in Strasbourg, France. He can be contacted at mroot@ltss.edu; Lutheran Theological Southern Seminary, 4201 N. Main Street, Columbia, SC, 20203, USA.

Associate Professor **Tracey Rowland** is the Dean of the John Paul II Institute for Marriage and Family (Melbourne) and a permanent fellow of the Institute in political philosophy and continental theology. She holds degrees in law, politics and philosophy from the Universities of Queensland and Melbourne and a doctorate from the Divinity School of the University of Cambridge. She is the author of *Culture and the Thomist Tradition: After Vatican II* (London: Routledge, 2003), a member of the editorial board of the international Catholic journal, *Communio*, which was founded by Pope Benedict XVI and others in 1972, and a member of the Centre for Theology and Philosophy at the University of Nottingham. She is also a regular book reviewer for Blackwell's *Reviews in Religion and Theology*. Her next book, *Keys to the Theology of Benedict XVI*, is to be published by Oxford University Press in 2007. E-mail address: trowland@jp2institute.org Institutional Address: John Paul II Institute, P.O. Box 146, East Melbourne, 3002.

Patrick Sherry has spent most of his teaching career in the Religious Studies Department at Lancaster University, England, where he is now Professor Emeritus. His recent work has been in theological aesthetics, exemplified in two books, *Spirit and Beauty* (2nd edition, 2002) and *Images of Redemption* (2003).

Francis A. Sullivan sj taught ecclesiology at the Gregorian for 36 years, serving also as dean of the faculty of theology from 1964 to 1970. After being declared *emeritus* of that faculty in 1992, he came to Boston College, where he is now an adjunct professor of theology. He is the author of eight books, the most recent of which are *Creative Fidelity. Weighing and Interpreting Documents of the Magisterium* (New York/Mahwah: Paulist Press, 1996) and *From Apostles to Bishops. The Development of the Episcopacy in the Early Church* (New York/Mahwah: The Newman Press, 2001). E-mail address: sullivft@bc.edu Institutional address: St Mary's Hall, Boston College, Chestnut Hill, MA 02467.

John E. Thiel is Professor of Religious Studies at Fairfield University, Fairfield, CT, USA, where he has taught for 30 years. He has served as Chair of the Department of Religious Studies at Fairfield and currently is Director of the university honors program. His most recent books are *Senses of Tradition: Continuity and Development in Catholic Faith* (Oxford University Press, 2000) and *God, Evil, and Innocent Suffering: A Theological Reflection* (Crossroad, 2002). He can be reached at jthiel@mail.fairfield.edu

D. Vincent Twomey, born 19.07.1941 in Cork, Ireland. Educated at the Christian Brothers' College, Cork. Joined the Divine Word Missionaries in 1963; studied for the priesthood at Donamon, Co. Roscommon, and St Patrick's College, Maynooth, Co. Kildare. After ordination (1970), postgraduate studies first at the University of Muenster, Westphalia, and then at the University of Regensburg, Bavaria, where his doctoral supervisor was the then Professor Joseph Ratzinger. Professor of Dogmatic Theology at the Regional Seminary of Papua New Guinea and the Solomon Islands (1979–81) and at the SVD Theologische Hochschule, Moedling/Vienna, Austria (1982–3). In 1983, appointed Lecturer in Moral Theology, and in 2004 Professor, at the Pontifical University, St Patrick's College, Maynooth (1983). Editor, *Irish Theological Quarterly* (1998–2006), Editor-in-Chief, *The Word* (2004–present), General Editor, *The Irish Theological Quarterly Monograph Series*. Founder (1986) and organizer of The Patristic Symposium, Maynooth, and the international Maynooth Patristic Conferences.

Susan K. Wood (PhD Marquette University) has taught at St John's University, Collegeville, and currently teaches systematic theology at Marquette University. She is an associate editor of *Pro Ecclesia* and serves on the editorial advisory board of *Ecclesiology*. In addition to articles in numerous journals, she has published *Sacramental Orders* and is editor of *Ordering the Baptismal Priesthood*. She is a member of the Sisters of Charity of Leavenworth. She can be contacted at susan.wood@marquette.edu

Wendy M. Wright holds a doctorate from University of California at Santa Barbara. She is currently Professor of Theology and holder of the John C. Kenefick Faculty Chair in the Humanities at Creighton University. She is author of *Francis de Sales and Jane de Chantal: Letters of Spiritual Direction*, *Heart Speaks to Heart: the Salesian Tradition*, *Sacred Heart: Gateway to God*, and *Caryll Houselander: Essential Writings*. She is married and the parent of three young adults. She can be contacted at wmwright@creighton.edu/ Creighton University, Theology, 2500 California Plaza, Omaha, NE 68178, USA.

Introduction

James J. Buckley, Frederick Christian Bauerschmidt, and Trent Pomplun

The *Blackwell Companion to Catholicism* is a volume in the series of Blackwell Companions. We intend this volume on Catholic life and thought to be neither a theological dictionary nor an encyclopedia on matters Catholic. A companion, in its etymological sense, is someone who joins us at the table, someone with whom we share bread, and someone whose conversation we enjoy. The companions in this *Companion*, then, seek to engage their readers in an informed and informative conversation about Roman Catholic life and thought.

The essays in this *Companion* are addressed to educated persons who wish to broaden and deepen their knowledge of Catholic life and thought – whether because they are Catholic or because they have an interest in matters Catholic for personal or other reasons. We hope that the combination of brief surveys and detailed analyses will make the book useful for beginners as well as interesting for those who already know a good deal about Catholicism.

Many readers of this *Companion* will no doubt browse its essays and read only those that interest them. Other readers will use it as an overview that, read in its entirety, can guide them through Catholic life and thought. To help these readers we have organized this *Companion* around two distinctions. The first is the distinction between time and space, and the second is the distinction between theory and practice. Parts I (Catholic Histories) and II (Catholic Cultures) address the first distinction. Parts III (Catholic Doctrines) and IV (Catholic Practices) address the second distinction. We have tried to develop a common structure within each section, even as we allowed authors freedom to develop their topics in ways they saw fit.

Thus we asked the authors in Part I (Catholic Histories) to keep in mind the other sections of the *Companion*, and therefore to describe the cultures, thoughts, and practices of Catholicism historically. The essays in this first Part, and indeed in the *Companion* as a whole, try to walk the line between general introduction and specialized study. We asked the authors to provide a brief survey of the time period being discussed as well as a more in-depth discussion of a person, movement, debate or event that embodies its distinctive aspects or tensions. We asked the authors in Part II (Catholic Cultures) to provide a "snapshot" or a "thick description" of Catholic life and thought in the diverse countries and cultures of a particular geographical area. Each contains a brief history of Catholicism in the area under discussion (supplementing the histories of Part I), some ethnographic descriptions, and pertinent economic and sociological data. To help strike a balance between a general survey and an in-depth study, we asked authors to devote part of their essay to one or two figures, movements, debates or events that illustrate the distinct shape of Catholicism in that area and the sometimes surprising traits it may share with others. The chapters in Part III (Catholic Doctrines) introduce readers to the major topics of Catholic theology, including both official doctrinal positions and important contemporary debates. We asked each author to address the roots of his or her topic in Scripture and tradition and today. Because the teaching office of the bishops, including the bishop of Rome, is essential to Catholic life and thought, we also asked that all essays should, where appropriate, clearly and accurately present the official teachings of the Church and, where appropriate, candidly recognize places where disagreement exists among the Catholic faithful. Part IV (Catholic Practices) contains chapters on selected activities that constitute Catholic life and thought. Because of Catholicism's long history and present diversity, these essays are even more selective than those in other sections. Nonetheless, we think they capture some of the breadth of Catholic life by showing how it has shaped and been shaped by art, politics, science, and spirituality, among other things. Again, we asked the authors to offer not only a general survey of their topic but also a more in-depth discussion of representative figures, movements, or debates.

The distinctions between Histories and Cultures, Doctrines and Practices are heuristic devices and do not name isolated areas of inquiry. These distinctions cannot be made too neatly. Thus the essays on Catholic histories will have reference to various cultures, doctrines, and practices; the essays on practices will appeal to particular times and places as well as the doctrinal foundations of practices, and so forth. While we recognize that all thought is shaped by life's practices, and all history by culture, we hope that this structure will guide both the reader who desires a comprehensive survey and the one who wishes to focus on specific areas of Catholic life and thought. We invite readers to think, talk, and debate the picture of Catholicism that emerges from these pages.

The cover has one sort of picture: a selection from the icon, designed by Marco Ivan Rupnik sj that constitutes the Redemptoris Mater chapel a few yards from the residence of the Bishop of Rome. Visitors can view the whole chapel from the website of the Holy See (www.vatican.va). Here they will see that the icon is, in some ways, very traditional: tessera of stone, with scenes from Old and New Testaments, incorporating past and contemporary saints, East and West. But it is in other ways very untraditional. The icon covers everything but the floor of the chapel with 600 square meters of mosaic with no traditional frame to constrain it. Further, the stones are of varying dimensions, placed in motion as if God is here in the process of transforming the material cosmos into the new heaven and new earth envisioned in the Book of Revelation.

This *Companion* makes no pretense to have the unity, much less the beauty, of the Redemptoris Mater chapel. But perhaps it hides a whispered echo. The unity of these distinctively human Histories, Cultures, Doctrines, and Practices will be complex and imperfect. For example, no *Companion* written in a single language at a single time can reflect the diversity of Catholic life and thought. We also wish we had more artists, activists, pastors, and journalists to complement the dominance of academic authors for Catholic theology and practices. But we remind readers that the unity of Catholicism is centered less on these Catholic Histories, Cultures, Doctrines, and Practices than on the triune God who creates the whole world for communion with God, who elects Israel to be a blessing for the nations, who is incarnate in Jesus Christ, and who sends the Pentecostal Spirit to form a community of Jew and Gentile, male and female, slave and free. Even at its best (which it usually is not), our companionship is mere image of that triune communion.

Our thanks to David Haddad (Vice President for Academic Affairs at Loyola College), Anne Young (Associate Vice President for Academic Affairs), and Loyola College's Center for the Humanities for supporting our work on this volume. Our thanks also in particular to Devon Lynch-Huggins for her invaluable help in preparing the manuscript for publication.

James J. Buckley, Frederick Christian Bauerschmidt, and Trent Pomplun
Loyola College in Maryland

PART I

Catholic Histories

CHAPTER 1
The Old Testament

Claire Mathews McGinnis

Introduction

Christian sacred Scripture – the Bible – consists of a collection of compositions in two major sections, known as the Old and New Testaments. For Roman Catholics, the Old Testament contains 46 books. Produced by the ancient Israelite and Jewish communities in a period spanning roughly from the thirteenth century BCE (for the earliest oral traditions) to the first century BCE, most of these books were written in Hebrew, except for small portions written in Greek and Aramaic. That 39 of the 46 Old Testament books also comprise the Bible of Judaism (often referred to as the Hebrew Bible) serves as a tangible reminder of the context of Christianity's origins.

The Old Testament witnesses to the Israelites' experience of God from the very earliest period, the period of the patriarchs, into the period of the Second Temple, at which point, in the Christian Bible, the New Testament picks up with the life of Jesus. The Israelites' experience of God is marked by a series of covenants through which God and Israel are bound by mutual love and obligation. A central question for the New Testament writers and for the Christian community from early on was how the new covenant that God enacts through Jesus relates to the covenants of the Old Testament, particularly the covenant made at Mt Sinai which serves as a foundation for Jewish observance.

The literature of the New Testament is woven through with allusions and explicit references to texts of the Old Testament. That this is so reflects the attempts of the very earliest followers of Jesus to comprehend the significance of his life and death by means of their (Jewish) Scripture. It also equally reflects their conviction that the "gospel" or good news of Jesus Christ is integrally related to the good news of what God has done for Israel and the world as recounted in the Old Testament. For Christians, the good news of Jesus is, on the one hand, a continuation of the story that begins in the opening chapters of the Old Testament, but, on the other, it is also more than this; for in Jesus is revealed the fullest expression of what God intended for the world in its creation and in the divine election of Israel. In short, Jesus reveals God's intention for humanity, but the meaning of Jesus for humanity is unintelligible apart from the Old Testament.

The Canon of the Old Testament

That the Catholic Old Testament includes more than seven books not found in either the Hebrew Bible or the Protestant Old Testament bears some explanation. The term Bible comes from the Greek *Ta Biblia*, which means literally, "the books," although originally the "books" of the Old Testament would have been written on scrolls constructed of parchment, that is, sheepskin. The size and weight of parchment defined to some extent how much material was included on one scroll. For example, while the 66 chapters of Isaiah could fit on one scroll, the writings of all three of the major prophets could not. As a result, the collected words of the prophets Isaiah, Jeremiah, and Ezekiel would each have circulated on their own scrolls, while the 12 smaller prophetic writings circulated on one. The various scrolls that became the Jewish Scripture evolved into a collection or "canon" over time. Into the first two centuries of the Common Era there was no fixed list of books deemed scriptural. While the contents of the first two sections of the Bible were already stable, that of the third division was not. Hence, we hear of Jesus referring to "the Law and the Prophets," the first two traditional divisions of the Hebrew Bible, but not to its third, "the Writings." (Luke 24:44 refers to the Law, the Prophets, and the Psalms.)

Because a sizeable population of Jews were living in the Greek-speaking Diaspora in the postexilic period it was necessary to translate the Hebrew texts into Greek. The Greek translation of the Hebrew Bible came to be known as the Septuagint because of a legend, recorded in the Letter of Aristeas to Philocrates, of its translation by 72 elders (or alternatively, by 70, hence its abbreviation as LXX). New Testament and early Christian writers primarily depended on the Greek translation of the Hebrew Scriptures, and continued to do so after the number of books in the Jewish canon was fixed. (The number settled on was 24, but this figure is based on a consideration of several two-part books as one (e.g., I and II Samuel); on the Book of the Twelve prophets as one; and on Ezra-Nehemiah as one. Were we to count each of those as individual books, the number would be 39. The Septuagint, counted similarly, contains 46 books, as well as portions of Daniel and of Esther not found in the Hebrew version of those books.) While, from the settling of the Jewish canon at 24 books on, Christian writers variously preferred either the longer (Greek) or shorter (Hebrew) canon of Old Testament books, even those who preferred the shorter canon continued to quote from those books contained in the longer list. At the Council of Trent, in 1546, the Roman Church officially recognized a list of biblical books based on the Septuagint. Martin Luther rejected the books in the Septuagint not found also in the Hebrew canon as Scripture, resulting in a different Old Testament canon for Roman Catholic and Protestant Christians, although Luther did publish these additional works in his German Bible as Apocrypha (non-scriptural works). In the Catholic tradition these books are referred to as deuterocanonical rather than apocryphal books.

A comparison of the contents and order of books in the Old Testament, based on the Hebrew Bible and on the Septuagint, is found in Table 1.1. The table illustrates the following differences between the canons of the Bible of Judaism and the Old Testament of the Christian Churches. First, both the Jewish and Christian canons begin with the five books of Moses and follow the same ordering of books through the "former prophets,"

Table 1.1 Canons of the Hebrew Bible/Old Testament

In the center list, * indicates a deuterocanonical book, i.e., one not counted in the Jewish or Protestant canons.

Hebrew (Jewish) Bible	Roman Catholic	Protestant
Torah		
Genesis	Genesis	Genesis
Exodus	Exodus	Exodus
Leviticus	Leviticus	Leviticus
Numbers	Numbers	Numbers
Deuteronomy	Deuteronomy	Deuteronomy
Prophets		
Former prophets		
Joshua	Joshua	Joshua
Judges	Judges	Judges
	Ruth	Ruth
I and II Samuel	I and II Samuel	I and II Samuel
I and II Kings	I and II Kings	I and II Kings
Latter prophets	I and II Chronicles	I and II Chronicles
Isaiah	Ezra	Ezra
Jeremiah	Nehemiah	Nehemiah
Ezekiel	*Tobit	
The Book of the Twelve	*Judith	
Hosea	Esther	Esther
Joel	*I and II Maccabees	
Amos	Job	Job
Obadiah	Psalms	Psalms
Jonah	Proverbs	Proverbs
Micah	Ecclesiastes	Ecclesiastes
Nahum	Song of Solomon	Song of Solomon
Habakkuk	*Wisdom of Solomon	
Zephaniah	*Sirach (Ecclesiasticus)	
Haggai		
Zechariah	Isaiah	Isaiah
Malachi	Jeremiah	Jeremiah
	Lamentations	Lamentations
Writings	*Baruch	
Psalms	Ezekiel	Ezekiel
Job	Daniel	Daniel
Proverbs	Hosea	Hosea
Ruth	Joel	Joel
Song of Songs	Amos	Amos
Ecclesiastes	Obadiah	Obadiah
Lamentations	Jonah	Jonah
Esther	Micah	Micah
Daniel	Nahum	Nahum
Ezra	Habakkuk	Habakkuk
Nehemiah	Zephaniah	Zephaniah
I and II Chronicles	Haggai	Haggai
	Zechariah	Zechariah
	Malachi	Malachi

ending with II Kings. In the Hebrew Bible, however, what follows is the collection of latter prophets – three larger and a grouping of twelve smaller prophetic collections; this collection of latter prophets comes last in the Protestant and Catholic canons. Second, while the Protestant canon contains the same number of books as the Hebrew Bible, the books are published in the same ordering as that of the Catholic canon. Third, the books of the Hebrew Bible that constitute the Writings appear in a slightly different order than in the Christian canons. The canons of the Orthodox Christian Churches, like the Roman Catholic Church, use the Septuagint as their bases.

Inspiration and Interpretation

A Catholic perspective on the divine inspiration of Scripture is set forth clearly in the Dogmatic Constitution on Divine Revelation, published during the Second Vatican Council. This document, more commonly known as *Dei Verbum*, recognizes that the books of the Old Testament were written by human authors who "made full use of their faculties and powers," but who, at the same time, were also writing under the inspiration of the Holy Spirit. Thus, although the books are written "through human agents and in human fashion," they also "have God as their author" (*Dei Verbum* 11–12, Béchard, 2002).

This understanding of the inspired nature of the biblical books has important implications for how Catholics approach them. On the one hand, it is important to understand the texts as the work of human authors, paying attention to their culturally conditioned ways of communicating – to language, genre, and modes of narration, for instance. On the other hand, if the Old Testament is to speak as a living text – as the word of God – then the mind of the reader must also be illumined by the work of the Spirit. This means that the task of understanding a biblical text on its own terms, as a document from a particular people, place, and time, is necessary to the process of interpretation but it is not sufficient. Scripture must also be interpreted in light of the Spirit that inspired it, and from this it follows that a reader must pay attention also "to the content and unity of the whole of Scripture" (*Dei Verbum* 12). Attention to the whole of Scripture represents a principle of Christian interpretation from the earliest days on: since the whole of Scripture is inspired by the Holy Spirit, any individual section of Scripture is to be understood in the light of all the rest. For Christians, then, the Old Testament is read in relation to the New, just as the New Testament is read in relation to the Old. *Dei Verbum*, drawing on the words of St Augustine, describes the relationship of the two Testaments such that the New is "hidden in the Old and the Old [is] made manifest in the New" stating further,

> For, although Christ established the New Covenant in his blood, nevertheless the books of the Old Testament, fully taken up in the Gospel proclamation, acquire and show forth their full meaning in the New Testament and in turn shed light on it and explain it. (16)

However, to say that the books of the Old Testament "show forth their full meaning in the New Testament" in no way implies that these books are not of significant and lasting value in their own right. The God who revealed God's self, in words and deeds, in the long history of Israel's covenantal relationships is the one true God, the same God who raised Jesus from the dead. Thus, not only does the Old Testament offer a compelling portrait of God, it also offers sound teaching about God, wisdom, and instruction for living, and, particularly in the book of Psalms, pedagogy in prayer (*Dei Verbum* 15).

As the living word of God, the Old and New Testaments offer nourishment for the faithful. Not surprisingly then, the reading of, and preaching on, Scripture plays a central role in Christian worship. A Catholic Mass includes both a Liturgy of the Word and a Liturgy of the Eucharist. The former will typically include a reading from an Old Testament book, recitation of a Psalm, a reading from a New Testament epistle or book other than a gospel, and a reading from a New Testament gospel, followed by a homily which expounds on the Word. Personal study of the Scripture is also encouraged for individual Christians, for "Ignorance of the Word is Ignorance of Christ" (St Jerome). However, the interpretation of Scripture is never a wholly personal affair, as a reader must also take into account "the entire living Tradition of the whole Church" attending to the coherence of the truths of faith that have grown out of that tradition (*Dei Verbum* 12).

The earliest Christian interpretation of the Old Testament is that found in the compositions of the New Testament. The interpretive techniques used by the various New Testament writers were generally no different than those of the writers' Jewish contemporaries. For instance, it was not uncommon to read the words of prophetic texts as addressing the situation of one's own day, or to interpret one passage of Scripture by means of another. Similar hermeneutical practices do not render identical results, however. The New Testament writers' conviction that Jesus is the Christ led them to understand various passages from the Old Testament books as pointing toward Christ, where their Jewish contemporaries did not. In as much as nascent Christianity was a Jewish sect rather than the distinct religion that it became, and in as much as the early Christian communities struggled to define themselves in relation to Judaism, it was quite important for the early Christians to search the Scriptures for those passages that illumined their experiences of the crucified and risen Lord, and to articulate the ways in which in him was found the fulfillment of the prophetic hope expressed in the Hebrew Bible. As important as this was, however, the Old Testament was not used simply as a prophetic pointer to Christ, but for ongoing instruction.

Both ways of reading the Old Testament, Christologically and otherwise, are evidenced in subsequent Christian interpretation. Early Christian writers described Scripture as having both a literal and a spiritual sense. These two senses of Scripture enable one to be enriched by the "plain sense" of the words, while also seeing in them prefigurations or allegorical references to the work of Christ. But the two senses have an added benefit: in the face of passages that confound the reader, as when, for instance, they seem to portray something unworthy of God, the reader is pointed beyond the literary obstacle to the spiritual sense of the text. (For a fuller history of the evolution of Christian interpretation in general, see chapter 2 on the New Testament.)

Unlike the New Testament which is uniquely Christian Scripture, the Hebrew Bible continued to serve as the Scripture of Judaism, and so alongside the Christian tradition of interpretation of the Old Testament stands a lively and robust tradition of Jewish interpretation of those same books, recorded, most prominently, in the Talmud. The acceptance by Catholic scholars of historical critical approaches to Scripture has created common ground for Catholic and Jewish scholars on which to work collaboratively, and official recognition that God's covenant with Israel has never been revoked commands respect among Catholics for the Jewish people and their tradition.

The Contents of the Old Testament

The Torah and former prophets

The Old Testament contains a variety of kinds of material, written over a large span of time. Even within the same book one sometimes finds the work of different authors from different time periods and points of view, along with very ancient material that assuredly circulated orally before being written down. A large segment of the Old Testament consists of narrative. Much of it is of historical value, while other pieces are apparently legendary. It contains a large corpus of legal material governing Israel's religious practice as well as the more mundane aspects of Israelite life, which are also seen as an important aspect of a loving response to God. A substantial portion includes collected sayings of Israel's prophets, proverbs, prayers, and other forms of discourse.

Tradition long held that Moses authored the first five books of the Bible, with the recognition that some parts – such as the report of Moses' death – could only have been added by another hand. These five books, often referred to as the Torah or Pentateuch, are, in Jewish tradition, considered to be the center of Scripture if one imagines the Prophets and the Writings as comprising two concentric circles around it. The reason for the primacy given to the Torah is that in these books are recounted the promises made to Abraham, the liberation of his descendants from Egypt, the covenant that God makes with them on Mt Sinai and the legislation pertaining to that covenant, all of which are foundational for the practice of Judaism. Biblical scholars now recognize that the Pentateuch as a whole could not have been authored by Moses, since, as was noted above, even within its individual books one may find material reflecting different perspectives and different historical periods. Nonetheless the Torah presents a coherent story of God's election of, and relationship to, the people of Israel from the call of Abraham to the eve of their entry into the Promised Land.

Creation and the Fall

The first book, Genesis, opens with accounts of Creation and the rise of civilization. It is clear that the biblical authors' accounts of Creation were not intended as an attempt to scientifically explain the origins of the natural world, if simply because a modern scientific perspective would have been quite alien to an ancient Israelite. Rather, as is the case with other ancient Near Eastern Creation stories, the biblical writers offered their account of *how* things came to be as a way of stating claims about *the nature of things as they are*. As Christians have understood the Creation narratives, included in these claims about the nature of things are: the conviction that the world and all that is in it depends for its creation and ongoing existence on the one God; that the Creation reflects the goodness of that one God; and – a conviction especially central to Catholic moral theology and social teaching – that human beings are created with an inherent dignity, the dignity of having been created in the image of God which remains even after the "fall" of humankind (Gen 1:26–7).

The first account of Creation is structured according to seven days, beginning with the formless void, progressing through the creation of plants, various groupings of animals, humans, and ending with the Sabbath day, on which God rests from the divine work of Creation and which God blesses and hallows. At Mt Sinai God will command the Israelites to similarly observe and hallow the Sabbath as a day of rest. The observance of the Sabbath also becomes central to Christian practice, although the Christian Sabbath is observed on the first or "eighth" day of the week, the day of Christ's resurrection from the dead. For Catholics, participation in the Eucharist is central to the Sabbath's weekly observance.

A second account of Creation, in Genesis 2, focuses more narrowly on the creation of human beings. These first humans – Adam and Eve – are placed in the Garden of Eden where they are allowed to eat freely, except for the fruit of one tree, "the tree of the knowledge of good and evil." Seduced by the serpent, they disobey God's command, and are sent forth from the garden lest they eat, in their new condition, of the fruit of the tree of life and live forever. In addition to being removed from the intimacy with God that characterized life in the Garden of Eden, their punishments include pain in childbirth and having to toil to eat of the earth's produce.

This account of what befalls the first two humans, frequently referred to as the Fall, has been important to the Church's understanding of the human condition and of Christ's role as savior. In his epistle to the Christian community in Rome the Apostle Paul describes Adam as a "type" of Christ: whereas through Adam sin and death came into the world, through Christ, the "new Adam," come justification and life for all (Rom 5:12–21). In 1 Cor 15:21–2 Paul similarly writes, "For since death came through a human being, the resurrection of the dead came also through a human being. For just as in Adam all die, so too in Christ shall all be brought to life" (New American Bible).

The typological connection that Paul makes between Adam and Christ is built on by Augustine, to whom is credited the classic expression of the doctrine of Original Sin, in his fifth-century writings against Pelagianism. The contours of this doctrine are further refined in the Middle Ages, and defined in relation to Protestant alternatives at the Council of Trent in 1546. From the perspective of this doctrine, summarized in paragraphs 396–409 of the Catechism of the Catholic Church, Adam and Eve's act of disobedience is at its heart a refusal to accept the limits placed upon them as creatures. In eating of the fruit they were commanded not to eat, they fail to trust their creator and they abuse their divinely-given freedom. As a result, not only does death enter into human history and not only is the harmony of the humans' relationship with one another and with the rest of Creation destroyed, but humans are deprived of the original justice and holiness with which they were created. Human nature is not completely corrupted but is wounded, and inclined to sin. This privation marks the condition in which all humans now find themselves from birth, the loss of which can only be restored through justification in Christ, through baptism. While Augustine, who read Genesis literally, understood this fallen nature to be transmitted from Adam and Eve to all of their human descendants through procreation, what the doctrine affirms is not dependent on a literal reading of Genesis.

The state of human nature after the fall, with its tendency to turn away rather than toward God, expresses itself in Genesis' subsequent chapters, beginning with the murder of Abel by his brother Cain. So wicked do humans become that in Genesis 6 the Lord would return the natural world completely to its primordial, uninhabited watery chaos were it not for Noah, who finds favor with God, and who with his family is delivered from the great flood to begin anew. Noah's offering of incense after the flood becomes the occasion for the first of the biblical covenants, made with Noah and his descendants and hence with all of humankind.

The covenant with Abraham

A second covenant is made with Abraham, to whom God promises blessing, descendants as numerous as the stars of the sky, and, to his offspring, the land of Canaan forever (12:1–3; 13:14–16; 15:4–5; 17: 9–19). Circumcision is given as the sign of this covenant. Abraham is blessed with two sons: Ishmael, through his wife's servant Hagar, and Isaac, the promised and long-awaited son of Sarah, who gives birth when she is 90 years old. Toward the end of Abraham's story he is commanded to offer his son Isaac as a sacrifice, a test which Abraham obediently passes, although at the last minute his son's life is spared in exchange for a ram caught in the thicket. This test becomes the occasion for the reaffirmation of God's promise and blessing.

The remainder of Genesis is concerned with the perils involved in transmitting the promise and blessing to subsequent generations. As was the case with Isaac and Ishmael, sibling rivalry takes center stage as the story of the next generations unfolds, first between Isaac's sons Jacob and Esau (and Jacob's wives Rachel and Leah) (Gen 25:19–33:17) and then between Jacob's favored son, Joseph, and his brothers (Gen 37–50). Genesis comes to a close with Joseph's and his brother's families in Egypt, having survived famine through Joseph's divinely-granted talents. On his deathbed, Joseph exacts an oath from his brothers to carry his bones up out of Egypt when God brings them "up out of this land to the land that he swore to Abraham, to Isaac, and to Jacob" (50:24–6).

Moses and the exodus

The story of Abraham's descendants continues in the book of Exodus, although it does so less by focusing on specific family groups than by telling the story of Abraham's "fruitful and prolific" descendants as a whole: the people Israel, bearing the name given Jacob in Gen 32, "he who strives with God." The first half of Exodus tells the story of Pharaoh's enslavement and oppression of the Israelites. It is in this context that the reader is introduced to Moses – Israel's preeminent prophet – who is to deliver his people. The divine personal name is revealed to Moses. The name given, YHWH (Exod 6:2), is thought to have been pronounced Yahweh (Hebrew was written without the vowels until the post-biblical period) and a play on the letters in the name is given, suggesting something of the divine nature: "I am who I am" (3:14). Through Moses, God sends plagues on Pharaoh and the Egyptians, after which Moses leads the people out of bondage, culminating in the miraculous passage through the Red Sea as if on dry ground. It is the death of the firstborn of Egypt that convinces Pharaoh to let the Israelites go, and intertwined with the account of this plague is the account of the institution of the first Passover and instructions for its celebration in the Promised Land. While Jewish families continue to celebrate the Passover annually, for Christians the Passover gives way to celebration of the Eucharist, since it was at the Passover Seder that Jesus instituted the practice "in memory of [him]." Christians, reading this section of Exodus typologically, have understood the Passover as a prefiguration or type of the Eucharist. The deliverance from Egypt is followed by accounts of several events that occur in the wilderness, including God's sending the manna, the bread from heaven which feeds the Israelites throughout their years in the wilderness (chapter 16) which Christians, again, have seen as pointing to Christ, the bread of life.

The Sinai covenant and ritual worship

When the Israelites reach Mt Sinai, God makes a covenant with them. On their part, the Israelites are to obey God's commandments, while God, on God's part, will hold them as a "special possession." They shall be a "kingdom of priests" and a "holy nation" (Exod 19:4–6). On the mountain God delivers the ten commandments, written in stone, along with a varied body of legislation. The covenant is ratified with the blood of sacrificial offerings (Exod 24:7–8).

Also given on Mt Sinai are instructions for building the Tabernacle, the portable shrine that will accompany the Israelites in the wilderness; for the Ark of the Covenant, into which the tablets with the Ten Commandments will be placed and which will serve as God's throne; for the various liturgical accoutrements to the Tabernacle; for the ordination of priests, the daily offerings and so on. The instructions are followed by an account of their fulfillment by Moses and the Israelites, which then leads to the book's climactic conclusion: the descent of the glory of the Lord, God's visible presence, filling the Tabernacle and thus accompanying and leading the Israelites on their journey through the wilderness. (Exod 40:34–8)

Once the Israelites are living in the Promised Land this portable sanctuary is eventually replaced by a permanent shrine, and the Jerusalem Temple becomes the official center of Israelite corporate worship. The building of the temple is envisioned by King David, but accomplished by his son, Solomon, as recounted in the early chapters of I Kings. It serves as the place of elaborate sacrificial worship, a destination of pilgrimage, and the place where Israel's God is preeminently present in the midst of the people and land. I Kings 8 describes the glory of the Lord filling the temple just as it had descended on the Tabernacle at the end of the book of Exodus (see also Isa 6).

The legislation that claims the authority of the covenant made at Sinai is not only found in the book of Exodus, but comprises the entirety of the book of Leviticus, part of Numbers, and most of Deuteronomy. Leviticus intimates the era of Solomon's temple with its instructions concerning the preparation and presentation of offerings and sacrifices, concerning foods that can and cannot be eaten (the kosher laws), and concerning bodily functions and diseases that necessitate a process of ritual purification. The operative categories in much of Leviticus' legislation are notions of holiness, of defilement and purification, of "clean" and "unclean." Also included are instructions concerning various observances – the Sabbath, the Passover, several feasts, the Day of Atonement, the Sabbatical and Jubilee year, among others.

As the book of Numbers recounts, the Israelites are in the wilderness for 40 years, until the initial, "faithless" generation of Israelites is succeeded by a new generation. A census at the beginning of the book, and then toward the end, marks the transition from the generation that left Egypt to the next. Here also are given instructions concerning the apportioning of the promised land among the 12 tribes (family groups descended from Jacob's 12 sons), and included are some classic stories of the Old Testament, including the spying out of the land of Canaan (chapter 13); Balaam's talking ass (chapters 22–4); and various rebellions and acts of unfaithfulness on the part of the Israelites (chapters 11–14; 16; 20; 25).

When Moses and the Israelites reach the border of the Promised Land, poised in the plains of Moab to enter into it, Moses looks backward to the exodus and forward to life in the land, in a series of speeches before his death. These speeches comprise the fifth book of the Torah, known as Deuteronomy. The speeches of Moses have a sermonic quality to them, and rather than simply reiterating the law they exhort their hearers to obey it, illustrating the blessings that come with obedience, and curses with disobedience. Prosperity and peace in the land are the benefits of keeping the covenant. Failure to keep it will result in hunger, illness, oppression, and loss of the land to foreigners.

The land, monarchy, and Davidic covenant

The actual conquest of the Promised Land, inhabited by other peoples, is recounted in two basic forms in the books of Joshua and Judges. One version suggests that the conquest was swift and thorough, while the other suggests that the process of taking the Promised Land was a more arduous task, and less than complete. Judges offers insight to the structure of the community at this time as a loose federation of tribes that came together under a single leader or "judge" only when a crisis necessitated it. The transition from a federated structure to a monarchy is recounted in the books I and II Samuel, and takes place under the leadership of the prophet Samuel, at a time of border skirmishes with the neighboring and more powerful Philistines. An ambivalence about monarchic rule is drawn especially sharply by the characterization of the people's request for a king as a rejection of YHWH as king over Israel, and as a desire to be "like the other nations." Fortifying this sense of ambivalence is the early rejection of Saul, YHWH's first "anointed" as king, and the designation, even before Saul's death, of David as his successor, described as a man "after [God's] own heart." While David is not without fault, he has much to commend him, and it is in response to his desire to built a permanent temple to house the Ark of the Covenant that God promises David "Your house and kingdom shall endure forever before me; your throne shall stand firm forever" (2 Sam 7:16).

God's promise to David is celebrated in the Psalms and it is in the Psalms that we get a glimpse of the idea of the king (the "Lord's anointed" or *mashiach*, rendered in English as messiah) as a savior in the sense that he brings justice and peace to his rule:

> He shall govern your people with justice
> and your afflicted ones with judgment.
> The mountains shall yield peace for the people
>   and the hills justice.
> He shall defend the afflicted among the people,
>   save the children of the poor
>   and crush the oppressor. (Ps 72:2–4, NAB)

In some cases, David's descendants did not fit this ideal, and so we find the prophet Isaiah, for instance, raising hopes for a future king, yet unborn, who will restore YHWH's rule to the kingdom. The symbolic name given to this one is Immanuel, which means "God is with us" (Isa 7:14). Later interpretations notwithstanding, in this passage the prophet most likely imagines a soon-to-be heir of the current king. However, several chapters later the prophet speaks of the reign of the future Davidic king in terms that seem to transcend history as we know it. During the reign of that king, he suggests, "The wolf shall be the guest of the lamb, and the leopard shall lie down with the kid . . ." (11:6a).

Upon David's death the succession of the throne to his son Solomon goes smoothly, but not so at the end of Solomon's reign, and the rest of the history of pre-exilic monarchic rule is the story of a divided kingdom, with David's heirs ruling over the southern kingdom, Judah, whose capital is Jerusalem, and a series of non-Davidic kings ruling over the northern kingdom, Israel, with its capital and shrine in Samaria. The northern kingdom fell to the Assyrians in 722 BCE. Jerusalem fell to the Babylonians in 587 BCE. Although the Israelites were allowed to return to Judah under the rule of the Persians and the temple was eventually rebuilt, the land of Judah was almost continuously under foreign rule from that time forward, without a Davidic king on the throne. Thus, while the hopes for a Davidic king who will once again establish YHWH's reign of justice and peace continued to be held, they were now held for an indefinite future. The New Testament literature makes a point of noting Jesus' Davidic ancestry, and asserts that in him are fulfilled, albeit in unexpected ways, the promises and hopes surrounding a Davidic king who will establish YHWH's reign of peace and justice.

Exilic and post-exilic concerns

A good portion of the literature of the Old Testament addresses the crisis of exile from the land in one way or another. The books of Kings recount the history of the monarchic period with a view to explaining Israel and Judah's misfortunes as resulting from the rulers' and peoples' sins, just as Deuteronomy, before it, suggested that loss of the land would be the result of disobedience. Most of the books of Isaiah, Jeremiah, and Ezekiel are devoted to addressing the crises precipitated by the incursions of the Assyrian and Babylonian armies whether before, in the events that would lead up to them, during, or after, as, for instance, when the prophet's audience is living in Babylon. The book of Lamentations, as its name suggests, records a series of laments on the fall of Jerusalem, while the Psalms reflect the same events in lamentation and prayer to God.

That the Old Testament literature does not end at this critical point in Israel's history is testament not only to God's faithfulness but also to the vitality of the faith life of the people of God. The biblical books stemming from the exilic and post-exilic periods demonstrate the Israelite community reflecting, on one hand, on what it means to "sing the Lord's song in a foreign land." On the other hand, return to the land of Judah under Persian rule and the rebuilding of the Temple and a community around it generated a body of literature reflecting another set of concerns and questions: who may belong to the community of the faithful and who is to be excluded? What constitutes authentic worship of YHWH? Why have the early hopes for restoration to an autonomous life in the land under a Davidic king not been fully realized? The synagogue, and inspirational stories about the problems of negotiating the demands of Jewish observance in the midst of a non-Jewish culture are generated out of life in the Diaspora, while the books of Haggai, Zechariah, Malachi, Ezra, and Nehemiah all provide information about the difficulties and controversies of the early years of reconstruction. Daniel and I and II Maccabees reflect the struggle under later Hellenistic rule, when attempts were made to have Jews abandon their religious practices for paganism.

The prophets

Throughout the period of the Israelite monarchy kings retained prophets as advisors, and the Old Testament contains a number of stories about prophetic figures. It is clear that "professional" prophets could find success in telling the king what he wanted to hear, but there were also strong prophetic figures that challenged and wisely advised the royal house. They also spoke prophetically to individuals and to the broader Israelite community. Samuel, Nathan, Elijah, and Elisha are among this group of prophets, about whom stories are preserved in the books of Samuel and Kings.

Equally important are the latter or "writing" prophets, that is, the prophets whose collections of oracles have been preserved in books that bear their names. Their prophetic invectives against social injustice continue to capture the imagination of readers today, and when someone is said to play a prophetic role what is usually meant is that they stand as a lone, and therefore courageous, voice of critique. But the prophets also spoke against idolatry and other forms of inauthentic worship, and enjoined trust in YHWH in the face of threats from more powerful nations when political alliances and dependence on military solutions threatened to undermine Israelite autonomy and identity as a people of God. The prophets frequently threatened divine judgment in response to their hearers' misdeeds in an attempt to effect repentance, and in some cases indicated that it was too late for the chance to repent. The prophets also held out a vision of hope when there otherwise was none, and in general, could be said to have interpreted their present circumstances from the divine perspective. As Moses and others have shown, a central role of the prophet was also to intercede on behalf of the people with God. The words of the prophets almost always are recorded in poetic form, and characteristics of prophetic speech include wordplay and the creative reuse of earlier narrative, legal, and poetic traditions. Of all the prophetic books Isaiah is one of those most quoted in the New Testament. His powerful words of comfort and hope, rendered in stirring poetry, continue to speak to readers today, while his descriptions of the Servant of the Lord (Isa 40–55 *passim*) found appeal among early Christian writers.

The wisdom literature

A handful of books in the Old Testament fall under the rubric of wisdom literature, which has a very different feel from both the prophetic and the narrative material discussed above. A comparison of these books, Proverbs, Job, Ecclesiastes, Sirach, and Wisdom, demonstrates that while they exhibit a variety of concerns and modes of expression, they also have much in common: an emphasis on practical instruction for successful living, conveyed often through short sayings or proverbs, along with exhortation, warning, and other forms of advice. What also distinguishes the Bible's wisdom literature is its lack of reference to the sacred traditions of Israel: to the stories of the patriarchs, to the exodus, and the Sinai covenant. Wisdom can be depicted as a divine gift, as is the case with Solomon (I Kings 4:29–34), but it also comes with experience, with observing how certain actions lead to certain outcomes, and especially, with taking heed of the instruction of one's elders. This is not to say that wisdom literature is devoid of talk about God or concern for things religious. On the contrary, as Proverbs 1:7 asserts, "The fear of the Lord is the beginning of wisdom." Wisdom comes in a variety of species. There is judicial wisdom, such as the sort exercised by Solomon in judging a difficult case (1 Kings 3:16–28), experiential wisdom, wisdom concerning nature, and theological wisdom which involves reflection on the very nature of wisdom itself.

One example of theological wisdom is her personification as a woman, begotten by the Lord and "the first-born of his ways" (Prov 8:22). And, while wisdom is very much seen as something to be handed down from one generation to another, and hence, as a traditional form of knowledge, one also sees an ongoing conversation within the wisdom tradition itself, as when, in the Book of Job the conventional view that the wicked suffer and the righteous are rewarded is, at least for much of the book, turned on its head. Just as other ancient Near Eastern cultures had their own Creation stories and their own traditions of prophecy, so also traditions of wisdom thrived among Israel's neighbors. And, while Israel's wisdom traditions had much in common with those of its neighbors, they are nonetheless consistent with and support her unique, monotheistic faith. Not surprisingly, certain of the New Testament literature reflects a familiarity with the wisdom traditions of the Old Testament. Of particular mention are the Letter of James and the prologue to the Gospel of John, which depicts Christ as the Word or *logos*, drawing both on the personification of Wisdom found in Proverbs 8, and on Greek notions of the term.

Psalms

It is fitting that this survey of the Old Testament literature should come to a close with the Psalms, which have rightly been characterized as Israel's response to the words and deeds of God revealed in the other books of the Hebrew Bible. The book of Psalms is a collection of 150 sung prayers that were used in Israel's worship of God. Some of the Psalms are composed as communal expressions, others as personal ones. They encompass a wide range of experience and sentiment, from thanks and praise to repentance, petition, and lament. Included among them are "historical psalms" recounting events in Israel's history, and "wisdom psalms" that offer the kind of theological reflection and counsel characteristic of literature of that sort. While the shape of the Psalter reflects its historical development – one finds in it several "books" added one to another – it also shows signs of intentional ordering, such as in the way that it begins with a wisdom psalm, and ends with a collection of fervent praise.

The Psalms have long served both the Jewish and Christian communities as a prayer book and pedagogue in prayer. They demonstrate the full range of experience and emotion that is to be brought before God and, equally important, they offer words for one to lift up to God on those occasions when one cannot formulate the words oneself. Over the centuries of their use by Christians the Psalms have been given a variety of musical settings, from Gregorian chant to the more contemporary melodies found in songbooks of Catholic parishes. It has long been the practice of Christian monastic communities to recite Psalms throughout the day, in what is known as the Liturgy of the Hours. This practice is replicated, in small part, in the practice of reciting or singing a psalm responsively during the Catholic Mass. When prayed consistently in this way over the course of the months and years, then, the prayers of the Psalms become an indelible part of one's mind and heart. They form believers in a life of prayer, and allow the word of God to take root in believers, dwelling in them richly.

References and Further Reading

Holy See (1994) *Catechism of the Catholic Church.* Mahwah, NJ: Paulist.

Béchard, Dean P. (2002) "Dogmatic Constitution on Divine Revelation, *Dei Verbum*," in *The Scripture Documents: An Anthology of Official Catholic Teachings*, ed. and trans. Dean P. Béchard. Collegeville, MN: Liturgical Press, 19–31.

CHAPTER 2
The New Testament

Luke Timothy Johnson

The New Testament consists of 27 compositions that, together with the Old Testament, make up the Christian Bible. Originally written in Greek between 50 and 150 CE, the New Testament has been translated into every major language and serves as a source of revelation and a guide to life for all Christians, even when they disagree on its precise meaning or application. Catholics read it (with the Old Testament) as the Word of God in worship, and consider the New Testament to be indispensable and normative for theological understanding, moral discernment, and spiritual nourishment. The New Testament's authority within the life of the Church is grounded in the conviction that its writings, composed by human authors of the ancient Mediterranean world, are also inspired by God's Holy Spirit, and are therefore a living word from God to humans in every place and time.

The New Testament contains four narratives that recount the ministry, death, and resurrection of Jesus (the Gospels of Matthew, Mark, Luke, and John), a narrative concerned with the first spread of Christianity from Jerusalem to Rome in the first generation (Acts of the Apostles), 13 letters attributed to the Apostle Paul, a leader in that first great expansion and the most important interpreter of earliest Christian experience and conviction (Romans, 1 Corinthians, 2 Corinthians, Galatians, Ephesians, Philippians, Colossians, First Thessalonians, Second Thessalonians, Philemon, 1 Timothy, 2 Timothy, Titus), eight letters from other apostles and teachers (Hebrews, James, 1 Peter, 2 Peter, Jude, 1 John, 2 John, 3 John), and a visionary work (Revelation).

The Process of Composition

The factors that shaped earliest Christianity are the same that shaped the writings of the New Testament. First, Christianity was born, not directly out of Jesus' teachings or actions, but out of the experience of Jesus' resurrection and exaltation to God's right hand as Lord. The resurrection experience – the experience of transforming, transcendent power from the Holy Spirit – is everywhere implicit in the New Testament compositions, inextricably linked to the conviction that Jesus is "Lord," that is, shares fully in the life and power of the one God (1 Cor 12:1–3). It was this power and conviction that energized and guided the proclamation of the "good news from God" that established communities across the Roman Empire in a matter of decades. And it is from the perspective of the resurrection of Jesus that every composition in the New Testament is written. Letters were written to communities gathered in the power of the resurrected one and living by his Holy Spirit. Gospels interpreted the story of Jesus from the perspective of his continuing presence in the community.

The second factor was the manner of Jesus' death. Crucifixion was shameful, and appeared to disqualify Jesus as a Son of God in Greco-Roman terms and as a Messiah in Jewish terms (see 1 Cor 1:18–30). If without the resurrection there would be no Christianity, without the crucifixion there would be no New Testament, for the cognitive dissonance created by the conflict between the experience of the resurrection and the symbolic world of Judaism, which declared that anyone who was hanged on a tree was cursed by God (Deut 21:23; see Gal 3:13), demanded resolution through the reinterpretation of the symbolic world shaped by the first believers. Other experiences also demanded interpretation – from the outside, rejection and persecution; from the inside, continuing experience of sin and death – but the manner of Jesus' death demanded urgent attention, not only so that believers could come to grips with his story but so that they could understand their own continuing experience. Thus, Jesus appears in the New Testament compositions not only as the powerful resurrected Lord, but also as the Servant who suffered a shameful death for the sake of others.

The third factor shaping the New Testament compositions is the cultural matrix within which the first believers interpreted their lives in light of a crucified and raised Messiah. Most important was the symbolic world of Torah, for the first believers were Jews, perceiving and interpreting even their most radical experiences within the framework of God's revelation in Scripture, so that, within a generation, even the scandalous death of Jesus was understood to be "according to the Scriptures" (1 Cor 15:3), and the entire story of Jesus was read as "promised beforehand through the prophets in the holy writings" (Rom 1:2). Every New Testament composition involves a re-reading of Scripture in light of Jesus the Messiah and Lord. Conversely, every interpretation of Jesus in the Letters and in the Gospels involves as well the appropriation of stories and symbols drawn from Scripture.

Greco-Roman culture also shaped Christian compositions. The New Testament was written in the *koine* Greek of the early empire, and the influence of Greco-Roman cultural realities and rhetoric pervade both Gospels and Letters. Indeed, New Testament authors read and quoted the Greek translation of the Hebrew Bible known as the Septuagint (LXX), which was widely used by Jews both in Palestine and the Diaspora since *c.*250 CE. The Septuagint quoted by the New Testament does not always agree with the Hebrew original, a disparity that continues in contemporary translations that are based on the original languages. Nevertheless, the "proof from prophecy" practiced by the New Testament authors depends – in many cases critically – on the Septuagint version. The Septuagint also contained more compositions than did the original Hebrew. Despite the Protestant Reformation's recognition only of the Hebrew collection, Catholic and Orthodox Christians continue to accept the Septuagint version of the Old

Testament as Scripture, even though they maintain a distinction between "canonical" and "deuterocanonical." Thus, a Catholic theologian can quote *The Wisdom of Solomon* as Sacred Scripture, whereas a Protestant theologian can quote it only as an "apocryphal" (that is, non-canonical) writing.

A fourth factor shaping the New Testament was the experiences of the diverse Christian communities out of which and for which these compositions were produced. The New Testament was written by individuals across the span of the empire to be read aloud in assemblies that faced a variety of social settings and problems. Some faced persecution and ostracism from outsiders. Others dealt with a variety of internal conflicts concerning community practices and beliefs. Authors not only addressed a variety of real-life situations, they each had their own perspective, and each employed distinctive forms of rhetoric. Because they interpreted the good news and its implications with reference to specific readers, they therefore also necessarily engaged the figure of Jesus and the symbolic world of Torah in distinctive ways. The New Testament's remarkable diversity in literary expression and in perspective – among the Gospels as much as among the Letters – is best understood as deriving from the diversity in the situation and experiences of the earliest Christian communities.

The process of composition within early Christian communities was complex. The earliest extant writings are Paul's letters, written between 49 and 68 CE, and they already make use of community traditions (confessional statements, hymns, the rituals of baptism and Lord's Supper). Despite the strong imprint of Paul's authority, his letters also show signs of communal effort in their production, which accounts in part for the variety of rhetorical expression in his correspondence, and the difficulty of detecting which of the 13 letters ascribed to him are authentic. A standard view of the matter considers Paul to have written seven letters himself, with the other six (2 Thess, Col, Eph, 1 Tim, 2 Tim, Tit) being pseudonymously composed by followers after his death. Another view of Pauline authorship emphasizes the presence of the Pauline School during his lifetime and regards Paul as the author (in the broad sense of the term) of all 13 letters.

Lacking firm chronological controls outside the few established by the Acts of the Apostles and the Pauline Letters that fit within its framework, other New Testament compositions are even harder to place within the early period. Some letters, such as Hebrews, James, and 1 Peter, might well be as early as Paul. Others, like 2 Peter and Jude and the Letters of John, are more reasonably dated toward the end of the century. The precise authorship of compositions other than Paul's is also notoriously difficult to establish with certainty. James, for example, may well be by "the Brother of the Lord" (see Gal 1:19) who was the leader of the Church in Jerusalem, but 2 Peter is almost certainly pseudonymous.

The process of Gospel composition was even more complex. During the decades when Paul and others were writing letters to communities, the memories of Jesus – in the form of sayings and stories – were simultaneously being transmitted in oral form within the common life of Churches. Some parts of the story, above all the Passion account, reached a stable, perhaps even a written state, early. A collection of sayings (conventionally called Q, for *Quelle*, "source") was also probably composed during the first decades of the Church. Communities made do without full narrative accounts of Jesus' ministry for some 35–40 years after his death. Narrative Gospels began to be written after the year 70: the death of eyewitnesses, the loss of the Temple, and the increasing split between Jews and Gentile believers made it urgent to put the memory of Jesus into more stable form. Mark's Gospel was first, possibly *c.*70 CE. Matthew and Luke used Mark's account in composing their own fuller narratives, sometime around 85 CE, each using shared additional material (Q) and adding distinctive material of their own. Because of the close literary relationship among them, these three Gospels are called Synoptic (able to be viewed together). John's Gospel (*c.*90 CE) shares some material with the Synoptics, but shapes it in a strongly independent manner. The true identity of the evangelists is neither known nor is necessary for the competent reading of their narratives.

The Process of Canonization

The way the Church became Catholic (in the sense of "universal") and the way these early Christian writings became Scripture are part of a single process of canonization. The exchange of Paul's letters already during his lifetime, and the use of Mark's Gospel in composing their own by Matthew and Luke reveal a form of fellowship already in the first generations in which communities were bound by the reading of shared writings. And the more diverse communities read compositions other than those written directly for them, the more they grew conscious of being a "Church" (*ekklesia*) larger than the local assembly.

The first stages of the process were natural and organic. Compositions used community traditions and were read aloud at worship. When a letter of Paul or a Gospel was read together with compositions from the Old Testament in the liturgy, the new Christian writings quickly grew to share the authority of what had always been regarded as "Scripture." When communities exchanged compositions, they signaled that what was written for one community in the past had authority for another community in the present and future. Soon, communities began to have collections of apostolic writings: more than one Pauline letter, more than one Gospel. At the end of the first century, Clement of Rome writes a letter to the Corinthian Church in which he appropriates the language of 1 Corinthians, Hebrews, and James, as well as sayings of Jesus. At this stage of exchange and collection, however, there was no need for an authoritative list, for there was as yet no challenge to the traditional understanding of the faith.

That challenge arose in the mid-second century when powerful teachers began to argue for a contraction or expansion of the Christian collection, in line with a narrower or broader understanding of the Christian truth. On the side of contraction, the dualistic teachers Marcion and Tatian argued for a smaller collection. Marcion rejected the Old Testament and everything in the New Testament apart from 10 Letters of Paul and the Gospel of Luke in order to have a Christianity free from Jewish elements. Tatian removed the scandal of four distinct Gospels by composing the *Diatesseron* ("through the four"), a Gospel harmony drawn from Mark, Matthew, Luke, and John. On the side of expansion, various Gnostic teachers wrote revelatory literature that claimed authority equal to the traditional texts that offered a Christianity also free of the Jewish God and strongly dualistic and individualistic in character.

The battle over books was therefore a battle over Christian identity, and the conflict of the second century made it the period of real Christian self-definition. The orthodox side, led by Tertullian and above all by Irenaeus of Lyons, based their understanding of an embodied, historical, sacramental, and institutional Christianity on a three-fold strategy of identity. To the new ideologies of dualism, they offered the Rule of Faith (or Creed); to the interpretations of recent teachers, they responded with the succession of public leaders from the apostles to bishops; to arguments for expanding or contracting Scripture, they responded with a canon of Scripture made up of the Old Testament and the traditional compositions included in the New Testament. Although they established the concept of canon as an instrument of Catholic identity, there remained some small flexibility in the actual makeup of the collection: the four Gospels and the 13 Letters of Paul were always there, but some communities added or subtracted or had doubts about some others. It was in the fourth century that the present canon of 27 writings was definitively established.

Paradoxically, the canon of the New Testament, which served to draw a circle around a certain understanding of the Christian truth in the face of radical deviance, and thus was an instrument of Catholic unity, nevertheless maintained a collection of compositions that retained all the perspectival, literary, and thematic diversity of the earliest Christian communities. Thus, the Catholicity of the New Testament is far from imposing uniformity of practice or outlook; its Catholicity, rather, is one of a deep unity of experience and conviction that embraces and even enables a healthy diversity in practice and thought.

History of Interpretation

As part of Sacred Scripture, the New Testament has been read continuously and interpreted within the life of the Church. During the longest period of this history of reception – some 1,600 years – interpreters paid little attention to the diversity of compositional perspectives or even to the New Testament in isolation from the Old Testament. Scripture was read as a unity, with each word and statement interpreted in light of the whole collection rather than within the context of a single composition. Inspiration meant that the meaning intended by the divine author transcended the intention of the human author. Because God spoke through Scripture, its words could bear meanings at several levels beyond the historical or literal: the living word of God could speak to the life of the Church and the individual through allegory.

The study of Scripture was, moreover, conceived as an act of piety, with authority always assumed to lie with the text as God's word rather than with the reader's human reason: difficulties or contradictions in the text appeared as invitations to a deeper wisdom more than as reasons for rejection. Finally, interpreters regarded Scripture as harmonious in its teaching, in two ways: first, a generous reading could always show a deeper unity among conflicting statements in the text; and second, Scripture as a whole harmonized with the understanding and practice of the Church (Tradition).

In the East, such premises guided interpretation of the Greek Bible (LXX + NT); in the West, a variety of Latin translations was replaced in the late fourth century by

Jerome's Vulgate translation. The fact that Jerome chose to translate from the Hebrew Old Testament rather than the Septuagint was camouflaged by his close attention to the Greek in critical passages, and a brilliant rendering that allowed readers to continue to read the Bible as an apparently seamless whole. In both East and West, moreover, interpretation of the Bible took place within the context of the Church's life: in the liturgy of the Eucharist and the Divine Office, through sermons, letters, theological treatises, monastic rules, and spiritual meditations. Biblical interpretation was less a pursuit of *scientia* (science, knowledge) than an expression of *sapientia* (wisdom) in *lectio divina* ("divine reading"), and its characteristic mode was the contemplative pondering of the *sacra pagina* ("sacred page").

Although these same premises and practices were at work in the medieval Church, above all in monasteries and cathedral chapters, a significant sociological shift occurred with the development of the medieval university. Now, scholars interpreted the Bible within a part of a universal system of knowledge whose apex was theology in a curriculum of professional education. In this social context, interpretation necessarily became more pragmatic and scientific: the Bible was read not as a means for the transformation of life, but as a source of information supporting theological propositions. Despite a tilt away from *sapientia* and toward *scientia*, however, university scholars – themselves monks and friars – continued to read Scripture within the context of the life of the Church.

A distinctively "Catholic" mode of interpretation – in the sense of "Roman Catholic" – arose in response to the Protestant Reformation, which, especially in Martin Luther, fundamentally challenged the premises that had governed earlier readers. Luther's principle of *sola scriptura* drove a wedge between the Bible and tradition; his rejection of allegory meant that the Bible's meaning must be found only within the literal or historical sense; the authority of the individual reader (enabled by the invention of the printing press) challenged a communal and eventually even creedal framework for interpretation; the choice of the Greek text over the Latin Vulgate privileged the scholar over the pastor; and the principle of *sachkritik* (content criticism) paradoxically challenged the authority of the very text that Luther had declared as the sole norm for Christian identity: only some of the writings of the New Testament were considered to truly "show thee the Christ." Most of all, the Lutheran premise that the original form of Christianity (revealed in the New Testament) is the measure for all subsequent forms of Christianity implied that development was a form of decline.

In response to this challenge, Catholic interpreters maintained the earlier premises, but in the context of polemic, patterns of interpretation were unavoidably altered. Catholic theologians insisted on the validity of both Scripture and Tradition, for example, but Tradition increasingly became something like a distinct source of revelation rather than the context for reading Scripture. The practice of theological proof-texting, which had begun in the universities, now was applied to the hardened theological positions occupied by Catholics and Protestants. Protestants emphasized passages that supported righteousness by faith (Gal 2:16–20) and freedom in the spirit (Gal 5:1–26); Catholics emphasized texts that supported the seven sacraments (James 5:13–18), the Catholic understanding of the Eucharist (John 6:52–8) and the authority of Peter (Matt 16:17–19). The sharp ideological and institutional division within

Christianity led, on both sides, to a polemical and partial reading of both the Old and New Testaments.

The spirit of rationalism that arose in seventeenth- and eighteenth-century Europe challenged biblical interpretation in a more fundamental way. World exploration showed that world history could not fit within biblical history, Enlightenment philosophy asserted the supremacy of human reason over divine revelation. Science asserted as true only what is capable of empirical verification; for the present world, this meant truth was found in the natural sciences, and for the world of the past, this meant critical historiography. Biblical accounts might be regarded as meaningful, but if they were not historically verifiable they could not be considered true. The world-view that has come to be called Modernity set the frame for all biblical interpretation since the eighteenth century, whether Christians accepted its premises or rejected them.

Protestant biblical interpretation has been deeply divided in its response to modernity. For more liberal forms of Protestantism, the historical-critical approach to the New Testament developed in nineteenth-century Germany was regarded as an essential tool of continuing reformation: the historian alone could uncover the origins of Christianity, and thereby reveal its essence. The Bible, and above all the New Testament, was valuable primarily as a historical source, and served only secondarily as a theological norm. The discipline called "New Testament Theology," indeed, arose as an effort to bridge what was assumed to be a fundamental chasm between the text's historical meaning and its possible significance for the life of the Church. The supreme example of this approach was the "Quest for the Historical Jesus," which sought to displace the traditional Christological doctrines of the Church on the basis of a historical reconstruction of the person and ministry of Jesus. Other Protestants rejected the "higher criticism" in favor of interpreting the Bible within the framework of a set of "fundamentals" of faith, such as the inspiration and inerrancy of God's Word. The Modernist/Fundamentalist conflict continues to divide Protestantism.

Until the middle of the twentieth century, Roman Catholicism firmly resisted Modernity, including the historical-critical study of the Bible, but in 1943, Pius XII's *Divino Afflante Spiritu* opened the way for Catholic scholars to engage Scripture with the tools of modern criticism, including history. The legitimacy of such historical study was reaffirmed by the Second Vatican Council in its Constitution, *Dei Verbum* III, 12 and by the *Catechism of the Catholic Church* 110. Catholic scholars energetically and creatively joined with Protestant exegetes in the historical-critical study of the Old and New Testament. At the beginning of the twenty-first century, however, some Catholic Scripture scholars and theologians are asking whether enthusiasm for historical analysis – together with other ancillary forms of criticism – has not adversely affected some traditional and characteristically Catholic perceptions of Scripture.

No one doubts the great benefit given by history: the study of ancient language and literature, of social world and economics, of rhetoric and philosophy, has enabled contemporary Catholics to know more about the world of the Bible than any previous generation and therefore to be more competent and responsible readers. But an exclusive preoccupation with history can serve to keep the text simply in the past and diminish its prophetic potential. In a period that some designate as "Post-Modern," therefore, Catholic interpreters seek for ways to rejoin in creative ways the long and living conversation with Scripture within the Church, and to reconnect the world imagined by Scripture with the world that Catholics continue to construct through their experience of God and their practices of faith.

The New Testament as Historical Source

Written by participants in a rapidly expanding religious movement that began as a Jewish sect but quickly gained the majority of its adherents among Gentiles, the writings of the New Testament, considered simply as human literature, are of great importance to anyone seeking an understanding of earliest Christian history, practice, and belief. Historians and scholars of religion must recognize, however, that the circumstantial character of the literature provides at best fragmentary evidence on the matters of greatest concern to present-day historical inquiry.

The nature of the Gospels, for example, inhibits easy access to a full or satisfactory reconstruction of the historical ministry of Jesus of Nazareth. The Gospels are all written from the perspective of the resurrection experience, and the memories of Jesus included in the Gospels are both selected and shaped by the continuing experience of the risen Jesus in communities of faith. The faith perspective of the Gospels pervades the entire narrative; there is no neutral data-base within the tradition. The Synoptic Gospels of Matthew, Mark, and Luke, furthermore, offer only a single historical witness because of their close literary interdependence. But even within that literary relationship, they differ in the wording of Jesus' sayings, as well as in the selection, shaping, and placement of stories concerning him. John's Gospel, in turn, differs more markedly in its portrayal of Jesus' ministry, not only in such matters as its duration and location, but in its depiction of Jesus' characteristic deeds and manner of speech. The four passion accounts, which provide a circumstantial and connected narrative of Jesus' last hours, show more agreement than other parts of the Gospel narratives, but they still have notable differences among them. As for the accounts of Jesus' birth, they are absent in John and Mark, and are completely different in Luke and Matthew.

Nevertheless, through the convergence of the evidence found in the four Gospels, the other New Testament compositions (especially Paul's letters, which are the earliest datable sources speaking of Jesus), and the handful of Jewish and Greco-Roman observers, responsible historical judgments can be reached about the human Jesus. The critical assessment of these sources enables us to say that Jesus was a Jew in first-century Palestine, that he was crucified under the Roman Procurator Pontius Pilate, and that a movement arose in his name after his death. More than that, the historian can confidently assert concerning the broad patterns of Jesus' activity that he was an itinerant teacher and wonder-worker among the Jewish people of Palestine, that he proclaimed the rule of God, that he spoke in parables and interpreted Scripture, that he associated with the marginal elements of his society, and that he chose 12 followers. The historian can make strong claims for certain specific incidents (e.g. the baptism by John, the cleansing of the temple) and for certain ways of speaking (e.g. using "Son of Man" as a self-designation).

Such judgments are significant. They make clear that Christianity is not based in a fantasy but in a real human being with specific characteristics, that the incarnation is not God "becoming human" in general, but God entering the human story through a specific Jewish man of the first century. Such historical rooting also serves as a negative check on possible theological deviance: the New Testament would resist, for example, any suggestion that Jesus is a non-Jewish savior. But as valuable as these historical findings are, they are limited. To ignore the intrinsic limits imposed by the New Testament compositions and push further, toward a full "historical Jesus" capable of standing outside the witness and interpretation of the Gospels, has proven to be both illusory and destructive.

The same modesty is appropriate with respect to the history of the earliest Christian movement. On one hand, the compositions of the New Testament are the sole and invaluable sources for that history. On the other hand, they are incapable, because of their circumstantial character, of yielding anything near to a comprehensive portrayal of that movement. Certainly, they fall short of providing adequate information for a chronologically precise account of development within the New Testament period (c.30 and 100). The Acts of the Apostles – the second volume of Luke's Gospel – provides the only relative chronology for the first generation, and fragments of an absolute chronology for the movements of some leaders (James, Peter, and especially Paul) between 30 and 60. Acts certainly provides genuine historical evidence. But that evidence is selected and shaped by Luke's distinctive religious and literary purposes, and at best provides a partial view even of the events it narrates. Only Paul's movements between 34/37 and 60/64 can be traced with any confidence, and only five of his letters (Romans, 1 and 2 Thessalonians, 1 and 2 Corinthians) can be dated with a fair degree of probability, leaving eight others open to dispute. And once we step outside the framework of Paul's ministry, the possibilities for a coherent historical narrative of Christian beginnings are even more limited. All the other writings of the New Testament, including the Gospels (and Acts itself!) fall outside that framework and can therefore be dated and located only through guesswork. It is not possible even to do a full "history of New Testament literature," much less a full history of the New Testament Church based on that literature.

As in the case of the Gospels, however, Acts and the Letters do contain good historical evidence for some broad patterns of early Christian mission and life. Converging evidence supports the conclusions that Christians organized themselves from the start in intentional communities (ekklesiai) in the large urban centers of the empire, that they had leadership roles both of a transient (apostles and prophets) and local (bishops, elders and deacons) character. The movement did not enjoy great success among Jews but drew its adherents from among Gentiles who had associated themselves with the Diaspora synagogue. For the most part, communities met in households, and this social setting, with its stratified structure, generated some tensions with the egalitarian impulses of the baptized (see Gal 3:28). Local Churches practiced baptism and the Lord's Supper. Explicit evidence for other sacramental activity, apart from the anointing of the sick, is scarce. Worship involved the reading of Scripture, hymns, confessional statements, prayer, preaching, and, in some places, speaking in tongues, the interpretation of tongues, and prophecy. The working of powerful deeds (such as healings) attested spiritual authority (see 2 Cor 12:12). And teaching, which probably included the transmission of the sayings of Jesus, took place in a variety of contexts.

The New Testament also bears witness to a variety of conflicts experienced by early communities: from the outside, rejection and persecution (probably of a local character); and within, a variety of disputes concerning authority and behavior. Christians with quite different cultural backgrounds in Hellenism and Judaism needed to negotiate the manner in which the resurrection life should be expressed in such quotidian matters as food, work, and sex, especially how much the Jewish Law should be normative for such decisions. The impression of conflict everywhere is probably due to some extent to the fact that the New Testament compositions were occasional and written precisely to address situations that were sometimes critical. Equally important is the way the New Testament witnesses to the celebration of diversity within communities (see 1 Cor 12–14; Rom 14), and the signs of a commitment to fellowship (*koinonia*) expressed through shared conviction and practice within and among communities. The impulse toward a sense of Church larger than the local assembly is attested already within the New Testament (see especially Romans, Colossians, and Ephesians).

In addition to providing historical evidence concerning Jesus and the early Church, the New Testament is also an invaluable source for the history of Judaism and Greco-Roman culture in the first century. It is appropriate to study the larger cultural matrix in order to be better readers of the New Testament. But it is also the case that the New Testament provides some of the earliest datable evidence concerning the character of Judaism both in Palestine and in the Diaspora in the first century, and is as well our best first-hand evidence for a successful foreign mystery cult and philosophical community within the early empire.

New Testament as Religious and Theological Witness

The New Testament provides evidence for historical reconstructions of Jesus or early Christianity only indirectly. It witnesses directly and powerfully to religious experiences and convictions, and provides models for theological reflection on those experiences and convictions. Certainly, this aspect of the New Testament is also of historical interest and importance, since its witness on these matters is also shaped by its ancient context. Yet two considerations make the religious and theological witness of the New Testament of particular importance to the present-day Church.

The first is that the experiences and convictions concerning Jesus Christ found in the New Testament are true also in the present for those who live within the same community of faith as those who wrote the New Testament. Believers consider the resurrection of Jesus to be as powerfully true in their own lives as it was in Peter's or Paul's. It is not simply that Paul thought he was living in a "new creation" (2 Cor 5:17), it is that present-day believers think (or ought to think) that they are also in a "new creation." When the New Testament speaks, therefore, of Jesus as Lord, or of the Holy Spirit dwelling within us, or of the Living God who raised Jesus from the dead, it is speaking the truth about the religious experiences and convictions of the Church. The second is that the New Testament is read in the Church as the inspired Word of God. It is therefore prophetic to every age of the Church, and normative for every realization of the Church through the ages. Believers are able to discern their experiences and convictions as the work of God through the lens provided by these texts.

When the Gospels are read in the Church, consequently, the very resurrection perspective that makes them problematic for the historian makes them most true to believers, who read, not so much for information about a man in the past as for insight into how the risen Lord works in the present. The miracles worked by Jesus in the Gospels do not offend the scientific sensibilities of the believer, who knows that by the name of Jesus people are being freed from unclean spirits and brought to health within the community of faith. Similarly, believers are not shocked by the differences in the four Gospels. They know that the reality of Jesus Christ cannot be contained within a single portrayal, and that the four Gospels witness to the same reality through their four distinct literary portrayals, just as the wonderfully diverse communion of saints all bear witness to the one Lord whose pattern of life they have embodied.

Believers recognize that the four Gospels converge most fully, not on the historical details concerning Jesus – details that in any case remain in the past – but in his human character. In all the Gospels, Jesus is portrayed as one totally and radically committed to God's will, and as one who expresses his faithful obedience to God through the deepest self-donation to others. Within the life of the Church, shaped by the celebration of the Eucharist and instructed by the lives of the saints, believers recognize in the character of Jesus as portrayed in the Gospels, the same "mind of Christ" described in the New Testament Letters. Indeed, everywhere in the New Testament, Jesus is at once the risen and powerful Lord, and the human being whose life of obedience and love defines the shape of discipleship for his followers. They understand, then, that the work of the Holy Spirit is to replicate in their own freedom the pattern of faith and love found in Christ.

Similarly, when the letters are read within the life of the Church, they are read not simply as ancient correspondence but as letters written by the Spirit to the Church in every age. Believers understand through the reading of these letters that they have been baptized into the death of Christ so that, just as Jesus was raised to new life, so are they to walk in a new and higher form of existence, through the power of the Holy Spirit at work in them (Rom 6:1–8:39). They learn that this power is not for their self-aggrandizement, but enables them to serve the needs of others and fulfill "the law of Christ" (Gal 6:2), just as they follow Jesus on the path of faith and learn obedience from the things they suffer (Heb 5:7–10; 12:1–3). They come to understand that, just as Jesus had to suffer and then enter into his glory (Luke 24:26), so their present sufferings prepare them for a share in God's presence (Rom 8:18; 2 Cor 4:17–18), so that their mortal life is a pilgrimage toward their true homeland (Heb 11:14–16; 12:18–24).

The process by which the New Testament was composed and canonized, together with the practice of its liturgical reading, suggest that the Church as Church is the intended and appropriate reader of the New Testament. It is the Church as such that is to cultivate "the mind of Christ" in each of its members so that they reciprocally look to the common more than the private good (Phil 2:1–5); it is the Church that is to be the temple of the living God that exemplifies holiness of life (1 Cor 3:16–17; 6:19); it is the Church that is to be the "Body of Christ" in which every member exercises spiritual gifts for the building up of the community (1 Cor 12–14). It is the Church that, as a place of reconciliation, is to be the sign of God's work in the world and the sacrament of the world's possibility (Eph 2:1–22; 3:10). This does not mean that the New Testament, together with the Old Testament, cannot be read for individual edification and transformation, but the most direct and powerful witness of the New Testament is to the common life of believers.

In addition to bearing witness to the religious experiences and convictions that structure and enliven the life of the Church, the New Testament also provides models of how the Church can think theologically. The phrase "to think theologically," means something more than "to collect theological propositions." The New Testament does contain a rich body of theological propositions that have been profitably studied and employed within theological and moral discussions and debates throughout the ages. Such propositions concerning Father, Son, and Holy Spirit have been of critical importance in developing the Creed as an instrument of Christian self-definition. But "thinking theologically" suggests a process rather than a product, a process that is demanded of the Church precisely because of the experiences and convictions that it claims to be true.

Four of these convictions form the premises of theology within the Church. The first is that ours is a living God, whose creative activity moves ahead human capacity to understand or control; the living God who is Spirit, furthermore, seeks expression through body. The second is that God's Holy Spirit works prophetically, that is, through humans, whose words and actions form a word from God to humans in embodied form. The third is that the living God acts in unexpected, surprising, and even shocking ways. That the Messiah should suffer the shameful death of crucifixion is the greatest example, but there are others: that Gentiles are to be part of God's people without first becoming Jews, and that a pharisaic persecutor of the Church who would not eat with Gentiles is to become the instrument through which Gentiles are to be invited into the people of God. The fourth conviction is that those touched by the power of the living God must seek to understand these experiences through the rereading of the Scripture. The manner in which the New Testament came into being in the first place is to be the model for theology within the Church. That these four premises are not arbitrary is shown through the narrative of Acts 10–15, which shows the process by which the Church in the first generation responded to the experience of God's initiative and, through difficult debate and discernment, came to recognize that the responsibility of the Church is precisely to respond, not to its own precedents, but to God's will.

Interpreting the New Testament in the Church

Interpretation in the proper sense means more than determining historical facts or ancient opinions; it means engaging the New Testament as Scripture, God's word to the Church. Such interpretation involves a complex and delicate conversation that is never completely closed, that remains faithful both to the texts of Scripture and the texts of human lives in which God continues to work, and that respects the embodied and historical character of the Church's tradition. Because God's work in creation never ceases, and because human experience constantly changes, there is always need for interpretation. Because God's Holy Spirit is at work both in the texts of the New Testament and in human lives, the interpretive conversation is both delicate and complex. The voices of Scripture and the voices of human experience are mutually interpretive and responsible interpretation demands being responsible to both.

For Catholics this complex conversation takes place within a tradition that is historical and institutionally embodied. The instruments of tradition include the canon of Scripture, the Creed, and the teaching office of the bishops. The ultimate responsibility for authoritative interpretation lies with the bishops (*Dei Verbum* X, 2), whose charism is to guide the Church faithfully through time. These instruments all work to protect from deviance or corruption "the deposit of faith" (1 Tim 6:20) that comes from the apostles. The interpretation of Scripture is therefore in the fullest sense ecclesial; it is not a matter of individual choice or taste.

At the same time, since God continues to speak through saints and prophets within the Church, and continues to act within the lives of humans both inside and outside the visible community of faith, interpretation must also pay the closest attention to other charisms within the Church that serve to interpret Scripture. The Second Vatican Council declares,

> Catholic exegetes then and other students of sacred theology, working diligently together and using appropriate means, should devote their energies, under the watchful care of the teaching office of the Church, to an exploration and exposition of the divine writings. This task should be done in such a way that as many ministers of the divine word as possible will be able effectively to provide the nourishment of the Scriptures for the People of God, thereby enlightening their minds, and setting men's hearts on fire with the love of God" (*Dei Verbum* VI, 23).

A proper balance of charisms in the Church is one in which the official teaching office works to protect the integrity of the tradition while biblical scholars and theologians work to energize the prophetic power of the word.

Catholic interpretation of Scripture therefore locates authority in several places, thus enabling a dialogical or conversational form of interpretation. Authority is vested in the official teaching office of the Church, to be sure, but bishops cannot be arbitrary in the exercise of that authority. They must be responsive to tradition. And since tradition in the fullest sense is a living process, this means that the official teaching office responds as well to the saints and prophets in every age through whom God challenges the hierarchy's natural tendency toward inertia.

All contemporary voices in the Church must respond, furthermore, to the authority of the Scriptural texts, which resist, when read faithfully, the rigid control of readers. The textual authority of the New Testament, in turn, can be described in three ways. First, the New Testament *authors* Christian identity. This is why it is read aloud to the assembly. The New Testament, read as a whole, shapes its readers into the authentic "mind of Christ." It is at this level that the New Testament can be said to be truly inerrant, for through the power of the Holy Spirit, it unfailingly creates humans in the image of Christ. Second, the New Testament also *authorizes* its own reinterpretation in light of the experience of God in human lives. Third, the New Testament presents readers in every age with a set of *authorities* on a range of specific issues having to do with discipleship. It does not speak to every issue, nor does it, at this level, speak with one voice. And this is a gift, for it enables Christians in different circumstances to find guidance in places where others have not.

In seeking to respond faithfully to the call of God in concrete circumstances, therefore, Catholics first seek to discern how God is calling the Church to decision, because of the work of sin or grace in human lives, as human experience rises to the level of ecclesial discernment. Then Catholics discern among the diverse authorities in the text of the New (and Old) Testament those that best speak God's Word in the here and now. They are authorized to do this by the example of the New Testament and by the practice of the Church in every age (even when not always explicitly acknowledged). The measure for determining the authentic Word must be "the mind of Christ" that leads to a form of discipleship in the image of the one who radically obeyed God his Father and freely gave his life as ransom for others. Finally, Catholics pay close attention to the official teaching office of the Church as it speaks to contemporary circumstances on the basis of Scripture. This is indeed a complex and delicate conversation. It is not always neat. Time and suffering are sometimes required for the Church – an ancient and cumbersome institution – to respond faithfully to God. But when it does, it is most closely in harmony with the writings of the New Testament, which witness in every page to the need to answer, with deep faith and generous love, the God who calls.

References and Further Reading

Brown, R.E. (1981) *The Critical Meaning of the Bible.* New York: Paulist Press.
Brown, R.E. (1997) *An Introduction to the New Testament.* New York: Doubleday.
Danielou, J. (1960) *From Shadow to Reality: Studies in the Biblical Typology of the Fathers,* trans. W. Hibberd. London: Burns and Oates.
Grant, R.M. and Tracy, D. (1984) *A Short History of the Interpretation of the Bible,* 2nd edition. Philadelphia, PA: Fortress Press.
Johnson, L.T. (1996) *Scripture and Discernment: Decision Making in the Church.* Nashville, TN: Abingdon Press.
Johnson, L.T. (1999) *The Writings of the New Testament: An Interpretation.* 2nd revised and enlarged edition, with the assistance of Todd Penner. Minneapolis, MN: Fortress Press.
Johnson, L.T. and Kurz SJ, W.S. (2004) *The Future of Catholic Biblical Scholarship: A Constructive Conversation.* Grand Rapids, MI: W.B. Eerdmans.
Lubac, H. de (1998) *Medieval Exegesis: The Four Senses of Scripture.* 2 volumes, trans. S. Sebanc and E.M. Macieroski. Grand Rapids, MI: W.B. Eerdmans.
MacDonald, L.M. (1995) *The Formation of the Christian Canon.* Revised edition. Peabody, MA: Hendrickson Publishers.
O'Collins SJ, G. and Kendall SJ, D. (1997) *The Bible for Theology: Ten Principles for the Theological Use of Scripture.* New York: Paulist Press.

CHAPTER 3
The Early Church

Angela Russell Christman

An introductory essay on early Christianity raises, at least implicitly, the question of why the history of the Church is important. While historians may offer a variety of answers to the more general question, "Why study history?," for Christians there is a fundamental reason for understanding and engaging the Church's history: Christianity is a thoroughly historical religion, one that rests on specific claims about the past. That is, Christians confess that in first-century Palestine, in the person Jesus Christ, God was reconciling himself to the world (cf. 2 Cor 5:18–19). The events of Jesus' life, Christians believe, but especially his passion, death, and resurrection, are decisive for human history. Moreover, many Christians, and in particular Roman Catholics, affirm that the proper understanding of Christ has been handed down, indeed safeguarded, by the Church. Because the Church's faith is grounded in these historical claims, a vigorous Christian identity cannot flourish without cultivating memory of the past. Further, the era of the early Church – usually considered to be the period extending from the early second century to the end of the fifth – is of particular interest to Christians in the twenty-first century. During this time many of the most fundamental Christian beliefs were hammered out, and likewise many basic Christian practices took root. Moreover, although early Christians composed their essays and treatises not on a computer but on a codex, their world was in many respects similar to ours, for the Roman Empire was thoroughly multi-cultural and often hostile to their beliefs and practices.

Although we possess a few writings from Christian women of this period, most of the literary works we have were written by men, who are often referred to as the Church Fathers. (Thus, this era is also known as the patristic period, from the Latin word for "father," *pater*.) Further, most of the patristic texts that have survived were written in either Greek or Latin, although there are a number of significant works in other ancient languages, such as Syriac and Coptic. An introductory essay such as this, covering more than 400 years, during which both Christianity and the Greco-Roman world undergo significant changes, cannot treat or even mention every important development. Thus, I have focused on those aspects of early Christianity which have been of enduring significance for Catholic life and thought. Of course, there is no substitute for

the actual words of the Fathers, so the primary purpose of this essay is to invite and encourage readers to turn to the Fathers themselves.[1]

Although Christianity began as a small movement within Judaism in the first half of the first century, within decades of Jesus' crucifixion and resurrection it was spreading throughout the Mediterranean world, and by the end of the fourth century, it was the official religion of the Roman Empire. Initially Christianity seems to have been primarily an urban movement, and in various cities Christians met for worship in private homes or "house churches." In the first three centuries, Christians were viewed by those outside the Church as members of a perverse cult who were hostile to their fellow human beings. Because they refused to worship the Greco-Roman deities they were deemed to be atheists and political subversives, since the gods were viewed as protectors of the state. As a result, Christians found themselves persecuted, sometimes simply for the crime of bearing the name "Christian" (cf. 1 Peter 4:14–16), and at others for despising the traditional Greco-Roman gods and refusing to sacrifice to them. While persecution was most often focused on Church leaders (e.g., the martyrdoms of Peter and Paul in Rome during the reign of Nero, and of Ignatius of Antioch in the early second century), it was not limited to them. Nor did it discriminate on the basis of gender: perhaps the most famous account of martyrdom is the *Passion of Perpetua and Felicity*. Both young women – the former from a well-to-do Roman family, the latter a slave – were catechumens preparing for baptism. However, only sporadically was there systematic persecution throughout a region or across the entire empire, so its severity should not be overestimated. Although there was significant and widespread persecution in the late second century, in the mid-third century, and at the beginning of the fourth century under the emperor Diocletian, it is likely that the total number of Christians martyred during this period was fewer than 1,000. (For a fascinating sociological analysis of how martyrdom, as well as various other factors such as the urban character of Christianity and the role of women, contributed to Christianity's rapid growth, see Stark, 1996.) Despite Christianity's status as a persecuted minority, it was not an underground movement, and from as early as the second century we have writings – such as Justin Martyr's *First Apology*, a work addressed to the emperor – which openly offer a defense of Christianity to its pagan critics. Justin and other apologists like him responded to the charges of atheism and anarchy as well as to other accusations such as cannibalism and ritual murder which were clearly based upon outsiders' misunderstanding of rituals such as the Eucharist.

Christians answered the objections not only of pagans, but also of Jews. The historical sources suggest that the relationship between Christianity and Judaism was particularly complex. Despite having suffered the destruction of the Temple (c.70 CE) and the defeat of the Bar Kochba revolt (132–5 CE), both at the hands of the Romans, Rabbinic Judaism presented Christianity with a vibrant and challenging partner in debate. Jews and Christians obviously disagreed on how the prophecies of the Jewish Scriptures (the Christian Old Testament) were to be interpreted, since Christians claimed that they were fulfilled in Christ and the Church. In such disputes Christians were at a disadvantage because, with few exceptions, they did not read the prophetic passages in the original language (i.e., Hebrew), but rather in translations into Greek (known as the Septuagint) and Latin (the Old Latin or later, the Vulgate). Few

Christians had the ability to consult the Hebrew text, and those who did were usually dependent on their Jewish neighbors for development of their linguistic skills. (In the early Church, Jerome had the greatest command of Hebrew, having devoted years to its study. He was tutored initially by a Jewish convert to Christianity and later by Jewish friends willing to risk the anger of their co-religionists.) Even as Jews and Christians argued about the correct interpretation of the Scriptures, the ancient traditions and language of Judaism possessed a definite allure for some Christians, particularly in cities such as Antioch (modern day Antakya in southern Turkey) with large, well-established Jewish communities. In writings from the third and fourth centuries, Christian preachers repeatedly express disapproval of members of their congregations who attend synagogue on the Sabbath and participate in Jewish festivals and rituals (see Wilken, 1983 and Simon, 1986).

The complexity of the relationships of Christianity with both Judaism and Greco-Roman religion can be illustrated by the example of Celsus, a second-century pagan critic of Christianity. Celsus stands out for his time because his criticisms, unlike those of others, are based not on rumor and hearsay – he does not repeat accusations of cannibalism, for example – but on his own careful study of Christianity, and particularly its sacred writings. The leading Christian theologian of the third century, Origen, later responded to him, and his apologetic work *Contra Celsum* (*Against Celsus*) preserves at least some of Celsus' charges against Christianity. Although much of Celsus' disapproval is articulated from a pagan philosophical perspective, he was perceptive enough to realize that some of the most cogent censures of Christianity could only be leveled by a Jew. Not surprisingly, then, Celsus places a number of his condemnations on the lips of a Jew who, for example, charges Jewish Christians with apostasy for abandoning the observance of the Torah (i.e., the Law). Celsus' strategy would only have been strengthened by the Greco-Roman view that the older an institution, the greater its authority. Although pagans disliked many aspects of Judaism (e.g., its rituals, including circumcision), they admired it for its ethical mores and granted it a certain respect because of its antiquity. By contrast, Christianity was a novel religion which while claiming to adhere to the Bible of the Jews, rejected the observance of Torah.

While *Contra Celsum* is filled with polemic, it would be a mistake to think that the attitude of Origen and other Church Fathers toward classical culture was only hostile. Tertullian's famous quip "What has Athens to do with Jerusalem?" notwithstanding, early Christian writers did not shy away from drawing on Greco-Roman culture and philosophy when it was consistent with the Gospel. Thus, for example, Origen draws attention to such points of contact, noting that Christian doctrines are "in complete accord with the universal notions" subscribed to by reasonable people (*Contra Celsum* 3.40).[2] The Fathers take such a fearless stance with regard to classical thought because of their conviction that wherever truth is found, it is God's. Moreover, the standard of truth is the Gospel, and thus it stands in judgment of Greco-Roman culture and philosophy, not vice versa, for as Origen writes, "the Gospel has a proof which is peculiar to itself, and which is more divine than a Greek proof based on dialectical argument" (*Contra Celsum* 3.40). A similarly confident attitude toward classical culture is seen in Gregory of Nyssa's interpretation of the despoiling of the Egyptians (Exod 12:35–6) in *The Life of Moses*. This passage, Gregory explains, commands Christians to equip themselves with the wealth of pagan learning by which foreigners to the faith beautify themselves. Our guide in virtue commands someone who "borrows" from wealthy Egyptians to receive such things as moral and natural philosophy . . . and whatever else is sought by those outside the Church, since these things will be useful when in time the divine sanctuary of mystery must be beautified with the riches of reason. (2.115; 1978)

Just as the Israelites, at Moses' command, took the gold and silver of the Egyptians as they departed and eventually used it to decorate the Ark of the Covenant, so too Christians ought to take the riches of classical culture and place them at the service of the Gospel. Of course, the gold for decorating the Ark could also be used to fashion the golden calf, a fact which underscores the importance of purifying Egyptian gold through the transforming power of the Gospel. Nonetheless, the comments of both Gregory and Origen suggest that they not only discerned a fundamental compatibility between faith and reason but also were possessed by a confidence that faith brings reason to fulfillment.

In their encounters and debates with Jews and pagans, Christians were establishing boundaries, however permeable these may have been at times. Within the Church, a similar process of self-definition was also at work. The early Church was varied and complex, and as Christians reflected on the implications of their belief in Christ, it was perhaps inevitable that disagreements in doctrine (i.e., Church teaching) would arise. Almost from the beginning, but especially in the second and third centuries, orthodox Christians found themselves in conflict with other Christian groups known as Gnostics. Although there were a number of Gnostic sects, their belief systems shared the same basic contours. They claimed that the god depicted in the Jewish Scriptures, the creator, was not the one whom Jesus addressed as Father, but rather a lesser deity. This lesser god was responsible for creation of the physical world which Gnostics generally viewed as evil. Rejecting the authority of the Old Testament, the Gnostics claimed that salvation could only be attained if one were an initiate into their secret and arcane tradition, that is, if one possessed their special *gnosis* (the Greek word for "knowledge"). Against these groups, Irenaeus of Lyons and others like him appealed to the Scriptures to demonstrate that the God who created the heavens and the earth was the same one whom Jesus called Father. In other words, the Old and New Testaments form a unified book. Moreover, Irenaeus asserts, Jesus' true teachings are to be found in the tradition handed down openly by the apostles to their successors, not in the secret beliefs and practices of the Gnostics. (See chapter 17, The Development of Doctrine.)

Such conflicts with the Gnostics were only the beginning. From the very first, Christians had confessed Jesus as "Lord" (*kyrios*, the Greek word which had been used in the Septuagint to translate God's holiest name, the tetragrammaton of the Hebrew Bible) and baptized in the name of Father, Son, and Holy Spirit. How were such claims and liturgical actions to be reconciled with belief in the oneness of God? That is, if God is truly one, how can Christians say that God is also Father, Son, and Holy Spirit, without becoming tritheists? Such issues exercised the minds of theologians throughout the fourth century. As a result of these theological debates, the Council of Nicea (325 CE) affirmed that the Son – the second person of the Trinity, the *Logos* – was of the same essence (*ousia*) as the Father, and at the Council of Constantinople (381 CE), the Spirit's full divinity was recognized. But the definitions set out by Nicea and Constantinople (which Christians proclaim to this day in what is known as the Nicene Creed) inevitably led to other questions. For example, what is the relationship between the human and divine in the person Jesus Christ? This and related issues were the focus of the Councils of Ephesus (431 CE) and Chalcedon (451 CE). (For a fuller discussion of these theological debates, see chapter 20, Jesus Christ and chapter 18, God.) While Christians in our day are sometimes incredulous at the amount of time and energy expended on such questions, it is crucial to realize that the Fathers did not devote themselves to intricate theological and philosophical discussion as an end in itself. Rather, they sought to safeguard, to understand more deeply, and hence to confess more fully, the truth of the salvation wrought by Christ. Indeed, the answers to such questions had (and still have) concrete implications for Christian life and practice, and we can marvel at the Fathers' tenacity in these struggles at least in part because we sometimes too casually take for granted their results.

While the fourth century was filled with theological debate, it also saw the end of persecution and the rise of both monasticism and pilgrimage. The threat of persecution ceased after Constantine, in 313 CE, declared freedom of worship for Christians. Constantine had become emperor in 312 after defeating his rival Maxentius, and according to the report of Eusebius of Caesarea, he attributed his victory to the Christian God after having had a vision of the Chi-Rho (the first two letters of "Christ" in Greek) on the eve of battle. Nonetheless, Constantine was not baptized until his deathbed (337 CE), and as a result historians have long questioned the sincerity of and motivation behind his conversion. There is no question, however, that he patronized the Church through his building programs. In late antiquity, emperors were expected to display their power through construction of grand buildings. Constantine was no exception, erecting a number of impressive, even ostentatious, public buildings, as well as the triumphal arch (the Arch of Constantine) that still stands in Rome next to the Colosseum. But he also built churches. The sensitive political situation in Rome prevented these from being built in the heart of the city, the domain of traditional Greco-Roman religion. Thus Constantine constructed churches initially only on his own property and with his own funds, and near the outskirts of the city. Eventually, frustrated, he would leave Rome and found a new capital in Constantinople (modern-day Istanbul), but not without having set in motion forces that would in time transform Rome's topography. (For a thorough discussion of these issues, see Krautheimer, 1983.)

Although monasticism and pilgrimage have their roots in earlier centuries, in the fourth century they flourished. In *The Life of Antony*, Athanasius tells us how the young Antony of Egypt (*c*.251–356), in church one day when he was barely 20 years old, heard the words of Jesus: "If you would be perfect, go, sell what you possess and give to the poor, and you will have treasure in heaven" (Matt 19:21). Taking these words as addressed to himself, Antony immediately gave all his possessions to the poor and committed himself to the ascetic life, a life of rigorous, often solitary, self-denial and prayer. Initially remaining on the outskirts of his small hometown, Antony soon ventured deep into the Egyptian desert to pursue the solitary life. For almost two decades he had little contact with others, though eventually he began to offer spiritual counsel and perform healings for those who came to see him. So many were persuaded to take up the ascetic life themselves, Athanasius tells us, that the once-empty desert "was made a city by monks" (1980: 14). (The word "monk" is from the Greek *monachos*, "solitary.") Literature from this period testifies to remarkable feats performed by both men and women: some ascetics practiced extreme fasting and limited their sleep, others wore iron chains, and still others lived atop pillars for years. Although such practices seem odd to us, Theodoret, bishop of Cyrrhus in the fifth century, remarks that these "athletes of virtue" as he called them were motivated by nothing other than the love of God:

> [I]t is clearly desire for God that has made [these ascetics] surpass the limits of nature ... It is this desire that nourishes, waters, and clothes them, gives wings and teaches to fly, makes them transcend the heavens, reveals the Beloved in so far as it is possible, and through imagination inflames yearning for contemplation, stirs up longing for it, and kindles the flame more fiercely. (1985, Epilogue: on Divine Love, 4)

Not all monks, however, were solitaries capable of incredible feats; not all who were drawn to the monastic life could endure the rigors of Antony's solitary regime. Beginning in the early fourth century, coenobitic (i.e., communal) monasticism was on the rise: Pachomius founded a monastery in Egypt, and others appeared throughout the Mediterranean world. By the sixth century, when Benedict of Nursia composed his "little rule for beginners" for the community he had established at Monte Cassino *c.*529, coenobitic monasticism had become the dominant form of ascetic practice.

The story of Antony and other ascetics captivated many, and Christians flocked to the desert to witness first-hand the dedication and commitment of these solitary men and women. But by the fourth century, Christians were traveling great distances to see not only holy people, but also holy places, that is, where Jesus had been born, where he lived, died, and was raised from the dead. A century before, Origen had insisted that the actual physical land of Israel and the particular city Jerusalem were of little theological significance for Christians. The New Testament, he pointed out, spoke of the "Jerusalem above" (Gal 4:26) and "the heavenly Jerusalem" (Heb 12:22), with both phrases clearly referring to a spiritual reality. Origen's biblical interpretation notwithstanding, early Christians developed ever greater interest in seeing the places where the awe-inspiring events of salvation history had occurred. The appeal of pilgrimage was only increased by Constantine's ambitious church building program which was not limited to Rome and Constantinople but also focused on the Holy Land. After erecting a church in Jerusalem over the site of Christ's tomb (the Church of the Anastasis), Constantine had built churches on the Mount of Olives (the site of the Ascension) as well as in Bethlehem. Toward the end of the fourth century, a Spanish nun, Egeria, went on a pilgrimage that took her to a host of holy sites, from Mt Sinai to Jerusalem, where she arrived in time to celebrate Holy Week. Her diary is a precious witness not only to the developing sacramental notion of place, but also to the liturgies celebrated at the holy places from Palm Sunday to Easter. But perhaps the most significant aspect of the rise of pilgrimage is what it suggests about the Christian understanding of the

Incarnation and human memory. Although the Church Fathers never ceased to insist that God is not confined to any one location, they also recognized the implications of the historical reality of the Incarnation: in Christ, God had dwelt in a particular place, thereby hallowing it. Seeing the location of momentous episodes in the Bible or the lives of the saints provides fertile soil for a robust Christian memory, the memory so necessary to support the claim that God has acted definitively in human history.

Scholars debate whether Constantine's patronage of Christianity caused a wave of increased conversions or whether it was instead the new emperor's prudent response to the Church's exponential growth. Even if we cannot know the answer to this question, by the end of the fourth century Christianity was well on its way to becoming the dominant religion in the Mediterranean world. However, Constantine's patronage of the Church as well as its growing appeal should not be taken to suggest (as they sometimes are) that relations between the Church and the State were entirely smooth during the fourth century. Constantine had called the Council of Nicea, largely out of concern for political unity and stability, but although the Council decided against Arius, in his later years Constantine tended toward the Arian position, receiving baptism shortly before his death from Eusebius of Nicomedia, a bishop with Arian sympathies. Although two of the sons of Constantine were Nicenes, his middle son, who reigned the longest, adhered to Arianism, as did a later emperor, Valens (d. 378), and on more than one occasion, Nicene bishops found themselves in conflict with these rulers. They would have faced many more struggles had not Julian the Apostate (the sole fourth-century emperor baptized as a child, only to convert to paganism later) died in battle after being on the throne only two years (361–3 CE). But Church leaders also found themselves in disputes with emperors who supported Nicene Christianity, as Ambrose did with Theodosius, whose edict of 380 established Nicene Christianity as the official religion of the empire. In 390, Theodosius had ordered a massacre of the people of Thessalonica as punishment for the murder of one of his generals in a riot in that city. In response, Ambrose excommunicated him, and he was not readmitted to the Eucharist until after he performed public penance months later.

Although this incident perhaps illustrates the Church's growing authority, many people still adhered to paganism and Christianity was not without critics, both inside and outside the Church. After the sack of Rome by Alaric and the Goths in August 410, the empire seemed more vulnerable, its boundaries less secure. At least some pagans blamed the new religion for this state of affairs, and there appear to have been Christians who shared their view. To respond to such criticisms, Augustine of Hippo wrote *The City of God*. A native of North Africa, Augustine had received baptism from Ambrose of Milan in 387. Returning home shortly thereafter, he was soon coerced into ordination to the priesthood, and then some five years later found himself bishop of Hippo (in what is now Algeria). *The City of God*, his longest work, is both a critique of paganism (the first 10 books) and a defense of Christianity (the remaining 12 books), and so comprehensive and wide-ranging as to resist easy summary. At its heart, however, is an understanding of the Church and the political state which undermines any facile identification of the two. Two (mystical) cities exist side-by-side in the present realm, Augustine explains, and each is defined by what it loves. The "earthly city" and its inhabitants are characterized by "self-love reaching the point of contempt for God," while the "heavenly city" (i.e., the city of God) and its citizens exemplify "the love of God carried as far as contempt of self" (1972: 14.28).

While *The City of God* treats theological questions on a grand scale, another of Augustine's masterpieces approaches them from an intensely personal perspective. *The Confessions*, a mixture of autobiography, prayer, and theological and philosophical reflection, was composed near the end of the fourth century and remains to this day an engaging narrative. Scholars speculate as to Augustine's motivations for producing this work which describes his conversion to the Catholic faith after a lengthy affiliation with the Manichees, a heretical Christian sect with certain affinities to Gnosticism. Some suggest that he penned *Confessions* to counter accusations that he remained a crypto-Manichee, for at the time of its writing, he was embroiled in conflict with the Donatists, a schismatic group in North Africa, who may have been trying to cast doubt on the authenticity of his conversion. The Donatists had separated from the Catholic Church in the early fourth century over the issue of clergy who had betrayed the faith in the face of persecution, and they maintained the rigorist position that sacraments celebrated by such clergy were invalid. Their ecclesiology (i.e., understanding of the Church) was thus one which emphasized the radical separation between the Church and the world. Against this, Augustine argued that in this age there was no clear line dividing Church and world, the holy and the sinful. Rather, the Church is a mixture of wheat and chaff, good and bad Christians, and the judgment as to which is which rests with God.

Even if we cannot be certain whether the Donatist controversy prompted Augustine to write his autobiography, it is clear that the understanding of divine grace and human fallenness articulated in *Confessions* placed him in the center of another major theological controversy, this time with the British monk Pelagius. In a number of other works but perhaps most vividly in *Confessions*, Augustine describes human beings as helpless not merely to carry out, but even to will, good and righteous actions without divine assistance. Thus in *Confessions* Augustine would say to God, "Grant what you command, and command what you will" (10.29.40). When quoted to Pelagius, these words roused his ire, for they seemed an invitation to moral laxity and passivity. The natural power for moral good, according to Pelagius, had survived the Fall. If it had not, human nature would cease to exist as such. Moreover, if human beings were powerless not to sin, this would mean that God condemned them for what they could not possibly avoid. Pelagius did not deny that God granted assistance to humans: the commandments, for example, were a gift that taught the virtuous life. However, for Pelagius, even after the Fall the will was capable of freely choosing the good, and divine gifts such as the commandments and the example of Christ merely facilitated that choice.

Against this position, Augustine argued that through the sin of Adam and Eve, human nature, although initially created good, was corrupted and our desires became so disordered that we lost the power to resist sin. Any good, willing, and righteous acts on our part stem from God's power at work in us, and so any human claim to merit is ruled out. Indeed, for Augustine, even the human response to God's grace is possible not by virtue of human capacity or merit, but only as an effect of grace itself. Further, Augustine realized that a person needed more than simply freedom of the will and knowledge of the commandments in order to live a virtuous life. In *The Spirit and the Letter* he explains that as a result of the Fall, human desires are so disordered that obedience to the fundamental command to love God is impossible without the transformation of our hearts, which is the work of the Holy Spirit:

> We must fiercely and strongly oppose those who think that the power of the human will can by itself, without the help of God, either attain righteousness or make progress in tending toward it. When these people begin to be pressed as to how they presume to claim that this is possible without God's help, they hold themselves in check and do not dare to make this claim, because they see that it is godless and intolerable. Rather they say that these things are not done without God's help, because God created human beings with free choice and, by giving the commandments, he teaches them how they should live. Moreover, they say that he certainly helps them, insofar as by his teaching he removes ignorance so that human beings know what they should avoid and what they should pursue in their actions. Thus, by following the path he pointed out to them, they may by the free choice implanted in their nature live chaste, righteous, and pious lives and merit to attain to the blessed and eternal life.
>
> We, on the other hand, say that the human will is helped to achieve righteousness in this way: Besides the fact that human beings are created with free choice of the will and besides the teaching by which they are commanded how they ought to live, they receive the Holy Spirit so that there arises in their minds a delight in and a love for that highest and immutable good that is God, even now while they walk by faith, not yet by vision (cf. 2 Cor 5:7). By this love given to them like the pledge of a gratuitous gift, they are set afire with the desire to cling to the creator and burn to come to a participation in that true light (cf. John 1:9), so that they have their well-being from him from whom they have their being. For free choice is capable only of sinning, if the way of truth remains hidden. And when what we should do and the goal we should strive for begins to be clear, unless we find delight in it and love it, we do not act, do not begin, do not live good lives. But so that we may love it, the "love of God" is poured out "in our hearts," not by free choice which comes from ourselves, but "by the Holy Spirit who has been given to us." (Rom 5:5) (2.4–3.5; 1997)

Augustine's argument against Pelagius, here and in other works, is grounded in his interpretation of the Bible. This is true more generally of all the Fathers, for in the patristic period, exegesis of Scripture (i.e., interpretation or explanation of the biblical text) and theology are one and the same endeavor. This approach contrasts with that currently dominant in academic circles, in which the enterprise of commenting on the biblical text is often separated from the task of theology.

This intimate connection between theology and exegesis does not originate with the Church Fathers, for it is found in the biblical tradition itself. In the Gospels, for example, much of Jesus' teaching ministry consists of a reinterpretation of the Jewish Scriptures (e.g., Matt 5–7). Indeed, after the Resurrection, when Jesus walks to Emmaus with two of his disciples (who do not yet recognize him), he explains to them the Christological meaning of the Old Testament: "And beginning with Moses and all the prophets, he interpreted to them in all the Scriptures the things concerning himself" (Luke 24:27). Moreover, in other New Testament writings one can see the beginnings of soteriology (the study of the doctrine of salvation) in texts which expound both the Old Testament and Jewish institutions in the light of Christ (e.g., Acts 10:26–40; Hebrews).

That theology and exegesis go hand in hand in the patristic period can be easily seen in the writings of Irenaeus of Lyons, often considered the first systematic theologian. Although probably a native of Smyrna in Asia Minor (modern Turkey), Irenaeus studied in Rome and served as a priest in Lyons (in modern France), eventually becoming bishop of Lyons after the persecution of 177 CE. He is best known for his work *Against Heresies*, a lengthy and detailed refutation of Gnosticism. Although Irenaeus' argument against the Gnostics is not made solely on the basis of Scripture, page after page of this treatise (particularly in Books III–V) is peppered with biblical quotations and allusions which Irenaeus comments on, thereby exposing the errors in the beliefs of the Gnostics and demonstrating that their heretical theology grows out of their (willful) misunderstanding of Scripture (see, e.g., *Against Heresies* IV.11.4). Irenaeus' use of the Bible, however, is not solely negative, the refutation of heretical views, but is also constructive. Thus, for example, his notion of recapitulation, in which Christ corrects all the mistakes made by human beings and both restores and brings to perfection all of Creation, is grounded in his exegesis of Romans 5:12–21 (Christ as the new Adam) and other New Testament texts.

In the course of his argument against the Gnostics, Irenaeus remarks that "the writings of Moses are the words of Christ" (*Against Heresies* IV.2.3). This pithy comment points to a fundamental assumption undergirding the exegesis not just of Irenaeus, but of all the Church Fathers. That is, the Bible is not a collection of discrete texts that can be understood independently of one another. Rather, for the Christian, the Old and New Testaments form a unified whole, and any particular book or passage can only be properly understood in that light. Even further, all of Scripture has Christ as its object. Or, as Augustine would later say, "The entire contents of the Scriptures are either directly or indirectly about Christ" (*Against Faustus*, 12.7).

Although Irenaeus and other second-century Christians affirm that the entire Bible witnesses to Christ, their interpretation is *ad hoc* insofar as the selection of texts that are interpreted is determined by the theological point under discussion. That is, while Irenaeus quotes from most of the books in the canon as we know it, he does not deal with any of them in a comprehensive fashion, but rather comments on particular passages as they relate to the issues he was debating with the Gnostics. As a result, at the end of the second century, large portions of Scripture, and especially of the Old Testament, had received little or no attention from Christian exegetes.

This situation changed dramatically in the third century due to the efforts of Origen, who revolutionized Christian exegesis in several ways. First, he employed the tools of linguistic analysis and exegesis, as taught in ancient schools under the headings of grammar, rhetoric, and oratory, in a more thorough and refined way than Christians before him. While every act of reading involves interpretation, it was especially true in the ancient world that reading presupposed interpretation because texts, whether sacred or secular, were written in *scriptio continua* ("continuous script"), that is, they lacked punctuation and word division. Because of this, the reader, upon first picking up a literary work, had to determine where words, phrases, and sentences began and ended, and whether a sentence was a question or statement.[3] After this initial "grammatical" dimension of interpretation was carried out, the reader turned to issues of language and vocabulary, such as the correct definition and etymology of unfamiliar words, the author's literary style, and the presence of figures of speech (e.g., metaphor, hyperbole, etc.). From this, the reader moved to actual explanation of the text, addressing questions concerning historical and literary references as well as the narrative itself (e.g., is the story plausible?). In his biblical commentaries, Origen put these interpretive tools to work in service of illuminating the biblical text.

Picking up on St Paul's mention of "spirit and soul and body" in 1 Thessalonians 5:23, Origen also developed a theory that the biblical text, mirroring the human person, had three levels of meaning: body, soul, and spirit. (He articulates this most fully in Book 4 of *On First Principles*.) The "body" corresponds to what might also be called the literal or historical meaning, the level most readily accessible. The two spiritual senses, which can be apprehended only by those more advanced in the Christian life, deal with the moral meaning, the "soul" of the text, and the deepest mysteries of God, its "spirit." Origen also held that the Holy Spirit prompts Christians to search for these deeper spiritual meanings through the specific details of the scriptural writings. Thus, when readers discover inconsistencies or historical errors in any given passage, this does not indicate a fatal problem with the biblical text, but rather signals the Spirit's promptings to search for meanings deeper than the literal or historical.

Finally, Origen had a profound impact on early Christian interpretation through his insistence that, since Christ is the key to Scripture, the Christian exegete ought to treat the *entire* Old Testament, not merely selected verses. Moreover, while granting that a preacher was limited in what he could cover in a homily, Origen insisted that the person writing a commentary should aim for a detailed explanation that omitted nothing. Through this insistence, Origen not only opened up for the Church the entire Bible, especially the Old Testament, but also inaugurated the tradition of verse-by-verse scriptural commentary.

Origen's exegesis was not without its detractors. In the fourth and fifth centuries a number of Christian interpreters, sometimes referred to as Antiochenes, severely criticized Origen's most extreme spiritual exegesis (also called "allegory"). Others, known as the Alexandrians, defended Origen's method. These two schools had for long been viewed as diametrically opposed, with the Antiochenes portrayed as eschewing all allegory in favor of literal interpretation and the Alexandrians as embracing allegory indiscriminately. More recently scholars have come to see that Antiochenes and Alexandrians had much in common in their exegetical methods, though the Antiochenes argued that the spiritual meaning of a text should be tied much more closely to its historical sense than was often the case with the Alexandrians. (For a helpful introduction to these issues, see Young, 2004.) Despite such criticisms, the notion that a biblical text is polyvalent (i.e., has more than one meaning) was affirmed virtually universally in the patristic era and is significant for what it suggests about Scripture's capacity to speak to all the members of the Body of Christ, in all times and places. That is, because the sacred text possesses various levels of meaning, two people of very different degrees of spiritual maturity could sit side-by-side reading it, and both would be nourished appropriately. Gregory the Great (*c*.540–604) expressed this in the preface to his *Moralia in Job*, a massive commentary on the Book of Job, by comparing the Bible to a river that is both shallow and deep, shallow enough that a lamb can wade in it and deep enough that an elephant can swim. Likewise, as individuals advance in the

Christian life, so too does their grasp of the Bible's meaning. Or, as Augustine put it, "The Bible was composed in such a way that as beginners mature, its meaning grows with them" (*Confessions* III.5.9). Further, following the lead of St Paul in 1 Corinthians 10:11 ("Now these things happened to them as a warning, but they were written down for our instruction, upon whom the end of the ages has come"), the Fathers believed that Scripture's message was not limited to those to whom it was initially addressed. Rather, the sacred text speaks across the generations to all those who hear it with humility and faith.

The legacy of the early Church is vast. These ancient Christians left future generations examples of fearless virtue in the face of persecution and an approach toward culture that is both sympathetic and critical. For the sake of their fellow believers they studied the biblical witness to Christ, laying out the implications of the Incarnation in treatises, sermons, and creeds. They built breathtaking churches that still have the power to focus our attention more clearly on God. They handed down a way of reading the Bible that has nourished the Church for centuries. But perhaps their greatest legacy is what the act of reading their works can do for Christians today. In his panegyric on Basil the Great, the fourth-century theologian Gregory of Nazianzus wrote,

> Whenever I handle his *Hexaemeron* [commentary on the days of creation], and take its words on my lips, I am brought into the presence of the Creator, and understand the words of creation, and admire the Creator more than before, using my teacher as my only means of sight. (*Oration* 43.67)

Above all else, these ancient Christians help us to see and know God.

Notes

1   Fortunately, a number of fine series present many of the most important works in English translation. The translations in the *Ante-Nicene Fathers* (ANF) and *Nicene and Post-Nicene Fathers* (NPNF), produced in the nineteenth century, while archaic, are reliable and still valuable. More recent translations can be found in *Ancient Christian Writers* (Paulist Press) and *The Fathers of the Church* (Catholic University of America Press). *The Classics of Western Spirituality* (Paulist Press) includes volumes on a number of important Church Fathers. *Cistercian Studies Series* comprises a number of texts dealing with monasticism, including works originally written in Syriac and Coptic. New City Press is currently producing a series of new translations of the entire corpus of Augustine, *The Works of St Augustine*. In the bibliography I have included several works that provide a helpful introduction to early Christian life and thought.
2   I have cited patristic texts according to standard practice, citing book and chapter. Where I have drawn upon a specific translation, it is listed in the bibliography. Many of the patristic texts mentioned are available in multiple translations in the various series listed in note 1.
3   For readers in the early twenty-first century, accustomed to the conventions of modern texts, the process of reading in the ancient world seems complex indeed. However, it is likely that the ancients found reading no more difficult than we do, since they were accustomed to *scriptio continua* (Gamble, 1995). Nonetheless, in working through a text, the ancient reader necessarily made more interpretive decisions than we do, decisions that could bear significantly on a passage's meaning. An example from the history of English translations of the

Bible can illustrate the sort of alteration of meaning that can arise solely from different judgments about where a few punctuation marks are to be placed. When translated into English, Jesus' words on the cross to the repentant thief (Luke 23:43) can be punctuated as, "Verily, I say unto thee, This day thou shalt be with me in Paradise." or as, "Verily I say unto thee this day, Thou shalt be with me in Paradise." As Lynne Truss observes, these seemingly minor changes in stress and punctuation dramatically alter the meaning of Jesus' words: "Now, huge doctrinal differences hang on the placing of this comma. The first version, which is how Protestants interpret the passage, lightly skips over the whole unpleasant business of Purgatory and takes the crucified thief straight to heaven with Our Lord. The second promises Paradise at some later date (to be confirmed, as it were) and leaves Purgatory nicely in the picture for the Catholics, who believe in it" (2003). One can imagine how much more complicated interpretation becomes when the text lacks not only punctuation but also word division.

References and Further Reading

Athanasius (1980) *The Life of Antony and the Letter to Marcellinus*, trans. Robert C. Gregg. New York: Paulist Press.

Augustine (1972) *The City of God*, trans. Henry Bettenson. London: Penguin Books.

Augustine (1991) *Confessions*, trans. Henry Chadwick. Oxford: Oxford University Press.

Augustine (1997) *Answer to the Pelagians*. Works of St Augustine, I/23, trans. Roland J. Teske SJ. Hyde Park, NY: New City Press.

Gamble, Harry Y. (1995) *Books and Readers in the Early Church: A History of Early Christian Texts*. New Haven, CT: Yale University Press.

Gregory of Nyssa (1978) *The Life of Moses*, trans. Abraham J. Malherbe and Everett Ferguson. New York: Paulist Press.

Krautheimer, Richard (1983) *Three Christian Capitals: Topography and Politics*. Berkeley: University of California Press.

Origen (1953) *Contra Celsum*, trans. Henry Chadwick. Cambridge: Cambridge University Press.

Origen (1973) *On First Principles*, trans. G.W. Butterworth. Gloucester, MA: Peter Smith.

Simon, Marcel (1986) *Verus Israel: A Study of the Relations between Christians and Jews in the Roman Empire (135–425)*. Oxford: Oxford University Press.

Stark, Rodney (1996) *The Rise of Christianity: A Sociologist Reconsiders History*. Princeton, NJ: Princeton University Press.

Theodoret of Cyrrhus (1985) *A History of the Monks of Syria*, trans. R.M. Price. Kalamazoo, MI: Cistercian Publications.

Truss, Lynne (2003) *Eats, Shoots and Leaves: The Zero Tolerance Approach to Punctuation!* New York: Penguin Books.

Wilken, Robert Louis (1983) *John Chrysostom and the Jews: Rhetoric and Reality in the Late 4th Century*. Berkeley: University of California Press.

Wilken, Robert Louis (1992) *The Land Called Holy. Palestine in Christian History and Thought*. New Haven, CT: Yale University Press.

Wilken, Robert Louis (2003) *The Spirit of Early Christian Thought: Seeking the Face of God*. New Haven, CT: Yale University Press.

Young, Francis (2004) "The Interpretation of Scripture," in Evans, G.R. (ed.) *The First Christian Theologians*. Oxford: Blackwell Publishers, chapter 2.

CHAPTER 4
The Middle Ages

Frederick Christian Bauerschmidt

The Middle Ages in the Catholic Imagination

The Middle Ages occupy a peculiar place in the Catholic imagination. For much of the first half of the twentieth century the Middle Ages were seen by Catholics as "our" era: a kind of golden age in which Church and society, humanity and God, faith and reason were all harmoniously ordered. Part of what makes this peculiar is that many non-Catholics also saw the Middle Ages as somehow belonging to Catholics, but they saw them as the "Dark Ages" of ignorance, priestcraft, crusades, and feudal servitude. One thing Catholics and non-Catholics agreed on was that the Catholics had claim to the Middle Ages, for good or for ill. But times change, and today we find many Catholics for whom "medieval" is a term of opprobrium. In the era of the Second Vatican Council, both those who advocated *ressourcement* – a return to the biblical and Patristic sources – and those who advocated *aggiornamento* – "updating" – seemed to find common cause in abandoning the Middle Ages, though they were fleeing in opposite directions.

Many of the attitudes that Catholics and non-Catholics have toward the Middle Ages, whether positive or negative, are founded on images of the period that are really carica-tures. While caricature is able to gain a firm purchase on the imagination, the murky complexities of actual history can help us better to appreciate how the Middle Ages were neither a golden age nor a low-water mark for the Catholic Church, but rather a part of the on-going conversation that is the Catholic tradition. They are an important period during which Catholicism attempted to resolve the problems bequeathed to the Church by its fourth-century transformation from an intermittently persecuted minority to the dominant social force in the lands that would become Europe. Particularly in the West, this struggle was determinatively shaped by Augustine's account of the "two cities" – the earthly city and the heavenly city – that he gives in *The City of God*. In what follows, I will explore how the tension between the demands of these two "cities" plays itself out in three realms: monasticism, the relationship of spiritual and temporal power, and the negotiation of the demands of faith and reason.

Delineating the Middle Ages

Before charting the fate of the two cities in these three realms, we must try to get some purchase on the time period itself. The term "Middle Ages" defines this period both by what came before and by what came after: something is "medieval" if it belongs neither to Antiquity nor to Modernity. Obviously, medieval people did not understand themselves to be "medieval." This does not mean that we ought not speak of a Middle Ages, but we ought to be alert to the fact that our attempts to characterize the Middle Ages are always contestable.

If we ask when the Middle Ages began, we might follow Edward Gibbon (1737–94), who locates the "fall" of Rome in the fifth century, specifically the abdication of the emperor Romulus Augustulus and the establishing of the Germanic tribal leader Odoacer as the *de facto* ruler of the Western Empire in 476, or we might follow Henri Pirenne (1862–1935) who, while not denying the Roman Empire's decline in the fifth century, argued that the true historical break begins with the Muslim conquest of much of the Mediterranean world in the seventh and eighth centuries, which shifts the center of Christian culture northward, beyond the Alps, making the coronation of Charlemagne on Christmas Day in 800 the true point of transition between the ancient and medieval worlds. In the end, perhaps the best we can say is that between the fifth and the eighth centuries there was a gradual shift from the Roman, Mediterranean world of Augustine to the Germanic, European world of Charlemagne. A sharp line of division between Antiquity and the Middle Ages simply cannot be drawn. The ending of the Middle Ages is no less disputed. When do the Middle Ages end and the Early Modern period begin? Numerous possibilities present themselves: the social and economic upheavals the followed the Black Death in the mid-fourteenth century; the fifteenth-century revival of interest in classical art and literature that we know as the Italian Renaissance; the fall of Constantinople to the Ottoman Turks in 1453 (which could also mark the end of Antiquity); the discovery of the New World in 1492; the beginning of the Protestant Reformation in 1517; the philosophical "turn to the subject" inaugurated by Descartes in his *Discourse on Method*, published in 1637; or the ending of the Thirty Years War with the Peace of Westphalia in 1648. As with the beginning of the Middle Ages, so too with their ending, perhaps the best we can do is to identify a centuries-long period of transition.

Common sense would seem to dictate that a thousand-year period of human history would be characterized by significant diversity, and, at least in this case, common sense is correct. The Middle Ages were neither unrelievedly "dark," nor were they simply the triumphant "Age of Faith." At the very least, we ought to replace the gross over-simplification of lumping the entire millennium into a single category, with the slightly less gross over-simplification of distinguishing at least four different periods.

The period from *c*.500–750 is one that, in the West, might warrant the adjective "dark." This was a time of decline in urban life and of political fragmentation. As the institutions of the Roman Empire began to disintegrate, the Church became an increasingly important source of stability and continuity. As Europe became increasingly "Germanized," the Germanic tribes, beginning with the baptism of Clovis in 496, were progressively Christianized and, in this process, they became the inheritors of much of the heritage of antiquity.

From c.750–1050 there is a resurgence of "imperial" power in Europe: the Carolingian Empire in the eighth and ninth centuries, and the Ottonian emperors of the tenth and eleventh centuries. These empires brought with them, particularly in their early years, a flourishing of scholarship and the arts, as well as significant patronage of the Church. At the same time, however, imperial patronage brought with it imperial control.

The period from c.1050 to 1350 is one of reform and renewal for the Church, encompassing reform of the clergy and attempts to strengthen papal power as well as movements manifesting the desire of lay and religious Christians to live their faith with greater fervor. In the twelfth century, the rise of the Franciscan and Dominican orders are examples of a spirit of renewal that produced new forms of religious life, forms better adapted to the revival of urban life sweeping Europe, producing the great gothic cathedrals and the first universities.

The century and a half from c.1350 to 1500 is sometimes seen as a period of decline, what the historian Johan Huizinga called "the autumn of the Middle Ages." It is certainly true that the mid-fourteenth-century plague known as the Black Death devastated the population of Europe and disrupted economic and social life for decades, but this same era saw important technological innovations and a flourishing of devotion among lay people. This was also the era of such artistic giants as Donatello and Brunelleschi in Italy and Jan van Eyck and Hans Memling in the Low Countries. Thus, rather than a period of decline, the late Middle Ages is better characterized as part of the long transition from "medieval" to "modern."

How do we find unity in such diversity? While we might approach this question in various ways, I propose that it is Augustine's account of the two cities – the earthly city ruled by pride and love of self, and the heavenly city rule by humility and love of God – that can serve as a framework through which to view this era. Augustine's account is irreducibly complex, for the line between the two cities is not one that can be fixed prior to the final judgment. In Augustine's phrase, even the Church is a "mixed body" of saints and sinners that "has in her midst some who are united with her in participation in the sacraments, but who will not join with her in the eternal destiny of the saints" (*Civ. Dei* 1.35).[1] While on "pilgrimage" through history, those chosen by God for salvation, the true citizens of the heavenly city, must "make use" of the peace of the earthly city, a peace often secured through warfare and the threat of violence, while never mistaking this for the ultimate eschatological peace of the City of God (*Civ. Dei* 19.17). The question faced by medieval people, then, was how to "use" the earthly city and its genuine but finite goods without losing one's citizenship in the heavenly city. This is an enduring tension throughout the Middle Ages, operative in a variety of realms.

Monasticism

We can see in the development of monasticism in the Middle Ages an example of the tension between the two cities. In monasticism, as represented in ideal form in the *Rule* of St Benedict, we see what might be called an attempt at giving social form to

Augustine's *City of God*, to outline what a Christian community on pilgrimage through history might look like. It was an embodiment of the kind of "otherworldliness" characteristic of those spiritual descendants of Abel, who founded no city (see *Civ. Dei* 15.1). Yet in the context of the crumbling institutions of the Roman Empire and the need to evangelize the people of northern Europe, monasticism rapidly took on the role of the preserver and transmitter of culture: what begins as a counter-cultural movement becomes a culture-sustaining force. Yet the persistent memory of monasticism's counter-cultural origins leads to a rhythm of reform within monastic institutions that yields a particular version of the tension between the two cities.

The monastic community, as envisioned by Benedict, is something like an outpost of the pilgrim city of which Augustine speaks, seeking to embody that which is most characteristic of Augustine's heavenly city: "the love of God carried as far as contempt for self" (*Civ. Dei*, 14.28). And the chief means by which we come to this love of God is that humility by which, paradoxically, our abasement becomes our exaltation (see Luke 14:11). Augustine writes that "there is something in humility to exalt the mind, and something in exaltation to abase it" (*Civ. Dei* 14.13). In a similar way, Benedict speaks of a "ladder of humility" upon which "we descend by exaltation and ascend by humility" (*Rule* 7.7).[2] At the heart of Benedictine monasticism is the fundamental Augustinian paradox of exalted humility and humiliated exaltation.

Yet there is something distinctive in the Benedictine appropriation of this Augustinian paradox. The image we have of Augustine – a certainly misleading image – is of one who achieves humility in a single heartrending moment in the garden. This is an image fostered not only by Augustine's highly dramatic account of it in the *Confessions*, but also by the fact that, even in his monastic rule, Augustine offers no systematic plan for the cultivation of this humility. Rather, he typically simply points to Christ, the King of the heavenly city who for our sake became incarnate, as the exemplar of humility. Benedict, however, spells out in great detail the concrete shape of the life in which this humility is cultivated. While not ignoring the inner life, Benedict focuses on the external structures within which the monk lives, not only the highly structured round of prayers that Benedict called "the work of God," but also relationships of hierarchical authority. The monk is enjoined to submit his will to another, just as Christ submitted his will to the Father (*Rule* 7.31–3). The abbot, who "holds the place of Christ in the monastery" (*Rule* 2.2), is a key figure in the path toward humility before God, by serving as an instrument through which God works to humble the monks through concrete acts of submission. The submission to human superiors is the chief means by which the monk gradually interiorizes the attitudes that are outwardly expressed (*Rule* 7.51). Further, the abbot's rule is not to be motivated by the *libido dominandi* (lust for domination) that for Augustine characterizes the earthly city (*Civ. Dei* 1.30, 3.14, 14.28, 15.7, 19.15). Rather, the monastery is to conform to Augustine's description of Christian households, in which "even those who give orders are the servants of those whom they appear to command. Because they do not give order because of the lust for domination, but from a dutiful concern for the interests of others, not with pride in taking precedence over others, but with compassion in taking care of others" (*Civ. Dei* 19.14). Benedict's vision of monasticism requires an abbot who is a loving father, concerned above all for the good of the souls entrusted to him.

The *Rule* cautions that the abbot, "must not show too great concern for the fleeting and temporal things of this world, neglecting or treating lightly the welfare of those entrusted to him. Rather, he should keep in mind that he has undertaken the care of souls for whom he must give an account" (*Rule* 2.33–4). This caution reflects a real tension: the abbot must look not only to the spiritual welfare of the monks, but also to their physical welfare. The monastery always has at least one foot planted in the earthly city and its demands. Each monastery required a "cellarer" (*cellarius*) who was in charge of the management of the worldly goods of the monastery (*Rule* 31). Further, the *Rule* pays careful attention to disciplinary procedures (e.g. chapters 23–30 and 43–6), indicating that the monastery shared the lot of the Church as a whole: during the time of the heavenly city's historical pilgrimage, the monastery can never be purely an outpost of the heavenly city; it too was a "mixed body" of saints and sinners. There is a bracing realism to Benedict's rule for monks that recognizes that until the consummation of history the earthly city can never be entirely left behind. Benedict's *Rule* still points us to the tension between the two cities: it still breathes some of the atmosphere of the early monasticism of the East, which Georges Florovsky characterizes as a "Resistence Movement" within the Christianized Roman Empire (Florovsky, 1957: 150), and at the same time it already recognizes the inevitability of worldly entanglements. In some ways the subsequent history of monasticism in the medieval West is the story of the repeated slackening and tightening of that tension, which is reflected in the reform movements that appealed to different elements in Benedict's *Rule*.

For monasticism during the Carolingian and Ottonian periods, we see the Benedictine *Rule* as simply one factor among several in a monastic ideal that also included, as one historian notes, "the Cassiodoran view (from the same period) of the monastery as a bastion of erudition; Germanic notions of authority in which princely and spiritual powers were closely linked; and a hierocratic vision of society, based on function, that exalted the liturgical role of the monks and thus placed them well above the peasants who had the task of working the monastic lands" (Little, 1978: 61). Monasticism was no longer a point of resistance to an essentially pagan earthly city, but rather found its place within the unified social reality of Christendom. Within the tripartite image of society as those who fight (*bellatores*), those who labor (*laboratores*), and those who pray (*oratores*), the monks held a preeminent place among the last. They also, drawing from the Cassiodoran part of the ideal, served a crucial function in Carolingian efforts in education and the dissemination of knowledge. The monk Alcuin of York (730–804), who was the head of Charlemagne's royal palace school at Aachen, was described by Charlemagne's biographer, Einhard, as "the most learned man anywhere to be found" (*The Life of Charlemagne* §25, in Thorpe, 1969: 79). This learning included not simply familiarity with Scripture and the Church Fathers, but also with the available classical sources. And in this Alcuin was unusual only for the degree of his knowledge, since classical authors had figured in monastic education since the seventh century as models for learning Latin (Leclercq, 1961: 118). Though the texts of pagan antiquity were approached with a certain wariness, they were ultimately seen as containing truth, which belonged by right to Christians (Leclercq, 1961: 129–31).

But as important as the educational and cultural activity of the monks was, it was

their role as *oratores* that was most valued by their contemporaries. Indeed, the celebration of liturgical offices, which in the *Rule* of Benedict occupied about a fourth of the
monk's day, grew by the late eleventh century to occupy the entire day in some monasteries (Little, 1978: 67). The abbey of Cluny, founded in 910, became famous for the
splendor of its liturgies and by the twelfth century was home to over 400 monks. Of
course, this devotion to prayer, and the sumptuousness of its setting, had certain economic consequences: the monks themselves had little or no time for the manual labor
that had been integral to Benedict's vision of the monastic life (*Rule* 48), and while
Benedict had seen this labor more as a form of asceticism than a source of wealth, the
large number of monks needed to carry out the various offices demanded some steady
income. One solution to this problem was found in the *Rule*'s mention of gifts given to
the monastery (*Rule* 58.24; 59.4). Benedict mentions this only in terms of "dowries"
given to the monastery when a monk entered, but this opened the door to other sorts
of gifts to the monastery, particularly the gift of land, which helped form the demesnes
from which monasteries drew income in the form of tithes and rents (Milis, 1999:
19–23). Thus, while the individual monks might be poor, the monasteries themselves
were often fabulously wealthy.

This "worldliness" led to a reaction in the twelfth century, with the foundation of
orders such as the Carthusians, the Premonstratensians, and, above all, the Cistercians.
The first Cistercian monks, in the monastery at Cîteaux, sought a return to primitive
Benedictine practice: "drawing the integrity of the Rule over the tenor of their life –
liturgical observance as well as daily living – they followed faithfully in its track, and,
having stripped off the old self, they rejoiced to have put on the new" (*Exordium Parvum*
§15, in Matarasso, 1993: 6). They focused particularly on a poverty that involved actual
deprivation. They withdrew into "wasteland" – uninhabited areas where they could
pursue contemplation undisturbed – and thus sought to reestablish something of the
tension between the earthly and heavenly cities.

Yet within a few generations the demands of the earthly city reasserted themselves.
Originally the Cistercians had sought to reestablish Benedict's rhythm of prayer and
work, *ora et labora*. But in order to provide the monks with more time for contemplation, the monasteries soon began admitting *conversi*, lay brothers who lived under
vows but followed a much-simplified monastic regimen, with less fasting and fewer
hours devoted to prayer, and much more time spent working in the fields. The indus-
try and ingenuity of these *conversi* soon turned the wasteland upon which they built
their monasteries into thriving agricultural concerns (Little, 1978: 93–6; Milis, 1999:
28–34). Furthermore, the zeal of the Cistercians soon turned them into the medieval equivalent of celebrities; a figure like Bernard of Clairvaux (1090–1153) came to
wield immense influence, including involvement in disputed papal successions and the
preaching of the second crusade. The intertwining of the earthly and heavenly cities
persisted even amid the austerities of the Cistercians.

As we move into the thirteenth century, the vital center of religious life shifts to the
new mendicant (i.e. begging) orders, the Franciscans and the Dominicans, who had
their own struggles with the tension between the earthly city and the City of God. But
it is in monasticism, rooted in the rejection of Christian compromise with the world,
that we can see most poignantly played out the medieval attempt to preserve the ten-

sion between the radical demands of Christian humility and the need to make use of the peace of the earthly city, penultimate as that peace may be.

The Investiture Controversy

The same reforming impulses that produced communities like the Cistercians were also at play in what has come to be known as the "Investiture Controversy." This conflict, which came to a head in the clash between Pope Gregory VII and the Emperor Henry IV, was the result of tensions that had simmered for centuries. It grew from the practice of the Emperor and other secular rulers reserving for themselves the right to appoint bishops and abbots, "investing" them with their office and property that went along with it. While this practice of "lay investiture" seemed quite natural in a context in which secular rulers had considerable interest in who controlled the vast wealth of the diocese and monasteries within their territories, lay investiture also led to the awarding of Church offices to men who were simply interested in the wealth and power that they brought. This was unacceptable to reform-minded leaders of the Church. At heart, this controversy was one more manifestation of the basic problematic posed by Augustine: how, during its pilgrimage through history, can the heavenly city make use of the peace of the earthly city without losing its identity as the City of God?

We have seen that monasticism pushed in the direction of answering this question by removing the monk as much as possible from the earthly city; we have also seen that this answer ran up against the worldly demands placed upon the monks, both by their own human natures, and also by their fellow Christians outside the monastery. Yet the ideal remained. But for the vast majority of Christians, whether peasants or nobles, bishops or kings, withdrawal could not serve even as an ideal. The Church was enmeshed in the world to the degree that there was no clear boundary between the two, particularly after Charlemagne was crowned and anointed as "Holy Roman Emperor." The Christian world, Christendom, was an organic whole, a social body made up of diverse members, so the question became how the various members of this whole ought to be ordered. In particular, the question came to focus on the proper ordering of the relationship to the two most obvious claimants to visible leadership of this body: the Emperor and the Pope.

In some ways the issue of the relationship between Emperor and Pope was an old one. In the late fifth century, Pope Gelasius I had sought to minimize the Emperor Anastasius' influence on the Church's formulation of doctrine, not least because he suspected the Emperor of monophysite sympathies, by drawing a distinction between different areas of authority. Writing to Anastasius, he says, "two there are, August Emperor, by which this world is ruled: the consecrated authority of priests and the royal power" (in O'Donovan and O'Donovan, 1999: 179). Gelasius' distinction is not exactly the Augustinian one between the two cities, but it still bears some of its elements. The Emperor is responsible for establishing the kind of limited peace that for Augustine characterized the earthly city, while, like every Christian, he must cultivate a spirit of humble service characteristic of the heavenly city. But the realm of action proper to the Emperor, the realm of wars and treaties and intrigues, is not the realm in which such a spirit is cultivated. Rather, it is the area ruled by the priestly power, the realm of the word of God and the sacraments, to which even kings must look for salvation. This is why, as Gelasius goes on to say in the same letter, "the priests have the greater responsibility in that they will have to give account before God's judgment seat for those who have been kings of men." Gelasius sees both spiritual and temporal power operating under God's providence in this world, but it is the spiritual power held by the priests, and above all by the Pope, that is the greater, because this is the power that is of ultimate significance, even to temporal rulers.

With the advent of the Carolingian Empire, the situation changes. Kingship was seen as no less sacred than the papacy. The Holy Roman Emperor is God's anointed, compared to David and Solomon and Christ himself. Indeed, the anointing of kings is numbered by some among the sacraments, and seen as investing the king with responsibility for, and power over, the Church. For a theorist of royal power like Jonas of Orléans (c.780–842/43), the task of the king was "to govern the people of God," a term that now referred, not to a group who have been called by God out of a larger social whole (1 Peter 2:9–10; Revelation 8:14), but simply to the people of Europe (*The Institution of the King* §4, in O'Donovan and O'Donovan, 1999: 218). Such an understanding of royal power reaches its height in the early twelfth-century writer referred to today as the "Norman Anonymous." He interprets Gelasius' reference to the two powers "by which this world is ruled" in a way quite different from Gelasius himself: "By 'this world' he means Holy Church, which is on pilgrimage through the world" (*The Consecration of Bishops and Kings* §664, in O'Donovan and O'Donovan, 1999: 252). Thus, for this school of thought, the Emperor, no less than the Pope and bishops, had a role in ruling the Church. Indeed, the royal power was the superior, since Christ was a priest on account of his humanity, while he was a king by virtue of his divinity (*The Consecration of Bishops and Kings* §665, in O'Donovan and O'Donovan, 1999: 254). The desire of lay rulers to exercise control over the Church was not "secular" interference in the realm of the "religious," because kingship itself was a sacred office within Christendom, and it was only fitting that this office be expressed liturgically by the lay lord "investing" the newly ordained bishop or consecrated abbot with his temporal goods by conferring upon him the pastoral staff, symbolic of his office.

In the eleventh century the spirit of reform was moving through Christendom and had received support from a number of lay rulers. Efforts were initially focused on forbidding clerical marriage, and thus the establishment of clerical dynasties, and simony, the practice of receiving Church offices in return for payment. But by the mid-eleventh century clerics interested in reform came to focus their efforts on the practice of lay investiture. So long as the conferring of the worldly wealth attached to Church offices remained in the hands of lay lords, other abuses could not be curbed; loyalty to the lay lord would invariably take precedence over the spiritual qualifications required by the office. While one might be tempted to see the forbidding of lay investiture as a cynical grab for power on the part of the Church, it was in fact rooted in a genuine desire to free the Church from the control of lay lords in order to reform it. It also reflected the Augustinian theological conviction that the power of even a Christian king was inevitably tainted by the desire for domination, and thus must be subordinate to the priestly power of popes and bishops (see letter 4.2 of Gregory VII, in Emerton, 1932: 104). This was true not only, as for Gelasius, in matters of doctrine, but also in matters having to do with the rule of the earthly city.

Pope Nicholas II had outlawed lay investiture in 1059, but it is really with the accession of Gregory VII to the papal throne that the controversy becomes a crisis. When Gregory again banned lay investiture in 1075, and made serious attempts at enforcement, he came into conflict with the Emperor Henry IV, who ruled what is today Germany, over the appointment of the bishop of Milan. When Henry refused to fulfill promises he had made to Gregory to submit to the ban on lay investiture, Gregory threatened him with both excommunication and deposition as Emperor. In response, Henry held a synod of bishops in Germany that declared the Pope deposed. In counter-response, Gregory excommunicated Henry in February of 1076, freeing Henry's subjects from their oath of allegiance to him. Gregory's nobles took this as an opportunity and within a few months Saxony was in revolt and a movement was afoot to elect a new Emperor. In one of the most dramatic scenes in medieval history, in January of 1077 Henry intercepted the Pope at the town of Canossa in northern Italy, and stood dressed as a penitent for three days in the snow outside the castle where the Pope was staying, asking for forgiveness. Gregory relented, lifting the excommunication, but leaving the deposition unresolved. Henry's repentance was short-lived when it became apparent that his nobles were going to continue with their plans to elect a new ruler. A civil war ensued in which Gregory backed Henry's opponents and by 1080 he had excommunicated Henry once again. Henry responded by having the German bishops elect a rival Pope and in 1081 he marched on Rome, laying siege to the city for several years and finally forcing Gregory into exile, where he died in 1085. Gregory's successor, Urban II, regained control of the city of Rome, but the conflict did not reach an official settlement until 1122 when, in the Concordat of Worms, Henry's son and successor, Henry V, relinquished all claim to the bestowal of the episcopal ring and pastoral staff. In turn, Pope Calixtus II granted Henry some measure of control over the choice of bishops and abbots within his realm, and also gave him the right to grant the worldly goods that were attached to Church offices, though this was to be seen as something clearly distinct from the bestowal of any spiritual power.

It may seem that the Church had simply won a ritual victory, retaining for itself the right to bestow the symbolic staff and ring. But the long-term effects were profound. We see in the resolution reached at Worms a delineation of the "sacred" and the "secular" that is clearer than ever before. Sacred items, such as the ring and staff, were under the control of the Church, while control over land and the people living on it was now seen as secular, the purview of lay rulers. This delineation brings a number of things in its wake. On the one hand, it tightens the tension between the two cities, making sharper, at least in theory, the line between the earthly power of lords, rooted in the desire for earthly glory, and the spiritual power of popes and bishops, rooted in the love of God and pastoral concern. This will serve as a basis from which to criticize a Church that makes too easy a peace with worldly power. On the other hand, it also undergirds a growing tendency to identify "the Church" with the clergy, and to see the laity as occupying a realm now rendered totally secular (see Florovsky, 1957: 145). Ironically, it is the Church's struggle to free itself from secular rulers that plants the seeds of the tendency in succeeding centuries to see the Church as the ruler of the soul and the State as the ruler of the body, leading to an interiorization and privatization of religious belief in Western society that poses one of the most significant challenges to Catholicism in the modern world.

Faith and Reason

In both monasticism and the investiture conflict we see Augustine's idea of the two cities at work in reflection on the shape of the Christian life in community. But the discordant harmonies between the two cities are also sounded in the relationship of human reason to divinely given faith. Augustine held that human reason could attain knowledge of God, as witnessed by the Platonists, who "found the cause of the organized universe, the light by which truth is perceived, and the spring which offers the drink of felicity" (*Civ. Dei* 8.10). Yet the reason of fallen human beings, which is "weakened by long-standing faults which darken it," is "too weak to cleave to that changeless light and to enjoy it; it is too weak even to endure that light." Thus the mind must be "trained and purified by faith," which is given by God through Christ the mediator, who as divine is our goal, and as human is our way (*Civ. Dei* 11.2). While the citizens of the earthly city trust in darkened human reason, the citizens of the heavenly city trust in Scripture, which "exercises sovereign authority over the literature of all mankind" (*Civ. Dei* 11.1). At the same time, human reason is not abandoned; rather, Christians can use "such powers of reason as we can apply for the benefit of unbelievers" (*Civ. Dei* 19.1).

The Middle Ages thus assigns a place for human reason, even in its fallen state, as one of those goods of the earthly city of which the citizens of the City of God can make use while on pilgrimage. We see this in the monastic involvement in the preservation and transmission of knowledge. The theology of the monasteries, however, most often took the form of a meditative appropriation of Scripture, rather than an investigation into the logical cogency of doctrine. It is with the rise in the late eleventh century of scholasticism – so called because it is the type of theology practiced in the new schools or universities that appeared as part of a more general urban revival of the time – that we really begin to see the dialectical tools of the earthly city brought fully to bear upon questions of faith. Anselm of Canterbury (*c.*1033–1109) was a Benedictine monk, and thus in some ways looks back to the older, more meditative forms of theology found in the monasteries. At the same time, in his theological project of "faith seeking understanding" he often appealed to logical argumentation rather than the authority of Scripture or the Church Fathers. A more purely "scholastic" approach can be found in the controversial theologian Peter Abelard (1079–1142), whose work *Sic et Non* ("Yes and No") collected and contrasted contradictory sayings of Scripture and the Fathers on a number of theological questions. For Abelard, Scripture and the Fathers were not a source for meditation, but rather a source of theological problems to be resolved by dialectic (i.e. logic). While Abelard simply collected and arranged conflicting passages from theological authorities, Peter Lombard (*c.*1100–60), in his similar collection of *sententiae* (opinions), sought to resolve the differences between the various authorities.

His work, commonly referred to as the *Sentences*, served as the standard theological textbook into the seventeenth century. It provided a common set of theological questions and authoritative sources with which virtually every scholastic theologian had to deal.

The thirteenth century is commonly held to be the high point of scholasticism, with such luminaries as Alexander of Hales (*c.*1186–1245), Albert the Great (*c.*1200–80), and Bonaventure (*c.*1217–74).[3] But the figure who has come to symbolize scholasticism is Thomas Aquinas (*c.*1225–74), the Italian Dominican friar who combined immense erudition with acute reasoning skills, producing one of the most enduring intellectual achievements of the Middle Ages. Thomas began his theological work, as most medieval theologians did, by writing a commentary on Lombard's *Sentences*. He went on to write commentaries both on Scriptural texts and on the major works of Aristotle, as well as several collections of "disputed questions" (a theological genre that reproduces the form of a classroom debate) and numerous smaller works. He is best known, however, for his two *Summae* or comprehensive treatments of theology: the *Summa Contra Gentiles* and the *Summa Theologiae*.

One of the chief intellectual problems of Thomas' day was the question of how, if at all, the philosophy of Aristotle could be integrated into Christian theology. Most of Aristotle's works had been lost to the West, and it was only in the twelfth century that Latin translations (initially made from the Arabic translations of Muslim philosophers) began to appear. This posed a vast intellectual challenge, because it represented the rapid introduction into the medieval Christian world of a rigorous and compelling philosophical system of great explanatory power that seemed to have no need for Christian revelation. Christianity had, in a sense, made its peace with Platonism over the course of the centuries, and read Platonic philosophy through Christian eyes in such a way that Platonism seemed to provide the natural philosophical basis for theology. But Aristotle contradicted Plato on any number of points; worse, he contradicted Christianity on key points such as whether the world was eternal or had a beginning in time. Some were fascinated by Aristotle and sought to adopt him wholeheartedly; others violently rejected his thought; still others sought to make judicious use of it.

Thomas is often presented as the one who brought about a synthesis of reason (represented by Aristotle) and faith by carefully delineating the realms proper to each. Reason had to do with the "natural" and faith with the "supernatural," and one could fairly clearly distinguish between the two. In reality, Thomas' position is a good deal more complex, and more ambiguous. At the very outset of the *Summa Theologiae* Thomas asks the question "Whether, besides philosophy, any further doctrine is required?" (1.1.1).[4] In essence, Thomas is asking whether the knowledge that human beings can attain simply through exercising their minds upon the data of the world can tell them all that they need to know in order to fulfill the purpose of their existence. Thomas answers "no," and gives two reasons for this. The first is that the goal of human life is to be united with God, which is something that exceeds the grasp of human knowledge. Thus if human beings are to reach their ultimate fulfillment, they must be taught by God. The second reason is that even those things concerning God that we could know simply by exercising our minds upon the data of the world – and Thomas does believe that there are such things; in particular, we can know that God exists (1.2.3) – "would only be known by a few, and that after a long time, and with the admixture of many errors" (1.1.1). Thus, it is fitting that God teach us through divine revelation. At the same time, reason has a role to play, even in our grasping of what it is that we believe. Thomas holds that "grace does not destroy nature but perfects it" meaning that what we are by nature, including our natural capacities, is not overridden by God's gifts but is transformed and elevated. Therefore, "natural reason should minister to faith" (1.1.8), and the way in which it does this is by enabling us to draw conclusions from what we have been taught by God in revelation. Reason helps us distinguish between genuine mysteries of faith and simple illogic and intellectual confusion. There are certain truths that we can affirm only on the basis of faith, particularly God's nature as Trinity and the Incarnation of God in Jesus Christ (2–2.1.8). Reason can in no way prove these things, yet once we have accepted these things on faith, reason can be employed to help us see how the various things that we hold on faith can be related to each other. It can also help answer charges brought against Christian faith by unbelievers, by showing that what Christians hold on faith is not *un*reasonable (1.1.8).

In practice, faith and reason overlap. Many things that could in principle be known by reason, such as God's existence, most people hold on faith; and many things that we hold on faith can be illumined and held more firmly through the exercise of reason. Though Thomas holds human reason in great esteem, he also recognizes that nothing it can tell us has the power to save. Human beings can know things simply by the exercise of their God-given reason (1–1.109.1), but true "understanding" (*intelligere*) of our ultimate purpose, by which we penetrate to the reality of things, is the gift of grace (2–2.8.5), and the fruit that comes from this gift is faith (2–2.8.8). Like the peace of the earthly city, reason untransformed by grace can be of use to citizens of the heavenly city (and Thomas certainly made ample use of Aristotle), but it can never substitute for the divine gift of understanding. This is perhaps why, at the end of his life, Thomas said that all he had written seemed like straw to him compared to the reality of God he had glimpsed.

The relationship of faith and reason that we find in Aquinas is neither a segregation of the two into separate realms, nor a synthesis in which faith and reason lose their distinctness, but rather an exquisitely poised and never-quite-resolved dialectical tension. The resolution of this tension must await the City of God's completion of its earthly pilgrimage, for "the more perfectly do we know God in this life, the more we understand that He surpasses all that the mind comprehends" (2–2.8.7). This is a point echoed by the fourteenth-century English anchoress Julian of Norwich (*c.*1342 to after *c.*1416). Having lived through the second half of the fourteenth century, with its plagues and wars and rebellions, she received a series of visions, in which she was assured that "all shall be well, and all shall be well, and all manner of things shall be well" (Long Text, chapter 27, in Julian of Norwich, 1998: 79). This seemed to her absurd in the face of sin and the damage that it has caused to human nature. Yet Julian trusted her visions and applied herself to resolving the conflict between God's promise that all shall be well and the reality of sin and its consequences. As the fruits of her reflection, Julian produced one of the most brilliant works of theology of the late Middle Ages, a work known today as *Revelations of Divine Love*. But Julian's true genius as a theologian is not in any intellectual resolution she achieves, but in her ability to know what must be left unresolved. At the end of her meditation on her visions, she writes:

> when the judgment is given, and we are all brought up above, we shall clearly see in God the mysteries which are now hidden from us. Then none of us shall be moved to say in any way, "Lord, it would have been very good if it had been like this," but we shall all affirm silently, "Lord, may you be blessed! For it is thus and it is good." (Long Text, chapter 85, in Julian of Norwich, 1998: 178)

Julian, like Aquinas and Augustine, is unafraid to push reason to, and even beyond, its natural limits, while recognizing the poverty of our knowing in the time between times of the heavenly city's pilgrimage.

Conclusion

Sometimes one hears reference to the "medieval synthesis," by which is presumably meant the seamless reconciliation of such dichotomies as contemplation and action, Church and State, faith and reason, and so forth. In this essay I have tried to argue that whatever characterizes the Middle Ages, it is not synthesis. Rather, this is a time of fraught and fruitful tensions, first mapped out by Augustine in *The City of God*. One might say that the Middle Ages ended when these tensions collapsed into dualisms. It is in the tension between monastic withdrawal and worldly involvement, sacred power and secular authority, grace-given faith and natural reason, that the Middle Ages produced their greatest achievements, and it is this tension that makes them of enduring interest.

Notes

1   Quotations from *De civitate Dei* [*The City of God*] are taken from Augustine 1984 and are cited by book and chapter.
2   Quotations from the *Rule* of Saint Benedict are taken from Fry (1981) and are cited by chapter and, where applicable, verse.
3   Representative texts of most of these figures, as well as those mentioned in the previous paragraph, can be found in Fairweather (1982).
4   All quotations are from Thomas Aquinas (1981) and are cited by the part of the *Summa*, the question, and the article.

References and Further Reading

Aquinas, Thomas (1981) *Summa Theologiae*, trans. Fathers of the English Dominican Province. Westminster, MD: Christian Classics.
Augustine (1984) *City of God*, trans. H. Bettenson. London: Penguin.
Emerton, Ephraim (ed. and trans.) (1932) *The Correspondence of Pope Gregory VII: Selected Letters from the Registrum*. New York: Columbia University Press.

Fairweather, Eugene (ed.) (1982) *A Scholastic Miscellany: Anselm to Ockham*. Philadelphia, PA: Westminster John Knox Press.

Florovsky, Georges (1957) "Empire and Desert: Antinomies of Christian History," *Greek Orthodox Theological Review*, no. 3, 133–59.

Fry, Timothy OSB (ed.) (1981) *RB 1980: The Rule of St Benedict in Latin and English with Notes*. Collegeville, MN: The Liturgical Press.

Julian of Norwich (1998) *Revelations of Divine Love*, trans. Elizabeth Spearing. London: Penguin.

Leclercq, Jean (1961) *The Love of Learning and the Desire for God: A Study of Monastic Culture*, trans. Catherine Misrahi. New York: Mentor.

Little, Lester K. (1978) *Religious Poverty and the Profit Economy in Medieval Europe*. Ithaca, NY: Cornell University Press.

Matarasso, Pauline (ed. and trans.) (1993) *The Cistercian World: Monastic Writings of the Twelfth Century*. London: Penguin.

Milis, Ludo J.R. (1999) *Angelic Monks and Earthly Men: Monasticism and its Meaning to Medieval Society*. Suffolk: Boydell Press.

O'Donovan, Oliver and O'Donovan, Joan Lockwood (eds.) (1999) *From Irenaeus to Grotius: A Sourcebook in Christian Political Thought 100–1625*. Grand Rapids, MI: W.B. Eerdmans.

Thorpe, Lewis (trans.) (1969) *Einhard and Notker the Stammerer: Two Lives of Charlemagne*. London: Penguin Books.

CHAPTER 5
The Reformation

Carlos M.N. Eire

Introduction

The word "Reformation" has been a troublesome one for Catholic historians since the sixteenth century, when Protestants first claimed exclusive rights to the term. In Protestant historiography – which served for centuries as the framework for the national histories of many northern European nations, including England and its North American colonies – "Reformation" meant only one thing: the rise and triumph of Protestantism. As Protestants saw it, Catholics could not speak of reform among themselves for the simple reason that they had remained Catholics. At its core, Protestant historiography was guided by a single paradigm: the notion that the Catholic Church was thoroughly corrupt, even demonic, and that it needed to be abolished and replaced.

Catholics had a very different story to tell, even when acknowledging the sins of their Church, for as they saw it, Protestants were not true reformers, but rebels and heretics. For centuries Catholics had conceived of genuine "reform" conservatively, as any improvement that did not challenge the Church's authority structure. More often than not, Catholic "reformers" were clerics who remained obedient to their superiors and whose agenda lined up with the teachings and traditions of the hierarchical Church. As far as the history of the pivotal sixteenth century was concerned, Catholic historiography focused on the Council of Trent – which had issued numerous decrees entitled *de reformatione* – and on the establishment and renewal of various religious orders. In other words, Catholics would boast of the many reforms that took place in their Church throughout the sixteenth and seventeenth centuries, but they shied away from speaking of any "Reformation" with a capital "R."

In the late nineteenth century, thinking about this issue began to change, thanks largely to the German historian Leopold von Ranke, and his use of the term *Gegenreformation*, or "Counter Reformation." Ranke, a Protestant, thrust Catholicism into the narrative of the Reformation in a negative way, by turning it into an opposing movement, as an obligatory dialectical symmetry of a Hegelian sort. Ranke's

German *Gegenreformation* was a Counter-Reformation in two ways: not just a nega-tion or antithesis of everything the Protestants asserted, but also an antagonistic force that was constantly engaged in mortal conflict with Protestantism. Ranke's new term caught on rapidly, giving rise to the acceptance of two distinct Reformations in the early modern period: one positive and Protestant, the other negative and Catholic. It was a big step toward the redefinition of the history of the early modern period, but not an entirely positive one from the Catholic point of view.

In the mid-twentieth century, however, Catholic historians began to reclaim the concept of "reform" in a positive way, giving it the same sort of meaning that Prot-estant historians had given it for so long. Hubert Jedin, a Catholic historian, first led the way by proposing that the term "Catholic Reformation" was far more adequate than Ranke's "Counter-Reformation." Gradually, the term gained acceptance, espe-cially after the Second Vatican Council (1963–65) ushered in a new era of reform and ecumenical goodwill, lessening the ages-old antagonism that had dominated Catholic–Protestant relations. Jedin and those who followed in his wake did more than simply employ a new term: focusing on continuities rather than discontinu-ities between medieval and early modern Catholicism, historians of the "Catholic Reformation" began to craft a new narrative, one in which a long and constant pat-tern of reform could be traced within the Catholic Church itself – a vibrant trajectory of improvement that was already in place before the advent of Protestantism and that continued to grow and flourish in spite of it. Changes in terminology and chronology are seldom accepted immediately, so throughout the final two decades of the twentieth century, a fair amount of disagreement over the terms "Counter-Reformation" and "Catholic Reformation." proved inevitable. Was either term adequate? Was one better than the other? This debate was intensified by other developments in the study of the early modern age that further redefined the meaning of "reformation" for this period.

In France, many historians began speaking of the *longue durée*, that is, of long-term patterns that transcended the conventional periodization of Western history. One French historian, Jean Delumeau, suggested that a defining characteristic of the Middle Ages was the gradual, but very superficial, Christianization of Europe, and that the religious divisions that arose in the sixteenth century could best be understood as a disagreement over how best to finally Chrisianize Europe for good. In this view of his-tory, the differences between Catholics and Protestants mattered much less than the common effort of their elites to instill certain Christian values in the common people.

At the very same time, historians in Germany also began to reassess their approach to large-scale changes in history, and their approach to the Protestant Reformation in particular. Gone was the simple concept of the Protestant Reformation as a sudden outburst of religious awakening. Gone too was the notion that religion itself should be the main focus of attention. Out of the ashes of post-war Germany came the new insight that what distinguished the early modern age most intensely was the pro-cess of state formation. In this view of things, the development of the modern state is seen as the driving force behind all reformations in society, including the reformation of religion. And it was precisely because the elites saw religion as an agent of change that Europe fell victim to intense religious disagreements, and why Germany in par-ticular underwent a "Long Reformation" that stretched into the seventeenth century, a reformation that was accomplished through "social disciplining" and "confession-alization," that is, through a molding of the common people into pliant good citizens who thought of themselves first and foremost as Christians who belonged to a specific "confession," or Church that related to the State in specific ways.

Taken together, the advances made by the French and the Germans – and the North Americans and Britons who followed them and blazed their own trails in the same direction – have brought about a wholesale redefinition of the meaning of "Reforma-tion" with a capital "R," changing it from the singular "Reformation" to the plural "Reformations," and stretching its duration to three centuries, roughly from 1400 to 1700. No longer bound to writing history as Catholics or Protestants, thanks to ecu-menism and secularization, the majority of historians of the early modern period now understand "Reformation" as a term that designates the attempts made by *both* Cath-olic and Protestant societies to lessen the gap between Christian ideals and social and political realities.

Reform in the Late Middle Ages

In the fifteenth century, Western European culture seemed obsessed with the idea of reform. Terms such as *reformatio, renovatio, restauratio, reparatio,* and *instauratio* were frequently used by ever-growing numbers of the elite. Rulers, clerics, and intellectuals alike seemed to share in a sense of dismay that was also filled with optimism about the possibility for change. Egidio da Viterbo, a very high-placed churchman, summed it up in the opening address to the Fifth Lateran Council in 1512, which had been convened by the worldly Pope Julius II. Warning that the Church needed to turn back to "its old purity, its ancient brilliance, its original splendor, and its own sources," Viterbo added that "celestial and human things . . . crave renewal" (in Olin, 1969: 44–53).

The idea of reform was not at all new, however; in fact, it was already an ancient tradition in the Catholic Church and European society. Paradoxically, the Church itself bred corruption and reform simultaneously, and this was an ongoing dialectic, as old as Christianity itself, which was driven by an intensely bipolar idealism: on the one hand, the Church taught that all humans are bound to sin, while on the other hand it encouraged all to obey Jesus' command "be ye perfect as your heavenly Father is per-fect" (Matt 5:48). Most often, it was the clerics themselves who strove to bridge the gap and bring Church and society closer to perfection. And as many of these reform-minded clerics saw it, the only way out of this dilemma was for the clergy to purify the Church in one way or another. To be a successful reformer, one had to discern the line between reform and rebellion, criticism and disobedience, dissent and heresy. It was a fine line at times, too fine or too wrongly drawn for some who chose to cross it. Consequently, while some reformers such as Saint Francis of Assisi (1182–1226) would be recognized as saints, others such as John Wycliffe (1330–84) and John Hus (1370–1415) could end up condemned as heretics.

Because religion was so intricately woven into nearly every aspect of life in medi-eval Europe, all religious reformers were also social, cultural, and political reformers. The phrase often used toward the end of the Middle Ages, *reformation in head and limbs* (*reformatio in capite et in membris*), which relied on a bodily metaphor and on medical theory, figuratively summed up the assumption that all reforms had to begin with the head, that is, at the apex of society, among the Pope and his clerics.

But reforming the Church was easier said than done, even for a pope or an emperor. By the beginning of the sixteenth century, despite all of the cries for reform, the Catholic Church was as rife with problems as the world itself. The situation was not necessarily worse than it had been for centuries – on the contrary, in some ways the Church and religious life were much more vibrant than ever. The difference was that during the course of the fifteenth century the abuses and failings of the Church became more conspicuous, more openly discussed, and more deeply resented by a wider spectrum of people. Also, after 1450, the invention of the printing press not only allowed for the wider dissemination of information and reforming ideas, but also speeded up the process of consciousness-raising, among both the clergy and the laity.

But, what, specifically, did reformers find objectionable about the late medieval Catholic Church? In what ways did they find the Church and its clergy corrupt? What were the failures and abuses singled out most often?

At the very top, in Rome, the papacy itself seemed the epitome of corruption, an office controlled by worldly men who seemed to embody sin rather than redemption from it. A popular Latin pun played on the meaning of the city's name, **Roma**, by suggesting that it was an acronym for the proverb *Radix omnium malorum avaritia*: "avarice is the root of all evil."

Beyond Rome, scattered throughout the map of Christendom, the bishops who were ostensibly in charge of the dioceses were a mixed lot in terms of their commitment to their vocation, but, overall, it was relatively easy to find fault with many of them. One of the worst problems at the episcopal level was absenteeism: that is, bishops who did not live within their dioceses, or even visit them. Another problem was pluralism, that is, the holding of two or more Church offices at once by some of the high clergy. Two other persistent problems in the episcopate were nepotism and simony. Nepotism is the practice of bestowing offices on one's relatives (from Latin, *nepos* = nephew). Though Church offices could never be made hereditary, there were no laws forbidding the appointment of relatives, and this sometimes placed certain offices in the hands of the same families for generations. Simony is the practice of selling Church offices (named after Simon Magus, who tried to buy influence from St Peter in Acts 8.18–24). Though simony was forbidden outright by the Church *de jure*, it was very much in place *de facto*, in various ways, thanks to dispensations and to some inventive loopholes in canon law.

Lower on the hierarchy, similar problems and abuses could be found nearly everywhere among the secular clergy. Preaching at a convocation of priests in 1512, the English humanist John Colet (1466–1519) complained about the lifestyle of many clerics:

> They give themselves to feasting and banqueting; spend themselves in vain babbling, take part in sports and plays, devote themselves to hunting and hawking; are drowned in the delights of this world; patronize those who cater for their pleasure . . . mixed up and confused with the laity, they lead, under a priestly exterior, the mere life of a layman.

Colet was no detached observer. As dean of St Paul's Cathedral in London, he had to deal with the failings of the clergy on a daily basis. He added: "Who is there who does not see this? Who that sees it does not grieve over it?"[1]

At the top of the ecclesiastical ladder, one step below the episcopacy, the cathedral clergy and the collegiate clergy were usually drawn from the various tiers of the upper class. These canons or collegiate clerics normally drew a larger income than parish clergy, and would prove to be among the most difficult to reform, given their privileged position in society. Below the cathedral chapters and collegiate Churches, most of the secular clergy were very poorly educated, or not educated at all. This meant that many parish priests lived lives that were barely distinguishable from those of their flocks, tilling the earth, minding the livestock, or drinking and brawling. In a list of complaints presented to Emperor Charles V in 1521, the lower clergy of Germany are described in the most unflattering terms:

> The majority of parish priests and other secular clerics mingle with the common people at inns and taverns. They frequent public dances and walk about the streets in lay garments, brandishing long knives. They engage in quarrels and arguments, which usually lead to blows, whereupon they fall upon poor folk, wound or even kill them, and then excommunicate them unless the injured parties agree to offer money for a settlement with the offending priest.[2]

The state of the monastics – the regular clergy – varied tremendously from place to place and house to house, but, overall, monasteries were not at all immune from the corruption that seemed to plague the secular clergy. Tales of mischief among monks and nuns abounded in the late Middle Ages. Often, as in Geoffrey Chaucer's *Canterbury Tales* (1390s), their failings were ridiculed in literature, reinforcing the myth that gluttony, drunkenness, greed, deceit, and lechery seemed to be as much a part of their lives as the habits they wore. It was a cheap shot, commonly taken. Yet, paradoxically, these signs of contradiction seemed to spark reform more intensely, for inasmuch as they were a cause for scandal, monks and nuns were also agents for change. Consequently, it is no accident that the man who sparked the Protestant Reformation was an Augustinian monk, and that so many of the leading reformers of the Catholic Church also belonged to the regular clergy.

Protestant Dissent and Reform

What we now call the Protestant Reformation was in large measure a revolt against the authority of the clerical hierarchy of the Catholic Church. Armed with the spiritual battle cry *Scripture Alone!*, some relatively young clerics – all in their thirties – began a reform movement around 1517 that eventually fractured the unity of the Church throughout Europe. Denying the authority of the Pope and redefining the nature and function of the clergy and the sacraments, these reformers would create new Churches and a tradition that would revere them as Reformers, with a capital "R."

Although no one at the time expected it, this epochal transformation of Western

Christendom began in 1517 as a simple "monkish squabble" – in the words of Pope Leo X. At issue was the topic of redemption, and more specifically of indulgences, that is, the remission of penalties in the afterlife that had been routinely granted by the popes since the time of the First Crusade in 1096. But what began as a theological dispute between two obscure clerics – Martin Luther, an Augustinian monk, and Johann Tetzel, a Dominican friar – rapidly escalated into a full-blown rebellion against Pope Leo X and the Catholic Church, larger in scope and more widespread and successful than any that the Catholic Church had ever faced.

Of course, Luther was not alone. Very quickly, as Luther's renown increased and as his list of complaints against the medieval Church grew longer, others began to step up their campaign against perceived errors and corruption. Some were close to Luther; others not, both literally and figuratively. Disagreement was rife among these reformers, and it quickly led to the birth of several new Churches. In essence, Protestants would evolve into four distinct families of Churches:

1 Lutherans: Confined to parts of Germany and all of Scandinavia, these state-run Churches adhered closely to the reforms outlined by Martin Luther (1483–1546).
2 The Reformed: Scattered throughout Europe, Reformed Protestants followed various leaders, but most notably Ulrich Zwingli (1484–1531) in Switzerland and John Calvin (1509–64) in many different places. Eventually, Reformed Protestants would end up controlling about half of Switzerland and all of Scotland and the Dutch Republic, and would also make up sizable minorities in France, England, Hungary, and Poland.
3 Anglicans: Established by King Henry VIII (1491–1547), with the English monarch as its supreme head, the Church of England would have a very complex history of reform.
4 The Radicals: Usually subdivided into Anabaptists, Spiritualists, and Anti-Trinitarians. "Radical" is a catch-all term that covers a very broad spectrum of religious dissenters who rejected not only Catholicism, but also the three other Protestant Churches just mentioned. Radicals tended to reject the symbiosis of Church and State and to believe in gathered Churches, that is, Churches composed only of true believers who had been baptized as adults. Some spiritualists, however, believed that genuine believers did not need a Church at all.

Despite all of this fragmentation, and all of their disagreements, Protestants shared several core ideas and goals that gave them a common sense of purpose. And their wholesale rejection of many of the key features of medieval Catholicism, in turn, also helped to shape how Catholics would react to them. Though there were many continuities between Catholicism and Protestantism, as one might expect among a people who continued to call themselves Christians and who professed belief in the same redeeming God and the same sacred texts, the discontinuities were immense and also numerous. Protestants rejected the authority of the Pope, the hierarchy of the Church, the institution of monasticism, the teachings of the medieval theologians, the validity of several sacraments, including that of confession, the existence of purgatory, the practice of praying for the dead and of praying to the saints as intercessors, the use of

Latin in ritual, the custom of clerical celibacy, the observance of fasts, vows, and pilgrimages, the veneration of images and relics, and belief in miracles and wonders. And that was just what they agreed on. There were even more items that Protestants rejected in different ways, sometimes vehemently disagreeing with one another about how best to reject them.

On a theological level, the most radical departure made by Protestants was the rejection of what Luther called "works righteousness," that is, the idea that individual Christians are either saved or damned on account of their behavior. All Protestants except for the Radicals denied the freedom of the will and the capacity of humans to influence God's judgment: one was saved by God's grace (*sola gratia*), freely given, and by faith alone (*sola fide*), not by any merit one could earn through virtuous deeds. Among the Reformed, the followers of John Calvin went furthest in following this teaching to its logical conclusion, elaborating a theology of predestination. Calvin's thinking, sometimes credited with having made Western capitalism possible, was as clear on this point as it was unflinching:

> Scripture, then, clearly shows that God once established by His eternal and unchangeable plan those whom He long before determined once and for all to receive into salvation; and those whom, on the other hand, he would devote to destruction.[3]

The Protestant Reformation was much more than theological dissent, however, and teachings such as predestination were inconceivable without a corresponding ecclesiology and a plan of action against the authority claims of the hierarchy of the Catholic Church. Armed with the spiritual battle cry " Scripture Alone!" (*sola scriptura*), Protestants everywhere rejected the office of the papacy and the notion of a permanent, indelible clerical office. As they saw it, clergy were *ministers* of the Word, not *priests* who mediated salvation to a subservient laity. The office of a cleric was determined solely by his function as preacher and servant of the community. At least in theory, if not always in practice, Protestants tended to uphold the notion that clerical authority was derived from the laity. In 1520, Martin Luther explained it this way:

> Now we who have been baptized are all uniformly priests in virtue of that very fact. The only addition received by the priests is the office of preaching, and even this with our consent.[4]

Moreover, Protestants also rejected the Pope's claims to supremacy and identified him as the Antichrist. In their view, the Pope and all of the Catholic clergy were abusive tyrants who had brought the Church to ruin. This charge struck a chord at a popular level, for even if they could not fully grasp the theology of the Protestant Reformers, the laity could easily understand the need for a reform of the clergy and a redefinition of their role.

Among the so-called "Radicals," a single concept prevailed: their belief that the Church should be a purely voluntary association and that baptism should not be forced on infants by the State. Beyond this point, there were wildly divergent opinions on authority. At one extreme, for instance, the militant Anabaptists of Münster took control of the entire city, and set up a "New Jerusalem" ruled despotically by a king-prophet and a court of elders. At the other extreme, the pacifist Hutterites and Moravian Brethren developed a more communal understanding of authority. And in another dimension altogether, spiritualists such as Sebastian Frank argued that there should be no visible Church at all, and no sacraments.

The Protestant Reformation was also a revolution in worship, and in thinking about the sacred and the way in which the natural and supernatural dimensions relate to one another. Though there was plenty of disagreement among Protestants on this point, all of them rejected the Catholic understanding of how spirit and matter relate to one another. Luther was much in favor of a sacramentally centered faith and even continued to believe in the real presence of Christ in the Eucharist, but nonetheless gave a much more spiritualized interpretation to ritual and reduced the sacraments from seven to two (baptism and Eucharist), reorienting the ritual life of his Church toward the Bible. Reformed Protestants, in contrast, were guided by the principle that the divine cannot be conveyed through finite matter (*finitum non est capax infiniti*), or as Ulrich Zwingli put it, that "they who trust in any created thing whatsoever are not truly pious."[5] Always on the lookout for "idolatry" or false worship, Reformed Protestants redefined every aspect of ritual, inside and out. This was no small point. As many anthropologists see it, the very essence of any religion is its ritual. And nothing could be further from Catholicism than the belief voiced by John Calvin: "Whatever holds down and confines the senses to the earth is contrary to the covenant of God; in which, inviting us to Himself, He permits us to think of nothing but what is spiritual" ("Commentary on the Last Four Books of Moses," in Calvin, 1863–80, volume 24: 387). This abhorrence of "idolatry" would turn all Reformed Protestants into determined political opponents of any state that supported Catholicism.

At the most radical end of the Protestant spectrum, spiritualists argued that ritual was unnecessary altogether. If the Spirit dwelt in every person, then everyone could deal with God directly. Sebastian Franck, for instance, would say: "Why should God wish to restore the outworn sacraments and take them back from the Antichrist [the Pope], yea, and contrary to his nature (which is Spirit and inward), yield to weak material elements?" ("Letter to John Campanus," in Williams, 1957: 154–5). An extremist to the core, Frank would also reject the Bible itself as "the paper Pope."

Catholic Reform

In many ways, an extremist like Sebastian Frank was a godsend to Catholic polemicists. As many Catholic apologists saw it, Franck's spiritualism was the logical conclusion of Luther's rebellion, and the ultimate testament to the slippery slope that lay on the other side of every challenge to papal authority. As one Catholic reformer put it,

> For already, since these men began, how many sects have torn the Church? . . . Truth is always one, while falsehood is varied and multiform; that which is straight is simple, that which is crooked has many turns.[6]

Faithful Catholics may have had a fairly simple guiding principle – to reform their Church from within while remaining obedient to its hierarchical authority – but carrying out the actual work of reform could be a very complex and difficult task, akin to the challenge of untying the fabled Gordian knot, little by little, with great patience, under highly stressful circumstances. Given the incredibly long history of the Church and the power, privileges, and wealth of its hierarchy, inertia and resistance were the rule rather than the exception. At the very top, the popes who were in charge of the Church just before and after the rise of Protestantism offered no solution. Scions of wealthy and powerful families, such as the Borgias (Alexander VI) and the Medicis (Leo X and Clement VII), rulers of much of central Italy, entangled in complex alliances with secular powers, these popes did little to thwart the Protestants or to reform the Church from within. Although many among the clergy and laity clamored for a council to handle the crisis, several popes balked at the suggestion, fearing their authority might be successfully challenged. Consequently, it took the papacy 28 years to convene a council. And when Pope Paul III finally used his authority to assemble a council at Trent in 1545, it would take another 18 years for it to complete its pressing business.

In the first half of the sixteenth century, then, Catholic reformers were more or less on their own. Some, like Cardinal Francisco Ximenez de Cisneros (1436–1517), Archbishop of Toledo, were lucky enough to hold powerful offices that enabled them to tackle some of the Church's worst problems. Ximenez de Cisneros not only expelled hundreds of unworthy clerics and monastics from their posts, but also encouraged biblical scholarship and vigorously supported the printing of devotional texts for the laity. As if this were not enough, he also used his vast income to establish a new university at Alcalá de Henares, the chief purpose of which was to properly educate the Spanish clergy.

Reformers who accomplished as much as Ximenez de Cisneros might have been rare, but there were still plenty of smaller-scale reforms afoot in Catholicism, especially among clerics and monastics of all types, both male and female, from the powerful Gian Pietro Caraffa (1476–1559), who became Pope Paul IV, to the humble Catherine of Genoa (1457–1510) and John of Avila (1500–69); from the very liberal and highly visible Bishop of Meaux, Guillaume Briconnet(1472–1534), to the very traditional Bishop of Verona, Gian Matteo Giberti (1495–1543), and the nearly invisible Carthusian monks of Cologne. And these reformers, in turn, influenced or gave rise to other reforms. It was a slow process, certainly when compared to the lightning-quick progress of the Protestant Reformation, but it was steady, and it eventually yielded significant results.

Catholic reform can be best understood as a collective and slow-moving effort that had been simmering throughout the Middle Ages, and began to gather strength in the late fifteenth century from the ground up, so to speak, thanks to the efforts of courageous and determined individuals, very few of whom wielded great power. It was also a movement that certainly had its share of leaders, but was never controlled by any single individual, not even by any pope. Roughly, it can be subdivided into five phases, keeping in mind that all chronological boundaries are permeable and that there were plenty of local variations to the broader developments that came along at any particular time:

1 From 1378 to 1517, when the challenges tended to be purely internal and heresies were contained.
2 Between 1517 and 45, from the advent of Luther to the opening of the Council of Trent, when Protestantism seemed unstoppable and responses to it were largely haphazard.
3 During the Council of Trent (1545–63), when Catholic reformers began to hit their stride and the leaders of the Church were forced to devise plans for genuine reform.
4 Between 1563 and 1618, when the reforms of Trent began to be implemented and Catholics began to win back territories that had previously become Protestant.
5 From 1618 to 1700, when Catholic baroque culture reached its apogee, and when religious wars, the witchcraft craze, and the rise of skepticism and empirical science all began to erode the Church's authority with ever-increasing intensity.

Though the reforms carried out by Catholics were so numerous and diverse and so intertwined (and sometimes also so slow and inperceptible) as to defy cataloging, they can be sorted out into 13 different areas. Ironically, even paradoxically, the reforms can be rightly considered the work of a large and ever more centralized institution, but it remains true nonetheless that the most effective and significant changes were often brought about at a local level through the efforts of specific individuals. It could be argued, then, that the reform in "head and limbs" was effected in large measure by the limbs themselves, thanks to a healthier head.

The Council of Trent, 1545–63

Arguably one of the most significant moments in all of Catholic history, this council reformed the Church from top to bottom, and set the course it would follow for the next four centuries. Due to the fact that the council met on-and-off over the space of 18 years, its work was carried out by different sets of representatives. Deeply influenced by Spanish reformers, especially in its later sessions, the Council of Trent clarified all points of doctrine, ritual, and ethics vis-à-vis the Protestant challenge and also sought to do away with the deeply ensconced corruptions and abuses that plagued the Church. As far as doctrine was concerned, the council made no compromises with Protestantism, denying the validity of most of their teachings and reaffirming the authority of the Pope and the Catholic hierarchy. In addition, the council not only defended traditional Catholic ritual and piety, but actually emphasized those aspects of worship that Protestantism had attacked most intensely, such as the veneration of saints, images, and relics.

Reform and standardization of ritual

Among the many achievements of the Council of Trent, one of the most significant was its reform of ritual, which gave a firm definition to Catholic identity as nothing else could. First and foremost, the council not only insisted on retaining Latin as the sole language for all Catholic worship, but also supplanted most local liturgies with a new universal ritual code. These changes were uniformly enforced through the publication and dissemination of the *Roman Missal* in 1570, which bound the faithful together in a common symbolic universe and also gave Catholicism a distinctive Latin voice. In 1614 the publication of the *Rituale Romanum* ensured even more consistency and universality by providing a standardization of all of the services performed by a priest that are not in the Missal, such as the rite of exorcism.

Reform of the secular clergy

In addition to drawing such clear boundaries for Catholic belief and practice, the council also set out to reform the clergy and to do away with abuses great and small, condemning all clerics who sold and bought appointments to office, held more than one post at a time, never or seldom set foot in their churches, or broke their vows of celibacy. Even more important, the council also called for bishops to be more involved in the education and oversight of the clergy who were under their charge, encouraging the creation of seminaries and the constant monitoring of clerical job performance.

Putting the decrees of the Council of Trent into effect proved to be a very long and difficult task, unevenly spread out over the Catholic world. In some dioceses, reforming bishops such as Milan's Carlo Borromeo (1538–84) implemented Trent's reforms immediately. Other dioceses were reformed much more slowly or gradually, or, sometimes, not at all. Resistance came from many quarters. In Milan, Cardinal Borromeo ended up being shot in the back by one of his priests while he said Mass. (Fortunately, the bullet bounced off his thick vestments.) In France, due to the crown's disagreement with Trent's affirmation of papal supremacy, the decrees of the council could not be published. Gradually, however, the reforms spread far and wide. By 1650 it would be difficult to find a diocese or parish that had not been touched by the reforms of the Council of Trent.

Reform of the regular clergy

Communities of monks, friars, and nuns could not usually be reformed by the Church hierarchy, but rather from within, by their own members. Even more so than in the case of the secular clergy, these reforms spread gradually and unevenly. In most cases, the reforms aimed to expel those members who were deemed unfit and to enforce a stricter application of the original rules. Some reforms, such as that of the Carmelite order, spearheaded by St Teresa of Avila (1515–82) and St John of the Cross (1542–91) involved the creation of new, distinct branches within an older order. Eventually, by 1650, the regular clergy as a whole were striving to meet their ideals more intensely than ever before.

Establishment of new orders

Throughout the sixteenth and seventeenth centuries the vigor of the regular clergy and of the Church as a whole was increased by the creation of new religious orders. Some, like the Discalced Carmelites, devoted themselves more intensely to the contemplative life, but others, such as the Theatines, Barnabites, Capuchins, and Ursulines dedicated themselves to ministering to the laity in new and innovative ways. And no new order achieved greater success all around than the Society of Jesus (the Jesuits), whose members are often described as the shock troops of the Counter Reformation. Founded in 1540 by Ignatius Loyola (1495–1556), the Jesuits quickly gained a reputation as superb teachers and missionaries. Organized like an army, run by a general who answered to no one other than the Pope, the Jesuits fanned out throughout Europe and the whole globe, winning over countless converts, gaining great power and influence, and imbuing the Church as a whole with a vigorous sense of purpose – and with the attitude summarized in the thirteenth rule of the "Rules for thinking with the Church" that Ignatius Loyola appended to his devotional manual, *The Spiritual Exercises*:

> To be right in everything, we ought always to hold that the white which I see, is black, if the Hierarchical Church so decides it, believing that between Christ our Lord, the Bridegroom, and the Church, His Bride, there is the same Spirit which governs and directs us for the salvation of our souls. Because by the same Spirit and our Lord Who gave the ten Commandments, our holy Mother the Church is directed and governed. (Ignatius of Loyola, 1914)

Tightening of censorship and vigilance

Having defined the contours of Catholic orthodoxy clearly at Trent, the Church could turn its attention more intensely to identifying and censoring questionable individuals and texts. Repression was most intense and efficient in Spain and Italy, where Inquisitions were already well established, but elsewhere in Europe Catholic authorities also did whatever they could to silence heresy. Far more universal in scope was the reach of the *Index of Forbidden Books* (*Index Librorum Prohibitorum*), first published in 1559 by the Sacred Congregation of the Roman Inquisition, and later expanded and updated periodically. Inclusion in the *Index* did not guarantee the disappearance of any title, but certainly hampered its circulation, for all books included in that list were ostensibly subject to confiscation and destruction. Suspicion of heresy was enough to land a title on the *Index*, and the lists grew to include an odd assortment of works, not all of which were explicitly heretical. Both the *Index* and the Inquisition worked together to stifle dissent rather effectively.

Promotion of saints and mystics

While Protestants tended to deny freedom of the will, and the possibility of mystical ecstasy in this life, Catholics did all they could to affirm them. Not surprisingly, then, one of the most direct challenges to the Protestant message was a gradual upsurge in the number of holy men and women that the Catholic Church promoted as saints, that is, as living proof of its teachings. These saints not only served as teachers and as servants of the poor and needy, but also confirmed the ultimate values of Catholicism through their heroic virtue and through their miracles. Their impact was immense, for everywhere throughout the Catholic world, texts that recounted the lives and miracles of these saints became very popular, especially between 1580 and 1680.

Promotion of miracles and shrines

Alongside the upsurge in the number of saints came a corresponding expansion of the miraculous, not just in terms of frequency and quantity, but also in terms of the kind of phenomena reported and accepted. As the sixteenth century gave way to the seventeenth the boundary between the natural and supernatural seemed to shift in Catholicism. From Teresa of Avila in Spain, whose corpse refused to decompose, to Joseph of Copertino in Italy, who flew through the air and read people's minds, to Martin de Porres in far-off Peru, who could be in two places at the same time and also talk to animals, the Catholic world pulsated with the expectation of everything that the Protestants ridiculed as impossible, and also with an eagerness to enshrine and venerate the miraculous with more fervor than ever before, thus intensifying the differences between Protestant and Catholic cultures.

Lay education and involvement

Ever conscious of the need to reform the Church "in head *and limbs*," the Council of Trent also gave a great boost to those lay movements that were already an essential part of the Church's life. First and foremost, the council sought to promote lay participation in confraternities, that is, in lay associations that devoted themselves to specific devotions and acts of charity. Another change, parallel to the growth of confraternities, was a gradual increase in the centrality of parish life in towns and cities, which brought the laity together more closely under a common roof and a common pastor. And along with this shift of attention toward the parish came also an effort to educate the laity, not just through more frequent sermons, but also through direct instruction. A key component in all this was the *Catechism of the Council of Trent* (1566), which neatly summarized the Catholic faith, and which pastors were supposed to use in the instruction of their flocks. Another key component was the publication of hundreds of devotional treatises aimed specifically at the laity, such as Luis de Granada's *The Sinner's Guide* (1565), Lorenzo Scupoli's *The Spiritual Combat* (1585), and Francis De Sales' *Introduction to the Devout Life* (1609), all of which went through many editions and translations.

Missionary expansion

The age of reforms was also an age of exploration and discovery, and an age of unprecedented missionary activity, especially in the Americas and in Asia. Early on, much of the missionary effort fell to the religious orders already well-established in Europe, such as the Franciscans, Dominicans, and Augustinians. But from 1540 on, the lion's share of the attention (if not of the work itself) began to be claimed by the Jesuits. Even more significant, Europe itself came to be viewed as a missions field, not just in those areas lost to Protestantism, but almost anywhere at all. Though it is difficult to measure success in these urban and rural European missions, many historians now accept it as an indisputable fact that this phenomenon needs to be seen as the ultimate "Christianization" of Europe.

Renewal of scholastic theology

Catholics responded to the Protestant rejection of medieval scholastic theology by reemphasizing the very methods that came under attack. One scholastic in particular who grew in stature during this period was Thomas Aquinas (1224–74). Not only was his *Summa Theologiae* placed alongside the Bible at the Council of Trent; in 1567 Pope Pius V proclaimed him a doctor of the Universal Church, and from 1570 on, well into the eighteenth century, numerous editions of his *Opera Omnia* continued to be published. But there was far more to the scholastic revival than this. A roster of brilliant theologians, most of them Spanish and many of them Jesuits, took on all subjects, moving Catholic theology into a new age, writing in Latin, relying not just on the Bible, but also on Plato and Aristotle, and the Church Fathers, and on all of the other scholastics the Protestants reviled. The most notable of these thinkers were Francisco de Vitoria (1486–1546), Melchior Cano OP (1509–60), Francisco Suárez SJ (1548–1617), Luis de Molina SJ (1535–1600), and Roberto Bellarmino SJ (1542–1621).

Promotion of anti–Protestant polemic

Although at first they never seemed to match their Protestant opponents when it came to polemics and propaganda, Catholics eventually managed to find their voice. The writing and publishing of texts that aimed to deny and demolish Protestant claims had been part of the Catholic Reformation from the start, as evidenced in the polemical works of Luther's early opponents, John Eck (1486–1543), Jerome Emser (1478–1527), John Cochlaeus (1479–1552), and Jacob Latomus (1475–1544), but it was not until 1550 or so that Catholics began to hit their stride in this area. Whether it was through histories such as Pedro de Ribadeneyra's *History of the Schism of the Church of England*, or through exegetical rebuttals of Protestant views, such as Peter Canisius' *Commentaries on the Corruption of the Word* (1585), or through more theological and catechetical texts, such as Francis De Sales' *Controversies*, Catholic authors would struggle to never again allow Protestants to gain the upper hand.

Promotion of religious art and music

Catholic reform was as sensual as it was spiritual, for at the core of the Catholic faith lay the claim that all of Creation is a gateway to the Creator and that matter and spirit are not antithetically opposed to one another. Exuberance is the hallmark of Catholic art and music from this period. In the nineteenth century, derisive moderns would dismiss this ebullience as "baroque"– a French word meaning "strange" or "bizarre"– but in the seventeenth century, especially, lack of restraint became a virtue in Catholic aesthetics and so did the blurring of distinctions between the heavenly and the earthly, and this "baroque" sensibility became the very essence of the faith. Nowhere could the senses be more overwhelmed than in a baroque church at High Mass, and nowhere else could the stark aesthetics of Protestantism and its *sola scriptura* principle be more thoroughly challenged or denied.

Conclusion

Scholarly opinion now leans heavily toward speaking of "Reformations," in the plural, rather than of a single "Reformation" or an opposite "Counter-Reformation," and also toward conceiving of these "Reformations" not so much as religious movements that reshaped society, but rather as indispensable tools in the process of social disciplining and state-building in early modern Europe.

Viewing all of the "Reformations" of the early modern period as a single movement has its advantages and disadvantages. On the positive side, when all of the religious changes of this period are seen as an interrelated set of movements that took a long while to unfold – as "Reformations" – it becomes easier to see how they shaped each other while they reshaped the Western world. In sum, this new perspective posits what Thomas Jefferson might have called a "self-evident truth": that one cannot fully understand the Protestant Reformation without taking Catholicism into account, and vice versa.

Another advantage of viewing all of the "Reformations" together over a period of two centuries is that such a perspective reveals what they had in common, in spite of all the strife and the bloodshed. This, in turn, helps to prove that theology alone is not the measure of all things, and that reductionism is as perilous an enterprise in this period as in any other. When all is said and done, one must admit, both Catholic and Protestant Churches tried to elicit the same kind of behavior from their members in the early modern period, and both also strove to create very similar kinds of "good" citizens for the new centralizing states of Europe.

But stressing the similarities between warring confessions and seeing them all as instruments of the state-building elites of this period also has obvious perils. One fact that is easily buried and forgotten when the various "Reformations" are all placed in the same frame of reference is one of the most conspicuous, and perhaps the most significant of all: the fact that Catholicism and Protestantism had vastly different world-views and produced very different cultures. The list of differences, in fact, will always be much longer than the list of similarities. And at the top of the list must stand the fact that the Catholic Reformation – or whatever one chooses to call the process through which early modern Catholicism redefined itself over and against Protestantism – was a reaffirmation of most of the principles rejected by the Protestants. Yes, one must admit, the ethics of Protestants and Catholics remained fairly similar, as one would expect from Churches that followed the same Ten Commandments and read the same Gospels. But beyond that, what? Beyond ethics, where are the similarities? No matter what Immanuel Kant might have said, religion is much more than ethics, and in *real* religion as opposed to *religion within the limits of reason alone*, metaphysics is what really matters, not just as an abstraction, but as the very foundation and framework of society. As most anthropologists and historians of religion still see it, that sacred triad of myth (theology), ritual, and symbol defines not just the religion of a people, but also their society, culture, and economy, along with their *Weltanschaung*, or world-view. And when it comes to that sacred triad, the very essence of religion, Catholicism and Protestantism remained worlds apart and created very different cultures, despite all of the similarities that linked them.

Yes, one must ultimately admit, there were multiple Reformations set in motion in the sixteenth century, and they had deep roots in the preceding centuries, and they gave shape to each other and to the West over a long period of time in what we now call the Early Modern age. In fact, these Reformations helped shape Modernity itself. Nonetheless, all of this should never lead one to assume that the Reformation that early modern Catholics undertook could be easily mistaken for that of the Protestants.

Notes

1   John Colet, "Oratio habita ad clerum in convocatione" (1512) in Seebohm, 1869: 230–47.
2   *Deutsche Reichstagakten*, II (Gotha, 1896), 670–704, translated by G. Strauss, *Manifestations of Discontent in Germany on the Eve of the Reformation* (Bloomington, IN: University of Indiana Press, 1971), 61.
3   *Institutes of the Christian Religion*, Book III, chapter 21.7, in Calvin, 1961, vol. 2: 931.
4   Martin Luther, "The Babylonian Captivity of the Church," translated in Luther, 1961.
5   Ulrich Zwingli, "Commentary on the True and False Religion," in Zwingli, 1929, vol. 2: 92.
6   Cardinal Jacopo Sadoleto, "To his dearly beloved brethren, the magistrates, council, and citizens of Geneva" (1539), in Olin, 2000: 40.

References and Further Reading

Primary sources

Calvin, John (1961) *Institutes of the Christian Religion*, 2 vols. trans. Ford Lewis Battles; ed. J. T. McNeill. Philadelphia, PA: Westminster Press.
Calvin, John (1863–80) *Joannis Calvini Opera quaesupersunt omnia*. ed. W. Baum et al. Braunschweig.
Ignatius of Loyola (1914) *The Spiritual Exercises of St Ignatius of Loyola*. trans. Elder Mullen SJ. New York: P. J. Kennedy and Sons.

Luther, Martin (1961) *Martin Luther: Selections from his Writings.* ed. John Dillenberger. New York: Anchor Books.

Olin, John C. (ed.) (1969) *The Catholic Reformation: Savonarola to Ignatius of Loyola.* New York: Fordham University Press.

Olin, John C. (ed.) (2000) *A Reformation Debate.* New York: Fordham University Press.

Seebohm, Frederic (ed. and trans.) (1869) *The Oxford Reformers,* 2nd edn. London: Longmans.

Williams, George H. (ed. and trans.) (1957) *Spiritual and Anabaptist Writers.* Philadelphia, PA: Westminster Press.

Zwingli, Ulrich (1929) *The Latin Works and the Correspondence of Huldrych Zwingli,* 3 vols. ed. and trans. S. M. Jackson. Philadelphia, PA: Heidelberg Press.

Reformation surveys

Bireley, Robert (1999) *The Refashioning of Catholicism, 1450–1700.* Washington, DC: Catholic University of America Press.

Bossy, John (1985) *Christianity in the West, 1400–1700.* Oxford/New York: Oxford University Press.

Collinson, Patrick (2004) *The Reformation: A History.* New York: Modern Library.

Delumeau, Jean (1977) *Catholicism between Luther and Voltaire.* London: Burns and Oates; Philadelphia, PA: Westminster Press; French edition: Paris, 1971.

Hsia, R. Po-chia (2005) *The World of Catholic Renewal, 1540–1770,* 2nd edition. Cambridge/New York: Cambridge University Press.

MacCulloch, Diarmaid (2004) *The Reformation: A History.* New York: Viking.

O'Malley, John (2000) *Trent and All That.* Cambridge, MA: Harvard University Press.

Ozment, Steven (1992) *Protestants: Birth of a Revolution.* New York: Doubleday.

Rublack, Ulinka (2005) *Reformation Europe.* New York: Cambridge University Press.

On late medieval religion

Bartos, F.M. (1986) *The Hussite Revolution, 1424–1437,* English edition prepared by John M. Klassen. New York: Columbia University Press.

Fudge, Thomas A. (1998) *The Magnificent Ride: The First Reformation in Hussite Bohemia.* Brookfield, VT: Ashgate.

Huizinga, Johan (1996) *The Autumn of the Middle Ages.* Chicago: University of Chicago Press; first published as *Herfsttij der Middeleeuwen.* Haarlem: H.D. Tjeenk Willink, 1919.

Rex, Richard (2002) *The Lollards.* New York: Palgrave.

On specific aspects of the Reformation era

Benedict, Philip (2002) *Christ's Churches Purely Reformed: A Social History of Calvinism.* New Haven, CT: Yale University Press.

Black, Christopher (2004) *Church, Religion and Society in Early Modern Italy.* New York: Palgrave Macmillan.

Chatellier, Louis (1989) *The Europe of the Devout: The Catholic Reformation and the Formation of a New Society,* trans. Jean Birrell. New York: Cambridge University Press.

Christian, William Jr. (1981) *Local Religion in Sixteenth Century Spain.* Princeton, NJ: Princeton University Press.
Dickens, A.G. (1989) *The English Reformation*, 2nd edition. London: Batsford.
Duffy, Eamon (2005) *The Stripping of the Altars: Traditional Religion in England, c.1400–c.1580*, 2nd edition. New Haven, CT/ London: Yale University Press.
Eire, Carlos M.N. (1986) *War against the Idols: The Reformation of Worship from Erasmus to Calvin.* New York: Cambridge University Press.
Forster, Marc (1992) *The Counter-Reformation in the Villages: Religion and Reform in the Bishopric of Speyer, 1560–1720.* Ithaca, NY: Cornell University Press.
Gordon, Bruce (2002) *The Swiss Reformation.* Manchester: Manchester University Press.
Gritsch, Eric W. (1994) *Fortress Introduction to Lutheranism.* Minneapolis, MN: Fortress Press.
Hsia, R. Po-Chia (1989) *Social Discipline in the Reformation.* London: Routledge.
Iserloh, Erwin, Glazik, Joseph, and Jedin, Hubert (1986) *Reformation and Counter Reformation*, trans. Anselm Biggs and Peter W. Becker. New York: Seabury Press.
Jedin, Hubert (1963) *A History of the Council of Trent*, trans. Ernest Graf. London: Nelson.
Kamen, Henry (1998) *The Spanish Inquisition: A Historical Revision.* New Haven, CT: Yale University Press.
Kingdon, Robert M. (1995) *Adultery and Divorce in Calvin's Geneva.* Cambridge, MA: Harvard University Press.
Marshall, Peter (2003) *Reformation England, 1480–1642.* London: Arnold.
Naphy, William G. (2003) *Calvin and the Consolidation of the Genevan Reformation.* Louisville, KY: Westminster John Knox Press.
Ozment, Steven (1973) *Mysticism and Dissent.* New Haven, CT: Yale University Press.
Ozment, Steven (1975) *The Reformation in the Cities.* New Haven, CT: Yale University Press.
Racaut, Luc (2002) *Hatred in Print: Catholic Propaganda and Protestant Identity during the French Wars of Religion.* Burlington, VT: Ashgate.
Rawlings, Helen (2002) *Church, Religion and Society in Early Modern Spain.* New York: Palgrave.
Scribner, Robert (1994) *For the Sake of Simple Folk: Popular Propaganda for the German Reformation.* New York: Oxford University Press.
Targoff, Ramie (2001) *Common Prayer: The Language of Public Devotion in Early Modern England.* Chicago, IL: University of Chicago Press.
Walton, Robert C. (1967) *Zwingli's Theocracy.* Toronto: University of Toronto Press.
Williams, George H. (1992) *The Radical Reformation*, 3rd edition. Kirksville, MI: Sixteenth Century Journal Publishers.

Anthropological approaches to religion

Geertz, Clifford (ed.) (1974) *Myth, Symbol, and Culture.* New York: Norton.
Turner, Victor (1995) *The Ritual Process: Structure and Anti-Structure.* New York: Aldine de Gruyter.

CHAPTER 6

Modernity and Post-Modernity

Peter J. Casarella

Joseph Cardinal Ratzinger's first papal decision concerned his name. After the presentation of a Pope named Benedict, reporters scrambled to uncover the hidden layers of meaning. One clue, later confirmed by the Pope himself, was the lonely figure of Pope Benedict XV, a largely forgotten advocate of world peace from World War I. In a world marred by an eclipse of cultural memory, Benedict XVI entered the media frenzy surrounding his election by broadening the world's view of its present troubles.

This essay covers a period of 256 years. As in the new Pope's selection of a name, I attempt to present issues in the Church today against the backdrop of a broader legacy. For example, there is currently a debate in the US Church regarding the difference of perspective between Catholics who underwent the experience of the Second Vatican Council in the 1960s as adults and those who came of age during the pontificate of Pope John Paul II (Casarella, 2003). The former identify with a brand of progressive Catholicism they consider to be stamped with conciliar authority. The latter group often finds that standpoint dated. Both sides need to deepen their historical memory. Progressives overestimate the novelty of Vatican II and too often ignore the painstaking recovery of the tradition that shaped the preparation of its decrees. Traditionalists commit the same myopia when they presume that the Polish Pope's interpretation of the Council circumvents the crucible of modernity or that his encyclicals are nurtured solely by premodern wisdom.

Conservatives and liberals in the Church are enriched (and neither extreme is vindicated!) by a consideration of the evolution of Catholicism in the modern era. These centuries will be treated in terms of four periods: (1) the French Revolution and its aftermath (1750–1815), (2) the initial struggle with the Industrial Revolution, modern atheism, Catholic liberalism, and the dissolution of the Papal States (1815–1914), (3) the questioning of modern progress (1914–78), and (4) the call for a new evangelization at the beginning of a new millennium (1979–2005). While there is no single thread that connects these four epochs with the current generation gap among US Catholics, two constants emerge. First, there arises already in the eighteenth century the issue of what Vatican II addressed under the rubric of the "rightful autonomy of earthly affairs." In other words, how are personal and political freedoms to be treated by the Church when society advocates a norm of secular reason? The precise nature of the Church's communion is an equally recurrent theme. In the late nineteenth century, the conflict focused on the juridical power of the Bishop of Rome. Today one might cite globalization as the context for a new catholicity (Schreiter, 1997). In either case, what is at stake is the distinctiveness of what Johann Adam Möhler considered to be a uniquely Catholic idea of unity (1996: 261–2).

The Church in an Age of Revolution: 1750–1815

In 1789 revolution broke out in France. An older scholarship focused on the "shock of augmented revolution" felt by the institutional Church in order to highlight that changes in European society at the end of the eighteenth century represented the first public engagement with de-Christianization in the history of the West (Latourette, 1965). But one recent study argues convincingly for the resilience and vitality of eighteenth-century Catholicism and demonstrates that certain Catholics at the epicenter of revolutionary politics, namely, the educated clergy in France, assimilated quickly and not without a certain eclecticism key principles of the new philosophy (e.g., the duties of Christian citizenship or the cultivation of religion as a personal sentiment) precisely in order to defend orthodox belief (Aston, 2000: 81–99). The confluence of high-minded ideals (e.g., "liberty, equality, and fraternity") and rabid anti-clericalism is so difficult to decipher that one can with good reason consider the historical event of the French Revolution as a palimpsest (Tracy, 1987: 3). For example, the declaration in 1790 of a "Civil Constitution of the Clergy" sought to bring the reorganization of the French Church directly under state control. Ecclesiastical property was nationalized, monasteries and religious organizations dissolved, and hundreds of faithful lay Catholics slaughtered. A condemnation of the new constitution by Pope Pius VI had little effect on France's Constituent Assembly, whose members were also dismayed at the high percentage of non-consenting clergy in rural areas. French Catholics were forced to choose between their loyalty to a Roman pontiff or a Parisian legislature. The subsequent policy of de-Christianization eliminated the Sunday Sabbath from the calendar, and the increasingly anti-clerical Assembly made any rapprochement unthinkable. The Assembly's decree of religious freedom in 1795 was more a matter of political expediency than the promotion of personal liberty for Catholics.

Napoleon Bonaparte (1769–1821), a Catholic from Corsica with the ambition to annex the Papal States, also had political gain in view when he promoted a religiously neutral state. He was successful in exploiting the religious feeling of Catholics and sought a papal alliance. After Napoleon's final defeat at Waterloo, the Council of Vienna in 1815 restored Pius VII's position as ruler of the Papal States. It seemed at first that the new alliance between the Pope and the Bourbon king of France would prevent future revolutions, but this did not prove to be the case.

The age was one not only of magnetic individuals but also of disputed ideals. The French Revolution was fueled by a modern concept of emancipation from tyranny, but its recourse to intimidation made it an object of ridicule by both defenders and critics of Enlightenment freedom. Conservatives like Edmund Burke offered qualified praise for some elements of the new democracy while exposing the internal contradictions in the Revolutionary program. The attitude of the Church toward the philosophy of the Enlightenment was less differentiated. The institution was not able to face the intellectual challenge posed by the secular elites who were forging a radically new view of the world. In spite of an occasional sign of papal acquiescence, the large majority of cardinals and prelates remained consistently opposed to modern philosophy and favored a return to established religion (Jedin and Dolan, 1981b: 91).

The ancient motto *Sapere aude!* ("Dare to know!") was revived in a programmatic essay by Immanuel Kant (1724–1804) (Kant, 1959) and echoed in intellectual circles throughout Europe. In France Voltaire (1694–1778) was a loyal standard-bearer *and* sharp critic of the Enlightenment. Early on Voltaire espoused a purely natural religion, i.e., a rational faith devoid of any tenets from revealed sources like the Bible. On the other hand, Voltaire defended the existence of God and the immortal human soul and could point to elements of his philosophy that were more traditional than the even more streamlined British Deism. The chief object of his acerbic wit was hypocrisy, whether carried out in the name of a revealed religion, the Catholic Church, or the new goddess of the Enlightenment, i.e., Reason.

There were more conservative Catholic thinkers in this period (Heimann, 1999: 471–6). René Francis Augustus, Viscount de Chateaubriand (1768–1848) was a French nobleman who had the leisure and temperament to pursue travel, poetry, fraternizing with the likes of George Washington and Napoleon, and overt skepticism regarding religion. A brush with death and the passing of his mother occasioned a change of heart. The immense popularity of his *The Genius of Christianity, or the Beauties of the Christian Religion* (1802) was helped by Napoleon's re-opening of the Catholic Church one year earlier. Chateaubriand challenged Voltaire's Enlightenment, and his lyrical defense of Christianity found an attentive audience among those who were still not convinced of the usurpation of faith by reason alone. The resurgence of traditional French Catholicism was not simply among intellectuals and nobility. For example, the number of nuns in the now restored or newly opened religious houses of France doubled between 1814 and 1830 (Heimann, 1999: 480).

Expansion in the missionary territories of the European monarchs was not progressing as rapidly as it had in the previous two centuries (Jedin and Dolan, 1981a: 135–325). A major period of missionary activity was brought to a sudden halt when the Jesuit missions were temporarily dissolved by the Pope in 1773, an order not lifted until 1814. A few stalwarts continued to build up the Church in the midst of the upheaval. For example, Blessed Junípero Serra (1713–84) was a professor of philosophy who traveled at the age of 36 from his native Mallorca to Mexico to join Franciscan missionaries who had benefited from the Jesuit expulsion. Because of his political and intellectual prowess, Br Junípero was sent up the coast of what was then the northernmost boundary of New Spain and is now California. He had great success in conversions, in founding missions as far north as what is now San Francisco, and in introducing agricultural commodities that remain vital to the economy of the region even today. But his methods of presenting the gospel have been evaluated in very different ways by contemporary historians (Sandos, 1988). It seems clear, for example, that Serra considered the newly baptized Indians his spiritual children and explicitly sanctioned the use of corporal punishment for their chastisement, but it is not clear that he himself went beyond established practices or encouraged forced conversions.

The Rise of Prometheanism: 1815–1914

The near century that runs from the Council of Vienna to the outbreak of World War I included a wave of revolutions that spread across Europe in 1848, an upheaval in technology that made rural folk endure intolerable working conditions in urban settings, Darwin's *Origin of the Species*, the invention of electricity, and the genesis of quantum mechanics. These are just some of the momentous events that contributed to the palpable sense that history was accelerating at an unprecedented rate and that the Euro-American of the late nineteenth and early twentieth centuries – like the mythical Prometheus in the ancient world – had finally succeeded in stealing fire from the gods. Catholicism in the nineteenth century was not completely beholden to the new Promethean spirit, for its internal development was often shaped by events that hardly contributed to a heightened sense of progress, e.g., the deployment of newly founded orders of European missionaries into Africa and Asia, waves of Marian piety that spread across the globe, and the decision of a Pope at the end of the century to brand St Thomas Aquinas as the author of the "true meaning of liberty." These contradictions represent the spiritual paradoxes of the age.

The conclusion of the first half of the nineteenth century brought the age of revolutions to a close and unleashed a new series of challenges to the political and spiritual authority of the Catholic Church. The epoch was one of national independence accompanied by an increasingly international brand of overt anticlericalism. The July Revolution of 1830 overthrew the Bourbon dynasty. That same year Pope Pius VIII died. His successor, a theologian who took the name Gregory XVI, faced the new climate by repudiating all forms of revolutionary thought. An economic depression fell upon the European continent in the mid-1840s, and the conditions of the working classes worsened. In February, 1848 Karl Marx (1818–83) and Friedrich Engels (1820–95) published their *Communist Manifesto*. The effect of the international Communist movement could be seen in the revolutions that spread across Europe. They failed to produce any long-term changes of a regime. Monarchies eventually resumed their former place in most of the European capitals. But the social consequences, albeit not exactly of the sort envisioned by Marx and Engels, were far-reaching. At the end of 1848, a new united Germany had been formed as a constitutional monarchy. Moreover, Europe came to recognize as a result of 1848 constitutional protections such as freedom of the press, universal male suffrage, and the freedom to form trade associations. In spite of the "spectre of Communism" announced by Marx and Engels, the educated elites in European society had made a definitive shift from the support for the aristocracy to a new loyalty in the bourgeoisie, a class that consisted of bankers, industrialists, and civil servants. As a rule Rome did not endorse the prognostications of either socialists or the equally secular representatives of the growing middle class. On the other hand, the conscious relativization of faith aggressively pursued by intellectuals both within and outside of the Church became a primary preoccupation of the hierarchy for the ensuing decades.

"Liberal Catholicism" first emerges as a coherent, albeit ecclesiastically suppressed reform movement in the wake of the revolutions of 1848. At first liberal Catholics defended freedom in order to protect the Church from external political encroachments. Félicité Robert de Lamennais (1782–1854) is a case in point. Lamennais originally defended the freedom of the Church so that the teachings of the Pope could be freely professed throughout Europe. He broke with the ultramontane group – so named for their allegiance to those beyond the Alps in Rome – during the 1830 revolution in France and founded a short-lived journal entitled *L'Avenir* ("The Future"). The journal was shut down after Pope Gregory XVI condemned Lamennais' ideas in the 1832 encyclical *Mirari Vos*.

Germany experienced a comparable theological revival. Franz Xavier von Baader (1765–1841) became a professor of philosophy in Munich after pursuing a career in medicine and engineering. His attraction to the Protestant mystic Jakob Böhme and to the Protestant theologian Schelling gave his thought a decidedly Idealist caste. Johann Joseph Görres (1776–1848) was a Catholic layman deeply affected by Romanticism and equally supportive of the French revolution until he visited Paris in 1799. Görres published a weekly newspaper that attacked Napoleon in the name of restoring the old German empire. He spent much of this time engaging liberal politics and trying to write the definitive Christian interpretation of world history. The Catholic Tübingen School of theology was founded by Johann Sebastian Drey (1777–1853). Among Drey's students are the Church historian Johann Adam Möhler (1796–1838) and the New Testament scholar Johann Evangelist Kuhn (1806–87). Möhler applied Drey's idealist notion of history as an organic living form to the Catholic tradition, the unity of the Church, and the differences between Catholics and Protestants. Kuhn was more critical vis-à-vis Romanticism than the earlier generation but still sufficiently modern to draw hefty criticism from Neo-Scholastic quarters. In Vienna the private scholar and priest Anton Günther (1783–1863) also attempted an influential synthesis of Catholic faith and post-Romantic philosophy. His works were placed on the Index of Forbidden Books by Pope Pius IX.

What, if anything, do these diverse figures hold in common? Steinfels has identified what he considers the movement's unifying features (1994: 31–7). First, Catholic liberals in the nineteenth century offered a nuanced assessment of the political ideals that the revolutionaries espoused. Second, liberals were convinced that the Old Regime was dead and the Church must prepare the way for a new form of Catholicism bereft of the trappings of the monarchical despots. Third, liberals endorsed the pursuit of secular learning, the civil liberties that were emerging in the revolutionary uprisings, and the idea that freedom of conscience could serve the end of a socially vigorous and fully independent Catholic Church. Finally, Catholic liberals of this period generally did *not* bind their impassioned endorsement of new democratic ideals to the internal reform of the Church. In spite of their attempts at moderation, the Catholic liberals were vilified for advocating principles inimical to the faith.

It took some time for the religious orders to recover from Napoleon's closing of monasteries and alienation of Church property, but new congregations eventually sprung up in large numbers. Canon law was changed in 1816 to allow the approbation for the first time of a female congregation with simple vows and whose members were not secluded. The revitalization of the orders often led to a spiritual revitalization of the laity. Lay revivals were sometimes sparked by a saintly individual, e.g., St John Marie Vianney (1786–1859). Popularly known as the Curé d'Ars, this pastor from a tiny French village became revered throughout the world for his persistent proclamation of Christ's gospel of repentance. Other times miraculous events intervened. In 1831 the Virgin appeared to a Parisian nun named Catherine Labouré (1806–76). Whereas reports of miraculous appearances were routinely dismissed by rationalists just prior to the Revolution, the vision of St Catherine became so widely diffused that a medal was struck to commemorate the event. Today the devotion to the miraculous medal continues as does the almost regular appearance of the Virgin in heavily Catholic countries, e.g., Lourdes (1858), Fatima (1917), and Medjugorje in the former Yugoslavia (1981) (Heimann, 1999: 482). Modern lay associations have their origins in this period of European history. In France the most successful effort at lay organization was named "Catholic Action," a term coined by Lamennais that maintained a strong currency through the Second Vatican Council.

The reign of Pope Pius IX (1846–78) was the longest of any pontiff in history. His decision to make a solemn declaration of the immaculate conception of the Blessed Virgin Mary is of one piece with the lay revival. Apart from the Pope's fervent piety, ecclesial life in these years was marked by a consolidation of power in the see of Rome, the creation of new centers of Catholicism throughout the American continent and in Australia, and dramatic political changes in Europe. In 1864 Pius IX issued the Syllabus of Errors, and in 1870 he witnessed the dissolution of the Papal States. The Pope refused to be compensated by the new Italian state and declared himself a prisoner of the Vatican, a situation that remained unresolved until 1929. Pius IX also endured Bismarck's anti-Catholic *Kulturkampf* (1873–8) as well as the French Third Republic's turn to anti-clericalism in 1877.

From 1869–70 Pius IX convened a council at the Vatican. For Pius the need for a council was twofold (Granfield, 1987: 37). The sudden restriction on the pontiff's temporal power was perceived as a threat to the Church itself. Moreover, there were theological currents questioning papal authority throughout the nineteenth century, e.g., Gallicanism, to which the ultramontane circle that supported Pius IX was adamantly opposed. Even though the criticism of a strong papacy was on the wane by 1870, the effect of a persistent critique added to the Pope's sense of entrenchment. The dogmatic constitution *Dei Filius*, which dealt with the Church's critique of modern rationalism, was approved fairly easily. The definition of papal infallibility, however, was hotly debated and provoked a small faction led by the historian Johann Josef Ignaz von Döllinger (1799–1890) to reconstitute itself as the Old Catholics. The constitution *Pastor Aeternus* declared that doctrines defined as infallible by a Pope who speaks *ex cathedra* are "irreformable of themselves and not from the consent of the Church."[1] This was a firm rebuke to Gallicanism as well, for it established as a juridical category the idea of a papal authority without any dependence on the consent of other bishops. The Second Vatican Council (1962–5) reaffirmed the legal formula but also reinserted the primacy of the Bishop of Rome back into the College of Bishops (Granfield, 1987: 37–44).

Pope Leo XIII reigned from 1878–1903. His encyclical *Aeterni Patris* (1879) dealt with the question of Christian philosophy and built upon the Neo-Scholastic approach laid out in *Dei Filius* (McCool, 1977: 216–40). Leo was convinced that Thomism was the proper response to the massive strides made by militant secularism as well as the recourse taken to rationalist manuals in Catholic seminaries. The encyclical praised the thought of Aquinas as a synthesis of the entire Catholic tradition (#17). In recommending Thomism, Leo was extolling above all the universal *wisdom* of the Angelic doctor, for he felt that Thomas' philosophy could even aid natural scientists and high school students. Thomism was thus envisioned as a program for cultural and social renewal, and if anything in the works of St Thomas was "too carelessly stated" in the light of advances made by more recent scholarship, then core Thomistic wisdom was to be heeded rather than any of its unnecessary and obviously dated subtleties (ibid.).

Leo's 1891 encyclical *Rerum Novarum* was the impetus for modern Catholic social teaching. To the dismay of progressive German Catholics, Leo had entered into an alliance with the Chancellor Otto von Bismarck. The conservative alliance did not, however, prevent Leo from employing Thomist ideas to formulate a Catholic alternative to the critique of capitalism made by Marx and Engels. Leo defended the inviolability of private property, the social value of the family, the right of workers to form trade unions, and the concepts of the dignity of work and a just wage. Leo thereby opened the door to a tradition of Catholic reflection on questions of social justice that extends to the 2006 encyclical of Benedict XVI (*Deus Caritas Est*).

When Leo's successor, Pius X, condemned "modernism" in 1914, he departed somewhat from his predecessor's broad humanism while still carrying forward the firm rejection of modern philosophy pursued by all previous popes. The official condemnation of modern thought and the enforcement of an anti-modernist oath were sharp blows to scholars like Alfred Loisy (1857–1940), a Biblicist who had written a cogent rejoinder to the mounting Protestant criticism of the way that the Catholic Church in its inception had departed from the norms of the apostolic community. Pius X's renewal of distrust toward modern ideas hindered the development of a theology that would adequately address the leading questions of the day.

Modernity as a Crisis, Platform, and Myth: 1914–78

Given its "oracular" role in international events of the twentieth century, papal history becomes a uniquely revealing lens through which the last hundred years of Catholic life and thought can be surveyed (Duffy, 2001). No less than in the previous century, the claim of the Pope to represent the entire Church was subject to dispute. At times, e.g., in condemning the relative silence of Pius XII during World War II, critical voices acted with reason. But there was also an equally clear wish voiced within the southward moving global Church that the Bishop of Rome speak out as Christ's Vicar on earth (Jedin, Repgen, and Dolan, 1989: 9).

Pope Pius X died on August 20, 1914. Mounting international tensions had already erupted in World War I, and the Church faced another crucial transition. Catholicism was led through these tumultuous decades by three pontiffs. The first was Benedict XV, who surprised the world by calling for a Christmas truce. Neither this gesture nor his even more ambitious Peace Proposal of 1917 was heeded. In fact, his bold stance led to the Vatican's exclusion from the Peace Conference of 1919.

Pius XI (who reigned 1922–39) began his pontificate by offering the traditional blessing from a window of St Peter's Basilica that had been closed to Italy for 52 years. He resumed the vigorous diplomatic activities and renewal of the Catholic missions of his predecessor. The opening of the window presaged the signing of no fewer than 18 Concordats, including the Lateran treaties with Mussolini in 1929. The latter agreements were difficult but established the Vatican City State. In return, the Vatican withdrew its support for the *Partito Popolare*, a political movement under the leadership of the socially progressive Fr Luigi Sturzo. Pius XI was aware of the dangers of fascism, but his decision to engage Mussolini and Hitler in dialog was based on a fear that an even greater threat to the Church lay in Communist atheism and the progressive, anti-clerical faction in the Spanish Civil War (1936–9). His 1937 condemnation of Nazism as a pagan form of idolatry, *Mit Brennender Sorge* (*With Burning Anxiety*), dispelled suspicion of a fascist Pope and led to his eventual elevation as a earnest champion of the unity of human race; however, his loathing of Communism, which dated back to a pre-pontifical journey to occupied Poland, remained far less restrained than the modest efforts at social unification (Duffy, 20001: 337–46).

In 1933 Pius XII (who reigned 1939–58) had negotiated the concordat with Hitler on behalf of Pius XI, an agreement the Nazis never honored. The new Pope was trained as a diplomat in the mould of Benedict XV and as such "believed that prophetic denunciations closed doors, narrowed room for manoeuvre" (Duffy, 2001: 348). Whereas Benedict's neutrality before the warring nations in 1914 seemed apposite, Pius XII's irenic stance seemed not to account for the changed circumstances in the world. Like his predecessors, he judged Communism to be the most serious threat for the Church and for the human family. He was not, as has been sometimes claimed, indifferent to the plight of the Jews, for it is well documented that the Vatican under his leadership gave safe refuge to many Roman Jews and that Pius justifiably feared the recriminations against both Jews and Catholics that would follow a public denunciation.[2] Nor were his pronouncements, e.g., the Christmas message of 1942 or a similar address of June 2, 1943, utterly devoid of condemnations of the genocide. As weighty as this matter was and remains today, it is still difficult to judge with any certainty what *may* have happened had Pius XII acted differently. Some rescued Jews have as a matter of public record praised the course he chose. In any case, his calculated decision to pinpoint the commission of atrocious deeds without a consistent branding of the individual perpetrators remains open to question.

Pius XII altered the course of Catholic theology. His encyclicals showed traces of recent developments in European Catholic thought, but his writings were also used to attack "new theologians" like Yves Congar OP and Henri de Lubac SJ. In *Divino Afflante Spiritu* (1943) Pius accorded significantly more freedom to modern methods of biblical scholarship than any previous Pope. The 1947 encyclical *Mediator Dei* spoke of "active and personal participation" in the Sacrifice of the Mass, which signaled a qualified endorsement of the Liturgical Movement flourishing in Belgium and Germany. In 1950 he made a solemn and infallible declaration of the bodily assumption of the

Virgin Mary into heaven and issued an encyclical (*Humani Generis*) that warned of the dangers in the new theology even while tacitly ratifying some of its key tenets.

Pope John XXIII (who reigned 1958–63) surprised the world by calling for an ecumenical council. The decades that preceded the Second Vatican Council (1962–5) are frequently cited as the moment in which the Catholic Church made its first steps to enter the modern world. For example, Pius XII's cautious consideration of modern biblical criticism and the very idea of evolutionary development in *Humani Generis* brought to a halt the thoroughly negative campaign against modernism waged by Pius X and can rightly be considered the path toward modernization pursued at the Council.

At the same time, the idea of a *modern* Catholicism needs to be analyzed more carefully. The very notion that the Church once and for all crossed a visible threshold is itself an interpretation of history. What is the "modernity" into which the Catholic Church entered? In what follows we will consider three possible answers to this question. These are not exhaustive categories but are meant to be representative of the wide range of twentieth-century Catholic thought on the question of modernity.

The crisis of modernity

Many Catholics in the twentieth century were shocked by the rapidity with which the modern world-view established itself. The crisis in the early twentieth century was very different from that of de-Christianization in the Enlightenment. The sparring with Deists over natural religion seemed pretty cerebral when compared to the combined effect of decades of global war, a severe economic depression, the spread of totalitarianism, and the dropping of an atomic bomb. Romano Guardini's *The End of the Modern World* consists of a series of lectures delivered between 1947 and 1949. Guardini was a post-modern theologian *avant la lettre*. The crisis of modernity for Guardini is not so much the denial of God's existence as the combination of a dissolution of nature, man, culture, *and* the resultant degeneration of divine revelation into an "unpagan paganism" (1998: 102). Guardini, however, counters the existentialist gloom of the postwar era by invoking the Christian theological virtue of hope. At the end of modernity, Guardini avers, the Christian will be permitted "to be a vital person within the mounting loneliness" (ibid.: 108).

Modernity as a platform

For others modernity is the impulse for *aggiornamento*, i.e., bringing the Church up to date. Modernization of this sort allows for a reform of internal structures but not without a simultaneous view of the whole. For example, Vatican II's *Gaudium et Spes* (*Joy and Hope*) states: "At all times the Church carries the responsibility of reading the signs of the times and of interpreting them in light of the gospel, if it is to carry out its task" (#4). According to *Gaudium et Spes*, the postconciliar Church will never again shrink from addressing the concerns of the world *on their own terms*. That much is clear. But the method for reading these signs has become a subject of far more debate than the Fathers of the Council had imagined. Take, for example, the idea of an "anony-mous Christianity," which was proposed by the German theologian Karl Rahner (1904–84). Rahner writes: "Christianity does not simply confront the member of an extra-Christian religion as a mere non-Christian but as someone who can and must already be regarded in this or that respect as an anonymous Christian" (1981: 219). There is much more to Rahner's construct than a simple equation of a non-Christian with an anonymous Christian. Rahner's tantalizingly simple declarations can obscure profound dialectics. Rahner nonetheless considered the new openness to reading the signs of the times as genuine liberation for the faithful. He maintained that even where the grace of God is not objectively affirmed among non-Christians, its presence cannot be denied. This openness to the modern world, he candidly asserts, could even be seen as a higher stage in the development of Christianity itself (ibid.).

De–mythologizing the modern age

There is a stark contrast between a crisis and an impulse for modernization. The first view treats the modern condition as a source of abandonment into which the Chris-tian must enter for purification. The second view sees openness to the modern world as *ipso facto* entry into new life for the individual and the Church. Attempts to ease the dialectical opposition between these views abound, but, in the end, theological iren-icism of this sort represents an unacceptable path of least resistance. There is, however, a view that moves beyond the opposition just depicted while still uncovering a truth in both paths. This third picture of the world problematizes the concept of modernity without rejecting its legitimate gains. This view became increasingly associated with what in the second half of the twentieth century became known as "late modernity" or even "post-modernity," but forerunners are already apparent in nineteenth- and early twentieth-century prophets of cultural fragmentation. The founder of the theology of liberation in Latin America, Gustavo Gutiérrez, recognized since the 1970s the need for a de-mythologizing of modernity's own dogmas (Goizueta, 1996). Gutiérrez showed how the cry for justice on behalf of the poor is enhanced through the early modern wit-ness of Bartolomé de las Casas, a Dominican defender of the rights of the Indians under colonial oppression (Gutiérrez, 1993). The modern critique of modernity that arises in a retrieval of this sort decries social injustice in a modern key without denuding the lived structure of Catholic belief (e.g., popular Catholicism with its visible Marian devotions) of its evangelical and prophetic strength. Moreover, first world Catholics like David Tracy and Charles Taylor formalize modernity's non-dogmatic relevance for modern Catholicism. They both suggest, among other things, a model of critical conversation gleaned from the philosophical hermeneutics of Hans-Georg Gadamer as a strategy for assaying the gains and losses incurred by modernity (Tracy, 1987; Taylor, 1990). "Postliberal" critics of Tracy's theology, focusing on his earlier work, highlight its roots in the Romantic idea of an expressive self, a charge that Tracy denies and sees not at all applicable to his later Gadamerian thought (Lindbeck, 1984: 43 n. 18; Tracy, 1985). In the sense that, for example, some sort of separation of faith and politics is an irrevers-ible outcome of the modern age, the notion of modernity as an indispensable myth is ingredient to all realistic proposals for Catholic life and thought put forward in the late twentieth century. The distinguishing characteristic of this third view lies in its deliberate enlargement of secular reason to include tradition, i.e., the formation of a modern notion of theological reason. Tracy and Taylor include within this synthesis both explanation through dissective analysis *and* the search for holistic meaning. Without ignoring the advent of progress, "transmodern" theologians like Gutiérrez, Tracy, and Taylor apply a uniform standard of rationality to Catholic faith and see Christian theology as a dialogical process that elicits riches old and new from the history of Christian praxis.[3]

Vatican II cannot be reduced to any one of these modern self-definitions. The documents contain elements of the three views of modernity just presented as well as diverse biblical, patristic, liturgical, and pastoral resources. The complexity of conciliar "traditioning" is apparent in the constitution *Gaudium et Spes*. Here the Council Fathers considered atheism "one of the most serious problems of our time" (#19). Surveying its diverse forms, they single out "a systematic form also which, in addition to other causes, so insists on man's desire for autonomy as to object to any dependence on God at all" (#20). What resources are to be found in the Christian message for addressing systematic atheism? After urging a careful scrutiny of the motives behind systematic atheism, the response in *Gaudium et Spes* singles out a divine person: "In reality it is only in the mystery of the Word made flesh that the mystery of man becomes clear" (#22). In opting for a response to modern atheism centered on the person of Christ, the Fathers are claiming that neither the advances nor the threats pinned on "modernity" can be adequately tested without a spiritual conversion. Concentration on the Word made flesh is not even mentioned when in the same document the Fathers carefully define and wholeheartedly affirm the "rightful autonomy of earthly affairs" (#36). It is "misleading" to oppose faith and science, they proclaim. Accordingly, when modern man claims to discover the internal workings of nature, he ratifies the desire of the world's own creator. When earthly autonomy is joined to independence from God and the natural moral law, then systematic atheism has usurped the just order of things. The Fathers envisioned no conflict between *Gaudium et Spes'* Christocentrism and its affirmation of creaturely autonomy. But this did not prevent Catholic theologians from focusing on one theme *at the expense of the other* in the postconciliar period.

Pope Paul VI (who reigned 1963–78) brought to completion the council John XIII convened and became the first to implement its reforms. His promulgation of a Roman Missal in 1969 was the actual beginning of the Mass in the vernacular. The most controversial act of his pontificate took place one year prior when Paul issued *Humanae Vitae (On Human Life)*. The encyclical reiterated the Church's ban on the use of artificial contraceptives by Catholic spouses. The Pope's decision not to follow the leaked majority report of his own lay commission added fuel to the fire that ensued. For decades to follow, progressive advocates of ecclesial reform singled out *Humanae Vitae* as the tinder that kindled lay disenchantment and erupted into a vocal opposition to the autocratic use of Church authority in the ensuing decades (Grabowski, 2003: 10–14).

"Put out into the Deep": 1978–2006

The successor of Paul VI died 33 days into his papacy. The conclave then stunned observers by electing a 58-year-old Pole named Karol Wojtyła. John Paul II was the first non-Italian Pope in 455 years, but in his first address from St Peter's Square he delighted the anxious crowd by speaking in "your . . . *our* Italian language." The new Pope was known for his capacity to marshal his intellectual prowess while speaking forthrightly about issues on the minds of ordinary lay people. In this regard, he not only defended Paul VI's teaching in *Humanae Vitae*, but provided on the basis of his 1960 book *Love and Responsibility* a "personalistic, humanistic response to the claims of the contemporary sexual revolution" (Weigel, 2001: 142). From the beginning of his pontificate, outside observers noted that his experience of persecution in a land controlled by a Communist regime gave him a unique qualification to speak to global abuses of human rights. Likewise, it was sometimes said that this Polish background fully explained his traditional stances. In fact, however, the complex enigma of John Paul II cannot be dismissed as the media-savvy, charismatic face of Eastern European nationalism even though his first trip to his native land in June, 1979 played a decisive part in the fall of the Iron Curtain in 1989 (ibid.: 291–325). A more revealing description of the Pope's thought can be gleaned from the opening chapter of his inaugural encyclical *Redemptor Hominis* (*The Redeemer of Man*, 1978). Having been Pope less than five months, the clarity with which he announced the future themes of his pontificate is astonishing: to carry forward the legacy of the two popes whose name he bore and the Council they led, to lead the Church into the great jubilee year of 2000, and to make "the first fundamental truth of the Incarnation" the mark of his pontifical service as a collaborative shepherd of the Catholic Church and promoter of Christian unity. As the leitmotif of an apostolic letter he penned at the end of the jubilee year 2000, he chose the words of Christ to the fisherman Peter and his first apostles: "Put out into the deep" (Luke 5:4; *Novo Millennio Ineunte*, #1), signifying the Pope's fervent desire to let the joy of Christ's gospel penetrate both the far reaches of the globe and the equally distant hearts of the spiritually weary Catholics in the First World. With regard to his view of modernity, the new Pope clearly sided with the teaching of *Gaudium et Spes* regarding the enlightenment that is brought to bear on the mystery of being human through the mystery of the Incarnate Word. He made this theme the key to his pontificate. In this way, the prophetic Christian humanism of John Paul II takes as its point of departure the conviction that the public but deeply inward repentance of the human person is the foundation for theology, Church life, and papal diplomacy.

John Paul developed a reputation as a traveling pope. No previous pontiff had displayed a comparable enthusiasm to traverse the globe. His 104 apostolic journeys outside of Italy attracted millions of the pious, every imaginable world leader, and even curious bystanders indifferent to what the Church taught. The Pope's long awaited trip to Cuba in 1998 is a good example. Prior to the Pope's arrival, Vatican officials had extracted promises from the regime to grant greater liberty to the Church. The world's curiosity about the historic encounter between Wojtyła and one of the world's last remaining Communist leaders was quickly diverted when the news broke on the day of the Pope's arrival that the US President was going to be implicated in a sex scandal. Consequently, the international press that had already assembled on the island was prevented from covering the Pope's historic address at the University of Havana. Standing in front of an assembly of distinguished intellectuals gathered by the Cuban regime, the former professor of social ethics spoke about the necessity of evangelizing the culture (John Paul II, 1998: 2). The Catholic Church, he said, identifies with no particular culture but approaches all in a spirit of openness. In each act of evangelization, Christ is present since he himself "entered into culture" (ibid.). The Church still does not *impose* anything upon any distinct culture. On the contrary, the Church "proposes" Catholic values in an effort to achieve "the greater humanization of society" (ibid.). To this end, the Church must plumb the mysterious element of transcendence in every culture and promote the full dignity of the human person in each cultural venue. The Pope turned to the question of intercultural dialog, a topic dear to Cubans on the island and in diaspora. The Pope praised Cuban *mestizaje*, i.e., the irreducible blend of Spanish Catholic, African, and native American identities that one encounters in the history and daily life of the island. The dialog that emerges from the promotion of Cuba's interculturality, he said, will ensure "a more harmonious growth and continuing development of the creative initiatives of civil society" (John Paul II, 1998: 6). As an enjoinder to hand over a pluralistic legacy to the next generation, the Pope concluded with these words of a mutually revered Cuban Catholic intellectual from the nineteenth century: "Tell them … that there is no motherland without virtue and no virtue without piety" (ibid.). In other words, without ever mentioning the regime by name, the Pope expressed his own hope to see Cuba freed from the oppression of a dictator. By the same token, few words could better express the Polish pontiff's long-standing vision that contemporary global Christianity could actively contribute to social renewal by planting seeds of hope within the constantly shifting soil of radically distinct and hybrid cultures.

In 2005 Cardinal Ratzinger became the first pope elected in Christianity's third millennium. In choosing his papal name, he expressed a sense of personal humility before an office that had been held so long by an internationally revered moral leader (*benedictus* means "blessed") and hearkened back to *two* earlier namesakes: St Benedict of Nursia and Benedict XV. The reference to the ancient founder of Western monasticism points to the new Pope's pledge to counter what he identified as the drift in the West toward a "dictatorship of relativism that does not recognize anything as definitive and whose ultimate goal consists solely of one's own ego and desires" (Ratzinger). The second namesake points to the need to rediscover Christian wisdom that counters growing threats to world peace, e.g., global Islamic terrorism and a potential conflict in the Middle East abetted by the instability that remains in the wake of a US-led invasion of Iraq. Only time will tell whether and how Benedict realizes these formidable goals.

Notes

1   *Ex cathedra*, meaning "from [his] chair and teaching office" refers to a special mark of infallibly decreed papal pronouncements.

2   In 1963 a play by Rolf Hochhuth entitled *The Deputy* appeared in Germany and London. In this play such accusations were leveled against Pius XII. A team of Jesuit historians appointed by the Vatican issued a report in eleven volumes refuting specific claims made by Hochhuth (Duffy, 349). It is not possible here to enter into the details of either the Hochhuth debate or the subsequent controversies that have ensued.

3   For an elaboration of the idea of "transmodernity," see Enrique Dussel, *The Invention of the Americas, Eclipse of the "Other" and the Myth of Modernity*, translated by Michael D. Barber (New York: Continuum, 1995).

References and Further Reading

Aston, N. (2000) *Religion and Revolution in France, 1780–1804*. Washington, DC: The Catholic University of America Press.

Casarella, P. (2003) "Not a Fusion of Liberal and Conservative," *Initiative Report, Catholic Common Ground Initiative*, vol. 7, no. 2, 3–6.

Duffy, E. (2001) *Saints and Sinners: A History of the Popes*. New Haven, CT: Yale University Press.

Goizueta, R.S. (1996) "Bartolomé de las Casas, Modern Critic of Modernity: An Analysis of a Conversion," *Journal of Hispanic/Latino Theology*, vol. 3, no. 4, 6–19.

Grabowski, J. (2003) *Sex and Virtue: An Introduction to Sexual Ethics*. Washington, DC: The Catholic University of America Press.

Granfield, P. (1987) *The Limits of the Papacy*. New York: Crossroad.

Guardini, R. (1998) *The End of the Modern World*. Wilmington, DE: Intercollegiate Studies Institute.

Gutiérrez, G. (1993) *Las Casas: In Search of the Poor of Jesus Christ*. Maryknoll, NY: Orbis.

Heimann, M. (1999) "Christianity in Western Europe from the Enlightenment," in Hastings, Adrian (ed.) *A World History of Christianity*, Grand Rapids, MI: W.B. Eerdmans, 458–507.

Jedin, H. and Dolan, J. (1981a) *The History of the Church*, vol. VI: *The Church in the Age of Absolutism and Enlightenment*. New York: Crossroad.

Jedin, H. and Dolan, J. (1981b) *The History of the Church*, vol. VII: *The Church Between Revolution and Restoration*. New York: Crossroad.

Jedin, H. and Dolan, J. (1981c) *The History of the Church*, vol. VIII: *The Church in the Age of Liberalism*. New York: Crossroad.

Jedin, H., Repgen, K., and Dolan, J. (1989) *The History of the Church*, vol. X. *The Church in the Modern Age*. New York: Crossroad.

John Paul II, Pope (1998) Address of John Paul II at the University of Havana, January 23, 1998, accessed on-line on August 31, 1998 at www.vatican.va/holy_father/john_paul_ii/travels/documents/hf_jp-ii_spe_23011998_lahavana-culture_en.html.

Kant, I. (1959) *Foundations of the Metaphysics of Morals and What is Enlightenment?*, trans. Lewis White Beck. Indianapolis, IN: The Liberal Arts Press.

Latourette, K.S. (1965) *Christianity through the Ages*. New York: Harper and Row.

Lindbeck, G.A. (1984) *The Nature of Doctrine: Religion and Theology in a Postliberal Age*. Philadelphia, PA: Westminster Press.

McCool, G.A. (1977) *Catholic Theology in the Nineteenth Century: The Quest for a Unitary Method*. New York: Crossroad.

Möhler, J.A. (1996) *Unity in the Church or The Principle of Catholicism*. Washington, DC: The Catholic University of America Press.

Rahner, K. (1981) *A Rahner Reader*, edited by Gerald A. McCool. New York: Crossroad.

Ratzinger, J. (2005) Homily delivered for Mass "Pro Eligendo Romano Pontifice" at Vatican Basilica on Monday, April 18, 2005, accessed on-line on August 31, 2005 at www.vatican.va/gpII/documents/homily-pro-eligendo-pontifice_20050418_en.html.

Sandos, J. (1988) "Junípero Serra's Canonization and the Historical Record," *American Historical Review*, 93, 1253–69.

Schreiter, R. (1997) *The New Catholicity: Theology between the Global and the Local*. Maryknoll, NY: Orbis.

Steinfels, P. (1994) "The Failed Encounter: The Catholic Church and Liberalism in the Nineteenth Century," in Douglass, R.B. and Hollenbach, D. (eds.) *Catholicism and Liberalism: Contributions to American Public Philosophy*. Cambridge: Cambridge University Press, 19–44.

Taylor, C. (1990) "Comparison, History, Truth," in Reynolds, F. and Tracy, D. (eds.) *Myth and Philosophy*. Albany: State University of New York Press, 37–55.

Tracy, D. (1985) "Lindbeck's New Program for Theology," *The Thomist*, 49, 460–72.

Tracy, D. (1987) *Plurality and Ambiguity: Hermeneutics, Religion, Hope*. San Francisco, CA: Harper and Row.

Weigel, G. (2001) *Witness to Hope. The Biography of Pope John Paul II*. New York: HarperCollins Publishers.

PART II
Catholic Cultures

CHAPTER 7
The Holy Land[1]

David B. Burrell

There had been a persistent presence of Christians in the Holy Land despite the fact that Jesus was hardly drawn to the land's symbolic center, Jerusalem. The turning point verse in Luke's Gospel underscores the tension: "he set his face resolutely toward Jerusalem" (9:51 New English Bible). Moreover, after his resurrection that same Gospel directs his disciples to proclaim "repentance bringing the forgiveness of sins . . . to all nations beginning from Jerusalem" (24:47), as they are sent (in the companion narrative of the Acts of the Apostles) to "bear witness for me in Jerusalem, and throughout Judaea and Samaria, and even in the farthest corners of the earth" (Acts 1:8). So the New Testament explicitly reverses the centripetal movement of all nations gathering to Jerusalem (in the messianic prophecies of Isaiah) to a centrifugal one, leaving Jerusalem to be a center whose role would remain ambiguous throughout Christian history. In her masterful account, *Jerusalem: One City, Three Faiths*, Karen Armstrong delineates these ambiguities through a history punctuated and shaped by diverse interactions with Jews and Muslims (Armstrong, 1996). Peter Walker provides an early set of reflections from Eusebius and Cyril in *Holy City, Holy Places? Christian Attitudes to Jerusalem and the Holy Land in the Fourth Century* (Walker, 1990; see also Walker, 1994), while Robert Wilken offers textual evidence of the richly theological exchange between Jews and Christians in the context of this holy city in his *The Land Called Holy* (Wilken, 1992). Frank Peters' *Jerusalem: The Holy City in the Eyes of Chroniclers, Visitors, Pilgrims, and Prophets from the Days of Abraham to the Beginnings of Modern Times* offers a rich compendium of texts (Peters, 1985).

A Brief Overview of the History

The earliest set of attitudes toward the land where Jesus lived, symbolized in Jerusalem, evinced in Origen and Irenaeus, reflect the end of Luke's Gospel by reminding us how Jesus' apostles, emboldened by their resurrection faith, "preached the good news from Jerusalem to the ends of the earth." As has often been remarked, the Romans' destruction of the Temple reinforced the convictions of contemporary believers in Jesus that they were to carry on as God's special people, preaching the God of Abraham, Isaac, and Jacob to the nations. The only Jerusalem relevant to that faith was the "new Jerusalem, coming down from heaven, adorned as a bride" (Rev 21:1). So Origen:

since we have been taught by Paul that there is one Israel according to the flesh and another according to the Spirit, when the Saviour says: "I was sent only to the lost sheep of the house of Israel" (Matt 15:24), we do not understand Him as [referring] to them who have an earthly wisdom . . . Rather, we understand that there is a nation of souls, named Israel. Even the meaning of the name suggests this, since Israel is translated "the mind seeing God" or "man seeing God." Moreover, the Apostle makes such revelations about Jerusalem as "the Jerusalem above is free, and she is our mother" (Gal 4:26). And in another of his letters he says: "but you have come to Mount Zion and to the city of the living God, the heavenly Jerusalem, and to innumerable angels in festive gathering, and to the Church of the firstborn who are enrolled in heaven" (Heb 12:22–3). If, therefore, there are certain souls in this world that are called Israel, and in heaven a certain city that is named Jerusalem, it follows that these cities that are said to belong to the nation of Israel have as their metropolis the heavenly Jerusalem. And we understand all of Judea in this way . . . therefore, whatever is either told or prophesied about Jerusalem, if we hear the words of Paul as of Christ speaking in him (cf. 2 Cor 13:3), we should understand according to his opinion to have been spoken of that city which he calls the heavenly Jerusalem and of all those places or cities that are said to be cities of the holy land of which Jerusalem is the metropolis. (*On First Principles* Book 4, chapter 3.8, in Origen, 1979: 194–6)

For Irenaeus, the matter was not simply transcendent: "in the time of kingdom, the earth has been called again by Christ [to its pristine condition], and Jerusalem rebuilt after the pattern of the Jerusalem above . . ." (*Against Heresies* 5.2, in Irenaeus, 1869). Although eschatological in character, this Jesus was to rule a literal kingdom from the geographical, if renewed, Jerusalem.

Eusebius (*c*.260–339) reflects the view of Origen, whom he personally admired. As bishop of Caesarea at a time when Jerusalem had been effectively replaced by the Roman garrison-town, Aelia Capitolina, after the successive destructions of the city in 70 and in 135, Eusebius consistently downplays the continuing theological significance of Jerusalem. Part of his motivation was doubtless to underscore the contrast between Christianity and Judaism, by emphasizing the way in which New Testament spirituality looked upwards to the "heavenly Jerusalem" rather than remaining focused on earthly realities. This attitude will be challenged, however, toward the end of Eusebius' life by the bishop of Jerusalem, Cyril (*c*.320–86?), who inherited the fresh perspective of the Edict of Constantine, and that emperor's personal intent to embellish the city as befits its proper dignity. His more positive assessment of Jerusalem reflected the change in spirit: "The 'Jerusalem mystique' was present and powerful, the potential of the city inviting, the presence of the pilgrims demanding and the possible increased status of the Jerusalem Church compelling" (Walker, 1990: 314). But bishops cannot initiate pilgrimage; there had to be other factors at work, not the least of which was an appreciation of an incarnate Christ, in opposition to the Arians. That the Word of God became flesh in space and time should give Jerusalem pride of place, for it was *here* that it all happened. This contrast, or better, opposition regarding the status of place would continue to mark Christian theology; holiness might attend place because of human association, but the free creator of all could hardly legitimize turf wars, as though this place and not that belonged to God. So Christians rather sought to establish a Jerusalem consonant with imperial recognition, a monumental presence fitting an imperial religion. Abetted by the Council of Nicea in the early fourth century, which would be elaborated into the celebrated Formula of Chalcedon in the mid-fifth century, the iconic status of Jerusalem mirrored the articulation of orthodox faith in Jesus as "one person with two natures, fully human as well as fully divine." That this formula was an imperial one, accepted by the bishop of Jerusalem, helped to restore that see to the original status it had lost after the Romans had destroyed it a second time (in 135).

Yet while the histories may have focused on the Basilica of the Anastasis [resurrection], constructed by Constantine, churches only function with communities to animate them, so it was the "church of Jerusalem" rather than its churches which began to elaborate and sustain the memory of this place as holy. Jerusalem became home to Christian communities, whose memory forged a bond between *place* and *people* which allowed Jerusalem to take its place among the "churches" of the East, indeed, as the first, the "mother church." So the earlier predilection for a "heavenly Jerusalem" became transmuted into a love and respect for this Jerusalem, where the "Word made flesh" had lived, preached, died, and risen from the dead – a place made holy by people whose presence kept alive the memories of the crucial facts shaping this personal revelation of the Word of God. Nor was Jerusalem itself to absorb all the "holiness"; in fact, it was the desire of monks and nuns to populate the desert, "that the prophecies made about it by the eloquent Isaiah be fulfilled" (Life of Sabas) – an about-face from the earlier set of attitudes (Cyril of Scythopolis, 1991: 88). It was in fact their presence that inspired the name of "Holy Land," as Robert Wilken has reminded us. That glorious chapter was to be abruptly truncated in 614, when the Persians took revenge on the Byzantines, slaughtering (by a contemporary account) some 66,000 Christians in the city alone, along with countless monks and nuns in the countryside. As Karen Armstrong tells the tale, "Christians [who] had sharply differentiated their experience in Jerusalem from that of the Jews, now . . . went into exile in their turn [and] turned naturally to the gestures and psalms of their predecessors in the Holy City, and like the Jews they spoke of God and Zion in the same breath" (1996: 214).

A scant 23 years later a Muslim army arrived outside its walls. The caliph Omar's peaceful entrance is legendary, along with his desire to rehabilitate the ancient Temple Mount, which the Byzantines had treated as a refuse site, following prevailing Christian conviction that the demise of the Jewish Temple simply confirmed the truth of Christianity. It was the Umayyad caliph, Abdul-Malik, who built the signature Dome of the Rock over the rock of Moriah in 691, both to establish Muslim hegemony as well as to commemorate Muhammad's celebrated "night journey" mentioned in the Qur'an. Between 637 and 1099, under a largely tolerant Muslim hegemony, Jerusalem became a coveted pilgrimage site, and the recorded travels of women and men fed the imaginations of Western Christians regarding the land where Jesus had lived. Pilgrimage could only enhance the theme of place made holy by the presence of faithful people, turning it into a "full-blown sacred geography [which saw] Jerusalem as the center of the world" (Armstrong, 1996: 216). When that imagination was encouraged to fuel an irridentist urge to "recover the holy places" from an upstart faith and to restore the "holy land" to Christianity, however, the Crusades were born. That urge was in turn fueled by the destruction of the Holy Sepulchre by the mad caliph Hakim, which precipitated a call for assistance from Byzantium to Western Christians – an appeal which they would soon regret. Beginning in 1099, power was to prevail over presence in Jerusalem and the Holy Land, and often brutally so, although those among the interlopers who stayed became themselves entranced by the land and its attraction to become a new breed of local Christians, Latin by persuasion.[2]

This "Latin Kingdom," however, was to last little more than a century. Following Saladin's decisive victory in 1187, and especially under subsequent Mameluke hegemony, the refurbished Temple Mount, Jerusalem's *haram ash-sharif*, became home to Sufi brotherhoods, while the city housed both Jews and Christians. Pilgrimage became expensive and often dangerous, however, due to the tenuous hold of the Egyptian political power over the countryside, and soon waned in the face of religious contention in Europe, as well as preoccupation with a freshly discovered continent by those seeking alternatives to the Silk Road. In fact, Santiago de Compostela tended to replace Jerusalem as the favored destination for pilgrimage. Yet transfer of the city to Ottoman hegemony led to Suleiman's reconstruction of the current walls in 1536, making it possible for communities of Abrahamic believers to continue to people Jerusalem, where their memories bonded them to the city, and the city to them, in ways peculiar to each religious faith. It was the Franciscans, inspired by Francis' dramatic journey to Damietta, who kept vigil in the "holy places," thereby assuring a Catholic presence to receive Western pilgrims who still found there way to them. The group denominated "Latin Christians/Catholics" stems from this period, so represents, ecclesiastically, a relatively recent group in the land. The title "Patriarch of Jerusalem" has been reserved to the Orthodox prelate from time immemorial, while the title "Latin Patriarch," for the bishop presiding over Latin Catholics, dates from the nineteenth century. Ecumenical efforts in Jerusalem and the Holy Land are often stymied by historical standoffs quite vivid in local memories, yet collaboration among faithful "on the ground" has been materially enhanced by their increasingly minority status. Lacking power, Christians of all persuasions are challenged to discover ways of being present, often as mediators between dominant Jewish and Muslim blocs.

The novel situation of the nineteenth century stemmed from Napoleon's landing in Alexandria in 1799, signaling the onset of a creeping colonization of the two major Islamic empires – Ottoman and Mughal – by Western powers. By the latter half of that century, European powers had managed to prevail upon one sultan after another to grant them privileges and place in Jerusalem, ostensibly to receive their pilgrims. A balance was struck between state and religious interests: the French were protectors of Catholic pilgrims, the British of Protestant, and the Russians of Orthodox. Yet in the cases where these ventures were spearheaded by religious men and women who were educators of health care workers, they settled into their accustomed role of serving the local Christian populations, and so enhancing the education and well-being of local communities of Christians, and decisively altering the local ecology of Jerusalem. Another strand of Western Christians descended on the "holy land" with tools of archeology, impelled to use these "scientific" explorations to further our understanding of the Bible. In time that very archeology would in call into question the biblical narratives of conquest of the land, but the principle of using archeology to reinforce a particular view of history and of identity had been established.[3] These Christians were less interested in the local communities, and more focused on the "holy sites," thereby setting a pattern for preoccupation with place which could ignore people. In fact, by reducing "holy land" to "holy places," this biblically inspired movement unwittingly set the stage for a set of policies toward local Christians on the part of the next ruling power, the state of Israel, often designed to dispossess them from Jerusalem while assuring "free access to the holy places" to Christians and Muslims alike who come from abroad.

Yet places cannot remain *holy* very long without a people whose memory and presence confirm that holiness. For while it is true that the Bible proclaims the holiness of the land because of the Lord's own presence: "the Lord will hold Judah as his portion in the Holy Land, and again make Israel his very own" (Zech 1:12), the same prophet urges Israel itself to "Sing, rejoice, daughter of Zion; for I am coming to dwell in the midst of you – it is the Lord who speaks" (1:10). Place needs people to affirm its specialness, and to confirm it with their lives. Indeed, the latest chapter in Jerusalem's history is intimately linked to the "return" of Jews to the land – *eretz Israel* – in the specific form of Zionism, a nineteenth-century socialist utopian movement which initially focused on peoplehood, but soon came to see how crucially symbolic was the attraction of this "holy land" to their constituency, however avowedly "secular" their Jewish audience might have been. The initial movements of people to the land – named *aliyahs* after the symbolic journey *up* to Jerusalem – began at the end of the nineteenth century, and continued in successive waves during the first half of the twentieth century (encouraged by the Balfour Declaration of 1917), only to become a poignant flood at the end of World War II when the Nazi extermination camps were liberated. The fears of local residents had found expression in a series of "Arab revolts" during the British mandate period between the two world wars, as the hegemonic consequences of the Zionist movement became increasingly clear. In the years just after World War II, however, pitched battles to establish that hegemony turned thousands of local Arab residents into refugees in their own land, while the stalemate left enough territory to establish the state of Israel in 1948 – a state which world opinion quickly embraced in the wake of the genocide at Auschwitz and elsewhere. The "holy land" remained so divided until 1967, when Israel occupied the rest of the land in a lightning war, begetting an immediate euphoria followed by decades of occupation contested by a series of United Nations resolutions comprising an international legal consensus.

So we are returned to the dialectic between presence and power in regard to place, and especially to a place deemed "holy." The Muslim caliph Omar sensed this when he took over Jerusalem, both in adopting an alternative site for worship from that of the Holy Sepulchre, and also by inviting Jews from Tiberias to return to the city. In each case, he realized that to take possession of a place which others not only deemed to be holy, but which their presence had sanctified in memory and often in blood, in such a way as to render them unwelcome, offered a needless provocation. Whoever holds the power – and place requires power if it is to be held – over a "holy place" will soon realize that embracing the presence of those whose lives and memory make it holy is the only way to peaceful co-existence. Place alone cannot be holy, as once-monastic sites like Mont Saint Michel testify so eloquently; a once-monastery turned into a national monument lacks its essential ingredient: place requires presence to be holy.

Indeed, the same could be said for Hagia Sophia: after its origins as a Christian basilica, transformed into a mosque when Constantinople became Istanbul, its final state as a monument inspires awe only by remembering all that it had been! Moreover, the power which holds a place fails to respect such a presence at its own peril. For in the end, presence may wield even more power than a power which tries to erase presence. And what a visitor to Jerusalem finds today is a vibrant Jewish presence, an imposing Muslim presence for Friday prayer, and Christians omnipresent as pilgrims, with fewer local Christians each year. In 1944 there were 29,350 Christians in Jerusalem, while in 2000 Christians living in Jerusalem numbered 10,000 at a most generous estimate. The Christians in Jerusalem make up 5.6 percent of the Arab population and 1.7 percent of the total population of the city, both Jewish and Arab. Whereas in 1967, West Bank Christians numbered 43,000 in the West Bank and Gaza Strip (2,000) or 3.9 percent of the total population; in 2000, Christians in the Palestinian Territories numbered 50,000, which makes only 1.8 percent of the total Palestinian population. In the same year, with respect to Israel, Christians numbered 130,000 or 13 percent of the Arab population and slightly less than 2 percent of the entire population of Israel.[4]

The diverse Christian groups who continue to reside in Jerusalem, however, are busy making common cause with Muslims to activate their presence to this city holy to them – and not merely the "holy sites." Jewish cultural life takes place for the most part in the institutions of the new city, which testify to the way in which a concentrated and articulate presence can foster deeper understanding of a tradition. Jewish society is divided on its willingness to accommodate others' convictions regarding this city. Debate on Jerusalem as the "everlasting and undivided capital of Israel" tends to be dominated by ideological concerns, while the facts of the matter present a city divided into neighborhoods almost as neatly as the Ottomans separated Armenians, Jews, Christians, and Muslims into the four sectors of the walled "old city." Storied Jewish return to *eretz Israel* often focused on "next year in Jerusalem" – *shana hava b'Yerushalayem* – even though many Israelis feel far more comfortable in Tel Aviv or in kibbutzim scattered throughout the land. The "holiness" of the Western Wall, however, is shared by all observant Jews, as the ever-present rituals there can attest. What is certain is that the city will remain holy to all three religious faiths, yet will effectively be so in the measure in which the respective faith communities display its special character in their life and work, and especially in their interaction with each other.

Reflections on a Continuing Christian Presence

How does this checkered history and divided geography affect Jerusalem today? And how can we assess the presence of Christians there as well as throughout the land where Jesus lived? We cannot begin to tackle these questions without reminding ourselves of the relevance of people, presence, and power to place. The "Holy Land" of today is a pastiche of peoples within a triad of faiths – Jewish, Christian, Muslim – whose presence to one another may only be glancing, yet the dynamic is unmistakably one of interaction with the place. Indeed, diverse communities of Christians co-exist in this land, living beside one another yet within Jewish and Muslim majorities. They have always accepted that part of their inbuilt mission, one might say, is to receive pilgrims to this land. Yet those who make the effort of pilgrimage will inevitably encounter the inscription above the tomb in the Church of the Holy Sepulchre: "He is risen; he is not here!" This motif, which epitomizes the faith of Christians worldwide, also relativizes the land itself. For here, as anywhere else, Jesus lives in the communities which bear his name. In that sense, there can be nothing special about Jerusalem, as the early witnesses – Origen, Irenaeus, and Eusebius – testified, yet the fact remains that there is something special about this land!

What seems to be the case is that what makes the place special is also what makes Jesus special – indeed, so special that it took four centuries to bring it to full articulation in the Formula of Chalcedon: "one person with two natures, fully human as well as fully divine." But formulae must always be re-appropriated in the light of shifting historical realities, and this one above all. For the full humanity of Jesus can neither be eclipsed by the universality of the "Christ-event," nor in reaction to that, be affirmed in such a way as to evacuate his theandric character. So Christians need always to be reminded of the Jesus of time and space, and where better than in the land which Jesus walked, and especially the city in which he was put to death. That he "rose from the dead," to foil the expectations of those who would have his person and subversive teaching out of the way, is of course a matter of faith. That is the faith which continues to animate those communities of Christians whose multiform presence has shaped Jerusalem over the centuries, and whose reception of each generation of pilgrims continues to make him present to those who come seeking Jesus in this place.

Let me propose that this presence is iconic, trying to suggest how it can be so. Icons are not ordinary pictures, we know, yet few Western Christians find it easy to appreciate the power which their presence bears for Eastern believers. The image seems appropriate to help introduce Western minds and hearts into the mystery of place which is Jerusalem, since the icon epitomizes the spirituality of its local Christians. An icon is so constructed as to suggest more than is presented, to gesture toward a transforming power at work in the persons depicted, and so to confront persons regarding it with a mirror revealing their own selves at this point in their call to be transformed. So to people of faith, icons initiate a transaction and invite a continuing transformation. To those who view them without that element of faith, they can seem hauntingly strange; at once enticing and off-putting. So it is with one's initial encounter of the congeries of communities of faith in Jerusalem, many of whom Western Christians have seldom encountered: Armenians, Melchites, Chaldeans, Ethiopians, Copts; along with the palpable presence of Jews and Muslims. Yet that variety itself poignantly displays the human condition with regard to faith: enticing but elusive; aggravating yet unavoidable. Moreover, none of the three Abrahamic faiths which share Jerusalem can dispense with time or space. If the land assumes a paramount position for Jews, for Christians the history of Jesus resonates with that land even when it does not tie Christians to it. Islam too, by orienting its daily prayer to Mecca, as well as by requiring, when feasible, pilgrimage there (and inclusively, to Jerusalem as well), reminds us where it was that Muhammad purportedly received the Word of God in flawless Arabic.

So certain places, and Jerusalem in a special shared way, are iconic for these three faiths. That is, this place is more than simply "a place," just as an icon is more than a representation. What marks it off, of course, is the irruption of eternity into time, as in the founding events of each of these faiths: the giving of the Torah to Moses, the incarnation of the Word in Jesus, and the "coming down" of the Qur'an. These events are unique in the way that no other historical event can claim to be, precisely because they represent (to believers) the presence of the creator in creation, eternity in time, in such a way as to make the eternal creator subject to temporal description. Only that "theandric" character can give a place iconic status. For just as any historical event must be comparable to others, so any place must be able to be mapped in space and in time. Yet just as some times serve to punctuate time itself – as creation (biblically calculated) does for Jews, the birth of Jesus does for Christians, and the *hijra* does for Muslims – so some places bear the mark of God's palpable presence. Merely stating this, however, raises the specter of "particularity" which threatens to send us all running for comfort into that "universality" which renders all time and space homogeneous. If Lessing's "ugly ditch" put the scandal of Abrahamic faith directly before our minds, this land presents it daily to our eyes. So we are returned, in a Christian context, to Chalcedon, and to the four-century struggle, often bloody, to craft that formula, for Jerusalem with the land it epitomizes confronts us with the "full humanity" of Jesus, and the shocking particularity of Jewish as well as Christian faith – for Jesus, after all, was not a Christian!

But what have icons to do with formulae? Very little, usually, but when the formula in question is one which attempts to articulate a community's faith, and in this case, faith in a person who is – in his very person – the revelation of God, then understanding the words themselves will require more than our intellects. The words must engage our very persons as well, and icons are meant to do just that. Yet if icons fail to do it for a Western sensibility, encountering a place like the Holy Land may awaken that untapped potential within us. For just as icons call us beyond the response reserved for mere pictures, so this land continues to have an uncanny effect on its visitors. In her attempt to capture this quality, Karen Armstrong recalls us to the ways in which (by the nineteenth century) "modernity was gradually changing religion [so that] people in Europe and the United States had lost the art of thinking in symbols and images, . . . yet the mythology of sacred geography went deep" (1996: 363). Moreover, among Jews facing their own modernity, "Jerusalem was still a symbol that had power to inspire . . . secular Zionists as they struggled to create a new world" (367). So a place that has been touched in the way this land has will confront our standing presumption that any place must be like any other, and open us to the "scandal of particularity" which characterizes Abrahamic faith. Moreover, in our time, this place shapes the interaction among those faiths in ways which would baffle the "nonviolent crusaders" of the nineteenth century. For the Jesus whom Christians meet here is unmistakably Jewish, even if the current Jewish presence for local Christians is more often oppressive than it is illuminating of the Gospels. Moreover, the hegemonic claims of the state of Israel over Jerusalem itself have awakened in Muslims their ancient attachment to this "third holy city of Islam," which Israel itself has effectively acknowledged since 1967, in accepting *waqf* jurisdiction over the *haram ash-sharif*, however pragmatic the motives may have been for doing so.

Here we touch, I propose, the current shape of Christian presence in the Holy Land. The legacy of the nineteenth-century "nonviolent crusade," establishing a variegated Western presence in the Holy Land, continues to affect its spiritual ecology, and through these standing institutions, the livelihood of countless of its Arab citizens. Moreover, these institutions are always more than buildings: they are staffed by dedicated women and men, many of whom are young volunteers drawn to serve in this special place, whose lives are animated by a faith which transcends all place but nonetheless draws sustenance here. Often enough, they will not possess categories sufficient to articulate the effects which the special presence of this place has on them, even though their own work and presence will go on to contribute to it for visitors who come. So once again, place and presence interact to produce a power which baffles our rational modes of discourse, much as icons do, and yet conspire to spell the charm of this land, and the special presence of the Jesus of history to the communities of Christians here. That presence today is closer to Jesus' own in his time, bereft as it is of political power, and confronted by Israeli hegemony and an increasing majority of Muslims, yet that very fact shapes the current witness Christians can give. What is becoming clearer in our new millennium is that Jesus' presence in these communities – themselves legacies from an earlier century and then current political visions of Christendom – will be found in the ways they learn to interact with their Jewish and Muslim compatriots to exploit the symbolic potential of Jerusalem as one city of three faiths, with the special allure of the land Jesus touched. If local Christians have benefited from the educational opportunities granted by institutions founded from the West, their telling contribution today will be to show Western Christians how to live in an environment shaped by many faiths.

Indeed, It may be the enduring presence of the Jesus of history which sharpens the interaction among the three faiths living in this land. Here especially will the shadow sides of faith-communities be played out: the demand that one's own *truth* must cancel out that affirmed by the other. It was that fierce intolerance, so often elicited and indeed sharpened by faith, which led the West into an enlightenment designed to circumvent these potentially conflicting particularities. Yet after passing through the crucible of a century in which more human beings were killed in the name of ideologies offered as secular alternatives to faith, we may be more inclined to return to those same faith-traditions to find how they also exhibit within themselves the capacity to criticize the abuses executed in their name, and thereby effect their own renewal. Here the Holy Land may offer the best test case, precisely because it always seems the most intractable. The landmark visit of John Paul II (in the early months of the year 2000) to this land, and especially to Jerusalem, may help bring these reflections to a clearer focus. He came as a "pilgrim" yet made explicitly political statements, as he had to have done since Jerusalem is a flesh-and-blood reality, iconic of three faith-communities, so can hardly be reduced to a "holy place." His statements were not calculatedly political, however, promoting special interests, but clearly emanated from principles imbedded in and redolent of each of the faith-communities whose composition mirrors extant political conflicts. In that way, groups currently at odds had to come together in affirming his presence, and although each would inevitably attempt to interpret his message in ways favorable to themselves, he supplied a discourse which all perforce could share.

The following reflections of Marcel Dubois OP can place the Pope's visit in the context of a lifetime of ministry in this land. And while they focus on Jerusalem, that special place remains emblematic of ways this entire land can resonate with people of faith:

> While it has become commonplace to speak of Jerusalem as a meeting point among the three monotheistic faiths, in fact, considering the history and the actual state of relations among these three religions, Jerusalem rather emerges as the "high place" of disunity. Its history represents one long path spiked with rivalries, conquests, revenge, and persecutions. The city is still marked by these secular battles, in its stones and in its hearts. The wounds of time have still not been cauterized. Today a situation of waiting which is neither peace nor war threatens to freeze into a lasting tension, a state of mutual ignorance and deaf hostility among three communities, each of which nonetheless believes in the same God and lays claim to Abraham.
>
> One feels this standoff in an especially striking and tragic way in a holy place in Jerusalem atop Mount Zion: the building which is celebrated by Christians as the Cenacle, by Jews as the tomb of David, and is now crowned by a minaret. We need only ponder this ancient edifice to understand how broken is the human world here. For the three major monotheistic religions manifest their division in the very place where, according to our faith, the Lord bestowed the sacrament of unity in the Eucharist, and where He sent the Spirit of Pentecost to be the leaven of love in the heart of each person – indeed, the very place where Love itself was manifested and communicated in a definitive way. The handsome large gothic room was constructed by the Franciscans and served as a church for nearly a century. Then it became what it still is: Muslim property used for many centuries as a mosque, as the décor testifies. Now it is an empty vessel where any official ritual is forbidden, according to the *status quo* [regulations governing the holy places since the Ottomans], administered by the Israeli ministry of religious affairs. This tension was even more striking before the 1967 war, when the Cenacle was situated on the border dividing the city, among ruined houses and fields laced with barbed wire, between a Jordanian and an Israeli military post which regularly exchanged fire. So the "high place" of the Eucharist and Pentecost stood as a counter-sacrament to a broken world and human divisions.
>
> Nevertheless, as we could say equally well regarding the chasms which continue to divide Christians here, the sharpness of the feelings testifies to the depth of the realities at work. The very vehemence of attachment to Jerusalem displays the import of a perception paradoxically common to all those which it seems to divide so radically: indeed, that perception reveals nothing less than the very vocation of Jerusalem.
>
> Why has this perception been the cause of such tragic conflicts, and why does it remain so? The reason is as simple as it is profound: it marks the very spiritual condition of humankind. We seem to be made in such a way that we fail to perceive the richness to which we are called until we have experienced our own limits and contradictions. We only discover the homeland of which we are citizens and for which we are made through feelings of exile. Happiness only appears to us in that nostalgia which lurks within our privation and our emptiness. Similarly, we only perceive the positive reality of unity among human beings in the suffering of division and conflict. All this is especially poignant in Jerusalem. It is unfortunately true that religion has for centuries offered the pretext for merciless wars and bloody persecutions. Human beings have faced off against each other in the name of their convictions and their religious identities. In our own time, intolerant and aggressive religious fanatics pose a signal danger to world peace, so that religion appears to many as a factor of division and hostility among us.
>
> Such a tragic error contradicts the very essence of faith, however, so it is incumbent upon people of faith to denounce this disastrous misreading by the witness of an encoun-

ter among believers animated by an authentic faith. If the differences among religions have provoked such rivalry and conflict, that can only indicate how impure was the faith which they claimed, and in whose name violence was perpetrated. Indeed, faith has too often been adulterated with other causes or interests of this world, for which it offered justification and a banner, thereby falsifying itself.

Indeed, rather than dividing human communities, the truth of the matter is that the spiritual attitude demanded by an authentic faith ought to unite believers, in a place beyond the object and content of their particular beliefs, by whatever signs and rituals these may be expressed. For in the hearts of human beings, faith provides, before anything else, an essential reference to the transcendent principle of the universe and of history: the One whom the monotheistic religions call God. On the part of one who believes, faith implies awareness of the glory and the limitations of the condition of creatures; that is, their radical dependence on the source of all being and every gift. That is why every authentic faith finds expression in prostration, humility, and thanksgiving. Opened in their spirit and their hearts to the transcendent principle of their being and their action, those who live by faith cannot but be open to all other human beings at the same time, whom they find called to that same recognition and the same openness. That is why the faith which inspires every authentic religious attitude is the very condition of love and peace among human beings. The fidelity of every believer to this spiritual dimension of their faith is the condition for that mutual respect among believers, and the most powerful factor bringing them together: "everything that rises must converge." Holy men and women of all spiritual traditions testify to this profound linkage between personal fidelity and openness to others: the very security of their religious convictions grounds their respect for believers of other faiths. Much more than in the past, and with an urgency ever more pressing and a scale as large as the world itself, our age needs to be awakened by the witness of such a spiritual attitude . . .

Indeed, this is the enduring spiritual vocation of Jerusalem. This city in which the three great monotheistic religions co-exist, recapitulates in its history and its very stones the tragedies, battles, and bloody events which have set Jews, Christians, and Muslims against one another over the centuries. It is the place in which the contradictions and divisions which separate these religions shine forth in the most visible and symbolic way. In this respect, Jerusalem has been and remains a sign of contradiction. Yet it is also a sign of hope. For believers of the three great monotheistic faiths, Jerusalem is the "high place" where God has intervened in the history of humanity. It is there where He revealed to us His proposal for unity and peace, and there where He has prefigured it. As the utterly unique point of contact between eternity and time, Jerusalem is called to be the laboratory of mutual comprehension and respect among human beings. For believers living in Jerusalem, in the fidelity each has to the interior light and in the joy of discovering that same fidelity among others, encounter among religions is an experience at once unique and exemplary, addressed to all human beings of good will: "Zion shall be called 'Mother,' for all shall be her children" (Ps 87,5) (Dubois, 1999, my translation).

Nearly 20 years ago, Yeheskel Landau and I co-edited a book, *Voices from Jerusalem* (New York: Paulist, 1980), whose subtext leaned toward showing how the very interfaith composition of this city gives it sufficient consistency to serve as capital of two states. Yet our perspectives (and available human resources) at that time were so restricted that we issued the collection without a Muslim voice! In fact, however, both our perspectives and the available resources have now shifted considerably, so no one can any longer conceive the issues in merely "Jewish–Christian" terms, but must always pose them in a triadic fashion: Jewish, Christian, Muslim. That is what the Holy Land does to one who lives there and imbibes its special spirit. The Spirit of Jesus will be found active in the diverse Christian communities which dot the landscape and serve its many peoples, yet especially in the ways those communities engage other faith communities to mine the resources each possesses. So seismic historical shifts have bequeathed a new mission to the Christian communities in this land: bring this sacred place, with its diverse Abrahamic faith traditions, to the point where it displays the power of each tradition to animate peace rather than justify conflict. A simple contrast with the Crusades will underscore the novelty of this mission; attention to comparable shifts in attitude toward "other religions," especially among Catholic Christians in the past half century, should alert us to the way these communities stand on the threshold of interfaith understanding, especially at the service of peacemaking. Will that happen? *Allah 'arafu*; God alone knows, yet the God of Abraham has left the execution of the "divine decree" in human hands – for better or for worse.

Notes

1   Much of the material in this essay was first elaborated in my "Jerusalem after Jesus," in *Cambridge Companion to Jesus* edited by Markus Bockmuehl (Cambridge: Cambridge University Press, 2001), 250–64; used with permission.
2   For an account based on historical documents, yet presented in narrative fashion, see Maalouf, 1984.
3   Note how an author like Michael Prior (1997) will be able to rely on archeological findings to query the accuracy of biblical accounts.
4   These telling statistics were supplied by Bernard Sabella, Associate Professor of Sociology at Bethlehem University, and serving as Executive Secretary to the Department of Service to Palestinian Refugees of the Middle East Council of Churches. See his "Socio-Economic Characteristics and the Challenges to Palestinian Christians in the Holy Land," in Prior and Taylor, 1994.

References and Further Reading

Armstrong, Karen (1996) *Jerusalem: One City, Three Faiths.* New York: Knopf.
Benvenisti, Meron (1996) *City of Stone: the Hidden History of Jerusalem*, trans. Maxine Kaufman Nunn. Berkeley: University of California Press.
Burrell, David, and Landau, Yeheskel (eds.) (1992) *Voices from Jerusalem: Jews and Christians Reflect on the Holy Land*, Mahwah, NJ: Paulist.
Cyril of Scythopolis (1991) *Lives of the Monks of Palestine*, trans. R.M. Price. Kalamazoo, MI: Cistercian Publications.
Dubois, Marcel (1999) "Jérusalem dans le temps et l'eternité," *L'Olivier de Jérusalem*, 2–3 (POB 1332, Jerusalem, Israel), 7–109.
Irenaeus (1869) *Against Heresies*, trans. Alexanders Roberts and W.H. Rambault, in *Ante-Nicene Christian Library* volume 9. Edinburgh: T. and T. Clark.
Lazarus-Yafeh, Hava (1974) "The Sanctity of Jerusalem in Islam," in Oesterreicher, J. and

Sinai, A. (eds.) *Jersualem*. New York: John Day, 211–25; reprinted in *Some Religious Aspects of Islam* (1981). Leiden: Brill, 58–71.

Maalouf, Amin (1984) *The Crusades through Arab Eyes*, trans. Jon Rothschild. London: Al Saqi Books.

McGarry, Michael and Landau, Yehesekel (eds.) (2005) *John Paul II and the Holy Land: Christian and Jewish Perspectives*. Mahwah, NJ: Paulist.

Origen (1979) *Origen: An Exhortation to Martyrdom, Prayer, and Selected Works*, ed. Rowan Greer. London: SPCK.

Peters, F.E. (1985) *Jerusalem*. Princeton, NJ: Princeton University Press.

Prior, Michael (1997) *The Bible and Colonialism*. Sheffield: Sheffield Academic Press.

Prior, Michael and Taylor, William (eds.) (1994) *Christians in the Holy Land*. London: The World of Islam Festival Trust.

Walker, Peter (1990) *Holy City, Holy Places? Christian Attitudes to Jerusalem and the Holy Land in the Fourth Century*. Oxford: Oxford University Press.

Walker, Peter (1994) "Jerusalem in the Early Christian Centuries," in P. W. L. Walker (ed.), *Jerusalem Past and Present in the Purposes of God*. Grand Rapids, MI: Baker, 79–97.

Wilken, Robert (1992) *The Land Called Holy: Palestine in Christian History and Thought*. New Haven, CT: Yale University Press.

CHAPTER 8
India

Charles J. Borges

Yours is a land of ancient culture, the cradle of great religions, the
home of a nation that has sought God with a relentless desire in deep
meditation and silence, and in hymns of fervent prayer.
Pope Paul VI while on a visit to India in 1964

A look at the history of the Church in India would be incomplete without a look at the
history of India itself. Indian history goes back 5,000 years to the Indus Valley civilization with its sophisticated urban culture as found in the cities of Harappa and
Mohenjo-Daro. The Indo-Aryan civilization probably came to India from central Asia
around 1500 BC and formed much of India's living tradition and impressive religious
system. Indian culture always was and continues to be a rich mosaic of new elements
and foreign influences merged into its ancient roots.

The oldest of India's religious traditions is Hinduism. Under the broad rubric of Hinduism, there existed an enormous fluidity of beliefs and practices which in turn evolved
by interacting with the other religions. Hinduism is really not a religion, but is a
way of life. It has no one single book as its sacred scripture nor does it have one god
or prophet. It is a religion of deep philosophy and metaphysics, existing side by side
with rituals and ceremonies that mark the days, seasons, and events in life. Gods can
be either distant or near, yet always part of every household and clan. One worships
them through silent meditation, communal singing, or joyful festivity. Closely linked
to this religious system is a social system. Society came to be divided into four castes,
the *brahmins* (priestly class in charge of the rituals and chants), the *kshatriyas* (war-
riors), the *vaishyas* (merchants), and the *sudras* (menial workers).

Besides Hinduism, three other great religions were born in India over the centuries: Jainism and Buddhism, founded in the sixth century BC, respectively by Mahavir
(the Great Hero) and Gautama Buddha (the Enlightened One); and Sikhism, founded
by Guru Nanak in the sixteenth century. But other major religions arrived from the
outside. Christianity appeared as early as the first or second centuries CE. Zoroastri-
anism arrived in the ninth century, taking refuge in India after fleeing persecution in

Persia. Islam first came to India in the tenth century through a series of raids on the subcontinent, but it established itself through a permanent dynasty in 1206. The great Mughal dynasty, established by Babur in 1526, ruled India for over 300 years. Mughal patronage of the arts brought a blending of the best of the Islamic, Hindu, and Christian traditions, thanks in large measure to the presence of Sufi preachers and the Jesuit priests stationed within its kingdom. By the end of the seventeenth century, however, the Mughals had been gradually weakened through a combination of religious wars and invasions from the northwest. Their political weakness allowed various European powers to establish their commercial and territorial sway in the subcontinent.

The first Europeans to come to India were the Portuguese, arriving in the persons of Vasco da Gama and his crew on May 27, 1498 at Calicut on the west coast. The Portuguese made substantial territorial gains in the following years, taking Goa in 1510. Though a strong power in the sixteenth century, they lost most of their territories, except for Goa, Daman, and Diu, to the Dutch and the English in the following century, a period during which French and Danish traders also arrived on the coasts of the subcontinent. By the eighteenth century, the Dutch had been largely pushed out by the English.

The English East India Company was created by a British royal charter in December 1600 and was granted a monopoly to trade with the whole of Asia and the Pacific basin. The Company established trading settlements, or factories, on the coasts of India, beginning with Surat on the western coast in 1608. It traded in Bengal from the 1650s. In 1702 it completed Fort William on the Hugli to protect its trading interests there. The city of Calcutta grew around Fort William, which by the later eighteenth century had become the center of British power in India.

The French, meanwhile, had set up the French East India Company in 1674 and by the early eighteenth century had made Pondicherry on the east coast of India, the base of its power. The eighteenth century saw a major confrontation between the English and the French, who fought three wars in India between 1740 and 1763. After the battle of Plassey (1757) the British Company established its Raj (rule) over Bengal, Bihar, and Orissa in eastern India. From 1773, Parliament in England started to exercise complete control over the Company's affairs, appointing Warren Hastings as the first Governor in 1772 and the first Governor General two years later. The Doctrine of Lapse ensured that lands belonging to any Indian ruler dying without a direct heir to the throne went into British hands, and ensured a steady expansion of British-held territory.

The Thomas Christians

According to tradition, Christianity first came to India in the person of St Thomas, said to have arrived on the western coast of Kerala about the year 52, and whose apostolate was preserved in the memory which his converts conveyed to later generations in India. This Christian community was in communion with the Syrian Church. Known as the Thomas Christians, they were largely upper class, and maintained their Hindu culture while they practiced the Christian faith with strong Syrian influences in their liturgy and worship.

Following their first encounter with the Thomas Christians at Cranganore on the western coast of Kerala, the Portuguese worked at bringing these communities more into line with the Roman Church and the Latin tradition. The Thomas Christians were initially willing to accept the primacy of the See of Rome, which they did formally at the Synod of Diamper in 1599, but great tension soon developed over the continuing attempts to alter their liturgy and remove other Eastern traditions from their Church life. According to the Portuguese, there could be only one law, that of Christ, and not two laws, one of St Thomas and the other of St Peter. The majority of the Thomas Christian priests (known as *kattanars*) met on January 3, 1653 at the Coonan Cross of Mattancherry and swore an oath never to accept the authority of the Archbishop of Cranganore, who was the head of the Roman Church in Kerala. These events led to the birth of a new Christian communion, the Malankara Syrian Orthodox Church, sometimes referred to as the Jacobites.

Rome acted promptly in response to this crisis. The Congregation for the Propagation of the Faith (Propaganda Fide) sent out Carmelites to India to attempt to deal with the situation. This initiative was forced on the Propaganda since the Thomas Christians refused to have anything to do with the Jesuits, with whom they had been dealing until then. Though often high-handed, the Carmelites were able to reconcile many of the Thomas Christians so that a majority of them returned to communion with Rome in 1662. This move had been possible because of Propaganda appointing in 1661 a vicar apostolic for Kerala, which gave the Thomas Christians in communion with Rome, known as the Syro-Malabar Catholic Christians, their own bishop.

At that time the separatist Malankara Church attempted to reestablish its links with the East Syrian patriarchate (or the Chaldean Church) but these attempts failed. Eventually the West Syrian Patriarch, based in Damascus, made contact with them and they became an autonomous Church within the Syrian Patriarchate, after having made some nominal changes in their customs to conform to the West Syrian as opposed to East Syrian traditions.

Meanwhile, the Syro-Malabar Catholics continued to complain to Rome about the Carmelites and to request an Indian bishop to replace the missionary vicar apostolic. In 1780 they even sent a delegation led by Fr Joseph Kariattil to Rome to petition personally for the appointment of an Indian bishop for their Church. Nothing came of this visit. But there was a change in their fortunes when the delegation arrived in Lisbon on its journey home to India. Under the powers of the Padroado, the Queen of Portugal appointed Fr Kariattil as Archbishop of Cranganore. When he landed at Goa, the excitement of the Thomas Christians was high but, to their despair, he fell ill and died before leaving Goa. Some have speculated that had he lived longer, the two communities of Thomas Christians, those in communion with the Syrian Church and those in communion with the Roman Church, might have come together again.

At this critical stage, the Archbishop of Goa made Fr Kariattil's companion, Fr Thomas Parreamakal, administrator of the apostolic vicariate, but this did not satisfy the people, who widely believed that Fr Kariattil had been poisoned. There was much agitation among the people and at a meeting in 1787 at Angamali in Kerala, the Thomas Christian leaders in communion with Rome vowed to recognize Fr Parreamakal and no other as their bishop. Goa refused to accept this. The agitation subsided but the Thomas Christians had to wait until 1887 to have bishops from their own communities to manage their affairs.

Catholic Missions in India

Goa

The Portuguese governor, Afonso de Albuquerque, had taken over the western coastal city of Goa in 1510 and it soon became the capital of the Portuguese possessions in the entire East, the *Estado da India* (as these possessions were called) spreading from Hormuz in the Persian Gulf to Malacca and Indonesia. Within Goa, the Portuguese made vigorous efforts to convert the people to the Christian faith. Along with the Portuguese government officials, merchants and soldiers, groups of religious priests and brothers and secular priests came to Goa each year from Portugal. Goa also became an important educational center, with priests and catechists receiving training there and then moving to missions in other parts of India and beyond. Goa was raised to the status of a diocese in 1534 and to that of an archdiocese in 1557.

The Franciscans arrived in Goa as early as 1510, the Jesuits in 1542, the Dominicans in 1548, the Augustinians in 1572, and the Carmelites in 1607. Among the well-known educational institutions located in Goa were the Colleges of St Aquinas (Dominicans), St Bonaventure (Franciscans), Populo (Augustinians), and St Paul's and St Roque (Jesuits). The many Goa churches (for example, Bom Jesus, Se Cathedral, St Francis of Assisi, Holy Spirit of Margao) remain rich expressions of the architecture, sculpture, painting, and wood-carving styles of the time. Unfortunately the Portuguese in the heyday of their evangelistic drive destroyed over 200 Hindu temples, some of them noted for their excellent craftsmanship. Besides being places of worship they had also been keepers of the land surveys and land registers of the Goan villages.

Various foreign travellers spoke in glowing terms of the Goa they saw, calling it the "Rome of the East" and "Golden Goa." Duarte Barbosa described it as a city inhabited by foreigners and rich merchants and to whose port sailed ships from Mecca, Eden, Hormuz, Cambay, and Malabar. It had large and imposing edifices and handsome streets surrounded by walls and towers. Tome Pires in 1511 had remarked that Goa was a great center of trade.

During the sixteenth century, Christianity made remarkable progress in the numbers of converts made both in the Portuguese-held territories and in the various Portuguese trading centers. There were, however, no close contacts with the higher classes of the Hindus. St Francis Xavier (1506–52) contributed much to evangelizing the people of India. Arriving in Goa on May 6, 1542, he was active in charitable works while he preached to the Portuguese settlers and catechized the local people. Within five months he had left Goa for the east coast of India and, by August 1549, he was in Japan. The Italian Jesuit Fr Alessandro Valignano (1539–1606) built on the foundations laid by Xavier and came to be known as the foremost organizer of the Indian missions of his day. He stressed the need for Jesuits to learn local languages and he set up schools for this purpose. He labored long on the problem of the Church in Malabar and did his best to bring its members fully back to the Catholic Church.

It was with Hinduism that the Jesuits waged a sustained and long relationship during the 200 years they were in India prior to their suppression in 1759. Contacts with the Hindus in Goa in particular had convinced them that the people were not illiterate but that many of them were well versed in Sanskrit, Konkani, and Marathi languages and literature. One Jesuit who took this insight seriously and who made sustained attempts to study Hindu literature deeply, was the English Jesuit, Fr Thomas Stephens (1549–1619). He had studied at Oxford and after joining the Society of Jesus in England, arrived in Goa on October 24, 1579. He worked as a priest in the Salcete area of Goa, an area which had been handed over to the Jesuits in 1560 by the Portuguese government but which could boast by that time only about a hundred converts. These converts lived close to the Portuguese stronghold of Rachol. Fr Stephens had witnessed the events connected with the revolt of the Hindus of the Cuncolim village against the Portuguese. The Hindus had felt highly provoked when their important temple was destroyed and pulled down a Jesuit chapel in reaction. The Jesuit superior, Fr Rudolf Acquaviva (who had earlier served at the court of Akbar in north India) and three other Jesuits who were on the scene to reopen the Jesuit mission and raise a cross in the area, were killed by the Hindus. Fr Stephens had to use his good offices to retrieve the bodies of the dead Jesuits which had been thrown into a well. This experience, it is said, became a turning point in his life.

Fr Stephens' major literary work was the *Kristapurana* (Epic on Christ), composed in Marathi and Konkani poetic style which was an attempt to translate the Christian message to Indian life. He presented Jesus Christ in the form of a *purana* (an epic), India's religious literature, thus helping his readers feel fully at home in their new faith as well as with the traditions of their native culture. The cultured new converts, who usually spoke Marathi, felt the absence and beauty of their former religious texts. It is said that they needed not only a catechism of doctrine but a literature that could feed their minds and hearts. Fr Stephens composed in a style that could be understood by the people and which would appeal to them.

If Fr Stephens appeared to be the one whose understood the needs of the new converts, there were other Jesuits who could be hard and unyielding. Among Jesuit parish educators, an important official was the *Pai dos Cristãos* (Father of the Christians) whose job was to take care of orphans and those in the process of being baptized. His other duties included punishing converts who took part in the Hindu festivals that were celebrated in their villages.

A Jesuit who had a harsh outlook toward the Hindus and Muslims, though a fine personality himself, was Fr Diego Gonçalves (1561–1640), author of the *História do Malavar*. To the end of his long life he is said to have strongly attacked Muslims in his sermons. With his knowledge of Malayalam he was able to understand Hinduism and its legends and myths well and admired all that he studied insofar as it was purely of a civil nature. He meant his *História* to be an instruction on how Hinduism with its corrupt morals and its polytheism could be overcome by Christianity.

Mughal Court

It was in 1581, during Fr Valignano's tenure as Provincial of the Province of Goa, that the enlightened Mughal emperor Jalal-ud-din Muhammad Akbar (1542–1605) invited the Jesuits to his royal court in north India. Akbar hoped to gather religious men from different faiths to help him found a new religion, the *Din-i-Ilahi*. Jesuits like Fr Rudolf Acquaviva (1550–83) and others took part in three successive Jesuit missions to the Mughal court over the next hundred years.

The missions to the court of Akbar had both a religious and a political purpose. As a religious enterprise, the missions aimed at the conversion of the emperor and the spread of Christianity in his dominions. The first never happened. But the small Christian communities needed the continued presence of the Jesuits at the Mughal court. Although the Jesuit missions failed to convert Akbar and the other emperors, they did help bring about a better understanding between Islam and Christianity. They built up a fruitful connection with the imperial courts, a connection which enabled them to open stations in various parts of the Muslim Empire and even in Nepal and Tibet. Akbar was succeeded by Jahangir (who aided British attempts to trade in India), then by Shah Jahan (builder of the Taj Mahal), and finally by the intolerant Aurangzeb whose death in 1707 marked the effective end of the Mughal Empire, although it continued in a much reduced form until the end of the rule of Emperor Bahadur Shah in 1858.

South India

Besides the Mughal court, Jesuits had an important presence at different times in the royal courts of the southern kingdoms of Vijayanagara, Gunji, Madurai, and Thanjavur. Jesuit superiors and subjects wrote regularly to Rome both from Goa and from various parts of south India, detailing their mission work, successes, failures, and needs. This system of regular correspondence within the Society of Jesus had been designed by St Ignatius, the founder of the order, as a way to strengthen the bonds of union among its members and facilitate good government. The *Litterae Indicae*, or Indian letters, soon became an effective instrument of propaganda in Europe for overseas missions.

The correspondence is revealing of the innovations and originality of the great Italian Jesuit missionary in south India, Fr Roberto de Nobili (1577–1656). He began his missionary work in 1606 at Madurai, one of the ancient centers of Tamil culture. In order to gain broad acceptance, he declared himself to be a member of the Italian nobility and of the raja (kingly) class, and a twice-born Roman Brahmin. He dressed in the Brahmin *sannyasi* (mendicant) mode, and wore the sacred thread (*kudumi*) and wooden sandals. He learnt Tamil, Telugu, and Sanskrit and began reformulating Christianity in the terms and thought patterns of Indian religious civilization. He eventually made over 30,000 converts and a century after his death, the mission he established could boast of over 200,000 Christians. His religious motto was, appropriately, "*Aperire portam*" (to open the door).

Fr de Nobili's intellectual gifts, his capacity to absorb and communicate the learning that he found in the land of his adoption, were outstanding. Though accused of being fixated on high caste, his perspectives went beyond caste and custom. He possessed an impressive spirit of penance and was called "*Tattuva Podagar*" (the Brahmin mendicant) by all. However, he encountered opposition from the Hindus, and even more from some of his fellow missionaries and Church leaders. Although the Jesuits in Rome and even Pope Gregory XV initially supported his innovations, eventually many of the practices he proposed for his new converts were banned by Rome. He had continually sought to understand Hinduism from within. His aim had been not merely to convert the high caste Brahmins, but through them to bring the whole of India to Christ.

The de Nobili method of mission remained a contentious issue through the seventeenth and eighteenth centuries. In 1703 Charles Maillard de Tournon was sent as papal delegate to China and then to India to settle matters of the "Chinese Rites" and "Malabar Rites." He ruled that there should be no compromise in the matter and that the two rites must be rejected. In 1739 Pope Clement XII required all missionaries to sign an oath to this effect. Pope Benedict XIV, by his instruction *Omnium Sollicitudinum* of September 12, 1744, ruled that all Catholics, whatever their caste, should hear Mass and receive communion in the same church and at the same time. The Jesuits adhered to the ruling, but they built separate entrances for believers from the low castes to enter the common churches and installed small divisions within the churches to separate the low from the high castes.

Not as intellectually gifted as de Nobili, yet equally sympathetic to Hinduism, was the Portuguese Jesuit, St João de Brito. He dressed in the garb of a Hindu *sannyasi* and worked exclusively with the low castes of south India. For his forthrightness he was tortured and then beheaded in February 1693 at Oriyur in Tamil Nadu. He was called a man of the rank and file, one who did not travel extensively as Xavier did, but was truly the second Xavier in India and because of his beheading, the second John the Baptist.

The Italian Fr Leonardo Cinnami (1609–76) was the founder of the Madurai, Kanara, and Mysore Jesuit missions in south India. He had come to recognize that his initial four years in the missions had not borne fruit, mainly because he had been viewed as a foreign priest. By 1649 he began dressing as a *sannyasi*, had his ears pierced and his head and neck smeared with ashes. The legacy of his great mission work was such that he was to the Mysore Mission what de Nobili was to the Madurai. He left several devotional works, the most notable of those being *Istoria del Canara* (1648).

Another great Italian Jesuit missionary was Fr Costanzo Giuseppe Beschi (1680–1747). He had come to India in 1711 and went on to work in the Madurai mission. He excelled in Tamil and wrote classical epics, philosophical treatises, commentaries, dictionaries, grammars, translations, and tracts for both Hindus and Christians. His epic three-volume poem *Tembavani* (Unfading Garland), a work on St Joseph, and his public disputations with Hindu scholars won him great renown, ensuring him a lasting legacy as a scholar of Sanskrit and Tamil literature. Christian teaching and philosophy are propounded in excellent Tamil verse. Hindu terms abound with Christ described as having *tulasi*-like hands, *tulasi* being a sweet smelling plant used in Vaishnava temples. There is also mention of the *nama japa*, the recitation of a thousand names of God.

In order to deal with fate and rebirth in Hinduism, he told the people that the sin of Adam and Eve was their "previous birth," and that fate actually meant "divine decree." He attacked the caste system and said that one can find it only on earth, for after death it is the spiritual life that will differentiate people. He condemned the tradition of not allowing the low-caste people to hear the Vedas. He used the idea of surrender (a theme in Vaishnavism) to speak of Our Lady as the refuge of all Christians. His church to the Virgin Mary had an Indian name (Periyanayaki) and in it Mary was shown as dressed in a sari, wearing bangles and earrings.

Other Jesuits who were equally proficient as writers included Fr Heinrich Roth (1620–68) who composed a Sanskrit grammar in Latin. He learnt the Kannada, Persian, and Urdu languages and wrote a work on the incarnations of Vishnu. Fr John Ernest Hanxleden (1681–1732) was author of *Mishiada Pana* (New Hymn), of a Sanskrit–Malayalam–Portuguese dictionary and a Malayalam grammar in Portuguese. He was popularly known as Arnos Padri. His *Mishiada Pana* was meant to inspire great devotion in his Christian community and the poem was composed on the lines of the Hindu *Ramayana* and puranas. Fr Gaston Coeurdoux (1691–1777) had served in Pondicherry, Kanara, and Tranquebar. He was well versed in Sanskrit and Telugu and wrote a Telugu–Sanskrit–French dictionary and was the first to show the linguistic connections of Sanskrit with Latin, Greek, German, and Russian. Fr Jean Calmette (1693–1739) served in the Tamil mission in Kanara and was the first European to get a copy of all the four Hindu Vedas, while Fr Francis Pons (1698–1752) was an astronomer, geographer, canonist, and a Sanskrit scholar who composed a Sanskrit grammar.

What is striking about the growth of the Church in seventeenth- and eighteenth-century India is the number of priests and laymen too who produced important literary and religious works. One recalls such sixteenth-century works as *Homem das Trinta e duas perfeições* (Archbishop Francisco Garcia Mendes), *Discursos sobre a vida do apóstolo Sam Pedro* (Estevão da Cruz), *Colóquios dos simples e drogas medicináis* (Garcia da Orta); and seventeenth-century treatises on Hinduism by Jean Venance Bouchet and Konkani grammar by Karel Prikryl.

Non-Jesuit religious orders and congregations also did commendable work but on a much smaller scale, given their limited numbers and paucity of funds. The activities of the Franciscans during the seventeenth and eighteenth centuries were directed more toward consolidation than expansion. By 1629 they had two provinces in India, with about 600 friars. They had houses in Goa and also in Bassein (near Bombay) and their houses suffered under the Hindu Maratha attacks in the eighteenth century. In 1766 they had to withdraw from the parishes they had held in the Bardez area of Goa, handing them over to local Goan secular priests who had become very numerous by that time and who were eager to run the parishes.

After their arrival in Goa in 1548, the Dominicans set up houses also outside Goa in places like Bassein, Mahim, Tarapur, Chaul, Daman, Diu (all in the so-called Portuguese Province of the North) and in Cochin, Nagapatanam, and Mylapore (south India) They were subsequently able to expand their missions to Mozambique and to Malacca, and to the islands of Timor and Solor in Indonesia. The Augustinians were the last to arrive in Goa, establishing the College of Our Lady of Grace between 1597 and 1602. From 1599 they expanded their mission into Bengal, the region which they viewed as their most successful missionary field. They also worked in Persia and on the east coast of Africa.

Other religious orders, like the Carmelites, the Capuchins, and the Theatines, arrived in India in the course of the seventeenth century. They worked under the direct supervision of Propaganda and had jurisdictional difficulties with the Portuguese Padroado. Both these units were structures of governance of the Church, with the Padroado system having worked well for a time. The Portuguese power had waned in the East with the rise of the Dutch and the English. The Church stepped in with the Congregation for the Propagation of the Holy Faith (1622), a unit that would oversee all Catholic mission work in the world. It established vicariates in places where the Portuguese had no territorial control. But in places like Bombay (ceded by the Portuguese to the British in 1661), Catholics found themselves under a double jurisdiction, either that of Propaganda or that of Padroado.

The Carmelites had charge of the vicariates of Malabar in south India and of the Great Mughal. The Capuchins worked in Surat, Madras, and Pondicherry, and the Theatines served in Golconda. Under the Padroado regime of Goa, there were both Portuguese and Goan priests. Under the Roman Propaganda system there were vicars apostolic in Bombay, Kerala, Pondicherry, and Tibet. Italian Carmelites served in Bombay and Kerala; French Capuchins and secular priests of the Société des Missions Étrangères in Tami Nadu; French Capuchins in Madras; and Italian Capuchins in north India.

The Theatines (Clerics Regular of Divine Providence of St Cajetan) were active in Goa although they lacked funds and personnel in comparison with other orders. However, the Oratory of the Holy Cross of Miracles, founded in Goa in 1682 and patterned on the Oratory of St Philip Neri, counted among its most illustrious members Blessed José Vaz (1651–1711). It grew to be an influential body, especially as it was the first religious congregation made up of clerics of local Goan origin.

In 1703, the Propaganda erected the Prefecture of Tibet-Hindustan, entrusting it to the Capuchins. They were able to maintain a presence in Lhasa from 1707 to 1745, when religious persecution forced them to move back to Kathmandu in Nepal, where the order had been established since 1715. But ultimately, in 1769, political unrest forced them to leave this kingdom as well and to relocate in India. In the meantime, many Nepalese Christians and catechumens relocated to Bettiah, Bihar in 1745. The Prefecture of Tibet-Hindustan was elevated into a vicariate in 1812.

The Jesuits moved into Tibet even earlier, with a mission at Tsaparang which ended in 1641. In 1713, a fresh start was made by two Jesuits, Frs Ippolito Desideri and Manoel Freyre, even though the Capuchins considered Tibet part of their mission field and out of bounds to all other orders. Fr Desideri was soon left alone in Tibet, and in the face of severe Capuchin opposition to his presence, he was ordered out of Lhasa in 1719. He was a great geographer, and his account of the mission was very reliable, revealing a deep understanding of Tibetan society and literature.

Though all of the orders and congregations mentioned above were engaged in the same general purpose of Christianization, a considerable amount of jealousy and exclusiveness existed among them.

The first convent for women in the East, the convent of Santa Monica, was established in Goa in 1606, largely through the efforts of Archbishop Dom Aleixio de Menezes. It was intended mainly for the widows of Portuguese soldiers. Although tensions prevailed for some years between two factions within the cloister, the nuns continued to perform their regular religious duties, excelled in literary and musical works, and were also known for their skill in the fine arts and in culinary innovations.

The year 1759 marked the beginning of a difficult period for the Jesuits in both Portugal and India. In that year, the Marquis of Pombal, virtual ruler of Portugal, managed to have the Society in Portugal and its colonies suppressed. The order's extensive landed properties and their houses in Goa were confiscated. In 1760, 127 Jesuits, working in various parts of India, were arrested and shipped back to Europe from Goa. Following the suppression, Pombal pursued a number of popular reforms in the colony. He disbanded the Inquisition in 1774 (it had conducted over 70 *Autos da Fe*, or sessions of examination, since its beginnings in Goa). He revamped the educational system and worked to improve conditions for the local clergy. Priests came to be selected for parish posts on the basis of their learning and virtue rather than on the basis of their racial backgrounds.

There were political disturbances in Catholic Goa. The Portuguese presence there did not remain unchallenged and there were many popular revolts In 1654, for example, Dom Mathias de Castro, unhappy over being bypassed for an episcopal post in Goa, joined with Adil Shah, ruler of Bijapur, in a failed attempt to overthrow the Portuguese. In 1787, the conspiracy of the Pintos of Candolim brought to the fore Caetano Francisco de Couto, José António Gonçalves, and Caetano Victorino de Faria – all Goan priests – who had developed an abortive plan to overthrow Portuguese rule in Goa, after they had failed to persuade the Holy See to fill vacant episcopal posts of the Padroado in Goa with Indian appointees.

Modern Missions

Modern Catholic missionary movement in India began from 1830 onwards, the preceding period often considered 70 years of mission decadence. The Jesuits had either left or been removed from their posts from Goa and various parts of India in 1759. The Paris Society for Foreign Missions came to the rescue of the Church though its members were soon involved in the crisis of the French Revolution. Tipu Sultan let loose a time of persecution on the Christians in the Kanara region.

The credit for setting in motion the missionary movement in India goes to Pope Gregory XVI. He set up apostolic vicariates in all non-Portuguese territories. Pope Pius VII had in 1814 restored the Society of Jesus worldwide. By 1838 various groups of Jesuits began arriving in India to start missionary work. English, Irish, and French Jesuits started work in Bengal and in 1859 the Belgians set up missions in West Bengal as well as in Orissa and Chota Nagpur. In 1854 German Jesuits took over Bombay from the Carmelites and proceeded to develop missions in Gujarat and Pune. Their arrival was made possible by the invitation of the Swiss-born Bishop Anatasius Hartmann of Patna. After serving the diocese there, he was called to Bombay where as bishop he supported Propaganda.

The Capuchin missions in North India continued over a wide area from Bihar to the Punjab. Their main mission center was at Sardhana, near Meerut, with Agra as their vicariate. In the south the Paris Society for Foreign Missions, based in Pondicherry, extended its work in Mysore, Coimbatore, and Kumbakonam. The Society of St Joseph (Mill Hill) took up work in the Telugu districts in 1875. Italian Jesuits came to Mangalore in 1877. As among the Protestants, so also among the Roman Catholics women's groups played an important part in building the Church in modern times.

Conflict between the Padroado and Propaganda continued during this time, leading to the signing of a Concordat between the Vatican and Portugal, first in 1857 and again in 1886, which recognized the rights of Portugal but defined their extent as clearly as possible. The Archbishop of Goa became known as the patriarch of the East Indies. All Indian vicariates in 1886 were raised to the status of diocese with six of them being raised to that of archdiocese.

Despite the Concordat of 1886, the issue of double jurisdiction remained, and in one and the same geographical place, churches under either the Propaganda or the Padroado bishops existed. In the archdiocese of Bombay, for instance, six churches belonged to the Padroado diocese of Daman and seven in Daman to that of Propaganda in Bombay. In 1928 a new agreement between Rome and Portugal abolished this process. In 1950 in view of Indian independence there was a new agreement between Rome and Portugal whereby Portugal renounced all of its Padroado rights.

In the last quarter of the nineteenth century, the Catholic missions increased substantially. There were some conversions among the higher castes, but the majority came from the sudras and the "scheduled" (i.e. outcaste) castes and tribes. The Jesuit missionary of the Belgian Province, Fr Constant Lievens (1856–93) was in India from 1885 to 1892 and realized the need to help the people in their quarrels with their zamindars (landowners) and moneylenders. He studied the history of land possession and British law and was able to defend the people in their lawsuits. He started a Mutual Help Society and a Cooperative Credit Society. He was followed in his work by Fr B. Hoffmann (1857–1928), a German-born Jesuit who had joined the Belgian Province and who had come to India in 1878. He founded the Catholic Cooperative Credit Society in 1909. Tribals were encouraged to deposit their savings and were able to receive moderate rates of interest. The tribals managed the Credit Society totally themselves and were slowly able to free themselves from the designs of the moneylenders. Fr Hoffman's efforts led to the drafting of the Chotanagpur Tenancy Act in 1908. His most important work was his contribution to the publication of the *Encyclopaedia Mundarica*.

The area popularly called the Northeast is made up of seven states: Arunachal Pradesh, Assam, Manipur, Nagaland, Mizoram, Meghalaya, and Tripura. Popular misunderstandings in the rest of the country hold that separatist tendencies in the region bordering China, Burma, Nepal, and Bangladesh, are largely a result of the Christian allegiance of peoples in these seven regions. Ethnically the people of these states are of Mongolian racial stock. Their beliefs are not influenced either by Hinduism or by Buddhism. As a result of the evangelizing work done by groups like the Baptist Missionary Society, the Welsh Presbyterian Missions, and various Catholic missionary groups (most notably the Salesians), large percentages of the states are Christian.

Catholic missionary work in the nineteenth century took account of the state of education in the country and worked actively at setting up nursery, primary, and secondary schools and colleges. Parishes and schools also had boarding hostels for Christians and non-Christians and orphanages. Various women congregations turned their attention to starting hospitals and dispensaries. Some of the most important colleges which were set up in the mid-1850s were St Joseph's College (Tiruchirapalli), St Xavier's (Bombay), St Xavier's (Calcutta), and Loyola College (Madras).

The modern period of Catholic mission history has been marked by an increasing number of Indian vocations to the priesthood and the setting up of seminaries for their training. In 1890 a Papal Seminary was started for Indian diocesan priests and though located at Kandy (Ceylon) it was shifted to Pune in 1954.

The first part of the twentieth century was a period of great political unrest with nationalist forces trying to win more political freedom from the British. The British eventually handed over power to the Indians in 1947. The French willingly relinquished their possessions of Pondicherry and other enclaves in south India. But the Portuguese continued with their possessions in Goa, Daman, and Diu until their forced eviction in 1961.

Since 1947, the Church has reflected hard on its role in free India while struggling to develop its own Indian face and understanding and living of theology and religion. There have been frequent calls for the Church to realize its Indian identity by adjusting itself to conditions prevailing in the country and develop an indigenous theology based on the responses to the Word of God in one's particular religio-cultural tradition.

In the aftermath of Vatican II, Indian theologians and thinkers are developing a deeper understanding of the Holy Spirit as present not only in persons but in all cultures and religions. They believe that elements of truth and grace are present in them due to the action of God's Word and Spirit. As a result of this understanding, the Church has laid great stress on the process of dialog with members of other faiths. There is a call for a theology that is inculturated and which will lead to the presentation of Jesus Christ as the fulfillment of the yearnings expressed in the mythologies and folklore of all people. Most of those involved in this dialogical process realize that when members of other faiths see Christians interested in the religious traditions of their faiths, they become more open to the process itself.

Catholic thinkers see God at work in all religions. The Christian kerygma reveals that Christ will not be fully discovered until the last moment of history. The hidden Christ of Hinduism – hidden and unknown – is presently at work and not far from being discovered. In God all differences which appear in nature and all distinctions known to the human mind are transcended. To share in the vision of God means that we have to pass beyond all concepts of the rational mind and all images derived from the senses. Christians can be confident that a healthy respect for those of other faiths will help the others to see the reality of Christ.

Socially, the Church is also now more aware of the plight of the various groups who have long suffered discrimination in one form or other in free India: the dalits and the tribals, all victims of centuries of oppression, exploitation, and discrimination. Though constitutionally all dalits are eligible for government benefits, dalit Christians are denied these benefits which are readily available to their counterparts in other faiths. The Church has realized the value of the folklore and religiosity of these dalits and tribal groups. Tribals and indigenous peoples, in particular, show great insights by their closeness to nature, their intimate family ties, and their respect toward elders. Dalit wisdom is wonderfully shown when it unfolds in their myths and folklore and spurs all who listen to them to work for a social solution to problems. Besides these issues, the Church has also to contend with various prevailing forces in the country, forces like Hindu revivalism (Hindutva and its various forms), Islamic fundamentalism, the caste system, discrimination against women, bonded labor and large-scale corruption. The Indian Catholic bishops at their Synod in February 2006 reiterated their commitment to educate the socially, economically, culturally, and politically marginalized people of India.

Many continue to find in the life and writings of Mahatma Gandhi (1869–1948) an inspiration for solving problems of social and political inequality. He was both eloquent in his writings and influential in his politics, seeing God as the basis of political and moral strategies. He spoke of using whatever was of value in other religions to enrich oneself spiritually. He did not advocate conversion to other faiths, and would advise Christians not to become Hindus but to absorb all that they could find of good value in Hinduism.

Conclusion

The Church in India has come a long way since the arrival of Christianity in the first century. Christians today represent 2.4 percent of India's population of over one billion people (Hindus form 80.5 percent and Muslims 13.4 percent). Legislation in at least three Indian states has made it difficult for people to convert to the Christian faith. The government continues to look with suspicion at foreign sources of funding for the Church, and attacks on churches and killing of missionaries at the hands of fundamental groups continue. The Church, however, has not faltered in its work of service to the people in the educational and medical fields. It runs 20,370 educational institutions of which over half are in rural areas, and 3,000 health-care institutions of which 85 percent serve rural populations, with 64 centers caring specifically for advanced AIDS sufferers.

The Church in India is justifiably proud of having five cardinals and 145 bishops along with a vast number of clergy and religious (12,000 diocesan priests, 17,000 religious priests and scholastics, and 85,500 sisters, the religious men and women belonging to over 300 congregations). There are six Blessed among the ranks of Indians raised to the altar (Mother Teresa being one of them), while nine others are designated "Servants of God."

References and Further Reading

Anand, Subash (2004) *Hindu Inspiration for Christian Reflection: Towards a Hindu–Christian Theology.* Anand: Gujarat Sahitya Prakash.

Anchukandam, Thomas (1996) *Roberto de Nobili's Responsio (1610): A Vindication of Inculturation and Adaptation.* Bangalore: Kristu Jyoti Publications.

Bayly, C.A. (ed.) (1990) *The Raj: India and the British 1600–1947.* London: National Portrait Gallery Publications.

Besse, L. (1918) *Father Beschi of the Society of Jesus: His Times and His Writings.* Trichinopoly: St Joseph's Press.

Charpentier, Jarl (ed.) (1933) *The Livro da Seita dos Indios Orientais of Fr Jacobo Fenicio SJ.* Uppsala: Almqvist and Wiksells Booktryckeri.

Clooney, F.X. (2003) "Hindu Views of Religious Others: Implications for Christian Theology," *Theological Studies,* vol. 64, no. 2, June, 306–33.

Correia-Afonso, John (1997) *The Jesuits in India 1542–1773.* Anand: Gujarat Sahitya Prakash.

Cronin, V. (1959) *A Pearl to India: The Life of Roberto de Nobili.* London: Rupert Hart-Davis.

D'Costa, Anthony (1965) *The Christianization of the Goa Islands.* Bombay: Heras Institute.

Dhavamony, Mariasusai (s.d.) *Hindu–Christian Dialogue: Theological Soundings and Perspectives.* Amsterdam: Rodopi.

DK Publishers (2002) *India.* New York: DK Publishing.

Dupuis, Jacques (2001) *Toward a Christian Theology of Religious Pluralism.* New York: Orbis Books.

Falcão, Nelson (2003) *Kristapurana: A Christian–Hindu Encounter (A Study of Inculturation in the Kristapurana of Thomas Stephens, SJ (1549–1619).* Anand: Gujarat Sahitya Prakash.

Fernando, Leonard and Gispert-Sauch, G. (eds.) (2004) *Christianity in India: Two Thousand Years of Faith.* New Delhi: Penguin/Viking.

Ferroli, Domenico (1939) *The Jesuits in Malabar,* vol. I. Bangalore: Bangalore Press.

Ferroli, Domenico (1951) *The Jesuits in Malabar,* vol. II. Bangalore: King and Co.

Ferroli, Domenico (1955) *The Jesuits in Mysore.* Kozhikode: Xavier Press.

Firth, C.B. (1988) *An Introduction to Indian Church History.* Delhi: ISPCK.

Frykenberg, Robert E. (ed.) (2003) *Christians and Missionaries in India: Cross-Cultural Communication since 1500.* London: Routledge/Curzon.

Griffiths, Bede (1973) *Vedanta and Christian Faith.* Los Angeles: The Dawn Horse Press.

Kunnumpuram, Kurien, D'Lima, Errol, and Parappally, J. (eds.) (1997) *The Church in India in Search of a New Identity.* Bangalore: NBCLC.

Mundadan, Mathias A. (1984) *History of Christianity in India,* vol. I: *From the Beginning up to the Middle of the Sixteenth Century up to 1542.* Bangalore: Theological Publications in India.

Naik, Gregory (ed.) (2000) *Understanding Our Fellow Pilgrims.* Anand: GSP.

Nevett, Albert M. (1980) *John de Britto and His Times.* Anand: GSP.

O'Neill, Charles E. and Dominguez, Joaquin, M. (eds.) (2001) *Diccionario histórico de la Compania de Jesus,* vols. I–IV. Rome: IHSI.

Pannikar, Raimundo (1981) *The Unknown Christ of Hinduism.* New York: Orbis Books.

Pathil, Kuncheria (1994) *Indian Churches at the Crossroads.* Bangalore: Dharmaram Publications.

Perumalil, H.C. and Hambye, E.R. (eds.) (1972) *Christianity in India: A History in Ecumenical Perspective.* Alleppey: Prakasam Publications.

Priolkar, A.K. (1961) *The Goa Inquisition.* Bombay: A.K. Priolkar.

Robinson, Rowena (1998) *Conversion, Continuity and Change: Lived Christianity in Southern Goa.* New Delhi: Sage Publications.

Ross, Denis and Power, Eileen (eds.) (1930) *Jahangir and the Jesuits.* London: George Routledge and Sons.

Sauliere, A. (1947) *Red Sand: A Life of St John de Brito, SJ, Martyr of the Madura Mission.* Mathura: De Nobili Press.

Smet, Richard de and Neuner, Josef (eds.) (1996) *Religious Hinduism.* Mumbai: St Paul's.

Souza, Teotónio R. de (1979) *Medieval Goa: A Socio-economic History.* New Delhi: Concept Publishing Co.

Souza, Teotónio R. de and Garcia, José M. (eds.) (1999) *Vasco da Gama e A India*, vols. I–III. Lisbon: Fundação Calouste Gulbenkian.

Thekedathu, Joseph (1982) *History of Christianity in India from the Middle of the Sixteenth Century to the End of the Seventeenth Century*, vol. II. Bangalore: Theological Publications of India.

Wicki, Josef (ed.) (1948–88) *Documenta Indica*, vols. I–XVIII (1540–97). Rome: IHSI.

Wicki, Josef (ed.) (1955) *História do Malavar 1615 by Fr Diogo Gonçalves, SJ.* Munster: Aschendorffsche Verlagsbuchhandlung.

Zapanov, Ines G. (1999) *Disputed Mission: Jesuit Experiments and Brahmanical Knowledge in Seventeenth-century India*. New Delhi: Oxford University Press.

CHAPTER 9
Africa[1]

Emmanuel Katongole

Within the Roman Catholic Church, northern dioceses are increasingly likely to use priests from lands in Africa or Latin America, which are still fertile grounds for vocations . . . African priests are appearing in – of all places – Ireland, that ancient nursery of Catholic devotion. Remarking on this phenomenon, an Irish friend of mine recalled, wryly, how as a child she had been told by the Church to collect pennies to "save Black babies in Africa." She wondered whether some of those babies might have grown up to save Irish souls in recompense. (Jenkins, 2002: 204)

A brilliant African student goes off to a European seminary. Here he learned German, French, Greek, Latin, Hebrew, in addition to English, Church history, systematics, homiletics, exegesis, and pastoralia. He reads all the great European Bible critics, such as Rudolf Bultmann. Returning home to his native village, the student is welcomed joyfully by his extended family but, suddenly, his sister falls dangerously ill. With his Western training, he knows that her illness requires scientific medicine, but everyone present knows with equal certainty that the girl is troubled by the spirit of her dead great-aunt. Since this fine student has so much theological training, the family knows that it is obviously up to him to cure her. The debate between the student and family rages until the people shout, "Help your sister, she is possessed!" He shouts back, "But Bultmann has demythologized demon possession!" The family is not impressed. (Jenkins, 2002: 124, citing Mbiti, 1974: 6–8)

These two quotations nicely capture everything I would like to say about African Catholicism. First, the two stories – of African Catholics re-evangelizing the West, and Westernized Africans trying to re-evangelize their homes – help to highlight the fact that the story of African Catholicism is indeed the tale of multiple stories. On the one hand, it is a story of great success, of surprise, and a story that holds great potential in terms of its gifts, dynamism, and contribution to the universal Church; it is also a story whose performance within Africa continues to be less than impressive, the cause of great frustration and, in some cases, even outright disappointment.

Understanding the dynamism of African Catholicism and its unique character requires exploring the intersection between these two stories of success and powerlessness, of gifts and challenges. Moreover, the more one does so, the more one appreciates the "catholicity" of African Catholicism. For, in Africa, the "universal" and the "particular," the "global" and the "local," the "Western" and the "non-Western," the ancient and new mesh, meld, collide, and synthesize in ways at once impressive and not so impressive, at times life-affirming and at other times life-draining. That is why, in order to get a sense of the African Catholic identity, as well as the gifts and challenges of African Catholicism, one must first highlight some of the intersections and apparent contradictions that shape Catholic life and practice in Africa. Only then can one appreciate the unique expression and complex performance of the African Church within Roman Catholicism.

PART I   CATHOLICISM IN AFRICA: A TALE OF MANY STORIES

Catholic Confidence – in a Distressed Continent

The story of African Catholicism is the story of unprecedented growth that has taken place in the past 100 years or so. While the growth has not been limited to Catholicism, but has been part of the general trend of the southern shift in World Christianity, African Catholicism is in many places at the center of this ferment. In 1900, there were slightly fewer than 2 million Catholics in Africa; by 2000 the number of Catholics had grown to over 130 million, representing a growth of 708 percent, (the population of Africa grew during the same period by 313 percent (Froehle and Gautier, 2003: 4–5)). The rise in African Catholicism is reflected in the number of vocations to the priesthood and religious life, with seminaries and convents in countries like Uganda, Nigeria, and Cameroon registering record numbers. It is also reflected in the number of African churchmen in prominent positions. In 1913, the first African Catholic priest (in modern times) was ordained; in 2000 Africa had 16,962 priests (Froehle and Gautier, 2003: 32). In 1939 Joseph Kiwanuka was consecrated as the first Catholic bishop in modern times. In 2000 Africa had 588 bishops and archbishops, and 16 cardinals – a fact that led to speculations about the possibility of an African pope in the April 2005 conclave.

While these developments have rightly led to optimistic projections and widespread confidence about Africa as the future of the Church, other developments have not led to the same confidence about Africa. The continent has continued to experience great social, economic, and political distress. Instability, civil unrest, war, violent clashes, poverty, and HIV/AIDS are the realities that African Catholics live with on a daily basis. Accordingly, if the growth of African Catholicism signals the confidence in "The coming of the Third Church" (Bühlmann, 1977), that Church is by and large a Church of the poor and marginalized. It is a Church characterized by the same unfulfilled dreams and frustrations; the same creative restlessness and destructive madness of a post-colonial Africa. No event depicts these contradictions more acutely than the 1994 genocide in Rwanda – a country that was and still is predominantly Catholic.

The Old and the New within African Catholicism

What is most striking about the growth of the Catholic Church in Africa is that most of this has happened in the past hundred years or so. It would be misleading, however, to think that Catholicism is "new" in Africa. As John Paul II notes in the Post Synodal Exhortation, *Ecclesia in Africa*:

> The spread of the Gospel has taken place in different phases. The first century of Christianity saw the evangelization of Egypt and North Africa. A second phase, involving the parts of the Continent south of the Sahara, took place in the fifteenth and sixteenth century. A third phase, marked by extra-ordinary missionary effort, began in the nineteenth century. (John Paul II, 1995: 30)

While the story of present day African Catholicism might appear to be "recent," the story of Catholicism in Africa is "ancient." That is why in reading various historical accounts of African Catholicism (e.g. Baur, 1994; Hastings, 1994; Sundkler and Steed, 2000) one must keep in mind that the three phases of Africa's evangelization are neither isolated nor self-contained – but rather moments within the same narrative. The historical continuity and connection between these phases must be constantly explored and highlighted. In this way, it becomes clear that though much of present-day African Catholicism has grown out of the missionary enterprise of the nineteenth century, what we have here is not "new," either in terms of its presence on the continent or in its key elements. What we see in the twenty-first century is just a recent expression of an ancient story – of Catholicism in Africa, which itself is part of a much bigger story of the universal communion of the Roman Catholic Church. Catholic identity in Africa is shaped and constantly negotiated at this intersection of new and old.

African Catholicism(s): A Tale of Many Stories

One often talks of African Catholicism as though it were a monolith. This, however, is not the case. In fact, anyone looking for a comprehensive historical guide to *African Catholicism* is often frustrated, for there is no single account that can capture the complexity of African Catholicism and its many (hi)stories. From this point of view, African Catholicism is more a patchwork quilt of diverse histories, traditions, and expressions, so it might in fact be more accurate to speak not of African Catholicism, but of African Catholicisms. Africa is a huge and complex continent; Catholics in Africa are spread over 54 countries, representing diverse colonial and missionary histories. Accordingly, Catholicism in Lusaphone Africa tends to look different from Catholicism in Francophone Africa, which itself looks different from Anglophone Catholicism. To be sure, even within a country or region that shares the same colonial history, the fact that African Catholics are spread over 2,000 languages and distinct cultures makes room for significant local differences within African Catholicism. Another factor that contributes to the complexity of Catholicism in Africa is the fact that the evangelization of Africa was undertaken by different missionary congregations that worked either side by side or in competition with one another. Whereas this may not seem to be a significant factor, the differences that the styles, devotions, and spiritualities of the evangelizing societies have had at the level of popular devotions, lay movements, and pious associations can be quite striking. Take the case of Uganda. The spiritual life of Catholics from the south (evangelized by the White Fathers) is organized around Marian devotion (with a grotto and a Marian chapel a regular feature in every parish); the spirituality of northern Catholics (evangelized by the Comboni missionaries) is centered around devotion to the Sacred Heart; and Catholics from eastern Uganda (evangelized mostly by the Mill Hill missionaries) practice a more cerebral type of Catholicism, without much devotional concentration. Similar differences exist in the Democratic Republic of the Congo where different Belgian orders, the Jesuits, Premon-stratensians, Redemptorists, and Benedictines were each responsible for evangelizing different regions of this huge country. This is what makes any talk of "African Catholicism" either unhelpful or a misleading generalization. On the other hand, the variety of traditions, histories, and expressions within Catholicism in Africa confirm the unparalleled "catholicity" of the African Church. Within the African Church one comes across every imaginable tradition within Catholicism represented in ways which at once affirm the rich diversity of Catholicism, and yet make African Catholicism such a hopelessly fragmented reality.

Western Missionary Dynamic and Local Transmission

The nineteenth century was a great era for both Catholic and Protestant mission as reflected in the growth of missionary fervor and the founding of new missionary congregations in Europe. Africa was the great beneficiary of this missionary movement. As Hastings notes (Hastings, 1994: 419) in 1910 there were nearly 4,000 Catholic missionaries, over half of them nuns, working in various places in Africa. Apart from the strength of the missionary movement, there were other factors – including increased mobility and even Catholic–Protestant rivalry – that contributed to the growth of the Church in Africa. In fact, in cases like Uganda's, the rivalry would even take violent forms, fermenting the religious wars of 1887–95. And as Hastings claims (Hastings, 1994: 421), without this rivalry, neither side would have worked so hard. Whatever other factors might have been at work, one has to admit that "the splendid growth and achievement of the Church in Africa are due largely to the heroic and selfless dedication of generations of missionaries" (John Paul II, 1995: 35).

Nevertheless, it is equally important to recognize that the evangelization of Africa was as much the work of Western missionaries as of local evangelists, who worked either as translators or catechists. These self-sacrificing and hardworking lay evangelists served as a crucial link between missionaries and local populations, between the parish center and the outlying rural missions. Often illiterate or semi-literate, the catechist depended greatly on memorization and his oral skills and often served as a story-teller. This overlooked factor marks the major difference between Catholic and Protestant mission. Whereas the translation of the Bible into the vernacular was essential to Protestant mission, memory (the question and answer drills around the catechism and set prayers) and story-telling were the most important factors in Catholic mission. Here, the case of Uganda is telling, though not unique. Matthias Mulumba and Noa Mawaggali (both of whom were to die as martyrs) were the leaders of a small group of Christians in Singo. Every Monday they would send one of their number to the capital to listen to the priest's sermon, attend the missionary's explanation of the catechism, so that he could repeat what he had learnt to his fellow Christians back home (Faupel, 1962: 180).

It is important to acknowledge how the rapid growth of Catholicism in Africa was and continues to be effected at the intersection of missionary transmission and local agency. African Catholicism today is still largely a coming together of missionary gifts and local talents. On the one hand, the Catholic Church in Africa remains very Western in its style and outlook, in its theology, and in its funding. On the other hand, its growth and dynamism, its leadership and expressions are the distinctive working of local gifts and charisms.

A Spiritual Message and Holistic Evangelization

A key feature of the nineteenth-century mission that helped the growth of Catholicism in Africa was the fact that the preaching of the missionaries addressed not just the spiritual, but the whole life of the person. The example of Comboni in the Sudan is very telling, though not unique. Daniel Comboni (1831–81) believed that "God wills the conversion of Africa." In his vision, however, the conversion went hand in hand with a clear determination to overthrow slavery and to end the slave trade in the Sudan. And like his predecessor Knoblecher in the Sudan mission, Comboni believed that education would help defeat slavery in the country. Thus, at mission centers, Comboni encouraged his missionaries to establish schools in which freed slaves would be taught how to read and write, as well as other simple skills like brick-making, mechanics, and farming. In some places (e.g. Malbes), the missionaries even set up model agricultural communities. Comboni's missions also included a number of sisters, who opened schools for girls (Baur, 1994: 155–86). A similar story was repeated by missionaries everywhere in Africa. Whether it was with the Oblates in South Africa, the Holy Ghost Fathers in Tanzania, or the Society of the African Mission in Ghana, the construction of mission schools, the setting up of health centers, and the development of technical institutes were key features and a hallmark of the holistic mission.

The growth, dynamism, and vitality of Catholic life in Africa today is closely connected with Catholic institutions and the provision of such services as education, health care, and development projects. In the diocese of Soroti in Uganda, the Catholic social services department (Soroti Catholic Diocese Integrated Development Organization SOCADIDO) is far more powerful and better known than the diocese itself. This is perhaps not surprising, for given the overall inefficiency, corruption, and mismanagement that characterize many public institutions in Africa, the impact of Catholic social institutions, which by comparison are fairly well run, is often very striking.

Double Identity within a Colonial Setting

By and large, the nineteenth-century evangelization of Africa coincided with its colonial occupation following the Berlin Conference of 1884–5. African Catholicism therefore arose from a colonial heritage. This of course is not unique to African Catholicism, for as Bamat and Wiest (1999: 1) note, "Most of those who identify as Catholics today inhabit lands that were once colonized by European powers. Foreign domination, enslavement, and processes of cultural uprooting are part of their historical inheritance."

It would thus be misleading to assume that the reason why Christianity has continued to grow in Africa is that the evangelization of the continent reflected a spiritual movement that had little or nothing to do with colonialism and imperialism that was going on at the same time. To make such a claim would be to overlook the obvious fact that missionaries were men of their time, shaped by Western history and conditions and values, and Western social networks and social, political, and intellectual discourse. As a result, they often found themselves collaborating with, and in some cases even explicitly advancing, colonial interests.

But it would be equally misleading, on account of the observations above, to dismiss the entire Christian mission as nothing but an extension of colonial exploitation. This overlooks the fact that quite often missionaries defended local/native interests against colonial annexation (especially in those places where the coming of missionaries predated the colonial advance). The claim would also gloss over missionary preaching, the study of local languages and customs, and the translation of the Bible/catechism into local languages as factors shaping and mobilizing local resistance to colonialism and the drive toward independence.

It is therefore more helpful to think of missionaries and mission work as bearing a "double identity" (Walls: 2004: xviii) within colonialism. Baur (1994: 284) captures this sense of ambivalence quite well when he notes, "Every mission station was an essay in colonization; every mission school was a step to independence." This is quite important, for it somehow helps to explain the "double identity" of many African Catholics, who find the Church at once empowering and frustrating, enabling, and inhibiting, affirming, and denigrating African ideals and aspirations – in much the same way as the colonial regime within whose imagination it took shape. It is this intersection that explains the ambivalent attitudes and relationships of many African Catholics to the Church they both love and hate; a Church that they will protect at all costs, but also a Church whose buildings they would have no qualms about burning down or looting during an insurgency.

Acknowledging the colonial heritage of African Catholicism is also helpful in understanding another aspect of the imagination that Catholicism shapes in Africa. Adrian Hastings is right when he notes:

All the conquerors claimed to be Christian, and at the end of the nineteenth century it seems overwhelmingly obvious that power, riches belonged to Christian nations. It would have been strange if Africans did not, in the situation of conquest, seek to share in the beliefs of their conquerors. If the process of Christianization was now to be greatly accelerated, it was not just that there were vastly more missionaries about, with plenty of privileged opportunities of proselytism, it was because African themselves had been placed in a situation of objective intellectual unsettlement and were thoughtful enough to seek appropriate positive answers of a religious as well as a technical kind to their current dilemmas. (Hastings, 1994: 405)

Having taken root within this context, African Catholicism shares and shapes the same imaginations of power, money, civilizations, and modernity that colonialism embodied.

Official and Popular Catholicism

Catholic identity in Africa is shaped at the intersection of two strong forces: the pull of "official" Catholicism on the one hand, and the equally strong appeal of "popular" movements and associations. The missionary evangelization of Africa coincided with the massive institutional revival of the Catholic Church world-wide in the post-Vatican II era (Hastings, 1994: 419). Accordingly, African Catholicism is a very highly hierarchical and, in many ways, stable institution. An account of African Catholicism is thus a story of the different hierarchies, dioceses, parishes, and mission centers, education institutions, charitable organizations, religious orders, secular institutes, and lay apostolate movements that make up institutionalized Catholicism. Such an account would however be incomplete without the many fringe movements which arise, more or less spontaneously, away from, and sometimes outside the bounds of officially acceptable Catholic practice.

Within such popular movements like the *Wanamawombi* in Tanzania (Bamat and Wiest, 1999: 157–82) or the *Movement for the Restoration of the Ten Commandments of God* in Uganda (Katongole, 2003: 108–43), the perennial themes of visions, prophecy, prayer, and exorcism are compressed into a Catholic spirituality defined by Marian piety and healing. That healing is at the heart of many of the popular movements is not only in response to a felt need (the unavailability of reliable and accessible medical care). It is also a reflection of the deep connection that many African Catholics feel between the spiritual and material world. For many Africans, problems of ill health, sickness, and even unemployment do not occur in a vacuum but are ultimately connected to the workings of spiritual forces, and therefore can only be solved through spiritual intervention.

That is why the tension between the official and the popular forms of Catholicism also reveals a tension between the "modern" and the premodern outlooks operating within African Catholicism. For while the theology and practice of the hierarchy are driven by the need to reshape Catholic life in Africa in relation to the reforms of Vatican II, what one witnesses in the popular movements is the resurgence of a traditional Catholic cosmology associated with such practices as exorcism, fasting, the use of holy water, the wearing of religious articles (rosaries, medallions and scapulas), and a deep, almost magical view of the Eucharist. Thus, in terms of outlook, popular Catholicism in Africa is more at home in a pre-Vatican II world. As Comoro and Sivalon (Bamat and Wiest, 1999: 170) note:

> The worldview and cosmology of pre-Vatican II Roman Catholicism were in fact an incul-
> turated understanding based on a culture and consciousness very similar to traditional
> African culture. Vatican II, while marking an opening up to the world in fact was open-
> ing up to a world, worldview, and culture of modernity that are quite different from
> African culture. As the culture accommodated itself to scientific and secularized culture
> it moved dramatically away from the cultures of indigenous people around the world.

It is this largely pre-Vatican II outlook centered on the world of spirits, demons, and spiritual forces that pits popular Catholicism against the official hierarchy and creates an element of constant tension within African Catholicism, as the controversy surrounding Archbishop Milingo's healing ministry reveals (Hastings, 1989). While the members of a popular movement may see themselves as a reform or revival movement, the hierarchy may perceive them as unorthodox, disruptive, and a challenge to their religious authority. On the other hand, many priests are, in their attempts to modernize the Church, accused of weakening Christian substitutes for the deep-rooted traditional rites. They may even be perceived as agents being used by Satan to destroy the Church (Kassimir, 1999: 270).

There are many other intersections to which one may point: sacramental versus non-sacramental versions of Catholicism, rural versus urban varieties, "traditional" versus charismatic expressions. Our treatment here is simply meant to provide an example of the kind of intersections that need to be explored if one is to get a sense of Catholic identity in Africa. Moreover, it is by exploring the complex intersections of Catholic life in Africa that one is able more fully to appreciate the gifts, and grasp the challenges, of African Catholicism.

PART II THE GIFTS OF AFRICAN CATHOLICISM

A Lived Experience of Hope

In a sermon at the canonization of the Uganda Martyrs in 1964, Pope Paul VI used the words of Tertullian to remind the Church that "the blood of martyrs is the seed of Christianity." This is especially true of Catholicism in Africa. The story of the Church in Africa is the story of a long witness of martyrs and saints, which is one of Africa's greatest gifts to the world. The list of African saints extends back to the great doctors, martyrs, virgins, and confessors (Athanasius, Tertullian, Cyprian, Augustine, Perpetua ...) of Roman North Africa; it includes St Charles Lwanga and companions of the late nineteenth century, and the more recently canonized martyrs and saints: Cyprian Michael Iwene Tansi of Nigeria (beatified 1998), Josephine Bakhita of the Sudan (canonized 2000), Irwa and Daudi Okello from Gulu in Northen Uganda (beatified 2002). The list also includes the eloquent witness of many unrecognized martyrs like Archbishop Christophe Munzihirwa of Eastern Congo, who was murdered in 1996 for his condemnation of violence in the region, and numerous Christians, many of them young people, who died resisting the genocide in Rwanda. The case of the secondary school girls at Kibuye in Rwanda is particularly striking. Hutu rebels attacked their dormitory, rousing the girls and ordering them to separate themselves, Hutu from Tutsis. When they refused, they were beaten and shot indiscriminately (Gourevitch, 1998: 353). The witness of such men and women constantly beckons the African Church, indeed the universal Church, to a sense of heroic witness in the face of trials and persecution. However, the fact that violence, poverty, sickness, HIV/AIDS are realities that African Catholics deal with on a daily basis means that "hope" is the very identity of African Catholics. Thus even more than heroic witness, what the African Church offers is a lived experience of hope. Where the topic of hope has so much become an academic one in Western theology, Africa offers the Church a lived theology of hope.

The Catechist

With his slender qualifications and very modest pay, the African catechist is the unsung hero of African Catholicism. Even with the growth of priestly vocations in Africa, the numbers are not sufficient to cover the wide geographical expanses of many parishes. And so, apart from the small amount of attention that a priest can give on his monthly visits, most local congregations depend on the pastoral leadership of the catechist. He teaches catechumens, instructs Confirmation candidates and First Communion classes, prepares the people for confession, collects tithes, visits the sick, sends out a call for the priest for those in need of anointing, attends parish meetings, and leads the Sunday worship, where he preaches and leads the prayers for the community. The village catechist therefore not only provides the necessary link between the community and the priest; he or she is the recognized pastoral leader and, in many ways, the "agent of conversion" for many African Catholics.

These selfless and hardworking men and women are a unique gift to the Catholic Church, and provide a confirmation, if one was ever needed, that the building up of the Body of Christ is sustained through the gifts and ministry of lay leaders, whose leadership and dedication need to be recognized, affirmed, and encouraged. Unfortunately, in Africa as elsewhere, the catechists are often the least appreciated and the most neglected in terms of training and remuneration. Unless this shortcoming is urgently addressed, there is the danger that educated young men and women will turn to more lucrative jobs, thus leaving the ranks of catechists to be filled with school drop-outs, who will lack the confidence and moral authority that the vocation of being a catechist demands.

Mission in Reverse – The Development of a New Catholicity

The gift of vocations (priestly and religious) is another gift of the African Church. The Bigard Memorial Seminary in Nigeria has over 700 young men training for the priesthood. In 2005, the Archdiocese of Kampala in Uganda ordained 16 priests, figures that are reflective of a general trend. It is not difficult to imagine that one or two of these priests may in a year or two find themselves spending some time at a parish in either Europe or the US. For a number of years now, the Comboni congregation has been sending African priests to Latin America and Asia. The quotation at the start of this essay – African priests appearing in (of all places) Ireland – is quite literally true, and very encouraging. Of course there are other ways that one might view this, including the fact that Africa itself might need those priests even more than Europe or the US does. But that would be to fail to recognize the essentially missionary nature of the Church, which means that a local church does not give only out of "excess." Mission is about the sharing of gifts and needs, which enriches both the one who gives and the recipient while advancing the communion of the whole.

That is why the issue must move beyond priests and definitely beyond the practice of merely recruiting vocations from Africa to staff needy parishes in the West. It is about forging greater interaction and the sharing of gifts in a way that builds up the Catholicity of the Church. It is only through this generous and genuine sharing in the gifts, vocations and otherwise, that the parochialism and isolation ("us" and "them") of nation-state loyalties will hopefully begin to break down and a new sense of catholicity will begin to take shape. But just as the presence of missionaries in Africa helps to push the imagination of Africans beyond its tribal limitations, the presence of African, Asian, and Latino priests in the West is now critical to push the Western Church beyond its tribal (national) loyalties, toward the formation of communities and practices that might genuinely be called catholic.

A Twenty-First Century Liturgical Movement out of Africa

Worship in Africa is always the occasion for deep celebration involving praise, singing, and dancing. For African Catholics, therefore, worship is not only an event to look forward to; it is the occasion and opportunity for the celebration of the deep spiritual, social, and bodily connection with God. It is therefore hoped that just as the pre-Conciliar liturgical movement helped to both revive and unify the Western Churches, the liturgical revitalization evident in the African Church may serve a similar role in the coming century. The gifts that come out of this rich dynamism of African liturgical life go beyond its fresh and lively expressiveness. They include a dynamic and ongoing engagement with Christian tradition. The old and new come together in ways which are both fresh and edifying. Latin songs are sung with a new beat, and to the accompaniment of drums. Old liturgical feast days, e.g. Corpus Christi, the Assumption, Christ the King, are marked with colorful processions; pilgrimages to holy shrines and other observances of Catholic traditions are celebrated with new contemporary African lyrics. Connected to this creativity is the gift of joy – spontaneous joy and celebration that the African Church displays so well through worship.

African Catholicism as an Embodied Experience

The refusal to separate the realities of body and soul is another distinctive gift that African Catholicism offers, which might draw the Church to a renewed appreciation of the deep connection between belief and practice, spiritual matters and material realities. Mostly arising out of their African background where there is no "secular" sphere, African Catholics live, work, and play within a religious environment. They are accordingly very much at home in a world of rituals, mysticism, sacraments, healing, exorcism, devotion, sacrifice, and prayer as a way of securing and sustaining the everyday interaction between the spiritual and material world. The full range of liturgical expression through music and dancing also bears witness to this reality of embodiment.

On another level, African Catholicism is not only a Sunday experience since it is as much about schools, health care, hospitals, development projects as it is about prayer and sacraments. This interaction between material and spiritual realities on a daily basis makes African Catholicism both dynamic and vibrant, and the Catholic parish a hub, a meeting point of bodily and spiritual concerns and realities.

The African Woman

African societies and nations have gone through a number of turbulent transitions and violent upheavals. Given this history, the resilience, resourcefulness, and sheer determination not to give up is simply remarkable. The real, if often invisible, pillars behind this determination and resourcefulness are the women. The most important category here are the mothers – those devout women, looking after their homes and families, often in the absence of the husband (due to war or migrant labor), and managing to raise and educate the children. They are the pillars, not only of society, but also of the African Church, in their care for the local church, in their involvement in its worship, in its leadership on the parish council, in their involvement in lay movements and associations, and even by their regularity in attendance. Increasingly, the leadership and impact of women in the Church is felt through the growing number of vocations to the religious life. In the face of Africa's social and political troubles, religious women have often provided a much-needed credible witness and alternative. What Paul Gifford says of religious women in Uganda is in many ways true of Africa as a whole:

> The real strength of Uganda's Catholic Church may turn out to be the congregations of sisters, which are attracting candidates in considerable numbers, and which have always been important for Ugandan Catholicism. The sisters are increasingly well trained, and their training is so un-clerical that they are less concerned with status than with service. They have certain independence and are beginning to organize themselves into an articulate group within the Church. The moral leadership that is not coming from the official Catholic Church may eventually come from this quarter. (Gifford, 1998: 150)

One can highlight a number of other gifts of the African Church – its youthful dynamism, hospitality, and warmth, its restless creativity and many others. The list here is not meant to be comprehensive, but to offer a sample of what to expect from the African Church. Such a sample would also include the challenges, frustrations, and limitations within African Catholicism.

PART III   CHALLENGES AND FRUSTRATIONS: IN SEARCH OF A WAY FORWARD

The single most critical challenge facing the African Church is theological, namely the absence of vibrant and well developed local theologies that can reflect the growing strength and liturgical dynamism of the African Church. The effects of this lacuna are felt in many areas, more particularly in the social and political area, where the African Church, its massive presence notwithstanding, is often powerless and thus unable to make any positive difference in the face of the many challenges facing Africa. In this way, African Catholicism often finds itself in the same predicament as the fictional character that Jenkins (Jenkins, 2002: 124) depicts at the beginning of this essay. First told by Mbiti (Mbiti, 1974: 6–8), the story recounts the homecoming of an African seminarian who, after many years of studying in Europe and receiving all the necessary training and degrees, is nevertheless disappointingly impotent in the face of the needs of his sister.

Just like Mbiti's fictional character who has extensive background and training in Western theology but has no ability to think creatively about the local situation (and therefore can only restate what Bultmann has said), the Church in Africa, in the face of Africa's social and political challenges, keeps harking back to outdated theological visions and practices. Part of the problem is that theological education in Africa has remained very Western. Both the orientation and content of courses in the seminary closely follow Western models, with just some token overture for "local relevance." As a result few seminaries have courses on such issues as AIDS, the Rwanda genocide, apartheid in South Africa, violence and nation-state implosions, tribalism, or popular Catholicism – challenges that African Christians face on a daily basis – and yet these seminaries have compulsory courses on critical theory, on Heidegger and on phenomenology.

This means that, its massive presence notwithstanding, the African Church is yet to become a genuine local Church. In talking about the conditions of a local Church, the Vatican II Decree on the Church's missionary activity notes: The task of developing a local church reaches to a definite point when

> the assembly of the faithful, already rooted in the social life of the people and to some extent conformed to its culture, enjoys a certain stability and permanence; when it has its own priests although insufficient, its own religious and laity and possesses those ministries and institutions which are required for leading and spreading the life of the people of God under their own bishop. (*Ad Gentes*: 19)

While the African Church seems to have attained most of these conditions, it has yet to develop "those ministries and institutions which are required for leading and spreading the life," particularly the ministry of thinking critically and creatively in relation to the challenges facing Africa.

Since Vatican II, inculturation has been the dominant theological trend in Africa, attracting the interest and contribution of many African scholars and theologians. Theologies of inculturation, however, have, on the whole, remained captive not only to issues of culture but to the predictable Western theological methodologies and cate-gories (translation, adaptation, indigenization). As a result, the transforming message of the Gospel has not been allowed to explode into the various areas of social life in Africa, in a way that provides for new visions and alternatives. A quick overview of the major challenges that African Christians face confirms the need and urgency for the development of such local theologies. The more explicitly political challenges include: political instability, civil war, and the general absence, in many African countries, of political structures that ensure a smooth transfer of power. Connected to this are the lack of transparency, blatant abuse of public office, corruption, and a general lack of accountability. Moreover, the abuse of basic human rights as well as the lack of respect for the rule of law makes life very cheap in many African countries.

The widespread reality of violence in Africa requires special attention. With many countries in Africa going through one kind of violent upheaval or another, there is an urgent need to focus on the political conditions and histories that create and perpet-uate violence in Africa. There is also an urgent need to understand the social effects of constant violence, particularly its tendency to percolate into a cultural pattern and thus become a "way of life." There are many indications that the Church in Africa has not only been unable to challenge this culture of violence, but has in some cases itself reproduced and intensified these patterns of life.

Economic challenges include extensive poverty characterized not only by the absence of basic necessities of life, but by the widening gap between the First World and Africa. Within Africa itself, the reality of poverty is heightened by the existence of massive poverty surrounded by pockets of wealth. The problem has to do basically with structures – political and economic structures which threaten a "programmed recolonization of the continent" (Ela, 1996: 133) by a combination of local economic warlords and international economic structures. The sense of powerlessness and increasing impoverishment combine to destroy any hope for a meaningful future and to make survival, mere survival, the only goal for the majority of Africans.

Among the key social challenges is the problem of AIDS. To date, AIDS has killed over 20 million Africans, and an estimated 26 million people are living with the con-dition. In sub-Saharan Africa, every individual is either infected or personally affected. The effect has not only been on the number of AIDS orphans, but also in the drastic reduction of life expectancy in Africa – to an all-time low of below 40 in many coun-tries. The reality of AIDS, making death an everyday occurrence, has raised many unanswered questions about sex and marriage, as well as questions about the mean-ing of friendship and fidelity, the meaning of life, the reality of the Church, and the existence of God.

Among the religious challenges is the one posed by the Pentecostal/Evangelical wave sweeping through much of Africa. Led by both foreign and local evangelists and charismatic preachers, the evangelical revival in Africa has attracted a large number of young people through lively services, a born-again spirituality, and the promise of miracles. One response to this Pentecostal/Evangelical wave has been the revival of the Catholic Charismatic Renewal. The effect of the renewal has on the whole been positive: a deepening of faith among members through greater knowledge of the Bible, more enthusiastic and expressive forms of religious practice, sharing of religious experience through small groups, a leveling of authority lines between clergy and laity, an emphasis on the Holy Spirit and the charisms, including the gift of healing. In this way, the Catholic Charismatic Renewal has re-attracted a number of Catholics who had been alienated from the Church. However, the Church has yet to find ways of facing the key challenges raised by Pentecostal revival in Africa, most significantly, the entrepreneurial imagination in which the message of the Gospel is uncritically hooked to the expectations and promises of modernity, progress, and prosperity.

No one institution in Africa has been undergoing so much change and has experienced so much uncertainty as the family. The endless regimes of civil unrest and violence, the genocide in Rwanda, the abductions of young children into rebel armies in Northern Uganda and Sierra Leone; the AIDS epidemic, the grinding poverty in the rural areas, growing urbanization, the rabid unemployment in the cities, the growth of cheap media entertainment, all have undermined the traditional values on which the African family is founded. The Synod Fathers proposed the African family as a model for the Church in Africa, reflecting the sense of communion, solidarity, and the affirmation of human life, characteristic of the African family (John Paul II, 1995: 64). With many of these values now threatened, serious attention must be paid to the area of marriage and family life in Africa, if the Church is to continue to be God's family in Africa.

Responding to these and many other challenges calls for nothing short of a new reality and a new way of being a church in Africa, a Church that can both faithfully discern the signs of the time and embody faithful and hopeful alternatives for the future. Doing so requires moving away from old pre-packaged theologies and calls for the "courage to reinvent Christianity so as to live it with [an] African soul" (Ela, 1980: 120). This is possible through the development of local theologies that reflect the yearnings and aspirations of African Catholics.

In order to respond to this challenge, theological education and seminary training in Africa must move away from the overly academic and the ivory tower approach of Western theology and move toward the development of what Jean Marc Ela (Ela, 1980: vi) has called "shade tree theologies" – theologies that develop "among brothers and sisters searching shoulder to shoulder with unlettered peasants for the sense of the word of God in situations in which this word touches them."

To be sure, there is already a great deal of this shade tree theologizing going on in informal, quiet, and unwritten ways as African Catholics unconsciously select and reject, mold, and transform certain beliefs and practices as they deal with issues of life and death, with AIDS and violence, marginalization and powerlessness, sickness and poverty. The challenge that the Church in Africa faces is how to let these shade tree theologies become the basis of a renewed program of Christian education in schools, in the training of catechists and the programs of the local parish, in the social teaching of bishops and in liturgical renewal at parish and diocesan level. The challenge is to allow these shade tree theologies to become an integral part of theological education and seminary training in Africa. In this way, as the future leaders of the Church in Africa study the rich resources of the Catholic tradition, they are able to press these ancient traditions and dogmas with new questions – questions reflecting the aspirations and frustrations of everyday life in Africa. In the same way as they are able to articulate and engage the yearning and restless ferment within popular Catholicism, they are able to press it into further clarity and consistence and help to reshape everyday life in Africa in ways that are life-affirming and liberating according to the spirit of the Gospel. Only through this mutual and ongoing interaction between the universal and the local, between the ancient and new, between the Western heritage and the African needs, will the African Church truly become a local Church – a genuine witness of God's presence in Africa. As this occurs, the results will not only benefit Africa, they will renew the practice and theology of the Church universal, while providing it with a fresh vision of the gifts and promises of Catholicism.[2]

Notes

1   In memory of Leo Kasumba, the dedicated catechist who first instructed me in the mysteries of the Catholic faith, even though at that young age, I did not understand much of the formulas and prayers he forced us to memorize.
2   I am grateful for my former student, Jay Carney, who through many conversations as I supervised his research, helped to give shape to the direction, contents, and final shape of this essay. Jay is currently pursuing a PhD research in missiology at the Catholic University of America.

References and Further Reading

"*Ad Gentes*, Decree on the Mission Activity of the Church," in *Vatican Council II: Constitutions, Decrees, Declarations*, edited by Austin Flannery. New York: Costello Publishing (1996).

Bamat, Thomas and Wiest, Jean Paul (1999) *Popular Catholicism in a World Church: Seven Case Studies in Inculturation*. Maryknoll, NY: Orbis.

Baur, John (1994) *2000 Years of Christianity in Africa: An African Church History*. Nairobi: Pauline Publications.

Bühlmann, Walter (1977) *The Coming of the Third Church: An Analysis of the Present and Future of the Church*. Maryknoll, NY: Orbis.

Ela, Jean Marc (1980) *African Cry*. Maryknoll, NY: Orbis.

Ela, Jean Marc (1996) "The Church – Sacrament of Liberation," in *The African Synod: Documents, Reflections, Perspectives*. Maryknoll, NY: Orbis.

Faupel, J.F. (1962) *African Holocaust: The Story of the Uganda Martyrs*. Kampala: St Paul Publications.

Froehle, Bryan and Gautier, Mary L. (2003) *Global Catholicism: Portrait of a World Church*. Maryknoll, NY: Orbis.

Gifford, Paul (1998) *African Christianity: Its Public Role*. Bloomington: Indiana University Press.

Gourevitch, Philip (1998) *We Wish to Inform You that Tomorrow We Will Be Killed together with Our Children*. London: Picador Press.

Hastings, Adrian (1989) *African Catholicism: Essays in Discovery*. London: SCM Press.

Hastings, Adrian (1994) *The Church in Africa 1450–1950*. Oxford: Clarendon Press.

Jenkins, Philip (2002) *The Next Christendom: The Coming of Global Christianity*. Oxford: Oxford University Press.

John Paul II (1995) *Ecclesia in Africa: Post-Synodal Exhortation*. Vatican: Libreria Editrice Vaticana.

Kassimir, Ronald (1999) "The Politics of Popular Catholicism in Uganda," in Spear, Thomas and

Kimambo, Isaria N. (eds.) *East African Expressions of Christianity*. Nairobi: East African Studies, 248–74.

Katongole, Emmanuel (2003) "Kannungu and the Movement for the Restoration of the Ten Commandments of God in Uganda: A Challenge to Christian Social Imagination," *Logos*, vol. 6, no. 3, 108–43.

Mbiti, John (1974) "Theological Impotence and the Universality of the Church," *Lutheran World*, vol. 2, no. 3, 251–60.

Sundller, Bengt and Steed, Christopher (2000) *A History of the Church in Africa*. Cambridge: Cambridge University Press.

Walls, Andrew F. (2004) *The Missionary Movement in Christian History: Studies in the Transmission of Faith*. Maryknoll, NY: Orbis.

CHAPTER 10
Europe

Emmanuel Perrier

In 2003 John Paul II concluded his apostolic exhortation *Ecclesia in Europa* with this urgent call: "Europe, as you stand at the beginning of the third millennium, find yourself again. Be yourself. Discover your origins. Revive your roots" (John Paul II, 2003, n. 120). These words were not new, for the Pope took them from a speech that he had given in front of European authorities in 1982 (AAS 75 (1983), p. 330). In the intervening 20 years the urgent need for renewal had not lost anything of its currency: the chasm between Europe and its heritage, in particular its Christian heritage, had continued to grow. Therefore, to study the situation of Catholicism in Europe, we will turn first to the features and causes of the veritable "silent apostasy" (John Paul II, 2003, n. 9) that is striking this continent. But even if European Catholicism is caught in the midst of a depression unprecedented in its breadth and irreversibility, a transformation has also begun in which a renewed Christianity that is freer in its movements is gradually shaking off the weight of a moribund Christendom. Therefore, we will also seek to grasp the most marked trends of this evolution, even if we cannot yet claim to determine its entire scope.

European Christendom in a State of Decay

The Second Vatican Council (1962–5) is distinguished from the other ecumenical councils by the fact that it was not convened to respond to a doctrinal crisis and, moreover, did not issue any condemnations. In considering the events that followed it, however, one is led to wonder whether it, like all the other great councils, is not closely related to a situation of crisis. The figures speak for themselves: in France, the regular practice of the faith went from 25 percent of the population at the beginning of the 1960s to a little more than 10 percent at the end of the 1970s; in Germany, Sunday practice was halved between 1960 and 1989, when it reached 23 percent; the same proportionate drop is found in Belgium between 1982 and 1997, when religious practice fell to 13 percent; in the Netherlands, the fall was 80 percent between 1960 and

2000. The coincidence of the Council's *aggiornamento* and the collapse of a more-than-thousand-year-old Christendom is disconcerting. For about 30 years, the discussions internal to European Catholicism pitted progressives, who felt that the internal reform of the Church had not gone far enough, against conservatives, who felt that it had gone too far, with each side claiming the other had thus precipitated the crisis. In hindsight, however, one can wonder whether this division along political lines took sufficient account of either the originality of the Second Vatican Council or the distinctive character of the process affecting European Christianity.

The Council's originality, on the one hand, must be taken into account because, beyond their calm and optimistic tone, the conciliar texts offer something of an assessment and a clarification of the way in which the Church, after 2,000 years of history, understands its own being and mission, particularly with regard to human societies and other religions. One does not, however, draw up an assessment without reason.

Thus, on the other hand, the distinctive character of the process of secularization in Europe must be taken into account, because even if it is obvious that the practical or theoretical materialism which prevails in the West is a powerful factor of irreligion – that is, of indifference with regard to spiritual realities – this materialism alone is not able to account for the extent and suddenness of the collapse of European Christendom. A rupture occurred in Europe, collective in nature, in which other factors came to be superimposed on materialism, giving European secularization an original and disquieting face. It is this originality that we must make explicit in the following pages, inasmuch as it forms the European face of contemporary Catholicism.

In search of a theory of secularization

Secularization, which with a few exceptions is general in Europe, was noted, theorized, and its expansion heralded, by the great sociologists of the early twentieth century. These theories all rest on a universal and deterministic causal explanation: because a cause ("rationality" in Weber, "the social function" in Durkheim) always produces the same effects, it was necessarily presumed that one would find that the trajectories of secularization were being homogenized in the various European countries. Whatever the starting point, the point of arrival could be only the completion of the very purpose of modernity, the advent of the autonomous subject, of whom the opposition to religion was a constitutive element (Seiwert, 1995). Religion was consequently to become a "private affair" (Luckmann, 1967), with each individual developing his own system of value independently of traditional communities and institutions (Polanyi, 1957). "If there is one truth that history teaches us beyond doubt, it is that Religion tends to embrace smaller and smaller portions of social life. Originally, it pervades everything; everything social is religious . . . Then little by little, political, economic, scientific functions free themselves from the religious functions" (Durkheim, 1949: 169). The process of secularization being linear, the degree of religiosity of a country came to constitute an inverse indicator of its degree of modernization.

Cracks began to appear in these deterministic theories when two things were realized. First, local cultures had more weight than had been imagined and because of this, trajectories of secularization were specific to each country (Arts and Halman, 2004b). Second, the industrial society characteristic of modernity tended to generate its own post-modern surpassing (Inglehart, 1977). In post-traditional societies the individual is constrained by a permanent questioning of his points of reference (Giddens, 1990) and, far from attaining to a pure rationality, becomes subject to an instrumental rationality, in which values selected from a traditional reservoir are recomposed according to their present utility. This utility is no longer determined only by the objective of the acquisition of goods, as in the beginnings of modernity, but also by fear of the risks generated by industrial society (Beck, 1992, 1999). This is why values are deeply ambivalent today: on the one side, they are expressed in attitudes that are no longer materialist but post-materialist – the flourishing of the self, democracy, solidarity (Inglehart, 1997); on the other side, they find themselves put to the test by the subject's lack of control over his life.

Further, it appears today that individualism is not the single key to European secularization: the individual does not set in motion the "marketplace" of religions by testing traditions in order to retain that which suits him (Kokosalakis, 1993) and, contrary to certain theories (Stark and Iannaccone, 1994; Stark and Finke, 2000), pluralism does not appear, at least in Europe, to be a religious stimulant. In reality, religion is above all conceived of as a social membership, situated in a tradition from which one feels more or less distant (Halman and Draulans, 2004: 313). This is what the recent large-scale sociological investigations into the values of Europeans teach us (Halman, 2001): at the turn of the new millennium, 72.2 percent of Europeans claimed to belong to some "religious denomination," which for 93.2 percent was Christianity; for 50.7 percent, religion remained "very or quite important." These figures should not mask the total increase of those "without religion," as well as the real continuation of the process of secularization: 77.4 percent of Europeans claim to believe in God, compared to 93 percent of Americans. The figures force us to revise, however, the idea of an inexorable detachment from religious institutions, as well as that of a complete decline in religious sensibility. Especially when looking at each country individually, one observes contradictory tendencies: whereas in France and Spain religiosity continued to drop between 1981 and 1999, it went up over the same period in Germany, Austria, Italy, Portugal, and Ireland, though these countries remain very diverse in their degrees of secularization. In addition, the classical distinctions between geographical "clusters" – with southern Europe being more Catholic, northern Europe more Protestant, and Eastern Europe more Orthodox – prove irrelevant with regard to current developments (Fulton and Gee, 1994; Gill et al., 1994; Halman and Riis, 2003). Thus, suggestive as the sociological profiles they produce may be, theories of modernity or secularization show their weakness precisely as theories, that is inasmuch as they propose evolutionary and predictive schemes with universal value (Bruce, 1992; Smith, 2003; Arts and Halman, 2004a). In other words, the various causal principles that these theories take as foundational – rationality, the social function, the disenchantment of the world, reflexivity, autonomy, the marketplace of religions, pluralism, etc. (Tschannen, 1992) – are not sufficient to characterize European secularization. In religious matters, there is no Law of History, of which Europe would be the inspired prophetess.

This crisis of the classical models of secularization calls for a more subtle approach to the process taking place in Europe, starting from four established facts. *First*, one can no longer hold to deterministic and universal principles stemming directly from the ideology of progress, and underestimating the richness and the complexity of the human element. *Second*, one must do a better job of taking into account both national cultural differences (Halman and Pettersson, 2003; Halman and Draulans, 2004) and the common cultural denominator of the European continent. Indeed, if the high level of religiosity in the United States was considered until recently to be a residual exception to secularization, it now seems, in light of the latest investigations, that it is "the singularity of Europe . . . that constitutes the enigma" (Davie and Hervieu-Leger, 1996; Hervieu-Leger, 2002: 11). *Third*, it appears impossible to understand secularization through the exclusive use of already secularized sociological concepts (tradition, worship, practice, institution, etc.), defined essentially by the reduction of religion to a utilitarian function, whether individual or social. It is indeed the real contents of these concepts that interest the subject, and not only their generic function: if one would comprehend its domain, European secularization must be studied, starting from its Christian soil. *Fourth*, it is essential to go beyond the modern dialectical oppositions between belief and reason, society and religion, institution and subject, wisdom and science or technology, if one would grasp the very root of these oppositions. Why is it that Europe and only Europe developed and then exported such dualisms? What are the cultural and religious roots of these dissociations?

These clarifications open up a renewed perspective on European secularization, around its three essential characteristics: it is common to the geographical territory of Europe, it is dependent on national cultures, and it is exportable. These characteristics betray the close link between secularization and Christianity. First, because Christianity is the common and traditional religion of Europe, transcending national identities, and because secularization is a phenomenon on a continental scale, we are led to suspect that it is a crisis proper to Christianity. Further, the Christian faith is distinctive in that it is not a culture, yet always incarnates itself in a culture. But this unique way of conjoining the universal and the particular – which is due to the fact that faith in Christ arises from the order of grace, which does not contradict but elevates the order of nature – explains the two other characteristics that we mentioned: trajectories of secularization are national and, at the same time, secularization is found in other countries of the world, which are influenced by the culture of Europe. The hypothesis which forces itself upon us, and which we will try to make more precise, is thus the following one: it is in the cross-fertilization of European culture and Christianity, in the extension by the Jewish–Christian tradition of the "eccentric" ambitions of Roman culture as enriched by the contribution of the Greeks (Brague, 2002), that the crucible of secularization resides. This reciprocal fecundation consists in this: European culture found in Christianity an amplifier of its universalist ideal, while at the same time it claimed to supersede Christianity (Gauchet, 1985). Ultimately, secularization seems an aberrant and self-destroying evolution of the evangelization of Europe. It is a Christianity without Christ or, more exactly, a Christian Europe – a Christendom – that judges itself to have so well culturally assimilated the fundamental features of the Christian Revelation that it is able to dispense with the faith to which this Revelation calls.

The correlation between practice and religiosity within national political structures

From the latest results of the *European Values Studies* (Halman, 2001), Halman and Draulans have established, nation by nation, a "scatterplot" of the relationship between the practice of religion and religiosity (Halman and Draulans, 2004: 309), which we include, with our own interpretation superimposed, in Figure 10.1. Let us start with two facts. On the one hand, there is a very strong correlation between practice and religiosity, indicated by the fact that all the countries are aligned on a diagonal. One does not practice without believing in God, even under societal pressure (one notes the exception of Sweden (se)), and one does not believe without practicing one's faith (one notes the exception of Russia (ru)). Consequently, secularization consists of a coherent crisis of religion; its impact on faith is reflected in practice, and vice versa. On the other hand, the countries are distributed all along the scale, with a stronger concentration around the coordinates (0:0). This confirms that there is no European homogeneity with regard to secularization, not even a geographical one (compare, for example, Germany (de), the Netherlands (nl), and Austria (at)), and that the different situations are in the first place dependent on national cultures.

Beyond these two facts, one is also led to notice that there is a cluster of countries with a strong dominance of Catholicism or Orthodoxy exhibiting a high degree of religiosity and religious practice: Ireland (ie), Romania (ro), and Poland (pl), followed closely by Italy (it), Croatia (hr), Slovakia (sk), Austria (at), Greece (gr), and Portugal (pt). The principle of unity of this cluster is not immediately apparent and, to make it clear, it is necessary for us to start from other significant correlations. But it is very clear what it is that connects Romania (ro), Greece (gr), the Ukraine (ua), and Russia (ru). These countries share a very old Orthodox tradition (or Greco-Catholic in the case of the Ukraine). They form a line running from highest to the lowest level of religiosity and practice. In other words, they present a trajectory of secularization proper to the Greek-Orthodox tradition, characterized by a religiosity more marked than the average. Beginning from this line, the most visible, one can distinguish two others, one for the Catholic tradition and another, more artificial, for the Protestant tradition. These trajectories of secularization show that the process that they describe is inscribed mainly within a tradition: it is not a particular sort of country that leaves its religious tradition; on the contrary, it is the religious tradition of the country that follows a path of decomposition. This fact clarifies the principle unifying the countries with strong religiosity and religious practice: whether in Ireland, Poland, Romania, Italy, Slovakia, Austria, or Greece, the religious tradition is tied to the political domain not by means of power but rather by its entry into the very definition of national identity. In other words, there is greater resistance to secularization when a people's affirmation of its political identity is indissociably bound up with the affirmation of its religious identity. On the other hand, secularization is exacerbated when the national identity has long been separated from religious identity (as in the Czech Republic), or when the political order has nationalized the religious identity. The former is the case in France, where secularism (*laïcité*) plays the part of a religion of the State, and the latter is the case in Russia, where declaring oneself Orthodox constitutes a profession of faith in Mother Russia. Paradoxically, the differences in the level of secularization between countries thus depends more on national identities

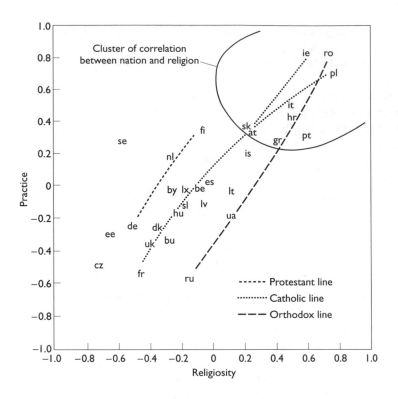

Figure 10.1   Country mean scores on religiosity and religious practice (source: Halman and Draulans, 2004: 309).

than on the religious factor itself. This means that, on a global foundation of secularization affecting all the "satisfied societies" (Hervieu-Léger, 2002: 16), the religious crisis is above all the epiphenomenon of a major restructuring of national identities. And, in its tendency to detach national identities from religion, which is part of their innermost foundation, this restructuring cannot but be a profoundly shattering one. In pursuing the hypothesis that we formulated earlier, could one not say that European culture, having assimilated Christian values to the point of thinking itself capable of dispensing with their basis – faith in Christ – and having instrumentalized these values in order to achieve its own universalist objectives, has seen its internal dynamism gradually being sterilized, in accord with its successes (the world-wide export of the democratic, technical and commercial model of the West) and failures (the self-destroying nationalism of the twentieth century, ideologies, the colonization of the world, dehumanizing economism, attacks on the environment, the Faustian drift of science, etc.)? In other words, has Europe not become the hostage of its own culture? Having thus assimilated and secularized the Christian conception of time and of salvation in the form of the ideology of progress, has Europe not been condemned to pursue to the point of exhaustion a project that constrains it to see its own tradition as ever more obsolete – because tied to the past – and relative – because it is particular vis-à-vis the universal? This configuration would explain the ambivalence of the relationship that Europeans currently maintain with their religious tradition and more generally with their history: a mixture of repulsion – since the Church is the last living institution recalling a past on which they have turned their backs – and of distant attachment – since Christian values are in the very marrow of the European soul.

Flaccid beliefs, the morality of justification, liturgical self–celebration, and cubist culture

European secularization, we have said, is characterized in particular by a strong feeling of attachment to the Christian tradition, coupled with a religious practice (which is the index of real membership in the Church) in free fall. Grace Davie has described this disjunction in terms of "belonging" and "believing": Europeans would always believe, but individually and in their own way, without belonging to the Christian community (Davie, 1990, 2000). In reality, the absence of belonging tends to lead more to unbelief than to alternative beliefs: only 27 percent of Europeans not belonging to a particular ecclesial denomination describe themselves as "religious," versus 57 percent who describe themselves as "non-religious" and 16 percent who are atheists. The profile of "believing without belonging" pertains only in a limited number of countries, primarily the Netherlands, Estonia, and Latvia. As for the opposite profile, "belonging without believing," one meets it only in Sweden, and to a lesser degree in Great Britain (Halman and Draulans, 2004: 310–11). As the preceding section has shown, the current phenomenon of secularization is better understood in terms of the progressive assimilation and neutralization of the Christian faith by European culture. This assimilation acts mainly on four levels.

First, a transcendent morality based in the natural law and in Christ, unifying all dimensions of human action in view of participation in the life of God (John Paul II, 1993), is reduced to a transcendental ideal of earthly achievement. Within a minimal social framework carried by shared values that are a secularized carbon-copy of the Christian Beatitudes (peace, justice, solidarity, equality, freedom . . .), the individual directs his life according to the interior rule of sincerity. Only personal experience is normative, with moral values being able to intervene only a posteriori, like an instrument for the justification of personal choices. In this context, it appears that the moral doctrine of the Church is displaced; it is received at best as an inaccessible ideal, at worst as an obstacle to freedom.

Second, deprived of existential import, faith in Christ gives way to the genial indifference of flaccid beliefs, where everything is of equal worth since nothing truly has importance (Campiche, 1993; Bréchon, 2001). One rests in the vague knowledge obtained from catechism class, thinking one knows the contents of the faith, while being in fact ignorant of even its historical basis: in 2006, close to one French person in four doubted that Jesus existed; in 1999, 52 percent of Austrians believed in a Spirit or a "vital Force" compared to only 32 percent who believed in a personal God, even though 87 percent claimed to belong to a Christian denomination. With the transmission of the faith no longer finding support in family life, and even less in social life, it will be a matter of only two or three generations before people will cease to regard themselves as Christian at all. Correlative to this ignorance, a dormant spiritual life maintains a faith that is immature, attracted by that which encourages the imaginary, the sentimental and, finally, the highly irrational. This is particularly manifest in questions regarding life after death, since personal human life tends to be no longer regarded as a unique destiny, willed by God, and consequently something for which one is responsible before God. Thus, if 44.7 percent of French believe in a life after death, while 55 percent claim to belong to a Christian denomination, there are only 19.6 percent who believe in the existence of hell, and 31.2 percent who believe in the existence of heaven, compared to 28.8 percent who believe in reincarnation. By way of contrast, among the Italians, 82 percent of whom are Catholic, 72.8 percent say they believe in life after death, with 49 percent believing in hell, 58.7 percent in heaven, and 17.8 percent in reincarnation. Such inconsistencies are explained by the fact that in a secularized world – that is, a world that has reduced its field of vision to everyday society – the hereafter is conceived only as an imaginary prolongation (if possible, an improved one) of the here and now. Reincarnation is thus never considered as a penalty, as it is in the Eastern tradition, but as a "new chance" to remake one's life.

Third, a weakening of the religious sense, joined to an incapacity to apprehend the world with any perspective other than that of utility or scientific technique, as well as the primacy of the instantaneous emotion, is at the root of a sterilization of the liturgical life of the Church. The repetitiveness of the rites is a source of boredom. Liturgical language becomes incomprehensible, since the signs no longer speak and the realities signified no longer have an influence on everyday life. Consequently, the celebration of the Christian mystery gives way to the self-celebration of the community. One remains Christian for the great events of life – baptism, first communion, marriage, burial – but the attachment is reduced to a purely traditional social ritualism, and before long this attachment is definitively attenuated. Thus, in France the number of baptisms of children fell 26 percent between 1990 and 2004, while the number of births remained stable. During the same period, the number of marriages celebrated in the Church dropped by 34 percent.

A fourth factor neutralizing the Christian faith results from the dislocation of European humanism. Sociologists have long noted that greater social complexity requires a stricter partitioning of competences and functions, with each sector having its autonomy and submitting itself only with difficulty to an extrinsic authority (Luckmann, 1967; Wilson, 1982; Martin, 2005). The Church's loss of influence results partly from this "functional differentiation": 67.6 percent of Europeans see the Church as providing adequate answers in the field of "spiritual needs" (47.4 percent in the Netherlands, 72.4 percent in Italy), but no more than 30.5 percent think this is true with regard to "social problems" (21.2 percent in France, 35.6 percent in the Netherlands). Notable in this respect is the question of the religious identity of the Church's charitable works. The apostolic religious congregations devoted to the service of children, the elderly, the sick, or the poor have seen a sudden and very often irreversible drying up of vocations (something distinct from the crisis in contemplative vocations), with one of the principal reasons being that these activities no longer are regarded as justifying a religious consecration. In the same way, Christian charitable associations have been gradually professionalized so as to meet the standards of social or humanitarian agencies, not only with regard to their methods but also, by bracketing their confessional nature, with regard to their values.

Beyond these findings, functional differentiation in Europe is distinguished by its radicalism, its inability to articulate the connection between differentiated sectors. The discussion that accompanied the development of the European constitution, beginning in 2001, provides a good example. A bitter debate began on the question of the recognition, in the constitution's preamble, of Europe's Christian heritage. We have already seen why such a recognition, obvious as it may be from an objective point of view, had become inopportune within the framework of secularization. The explicit reference to God was rather quickly drawn aside, even though 77.4 percent of Europeans say that they believed in God. This point is significant: in the minds of the writers of the proposed constitution, the fact that a vast majority of Europeans believed in God did not in itself imply that this faith should have consequences on the political level. God could not have his place in the European constitution because this place, if it had been recognized, would have appeared to initiate a confusion of the political and the theological. In other words, the distinction of orders, instead of allowing a better comprehension of their connection, led only to their artificial separation. The recognition of complexity played against unity. However, the case of the political is not an isolated one. On the contrary, European culture is currently presented as a culture fragmented into a multitude of dissociations conceived of as oppositions that, since they cannot be overcome, are compartmentalized artificially: faith and reason, nature and culture, morality and law, love and sexuality, the individual and the State, fact and meaning, freedom and duty, matter and spirit, public sphere and private sphere, tradition and progress, experts and decision makers, etc. The chief victim of this "cubist culture" is European humanism, for all these oppositions prevent a unified and unifying vision of the human being, of our *raison d'être* and our end. In this, European secularization is first of all a cultural crisis, an anthropological crisis, whose religious component is only the most visible aspect.

Toward the end of secularization?

These various elements make it possible to appreciate better the change that occurred following the Second Vatican Council. In order to comprehend its suddenness and breadth, this change must be contextualized within the broad sweep of history. Schematically, the structuring of national identities around the modern conception of the State underwent a radicalization in the nineteenth and the first half of the twentieth centuries. The Church, called to give up any competition with the State (by the German *Kulturkampf*, Austrian Josephism, the Italian *Risorgimento*, and French anticlericalism), and having tried vainly to resist, had to accommodate itself to the new order and sought to influence it from within. It privileged a policy of conciliation-in-equality with the various European States by means of concordats, while encouraging the development of a Catholic counter-culture based on the idea that, if states were no longer Christian and were even hostile toward Christianity, at least society ought to continue to receive the imprint of Christianity (Leo XIII, 1892, 1901). This project culminated in the introduction of the festival of Christ the King (Pius XI, 1925), a veritable liturgical rebuttal to nationalist ideologies, and the organization of Catholic Action (Pius X, 1905), a mass movement with a militant vocation – the call to unify the action of Catholics in society, under the supervision of the clergy. It was a question of preserving a relation between temporal power and spiritual power, in the context of a Europe where the nation was seen as the only source, autonomous and absolute, of political power.

This adaptation to the new political reality found itself out of date when the Western nations, seized by doubt after the experience of totalitarianism, began another political project – which one might call "post-national" – whose organizing principle was the development of a mass society of well-being and economic success. The Church's counter-culture collapsed along with the culture to which it was opposed, in a crash proportionate to the enthusiasm that had borne it along. The failure of the Christian Democratic parties; the disappearance of Christian militancy – which tried for a time to outlive itself in coalition with the Communists ; the abandonment, whether voluntary or not, by religious congregations of hospitals and schools; the obsessive leitmotiv of "opening in the world"; the exaltation of the "anonymous Christian"; the identity crisis of the clergy and religious (13 percent of the French priests ordained between 1945 and 1978 left the ministry); the rejection of popular devotions; the frenzy of liturgical innovation; fascination with the social sciences; the contesting of all authority, whether it be hierarchical, doctrinal, or moral; the opposition between action and contemplation, tradition and modernity, institution and community, truth and tolerance . . . such were the religious consequences of a crisis that was above all the crisis of a cultural model, but which affected European Catholicism because it had defined itself in relationship to this model. Christendom, which had fashioned and unified Europe, initially in its "sacral" medieval form, then in its humanistic and national form (Maritain, 1996), had taken a step that increased its capacity for universalization and, correlatively, its rupture with its past.

This rupture is consummated today: the phase of secularization which moved away from the Christian tradition has been succeeded today by a phase which no longer has any contact with it. Statistics show that the second generation born after the crisis of the 1960s, even in countries more resistant to secularization, manifests a new rupture in the transmission of the Christian tradition. Thus in West Germany, 40 percent of those over 60 years old have confidence in the Churches, compared to 14 percent of the 18- to 29-year-olds; conversely, 28 percent of the former compared to 49 percent of the latter have no confidence in the Church. One finds the same inversion in Spain, where the ratio of those with confidence in the Church to those without confidence is 55 percent/16 percent among those over 60 while it is 17 percent/53 percent among those aged 18 to 29. In Ireland, we find the same ratio between the same generations: 49 percent/14 percent compared to 7 percent/49 percent. A similar phenomenon is found in France, West Germany and Switzerland when these two age groups are asked if they consider themselves religious (Bréchon, 2001). The intergenerational rupture is obvious and, in a way, it indicates the completion of the process of secularization that we described in the preceding pages. Consequently, the currently fuzzy boundary between a minority of practicing Catholics and a majority who are strangers to Catholicism, must become clearer in the coming years, taking into consideration the specificities of each country. The Christendom which dies is detached, like bark from a tree, from a heart that rediscovers the possibility of a new vitality freed from a weight that it was no longer able to carry.

Being a Catholic, After All: Three Challenges for the Church in Europe

Memory

The contemporary redefinition of the place of religion in European societies was not a perfectly synchronous process. In the Western democracies, the turning point is located in the mid-1960s, when the development of consumer society and the export of the humanistic but areligious model of democracy became the new political project of the nations, supported by the baby-boom generation's arrival at adulthood. This was the case in Holland, West Germany, France and to a certain extent Italy, where the political alternative between Communists and Christian Democrats favored the latter for a time. The turning point was pushed back in Spain until the death of Franco in 1975, and in Belgium, Switzerland, and Austria until the 1980s, because the place of the Church was socially and institutionally better established. In Ireland and Portugal the turning point did not occur until close to the middle of the 1980s, when European integration brought about their economic takeoff. Lastly, in the countries of the former Eastern bloc, the Church found its freedom in 1989, but the long religious persecution had left it bloodless, except in Poland, Lithuania, and Slovakia where resistance to totalitarianism was inseparable from spiritual resistance.

The last half-century was thus, in all the European countries, a period of profound change – change that outflanked the internal reforms with which the Church was engaged. This explains the discouragement or giddiness which seized Catholics, and particularly the clergy, with regard to a situation that had become uncontrollable. The optimism characterizing the first years after the Council mutated into an interminable management of crisis. It was thought at first that the Church was paying for its delay in adapting to the modern world; people thus engaged in an unrestrained quest for new forms of Christian life, in which the catchphrase was rupture, even concerning fundamental assertions of the faith. Wasn't it, for example, necessary to forsake the parish organization? Did the distinction between clergy and laity hold any meaning? Was religious life still justified? This first, groping phase quickly showed its limitations as much by the excesses to which it led as by its incapacity to stop the decline in religious practice, since it had not taken the true measure of the crisis and its causes. It was not, however, sterile insofar as it supported the expansion of new communities, some of which experienced great development: Communion and Liberation in Italy, L'Emmanuel or Les Béatitudes in France, and the Neocatechumenal Way in Spain. This last, founded by Kiko Argüello and Carmen Hernandez in a shantytown of Madrid, today gathers one million people across the world and offers a path for the rediscovery of baptism and the proclamation of the Gospel within a para-parochial experience of community, nourished by lively and participatory liturgies. These characteristics are found more or less in all the new communities: a strong communal and liturgical accent; the primacy of the spiritual experience of a living relationship with Christ in the Holy Spirit; attachment to the Church and to an integral confession of the Catholic faith; a revamping of the Tradition; biblical rootedness;

the revival of Eucharistic adoration, the rosary and confession; kerygmatic preaching; and the practical expression of the Christian life through evangelization and works of justice and charity. It is striking to note that the success of these new movements (which also include the Focolari of Chiara Lubich, the Community of San Egidio or the cells of parish evangelization of Don P. Perrini in Italy, Opus Dei in Spain, Taizé, the Foyers de Charité of Marthe Robin or the Équipes Notre-Dame in France) is not rooted so much in the novelty of what they propose as in their capacity to elicit a living and life-giving experience of encounter with Christ. This contrasts with the phase of systematic questioning in the post-conciliar years: rather than requiring a rupture with Tradition, innovation is actually better achieved through a reappropriation of Tradition. The expression "the New Evangelization," launched by Jean-Paul II in the first years of his pontificate on the basis of Paul VI's 1975 encyclical *Evangelii Nuntiandi* (Second Vatican Council, 1995) summarizes well the challenge that European Catholicism must take up in the next decades: how to proclaim Christ in a continent that believes it already knows him, and has reduced him to a past moment of its history? How to reappropriate the Tradition, the indispensable mediation in the encounter with Christ, when this Tradition was, in large part, developed in a two-thousand-year culture that Europe is forgetting?

During the last few decades, in the midst of the storm, the difficulty has been sidestepped. European Catholics drew from the exotic treasury of Christian memory those things whose rediscovery released a fragrance of novelty (the art of the icon, Orthodox liturgy or Negro spirituals, the Desert Fathers, the *Philokalia* or Meister Eckhart, the Fathers of the Church or Jewish theology, etc.). But today, for a new generation, so much of Christian culture is unknown that all of it appears new. Catechesis was in effect the first great victim of the crisis of European Catholicism: from the "Dutch Catechism" of 1966, through the course *Pierres vivantes* (Living Stones) that appeared in France in 1981, up to the catechetical courses established in the Polish schools after Communism's fall from power, the repeated failures of catechetical reforms showed how difficult it had become to transmit the faith in a society characterized by the refusal of that transmission and the overturning of all points of reference. If the *Catechism of the Catholic Church*, promulgated by John Paul II in 1992, offers hope for improvement in the future, the fact remains that for at least 40 years young Catholics have received the barest minimum of Christian formation. Consequently, there is a clear difference in spiritual expectations and behaviors between the generations: the older generation worries about the younger generation's calls for identity, and the confidence-without-complexity regarding the Magisterium that they develop when they discover the unsuspected riches of the Tradition; meanwhile the younger generation, not having known anything of pre-conciliar Christendom, do not understand the reservations of the older generation. This hiatus is only one manifestation of the current stratification of European Catholicism, where the remainders of the Christendom model coexist with the forces of renewal. To recover a Christian memory on a continent at war with its own memory, without making a communitarian retreat but with a view to a revitalization of the faith, thus constitutes a first challenge for the Church in Europe.

Mission

If the abrupt change of the 1960s was not perfectly synchronous, it was even less uniform because of the more or less rapid adaptation of institutions connected with the Church. The German case is exemplary: beginning in the nineteenth century, Catholicism affirmed its identity in the face of Protestantism by mobilizing and gathering the laity into large organizations independent of the bishops. The *Katholikentag* – a kind of annual congress – remains today their showcase (40,000 participants in 2004). It also benefited from the system of the Church tax, which allowed it to implement a remarkable policy of solidarity, focused on five principal organizations: Misereor, Missio, Adveniat, Renovabis, and Caritas. This last today includes 500,000 collaborators in 26,000 local institutions. This is why parishes are not only places of worship, but also provide multiple services and call upon the work of many salaried laypeople: in 2005, for 16,700 priests there were 2,900 lay pastoral assistants who trained in theology at one of country's 60 university faculties, and 44,000 parish assistants trained in religious education. This formidable ecclesial structure, however, has became oversized: in addition to its operation now being too expensive, since many Germans have given up paying the Church tax, its maintenance absorbs the energy of the laity, and its inertia prevents the appearance of the movements of renewal found in other European countries.

This example is emblematic of the dilemma of Catholicism in Europe: should it continue to respond to the traditional expectations of an increasingly distant population – that is, continuing to exercise the mission of public usefulness that Christendom assigned to the Church within the framework of national identities; or should it recognize that this system is disappearing and recover a sense of mission focused on the proclamation of the Gospel to those that thirst for it? For, in contrast to even 50 years ago, the two choices are no longer evenly matched, and one can, to exaggerate a little, reduce them to the following: which is most important for the Church, Christendom or Christ? A recognized place in society or supernatural vitality? Time is working against the first alternative insofar as the younger generations generally do not expect anything from the Church; the privileged place that is granted to Christians in European societies is dearly paid for with contempt and growing scorn; and, finally, the Church is becoming unable to maintain a social presence according to the Christendom model because this model is sterile (by 2015, the number of active priests in France will be one third of what it is currently).

The experience of the new communities, like the recent success of evangelical Protestant groups, has shown that, as John Paul II and Benedict XVI have understood so well, the future of the Church in Europe requires a clear and explicit assertion of the faith and Christian life, founded on a call to conversion in Christ. The hour of the New Evangelization has truly come: the dynamism incited by the World Youth Days since Santiago de Compostela in 1989 and by the immense impact of the death of John Paul II, not restricted simply to practicing Catholics, attest to the fact that the Church does not have anything to lose by focusing on its own mystery, depending on Revelation, the sacraments, and apostolic succession as its only weapons, and by inviting men and women to respond to their supernatural vocation, as the Second Vatican Council called for in the dogmatic constitution *Lumen Gentium* (Second Vatican Council, 1996b).

Anthropology and holiness

Another text from the Second Vatican Council quite naturally evokes the third challenge with which the Church in Europe is confronted. In *Gaudium et Spes*, the Council clarified the relationship between the Church and the contemporary world, using two central ideas: "only in the mystery of the incarnate Word does the mystery of man take on light" (Second Vatican Council 1996b: n. 22); terrestrial realities (societies, human activity) cannot develop in accord with their own autonomy and with respect for the human person without the recognition of God, creator and savior. In other words, it was the conviction of the Council that forgetting God leads not only to a truncated image of humanity but also, in the long term, to the impossibility of having a unified image of what it means to be human and to live in society. A lasting peace between peoples, a durable democracy, the free development of individuals, and respect for the weakest require an anthropology that is conscious of the origin, limitations, and end of the human person. But on all these points Europe has accumulated successes without having in any way settled the question of anthropological foundations. On the contrary, as we have seen, humanism has entered into a "cubist" phase of fragmentation, of which secularization was once the most visible aspect, but which today has overflowed purely religious values so as to embrace all dimensions of human life. Mechanistic models, proceeding from a physical or biological framework of interpretation, manage to propose a unified and ordered vision of the human person and society only at the cost of a reductionism that ignores the specificity of the spiritual faculties of intelligence and will. This reductionism has its price: reason separated from the *Logos* deconstructs itself, and the will imprisoned in the illusion of its pure spontaneity is swamped in the ceaseless flow of desires.

The acceleration in the two last decades of the loss of conscience in European society – one thinks for example of bioethics or the rights of the family – led John Paul II to speak of a "culture of death" (John Paul II, 1995: n. 12) in the sense that, like a depressed person developing morbid impulses, European culture had started gradually to integrate regressive tendencies. The effects of this cultural evolution are already perceptible in the younger generations of Catholics, in the difficulty they have in unifying their lives, in rendering them coherent and, despite a great generosity, in translating into concrete action a faith that is otherwise strongly rooted. This is visible, for example, in their reluctance to make a permanent commitment to a state of life, whether through marriage or religious vows, in the tendency to live their faith at the level of felt experience, in their lack of a critical view with regard to the dominant social models, and in their difficulties in exercising clear discernment. John Paul II was very conscious of this challenge. His teaching engaged in a true theoretical reflection that aimed at producing a coherent Christian anthropology, relevant to the present era, and he accelerated the procedures of canonization because he was convinced that the saints are the primary witnesses to what it means to lead a fulfilled human life.

However, if the impulse has been given, if magisterial discernment has been brought to bear on a significant number of current questions in moral theology, if their extension into the pastoral realm has begun to acquire a certain consistency – for example, in the realm of the spirituality of marriage – much still remains to be done in offering to European Catholics well-marked and coherent paths to life with Christ. We can trust that the Holy Spirit will aid us by raising up great figures of holiness in the coming years, as has always been the case, at the crucial turning points of the Church in Europe. Already two names come to mind: Mother Teresa of Calcutta and John Paul the Great.

Translated by Frederick Christian Bauerschmidt

References and Further Reading

AA (Acta Apostolica Sedis) 75 (1983)

Arts, W. and Halman, L. (2004a) "European Values at the Turn of the Millennium: An Introduction," in Arts, W. and Halman, L. (eds.) *European Values at the Turn of the Millennium.* Leiden: Brill, 1–24.

Arts, W. and Halman, L. (2004b) "European Values: Changes in the Second Age of Modernity," in Arts, W. and Halman, L. (eds.) *European Values at the Turn of the Millennium.* Leiden: Brill, 25–53.

Beck, U. (1992) *Risk Society: Towards a New Modernity.* London: Sage.

Beck, U. (1999) *World Risk Society.* Cambridge: Polity Press.

Brague, R. (2002) *Eccentric Culture: A Theory of Western Civilization,* trans. Samuel Lester. South Bend, IN: St Augustine's Press.

Bréchon, P. (2001) "L'Évolution du Religieux," *Futuribles,* vol. 260, 39–48.

Bruce, S. (1992) *Religion and Modernization: Sociologists and Historians Debate the Secularization Thesis.* Oxford: Clarendon Press.

Campiche, R. J. (1993) "Individualisation du croire et recomposition de la religion," *Archives de Sciences Sociales des Religions,* vol. 81, 117–31.

Davie, G. (1990) "Believing without Belonging: Is This the Future of Religion in Britain?" *Social Compass,* vol. 37, 455–69.

Davie, G. (2000) *Religion in Modern Europe. A Memory Mutates.* Oxford: Oxford University Press.

Davie, G. and Hervieu-Léger, D. (eds.) (1996) *Identités religieuses en Europe.* Paris: La Découverte.

Durkheim, Emile (1949) *Division of Labor in Society,* trans. George Simpson. Glencoe, IL: The Free Press.

Fulton, John and Gee, Peter (eds.) (1994) *Religion in Contemporary Europe.* Lewiston, NY: Queenston and Lampeter: Edwin Mellen Press.

Gauchet, Marcel, (1985) *Le Désenchantement du monde. Une Histoire politique de la religion.* Bibliothèque des Sciences Humaines. Paris: Gallimard.

Giddens, Anthony (1990) *The Consequences of Modernity.* Cambridge: Polity Press.

Gill, S., D'Costa, G., and King, U. (eds.) (1994) *Religion in Europe: Contemporary Perspectives.* Kampen: Kok Pharos.

Halman, Loek (ed.) (2001) *The European Values Study: A Third Wave. Sourcebook of the 1999/2000 European Values Study Surveys.* Tilburg: EVS-WORC–Tilburg University.

Halman, Loek and Draulans, Veerle (2004) "Religious Beliefs and Practices in Contemporary Europe," in Arts, W. and Halman, L. (eds.) *European Values at the Turn of the Millennium.* Leiden: Brill, 283–316.

Halman, Loek and Pettersson, Thorleif (2003) "Differential Patterns of Secularization in Europe: Exploring the Impact of Religion on Social Values," in Halman, Loek and Riis, Ole (eds.), *Religion in Secularizing Society. The Europeans' Religion at the End of the Twentieth Cen-*

tury. Leiden: Brill, 41–65.

Halman, Loek, and Riis, Ole (eds.) (2003) *Religion in Secularizing Society. The Europeans' Religion at the End of the Twentieth Century*. Leiden: Brill.

Hervieu-Léger, Danièle (2002) "Les Tendances du religieux en Europe," in *Croyances religieuses, morales et ethiques dans le processus de construction Européenne*. Paris: Commissariat general du Plan, Institut universitaire de Florence and Chaire Jean Monnet d'Études Européennes, 9–22.

Inglehart, Ronald (1997) *Modernization and Postmodernization: Cultural, Economic, and Political Change in Forty-three Societies*. Princeton, NJ: Princeton University Press.

Inglehart, Ronald (1977) *The Silent Revolution: Changing Values and Political Styles in Advanced Industrial Society*. Princeton, NJ: Princeton University Press.

John Paul II (1993) *Veritatis Splendor*. Rome: Libreria Editrice Vaticana.

John Paul II (1995) *Evangelium Vitae*. Rome: Libreria Editrice Vaticana.

John Paul II (2003) *Apostolic Exhortation Ecclesia in Europa*. Rome: Libreria Editrice Vaticana.

Kokosalakis, Nikos (1993) "Religion and the Dynamics of Social Change in Contemporary Europe," *Archives de Sciences Sociales des Religions*, vol. 81, 1334–8.

Leo XIII (1892) *Au Milieu des sollicitudes*. Rome: Libreria Editrice Vaticana.

Leo XIII (1901) *Graves de Communi Re*. Rome: Libreria Editrice Vaticana.

Luckmann, Thomas (1967) *The Invisible Religion: The Problem of Religion in Modern Society*. New York: Macmillan.

Maritain, Jacques (1996) *Integral Humanism; Freedom in the Modern World;* and *A Letter on Independence*, trans. Otto A. Bird. Notre Dame, IN: University of Notre Dame Press.

Martin, David (2005) *On Secularization: Towards a Revised General Theory*. Aldershot, UK and Burlington, VT: Ashgate Publishing Company.

Pius X (1905) *Il Fermo Proposito*. Rome: Libreria Editrice Vaticana.

Pius XI (1925) *Quas Primas*. Rome: Libreria Editrice Vaticana.

Polanyi, Karl (1957) *The Great Transformation. The Political and Economic Origins of Our Time*. Boston: Beacon Press.

Second Vatican Council (1995) *Evangelii Nuntiandi*.

Second Vatican Council (1996a) "The Pastoral Constitution on the Church in the Modern World," *Gaudium et Spes*.

Second Vatican Council (1996b) "The Dogmatic Constitution on the Church," *Lumen Gentium*.

Seiwert, Hubert (1995) "Religion in der Geschichte der Moderne," *Zeitschrift für Religionswissenschaft*, 3, 91–101.

Smith, Christian (ed.) (2003) *The Secular Revolution: Power, Interests, and Conflict in the Secularization of American Public Life*. Berkeley: University of California Press.

Stark, Rodney and Finke, Roger (2000) *Acts of Faith: Explaining the Human Side of Religion*. Berkeley: University of California Press.

Stark, Rodney and Iannaccone , Laurence R. (1994) "A Supply-Side Reinterpretation of the 'Secularization' of Europe," *Journal for the Scientific Study of Religion*, vol. 33, 230–52.

Tschannen, Olivier (1992) *Les Théories de la sécularisation, travaux de droit, d'économie, de sciences politiques, de sociologie et d'anthropologie*. Geneva: Droz, 165.

Wilson, Bryan R. (1982) *Religion in Sociological Perspective*. Oxford and New York: Oxford University Press.

CHAPTER 11
Great Britain and Ireland

Fergus Kerr and D. Vincent Twomey

CATHOLICISM IN ENGLAND, WALES, AND SCOTLAND by FERGUS KERR

Catholicism in England and Wales

Catholicism in England and Wales has a significantly different character from Catholicism in Scotland. While the United Kingdom is of Great Britain and Northern Ireland, it has to be said that, for most Catholics in England, Wales, and Scotland, as for most people in these countries, Northern Irish Protestants (let alone Northern Irish Catholics!) do not seem at all "British." There is more sympathy for Northern Irish Catholics in Boston and New York (not to mention financial support for the Irish Republican Army) than among British Catholics. Modern Catholicism, in England and Wales as well as in Scotland, owes a great deal to Ireland – links, however, which are predominantly with the Republic.

The Catholic population of England and Wales, estimated at over 4 million, constitutes about 12 percent of the total population. Over 900,000 attend Mass weekly. There are 3,869 diocesan priests, nearly 700 retired priests, and over 500 permanent deacons. There are 1,548 religious priests. The biggest diocese is Liverpool: about 500,000 Catholics, of whom about 80,000 attend Mass regularly. Westminster, the next largest diocese, with 460,000 Catholics, records about 150,000 practicing. Catholicism, formerly strong in the northwest and northeast urban areas, now shows significantly greater vitality and level of practice in the London area.

For comparison, in the United Kingdom as a whole, the estimated Muslim population is from one million to 1,500,000; with about 500,000 Hindus, 500,000 Sikhs, and 283,000 Jews.

Catholicism in England and Wales is largely a nineteenth-century creation, with little historical continuity with the pre-Reformation Church. After two centuries of persecution and repression, Catholics were allowed, by the Papists Act of 1778, to own landed property on taking an oath of loyalty to the monarchy which did not involve a denial of their religion, and priests ceased to be subject to arrest for exercising their ministry. The passing of the Act was followed by anti-Catholic riots in London, no doubt fomented by a minority of extreme Protestants. By the Roman Catholic Relief Act of 1791 Catholics who took the prescribed oath were allowed further freedoms, including access to certain posts in the legal and military professions. Finally, by the Roman Catholic Relief Act of 1829, which was provoked by unrest in Ireland and intended to placate Irish Catholics, almost all remaining disabilities were removed. The most significant disability remaining to this day is that the King or Queen of Great Britain may not be, or marry, a Roman Catholic, on pain of losing the throne.

In the middle of the nineteenth century the tiny surviving Catholic population was greatly increased by waves of incomers, mainly from Ireland. The new industries required large numbers of unskilled labourers, mostly drawn in from the rural counties of England and Wales, but with significant numbers of Irish immigrants. The potato blight appeared in North America in 1844, reached Europe the following year, and had the most devastating effects especially in Ireland. The British government did a great deal to relieve the distress (whatever the myths to the contrary). The United States also sent substantial supplies across the Atlantic. But there were many deaths from starvation (21,770 by 1851). In the decade that followed 1847 more than 1,500,000 persons emigrated from Ireland, mostly to North America and Australia, but also to Britain.

Right into the middle of the twentieth century the Catholic population, mostly distributed in the great industrial cities, with its own schools and colleges of education, stood quite consciously apart from the "establishment": the Church of England by law established but also, in a looser sense, the political, social, and intellectual classes, mostly educated at private schools and Oxford or Cambridge. Often with Irish dancing and folk music, and regional Irish newspapers on sale, Catholic parishes created an Irish Catholic environment. Generations of priests from Irish seminaries served in England and Wales, though seldom being appointed as bishops. Many of the nuns and religious sisters in Catholic convents, schools, and hospitals were "missionaries" from Ireland.

It was only in the 1890s that upper-class Catholics were able to send their sons to Oxford and Cambridge. As a whole, English Catholics kept their distance from Anglicanism, with a conscious sense of superiority mixed with a much less conscious sense of social inferiority. In 1896, for example, most Catholics were delighted at the condemnation by Pope Leo XIII of Anglican orders as invalid. Many Catholics, even today, would say that Anglican bishops and priests are not "real" bishops or priests (which means, of course, that whether the Church of England ordains women priests, or the Anglican Communion women bishops, are matters of no consequence).

As for social status, it was only during the years when Basil Hume was Cardinal Archbishop of Westminster (1976–99) that middle-class Catholics felt, and were perceived as being, fully at home. Formerly abbot of the largest Benedictine monastery in the country, with a highly successful fee-paying school, Hume had a French Catholic mother and a Scots Protestant father, and a sister married into the upper echelons of the civil service. The picture of the gaunt figure, dying of cancer, seated beside Queen Elizabeth II, as she promoted him to the Order of Merit (the only honour in her own gift), was the final symbol of this astonishingly recent acceptance of Catholicism in mainstream British culture.

Before the reforms introduced by the Second Vatican Council, devotion to the Mass in Latin, the service of Benediction, and many subsidiary devotions, gave a distinctive character to Catholic worship in England and Wales. Most significantly, however, in the creation of English and Welsh Catholic identity was the memory of the hundreds of Catholics put to death by the State between 1535 and 1680, the cult which culminated in 1970 with the canonization of the Forty Martyrs of England and Wales. Among these were remarkable Jesuit priests such as Edmund Campion and Robert Southwell, as well as four laymen and three women, including Margaret Clitherow.

For Catholics, the wounds of the Reformation go deep. King Henry VIII threw off papal jurisdiction in 1534 when Pope Clement VII refused to grant an annulment of his marriage to Catherine of Aragon (unsurprisingly: Clement was a creature of her nephew Emperor Charles V). Nevertheless Henry remained staunchly Catholic in many other ways, even passing laws which included the death penalty for denying the doctrine of transubstantiation. He inaugurated the despoliation of the monasteries, widely perceived to be rich, with their property envied by other great landowners. However, during the five years' reign of his uncompromisingly Catholic daughter Mary Tudor (1553 to 1558) some 300 of her subjects were put to death for heresy. This included two bishops, Hugh Latimer and Nicholas Ridley, burnt at the stake in Oxford in 1554; and Thomas Cranmer, in 1556, archbishop of Canterbury. Henry VIII's chief instrument in the failed negotiations with Rome, Cranmer created the Book of Common Prayer, one of the glories of the English language. This book makes Cranmer the chief architect of Anglican liturgy and spirituality. With such memories of barbarously cruel martyrdoms on both sides, it has to be said that, at grass roots level, Catholics and Anglicans have not yet achieved anything like full reconciliation.

In the so-called Gunpowder Plot of 1605, a group of Catholic gentry sought to blow up the Houses of Parliament, with King James I, the Lords and the Commons, including many of their fellow Catholics, in order to seize control of the government. This stupendous act of terrorism was foiled but consolidated the hatred of Popery which has characterised the majority of the inhabitants of England and Wales until very recent times – so recent, indeed, that the immense media interest in the funeral of Pope John Paul II in 2005 was hailed by some commentators as evidence, only now, of the end of the Reformation. More plausibly, it was evidence of a celebrity cult. Few even of the Catholics who were inundated with media coverage of his death had much sympathy with most of the doctrines which the Pope held so dearly and preached so often.

While there was, by North American and western European standards, relatively little dissent after the appearance of the encyclical *Humanae Vitae* in 1968, which reaffirmed the Church's condemnation of contraception, Catholics plainly no longer have any more children than anyone else. The Society for the Protection of Unborn Children (SPUC) is regarded by many as perhaps somewhat provocative in some of its campaigning; yet it seems clear that the vast majority of Catholics in England and Wales are pro-life in their views, though doing little about it. Catholics are more likely to be active in various projects engaged in providing aid for famine relief, education, and medical programs, in parts of Africa and elsewhere. This concern for overseas aid programs is deeply rooted in Catholic schools, most of which are at least partly state funded.

The unusual feature of Catholic education in England and Wales, and for that matter in Scotland also, is that, while there is a flourishing tradition of Catholic schools, often now admitting non-Catholic and sometimes Muslim children, there are very few Catholic institutions at tertiary level.

There is no Catholic university. An attempt was made in the 1890s, and more recently the issue has been raised again; but Catholics have opted, more or less consciously, perhaps quite pragmatically, to enter the mainstream of British university education.

A handful remains of Catholic colleges of education, mainly engaged in educating schoolteachers, out of more than a dozen before Vatican II. For ecumenical reasons and also because of the drop in entrants and especially of religious sisters as teachers, several have amalgamated with non-Catholic institutions and become absorbed in university education faculties.

Heythrop College, set up in 1614 to train Jesuits, has, since 1970, been a constituent college of the University of London. It houses one of the finest libraries in the country, on a splendid central London site. Conducted by members of the Society of Jesus, who also hold some of the principal teaching posts, it is of course no longer exclusively Jesuit or Catholic in either staff or students. *The Heythrop Journal*, founded in 1960, is the most important Catholic theological periodical, particularly impressive for the comprehensive book reviewing, and hospitable to articles from beyond the British academic scene.

The most prolific Catholic theologian, Aidan Nichols, is a friar of the Dominican order. Theologians, such as Nicholas Lash, Eamon Duffy, Denys Turner and Oliver Davies, have held, or still hold, divinity chairs in leading universities (Cambridge and London). Most theology departments are now happy to hire a Catholic, if not in an ecumenical spirit then at least on the principle that minorities should be represented. Often enough the Catholic is the strongest candidate academically.

There have recently been proposals to establish "Roman Catholic studies" in two or three universities, sometimes in the context of "Religious studies," or alongside lectureships in "Islamic studies." On the whole, these proposals have not been warmly welcomed by Catholic academics. At least in one instance the proposal seemed to envisage "Catholic studies" as concerned principally with Mariology and Vatican II. What would seem more attractive, is a course in Christian doctrine simply taught from a Catholic point of view. In every British university at present, students (including Catholics) graduate in Christian theology without studying any theologian between Augustine and Schleiermacher. Students are much more likely to have read Karl Rahner or Hans Urs von Balthasar than Thomas Aquinas or even Augustine.

There is no such thing as a specifically British, or even an English, Catholic theological tradition or school, let alone the range of rival and often mutually hostile faculties that exist in the United States of America. On the other hand, there are many Catholic voices in academic posts: in a dispersed, perhaps often half hidden, way, fairly classical and orthodox versions of Catholic Christian doctrine are allowed to flourish and perhaps to interpenetrate the wider theological enterprise.

Catholicism in Scotland

The population of Scotland is just over 5 million. The Catholic population is estimated at 650,000: over 200,000 attended Mass on the first Sunday of Advent in November 2003. At the same date Scotland had 820 priests, of whom 142 were members of religious orders. There were 27 students in training in the major seminaries (Scots College in Rome, founded in 1600; Royal Scots College, Salamanca, founded in 1627; Scotus College, Glasgow, founded in 1993 when the Glasgow and Edinburgh diocesan seminaries in Scotland united). More than half the estimated Catholic population lives in the highly urbanized central belt of the country: Glasgow, Motherwell, Paisley, and Edinburgh. There are only some 35,000 Catholics scattered in the vast dioceses of Aberdeen and of Argyll and the Isles.

Catholics in the central belt are mostly descended from Irish immigrants, first drawn by the Industrial Revolution and then, in much greater numbers, forced to leave Ireland as a result of the Great Famine (1845–50). Native-born for over a hundred years, and perceiving themselves as ethnically and culturally Scottish, Catholics in the urban central belt, particularly in the Glasgow region, suffered from anti-Irish and anti-Catholic prejudice well into the twentieth century. Some, indeed, complain of such prejudice even today. In the sometimes isolated communities in Aberdeen diocese, as well as in the Gaelic-speaking islands, to which there was no significant immigration from Ireland, Catholics never experienced such hostility.

The collapse of Catholicism in Scotland in the sixteenth century is not easy to account for. In May 1559, with the support of English money and troops, a group of Scottish noblemen, led by the illegitimately born half brother of the young Mary Queen of Scots, instigated military action against the French-dominated government. This culminated in August 1560 in the "Reformation Parliament" and the adoption of legislation purporting to replace Catholicism by a nation-wide Protestant church. However, it took another generation before the Protestant church took the form of Presbyterianism. Only in 1688–9, as part of the "Glorious Revolution," did the reformed Church become at last fully Presbyterian. The substantial minority with episcopalian sympathies seceded, or was expelled, to form the Scottish Episcopal Church.

For all the dramatic results, the sixteenth-century *coup d'état* by a handful of great landowners involved little bloodshed and few martyrs. Many of the clergy turned Protestant overnight. Catholic priests and Protestant ministers even worked in parallel for some years. Some priests and religious went into exile abroad; but many continued to live in their monasteries, on government pensions, left in peace though not allowed to recruit.

John Knox (*c.*1513–72), hailed as the greatest Scottish Reformer, ordained priest in 1536 but apparently working as a lawyer, was converted to Protestantism in 1543 by the preaching of a former Dominican friar, Thomas Gwilliam.

Why the Reformation in Scotland was so much less bloody than in England is difficult to explain. However, the material destruction was far greater, with most of the many cathedrals and abbey churches ruined (quite unlike the situation in England). Mob violence directed against the friars, Franciscans, and Dominicans, began in the 1540s; they derived their income from rents and, in the economic depression of these years, were resented as harsh landlords. Zealous believers in the new Lutheran doctrines instigated a good deal of iconoclasm in city churches. Yet, most of the destruction had little or nothing to do with doctrinal innovations. The finest abbeys, such as Jedburgh, Coldingham, Kelso, Dryburgh, and Melrose, were looted and burned by the invading English troops in 1544–5. After 1560, however, by government initiative, cathedrals, abbeys, and priories were systematically unroofed, so that, by 1580, few, if any, of the larger ecclesiastical buildings remained intact. They became quarries for the grand houses of the nearby landowners. Whole libraries were burnt and works of sacred art destroyed. The result is that, today, only a handful of the great cathedrals remain standing. The most remarkable monument of ecclesiastical architecture in Scotland, Rosslyn Chapel (of *Da Vinci Code* fame), survives almost unscathed, protected by a Scottish Episcopal family.

Of pre-Reformation Catholicism very little survives, materially, less than in any other country in western Europe affected by the Reformation, and much less than in England. On the other hand, there were far fewer deaths. In the first half of the sixteenth century, some twenty Protestants were executed for the crime of heresy, mostly in the 1530s, with Walter Milne the last in 1558, formerly a priest, by then aged about 82 – an act of cruelty which backfired. There was nothing comparable to the executions of Protestants in England under Mary Tudor, let alone the burning of such unforgettable figures as Cranmer. Her equally devout Catholic cousin Mary Stuart (Queen effectively from 1561 to 1567) had no one put to death for heresy. Correspondingly, there was nothing like the reign of anti-Catholic terror that produced the English Martyrs. There was no equivalent in Scotland to the Gunpowder Plot (1605), to consolidate fears of Catholic disloyalty to the Crown. Some regard the beheading of Mary Queen of Scots in 1587, at the behest of Elizabeth of England, as a martyr's death, as she no doubt did herself. But the only martyr of the Reformation era in Scotland was John Ogilvie, a Jesuit priest, condemned for treason and hanged in Glasgow in 1615, because he refused to acknowledge royal jurisdiction (a process for beatification, started in 1628–9, lapsed but he was eventually canonized in 1976).

This does not mean that the Scots, in those times, were uniquely averse to bloodletting for religious reasons. During the "Killing Times," from 1660 to 1688, estimates of those killed have been as high as 18,000. But these were Presbyterians who, disowning the king and the State as "uncovenanted," certainly then for theological reasons, were hunted down and shot by royalist Protestant troops with Episcopalian sympathies. Relatively speaking, the Reformation era in Scotland was bloodless, with no legacy of inter-Christian slaughter.

That the Mass and associated popular devotion disappeared so completely is difficult to explain. The last Dominican friar was arrested for saying Mass as late as 1670, in Banffshire: he was banished, though died before he could leave the country, and was discreetly buried in a pre-Reformation graveyard. This graveyard was recognized as of special significance to Catholics well into the eighteenth century. There were pilgrimages to nearby waters to seek healing. Without Mass or priests, a good deal of folk religion of traditional Catholic character survived, in the northeast lowlands (Aberdeen and Banff), and in the Gaelic-speaking west, all relatively inaccessible to the Presbyterian ministers from Edinburgh.

In the late eighteenth century, despite anti-Catholic feeling in Edinburgh and other of the larger towns, new chapels were being built, the hitherto clandestine seminary at Scalan moved from the Banffshire hills in 1799, the Relief Act of 1793 and then Emancipation in 1829 marked the reappearance from "interior emigration" of the tiny but distinctive Catholic community. By then, and especially in the 1840s, with the waves of immigration by Catholics from Ireland (almost equalled by Protestants from Ulster), the Catholic Church in Scotland began to assume the shape that it has today. By 1878 Catholics numbered 325,000, about 9 percent of the population. In the urban-industrialised west there was great tension: the immigrants from Ireland resented the control of church affairs exercised by Scottish-born clergy, while the latter, for their part, feared the political overtones of popular Irish Catholicism. (Prime Minister W.E. Gladstone sought by his Home Rule bill of 1886 to solve "the Irish problem," and failed again in 1893; it would be 1921 before Britain conceded the creation of the Irish Free State, excepting the province of Ulster.)

Schism within Scottish Catholicism seemed a possibility, headed off only by the mediation of Charles Petrie Eyre (1817–1902), an Englishman nominated by Rome in 1868 to bring peace between Scots and Irish Catholics. He became the first archbishop of Glasgow when Rome restored the hierarchy in 1878.

The Education Act of 1918 gave state support to Catholic schools, facilitating the consolidation of the Catholic community, enhancing its self-identity. At the same time, however, the existence of Catholic schools and their associated activities, in sports especially, is perceived as isolating Catholics, if not in a self-chosen "ghetto," at any rate in their own sub-culture. Catholics have been slow to find a place in the mainstream of intellectual, academic, and cultural life in Scotland. James MacMillan (born in 1959 in the west of Scotland), a composer and conductor with an international reputation, recently denounced the anti-Catholic sectarianism which he detects in Scotland even today. It has to be said that, in the senior ranks of the legal profession and in financial services, both extremely influential in Scotland, the alumni of Catholic schools are noticeably under-represented. On the other hand, in local and national politics, certainly in central Scotland, Catholics play a significant part. Several prominent politicians in the recently devolved Scottish government went to Catholic schools. The late Cardinal Thomas Winning, and the present Cardinal Keith Patrick O'Brien, have not been reluctant to attack government priorities and policies, especially as these affect abortion and the sexual education of children.

It may be noted, whatever the symbolic significance of this, that Cardinal O'Brien was born in Northern Ireland though brought up in Scotland and educated at a Catholic school and then at the University of Edinburgh, while the Archbishop of Glasgow, Mario Joseph Conti, grandson of Italian immigrants to the northeast lowlands of Scotland and educated at a non-denominational school and at the Pontifical Gregorian University in Rome, has the rare distinction of being an elected Fellow of the Royal Society of Edinburgh (Scotland's national academy, founded in 1783).

The visit of Pope John Paul II in 1982 brought favorable media attention and

assembled the largest and most enthusiastic crowds in Scottish history. There was a
brief meeting between the Pope and the then Moderator of the Church of Scotland,
out of doors, on a chilly evening, under the statue of John Knox in the courtyard of
what was at the time the essentially Presbyterian divinity faculty of the University of
Edinburgh – nothing comparable to the shared prayer and elaborate ceremonial of
the Pope's visit to Canterbury.

Catholics in Scotland cannot be described as keenly ecumenical in their outlook or
practice. On the other hand, as their generosity to the Scottish Catholic International
Aid Fund (SCIAF) indicates, they are perhaps significantly more international and
European in their interests and sympathies than other churches. While once over-
whelmingly industrial working class and naturally supporters of the Labour Party,
locally and in United Kingdom elections, there is evidence suggesting that younger
Catholics at least are increasingly attracted to the policies of the Scottish National
Party. Perhaps somewhat ironically, the descendants of Irish immigrants now feel so
much at home in Scotland that they dream of an independent Scotland within the
European Union. As might be expected, they have none of the fears of Brussels, and of
Rome, characteristic of ultra-Protestants in Northern Ireland and of many Anglicans
in England.

It should perhaps be noted that there is a good deal of writing about "Celtic Christianity": the Christianity established by Saint Columba (c.521–97) and his followers,
centered at Iona, which had its own traditions and customs, and was – so the story
goes – entirely indifferent to Rome, and thus non-authoritarian, not to mention closer
to nature, the sea and the birds, and so on.

Catholics in UK Politics

The religious vote plays a significant part in British elections. Two-thirds of the population identify themselves as Christians, although only a tiny minority frequent church
services. According to MORI surveys [see *The Tablet* May 21, 2005: 4–5], while a majority of Anglicans voted Conservative, the Labour Party received 53 percent of the
Catholic vote at the 2005 General Election, the Conservatives 23 percent and the Liberal
Democrats 22 percent. As a group, Catholics remain among Labour's strongest supporters. Contrary to what was no doubt the case some decades ago, when Catholics were
mostly industrial workers, there is now little difference between Catholic and Anglican
congregations in respect of their social class composition. Indeed, 55 percent of Catholics, but only 51 percent of Anglicans, are "middle class" in market research terms.

Early in the 2005 campaign Cardinal Murphy-O'Connor spoke out approving a
pledge by the Conservative leader Michael Howard to make parliamentary time for
a bill to reduce abortion time limits. This seems to have had little effect on Catholic
voting intentions. The Labour Party, on the other hand, lost the votes of a significant
number of Catholics who believed that Prime Minister Tony Blair's support for the
American invasion of Iraq was mistaken, either because the war had no justification
in international law or because he lied about the reasons for British involvement.

Before 1990 all abortions were illegal in Britain where the child concerned was "capable of being born alive" [Infant Life (Preservation) Act 1929]. This was swept aside by the Human Fertilization and Embryology Act of 1990, passed by Parliament on a free vote and thus not treated as a party-political issue. In fact, however, the bill was strongly promoted by members of Margaret Thatcher's government. After much debate the majority in the House of Commons voted for a limit of 24 weeks' gestation. While there is some talk of revisiting the subject, in the light of recent medical advances, it does not seem likely that any Labour government would reduce the limit. On the contrary, since 1990 Britain has had the most liberal legislation in the world on stem cell research. This attracts scientists from elsewhere. Most states in the European Union, however, oppose such research because it involves the destruction and cloning of human embryos. Although an outright ban by the EU on member states is unlikely, EU directives and funding decisions could affect research so much that it might no longer be practicable. Britain, however, under the re-elected Labour government, seems eager to continue the policies of the previous Conservative administration in allowing the development of stem cell research and human cloning – well beyond the limits of Catholic ethics.

IRISH CATHOLICISM
by D. VINCENT TWOMEY

Scattered Christian communities existed in Ireland before Patrick the Briton came, first as a slave and later as a missionary bishop (c.432–61/492). Such was the impact of his personality and his evangelizing mission that he is known as the Apostle of Ireland. The inchoate diocesan structure set up by Patrick was soon transformed into a monastic Church by the sixth and seventh centuries, with major centers based on the reputation of great founders – such as Finnian of Clonard, Brigid of Kildare, Brendan of Clonfert, Ciaran of Clonmacnois – and/or the political strength of the associated tribal dynasties. Early Irish Christianity was marked by asceticism and a high moral sense, as found, for example, in the Irish Penitentials. These, in turn, led to a revolution in the universal Church's penitential system that eventually produced the practice of private confession. Paradoxically, early Irish spirituality was also marked by the joy of perceiving nature as speaking of the divine presence and of an art whose exuberance found expression in a distinctive iconography that transformed pagan Celtic art into new forms. The lavishly illuminated manuscripts, delicate chalices, and other metal work – those which survived the Reformation – are the glory of the early Irish Church. The original contribution of Irish scholarship to canon law (cf. the eighth-century *Collectio canonum Hibernensis*) is well known, though the rich ecclesiastical literature in Latin and the equally rich secular literature in the vernacular, the first in Europe, are still largely undiscovered. The missionary activity of Irish monks such as St Columba and St Columbanus to Britain and continental Europe, with its origins in the sixth- and seventh-century spirituality of *peregrinatio pro Christo*, profoundly marked the history and culture of Europe, making Ireland, in the words of Ludwig Bieler, the harbinger of the Middle Ages.

The first great spiritual reform movement *c.*800, the Culdees (*Céli Dé*, meaning Servants of God), almost coincided with the start of the Viking invasions (795–1014). The Norse plundered those monasteries which could be accessed by water. The typical Irish round towers probably originated as watch towers and places of refuge. The Vikings founded the first towns, such as Dublin, Waterford, and Limerick, eventually intermarried with the native Irish, and were converted. Their influence was considerable, even in the language – the name Ireland, for example, is of Norse origin. The new towns established bishoprics with ties to Canterbury. It was also during this period that the art of the Irish High Crosses reached an artistic perfection unknown in the rest of Europe. However, two centuries of Viking wars and political upheaval eventually led to spiritual and moral laxity.

A new reform movement followed, not only spiritual but also structural, thanks to contact with the great reform movements on the continent brought about by the final wave of missionaries to Europe (compare *Schottenklöster* in Regensburg and Vienna), increased pilgrimages to Rome, and the Norse links to Canterbury. The present diocesan structure of the Irish Church was established at the reforming Synod of Ráth Breasail (near Cashel) in 1111. Based on seventh-century claims to be the See of Patrick, Armagh emerges as the chief see. The great reformers were Cealach and Malachy, both of Armagh. Malachy was the intimate friend of St Bernard of Clairvaux and introduced the first non-native monastic rule to Ireland, the Cistercians.

The need to reform the Irish Church was used by the Anglo-Normans to justify their invasion (1169-*c.*1300) – with papal approval. The Papal Bull, *Laudabiliter*, issued by the only Englishman to become Pope, Adrian IV, granted dominion over the country to the English kings. Ireland lost its independent status, though its towns gained in importance. The Normans facilitated the introduction to Ireland of the older Benedictines (from England), as well as the new mendicant orders of Augustinians, Carmelites, Dominicans, and Franciscans into the towns. English bishops were appointed to a number of Irish sees, most of which were proximate to Dublin. They also introduced into their sees practices and customs peculiar to the Church in England (and the continent), such as cathedral chapters and ecclesiastical courts, as well as territorial lordship over great estates. Discrimination against the native Irish clergy was not unknown in episcopal elections. On the other hand, the mendicant orders, in particular the Franciscans, were hugely influential, especially after they underwent an intense movement of reform themselves in the fourteenth century. Among the effects of this reform were, on the one hand, a strong current of spirituality to offset medieval malpractices (used in other countries to justify the Reformation), and, on the other, the loyalty of the majority to the Pope in the sixteenth century, when the Crown tried to impose its State religion.

Even though the State took over all the institutions and buildings and entrusted them to the new Anglican Church, the Reformation failed in Ireland. This was due to a number of factors, some religious, others sociological and political. By way of contrast, the underground Counter-Reformation movement almost immediately found an echo among the faithful, native Irish and Old English alike. The result was the legal proscription of Catholicism (the Penal Laws), "frequently escalating into persecution, civic pressure on Catholics, and wars of conquest that in the end left Catholics largely despoiled of their property and without a political voice" (P.J. Corish, oral remark to author). Some 259 martyrs have been identified for the period between the accession of Elizabeth I in 1558 and the restoration of Charles II in 1660.

Apart from being economically and politically impoverished, Catholicism became the chief characteristic of being Irish. In the early seventeenth century, the era of confessional states – *cuius regio, eius religio* – Ireland found itself in the anomalous position of being a predominantly Catholic country ruled by a Protestant king. To make sense of the situation, Irish émigré theologians in the Sorbonne, such as David Rothe, created the notion of the Irish nation as Catholic by divine right, a people specially chosen by God. By the beginning of the eighteenth century, the Catholic Church had been legally proscribed but was in practice increasingly tolerated – on condition that it did not threaten what was called "the Protestant interest," namely the complete control of the Protestants over every aspect of public life.

With the destruction of the Irish monasteries and schools, Irish Colleges opened in various centers of Catholic learning in Europe, such as Louvain, Paris, Bordeaux, Salamanca, Valladolid, and Rome, to educate priests and laity. Novices for the religious orders were formed in their own houses from Lisbon to Prague. For almost 200 years, communities, mainly of male religious, also continued a furtive existence within the country. Right up to the early part of the nineteenth century, elementary education for Catholics was provided by an unofficial network of "Hedge Schools," which achieved an astonishingly high standard of education, especially in ancient classics, and which were marked by tolerance of other faiths.

Beginning at the end of the eighteenth century, developments of enormous consequence took place. Young Irishmen and women of some personal means and education, and of even greater piety, such as Edmund Rice, Nano Nagle, and Mary Aikenhead founded new religious congregations of brothers and nuns to educate the poor and to care for the needy and the sick. In the 1830s, the State-sponsored school system replaced the Hedge Schools but came under the control of the local parish, becoming denominational schools in all but name. Thus was born the Irish educational and health-care systems run by Church institutions, which in turn greatly shaped "traditional Irish Catholicism," even when exported abroad. Other significant factors included the opening of seminaries in Ireland, the most important being the foundation of the Royal Catholic College of Maynooth (1795), in which Edmund Burke was greatly influential. Thanks to the political agitation by Daniel O'Connell, the Liberator, Catholic Emancipation was achieved in 1829 by means of the first peaceful mass demonstrations in history that helped to define modern democracy. After Emancipation, the Catholic Church emerged fully out of the underground and engaged in massive building projects, including the many magnificent cathedrals and churches that replaced the Mass Rock on the hills and the humble chapel in a back lane.

With the closure of the Irish Parliament in Dublin in 1800, Ireland was reduced to a province of the newly created United Kingdom of Great Britain and Ireland. This had two main consequences. Irish Catholicism took on a new worldwide significance, while at the same time it became culturally provincial. Famine brought large-scale emigration, especially the Great Famine (1845–7). Beginning in the eighteenth century, colonies of poor Irish emigrants sprung up in Britain, America, Australia, and

New Zealand, with Catholicism as their defining characteristic. It became the Irish Catholic Diaspora. Priests and Religious followed to minister to their needs. All Hallows College, Dublin, was founded in 1842 to train priests for these "missions." Rome used the new political situation to break the Portuguese control over appointments of bishops in India by appointing priests from Maynooth as Apostolic Vicars to various sees there.

In Ireland itself, Catholicism was profoundly changed after the Great Famine, initially by the displacement of large sections of the population. This upheaval was compounded by the loss of their language by those who previously had spoken Irish and now spoke an impoverished English. The Irish language was the last living contact with the autochthonous, medieval Catholic tradition. Faced with a dispirited people, Cardinal Cullen, Archbishop of Dublin, introduced reforms that in fact amounted to what the historian Emmet Larkin has called a "devotional revolution," which radically marked the practice of the faith. In the towns in particular, the ethos of Victorian Puritanism (based on the notion of respectability) became the measure by which Catholics were measured – and measured themselves. The increasingly rigorist legalism of Catholic moral theology, with its emphasis on sin, especially sexual sin, played its role, as did the economic situation that discouraged marriage. Parish missions and popular devotions, mainly of French or Italian origin, revived personal piety, but also produced an emotionally charged, non-intellectual Church, while the increasingly centralized organization of the Church favored an authoritarian one.

More positively, the devotional revolution did produce a striking growth in vocations, in particular to the overseas missions, the territory of which was as extensive as the British Empire. Early in the twentieth century, two indigenous missionary congregations, one to China and one to Africa, were founded from Maynooth, in addition to the many continental missionary congregations which attracted thousands of vocations to the overseas missions. The strength and influence of Irish Catholicism was noted at the First Vatican Council, where bishops of Irish origin or background played a leading role.

The public standing of the Catholic Church in Ireland was to a great extent due to the close identity of Catholic Church and nationalist cause since the time of Daniel O'Connell. It increased enormously with political independence from the UK in 1922, and remained so until shortly after the Second Vatican Council's reforms began to be felt in Ireland. Though largely unprepared for the reforms, the Irish Church obediently implemented them all according to the letter, if not the spirit, of the law. But the canker of doubt had entered what had been a very self-satisfied, indeed successful, Church. Increasing material prosperity and, inspired by Vatican II, a more vocal lay voice – at times more educated than the clerics – began a process of criticism of traditional Irish Catholicism, which ended in disillusion and weakened the convictions of many. The civil war in the North gave a bad name to both the terms "Irish" and "Catholic." To counter claims by Northern Protestants that the Republic of Ireland was a "sectarian" state, a referendum was held on December 7, 1972 to delete the (in fact, innocuous) article from the 1937 Constitution, which recognized the special status of the Catholic Church as the Church of the majority. Supported by the Irish hierarchy, the amendment was approved by 84.4 percent of those who voted (50.7 percent of the electorate).

From 1968 onwards, Ireland was overwhelmed by two developments it was ill prepared to counter: modernity's intellectual scepticism and an unprecedented surge in
prosperity that produced the Celtic tiger, making Ireland one of the richest countries
in the world. Catholic Ireland had become publicly secular.

1968 was also the year *Humanae Vitae* was published. It was effectively rejected in
theory by theologians and ignored in practice by laity. Mass attendance began to fall,
as did vocations, at first slowly but more recently quite dramatically. Having been too
subservient to the bishops after Independence, a reaction set in and politicians began
to assert their autonomy. The once-sympathetic media became increasingly hostile,
leading to the effective privatization of the Church in recent decades and the imposition on the country of the so-called "liberal" moral agenda by a vocal minority.
Shocking revelations in the media of child abuse in institutions run by religious brothers and sisters, and then a whole spate of clerical sexual scandals all took their toll.
The inadequate response by the bishops to the scandals, together with their own low
profile in the media, have helped to undermine their credibility and so their authority.

And yet, Church practice, measured in term of Sunday Mass attendance, remains
among the highest in the world, as is the ratio of priest to people. Irish missionaries abroad are still relatively numerous, while the missionary spirit has, to a certain
extent, been channelled into NGOs like Trócaire, Concern, and Goal, which are among
the biggest aid and development organizations in the world. Vocations to the priesthood seem to be again on the increase. New youth movements with great vitality are
beginning to appear. Study of theology at university level is now possible for laity, and
courses are well subscribed, with not a few lay professional theologians teaching for
the first time. Prayer groups and Bible study groups have multiplied. In many parishes, lay involvement in parish life has increased and lay ministries have become the
norm. Lay chaplains are found in hospitals and schools. Immigration into Ireland is a
recent phenomenon; a large percentage from Eastern Europe and Africa are Catholic.
How they will integrate and affect Irish Catholicism is an open question. The increasingly fragile nature of society and traditional communities, as well as increased crime,
drugs, excessive drinking, and suicide rates have prompted many thinking people,
otherwise sceptical of religion, to recognize the danger to Irish society, if the Catholic
Church does not renew itself today as it did in the past.

Recent scandals have made it clear that a new reform of the Irish Catholic Church is
urgently needed at the spiritual/theological level and at the structural/pastoral level.

References and Further Reading

Bieler, Ludwig (1966) *Ireland: Harbinger of the Middle Ages*. Oxford: Oxford University Press.
Bossy, John (1975) *The English Catholic Community, 1570–1850*. London: Darton, Longman, and
    Todd.
Bradshaw, Brendan and Keogh, Daire (eds.) (2002) *Christianity in Ireland: Revisiting the Story*.
    Dublin: The Columba Press.
Corish, Patrick J. (1985) *The Irish Catholic Experience: A Historical Survey*. Dublin: Gill and
    Macmillan.
Corish, Patrick J. and Millett, Benignus OFM (2005) *The Irish Martyrs*. Dublin: Four Courts Press.

Duffy, Eamon (1992) *The Stripping of the Altars: Traditional Religion in England, 1400–1580.* New Haven, CT: Yale University Press.

Fallon, Brian (1998) *An Age of Innocence: Irish Culture 1930–1960.* Dublin, New York: St Martin's Press.

Fuller, Louise (2002) *Irish Catholicism since 1950: The Undoing of a Culture.* Dublin: Gill and Macmillan.

Ker, Ian T. (2003) *The Catholic Revival in English Literature, 1845–1961: Newman, Hopkins, Belloc, Chesterton, Greene, Waugh.* Leominster: Gracewing.

Johnson, C. (1983) *Developments in the Roman Catholic Church in Scotland 1789–1829.* Edinburgh: John Donald Publishers Ltd.

McRoberts, D. (ed.) (1962) *Essays on the Scottish Reformation 1513–1625.* Glasgow: John S. Burns and Sons.

McRoberts, D. (ed.) (1979) *Modern Scottish Catholicism 1878–1978.* Glasgow: John S. Burns and Sons.

Moody, T.W. and Martin, F.X. (eds.) (1967) *The Course of Irish History.* Cork: Mercier Press.

Stanford, Peter (1993) *Cardinal Hume and the Changing Face of English Catholicism.* London: Geoffrey Chapman.

Twomey, D. Vincent SVD (2003) *The End of Irish Catholicism?* Dublin: Veritas Publications.

CHAPTER 12
Latin America

Angel F. Méndez Montoya

At the beginning of the second millennium, half of the Latin American population still suffer from poverty, and a quarter live in extreme poverty. Racism, sexism, and classism abound. Amerindians, blacks, women, and the poor are systematically marginalized. The vast majority (about 88.8 percent) is Catholic, followed by other Christian denominations. The number of Catholics, however, is waning, whereas Protestants and Muslims are on the increase. Hinduism, Buddhism, Jewish, and indigenous religions are also practiced.

What do these aspects of the Latin American reality mean to Catholicism, particularly to Latin American Catholicism? How can the Latin American Church preach today a truly redeeming and fully liberating message with self-integrity in word and action? To answer these questions one first needs to address the many narratives of an itinerant church that has been giving shape to the Latin American reality for over 500 years. One of these narratives recalls that the origins of Latin America were neither Catholic nor European. European Christianity arrived in Latin America in 1492, when Christopher Columbus first set foot on these lands. Since then, Latin American Catholicism has become a "contradictory sign of hope and oppression" – as expressed in the Fourth General Conference of Latin American Bishops in Santo Domingo (October 1992). In 1989, the Pontifical Commission for Justice and Peace had already acknowledged European domination and destruction in *The Church and Racism*:

> The first great wave of European colonization was indeed accompanied by a massive destruction of the pre-Colombian civilizations and a brutal subjugation of their populations . . . Soldiers and traders killed to establish themselves; in order to profit from the labour of the indigenous population and later, of the blacks, reducing them to slavery. (Boff, 1990: 133)

More than 500 years later, the Latin American people still suffer the destructiveness of colonial power with which the Catholic Church often become complicit while embracing the Gospel's redeeming message. If the Catholic Church is truly committed to offer a salvific word through its own action (its own daily practice), Latin American Catholicism needs to heal the wounds left first by Spanish and Portuguese colonization and then by the neo-colonial US policies and global capital that continue to oppress Amerindians, blacks, *mestizos*, *mulattos*, and women throughout Latin America. More than ever, the Church must engage in a decolonizing prophetic project, a "new evangelization" that speaks of humanity's participation with a God that is true relationality (a communion that is unity in difference; a perpetual, ecstatic expression of reciprocal love).

To understand this new evangelization, as well as the development and meaning of Catholicism in Latin America, we must look at the historical trajectory of these contradictory signs of hope and oppression shaping Latin American Catholicism.[1] The Catholic Church in Latin America has often been complicit with oppression and destruction, but at the same time it has also been a prophetic voice, bringing the Latin American people and the entire Church signs of hope and liberation.

Impact of Colonial Christendom

In *Ecclesia in America*, John Paul II calls the Amerindian cultures the "seeds of the divine Word." However, few seeds remained after the dreadful discovery – in fact, *invasion* – of the Latin American lands and people.[2] With the arrival of the Europeans, cultures and powers collided, cosmologies clashed – specifically the Amerindian cosmologies were systematically obliterated.

Amerindian religiosity has been claimed to be essentially shamanistic and to have greatly influenced the everyday life of the Amerindian people (Schobinger, 1992). In this shamanistic world-view, spirits interact with the ordinary world. Liturgical rites were significant practices of communication (both in this life and with after-death life) with a myriad of deities and spirits (mainly of animal origin: bats, eagles, serpents, and jaguars). Religious symbolism, believed to be shaped by divine, cosmic, otherworldly powers, also permeated agriculture, social, and political life. Reciprocity and the recycling of gifts both within the community and between humanity and spirits were exercised through the communal practice of offering gifts and counter-gifts (Mauss, 1990). Gods and goddesses were fed – just as they were thought to first feed humanity – with a variety of offerings, including, in special Aztec rituals, the highly honored human blood and hearts (Carrasco, 1999). The Amerindian religion searched for intense religious/sacred experiences, often including "trance" states, and for supernatural, divinizing powers. These experiences were triggered by performing bodily rituals, ingesting psychotropic plants, and by individual and communal practices of feasting and fasting, travelling to "other" worlds or cosmic dimensions (like *Mictlan*, the Aztec underworld). The Amerindian cosmology was, indeed, a rich and sophisticated "seed of the divine Word," full of symbolism, and deeply oriented towards the sacred.

The Spaniards and the Portuguese found three major centres of political and religious power: the Mayans, the Aztecs, and the Incas. Great temples and cities had already been built in Peru (Chavín, Cuzco, Pachacámac, Kotosh, Sechín Alto and Cerro Sejín, Moche); Argentina (La Aguada); the Olmec region (San Lorenzo, Mexico);

the Mayan region (Tikal, Copán, Palenque, Uxmal, Chichén Itzá in Central America and Mexico); and the Toltec regions which later became the great Aztec Empire (Teotihuacán and Tenochtitlán, mainly in central Mexico). These cities were the centres of religious ceremonials, political activities, trade (*mercados*), and civil, religious, and military education. Integrative learning (integrating mind, body, spirit, and heart) played a high role in the shaping of these communities.

With the arrival of Christendom, the greatness and sophistication of these centers of power came under attack. Many cities were partially or totally destroyed. The Amerindian people were cruelly humiliated, tortured, killed, and the survivors who could not escape were imprisoned or enslaved. Women were often raped and killed by the conquistadores (Esquivel, 1990). In addition to the genocide, many fell ill and often died from epidemics brought by the Europeans. Boff and Elizondo thus illustrate the devastation the Aztecs suffered: "Of the 22 million Aztecs in 1519 when Hernán Cortéz entered Mexico only a million were left in 1600" (Boff and Elizondo, 1990: vii). The Aztec devastation was by no means an exception.

The entry of Catholicism into the so-called "New World" left profound wounds. The Mayan *Chilam Balam de Chumayel* avows: "Sadness was brought among us, Christianity was brought among us. This was the beginning of our distress, the beginning of slavery" (Boff and Elizondo, 1990: vii). The sign of the cross that the first missionaries brought to the Americas became the mark of the "crucified people" (Ellacurría, 1989), who at first were Amerindians, but later included African slaves. More than 500 years later, the crucified people are still poor and outcast and include indigenous people and a great number of African descent.

From the perspective of the invaders, the Catholicism brought to the New World was the result of a long historical project of expanding Western Christendom which, by the late fifteenth century, reached a peak particularly with the strengthening of, and the recentring of Western power around the Spanish-Portuguese empires. This project, linked with mercantile capitalism and the legalization of "massive exploitation of labour to produce commodities for a newly global market" (Mignolo, 2005: 30) was achieved by taking over lands, and imposing a "universal" history of salvation under one religion. Although gold and silver were among the primary goods that the Europeans lusted for, their insatiable craving for spices was "even greater than their greed for gold" (Armelagos, 2003: 108). Whether it was gold, silver, or spices, the European greed justified expansion and created a colonial system that exploited the Latin American lands, cultures, and peoples.

By the late 1500s, the Church had allied, and even identified with the State. It often approved of the mercantilist zeal – slavery included – and joined the twofold project of evangelizing and "civilizing" a world beyond the Western borders. The Church granted legal powers to the Spanish-Portuguese crowns, allowing the monarchs to appoint bishops over the Latin American lands. The Church also accepted that the Spanish-Portuguese crowns create a system called *encomiendas* that granted the conquerors' property rights and total management – including the ownership over Amerindian slaves – over the conquered lands. With the rapid increase of epidemic illnesses and deaths, African slaves were brought to Latin America to labor in the new export-oriented plantations and mines. The weakening of the Church vis-à-vis these unjust moves granted the Crown more power over the Church. The Catholic Church often became complicit in the atrocities committed in this New World. To the eyes of many Amerindians and African slaves, the Church was part of the same dark power, the *encomenderos* and slave owners.

The dark origins of Latin American Catholicism coexist with seeds of light, hope, and liberation. By 1524, more systematic evangelization in Latin America was brought forth by Franciscans friars, followed by Dominicans, Augustinians, and later Jesuits. New dioceses and archdioceses were formed, and the Catholic Church started to spread. Many friars learned native languages, studied their narratives, symbols and rituals, translated the Bible and catechism, and taught European languages to the Amerindians and Africans. Some Dominican friars (like Antonio de Montesinos, Francisco de Vitoria, and Bartolomé de las Casas) became strong defenders of the Amerindians, and consistently denounced the cruelties and injustice committed against the people – God's children – to both civil and ecclesial authorities.

In this New World, Catholic theology faced new questions regarding the methods, principles, and techniques for spreading Christianity in a non-Western world. At this point in the history of Western Christian thought (the so-called beginnings of "Modernity"), the nature/supernatural, body/soul, immanence/transcendence divide suffered a greater division – even antagonism – than that of the Middle Ages that emphasized the notion of participation and co-arising of parts, a more dynamic understanding of individuality and difference as being mutually constitutive (Milbank and Pickstock, 2001). But the early modern Western colonial construction of such a strong divide became the main justification for the exploitation of Amerindians and Africans who were considered soulless "barbarians" on the other side of "civilization" (that sphere of the "natural" world that is to be dominated and eventually civilized). Preaching the Gospel requires facing these questions, and many missionaries and theologians started to articulate a vision of the Church that recognized the dignity of every single child of God, and demanded respect for all cultures and lands. These exemplary missionaries and theologians often risked their reputations, and became target of heavy criticism by Europeans within the Church and the State. At times, many of them were removed from their missions (a tendency that increased with the expulsion of the Jesuit order during the Enlightenment period), and some even met death because of their alliance to the disposed people. Thus, at the same time as a colonial and oppressive Church was imposed upon the Latin American people, a new Church integrated the new voice of the new races, *mestizaje* (the racial interbreeding of European and Amerindians) and *mulataje* (of African descent and interbreeding): a voice committed to dialog and reciprocal exchange, a voice of liberation for the voiceless. This prophetic voice was first pronounced in Latin America by the Dominican Fray Antonio de Montesinos, who in his 1511 sermon, used the same words as John the Baptist: "the voice of one crying in the wilderness" (Matt 3:3).

Wilderness they did find. This prophetic voice was difficult to hear, particularly with the deeply hierarchical colonial social structure. Europeans and *criollos* (Europeans born in Latin America) were at the top, enjoying many privileges and honors – most clerics belonged to this class. *Mestizos*, *mulattos*, blacks, and indigenous people were at the bottom and considered "inferior" soulless beings. Social class was habitually equated with skin color and ethnic background, for which people suffered violent discrimination. The more clearly someone was set at the bottom of this social class pyramid, the less likely he was to join a religious order or, even less so, to become a priest. Although there are cases of saints during the colonial times who eventually became canonized despite being considered of an "inferior" cast or race, many suffered great harassment and discrimination (like the *mulatto* St Martin de Porres in Peru, 1579–1639).

However, much fertility and superabundance were also found. Another interesting aspect of Catholicism during the colonial times is that religious experience and practices gradually became more intertwined, more hybridized with Amerindian religiosity. Because of the Amerindian deep sense of sacredness contained in their rituals and symbols, Catholicism fused with the Amerindian religions. Spanish-Portuguese Catholicism in those days was also full of rituals, processions, sacramental celebrations, popular feasts, and devotions – religious expressions that found fertile ground in Latin American lands. Catholic churches were often erected on ancient sacred sites. Pre-Hispanic deities were "baptized," while Christian symbols echoed Amerindian ones. Originality and creativity of expression from both Catholic and Amerindian cosmologies started to fuse with each other, not without clashing and destruction (particularly of Amerindian and African contents). Religious syncretism became inevitable and even innovating (Marzal, 1992). The apparition of Our Lady of Guadalupe (whom Pope John Paul II called the "Mother of America" in *Ecclesia in America*, 1999: 11) is an example of this new hybrid *mestizo* Catholicism. She appeared in 1531 as a dark-skinned Amerindian woman speaking Náhuatl to the Amerindian Juan Diego on the hill of Tepeyac (a site formerly devoted to *Coatlicue*, the Aztec "venerable mother"). This hybrid religion was perhaps better captured during the colonial baroque period, which US Latino theologian Roberto Goizueta characterizes as a "sensually rich" expression deeply embodying divine nearness (Goizueta, 2004). In this organic, embodied, and symbolic religious world, intellect and affectivity, rationality and sensuality, the human and the divine were intimately connected.

The Neo-Colonial Period and the Struggles for Emancipation

The direct Spanish-Portuguese power over the Latin American lands and people eventually weakened. Dussel points out that after the colonial hegemony of Spain and Portugal, Latin America entered a further neo-colonial period (from 1807 to the present) with a major "dependency on Anglo-Saxon industrial capitalism, first English and then North American" (Dussel, 1992: 9). However, influenced by the principles of the Enlightenment and the French Revolution, movements of independence and emancipation emerged in which, at times, Church leaders – clerics, religious and lay men and women – inspired and supported the people. Some clergymen were not only decisive in animating these movements, but also, as Bidegain notes, "there were even army engineers among them [clergy], such as Friar Luis Beltrán, who melted down convent bells to make cannons for the liberating army of San Martín which set Chile and Peru free" (Bidegain, 1992: 94). Some priests took up arms (like Frs Hidalgo and Morelos in Mexico). In the first half of this neo-colonial period, the Church witnessed a series of independence movements in most Latin American countries starting from River Plate, then New Granada, followed by Argentina, Chile, Peru, Venezuela, Colombia, Ecuador, Bolivia, and finally Mexico and Central America. Brazil's emancipation came later (1899). The process of independence in the Caribbean was more complex. Countries such as Haiti gained independence very early in the nineteenth century (in fact, Haiti was the first colony to achieve independence in Latin America; and was also the strengthening site for the great liberator Simón Bolívar), while others still depend on other countries, like Puerto Rico, now under US control, and other Caribbean islands still under English, French or Dutch rule.

While these independent movements favored the Latin American people's independence from direct European rule, many independence movements created a deeper division between the Church and the State, which weakened the Church's political and economic power to the point that the State would often claim patronage over the Church. Religious persecution against those who did not conform to the new rules led to the closure of churches, seminaries, and libraries. The gap between the members of the Church loyal to the European monarchy, and those favoring independence, freedom, and democracy widened. Most Dominicans and Jesuits were among the latter and continued teaching these principles in their new universities in Latin America. This created a sense of ambiguity regarding the position of the Church and its involvement in political decisions, and its alliance either to royal authorities or to the independence struggle. Despite persecution and division, in some Latin American countries, Catholicism became more identified with the people's struggle for emancipation. During this process of Latin American independence, theology experienced a further turn which envisioned salvation history as a continuum, taking place within the historical context of struggle for worldly emancipation: as a sort of "holy war," in which even the Virgin Mary (often Our Lady of Guadalupe on Tepeyac) was the main protector siding with emancipation and independence (Bidegain, 1992: 95).

The movements of independence and the creation of nation states also coincided with the violent annexing of Mexican lands to US territory (a result of US Western expansion). By 1848, Texas, New Mexico, Arizona and California had become part of US territory, and thus created a new class of Latino men and women, often called "chicanos," and a "Hispanic" or "Latino" Church. Dussel notes that this community in the US was "dominated by Anglo-American Catholicism: French and English-speaking bishops were appointed, Mexican priests were excommunicated, and it was not allowed to express itself through its own language or culture until the late 1960s" (Dussel, 1992: 11). The history of Latinos in the US reflects the same colonial and neo-colonial oppression that Latin Americans have suffered in their own countries (Sandoval, 1992).

Despite these movements of independence and the creation of nationhood that attempted to move beyond the predominant colonial hegemony, Latin America continued under the dominion of neo-colonial economic powers (Dutch, German, and French, but predominantly British and increasingly US hegemony). Between 1880 and 1930, Latin America experienced complex changes that impacted on the social, economic, political, and religious structures. Beozzo thus summarizes some of the economic changes:

The half-century 1880–1930 incorporated the whole of Latin America and the Caribbean, sometimes silently, but more often violently, into the changing market. The
connections were made through the new transport and communication system, steam-
ships, railways, cars, and lorries, telegraph, press and, in the 1920s, radio; through
new technology, steam-powered machines and electricity and internal combus-
tion engines; through the region's agricultural goods, such as cotton, cocoa, tobacco,
coffee, sisal, wheat, or animal goods, especially wool and beef, extractive goods, such
as guano and rubber or minerals, saltpetre, copper, iron, silver, oil; through its labour
relations, in the replacement of slaves or tenant farmers and share-croppers by rural
and urban wage-earners; in the diversification of classes, in the make-up of the population, as the import of African slaves was ended and was replaced by "indentured
servants" brought from India by the English and from Indonesia by the Dutch, or by
colonists and immigrant workers from Europe, the Middle East, China and Japan.
(Beozzo, 1992: 117)

After the success of the British Industrial Revolution that started to take control over
the world market, increasing its capital at the expense of Latin American soil, animal
goods, and labour, the US increased its economic and political power and control over
the continent – mostly after World War I and the systematic application of the Monroe
doctrine: "America for the Americans."

The creation of a new sense of nationhood led the Latin American Church to a deeper
questioning of identity, particularly the relationship between national and ecclesial
identity. By the end of the nineteenth century, Latin American Catholicism explored the
practice of ecclesial locality more in depth. Since national identity could imply a less
"Roman" Church, there was often a struggle to define the meaning of the Catholicity of the Church by opting for the predominance of either locality or universality. A
more conservative part of the Church and the higher ecclesiastical authorities usually
identified with the ruling classes (the rich, white Europeans, and *criollos*); and these
sectors within the Church usually favored the "Romanization" of the Church: i.e., a
more universalizing Christendom often suspicious and critical of local and popular
religious expressions. But at the same time, there were also exceptional cases of parish
priests, and religious and lay men and women who accompanied the forgotten people
– the poor, women, children, Amerindians, blacks, and *mulattos* – and thus identified
with a local Church while supporting and promoting popular religious symbolisms
and rituals (Dussel, 1992: 105–16). This sense of national identity and locality also
meant a questioning of the relationship between the secular and the ecclesial spheres.
During the early development of nationhood, a greater ambiguity arose between the
new secularity that the State enjoyed. The emergent separation of state and Church
created a clash between the secular/civil world and the ecclesial vision of society and
politics.

Between the late nineteenth century and the early twentieth century, liberal ideology in Latin America mixed Enlightenment, positivist, and socialist ideals with political
and philosophical theories taken from the French Revolution and the increasing blending of US capitalism with Protestantism. Again, the Church was divided between this
new liberal commitment to "civilizing" "Europeanizing" sectors and the "barbarian,"
lower-level sectors (Amerindians, African, and *mestizo/mulatto* groups). Liberal states

also legislated freedom of religion, often taken as an opportunity for the US to introduce capitalist ideals and for the immigration of US Protestants and European Anglicans, Lutherans, and Calvinists. The harder oppression towards the marginalized sectors often triggered resistance movements (even armed revolts) against the enforcement of this "civilizing" agenda. In the early twentieth century, countries like Mexico, Brazil, Argentina, and Chile experienced bloody conflicts, revolutions and revolts, particularly in rural areas. Many liberal governments expressed an anti-clerical zeal, expropriating Church property, and expelling many clerics and religious orders, thus creating a rift between Church and State.

Rome reacted against liberalism with the 1864 *Syllabus of Errors* by Pius IX and the First Vatican Council (1869–70) in which 42 Latin American bishops participated for the first time ever. The efforts to "Romanize" and "Europeanize" Latin American Catholicism were re-enforced by the foundation by Pius IX of the Colegio Pio Latino-Americano in Rome in 1859, which became a primary centre of doctrinal (Roman-Latin) education for future ecclesial authorities in Latin America. The Latin American Plenary Council, called by Leo XIII in 1899 was another effort to implement an agenda entirely centered in and controlled by Rome, as a systematic move to Europeanize Latin America and overcome the "evils" of modernity and liberalism. This strongly Roman and European Church aimed to reach out to all social sectors, but it became most effective among the upper class and the new European and Asian immigrants. By the early twentieth century, Latin American Catholicism was a more "introspective" religion, prioritizing personal salvation and devotional and sacramental practices (especially baptism, the Eucharist, and matrimony) over social transformation.

The Church's promotion of a more introspective and cultic religion was about to experience a crisis. The results of two world wars strengthened the British economic and political power, soon taken over by the US. At the same time, "the Russian Revolution (and the Mexican Revolution of 1910) raised the spectre of communism in the organs of the Roman Church" (Dussel, 1992: 139). A strong anti-Communist ideology spread among many Church authorities. Fascist regimes were also rising (mainly Germany, Japan, and Italy). Under Pius XI (1922–39) and Pius XII (1939–58), the Church adopted a more public voice, eventually raising questions around national and international politics, economics, and social justice in the light of an ecclesial vision. During his papacy, Pius XI wrote three important documents presenting an official ecclesial stance regarding the new world realities: *Quadragesimo Anno*, strongly criticising socialism; *Mit Brennender Sorge*, condemning Nazism; and *Divini Redemptoris*, setting "limits to socialism" (Dussel, 1992: 139). His successor, Pius XII, was committed to a "New Christendom" program. Keen on organizing Church congresses, he also promoted the ecclesial dimension of "social action" in *Quadragesimo Anno*. This ecclesial stance impacted on the new "populist" regimes in Latin America: Eucharistic and "Christ the King" congresses were held in many Latin American countries. Catholic social action and an emphasis on pastoral practice inspired many in the Latin American Church, particularly among the laity. The theological positions of Blondel and Maritain influenced the intellectual configuration of the New Christendom Church in Latin America. Student movements, intellectual leadership, Catholic universities, philosophical and theological journals flourished throughout the continent:

Jackson de Figueiredo and Tristão de Atayde (Amoroso Lima) in Brazil, José Vasconcelos and Antonio Caso in Mexico, and Victor Andrés Balaunde. Students formed movements: the first Ibero American Congress of Catholic Students was held in Rome in 1933, the second in Lima in 1938 and the third in Bogotá in 1944. Catholic universities multiplied . . . Major philosophical and theological reviews . . . underpinned the intellectual renewal of the new generation. In 1959, the Jesuit Juan Luis Segundo studied *The Function of the Church in the Conditions of the River Plate Area*, published in Montevideo in 1962, marking the start of contemporary Latin American theology, based on observation and analysis of current conditions. (Dussel, 1992: 142)

During this period many conferences of bishops were held both nationally and internationally (within Latin America); Dom Helder Camara with Manuel Larraín greatly influenced these official gatherings. CELAM (the Episcopal Council of Latin America) was founded at the First Conference of the Latin American Episcopate held in Rio de Janeiro in 1955.

These slow changes created a broader understanding of what it was to be *ecclesia* in Latin America: a Church deeply rooted in the historical (spiritual and material) transformation of society. Pope John XXIII, elected in 1958, was committed to continue with this renewal. He wrote "the encyclicals *Mater et Magistra* (1961) and *Pacem in Terris* (1963), which encouraged the process of renewed political commitment in Latin America. The Pope himself spoke of a 'Church of the poor'" (Dussel, 1992: 153). The election of John XXIII also coincided with the triumph of Fidel Castro in Cuba. The fear Church authorities felt vis-à-vis the potential spread of Communism was accompanied by a criticism of the rapid spread of capitalism and the greater dependence of poor countries on capitalist firms. The successor of John XXIII, Paul VI (1963–78), published his *Populorum Progressio*, denouncing the "international imperialism of money" (Dussel, 1992: 153).

Latin American Catholicism in the Post-Vatican II Period

The Second Vatican Council in 1962, attended by 601 Latin American bishops, is perhaps one of the most important contributions to the Church of the twentieth century, and particularly to the Latin American Church. Dussel thus expresses the Council's impact on the shaping of the Latin American Church:

The change was felt first by several minority but prophetic bodies. The first significant encounter was the Meeting of Latin American Bishops in Baños in Ecuador in June 1966, with those responsible for the commissions on education, the lay apostolate, social policy and general pastoral practice. Then came the Tenth CELAM Assembly in Mar del Plata on "The role of the Church in the development and integration in Latin America," in October the same year – which the dictatorial government of Onganía prevented Helder Camara from attending. There followed the University Pastoral Encounter in Buga in Colombia in 1967, which proposed reform of Catholic universities and opened the way for a major restructuring of important intellectual centres (leading to strikes, sit-ins and student demonstrations in Chile and other countries). Then theological seminaries were reformed after the Vocations Encounter in Lima in 1967; the indigenous question entered the Church's consciousness with the First Pastoral Encounter of Indigenous Missions in 1968; social policy was examined in Brazil in May 1968. All this prepared the ground for the central event in the Latin American Church in the twentieth century: the Second General Conference of the Latin American Episcopate in Medellín, on the theme of "The Church in the Present-day Transformation of Latin America." (Dussel, 1992: 154)

The *comunidades de base* ("grassroots church communities") were perhaps the most important Church-related popular movements created in Latin America. They aimed at a greater integral practice of becoming ecclesia, "the People of God" as defined in *Lumen Gentium*. Mainly inspired in Paulo Freire's work, new pedagogical methods were developed for a catechesis rooted in faith grassroots communities, reciprocal learning, integrative of the whole spectrum of the human learning experience: affectivity, embodiment, intellect, including the social, spiritual, and cultural dimension of personhood. Boff describes and comments on these grassroots church communities as follows:

> Connected with each other, and with the presence of priests, religious leaders and bishops who take part in their journey, they form the popular church, the church of the poor, with a particular style of living faith, distributing sacral power among their members, organizing the celebrations of the sacraments and the struggles of the community. This model of the Church makes it possible for women to exercise leadership, and is not felt as a break but as a communion with the model of the Church which comes from tradition and persists today. We cannot say what the future of this type of communitarian Christianity will be, but it represents the expression of Christianity appropriate to the new culture emerging in the continent, a Christianity which is ecumenical, democratic, militant in the struggle for a new society, that incorporates the feminine dimension and is in communion with other historical forms of Christianity. (Boff, 1992: 137)

Latin American Catholicism entered a new phase that promoted and engaged in popular culture and religion, greater awareness of the past (including the Amerindian past), political analysis and involvement, and the commitment to the exploited, the poor and the marginalized in our midst.

"Liberation theology" emerged out of these new practices and reflections (around 1968) – mainly in the earlier works of Gustavo Gutierrez, Juan Luis Segundo, Richard Schaull, Hugo Assmann, and Ruben Alves that greatly influenced the shaping of the Latin American Church as well as post-Vatican II theological and ecclesial thinking. From its foundations, liberation theology articulated a trajectory that read salvation history from the specificity of the experience of the marginalized and the victims with whom Christ identified on the Cross. Ellacuría articulates the event of the Cross as pointing to a twofold movement: the passion of Jesus as seen from the perspective of the crucified people, and the crucifixion of the people as seen from the perspective of the death of Jesus (see Ellacurría, 1998). Resurrection for both Jesus Christ and the "crucified people" is a sign of God's solidarity with his suffering son, and hope for those who suffer: a solidarity and hope that, while being open to a future eschatological promise, it is to be incarnated in the everyday life of the itinerant Church guided by the Holy Spirit. To speak of liberation in these terms is thus to integrate not only a transhistorical and transcendental element of emancipation into the horizon of faith, but also to materialize Christ's solidarity within the historical physical reality of people's lives. Liberation theology thus emphasizes the trajectory of the "practice" of God's kingdom enacted in mutuality and solidarity particularly toward those in most need. Because of this commitment to situatedness, liberation theology also focuses on popular religious expressions from "the bottom," the life of the community at a grassroots level. Liberation theology has particularly inspired Third World, Southern Cone, and Border Thinking theologies that are particularly engaged with the struggle for spiritual and material liberation for everyone with a preferential option for the poor and marginalized. This is also why liberation theology has directly and/or indirectly inspired new developments of theological thinking such as feminist, *mujerista*, Latino, black, gay/lesbian and "queer," indigenous, popular, and ecological theologies.

This Church renewal with its new and greater awareness of becoming a "prophetic voice" soon met harsh criticism and rejection. Not surprisingly, the most critical voices against this engagement with God's people were the "traditionalist" and privileged sectors within the Church. Strongly opposing this liberationist and "progressive" Church, some bishops tried to obstruct – if not end – these movements and forms of thinking. Priests, religious and lay men and women were often harassed, and even excommunicated because of their "radical option for the poor." The Church in Cuba under Fidel Castro, and in Chile during its "developmentist" period (1959–68), also suffered harsh criticisms from members of the Church hierarchy. Church members were split between those for and those against reform and revolution. Tension emerged between those committed to the popular classes and to social, political, and economic transformation and those committed to the ruling classes often aloof to these issues.

This tension intensified as the political arena in many Latin American countries experienced the painful wounds of violent dictatorial regimes (particularly between 1969 and 1976) that coincided with the strong "U.S. presidencies of Richard Nixon (1969–74) and Gerald Ford (1974–7), with the State Department in the hands of Henry Kissinger," during which "Latin America underwent a reign of terror" (Dussel, 1992: 165):

> Dependent capitalism cannot function without repressing the people: this was recognized in the anti-insurrectional, National Security regime model proposed by Kissinger to Presidents Nixon and Ford. Key dates for the installation of such regimes are: 31 May 1964, *coup d'état* by Castelo Branco in Brazil; 21 August 1971, by Hugo Banzer in Bolivia; 27 June 1973, dissolution of the Congress in Uruguay; 11 September 1973, military coup by Augusto Pinochet in Chile; 28 August 1975, by F. Morales Bermúdez in Peru; 13 January 1976, by G. Rodríguez Lara in Ecuador; 24 March 1976, by Jorge Videla in Argentina. (Dussel, 1992: 167)

A later period of US repression over Latin American countries came under Reagan (1981–9), Bush (1989–93), and Bush Jr. (2000–). People within the Church actively involved and committed to liberation were often repressed, persecuted, imprisoned, tortured, and even assassinated. The Latin American Church witnessed the martyrdom of many priests and bishops, such as Fr Antonio Herique Pereira Neto (1969), Fr Rodolfo Lunkenbein, and Fr João Bosco Penido Burnier (1976) in Brazil; Fr Héctor

Gallegos (1971) in Panama; Fr Arthur Mckinnon in Santo Domingo; Bishop Enrique Angelelli (1976), and Fr Carlos Mugica (1974) in Argentina; Fr Adolfo Aguilar (1977) in Mexico; Fr Nicolás Rodriguez (1970), Bishop Oscar Romero (1980), Fr Rutilio Grande (1977), Fr Alfonso Navarro (1977), Fr Barrera Motto (1978), Fr Octavio Ortiz (1979), Ignacio Ellacurría (1989) in El Salvador; and Fr Augusto Ramírez (1983) in Guatemala. Many others *desaparecidos* ("missing people") were never found. Religious and lay men and women were also tortured and martyred.

While some Church authorities remained indifferent to these cruelties – even criticizing the more progressive and socially active groups – different church members came up with a strong prophetic denouncing voice, like Mgr Romero, martyred in El Salvador, who had the courage to identify and give voice to the voiceless and to confront an unfair system, together with many bishops in Latin America who collaborated with the people. The Latin American Episcopal body issued documents such as those in Rio de Janeiro (1955), Medellín (1968), Puebla (1979), and Santo Domingo (1992) where the bishops gathered together to attend to most urgent pastoral matters, unanimously condemned the injustice and violence of dictatorial regimes and extreme poverty, speaking of a new evangelization mission urging conversion from both personal and social/institutional sin, and calling for a radical alliance to the Church of the Poor. Demonstrations, social movements, writings, and liturgies were also public manifestations against these oppressive evils. John Paul II's visit to Mexico (1979) and his encyclical *Laborem Excercens* (1981) were also signs of hope and encouragement to those in favor of social action – yet in his visit to Nicaragua in 1984, he was critical of Nicaragua's revolutionary process and of some aspects and thinkers within liberation theology (as with Leonardo Boff). Despite these ambiguities, the Latin American Church was identified with an earlier period of persecution. Even more radically so, they identified with the crucified Christ, and envisioned God's solidarity with the suffering Christ – manifested at the resurrection – as the Church's vocation to identify with those who most suffer and look for the risen Lord.

Dussel refers to the period from 1984 to 1992 as the "opening to democracy" (Dussel, 1992: 177–81) during which democratic governments gradually overcame dictatorial regimes. At the beginning of the second millennium, Latin America continues to struggle for a process and understanding of democratization, a challenge still to be faced. Some Latin American countries – like Mexico – have yet to overcome the corrupt political systems that hinder the opening to democracy. The people's political awareness of the need for more involvement in the political shaping of their countries must also be raised. Democracy in Latin America is at times closely "guided" and controlled by the interests of national and transnational capital, without much concern for the improvement of society at large, and even less so, for the poorest sectors. This attitude widens the gap between the rich and the poor, the privileged and the unprivileged. A few countries (Argentina, Brazil, Uruguay, and Venezuela) are moving towards a "left-oriented," participatory socialist-democratic vision. In my opinion, this tendency seems more attuned to the Gospel values since it promotes and celebrates diversity in the community, favors development with equal opportunities and benefits for everyone, and has a vision of social change founded upon the common good and respect for the dignity of every human being. Capitalism in Latin America, as currently orchestrated by the US, continues to fail to meet the needs and vision of an inclusive society. Corrupt administrative and political systems united with capitalist interests have also left some countries under the fear and burden of potentially being in a state of perpetual foreign debt (*Ecclesia in America*: 22 and 23). Global capitalism makes Latin American soil and labour a commodity to meet the needs of a few (*Ecclesia in America*: 20). With the rapid spread of the US global empire, and the more aggressive and unilateral international policies enforced by US president George Bush Jr., Latin America is struggling against the burden of neo-colonial hegemony. For Latin American Catholicism, these times require joining forces for a shared project that no longer ignores the great diversity of this continent, but embraces diversity thus enriching, transforming, divinizing the Church with these "seeds of divine Word."

Conclusion

Latin American Catholicism still needs to heal its colonial and neo-colonial wounds and, in doing so, envision and engage in a decolonizing process that preserves the integrity of the Gospel values: committing to intra-cultural dialog, mutual service and reciprocity, and greater inclusion of Amerindians, Afro-Latinos, women, and all those on the margins of society (Mignolo, 2005). The Church must face this challenge to self-integrity. The Church at times has also been part and promoter of oppressive and coercive colonialism over Latin American lands and people. Guided by the Holy Spirit, may the Church embrace a spirit of *metanoia* (conversion) and thus empower the Latin American people to re-orient every community toward God and each other.

This challenge also includes the increasing voice of Latino men and women, currently the largest "ethnic minority" in the US (nearly 40 millions). The struggle of many Latinos in the US is also a source of inspiration for Latin American Catholicism to learn new strategies for decolonization and mutual empowerment. The Latino experience shows Latin American Catholicism that Latin America is not a homogeneous category (as has been systematically constructed under the European and the US hegemonies that homogeneously sets the continent on the "other" side of the dominating Western horizon). Latin America is quite diverse, full of particular narratives, localities, and forms of self-expression such as gender, sexual orientation, histories, cultures, traditions, symbols, popular expressions, languages, and ethnicities. By attending to the specific requirements of the Latino communities, Latinos are able to outline the ecclesial embodiment of creation's affinity with God and the call to solidarity with our sisters and brothers, particularly those who suffer in this world. This serious attention to people's lives, experiences, and everyday-life expressions is a starting point and theological source for Latinos both in Latin America and the US (Isasi-Díaz, 2002). This form of theologizing is not mere "internalizing." It is a theology that speaks at the platform of the public life and of coalition building (Valentin, 2002).

This decolonizing prophetic project, this "new evangelization," is rooted in Latin America's prophetic tradition, committed to reciprocal relationships that open up a space for the liberation of its people. With and beyond liberation, this new evangelization further envisions God's redemption as enabling agapic communities (Pope

Benedict XVI's first encyclical *Deus Caritas Est*), i.e., communities where love and charity, compassion and reconciliation, justice and peace, and mutual sharing are a daily practice. Yet, in Latin America, there is oppression and injustice, hunger and violence, particularly towards those who are voiceless and considered "objects" to be manipulated and exploited. Women and children are most vulnerable to the sinful agenda of an unhealthy patriarchal structure, often expressed through seriously damaging *machismo* (*Ecclesia in America*: 45).

From a Catholic perspective, a decolonizing project of this new evangelization should no longer treat God's children as objects of manipulation and exploitation. To God, they are not the "alien other," for they are *of* God, members of a divine community beyond strictly mapped borders (whether social, political, racial, ethnic, or gender). This new evangelization can re-envision and recapture the Church's intrinsic political dimension: a communal project that announces God's participation in the shaping of a perpetually new embodiment of a new *polis*: coalition-building and harmonious communities empowered with God's *caritas*. The source of this new *polis* is divine *caritas*, expressed with a radical gesture of *kenosis*, reciprocity, and concrete communal practices of love and justice, mutual healing, nurturing, and interdependence. God is relationality, a community of loving individuals: a harmonious relationship of unity-in-difference shared as love, exchange (receiving and returning the divine gift of love), and ecstatic celebration. The Church is a communal feast, a "sacrament of communion" that participates in this prior Trinitarian community (*Ecclesia in America*: 33). The project of theology and politics, both at once, relies on this Trinitarian community the Church is called to imitate. The Latin American Church may become a model of recapturing the political dimension of being ecclesia: the enactment of the politics of a relational God who is love and solidarity to all, and radically identifies with the hungry, the marginal, and the outcast (Matthew 25). Boff tells how this new evangelization is giving rise to a unique Christianity, bearing the stamp of ordinary people, brown, white, Latino, indigenous, and black, as one of the forces for social change that points the way to new Church structures (Boff, 1992: 130).

In order to heal the wounds of colonialism and neo-colonialism, the Latin American Church also needs to recover the ecological dimension of God's creative project. Forests and jungles, water and soil, animals and plants, deserts and mountains, are also God's self-expression. At the Eucharist, the natural elements of bread and wine become Christ's own body and blood shared by all, particularly those who most thirst and hunger. Yet, abuse and ecological damage are widespread in many regions (*Ecclesia in America*: 25). The massive exploitation of its natural resources (often driven by national and transnational interests) is leading Latin America towards great ecological perils that could create famine, drought, extreme climatic imbalance, and health-related problems. More than ever, the Latin American Church must heal the wounds of this sinful application of domination such as suppression and destruction. The Latin American Church must become truly Eucharistic – the communal practice that nourishes and deifies Creation at the breaking and sharing of bread, when the Church, with Creation, become the sacred body of Christ.

The Gospel is mediated by situatedness: the body, culture, language, and symbols. In a way, the Gospel is a "hybrid," the *logos* of God made one with humanity – the in-betweenness of humanity and God. The Latin American Church is a hybrid church: *mestiza* and *mulatta* with a rich liturgical tradition reminiscent of this in-betweenness, the communal aspect of the divine human feast of co-abiding. Liturgies, sacramental celebrations, rituals, and popular religious expressions should be promoted rather than suppressed, for they are expressions of the Catholicity of the Church that is between locality and universality, between Creation and its Creator. Since Catholicity implies diversity and specificity, the Church should also continue engaging in dialog and communal projects with the many Christian and non-Christian communities throughout the continent. This requires a welcoming spirit and the encouragement of the myriad religious expressions and sacred practices of Amerindians, blacks and *mulattos*, and other hybrid expressions (like *santeria*).

The renewal and self-integrity of Latin American Catholicism, in the continuous act of becoming prophetic, indeed faces numerous challenges. May the voice of the Lady of Guadalupe, the voice of the voiceless, assist the Church in facing current and future challenges. May the Mother of the Americas guide the Church's daily liturgical and public practices to become a prophetic, fully divinizing voice "a voice crying in the wilderness" – within Latin America and the entire Church.[3]

Notes

1   Latin America consists of 20 countries: Argentina, Belize, Bolivia, Brazil, Chile, Colombia, Costa Rica, Cuba, Dominican Republic, Ecuador, El Salvador, Guatemala, Honduras, Mexico, Nicaragua, Panama, Paraguay, Peru, Uruguay, Venezuela, two French dependencies: French Guiana Guadeloupe, and Martinique; and one US dependency: Puerto Rico. The total population is 541,331,000: 268,328,000 men, and 273,092,000 women; 157,329,000 are under 15 years of age, and 475,523,000 are over 60. About 25 percent of the population is white; 24 percent *mestizo* (a blending of Amerindian and European); 19 percent *mulatto* (a blending of black African and European or Amerindian); 14 percent Amerindian or native people; 9 percent white/*mestizo*; 8 percent black; and 1 percent Asian. Some of the spoken languages are: Spanish, Portuguese, French, Quechua, Aymara, Nahuatl, Mayan languages, Guaraní, Italian, English, German, Welsh, Dutch, and Haitian creole. About 230 million people (almost half of the population) suffer from poverty, and 100 million live in extreme poverty. There is racism, sexism, and classicism in Latin America. Mainly Amerindians, blacks, women, and the poor are target of systematic marginalization. The great majority (about 88.8 percent) is Catholic, followed by other Christian denominations. Although there is a majority of Catholics in Latin America, it is decreasing/waning, while some other Christians and Muslims are increasing. Hinduism, Buddhism, Jewish, and indigenous religions are also practiced in the continent.

This above data correspond to the year of 2005, and it is mainly taken from *Anuario 2005 Iberoamericano* (Madrid: Ediciones Pirámide, 2005), and from CEPAL (*Comisión Económica para América Latina y el Caribe* – Economic Commission for Latin America and the Caribbean, from the United Nations): www.cepal.org. Also from *America Latina XXI: Avanzará o Retrocederá la pobreza?* Fernando Solona (ed.) (Mexico: Fondo de Cultura Economica, 2002).

My particular historical reading of the history of the Church in Latin America is mainly inspired by the works of Enrique Dussel and others who work within CEHILA (the Commission for the Study of Church History in Latin America) (Dussel, 1992).

2   Dussel argues that what actually took place at the arrival of the *conquistadores* was not a "dis-

covery," as has been commonly understood, but rather a "covering up" (*encubrimiento*), owing to the systematic obliteration of native customs, belief systems, and lives. See Enrique Dussel, *The Invention of the Americas: Eclipse of "The Other" and the Myth of Modernity*, trans. Michael Barber (New York: Continuum, 1995).

3   I would like to express my most sincere gratitude to Leslie Pascoe Chalk for his punctual editorial suggestions.

References and Further Reading

Armelagos, George (2003) "Cutura y Contacto: El Choque de Dos Cocinas Mundiales," in Long, Janet (ed.) *Conquista y Comida: Consecuencias del Encuentro de Dos Mundos*. Mexico: UNAM 105–29. Citation in text, 108 (my own translation from the Spanish original).

Beozzo, José Oscar (1992) "The Church and the Liberal States (1880–1930)," in Dussel, *The Church in Latin America: 1492–1992*, vol. I.

Bidegain, Ana María (1992) "The Church in the Emancipation Process (1750–1830)," in Dussel, *The Church in Latin America: 1492–1992*, vol. I.

Boff, Leonardo (1990) "The New Evangelization: New Life Burst In," *Concilium*, 130–40.

Boff, Leonardo and Elizondo, Virgil (1990) "The Voices of the Victims: Who Will Listen to Them?," *Concilium*, vii–x

Carrasco, David (1999) *City of Sacrifice: The Aztec Empire and the Role of Violence in Civilization*. Boston: Beacon Press.

Dussel, Enrique (ed.) (1992) *The Church in Latin America: 1492–1992*, vol. I. New York: Orbis Books.

Dussel, Enrique (1995) *The Invention of the Americas: Eclipse of "The Other" and the Myth of Modernity*, trans. Michael Barber. New York: Continuum.

Ellacurría, Ignacio (1989/18) "El Pueblo Crucificado. Ensayo de Sotereología Histórica," *Revista Latinoamerica de Teología*.

Ellacurría, Ignacio (1998) "The Crucified People," in Sobrino, Jon and Ellacuría, Ignacio (eds.) *Systematic Theology: Perspectives from Liberation Theology*. New York: Orbis Books, 257–78.

Esquivel, Julia (1990) "Conquered and Violated Women," *Concilium*, 68–77.

Goizueta, Roberto (2004) "The Symbolic Realism of U.S. Latino/a Popular Catholicism," in *Theological Studies*, vol. 65, no. 2 (June), 225–74.

Isasi-Diaz, Ada María (2002) *Mujerista Theology*. New York: Orbis Books.

Marzal, Manuel (1992) "Daily Life in the Indies (Seventeenth and Early Eighteenth Centuries)," in Dussel, *The Church in Latin America: 1492–1992*, vol. I.

Mauss, Marcel (1990) *The Gift: The Form and Reason for Exchange in Archaic Societies*, trans. W.D. Halls. London: W.W. Norton.

Milbank, John and Pickstock, Catherine (2001) *Truth in Aquinas*. London: Routledge.

Mignolo, Walter (2005) *The Idea of Latin America*. Oxford: Blackwell Publishing.

Schobinger, Juan (1992)"The Amerindian Religions," in Dussel, *The Church in Latin America: 1492–1992*, vol. I.

Valentin, Benjamin (2002) *Mapping Public Theology: Beyond Culture, Identity, and Difference*. New York: Trinity Press International.

CHAPTER 13
North America

Sandra Yocum Mize

The Canadian philosopher, Charles Taylor, in his 1996 Marianist Award lecture, "A Catholic Modernity?" attempts to capture the complexity of "Catholicism." He turns to "the original word 'katholou'" to emphasize two meanings "universality and wholeness; one might say: universality through wholeness." Its theological import is revealed in the redemptive power of "Incarnation, the weaving of God's life into human lives." Taylor distinguishes a "katholou" of "unity-across-difference" from a "unity-through-identity" and suggests "that the life of God itself, understood as trinitarian, is already a oneness in difference. Human diversity is part of the way in which we are made in the image of God." Admitting the danger of being "over-rigid," he offers "a Catholic principle . . .: no widening of faith without an increase in the variety of devotions and spiritualities and liturgical forms and responses to Incarnation" (Taylor, 1999: 15). North American Roman Catholicism manifests much of what Taylor describes. Examples of failure to create "unity-across-difference" abound in the Catholic Church's efforts to widen the faith. At the beginning of North American Catholicism, one discovers Spanish missionaries' attempts to create "unity-through-identity" by "Spanishizing" the Indians. One also encounters "unity-across-difference" and dedication to the "Catholic principle" evident in a "variety of devotions and spiritualities and liturgical forms and responses to the Incarnation," (ibid.) beginning in New Spain and enduring from south to north, east to west, across the vast and changing landscapes of North America.

The Catholicism here described begins just as the fifteenth century spilled into the sixteenth and ends as the second millennium spills into the third. The spatial limits are more circumscribed than "North America" suggests since Mexico is coupled in this volume with its linguistic partners in "Latin America." Of course, in southwestern United States, such linguistic distinctions quickly blur on the borderlands that today seem to extend into the Midwest and beyond. North American Catholics make their first appearance as Spanish, then French, and finally English Catholics who in their efforts to colonize and missionize begin the dramatic transformation of a people and their lands.

North America as Catholic Mission

Catholicism arrived in North America on an island off the coast of Florida in 1492. Here Christopher Columbus landed in his trek across the Atlantic, seeking wealth for himself and his patron, Queen Isabella of Spain. This Italian adventurer's diary reveals a man convinced of his own providential mission. So when he and his crewmen encountered a people who had no knowledge of Christ in a land tantalizing in its economic promise, Columbus felt confirmed in his sacred mission. Columbus' religiously informed colonizing zeal is suggestive of why sixteenth-century Catholic missionary efforts cannot be easily distilled from the economic and political goals of early modern western Europe.

The historical timing of Spain's initial colonization coincides with critical transitions in Europe. While sixteenth-century Spain felt little of the religious upheavals experienced in France, the German principalities, and across the sea in England, its people certainly felt the force of Catholic reform movements, from Spanish influenced humanism to Teresa of Avila's spiritual renewal to Ignatius of Loyola's religious fervor. Intense religious renewal occurred in conjunction with military and thus political and economic victories and constraints of Spain's monarchs, Ferdinand and Isabel, who expelled Muslims and Jews to consolidate their rule over the Iberian peninsula. Such a combination of religious, political, and cultural ferment created a potent mix of desire. Spanish adventurers sought to extend their newly realized military, political, and economic power beyond Iberia. Missionaries also had visions of expansion, though in this case of faith in Christ and his Church. Among Loyola's first companions was Francis Xavier who had traveled to India, China, and Japan. North America was only one among many mission fields for the intrepid men of the newly formed Society of Jesus.

The multiple tragedies that ensued from the contact of America's indigenous peoples with Spaniards leave several questions difficult to answer. All center on one basic question: How could a people who claim to follow Christ treat vulnerable persons so cruelly? This essay stops short of describing the displacement and eventual destruction of indigenous cultures, nor does it seek to mitigate the realities of massacre, rape, enslavement among those peoples that the Spanish conquered. In other words, the harsh realities of conquest cannot be excused or ignored and become blasphemous when identified with spreading the Gospel of Jesus Christ.

At the same time, it would be equally unfair to the memory of the peoples who met the Spanish and to their descendants to reduce them to mere victims. Certainly, some of the Indians, as they came to be called, selectively adopted Spanish ways that worked to their advantage, such as the use of horses and military arms. Generalizations about the missionaries prove equally elusive. These men brought the various Indian peoples into missions for a complex set of reasons. Undeniably prevalent was a willingness to coerce if it succeeded in "Spanishizing" for the purposes of "civilizing" and ultimately converting the Indians. Expecting missionaries to distinguish easily between the cultural and essential dimensions of religious practices presupposes that they knew "religion" as an abstract form to be taught to the Indians. Even basic tasks, like translating Christian doctrines into indigenous language, proved difficult. Strategies varied from teaching through images until potential converts learned Spanish to the missionaries learning various indigenous languages, creating a written form, translating a catechism, and then instructing the potential converts and other missionaries. Both linguistic strategies met with only limited success. For some of those catechized, however, the Christian message opened up a spiritual world that resonated with, expanded, and on occasion even transformed their own.

Many missionaries took seriously their role as protector of the Indians. The paternalism notwithstanding, the missions offered some protection against the cruelties of *conquistadores* and plantation owners. Among the Spanish Dominicans arose actual defenders of the native peoples. One of the most elegant defenses came from Bartolomé de las Casas (1474–66) who argued for native person's dignity as a human being created in God's image with reason and free will. This defense served both as an argument against enslavement and as the basis for excluding coercion in Christian conversion. Paul III, in the papal bull *Sublimus Deus* (1537), affirmed the fullness of Indians' humanity. Such debates indicate the complexity of theological questions that the missionary fields had wrought from the possibility of universal salvation to the challenge of what today is identified as "inculturation." The passage of time through the lives of the offspring of Spanish and native women created the Catholicism so distinctive in southwestern United States. To make that observation is not to take lightly either the maltreatment of women whom Spanish men forced into sexual relations or the continuing Anglo prejudice against *mestizos*. There is, however, more to this story as evident in the remarkable literature of Sor Juana Inés de la Cruz (1651–95). Her writings reveal the complexity of *mestizaje* in the emerging Mexican culture. Far more definitive is the Virgin of Guadalupe's appearance to the poor Indian, Juan Diego. La Morenita dramatically confirms Taylor's Catholic principle of "increase." The graceful image of Guadalupe validates the sanctity of Indian-Spanish blending into something new, a *mestizo* culture, the result of much suffering but not without great beauty, compassion, and even joy.

The seventeenth century marked the beginning of French influence, especially evident in the northeast, particularly Quebec. The first official Catholic presence, Jesuits, Franciscan Recollets, and a few diocesan priests, served as missionaries to native peoples, including the Mi'kmaw, Hurons, Algonquins, and Montagnais. The Jesuits and Recollets had evidently learned from the Church's century of missionary work. As in China, India, and Japan, the missionaries made concerted efforts to catechize in the native peoples' languages and to develop further strategies that drew from diverse cultural practices of the peoples with whom they lived.

French missionaries encountered a landscape and peoples quite different from that of the southwest where peoples had adapted to life in colorful deserts, mesas, and mountains. The northeast's beauty lay in its rivers and lakes with dense forests all around. Fur trading and fishing proved lucrative enough to entice the French, like the Indians among whom they settled, to endure frigid winters and cool springs and falls. Unlike the Spanish who enslaved Indians to work in *encomiendias*, the French sought to keep the native peoples in their own communities to maintain the fur trade. While not entirely sanguine about their potential converts' nomadic lives, the French missionaries, like their Spanish counterparts, adapted their work to their own particular and imperfect context.

The Holy See also took a new role in mission work. It established in 1622 the Congregation for the Propagation of the Faith to oversee missionary work in Asia, Africa, and the Americas. In retrospect, the decision contributed to the gradual centralizing of ecclesial authority that so characterizes modern Catholicism. Propaganda is of a piece in the Church's centuries-long response to the dissolution of a Catholic Europe and the emergence of nation states seeking to expand their authority throughout the world.

Clearly Europeans transported their political, economic, and social problems as well as their religious convictions to the "New World," which was a "world" with its own social, cultural, and religious history including conflict and domination as well as peaceful co-existence. Iroquois' dominance shaped French missionary work, evident in the life of native American Catholics' patron, Blessed Kateri Tekakwitha, and the memorable martyrdoms of Isaac Jogues, Jean Brebeuf, and Jerome Lalemant. Blessed Kateri, like the French Jesuits who catechized her, embraced austere religious practices including fasting and self-flagellation along with prayer. Kateri's brief life of extraordinary religious devotion made her tomb a site of religious pilgrimage almost immediately after her death in 1680. Renewed interest in her sanctity has emerged among some native American Catholics who celebrated her 1980 beatification by John Paul II, 300 years after her death – more evidence of Taylor's Catholic principle coming to fruition.

English Catholics under the sponsorship of the Calvert family arrived on the mid-Atlantic coast in 1634. Unlike the French and Spanish, the English Catholics were a distinct minority among a variety of Protestant traditions – even on the two Calvert-sponsored ships, the *Ark* and *Dove*. A Jesuit, Father Andrew White, accompanied the colonists who named the territory granted to them, Maryland, in honor of their homeland's queen. Most Catholics, including the Jesuits, settled on plantations where they exploited the labor of African slaves. By 1785, about 20 percent of all Catholics in Maryland were of African descent, almost all enslaved on Catholic plantations. The Catholic colonists, mostly landed gentry, adapted to their political context to prevent civil enactment of anti-Catholic prejudice that might prohibit their engagement in the colony's social and economic life.

Emerging National Identities

From these Maryland Catholic families came notable contributors to the colonists' break with English rule. Charles Carroll actively engaged in the movements leading to the American Revolution. His cousin, John, became Bishop of Baltimore and *de facto* of the United States of America in 1789, the year of the US Constitution's ratification. America's rebellion also impacted Canada's Catholics when the British Parliament passed the Quebec Act (1774) guaranteeing religious tolerance of Canadiens, i.e., Quebec's French-speaking Catholics. The guarantee short-circuited the efforts of American Catholic emissaries, Charles Carroll and Fr John Carroll who, with Benjamin Franklin, attempted to secure Quebec's support for revolution.

The US Constitution's First Amendment's coupling of religious liberty with non-establishment permitted Catholics not only to practice their religion without fear of reprisal but also to found a variety of institutions through the voluntary agency of its lay, religious, and clerical members. Following the directives of the Council of Trent,

John Carroll established a seminary for clerical education as one of his first official acts. He also called a diocesan synod, as Tridentine reforms recommended, in 1790, the year after his installation. Yet Carroll, and other Maryland Catholics, understood Tridentine Catholicism in light of moderate Enlightenment ideals expressed in John Locke and translated into Scottish Common Sense Realism. Evidence of deeply rooted influence comes from the popularity of Richard Challoner's guide to personal lay devotion, *Garden of the Soul*, emphasizing interiority and an individual's cultivation of virtues consonant with rationality rather than affections.

Life in the early Republic demanded more of Catholics than personal piety. Given the absence of the institutional structures and the fact that the clergy were forbidden to own land, enterprising Catholic laity purchased land, built a church building, secured a pastor, and thus founded a parish. The practice, identified as "lay trusteeism," resembled certain European practices and, more obviously, the dominant US congregational polity. Canadian Catholics' adaptation of trusteeism to establish parishes challenges any simple equating of trusteeism with American democracy. Trustees defended the practice by appealing to a wide tradition, inclusive of scholastic theology, canon law, and American civil law. In US Catholic historiography, trusteeism's bad reputation arose from those intractable conflicts that led some local ordinaries to place parishes under interdiction. Yet, trusteeism more often succeeded than failed in establishing parish life during the early Republic.

Establishing Catholicism in a Foreign Land

Concerns for providing Catholics access to the Church's sacramental life quickly accelerated in the United States and the Canadian provinces. The small and scattered population of English and Irish Catholics transformed rapidly in 1820 with the first major immigrant influx from Ireland and Germany. Besides meeting basic sacramental needs through strong parish communities, Catholic leaders quickly recognized the acute need for alternatives to the common schools, that reflected the dominant Protestant culture, particularly in its Reformed expression. Strident battles between Protestant-run boards of education and Catholic officials, such as John Hughes, Archbishop of New York, and Francis Kenrick, Bishop of Philadelphia, frequently centered on a school's reading from the King James rather than the Douai translation of the Bible. Animosity erupted into riots in Philadelphia in 1844 with a similar threat soon afterward in New York City. The most significant outcome to Protestant dominance in common schools was the founding of Catholic school systems.

Education was only one among many pastoral needs that bishops, clergy, religious, and laity had to address as immigrants settled across the growing nation, from urban centers like New York City to rural areas of today's Midwest. Women religious often met the challenges directly. Some cared for orphans and abandoned children including infants; others provided basic hospital care to those most in need; some even visited the imprisoned and many taught the ignorant regardless of age. To put it briefly, these religious communities dedicated their lives to the corporal and spiritual works of mercy.

Women religious also judged themselves against nineteenth-century's ideal woman dedicated to the domestic sphere. They described themselves as living this ideal as brides of Christ and spiritual mothers caring for children in the household of God. From another vantage point, women religious gained educational opportunities seldom available to immigrants' daughters and worked as professionals, usually teachers or nurses. Many found such opportunities especially attractive because of the deeply religious meaning with which the community's apostolic mission imbued their daily labor.

The stories of the literally thousands of women religious who served North America's Catholic communities remain unheralded. Yet the early modern women's religious communities became key in establishing a local Catholic presence throughout North America. Marguerite d'Youville, for example, accepted for her community, the Grey Nuns, responsibility for a hospital in Montreal. Their hospital work spread throughout Canada and the northern US. The convert, and first American-born canonized saint, Elizabeth Ann Seton, founded the Daughters of Charity of St Joseph, in Emmitsburg, Maryland, in 1808. Her community receives credit for establishing the first among the many parochial elementary schools staffed by women religious. More remarkable is the story of Mary Elizabeth Lange who founded the Oblates of Providence in antebellum Maryland for women like herself, free women of color. They dedicated themselves to the African American communities, mostly slaves or former slaves. Remarkable is these women's devotion to the Gospel in the face of racist-motivated opposition to their community's existence. An often overlooked effect of these various communities' work is their interaction with laity, particularly lay women, who accepted the public roles in the sisters' charitable enterprises. These women religious, along with their lay collaborators, created local expressions of the Church's "universality through wholeness" in practicing the works of mercy in service to poor and working-class families – a "widening of faith" through "an increase in the variety of . . . responses to the Incarnation."

The sacramental life of the local Church obviously depended on the ordained. In the early Republic, a severe shortage of clergy limited access to the sacraments. This situation began to change at the end of the eighteenth century, when French clergy, forced to flee the threat of execution, arrived in Canada and the United States. Bishops like Carroll appointed French clergy to serve in parishes. A few received episcopal appointments including John Cheverus in Boston, and Joseph Flaget ss in Bardstown, Kentucky, both in 1808 and both the first in those sees. Flaget's community, the Sulpicians, took over St Mary's Seminary that Carroll had founded in Baltimore. Next came Irish and German priests, who departed their homelands for reasons similar to the lay Catholic immigrants whom these clergymen intended to serve. As Canada and the United States expanded westward, so did Catholics and the clergy and sisters who ministered to them. By the twentieth century, North American born clergy and religious increased and the European born became the exception.

Identity and Difference in a Roman Church

The political and social turmoil of nineteenth-century Europe had a more subtle and pervasive influence on North American Catholicism. Among European Catholics, especially among the hierarchy, the papacy's authority played a greater role as counter to modern states' attempts to disestablish or control the churches. In Catholic Quebec, Church officials eschewed government interference. Inspired by French populist ultramontanist Félicité de Lamennais, Jean-Jacques Lartigue (1821–40) no longer sought approval from both the British colonial government and Rome to establish ecclesial entities. He became Montreal's first bishop and appointed his successor solely on Rome's approval.

Among North American Catholics, the papacy acquired a complicated set of symbolic meanings that gave a distinctive religious identity to a displaced people. By the mid-nineteenth century, for example, Catholics in both the United States and Canada participated in a devotional culture that provided a "unity-through-identity" centered in Rome. The new, quasi-international religious-cultural context reinforced an ultramontane ecclesiology with its emphasis on the Pope's transnational authority, further affirmed with Vatican I's declaration of the papacy's infallible spiritual authority. The emphasis on the pontiff's spiritual power coincided with the collapse of his temporal power.

Still, no single cause, including ultramontanism, explains populist-devotional forms in parish life. In Toronto's neighborhoods, for example, Irish nationalism had long found expression in voluntary Church organizations. Encouraged by Toronto's second bishop, Armand de Charbonnel (1850–60), the Irish joined in Church-related, usually parish-based, voluntary associations similar to European confraternities or sodalities. Yet, enthusiasm for these organizations is, at least in part, a function of immigrants' communal dislocation. Urban neighborhood parishes signified a localized unity-through-identity. Yet, stepping back further allows one to look at the variety of parishes as they developed, particularly in major urban areas from Toronto to Montreal to New York to Baltimore to Chicago to New Orleans to Los Angeles. To do so produces a slightly different vista, of a unity-across-difference, even amid the centralization and growing uniformity of devotional practices.

During this same time, both Canada and the United States continued westward expansion. Even the most intrepid missionary must have found the geographical realities of the Canadian Northwest difficult to comprehend. Modern Canada is second only to Russia in land mass. If the 1840 journey of Oblate sub-deacon Alexandre-Antonin Taché is any indication, the era of missionary adventurers was hardly over. He and a companion, Pierre Aubert, made the 1,400-mile trek in a canoe powered by their own efforts. Over the next century, nearly 300 Oblates of Mary Immaculate confrères followed Taché and Aubert to this vast missionary country where they labored tirelessly to protect Québécois Catholics' rights in these territories dominated by English-speaking Protestants.

Passing on the Faith

The connection between language and faith was and remains a source of contention between English-speaking Catholics and every other linguistic group in the US and Canada. In countering the Americanizing insistence of Irish American prelates like the ever-vocal John Ireland, Archbishop of St Paul, German Catholic immigrants declared: "the language saves the faith." The deep intertwining of language, culture, and religious commitment evident in the German Catholics' rallying cry helps one to understand the complex emotions expressed in the debates.

Canadian and American Catholics debated language issues as part of wider religious–national battles, epitomized first in English penal laws. Forty years after the US Constitution with its Bill of Rights was ratified, Great Britain passed legislation guaranteeing Catholic emancipation throughout its empire. In North America, an anti-Catholic rhetoric, imported from Great Britain, endured well into the twentieth century despite legal protection for Catholics. As Jenny Franchot has shown in *Roads to Rome*, Protestant-produced literature communicated a fascination with and repulsion against Catholicism. Few rival Maria Monk's harrowing account of Montreal's Hôtel Dieu. This fictional tale, purporting to be true, titillated readers with accounts of everything from exotic devotional practices to innocent girls at the mercy of lascivious priests, to infanticide, with the progeny of illicit relations between priests being smothered and thrown into a lime pit conveniently located in the convent's basement. A nineteenth-century best-seller, Maria Monk's tale continues to be published, even as a late twentieth-century comic book.

Anti-Catholicism in Canada and the United States, though having much in common, flourished in very different political contexts. In the United States, political movements emerged to challenge Catholicism's right to exist in the republic. The most notable groups include the Know Nothing Party, the American Protective Association, and the Ku Klux Klan. Their greatest effect was on local and state politics. The First Amendment afforded important protection against the groups as clearly seen in the 1925 Supreme Court decision in *Sisters of the Holy Name vs. Pierce et al.* The decision struck down a Ku Klux Klan-sponsored Oregon law making public school education compulsory. The case of Louis Riel (1844–85) serves as a Canadian example of how Protestant–Catholic coupled with anglophone–francophone animosity could have far-reaching and tragic consequences in provincial politics. Louis Riel emerged as a charismatic leader among his people, the *métis*, those of French-Indian heritage. On July 1, 1867, the provinces of Ontario, Quebec, Nova Scotia, and New Brunswick formed a federation, marking the beginning of modern Canada. Two years later, the Hudson's Bay Company agreed to transfer their land holdings to form a new province, Manitoba. Riel defended the *métis* who feared confiscation of their land and acted as their negotiator until the military under his command executed an Englishman, Thomas Scott. The controversy that followed forced Riel to flee. After living as an exile in the US, Riel returned to lead the Northwest Rebellion (1885). The *métis* were defeated, Riel captured and executed by hanging. Though rare in Canada, the eruption of violence highlights the intensity of enmity despite two centuries of co-existence.

Canadians' varied loyalties made for interesting intra-ecclesial divisions between the French- and English-speaking Catholics, who defined themselves not only by parish boundaries but also by provincial ones. As in the United States, the school system prove to be a site of high anxiety and thus frequent conflict over preserving communal identity, but responses to intra-ecclesial conflicts shifted from province to province. So, for example, francophone Catholic dominance in Quebec extended well beyond the school system to social service agencies, health care, and even trade unions until the mid-twentieth century. In Ontario, by way of contrast, Bishop Fallon sought to eliminate bilingual education. Despite fierce opposition among French Catholics living in Ontario, he remained adamant that the Catholic schools needed to provide a unilingual education to those in the English-speaking provinces to ensure their success in Canadian society.

The debates concerning language followed the westward migration of recently arrived eastern Europeans as well as French and English Canadians. Several anglophone bishops and clergy sought to make English the language of the Prairies. The Canadian Catholic Extension Society served as a primary agent for promoting English as the official language across the Prairies. Despite such efforts, the francophone Catholics remained unwavering in their commitment to bilingual education.

English-speaking Irish Catholics and their German counterparts engaged in comparable debates in late nineteenth-century America. Archbishop John Ireland of the St Paul diocese and Rev. John Keane spoke for Americanization; on the other side was Father Peter Abbelen of the Milwaukee diocese. Both brought their cases to Rome. Like Ontario's Bishop Fallon, Ireland and Keane insisted on Americanizing Catholic immigrants to guarantee a Catholic influence in American society. Unlike the Canadiens, the German representative, Peter Abbelen, argued for a gradual process of Americanization, maintaining that the intimate ties between language and faith required careful attention. A hundred years later the most prominent battles are between Latino/Latinas and Anglos.

The conflicts generated around language in parish and school among Catholics on both sides of the Canadian/US border are instructive. They highlight the critical role education, religious and otherwise, plays in passing on faith, culture, language, a communal identity. Battles over parish life and schooling are so fierce precisely because they are so important for the ongoing life of local Catholic communities. At the same time, immigrants recognized that their children's success depended upon an ability to negotiate the dominant culture of their adopted homeland. Supporting this kind of education challenged parents to allow their children to adopt as their principal language one that the parents often barely understood. The obvious pathos in the experiences of parents and children makes clear why the transitional generation has been the inspiration for novels, plays, films, memoirs, and autobiographies.

Americanist and Catholic

The immigrant character of US Catholicism coupled with the nativist hostility makes more understandable Church leaders' frequent and expansive claims about the unique relationship between Catholicism and the American nation. Such assertions have abounded from the days of the early Republic to the present. Many an English-speaking prelate claimed that the republican defense of equality and liberty had Catholic roots. Even the most ardent Catholic proponents of American exceptionalism, like Isaac Hecker and John Ireland, maintained that ultimately America would recover its roots in converting to Catholicism.

John Ireland proclaimed American democracy's growing dominance in the world and the Church's ability to adapt to the age of democracy, liberty, and new knowledge without affecting its essence. He and John Keane exported these claims to Europe with disastrous results. Many European Catholics still identified democracy, liberty, and new knowledge with the French Revolution and the consequent collapse of social, economic, cultural, political, and religious structures. In France, a controversy arose after the 1897 publication of the French translation of *The Life of Isaac Hecker*, by Walter Elliott, a Paulist, the order Hecker founded. French controversialists challenged the biography's perceived conflation of American-style democracy, the inner workings of the Holy Spirit among the faithful, and a renewed commitment to active rather than passive virtues.

The controversy culminated in *Testem Benevolentiae*, Pope Leo XIII's letter condemning a disposition, named "Americanism." Addressing the letter to James Cardinal Gibbons, Baltimore, the Pope distinguished theological from political forms of Americanism and condemned only the theological form with its exaggerated accommodation to US society, emphasis on subjective qualities of religious commitment, and promotion of a national Church akin to Gallicanism. US Catholic prelates, including John Ireland, denied holding these theological views. Less than a decade later, Leo's successor, Pius X, promulgated the encyclical *Pascendi Dominici Gregis*, condemning the heresy "Modernism," a term that encompassed several theological trends, particularly those identified with biblical higher criticism. Interestingly, Pius X in the following year, 1908, ended Canada's and the United States' missionary status. They now dealt directly with the Holy See rather than going through Propaganda.

Catholic Intellectual Traditions on Site

According to most scholars of US Catholicism, the Americanist combined with the Modernist condemnations halted creative theological scholarship in the United States. One can offer little evidence to counter this judgment. The condemnations followed the 1879 papal document *Aeterni Patris* – Leo XIII's call for a return to Thomas Aquinas' works to counter modern philosophical systems such as Marxism. While much of what is identified in the United States as neo-Thomism reflects the seminaries' use of a manual in compliance with the 1917 Code of Canon Law proscribing the study of Thomas, several instances of other kinds of Thomistic-inspired intellectual creativity emerged. Key to these efforts was the founding of the Catholic University of America (CUA) in Washington, DC, in 1889. Ireland and Keane, in this case, succeeded in winning Roman approval to establish a US Catholic university as a center for graduate studies. Despite the papal condemnations of Americanism and Modernism, and perhaps because of them, the university produced a coterie of intellectuals not in theology *per se*, but in emerging disciplines, especially social sciences.

Numerous examples can be noted. Edward Pace, like William James, crossed the still permeable boundaries of emerging academic disciplines. Pace studied with the experimental psychologist Wilhelm Wundt in Germany, returned to the US, and established an experimental psychology laboratory, giving CUA the second such facility in the US. After serving as professor of psychology (1891–4), he founded CUA's School of

Philosophy (1895), and also collaborated in founding its School of Education. Thomas Shields taught in the School of Education from 1902 until his death in 1920. Familiar with the work of educational innovator John Dewey, Shields developed an innovative Catholic philosophy of education with religion providing the central integrating force of a child's psychological development. Shields founded the Sisters College at Catholic University to provide women religious with opportunities to become educational innovators. Another disciplinary-crossing CUA professor, John Montgomery Cooper, founded CUA's Religion and Anthropology Departments. Cooper's four-volume *Course Outlines in Religion* set the terms of the debate about college religion courses until the mid-1950s. The American Anthropological Association elected him as president in 1940.

Two other influential thinkers from this period are William Kerby, CUA sociology professor, and John A. Ryan, CUA political science and moral theology professor. Kerby founded the National Conference of Catholic Charities (1910) and the National Catholic School of Social Service (1918) to secure Catholic influence in the emerging social work profession. John Ryan, author of *A Living Wage* (1906) and *Distributive Justice* (1916), exerted a national influence through the Social Action Department of the National Catholic Welfare Conference, his education of clergy and women religious on matters of social justice, and most notably his writing of the 1919 Bishops' *Program of Social Reconstruction* and subsequent influence on Franklin Roosevelt's New Deal programs. All of these men to some extent saw themselves as responding to Leo XIII's call to reinvigorate Catholic intellectual life by bringing to bear Catholic thought, especially Thomistic-inspired natural law, on contemporary life.

North American Catholic Social Teaching and Action

Leo XIII's publication of *Rerum Novarum* (1891) inspired many Catholics to respond to social injustices. John Ryan understood his defense of the living wage as an American application of Leo XIII's social teachings. Canadian Catholics also began social movements inspired by *Rerum Novarum* within their provinces. Drawing from his London-based education, Father Jimmy Tompkins initiated Nova Scotia's Antigonish Forward Movement, "knowledge for the people movement," at St Francis Xavier University in Halifax. After an episcopal reassignment to a remote village, Canso, an undeterred Tompkins educated local maritime workers who by the 1930s had established a packing plant to process and deliver their wares. Another priest, a cousin of Tompkins, Moses Coady, directed St Francis Xavier Extension Program to disseminate the Antigonish movement practices: adult education and cooperative movements.

Quebec, with its French Catholic majority, also took its cue from European Catholic reform movements. Early twentieth-century Quebec Catholics established several *caisses populaires*, parish-based credit unions. Jesuits inspired Quebec youth to translate Sacred Heart devotion into social action on behalf of the working class and the poor. Other grassroots movements in the 1930s utilized the Belgian priest Joseph Cardijn's method, "see, judge, and act." This "specialized Catholic Action" extended throughout North America. Chicago Catholics learned the Cardijn method through Father Reynold

Hillenbrand, who learned it from Oklahoma clergyman Donald Kanaly. Applications include the Christian Family Movement, Young Catholic Students, and Young Catholic Workers. Such movements spread to Catholic college campuses and guided the laity's organization on behalf of social justice. In Quebec, these movements translated into explicitly political movements such as the *Action libérale nationale*, whose platform became part of the *Bloc populaire canadien*, a catalyst for Quebec's neo-nationalist movement.

Lay Catholic Movements Respond to the Twentieth Century

Rarely did US Catholic social movements find expression in founding a political party though many had political concerns. None has been written about more than the Catholic Worker movement founded by Dorothy Day and Peter Maurin in 1933. The Worker movement found inspiration from the Gospel, particularly the Sermon on the Mount, and the corporal and spiritual works of mercy. These practiced teachings informed a Christian personalism, a call to personal responsibility for neighbor and stranger as Christ. Hence, the Worker established Houses of Hospitality (not homeless shelters or missions) to provide food, clothing, and shelter. Day, encouraged by Maurin, founded a newspaper, *The Catholic Worker*, to teach or, as Day wrote, "indoctrinate" the ignorant in Catholic Worker philosophy. "Round table discussions for clarification of thought" were another means of indoctrination. Finally, the Worker established farms, what Maurin called "agronomic universities," as locally-based, self-sufficient economic alternatives to capitalism. Like every other Catholic Worker practice, the farms depended on a commitment to voluntary poverty.

Another distinctive feature of the Worker movement came from Day's absolute commitment to pacifism. It never wavered from the Spanish Civil War to World War II to Vietnam. Day, along with other Catholic Workers, participated in non-violent resistance to protest nuclear armament and to support the civil rights movements among African Americans and the United Farm Workers. She helped to establish pacifism as a viable Catholic position. A quarter century after Day's death in 1980, Catholic Worker houses and farms exist throughout North America.

Another important movement under a woman's leadership is Friendship House, founded by a Russian emigré, Catherine de Hueck. She fled revolutionary Russia, eventually came to Toronto, and founded Friendship House in the city's depressed downtown. Its primary apostolate was to serve the poor. Inspired by *Quadragesimo Anno*, de Hueck joined workers' picket lines to demand a fair wage. In this case, the employer proved to be a major benefactor to Ontario's archdiocese. Besides receiving the archbishop's reprimand in this matter, de Hueck became the butt of increasingly severe criticism. Priests and laity alike challenged everything from her authority to engage in her apostolate to her ability to be a good mother to her son. Crushed under the criticism, she closed Friendship House in 1936 and came to New York City where she founded Harlem's Friendship House to promote interracial justice. In the early 1940s, she moved to rural Ontario to found Madonna House, a quasi-monastic community with a contemplative focus on Jesus combined with an active commitment to serving the poor. In 1968, the community became the first in Canada to embrace the charismatic renewal. As of 2006, the community continues the legacy of de Hueck.

Other movements that engaged lay people, the ordained, and members of religious communities increased at a remarkable rate through the twentieth century. Virgil Michel osb from St John's Abbey, Collegeville, Minnesota, introduced US Catholics to the liturgical movement. He offered a unique vision that integrated social action into a life defined by the liturgy, especially the Eucharist. Paul Hanley Furfey, shortly after ordination, began his long career as professor and chairperson of CUA's Sociology Department. Like Day, Michel, and countless other mid-twentieth-century Catholics, Furfey embraced the Church as the Mystical Body of Christ. This ecclesiology, along with his Christian personalism, inspired him to formulate a "supernatural sociology" to which he gave concrete expression at Fides Neighorhood House and Il Poverello House. Both served the poor in the nation's capital.

Across the landscape of North American Catholicism many other organizations and movements invited Roman Catholics to express their faith. Familiar examples deserve notice, including altar societies, Marian sodalities, and the Knights of Columbus and so too do the not so familiar, like New Mexican *cofradías*, the Knights of Peter Claver, an African American Catholic fraternal society, and the Grail, a women's lay apostolic movement transplanted from Europe to Loveland, Ohio. Invitations came from official ecclesial organizations like National Catholic Rural Life Conference in Des Moines, Iowa, Catholic Interracial Councils, Catholic Charities, and Confraternity of Christian Doctrine. One can find similar Canadian examples. All of these are suggestive of a richly textured Catholic life whose legacy has brought the "weaving of God's life into human lives" into the twenty-first century.

The Second Vatican Council: Here and There

Understanding North American Catholics' reception of the Second Vatican Council requires recognition of the social, political, and cultural, as well as the religious ferment already occurring among Canadian and American Catholics. Post-war America responded to a severe housing shortage by building suburbia, to which Catholics moved in droves. Some were escaping a ghetto, others reluctantly leaving the old neighborhood. The GI Bill allowed many veterans, now suburbanites, to attend the college of their choice including Catholic ones. Certainly suburbia redefined US parish life. As Will Herberg suggested, the Catholic fell into line with the Protestant and Jew as part and parcel of America's landscape of middle-class religiosity.

Such observations should not be read in a nostalgic light of an earlier, pristine Catholicism in decline. Every period has pockets of intense devotion, deep commitments to works of mercy and justice, and liturgical vitality. Examples also abound of Catholic commitments barely distinguishable from other social obligations like joining the local Elks Club. Yet, uniquely new events impinged upon Catholic lives in the 1950s as television brought into living rooms such disparate characters as charismatic Fulton Sheen and an attractive Catholic presidential candidate, charming enough to overcome America's persistent anti-Catholic fears. The decade that began with John F. Kennedy's election to the presidency ended on a very different note. Catholics joined with other Americans to watch endless hours of coverage of Kennedy's assassination, and soon to follow were scenes of brutality perpetrated by law officers against African Americans seeking basic civil rights, and then the horrors of a war in distant Southeast Asia. Catholics saw sisters in full habit and priests in clerical garb walking arm-in-arm with civil rights leaders or pouring blood on draft records and knew for certain that something was indeed happening here, even if what was happening was not "exactly clear."

In Quebec, the 1950s marked the period identified with the "Quiet Revolution." The phrase refers to the nearly imperceptible shift from Church to lay control of social service agencies including schools, and hospitals as well as trade unions and cooperatives. The movement had a long preparatory history including youth participation in Catholic action and devotional Catholicism in the late 1940s and early 1950s. With the 1960 election of Jean Lesage's Liberal government, Quebec's Quiet Revolution took hold. In the decade that followed, Québécois turned their focus toward a nationalism based upon secularized social institutions under the control of neither the Church nor wealthy Anglophone businessmen.

Of course, in the midst of Canada's Quiet Revolution and the violence occurring near and far with Americans' full participation, a second ecumenical council was held in the Vatican, with sessions in 1963, 1964, and 1965. One can point to North American contributions to some of the most influential conciliar documents. US theologian John Courtney Murray, silenced prior to the council for his views on Church and state relations, became a principal architect of the document on religious liberty with its focused defense of a right to freedom from state coercion in religious matters. Canadian Bishops Charbonneau, De Roo, Power, and Carter influenced the document on the Apostolate of the Laity, particularly its emphasis on the laity's mission in bringing Christ's redeeming love into the world in which they live.

Clearly, no simplistic terms of cause and effect relative to the Second Vatican Council fully explains Catholics' changing understanding of themselves as members of Church and world. No doubt the Council remains a part, indeed a significant part, of the shifts in Catholic beliefs and practices. Even those Catholics only minimally interested in the Council knew from attending Mass that change was coming. The priest faced the congregation and spoke not in Latin but in English or Spanish or French. Others engaged in ecumenical and even interfaith dialogs. Still others heard repeatedly of their identification now as the People of God called in a direct way to be the Church in the modern world.

The reception and implementation of the Vatican II documents seemed to open a floodgate of innovation in North American Catholic life and thought. Innovations included experimental Eucharistic liturgies, new forms of lay ministries from directors of religious education to social justice coordinators, and certainly new forms of theological discussion. Groundbreaking work in feminist theology, for example, began with Mary Daly's *The Church and the Second Sex*. Liberation theologies among US Hispanics, Black Catholics, Native Americans, and other groups further expanded theological boundaries. America's religious pluralism fostered ecumenical and interreligious engagement, producing influential work from theologians such as Canadian Gregory Baum and American Paul Knitter.

North America's "Post" Generation of Catholics

The year 1978 began a new era in the Church with the election of John Paul II. Well into the third millennium, this Pope's charismatic leadership has shaped Catholicism's understanding of itself. For some, it represented an unfortunate return to pre-conciliar authoritarian ecclesiology. For others, his pontificate restored a church confident in faith and its moral stance. For others again, especially those born after 1975, John Paul II held a status that combined celebrity, religious heroism, and spiritual inspiration. Among a small but vocal minority of younger Catholics, he inspired a renewed interest in Catholic apologetics, appropriation of devotions such as Eucharistic adoration and praying the rosary combined in some cases with a deep commitment to social justice.

Episcopal leadership in the United States and Canada has taken a more definitive form in national conferences, the United States Catholic Conference of Bishops, and the Canadian Catholic Conference of Bishops. The US bishops, for instance, have issued statements opposing the Vietnam conflict, condemning racism, supporting immigrants, opposing abortion. *The Challenge of Peace* (1983) and *Economic Justice for All* (1986), produced after extensive consultation with the laity, received attention even in the secular press. Joseph Cardinal Bernadin, a nationally recognized episcopal leader, has argued for a consistent ethic of life, as a powerful response to a set of issues from abortion to war to capital punishment to unjust economic systems. His exemplary leadership stands in sharp contrast to a failure of episcopal leadership in response to the clerical sexual abuse of minors. The tragic consequences of the crisis continue to unfold well into the twenty-first century because the scandal is of biblical proportions if one recalls Jesus' advice to those who do harm to the "little ones."

Does twenty-first century North American Catholicism, in light of current difficulties, still exemplify Taylor's Catholic principle? US and Canadian Catholicism seems more fractured than ever, especially when viewed through the liberal/conservative lens. Regular attendance at Mass has dropped precipitously in Quebec and other parts of Canada, and US Catholics seem to be moving in a similar direction. Younger Catholics with deep commitments to their faith appear to some as too narrow; though from another perspective, most seem to negotiate the hybridity of post-modernity with great ease. If one could transform Charles Taylor's "Catholic principle" into a kaleidoscope with a lens wide enough to see all of North American Catholicism on any given day, what might one see? Perhaps five elderly people at daily Mass in a Detroit parish, or Benedictine monks reciting the Liturgy of the Hours in Indiana's farmlands, or New Mexico's desert, or a Rwandan dancing her liturgical prayer at Mass, or first graders hearing about Jesus the Good Shepherd, or college students considering the merits of just war theory, or an *abuelita* praying to her beloved Guadalupe, or a Vietnamese priest praying for his parishioners, or an African American calling the Church to its catholicity, or a young woman uncertain in faith lighting a candle at St Anne's shrine in Montreal, or a native American man praying to Blessed Kateri, or a pilgrim, nearly lost, finding his way to Chimayo for a bit of holy dirt, or a social action committee meeting in a suburban parish, or men frying fish for the fiftieth annual parish fish fry, or an elderly sister receiving the Eucharist for the last time, or a young woman seeking the fullness of Catholic ministry, or another baby being baptized, or the least among us revealing Christ previously hidden . . . At the end of such a day, the view from the kaleidoscope suggests that however imperfect each individual's action, it seems hard to ignore a "widening of faith" in a "variety of devotions and spiritualities and liturgical forms and responses to the Incarnation" (Taylor, 1999: 15).

References and Further Reading

Carey, Patrick W. (1996) *Roman Catholics in America*. Westport, CN: Praeger.
Fey, Terence J. (2002) *A History of Canadian Catholics: Gallicanism, Romanism, and Canadianism*. Montreal: McGill-Queen's University Press.
Fisher, James T. (2000, 2002) *Communion of Immigrants: A History of Catholics in America*. New York: Oxford University Press.
Franchot, J. (1994) *Roads to Rome: the Antebellum Protestant Encounter with Catholicism*. Berkeley, CA: University of California Press.
Murphy, Terrence and Stortz, Gerald (eds.) (1993) *Creed and Culture: The Place of English-Speaking Catholics in Canadian Society, 1750–1930*. Montreal: McGill-Queen's University Press.
Taylor, Charles (1999) "A Catholic Modernity?" in James L. Heft SM (ed.) *A Catholic Modernity? Charles Taylor's Marianist Award Lecture*. Oxford: Oxford University Press..

CHAPTER 14
Asia

Peter C. Phan

Two expressions need preliminary clarification to circumscribe the scope of this essay. "Asia" is now usually taken to comprise four regions: East Asia (the Far East), West Asia (the Middle East), South Asia, and North Asia (Central Asia). This survey is however limited to East and South Asia only and, more narrowly, to five countries in them, namely, China, Vietnam, Korea, Japan, and the Philippines, other regions being studied elsewhere in this volume. By "Catholicism" or "Catholic Church" is here meant the form of Latin/Roman Christianity (excluding therefore the "Eastern Catholic" Churches) that emerged after the sixteenth-century Protestant Reformation, without of course discounting its claims of historical origination from and continuity with Jesus of Nazareth through Patristic and medieval Christianity.

Of all the Christian Churches in Asia, the Catholic Church is the largest and, in spite of its tendency toward uniformity and centralization, also the most diverse. This diversity is a function of the geography of Asia, the world's largest and most varied land mass; its teeming people, who constitute two-thirds of the world population; its immense array of languages, ethnic groups, cultures, and religions; the extreme differences in its economic and social realities represented by some of the richest and the poorest countries on earth; its opposite political systems, comprising the largest democratic and the largest Communist states in the world. Within the Catholic Church itself, there are ancient and at times competing "rites," or more precisely, vastly different theological, liturgical, and canonical traditions.

This survey offers a historico-theological analysis of Asian Catholicism. First, it presents a brief history of the Catholic Church in the five countries mentioned above, with an emphasis on how Catholicism has been received and transformed locally. These countries are treated together both because they have a common mission history and because they, especially the first four, share a similar cultural and religious heritage. Next, it studies the two recent events that have defined the course of contemporary Asian Catholicism, namely, the founding and activities of the Federation of Asian Bishops' Conferences and the Special Assembly for Asia of the Synod of Bishops. It concludes with a discussion of the salient characteristics of Asian Catholicism and the challenges facing the Catholic Church's evangelizing mission in Asia.

A Native Religion Came Home

It is an irony of history that Christianity, which was born in (West) Asia, came back to its birthplace as a foreign religion and is still widely regarded as such by Asians. More tragically, setting aside the arrival of East Syrian (Nestorian) monks and of the first Catholic missionaries to China, the former in the seventh century and the latter in the thirteenth century, Catholic Christianity in the five countries under study, except Korea, was irreparably tainted by its association with Western colonialism. Indeed, from the sixteenth to the twentieth century, in its conquest of Asia, every single Western power – Portugal, Spain, France, Holland, Britain, and the United States of America –enlisted the help of missionaries, who in turn reaped financial and political benefits for their work. The history of Christian missions in Asia, as is clear from the following survey, is a mixture of light and shadow, selfless service and imperialistic colonialism, evangelical humility and cultural chauvinism. It is imperative to acknowledge both the magnificent achievements and the abject failures of the Catholic Church in Asia; only thus can the Church understand its past and prepare itself to meet the challenges facing its mission in the future.

China

Nestorian Christianity under the Tang Dynasty

The famous Xi'an stele records the fact that East Syrian (Nestorian) Christianity, known as "The Ta-chin [Syrian] Luminous Religion," under Aluoben's leadership, was welcomed to China by Emperor Taizong in 635. For the next 210 years, it enjoyed imperial support, except under Empress Wu Zetian (reigned 650–705), until 845, when Emperor Wuzong expelled all foreign religions, including Christianity, from the country. Christians withdrew from the mainland to the northwest border. There they survived among the minority peoples and possibly were absorbed into the Muslim community. During the Yuan (Mongolian) dynasty (1260–1368) Nestorians returned and Roman Catholics came to China for the first time.

The Catholic Church under the Mongol/Yuan Dynasty

Under the reign of the fourth Great Khan, Mongke (or Mangu), the grandson of Genghis Khan and son of the Christian princess Sorkaktani, a Franciscan missionary, Giovanni dal Piano del Carpini and his companion, Benedict the Pole, penetrated the Mongolian empire. They had been sent by Pope Innocent IV in 1245 to the Mongol capital, Karakorum, with the double mission of averting further Mongol attacks on Western Christendom and converting the Mongols to the Christian faith. In the next hundred years, several Catholic missionaries, the most noteworthy among whom was Franciscan friar William of Rubruck (in 1253–5), were dispatched to Mongolia. The first Catholics to enter China, as distinct from Mongolia, under the reign of Kublai

Khan, were the two Polo brothers on their first journey (in 1260–9) and on their second journey, with their nephew (in 1271–95). The first Catholic missionary to enter China was Franciscan friar John of Montecorvino, who reached Khanbalik (Beijing) in 1294, shortly after the death of Kublai Khan. John built a church there and reported in 1305 that there were 6,000 converts. In 1307, Pope Clement V appointed him archbishop of Khanbalik and primate of Cathay (North China) and the entire Far East. When John died in 1328, it was estimated that there were more than 10,000 Catholics. In 1338, at the request of the last Mongol emperor, Toghan Timur, Pope Benedict XII sent a group of missionaries, among whom was John of Marignolli. But when the Yuan dynasty collapsed in 1368, the Catholic Church, which then numbered about 30,000 and had enjoyed imperial support, disappeared with it. To the Chinese, the Catholic Church, even more than the Nestorians, appeared as a foreign religion, protected by a foreign government, the Yuan, and financially supported by a foreign power, the West.

Catholic presence under the Ming Dynasty

Almost 185 years later, the Catholic Church attempted once more to enter China, which, under the Ming dynasty (1368–1644), had become isolationist, nationalist, and rigidly Confucian. Francis Xavier (1506–52) left Japan for mission in China in 1551 but died the following year on the small island of Sancian, within sight of the China coast, near Guangzhou. Under the Padroado (patronage) of Portugal, Xavier's missionary dream was fulfilled by a small band of Jesuits, particularly Alessandro Valignano (1538–1606), Matteo Ricci (1552–1610), and Michele Ruggieri (1543–1607). From Macau, a small Portuguese colonial enclave (with a diocese established in 1576), Ricci and Ruggieri entered mainland China. Following Valignano's accommodationist method, the two missionaries, Ricci in particular, learned the language, studied the Chinese classics, dressed in Confucian scholars' garb, and tried to convert the Chinese through science (especially mathematics, astronomy, and map-making). Ricci's goals were to reach Beijing and to convert the emperor. Though he failed in his latter goal, he was allowed by Emperor Wanli to reside in Beijing in 1600. In the last ten years of his life, Ricci, known in Chinese as Li Matou, was much more successful than in his previous 17 years. Among his converts were the so-called "Three Pillars of the Chinese Church": Paul Hsu (Xu Guangshi), Leon Li (Li Zhizao), and Michael Yang (Yang Tingyun), though the last was not taught by Ricci.

Other prominent Jesuits who worked in Beijing until the fall of the Ming dynasty (1644) and beyond include Nicholas Longobardi (1559–1654), Adam Schall (1592–1666), and Ferdinand Verbiest (1623–88), the latter two directing the prestigious Bureau of Astronomy. At the end of the Ming dynasty there were 150,000 Chinese Catholics.

The decline of the Catholic Church under the Manchu (Qing) Dynasty

At the beginning of the Manchu dynasty, the prospects of Catholic missions were promising. Thanks to his accurate prediction of the solar eclipse on September 1,

1644, Schall was appointed by the second Manchu emperor, Shunzi, to be director not only of the Bureau of the Calendar but also of the Institute of Mathematics. The emperor also gave the Jesuits a piece of land, a church, a residence in the capital, and an annual subsidy. Verbiest, who succeeded Schall and served for 20 years, was much decorated by the third Manchu emperor, Kangxi (reigned 1662–1723).

Unfortunately, internal struggles among missionaries soon threatened to unravel Catholic missions in China. Until 1631, the Jesuits had enjoyed a monopoly in China. From the 1630s, however, other religious orders arrived, in particular, Dominicans (1631), Franciscans (1633), Augustinians (1680), and Missions Étrangères de Paris (1683). These newcomers brought with them not only conflicts between the two rival patronage systems – the Spanish and the Portuguese – but also the nascent colonizing ambitions of France. More tragically, they adopted different attitudes toward Chinese cultural and religious practices, in particular the sacrifice offered to Confucius and the veneration of ancestors. In Ricci's footsteps, most Jesuits, who worked mainly with the elite, tolerated these customs as non-superstitious acts of political and civil nature, whereas the newly-arrived missionaries, who labored among the uneducated masses, condemned them as idolatry. These contrasting positions brought about what is known as the Chinese Rites Controversy, which began in 1633 and did not end until 1939. Popes Clement XI (in 1715) and Benedict XIV (in 1742) proscribed the Chinese rites. These condemnations proved disastrous for Catholic missions in China. In retaliation, Emperor Kangxi banished missionaries from China in 1722 unless they followed Ricci's policy, and his decision was confirmed by his successor Yongzheng. In the next 160 years sporadic persecutions broke out, Christians were ordered to apostatize, churches were seized, and native priests forced to secularize. Nevertheless, the Chinese Catholic Church survived. In 1800, there were reported to be 200,000 Catholics in all of China.

Catholic missions in the nineteenth century

At the beginning of the nineteenth century, Catholic missions in China were complicated by the arrival of Protestants, mostly British, who devoted much of their energies to education and medical welfare. With the new missionaries, other colonial powers appeared on the scene. The Opium War of 1839–42 and 1856–60, which humiliated China, concluded with favorable treaties for Britain, France, Russia, and the United States. These unequal treaties, besides forcing China to concede economic advantages to Western powers, stipulated the legal right of missionaries to preach and to erect churches in Chinese territories. Even the Chinese Christians were protected by the treaties as a special class, immune from Chinese laws. Catholic missions, in particular, were protected by France. Catholics were often segregated in isolated communities and were often regarded as foreign colonies, completely dependent on missionaries. In 1841, a Catholic mission prefecture was established in Hong Kong when the island was ceded as a British colony in that same year. From 1860 on, Catholic and Protestant missionaries flocked in great numbers to China which soon became the world's largest mission field.

Eclipse of the Catholic Church under the Communist regime in the twentieth century

By the middle of the nineteenth century, Christianity had been compromised by the Taiping Rebellion (1851–64), led by Christian-inspired Hong Xiuquan, against the Qing dynasty. At the beginning of the twentieth century, anti-foreign sentiments were rumbling and exploded in the Boxer Uprising (1898–1900). Identified in the Chinese eyes with Western imperialism, Christianity suffered heavily. With the overthrow of the Qing dynasty (1912), in which Christians played a role, and with the establishment of the Republic of China, led by the Christian Zhongshan (Sun Yat-Sen), Christianity enjoyed what may be called its Golden Age (1900–20). The number of Chinese Christians was estimated at 366,00 in 1920, and in 1926 six Chinese bishops were consecrated. Now Christianity was welcomed as an antidote to Chinese traditionalism. However, its victory was brief. In 1920, it was denounced by a group of college students as an anachronistic obstacle to China's modernization, and Christian missions were accused of being a tool of Western imperialism. Again, anti-Christian movements broke out in 1924 and lasted until 1927, this time supported by political parties, both Nationalist and Communist. Thousands of missionaries had to leave, mission schools and hospitals had to be closed, and properties were damaged.

With the victory of the Communists over Jiang Jiashi's (Chiang Kai-shek) Kuomingtang in 1949, Christian, and in particular Roman Catholic, missions ended. The Three-Self Patriotic Movement Committee was founded in 1954, and all Churches were required to join it. In 1956, the Chinese Catholic Patriotic Association was established. As a result, there are two Catholic groups in China: the government-approved Patriotic Catholic Association, with more than 100 official bishops and roughly five million members, and the so-called "Underground Church," loyal to Rome, with possibly eight million members and 60 bishops. There are encouraging signs that the Vatican and Beijing are working toward a rapprochement

Taiwan

In the sixteenth century the small island located 100 miles off the southeast coast of China, then known as Formosa, was often used as the launching pad for missions to mainland China. The Dominicans came and settled at the northern tip of the island in Jilong in 1626 and in Danshui in 1629. They were soon followed by Franciscans and Augustinians. The missionaries were active in Taiwan until their expulsion by the Dutch in 1642. Ecclesiastically, Taiwan belonged successively to the dioceses of Macau (1576), Nanking (1660), Fukien (1696), and Amoy/Hsiamen (1883). In 1913, Taiwan was detached from Amoy and was made an apostolic vicariate. Currently, the Catholic Church in Taiwan has seven dioceses and 307,000 members (1.39 percent of the population of 22 million). Since 1949, the Vatican has maintained a nunciature in Taiwan, and it has not complied with the demands of the People's Republic of China to sever its diplomatic links with the Republic of China.

Vietnam

The beginnings of catholic missions in the seventeenth century

Christianity first appeared in Vietnam in 1533 with the coming of a Westerner by the name of I-Ni-Khu (Ignatius). In the next several decades a small number of Dominican and Franciscan missionaries briefly visited the country. Vietnam, then known as Annam, was considered part of the China mission and lay under the jurisdiction of the Portuguese Padroado. Systematic missions were begun by the Jesuits in 1615, and until 1659 the bulk of missionary work was carried out by them. Among these the best known is Alexandre de Rhodes (1593–1660), who worked in both the northern (Tonkin) and southern (Cochin China) parts of Vietnam, off and on, from 1624 to 1645. In 1645, de Rhodes left Macau for Rome to recruit more missionaries, and more importantly, to promote his plan of establishing a local hierarchy, since no amount of missionaries would be sufficient for the number of Vietnamese Catholics which he reported, not without exaggeration, to be 300,000. Because the Portuguese Padroado was no longer able to provide for missions and to avoid its many abuses, de Rhodes proposed that bishops be appointed as vicars apostolic directly responsible to the Congregation of the Propagation of the Faith (*Propaganda Fide*). Two French priests, François Pallu and Pierre Lambert de la Motte, were made bishops, the former for Tonkin and the latter for Cochin China.

This action proved momentous for the future of Catholic missions in Asia, and in Vietnam in particular. It freed them from the interferences of Portugal; it introduced into the Asian mission field a new group of missionaries, the Missions Étrangères de Paris, one of whose founders was Pallu; and it eventually provided France with an excuse to colonize Vietnam.

The Church steeped in blood

From its very beginnings the Vietnamese Catholic Church suffered heavy persecutions from political rulers. In the seventeenth and eighteenth centuries, 30,000 Catholics were killed, followed by a further 40,000 under three emperors, Ming Mang (1820–40), Thieu Tri (1841–7), and Tu Duc (1848–83); and 60,000 by the Van Than movement (1864–85). Of these, 117 were canonized by Pope John Paul II in 1988. The reasons for the persecutions were complex. Politically, Catholics were regarded as collaborators with France, which used the persecution of French missionaries as an excuse to invade Vietnam in 1859. Religiously, Christianity was branded as the *ta dao* (false religion) insofar as it was perceived to undermine the moral and religious foundation of Vietnamese society.

The Church in a divided country until 1975

In 1954, French colonial rule was ended, and Vietnam was provisionally divided into two parts at the 17th parallel, with general elections stipulated in 1956 to decide about a unified government. Such general elections however did not take place, and Vietnam was permanently divided into the Democratic Republic of Vietnam (Communist) in the north and the Republic of Vietnam in the south. As a result, some 700,000 Catholics emigrated from the north to the south, causing a dramatic loss for the Church in the north. Under the Communist regime the Church's activities were severely curtailed. The permanent division also brought about the so-called Vietnam War, which ended in 1975, with the victory of the Communists.

The Church under the Socialist Republic of Vietnam

With the country reunited under the Communist government, the Church suffered great losses. Its educational and social institutions were confiscated and all its religious organizations disbanded. Hundreds of priests were sent to "reeducation camps." Pastoral activities were strictly regulated. Several hundred thousand Catholics emigrated, causing another hemorrhage in the Church. Since 1988, the Communist government has adopted a somewhat more relaxed attitude, allowing the opening of six major seminaries and other public Church activities. Though freedom of religion is officially guaranteed, religious persecutions still occur. Currently, the Catholic Church in Vietnam has 25 dioceses and 5,539,000 members (6.7 percent of the population of 82,319,000).

Japan: "The Christian Century"

The arrival of Francis Xavier and his Jesuit colleagues in Kagoshima in 1549 marked the beginning of Christianity in Japan, then convulsed by civil war. The Jesuit missions continued after Xavier's departure in 1552 and encountered spectacular success, thanks partly to warlord Oda Nobunaga's favorable attitude toward the Christians and to Alessandro Valignano's accommodationist policies. By 1581, there were more than 100,000 converts. Thirty years later, there were 300,000. Indeed, 1549–1650 has been called the "Christian Century" of Japan.

This does not mean that the Church did not meet with great difficulties. When Nobunaga was killed in 1582, he was succeeded by Toyotomi Hideyoshi (1537–98). At first, Hideyoshi seemed well-disposed toward the Jesuits, but in 1587 he suddenly issued an edict of exile against all missionaries. Mission properties, especially in Nagasaki, Osaka, and Fukuoka, were confiscated. Toleration was however practiced in the next decade, though Hideyoshi introduced execution and had 26 Christians put to death in Nagasaki in 1597. In 1593, the Franciscans were allowed to enter Japan from Spain and the Philippines; also so were the Dominicans and Augustinians in 1602. These new arrivals, as happened in China, adopted a different view of the Japanese culture and religions and soon rivalries and antagonism broke out between them and the Jesuits. Hideyoshi's successor, Tokugawa Ieyasu (1542–1616) at first tolerated Christians, but in 1614 he issued an anti-Christian edict in which Christianity was accused of undermining Japan's three great religions, i.e., Buddhism, Shintoism, and Confucianism. More ruthless persecutions were unleashed by Ieyasu's son, Hidetaka (1605–23) and grandson, Iemitsu (1621–51). The final anti-Christian edict of 1639, which declared Japan off-limits to all missionaries, brought the Japanese "Christian Century" to an end.

The Catholic Church returned

The Tokugawa shogunate, which had attempted to eradicate the Japanese Catholic Church, disintegrated in 1868, nine years after the United States forced Japan to open its ports to the West. Power was restored to the emperor Meiji (1852–1912). During the final years of the Tokugawa shogunate and especially during the Meiji Restoration (1867–1912) Catholic missions returned to Japan. Theodore Augustin Forcade of the Missions Étrangères de Paris opened a mission at Naha in 1844 and Prudence Gerard in Tokyo in 1859. It was shortly afterward that an intriguing discovery was made in Nagasaki. In 1865, Bernard Petitjean was met by a group of the descendants of Christians who had apostatized during the persecutions of 1615–34. These Christians, called "Hidden Christians" (Kakure Kirishitan or Kirishitan no Senpuku) or "resurrection Christians," hid their faith by adopting certain beliefs and practices of Buddhism and Shintoism and village customs. Many but not all returned to the Church after they were discovered; those who did not do so feared that their religious practices would be condemned as superstitious. The Meiji government once again cracked down on the Hidden Christians and executed 200 of them before the prohibition of Christianity was revoked in 1873.

The Church after 1945

With the disestablishment of state Shinto after Japan's defeat in 1945, full religious freedom was given to all religions. The renewal of the Church was not only facilitated by the new political conditions but also spearheaded by Vatican II's reforming impulses. Liturgical reform, ecumenical dialog (a common translation of the Bible), inter-religious dialog (particularly with Zen Buddhism), activities in favor of justice and peace (with special attention to migrant workers, Buraku minorities, and Korean residents), and efforts at making the Catholic Church a local/Japanese Church have been energetically undertaken. Deserving special attention is the National Incentive Convention for Evangelization (NICE) which seeks to establish the basic orientations and priorities for the Japanese Catholic Church in the twenty-first century. Currently, the Japanese Church has 16 dioceses, divided into three ecclesiastical provinces, and 506,000 members (0.38 percent of the population of 133 million).

Korea

Already in the sixteenth century, during the Japanese invasion of Korea (1592), some Christians had penetrated into the "Hermit Kingdom." The Spanish Jesuit Gregorio de Cespedes and the Japanese Jesuit brother Leon Hankan accompanied the invading army led by the Christian *daimyo* Konishi Yukinaga. When Korea fell to Japan, several Koreans, among them a 12-year-old boy, were brought back to Japan. The boy was baptized as Vincent in 1592, and a small Korean Catholic community was set up in Nagasaki. Another sign of the presence of the Christian faith in Korea was the summary of Ricci's *The True Meaning of the Lord of Heaven* by a Korean Confucian scholar, Yi Syu-Kwang. The third opportunity for Christianity occurred when the Manchus, after their defeat of the Ming dynasty, took to Beijing as hostage So-hyun, the crown prince of Korea, which had sided with the Ming. While in Beijing, the young prince was befriended by the Jesuit Adam Schall. On his return to Korea in 1645, the prince took with him eight Chinese Catholics. Unfortunately, he died 60 days after his return, and the Chinese Catholic entourage went back to China.

Missions by Koreans to Koreans

It was not until 1784 that Catholic Christianity came to Korea. Every year Korea sent two embassies to the imperial court of Beijing. The winter embassy of 1783 included a young scholar, Lee Seung-Hun (his family name is also transliterated as Yi, I, Rhee, and Ni), who had been asked to bring back Western books on religion and mathematics to a group of Confucian scholars. Lee met with the Jesuit Jean-Joseph de Grammont, who baptized him as Peter. Upon his return to Korea, Peter Lee baptized his friend Lee Pyok (Lee Tok-jo) as John Baptist and together they baptized a thousand others. They "ordained" leaders and commissioned them to celebrate the sacraments. Soon, the new religion suffered persecution by the Confucianists. Ten Catholics were martyred, though the two Lees apostatized. Peter Lee repented, and in 1789 and 1790, he wrote letters to de Gouvea, the bishop of Beijing, begging forgiveness for his apostasy and the canonical irregularities of his sacramental celebrations. Soon, the Korean Catholic community suffered another wave of persecution, and once again, Peter Lee apostatized. In spite of these setbacks, the number of Catholics grew to 4,000 in 1795. Meanwhile, Bishop de Gouvea had dispatched a Chinese priest, James Chou Wen-Mo, who arrived in 1795. Persecutions broke out repeatedly for 60 years, in 1801, 1815, 1827, 1839, 1846, and most cruelly of all, in 1866–7. Of the 10,000 estimated to have been martyred, 103 were canonized by Pope John Paul II in 1984.

The Church and Korean independence

From 1876 Korea ceased to be the Hermit Kingdom and began the so-called "Open Door Policy Era" by concluding treaties with Japan, the United States, Britain, Germany, Russia, and France. Thanks to this openness the Church enjoyed freedom and experienced a significant growth. The number of Catholics increased from 13,625 in 1885 to 73,517 in 1910. In this same year, Korea was annexed by Japan, which exerted a rash and exploitative rule until 1945. During this colonial period, Catholic authorities were in general opposed to armed resistance against Japan, though some Korean Catholics participated in the independence movement. In addition to foreign domination, the Catholic Church was also challenged by three new forces, namely, the imposition of Shintoism, Protestant missions (which arrived in 1884), and the Korean Communist Party (founded in 1925).

The Church in a divided country

At the end of World War II, Korea was divided into two parts at the 38th parallel. The division became permanent in 1948, with the Republic of Korea in the south, and the Democratic People's Republic under Communist rule in the north. At the time, there were 180,000 faithful (50,000 in the north, 100,000 in the south, and 20,000 in the Diocese of Yenki of Manchuria) or 0.7 percent of the population. In 1950, North Korea launched an attack on South Korea, initiating the Korean War. As a result, the Church in North Korea was destroyed, while it was supported by the government of South Korea because of its strong anti-Communist stance.

After the Korean War, while the Church in the north languished, it prospered in the south, though at first, it was repressed by the first president, Rhee Syngman, whose dictatorial and corrupt government was strongly opposed by Paul Rho Gi-nam, Bishop of Seoul. Rhee's government was toppled in 1960 and was succeeded by the long presidency of General Park Chung-hee (1963–79). During this time the Church experienced phenomenal growth, with 800,000 members in 1980.

The Church after Vatican II

Like the Japanese Church, the Korean Church received a significant impetus for renewal from the council. Special attention was given to inculturation, ecumenical and interreligious dialog, justice, and peace, and the reunification of North and South. The influence of the Church is evident in the fact that a Catholic, Kim Dae-jung, became president in 1998. Currently, the Catholic Church in South Korea has 16 dioceses and one military ordinariate and 4,308,000 members (8.7 percent of the population of 49,392,000).

The Philippines

Unlike the other countries discussed here, the Philippines is the only Asian country with an overwhelming Christian population. Furthermore, Catholic missions in the Philippines were under Spanish rather than Portuguese patronage, since Ferdinand Magellan was the first European to discover the country, in 1521. The Magellan expedition baptized a few thousands on the island of Cebu, but the Christianizing of the Philippines was cut short by Magellan's death in April of the same year.

The Church under Spanish rule

Real evangelization of the Philippines commenced only with the arrival of the Spanish expedition from Mexico under the command of Miguel de Legazpi in 1565. At first, conversions on Cebu island were few, only a hundred up to 1570. However, the pace picked up significantly after Legazpi moved his headquarters to Manila on the island of Luzon in 1572. The Spanish character of the early Filipino Church was accentuated by the arrival of the Franciscans in 1578, the Jesuits in 1581, the Dominicans in 1587, and the Recollects in 1606. Manila was made a diocese in 1580, with the Dominican Domingo de Salazar as the first bishop, and in 1595 it was raised to an archdiocese with three suffragan sees (Cebu, Nueva Caceres, and Nueva Segovia).

Because of the large number of missionaries and in order not to neglect less accessible islands, in 1594 religious orders were assigned different fields of missions. The Augustinians held on to their missions in Cebu, Panay, and the Tagalog and Pampango regions in Luzon. The Franciscans took the Bicol Peninsula and the Laguna de Bay. The Dominicans received the provinces of Bataan, Pangasinan, Zambales, and northern Luzon. The Jesuits were given the islands of Bohol, Leyte, Samar, and parts of Mindanao. Finally, the Recollects, who came after the apportionment, were assigned to different parts of the archipelago.

The most lamentable deficiency of the Filipino Church in the first three centuries – until the end of the Spanish rule in 1898 – was the lack of systematic efforts to train a Filipino clergy. The Spanish crown preferred to maintain a direct line of ecclesiastical power from the Spanish kings to Spanish bishops to Spanish priests, a policy sanctioned by the hierarchy in the Philippines. It was only in 1621 that the first ordination of a Filipino (Augustin Tabuyo) to the priesthood took place, and it took another 34 years before the second (Miguel Jeronimo) occurred. Fortunately, the Church created a network of excellent educational institutions, from elementary schools to universities (e.g. the University of San Ignacio and the University of Santo Tomas), from which an indigenous clergy eventually emerged.

The Church and national independence

Despite the fact that Spanish Catholic missions had fused the various peoples and islands of the Philippines into one country with a common national identity and faith, and in spite of the many educational, medical, social, and material benefits they had brought to the country, by the 1870s there were rumblings of discontent against not only the Spanish colonial rule but also the foreign-dominated Church. Spanish political domination, economic exploitation, and arrogance fueled movements of national independence in which Filipino clergy took part. In 1872, three Filipino priests (Burgos, Gomez, and Zamora) were put to death on a charge of sedition and treason. Widespread, at times violent, opposition was directed against the Church and the missionaries. Patriotism developed into anticlericalism. This was nowhere clearer than in José Rizal (1861–96). In 1896, a revolution was begun in the province of Cavite under the leadership of Emilio Aguinaldo (1869–1964) and the struggle for independence was brought to a successful end by the US naval victory over the Spanish fleet in Manila Bay on May 1, 1898. Sadly, the dreams for national independence were crushed when the Philippines was transferred from Spain to the United States in the Treaty of Paris which concluded the Spanish–American War. Full independence from the US was not achieved until 1935.

The rise of the independent Philippine Churches

The dream of an independent Filipino Church was carried out by Gregorio Aglipay (1860–1940), a priest of the archdiocese of Manila, who wanted to be a Filipino not a Spanish Catholic. In 1898, he joined the revolution of Emilio Aguinaldo and was made military vicar general of the revolutionary army. He went on fighting against the Americans as the US occupied the Philippines. In 1899, he was excommunicated by Archbishop Nozaleda on the charge of usurping the episcopal office. Meanwhile, another Catholic, Isabelo de los Reyes Sr (1864–1938) also attempted to organize a Filipino Church separate from Rome. In 1902, de los Reyes persuaded a reluctant Aglipay to be the first supreme bishop (Opispo Maximo) of the Philippine Independent Church (Iglesia Filipina Independiente).

In the Aftermath of Vatican II

Like other Asian Churches, the Catholic Church in the Philippines underwent a transformation after the Second Vatican Council. The difference, of course, is that it had both the personnel and the resources to carry out the reforms mandated by the council. Needless to say, of the five countries surveyed, the Philippines can rightly boast of the most numerous and influential Catholic Church in Asia. Its impact on the society is enormous, as political events during the Marcos regime amply demonstrate. Currently, it has 85 dioceses and one military ordinariate and 68,721,000 members (78.2 percent of the population of 87,876,000).

Asian Catholicism Renewed

It has been noted above that the Catholic Church in the five countries under study (to a lesser extent, China) has been transformed by the reforms mandated by Vatican II. Indeed, one helpful way to understand Asian Catholicism is to examine the ways in which the Catholic Church in each of these countries has attempted to carry out the renewal mandated by the council. Two events can serve as the gauge of this renewal, i.e., the founding of the Federation of Asian Bishops' Conferences (FABC) and the Special Assembly for Asia of the Synod of Bishops (the Asian Synod).

The Federation of Asian Bishops' Conferences: "A new way of being Church"

The application of Vatican II to Asia was carried out immediately after its conclusion in 1965, but it was not undertaken systematically and comprehensively until after 1972 when the Federation of Asian Bishops' Conferences was brought into being. The FABC's stated purpose is "to foster among its members solidarity and co-responsibility for the welfare of Church and society in Asia, and to promote and defend whatever is for the greater good."

The pastoral goal of the FABC is to realize what it calls a "new way of being Church," an ecclesial mode of being which is inspired by Vatican II's vision and at the same time goes beyond it to respond to the various contexts of Asia. As the FABC's Fifth Plenary Assembly states: "Our challenge is to proclaim the Good News of the Kingdom of God: to promote justice, peace, love, compassion, equality, and brotherhood in these Asian realities. In short, it is to work to make a Kingdom of God a reality."

Making the reign of God the sole *raison d'être* of the Church entails important changes in the way the Church carries out its mission. The FABC makes dialog the comprehensive *modus operandi* of the Church in Asia. It is vitally important to note that for the Asian Churches dialog is not simply one activity among many others that the Church performs, but rather the basic and overarching *modality* in which the Church's entire mission and all its manifold and complex activities – witness, proclamation, conversion, and baptism, building up local Churches, forming basic ecclesial communities, catechesis, worship, incarnating the Gospel in peoples' cultures, promoting social justice and peace, interfaith dialog, theologizing, to name a few – are carried out.

Christian mission involves a fourfold presence. First, there is *dialog of life*, where people strive to live in an open and neighborly spirit, sharing their joys and sorrows, their problems and preoccupations. Second, *dialog of action*, in which Christians and others collaborate for the integral development and liberation of people. Third, *dialog of theological exchange*, where specialists seek to deepen their understanding of their respective religious heritages, and to appreciate each other's spiritual values. Finally, *dialog of religious experience*, where persons, rooted in their own religious traditions, share their spiritual riches, for instance, with regard to prayer and contemplation, faith and ways of searching for God or the Absolute. This fourfold presence takes place, according to the FABC, in three dialogs, i.e., liberation, inculturation, and interreligious dialog, corresponding to the three contexts of Asia: massive poverty, cultural diversity, and religious pluralism.

The Asian Synod: The Church as communion of local churches

An occasion for the Asian Churches to exhibit their new way of being Church occurred when Pope John Paul II convoked a Special Assembly of the Synod of Bishops for each of the five continents to celebrate the coming of the third millennium of Christianity. A special theme was chosen for each, the one for Asia being "Jesus Christ the Savior and his mission of love and service in Asia."

During the synod, which began on April 19 and concluded on May 14, 1998, there were 191 "interventions" on the floor, of eight minutes each. Needless to say, there is a great diversity in the contents of these short speeches as they represented the vastly different faces of the Church in the immense continent of Asia. Nevertheless, on the whole, the Asian bishops did speak with a remarkably consistent voice about the basic needs and tasks of Christianity in Asia. As the FABC has repeatedly insisted, Christian mission in Asia can only be carried out in the form of dialog in three intimately inter-related areas: with Asian cultures, Asian religions, and Asian poor. Furthermore, to perform this dialog successfully, the Asian bishops believed that a legitimate autonomy of the local Churches, which is proper to and required by the principle of subsidiarity, is necessary. This autonomy enables the local Churches to decide, in consultation with the other Churches of the same region, what pastoral policies and practices are most effective for their evangelizing mission and for the life of the Christians, without undue control by or interference from the Roman Curia. This autonomy, the Asian bishops believed, is not opposed to the supreme authority of the bishop of Rome. On the contrary, it promotes collegiality and communion among the bishop of Rome and the other bishops and thus brings forth the manifold riches of the universal Church.

Speaking in the name of the Indonesian Bishops' Conference, Francis Hadisumarta, the Carmelite bishop of Manikwari, said that "the Catholic Church is not a monolithic pyramid. Bishops are not branch secretaries waiting for instruction from headquarters! We are a communion of local Churches." He pointed out the absurdity of the practice of having liturgical translation and adaptation of the Asian Churches approved by Roman officials, "who do not understand our language." Another way to achieve the new way of being Church in Asia is to bring back the ancient tradition of patriarchate rooted in communion, solidarity, and collegiality. Hadisumarta urged that the Church move from adaptation to inculturation and create new, indigenous patriarchates in Asia. He went on to suggest that "in many crucial pastoral areas we need to adapt Church law. We need the authority to interpret Church law according to our own cultural ethos, to change, and where necessary, replace it."

Another oft-repeated point in the interventions refers to the need to expand the roles of the laity, especially women, in the life of the Church. The ecclesiological model which the Asian bishops tried to promote is what has been called "participative Church," namely, a Church in which all members are fundamentally equal in dignity and share responsibility for the whole Church, though with different functions and duties.

The Future of Asian Catholicism

On November 6, 1999, Pope John Paul II came to New Delhi to promulgate his post-synodal Apostolic Exhortation *Ecclesia in Asia*. In a sense, the exhortation embodies some – but not all – of the achievements as well as the desiderata of the Asian Churches. The Asian Synod was the first official recognition that the Churches of Asia have come of age. To Rome the Asian bishops came back as a body after Vatican II, this time to teach – and not only to learn from – Rome and the universal Church, from their rich and diverse experiences of being Church in Asia, with surprising boldness and refreshing candor, with what the New Testament calls *parrhsia*.

The Asian Catholic Churches that participated in the Asian Synod were almost beyond recognition since they sprouted from the first seeds of the Gospel sown in the Asian soil four centuries earlier. Until the middle of the twentieth century, all the Churches of the five countries under study had remained mission Churches, heavily dependent on foreign missionaries, without a liturgy and theology of their own, with an underdeveloped laity, with the shameful legacy of entanglements with colonialism and imperialism, a stranger in the midst of their own people. Of course, any fair-minded historian will recognize the tremendous contributions of the Catholic Churches to their host countries in terms of technology, social services, education, health care, and culture, despite the misguided nature of the *mission civilisatrice* that Catholic missions at times took upon themselves. There is also the history of heroic witness to the Christian faith of so many martyrs, both foreign and native, whose blood is the seed of Christians. Nevertheless, it is no exaggeration to say that the Asian Churches were still experiencing growing pains as these countries were moving toward independence.

In light of this, what occurred in the Asian Churches in the 40 years after Vatican II was truly amazing. However, the Asian Churches know that there is still much to be done and that the journey is long. The number of Catholics in Asia remains minuscule. But, for the Asian Churches, the way forward is clear and well-defined. "If the Asian Churches do not discover their own identity, they will have no future." So declared the Asian Colloquium on Ministries held in Hong Kong on March 5, 1977. This search for self-identity, the Colloquium went on to suggest, consists in "the process of re-discovering that the individual Christian can best survive, grow, and develop as a Christian person in the midst of self-nourishing, self-governing, self-ministering, and self-propagating Christian community" (Eilers, 2002: 77). This self-discovery by the Asian Churches as *Asian* Churches capable of self-government, self-support, self-propagation, and self-theologizing was achieved by following Vatican II's inspiration *and* going beyond it, under the guidance of the FABC. The modality in which this self-identity is achieved is the fourfold presence in the threefold dialog as explained above: shared life, action, theological reflection, and religious experience with Asia's poor peoples, cultures, and religions.

A final note: This chapter focuses on Asian *Catholicism*. However, the picture of Asian *Christianity* would be seriously skewed if adequate attention is not given to the presence of Protestants, and to a lesser extent, Orthodox, in Asia. Indeed, the fortunes of Asian Catholicism have been intimately intertwined with Protestant missions, particularly in China, Japan, Korea, and the Philippines. This proves even truer today, especially in view of the activities of Pentecostals, and indeed, the future of Asian Christianity, at least in these countries, depends very much on how different Christian denominations relate to each other in their missions. Jesus' words, "That they may be one, even as you, Father, are in me and I in you, that they also may be in us, so that the world may believe that you sent me" (John 17: 21) have never been more urgent.

References and Further Reading

Eilers, F.-J. (2002) *For All the Peoples of Asia: Federation of Asian Bishops' Conferences. Documents from 1997 to 2002.* Quezon City, Manila: Claretian Publications.

Moffett, Samuel Hugh (1998) *A History of Christianity in Asia,* vol. I: *Beginnings to 1500.* Maryknoll, NY: Orbis Books.

Moffett, Samuel Hugh (2005) *A History of Christianity in Asia,* vol. II: *1500–1900.* Maryknoll, NY: Orbis Books.

Phan, Peter C. (ed.) (2002) *The Asian Synod: Texts and Commentaries.* Maryknoll, NY: Orbis Books.

Phan, Peter C. (2003a) *Christianity with an Asian Face.* Maryknoll, NY: Orbis Books.

Phan, Peter C. (2003b) *In Our Own Tongues.* Maryknoll, NY: Orbis Books.

Phan, Peter C. (2004) *Being Religious Interreligiously.* Maryknoll, NY: Orbis Books.

CHAPTER 15
Oceania

Tracey Rowland

The region of Oceania includes the many island "paradises" of the Pacific – Guam, Kiribati, the Marshall Islands, the Federated States of Micronesia, Nauru, the Northern Mariana Islands, Palau, and Wake Island (all classified as parts of Micronesia); American Samoa, the Cook Islands, French Polynesia, Niue, Pitcairn Island, Samoa, Tokelau, Tonga, Tuvalu, and the Wallis and Futuna Islands (all classified as parts of Polynesia); Fiji, New Caledonia, Vanuatu, and the Solomon Islands (all classified as parts of Melanesia) – as well as the larger island nations of Papua New Guinea (the largest of the Melanesian islands), New Zealand (the largest of the Polynesian islands), and the island continent of Australia.

This region first came to the attention of the Church in the sixteenth century when the Pacific islands fell under the Spanish sphere of influence, centered juridically in the Archdiocese of Mexico and later in the Diocese of Manila in the Philippines. The first Apostolic Prefect of "Terra Australis," Fr Vittorio Ricco OP, was appointed in 1681 but he died before any missionary initiatives were undertaken. For the next century and a half political events in Europe (the suppression of the Jesuits, the French Revolution, and the Napoleonic Wars) impeded the missionary efforts of the Church until the Congregation for the Propagation of the Faith was revived by Cardinal Bartolomeo Cappellari, prior to his election as Pope Gregory XVI in 1831. In 1835 he divided the region into the Vicariates of Eastern and Western Oceania, entrusting the first to the Congregation of the Sacred Hearts of Jesus and Mary (the Picpus Fathers) and the second to the priests of the Society of Mary (the Marists). In 1848 the name Eastern Oceania disappeared with further sub-divisions and from the late nineteenth century onwards numerous further divisions took place as dioceses and local hierarchies were established. Throughout this period the Roman Curia used Philippe Vandermaelen's six-volume *Atlas universel de géographie physique, politique, statistique et mineralogique*. Vandermaelen's choice of the word Oceania for one of the volumes gave rise to the use of the term for the mission fields of the Pacific. Australia was initially excluded from within its ambit but in recent times the Australian hierarchy has been included in the Synod of Oceania, a consultative body established by Paul VI in 1965 at the end of the Second Vatican Council.

The name "Australia" was first used by the Portuguese sea captain Pedro Fernandez de Quiros (1555–1614). In 1606 he left the Spanish harbor Callao, in Peru, to go west, hoping to find the southern continent. He thought he had done so when he arrived in Vanuatu. He named the island *Australie del Espiritu Santo* (the South Land of the Holy Spirit). His dream to take possession of the southern continent in the name of the Spanish crown and the Holy Spirit is the subject of an epic poem by the Australian poet, James McAuley (1917–76), entitled "Captain Quiros." An opera on the same theme has also been written by Australian composer Peter Sculthorpe. The epic begins with the voyage of Alvaro de Mendana, the 25-year-old nephew of the governor of Peru, to the Solomon Islands in 1568. Mendana was looking for gold. Quiros was with Mendana and later set out on his own mission to take possession of the South Land so as not to lose "those fields where grace might win the fairest harvest-yields" to the Protestant Dutch and English.

Notwithstanding the dream of the Spanish and a number of accidental landings by French and Dutch explorers, it was the British who were to colonize Australia in 1788, following the voyage of Captain James Cook in 1770. The first British settlement, a penal colony for British (including Irish) convicts, was at Port Jackson. The British also settled New Zealand and became the colonial administrators of Fiji, Tuvalu, parts of the Solomons, parts of Papua New Guinea which is now entirely within the British Commonwealth, though it was for a time divided into British and German regions, and numerous other smaller islands in the Pacific. Their colonial competitor, the French, took New Caledonia (after 1853), Vanuatu, and the Wallis and Futuna Islands as well as numerous smaller islands and atolls classified as French Polynesia.

During this early period of colonial history the British authorities looked to the Catholic Church in England for the provision of clergy to service the spiritual needs of a largely Irish Catholic population in Australia, while canonically Australia was under the ecclesial governance of the Vicar Apostolic of Mauritius, Dr William Morris OSB. In 1833 Dr Morris appointed fellow Benedictine, William Ullathorne OSB (1806–89) – lineal descendent of St Thomas More – as Vicar-General in Australia. He brought with him a library of some 1,000 books. Two years later, another Benedictine, Bishop John Bede Polding OSB (1794–1877), arrived. He carried the title of Vicar Apostolic for New Holland and van Diemen's Land until his appointment as Archbishop of Sydney in 1842. In 1842 Rome also approved the appointment of episcopal sees in Hobart and Adelaide, followed by Perth in 1845 and Melbourne in 1847. In 1877 Bede Polding was succeeded as Archbishop of Sydney by Roger Vaughan (1834–83), younger brother of Cardinal Herbert Vaughan, Archbishop of Westminster (1832–1903).

This group of Benedictines – Ullathorne, Polding, Vaughan – are associated with an era in Australian Catholic history known as the "Benedictine dream." They were highly educated men who carried a vision of Catholic culture and spirituality centered around monastic life, including the monastic emphasis on scholarship and solemn liturgy. The "dream" however was never realized because the English Benedictines and the English Church in general were unable to supply sufficient numbers of priests to meet the pastoral needs of the colony. Leadership of the Church in Australia fell into the hands of Irish clergy with other priorities and visions. While Polding took the view that the Australian Church had to develop its own identity, the predominantly Irish laity, led by Archdeacon John McEnroe, wanted "an Irish clergy for an Irish people." Even Polding's attempt to establish a choral society was opposed by Irish clergy and laity who insisted on Irish hymns in preference to Gregorian chant.

On the opposite side of the Australian continent, in the Western Australian diocese of Perth, the Irish–Benedictine conflict was so intense that the Irish bishop, John Brady, was eventually suspended from office by Pius IX, in part because of disputes with the Spanish Benedictine Dom Serra. Brady's vision was to settle the nomadic aboriginal peoples into villages and mission stations. The only one to succeed was that of New Norcia, founded by Dom Serra and Dom Salvado. Brady's supporters clashed with Serra and when they fought for possession of the bishop's house, Brady's supporters were defenestrated. Historian Patrick O'Farrell has written that the primary cause of the troubles was not national identity but temperament: "Serra was aristocratic in temperament, touchy and alone . . . driven by an imperious dream, that of a great network of Spanish Benedictine missions similar to that which the Franciscans had established on the west coast of America," while Brady was "a flamboyant demagogue" (O'Farrell, 1985: 76–7). The laity however did perceive the conflict in terms of Irish and secular clergy against Spanish and Benedictine clergy.

The Benedictine dream is said to have ended with the appointment of Francis Patrick Moran (1830–1911) as the third Archbishop of Sydney in 1884. Moran was part of the "Cullenite network" – a group of bishops who were either students or relations of Paul Cardinal Cullen of Ireland (1803–78). Cullen was Rector of the Irish College in Rome (1832–50), and for a time also Rector of Propaganda Fide and a friend of Gregory XVI and Pius IX. The Cullenite network was very influential. It included: James Quinn (Brisbane), Matthew Quinn (Brisbane), James Murray (Maitland), William Lanigan (Goulburn), Thomas Croke (Auckland, New Zealand), Patrick Moran (Dunedin, New Zealand) and Michael Verdon (Dunedin, New Zealand). Moran accompanied Cullen to the First Vatican Council. His era as Archbishop of Sydney is most remembered for developments in the field of education. In the 1870s a series of Education Acts made public education free, compulsory, and secular (Victoria: 1872; Queensland: 1875; New South Wales: 1880). This followed upon the establishment of the University of Sydney (1850) and the University of Melbourne (1853), both of which expressly excluded theology from the curricula. The response of Cardinal Moran to the problem of secular education was to set up a Catholic School system. He had the curriculum of Catholic schools constructed so that they taught the secular subjects to be found in the government schools, with the addition of a subject called religious education. This allowed him to claim that Catholic schools were doing the same job as government schools. In Melbourne, Archbishop Thomas Carr followed Moran's lead.

Moran's predecessor, Archbishop Vaughan, had however taken a different position. He believed that all secular education was a travesty, and that every subject needed to be delivered in a Catholic framework. His critique of the Moran style strategy anticipated the educational ideas of the twentieth-century English historian Christopher Dawson, and also the criticisms of the two-tiered account of the grace–nature relationship that flowed from the work of mid-twentieth-century scholars such as Henri de Lubac and Hans Urs von Balthasar. Contemporary scholars commonly identify the notion of an autonomous secular order as a post-sixteenth-century development inconsistent with Patristic and medieval notions of the secular as simply time this side of eternity.

In the effort to avoid sending Catholic children to government schools, numerous orders of religious were imported to found and staff Catholic schools. The most significant were the Sisters of Mercy, the Brigidines, the Presentation Sisters, the Loreto Sisters, the Dominican Sisters, the Christian Brothers, and the Marist Brothers. An Australian order, the Sisters of St Joseph, was founded by Blessed Mary MacKillop (1842–1909) in 1867. By the end of 1869 more than 70 of her sisters were educating children at 21 schools in Adelaide and in the countryside. The sisters followed farmers and railway workers and miners into the isolated outback. They made a major contribution to the social and educational life of the country towns. They built impressive convent buildings on prominent sites and they often taught Protestant children whose parents were prepared to pay the extra fees for what they judged to be a better education than that provided by the State system. This was particularly so in the field of music. This set a framework for ecumenical cooperation long before it became fashionable after the Second Vatican Council.

The Irish stamp on Australian Catholic culture was further embedded in the 1850s with the influx of Irish migrants to the goldfields. Whereas in the 1840s Victoria had 9,000 Irish born, by 1870 Victoria had 170,000 Catholics of whom 100,000 were Irish born. The first three archbishops of Melbourne were Irish: James Alipius Goold (1812–86), appointed in 1847, Thomas Joseph Carr (1839–1917), appointed in 1886, and Daniel Mannix (1864–1963), who was appointed as coadjutor Archbishop in 1912, and Archbishop in 1917. Mannix remained the Archbishop of Melbourne until his death in 1963. His episcopacy therefore spanned some five decades in Australian history. It is said that he never used a telephone or traveled in an aeroplane but he was the absolute monarch of his archdiocese. His episcopal style was in every sense regal. Although he was initially well received by the Protestant establishment when he arrived in Melbourne wearing top hat and tails, his early warm reception in such circles cooled because of his opposition to conscription during World War I. At the conclusion of the war Mannix told returned soldiers that they went to war for no unworthy ends, but that the objects for which they fought and won had been discarded at the Paris Peace Conference. In 1920 a wealthy Catholic layman, John Wren, organized a guard-of-honor of 14 Victoria Cross winners, each mounted on a white horse, to accompany the Archbishop's carriage at the St Patrick's Day procession through the center of Melbourne. Behind the carriage, 10,000 returned soldiers, accompanied by detachments of sailors and nurses, all in full uniform, marched eight abreast, before a crowd of 100,000 spectators. For some it was a dramatic demonstration that one could be both a Catholic and a supporter of the war effort, without being in favor of conscription; for others it was an ostentatious display of Irish Catholic social power for which a couple of generations would pay dearly for Protestant resentment and opposition to a Catholic ascendancy.

Primarily through the agency of the Jesuits at Newman College (University of Melbourne), Mannix promoted a new class of laity whose professional skills he valued. His scholarly interests won him the respect of many outside the Catholic community, though his Irish nationalism continued to be a source of contention, and his interest in

Irish politics got him arrested off the coast of Ireland by Scotland Yard detectives when attempting to visit Ireland in 1920. The British government feared his presence in Ireland would only exacerbate an already tense situation. When arrested he remarked that "since the Battle of Jutland the British navy has not scored a success comparable to the capture of the Archbishop of Melbourne without the loss of a single British sailor" and he added that "the Royal Navy has taken into custody the Chaplain-General of His Majesty's Forces in Australia."

The middle years of the twentieth century were a period of enormous growth for the Catholic community in terms of the numbers of parishes and schools and hospitals established, the numbers of men and women entering the priesthood and religious life, and the numbers of Catholics being born. As a typical example, in Queensland Archbishop James Duhig (1871–1965) presided over the foundation of 32 new parishes, 30 primary schools, 18 secondary schools, two university colleges, and a seminary, and he imported 35 new orders of religious to staff the diocesan expansion. By 1940 there were some 10,000 Catholic women in religious life. The parochial and secondary Catholic schools were supplemented at the tertiary level by a network of Catholic residential colleges at all seven of the secular universities. The most prominent of these were St John's and Sancta Sophia at the University of Sydney, and Newman and St Mary's at Melbourne University.

The issues that dominated the years prior to the Second Vatican Council (1961–5) were those of the campaign for state aid to Catholic schools, and the problem of the infiltration of the trade union movement by Communists and the consequent Australian Labor Party "split" of 1955. When Communists began to take control of the country's leading trade unions in the coal, steel, engineering, and shipping industries, working-class Catholics under the intellectual leadership of Bartholomew Augustine (B.A.) Santamaria (1915–98) fought against them. In 1954, Dr H.V. Evatt, the leader of the Australian Labor Party, blamed Catholics involved in this fight for Labor's loss at a federal election. At a national conference in Hobart in 1955, Santamaria's parliamentary supporters (some 104 members) were expelled from the Labor Party. This led to the formation in 1956 of the Democratic Labor Party (DLP). Its policies were explicitly anti-Communist and in favor of state aid to non-government schools. Although only ever achieving minor party status and eventually losing almost all of its influence in the 1970s, the DLP effectively kept the State aid issue alive. During this period DLP preferences went to the Liberal Party, whose leader, Sir Robert Menzies, eventually supported the principle of state aid to non-government schools. During the 1960s increasing amounts of state aid became available, culminating in the Karmel Report of 1973, after which both federal and state governments offered assistance to Catholic and other denominational schools. The Catholic Education Offices of dioceses that were once run by a handful of religious are now vast bureaucracies.

The "split" not only divided the Labor Party but it also divided the Catholic community and in particular the archdioceses of Sydney and Melbourne. While Mannix publicly supported Santamaria and the DLP, Norman Cardinal Gilroy of Sydney (1876–1977), the first Australian-born cardinal and veteran of the Gallipoli campaign in 1915, continued to support the ALP and eventually used his influence in Rome to have official Church support for Santamaria's Catholic Social Studies Movement withdrawn. The legacy of this division continues. Catholic parliamentarians who may have similar policy objectives are found in different and competing parties. While this means that the Catholic influence over policy formulation is rather more thinly spread, it also means that no one party can take the Catholic vote for granted.

In an ABC interview in 1961 Mannix described the Communist problem as "the most serious problem I have had to face in the hundred long years of my life." It was not only a problem for Australian Catholics in the trade union movement, but it became a central issue in public life in the mid-1960s as Australia was drawn into the Vietnam War. The appropriate response to the war became the source of another division within the Catholic community. Many of the 1960s generation of Catholic intellectuals were less concerned about Asian Communism than they were about US capitalism. They opposed Australia's involvement in the war and many of their number were later influenced by the liberation theology movement which gained popularity in the late 1970s and 1980s, though this movement waned somewhat after the fall of Communism in Europe in 1989, and the consequent intellectual displacement of Marxism by varieties of post-modernism, among the intellectual avant-garde.

The late 1960s and 1970s was also the era of post-Conciliar trauma as religious orders and seminaries went through an introspective phase of questioning their missions with reference to various interpretations of the documents of the Second Vatican Council. In 1968 Paul VI published the encyclical *Humanae Vitae* which affirmed the Church's opposition to contraception, and he also promulgated the *Novus Ordo Missae* (the "new" Mass) which not only made provision for liturgy in the vernacular, but substantially altered the form of the Tridentine Rite. While some laity dissented from the teaching against contraception, others lamented the loss of solemn liturgy. Over the next 30 years the laity tended to divide into factions, with one group promoting the liberalization of the Church's teachings across a range of issues; and another group maintaining loyalty to the magisterial teachings but being generally demoralized and disgruntled over the failure of the episcopacy to discipline dissenters, and over what they saw as the dumbing down of religious education in Catholic schools and the banalization of the liturgy. During this time many priests and religious sought laicization, vocations plummeted, and the numbers of those regularly attending Mass also dropped dramatically, while the numbers of Catholics availing themselves of liberal divorce laws, and what was in effect abortion on demand, increased just as dramatically. The era of strong episcopal influence over lay opinion and practice had ended. At the turn of the twenty-first century Catholics make up approximately 27 percent of the Australian population, but practicing rates are below 15 percent in many dioceses. The number of women joining teaching and nursing orders has declined so dramatically that the governance of the vast national network of schools and hospitals is in the process of being transferred to a new class of professional laity. Women religious who remained in their orders after the changes of the 1960s are now more commonly found running retreat and conference centers and engaged in other forms of pastoral care. The orders more popular with young women are Mother Teresa's Missionaries of Charity and the traditional contemplative orders such as the Carmelites whose numbers have remained stable. A high proportion of younger men and women in training for religious life come from Asian backgrounds. For many, their first association with the Catholic Church was as refugees or they are the children and grandchildren of refugees.

In 1996 Oxford-educated Dr George Pell was appointed Archbishop of Melbourne. He was an outspoken admirer of John Paul II and the late Archbishop Mannix, a member of the Congregation for the Doctrine of the Faith under the leadership of Cardinal Joseph Ratzinger (now Benedict XVI), a friend of Bob Santamaria at whose state funeral he presided in 1998, and a bishop who had publicly defended the unfashionable magisterial teachings against contraception and the ordination of women. His installation was attended by some 10,000 people, mostly loyal supporters, who had long regarded him as the *de facto* leader of the Church in Australia. His four short years as Archbishop of Melbourne are remembered as a period of expansion for Catholic educational institutions and for his support for lay initiatives and new ecclesial movements. He moved the diocesan seminary from outer suburbia into the center of the city between the University of Melbourne and St Patrick's Cathedral. The two Melbourne campuses of the Australian Catholic University were also brought in from the suburbs and consolidated in a new building one block from the cathedral. The Catholic Theological College was moved into new buildings two blocks from the cathedral and a session of the John Paul II Institute for Marriage and Family, a post-graduate theological institution founded by John Paul II at the Lateran University in Rome in 1981, was established on the same site. The overall effect was the creation of a Catholic educational precinct dubbed the "Pelican" – a pun on Vatican, the Archbishop's surname, and the pelican symbol on his coat of arms. Lay ecclesial movements such as Opus Dei and new congregations such as the Fraternity of St Peter were welcomed into the archdiocese, and a new religious education curriculum with doctrinal content was mandated for use in Catholic schools. Just as Mannix had interested himself in the ideas of young Catholic scholars at Melbourne University, Pell surrounded himself with a young post-Conciliar generation of intellectuals, and appointed one of their number, Dr Michael Casey, as his private secretary.

In 2001 Dr Pell was translated to the position of Archbishop of Sydney. Although Melbourne is the larger archdiocese, and historically the center of Catholic intellectual life in Australia, for historical reasons Sydney is the primatial see and in 2003 Dr Pell's *de facto* leadership of the Church in Australia was made *de jure* by his appointment as a cardinal. His years in Sydney have followed the same pattern as those in Melbourne, with emphasis given to the building of tertiary Catholic institutions, including a medical school under the auspices of the University of Notre Dame, and the encouragement of lay-led initiatives, such as the arts movement *Carnivale Christi*, an initiative of students from the University of Sydney which seeks to foster art, music, drama, and literature infused with a Christian metaphysic; as well as an intense engagement with the issues of contemporary public life, especially in the field of bioethics. Dr Pell's reputation in Rome as an institution builder and competent entrepreneur also helped to win the Sydney bid to be the site of World Youth Day celebrations in 2008.

Pell's leadership and educational interests were bolstered in 2003 by the appointment of Anthony Fisher OP as an auxiliary bishop of the Archdiocese of Sydney. Fisher is the first post-Conciliar generation bishop in Australia. He has played a prominent role in public bioethical debates and along with Bishop Eugene Hurley of the diocese of

Port Pirie, he has presided over the establishment of a national network of Respect Life Offices promoting John Paul II's vision of a culture of life. The work of these offices is primarily focused on cultural and spiritual change rather than direct political engagement, and as such represents a shift in emphasis from the pro-life strategies of the previous three decades. Implicit within the work of these Offices is the understanding that the laws of any given nation have a foundation in the moral values of the culture, and that unless the culture of countries such as Australia and New Zealand has a pro-life, pro-family and pro-marriage orientation, legal and political changes will be at best ephemeral.

At the beginning of the twenty-first century, the influx of Catholic refugees from Vietnam and China is changing the cultural profile of Australian Catholics. The dominance of the Irish is ceding to the emergence of a numerically powerful Catholic population of Asian extraction. The importance of the parish structure as the primary organ of Catholic social organization is ceding to the emergence of numerous lay ecclesial movements which operate across parochial boundaries and which have a small number of centers in the cities, while in country towns the shortage of priests is such that people commonly have to travel a long distance to attend Sunday Mass regularly. In the late 1990s the authority of the priesthood was tarnished by numerous sexual scandals and this has had a particularly devastating effect on Catholic morale and Mass attendance in country dioceses such as Ballarat. Although practicing rates remain low, those who are practicing tend to do so for reasons of intellectual conviction rather than tribal or nationalist loyalty. Among those in the under-30 age group the major influential factors tend to be an association with a new ecclesial movement and/or a World Youth Day experience.

Notwithstanding the decline in religious vocations, the Catholic Church is the largest non-state provider of social welfare in Australia. The St Vincent de Paul Society alone has 40,000 volunteers and 2,900 paid staff who assist around 800,000 people each year; this is in addition to the welfare provided directly through the Church's own agencies. The Missionaries of the Sacred Heart, the Pallotine Fathers, the Sisters of Mercy, the Missionaries of Charity, and other orders have been actively involved in the care and education of the Aboriginal peoples in northern Queensland, the Northern Territory and the Kimberley region of North-Western Australia. As early as 1868 Pius IX exhorted the Australian hierarchy to do more for the Aborigines. Notwithstanding their best efforts, however, the Aborigines remain the most socially disadvantaged section of the Australian community. Intense social trauma has been experienced by tribal communities trying to hold together a culture incompatible with the social and economic practices of late modernity.

To the southeast of Australia lies New Zealand, which shares with Australia the status of being a member country of the British Commonwealth, though unlike Australia, New Zealand was never a penal colony. The first Catholic settler was Thomas Poynton who landed in Hokianga in 1828. He and his wife pleaded for priests to be sent to New Zealand and in 1838 the French Marist Jean-Baptiste Pompallier, the Vicar Apostolic of Western Oceania, arrived in New Zealand. Pompallier built up good relations with the native Maori chiefs, learned their language, composed hymns in Maori, insisted that there should be no taking of Maori lands, and that people should come to worship in native dress. His basic approach to the Maori mission was given in his *Instructions pour les Travaux de la Mission*, completed in 1841. He advocated a gradual approach to the introduction of Christian morality such that only those ideas and practices which were quite contrary to Christian principles needed to be condemned. His work was assisted by Sister Suzanne Aubert (1835–1926), a Marist tertiary and nurse. In France she had received spiritual direction from the Curé of Ars, St Jean Vianney. Her noble background was a great asset, enabling her to negotiate with bishops. In 1892 she founded a women's religious institute of Our Lady of Compassion to staff an orphanage and a Home of Compassion in Wellington.

The Maori missions were also of special interest to Bishop Henry William Cleary of Auckland (1910–29) who was the first bishop after Pompallier to speak their language. He was also the first bishop to use air travel for episcopal visitation, he was a foundation member of the Auckland Aero Club, and he held a general fascination for cars, aeroplanes, and new forms of machinery. In 1916 when abroad for medical treatment he discovered that there was no chaplain with the New Zealand Second Brigade in France, so he volunteered and served with distinction on the front line. In 1918 he founded the journal *The Month* and had earlier been the editor of the *New Zealand Tablet*. His urbanity it said to have improved the standing of Catholics among Protestant leaders.

Just as in the early period of Australian history there was conflict between the Irish clergy and the English Benedictines, in New Zealand the Church was beset with an analogous conflict between the Irish clergy and the French Marists. Bishop Patrick Moran of Dunedin, another member of Cardinal Cullen's Antipodean network, not to be confused with fellow Cullenite Francis Patrick Moran, Archbishop of Sydney, founded the *New Zealand Tablet* in 1873 and used it as a vehicle for the promotion of Irish nationalism. In 1877, in a decision which was read as a response to British government pressure, Rome set aside the recommendation of the bishops of Australasia that Dunedin should be the Metropolitan diocese of New Zealand with Moran as its archbishop, and instead chose Wellington with Francis Redwood (1839–1935), an English Marist, as archbishop. Auckland (1848), Dunedin (1869), and Christchurch (1887) became the suffragan dioceses of Wellington. However the influx of Irish Catholics to the gold fields around Otago, and the increasing predominance of Irish clergy and religious teachers in the schools, meant that the Irish influence on the Church in New Zealand continued to be strong into the twentieth century.

Further similarities between the Church in Australia and that of New Zealand may also be found in their common opposition to secular education and fight for state aid to non-government schools. In 1877 the New Zealand government passed an Education Act guaranteeing that education would be "free, compulsory and secular." The New Zealand bishops responded in the same manner as the Australians, setting up a national network of parochial and secondary Catholic schools. The fight for state aid to Catholic schools was finally won in New Zealand in 1975 with the passage of the Conditional Integration Bill.

Today Catholics make up only 12.6 percent of the New Zealand population, including some 44,000 who have come from other Pacific islands, making New Zealand a more culturally Protestant country than Australia. However, within the Catholic community there are sociological sub-divisions similar to those in Australia, such as the division between those who accept the official magisterial teachings of the Church, and those in dissent, and between those who are members of the new ecclesial movements and those who rely on the parish system for their spiritual support.

To the north of Australia lies the large Melanesian island of Papua New Guinea, also a member of the British Commonwealth. In 1855 the Foreign Missionaries of Milan (PIME) attempted to establish a mission on Woodlark Island but those on board their boat, including Blessed Giovanni Mazzuconni, were massacred. In the 1880s groups of Missionaries of the Sacred Heart (MSCs) landed at Matupit Island and Yule Island and in 1889 Bishop Navarre MSC became Vicar Apostolic of British New Guinea and Father Henri Verjus MSC was named Vicar Apostolic of New Britain responsible for all of the colonial German New Guinea.

In 1899 Nevarre got a new auxiliary, Bishop Alain de Boismenu MSC – a friend of the French poet Paul Claudel who described him as a "man with the heart of a lion." He had been brought up by his sister Augustine, whom he joked was the only person in the world, other than the Pope, to whom he was unquestioningly obedient. He also befriended the Australian poet James McAuley, who worked in New Guinea, and was largely responsible for McAuley's conversion to Catholicism. De Boismenu opposed the Papuan administration's policy of allotting different denominational spheres of influence to missions and attempted to expand as much as possible. His work was ably assisted by Marie-Thérèse Noblet (1889–1930) who had been cured of tuberculosis of the spine at Lourdes. She suffered from bouts of demonic attacks similar to those recorded by the Curé of Ars, and indeed many missionaries who have spent time in New Guinea report that apparent demonic possession is a common phenomenon. Noblet and de Boismenu founded a Papuan society – The Handmaids of the Lord – to complement the work of the French sisters in 1918. De Boismenu also founded a Papuan society of Brothers of the Sacred Heart which included Louis Vangeke, an orphan brought up on a mission. Vangeke was to become the first indigenous priest (1937) and the first indigenous bishop, ordained by Pope Paul VI in 1970.

In 1889 Fr Louis Couppe was appointed Vicar Apostolic for the German Colonial area with its center at Kopoko. Like de Boismenu, he successfully opposed the policy of separate mission zones for different denominations. He also transferred the mission center from the colonial administrative center at Kopoko to a place he named Vunapope – the place of the Pope. In 1896 the Society of the Divine Word (SVD) took up the work of evangelization on the New Guinea mainland under the leadership of Eberhard Limbrock. By 1901 the Catholic Church had four centers for its missionary activity – Yule Island in the British section administered by Australia, and Vunapope, Alexishafen, and Kieta which fell under German jurisdiction.

The work of the missionaries was often highly dangerous. Ritual cannibalism was practiced as a means of protection against the spirit of an enemy killed in battle and often the head was not eaten but decorated and hung in the doorway of a "spirit house," a sacred hut that could only be entered by males who had passed their initiation rites. Inter-tribal warfare was also common. In 1904, ten missionaries and seven laity from the Vunapope Mission were massacred when trying to reconcile the Tolai and Baining peoples.

During the period between the late nineteenth century and the outbreak of World War I, the missionaries produced major anthropological and ethnological studies. The war however severely impeded their progress since they relied so heavily on financial assistance from Catholics in France and Germany. It was not until the 1930s that new milestones were achieved with the introduction of aeroplanes in 1935 making travel much easier for the missionaries, especially those in the highlands, and the foundation of the first major regional seminary at Vunapope in 1937.

These advances were followed by a period of persecution during World War II. The Divine Word Missionaries from the Vicariate of Central New Guinea (Wewak) with their bishop, Joseph Loerks, were interned on Kairiru Island and then sent by sea to Rabaul. On the way more missionaries were picked up by the Japanese and murdered on March 17, 1943. In February 1944 all the missionaries from the Vicariate of East New Guinea along with Bishop Wolff (seven priests, 16 brothers, 30 sisters) were being transported by sea to a Japanese prisoner-of-war camp when the Americans bombed their boat. Many of the missionaries, including the bishop, were killed. The Japanese tried to wipe out Christianity and to restore the practice of polygamy. A lay catechist who opposed both, Blessed Peter To Rot, was arrested in 1945 and sent to a concentration camp where he was given a lethal injection.

After the war new Missionaries of the Sacred Heart came from Australia, Ireland, and the United States. Australian Franciscans also came to assist in the work around Aitape and the Divine Word Missionaries went into the highlands around Goroka and Mount Hagan. In 1954 American Capuchins took responsibility for the southern highlands area, and in 1959 the Canadian Montfort Fathers (SMM) took over the new Prefecture Apostolic of Daru. In 1966, the hierarchy of Papua New Guinea was erected and Port Moresby was raised to the status of an archdiocese.

Today there are some 1.5 million Papuan Catholics spread across four metropolitan sees (Madang, Mount Hagan, Port Moresby, and Rabaul) with 12 bishops, 1,791 mission stations, and 339 parishes. Two-thirds of the Papuan population is in some sense Christian, with Catholicism being the dominant form, though half a million Papuans are Lutherans as a legacy of the German colonial administration, and one-third of the population continues to follow some form of animism and ancestor cults. The influence of the latter is especially felt in remote villages where certain people will have a reputation for healing and sorcery powers. The Sorcery Act (1971) makes it an offense even to claim to have magic powers for harmful practices, but the practice of sorcery continues to be a major source of civil disturbance.

Extending from New Guinea to the New Hebrides is the Solomon Islands chain. The first missionaries (Marists) arrived there in 1845 and soon afterward Bishop Jean-Baptiste Epalle was murdered when he refused to exchange his episcopal ring for two pieces of fruit. When Catholic missionaries, again Marists, returned to the Solomon Islands in 1898, it was as part of a steadily growing movement of European contact. By 1942 the Marists had 124 missionaries stationed at 34 posts – 22 in the North Solomons and 12 in the South and well over 30,000 Solomon Islanders were baptized Catholics, two-thirds of them in the North Solomons.

During the Second World War the Marists decided to stay on their missions and not abandon their people. In all two priests and two nuns were killed in the South Solomons while the northern vicariate lost four priests, six brothers, and two nuns. In 1950, 12 Anglican nuns swelled the numbers of Catholic missionaries when they were received into full membership of the Catholic Church. They were led by Mother Margaret of the Cross, a Cambridge-educated Englishwoman of 81 and her friend, Sister Gwen of the Cross, a graduate of London University. Later in the 1950s the Capuchins and the Dominicans sent priests to the Solomons and today some 75,000 Catholics are under the leadership of the Archbishop of Honiara. They make up approximately 20 percent of the population. Largely due to the work of missionary schools, they tend to be the better educated members of a community in which literacy rates are below 20 percent. Since an armed coup in 2000 the Catholic Church has been a major provider of emergency relief in a country whose infrastructure has broken down, where infant mortality and tuberculosis rates are high, and where Australian armed forces and police have been deployed to restore public order.

The situation is much better in the islands of New Caledonia where the Marists began work in 1843, led by Bishop Douarre. Today there are some 110,000 Catholics (60 percent of the total population) under the leadership of the Archbishop of Noumea, while in the neighboring Republic of Vanuatu, where the Marists arrived in 1847, there are now some 26,000 Catholics, comprising only 16 percent of the population. French is the official language of New Caledonia and some one-third of the population are descended from French settlers.

The islands of Wallis and Futuna also have a strong French culture and are self-governing (by a local king) French territories. Fr Pierre Chanel was martyred on the island of Futuna in 1841 after a chieftain's son asked for baptism, and within two years of his death the whole island had became Catholic and has remained so. The combined population of the two islands (some 14,000 people) is totally Catholic. French is the official language and the euro the unit of currency, champagne, and croissants are on the hotel menus, but for the most part the Polynesian rural way of life remains unspoilt by Western influence and tourist developments.

The traditional communal way of life has also remained strong is Samoa. On many of the Samoan islands there are no televisions, no contraceptives, and no other staples of modern Western culture. Christianity has replaced animism, and on Sundays churches are crowded and religious services are followed by family feasts. The Samoan vicariate, which was also a Marist mission from 1845, became a diocese in 1966 at the same time as the establishment of local hierarchies in other parts of the Pacific. Pio Taofinu'u was appointed its first bishop in 1968 and cardinal in 1973. Today there are some 37,000 Catholics in Western Samoa and some 9,000 Catholics in American Samoa.

In neighboring Fiji the Marists arrived in 1844 to find that the Methodist Church was already firmly established and in the period 1888–1927 Catholicism was officially outlawed. There are now 80,000 Catholics in Fiji under the leadership of the Archbishop of Suva, but they make up only 9 percent of the population. The Methodists make up 52 percent, and 38 percent of the population follow the Hindu religion as they tend to be descendants of Indian contract laborers brought to the island by the British in the nineteenth century. Political tensions between the native Fijians (who are mostly Christian) and the Indians resulted in military coups in 1987 and 2000. Archbishop Petero Mataca of Suva condemned the coup in 2000 and expressly rejected the close association of pro-Christian and pro-coup positions.

In other parts of the Pacific, the Federated States of Micronesia (some 600 islands and atolls) are the home of some 57,000 Catholics, the Republic of Kiribati 40,000 Catholics, the Republic of Pelau 8,000 Catholics, and the Republic of Nauru and the Republic of the Marshall Islands each include some 4,000 Catholics. In Guam, where the history of the Church began with the publication of a catechism by Fr Santidores in 1667, and the martyrdom of Blessed Diego Luis de San Vitores and Blessed Pedro Calungsod in 1672, there are now 119,000 Catholics. Although the mission in Guam was paralyzed by the Japanese presence during World War II and suffered the martyrdom of Fr Jesus Duenas by the Japanese in 1944, the island produced the first Micronesian bishop in 1970, and since 1984 the diocese of Agana has been the metropolitan See. In the Northern Marianas where Fr San Victoire SJ was martyred in 1668, there are now some 56,000 Catholics under the leadership of the local-born bishop, Thomas A Camacho, of the diocese of Chalen Kanoa. They make up 89 percent of the population. In French Polynesia where the Picpus Fathers began to evangelize in 1831 and where in 1838 the King and Queen of the Marquises became Catholics there are now 89,000 Catholics under the leadership of the Archbishop of Papeete (Tahiti). The Polynesian Cook Islands under the governance of New Zealand are the home to 3,000 Catholics, and the Polynesian Kingdom of Tonga Includes some 14,000 Catholics.

In an essay published in 1954 in which he reflected upon his experiences as an Australian government official in Papua New Guinea, James McAuley wrote that it was not the Western world's "sterile secularism with its will to desecrate, literally, all departments of life," nor its "disinterested liberalism with its inability to rationally affirm or practically defend its own values," that would help the peoples of the Pacific islands. He described these things as the "late luxury products or parasitical features of a Western civilization which had been founded and formed and maintained by far other commitments and disciplines, enthusiasms and sacrifices."

McAuley's judgments were echoed in the 2001 Apostolic Exhortation of John Paul II entitled *Ecclesia in Oceania*. With obvious reference to countries such as Australia and New Zealand, John Paul II noted that "the challenges of modernity and post-modernity are experienced by all the Churches in Oceania, but with particular force by those in societies most powerfully affected by secularization, individualism and consumerism." He acknowledged that many bishops identified the signs of a dwindling of Catholic faith and practice in the lives of some people to the point where they accept a completely secular outlook as the norm of judgment and behavior. Some scholars trace this development to decisions made in the nineteenth century during the education debates to offer in Catholic schools the same curriculum as that followed in the government "secular" schools with the addition of an added subject called religious education. It is argued that this gave rise to a way of thinking which was essentially secular and according to which one's theological beliefs in no way permeated all areas of life. This intellectual orientation was compounded by the not unreasonable desire on the part of Catholics to be accepted as part of the mainstream of their societies. The intensity of this desire however often gave rise to behavior and social strategies which have been described by Cardinal Francis George as the tendency to be "Catholic in faith, but Protestant in social practice." In sociological terms, religion in countries such as Australia and New Zealand tends to be merely "superstructural" (something privately added on by individuals) rather than infrastructural (something formative of cultural practices).

In the Pacific islands however, religion does tend to be more infrastructural and the major threat to this way of life comes from external factors such as the economic practices of the more modernized Western nations. Thus, John Paul II's Apostolic Exhortation included a warning that "the smaller nations of Oceania are particularly vulnerable to economic policies based on a social philosophy of economic rationalism"; and a plea that the natural resources of Oceania be protected against the harmful policies of some industrialized nations and transnational corporations which can lead to deforestation, the pollution of rivers by mining, the over-fishing of profitable species, and the fouling of fishing-grounds with industrial and nuclear waste.

At the beginning of the twenty-first century, the major problems faced by the Church in the region of Oceania are not so much those of a pre-Christian paganism as a post-Christian decadence, at least in Australia and New Zealand, while animism and tribalism, along with Western economic practices, remain a problem for the Catholic leaders of the smaller island nations. Leaving aside the Spanish dimensions of de Quiros' dream, the rest of his project remains partially fulfilled and partially yet to be realized.

References and Further Reading

Aerts, T. (1994) *The Martyrs of Papua New Guinea*. Port Moresby: University of Papua New Guinea Press.

Breward, I. (2001) *A History of the Churches in Australasia*. Oxford: Clarendon Press.

O'Farrell, P. (1985) *The Catholic Church and Community: An Australian History*. Sydney: UNSW Press.

Pompellier, J.-B. (1888) *Early History of the Catholic Church in Oceania*. Auckland: ET.

Wiltgen, R.M. (1979) *The Founding of the Roman Catholic Church in Oceania 1825 to 1850*. Canberra: Australian National University Press.

PART III
Catholic Doctrines

CHAPTER 16

The Practice of Catholic Theology

Joseph A. DiNoia

Readers of the final chapters of the Gospel of St Luke are treated to the remark-able story of an encounter between the risen Christ and two disciples on the road to Emmaus. The two disciples do not recognize Jesus as he joins them on their journey, and are amazed at how little this stranger knows about the troubling "events of the past few days." As they walk along, they inform him of the events surrounding the trial and execution of Jesus of Nazareth in Jerusalem. After hearing them out, Jesus rebukes them for being "foolish . . . and slow of heart to believe all that the prophets have declared!" "Was it not necessary that the Messiah should suffer these things and then enter into his glory?" Jesus asks. Then, "beginning with Moses and all the prophets, he interpreted to them the things about himself in all the Scriptures" (see Luke 24: 13–35).

Among the many interesting features of this story, there is something particularly instructive for our purposes here. The way in which Christ poses the question and then goes about answering it sheds light on very basic elements of the field of inquiry that has come to be called theology and that is our subject in this essay.

Theology as *fides quaerens intellectum*

Why was it necessary for Christ to suffer? The question is a cogent and difficult one, and once we start thinking about it we find ourselves asking additional questions. Why did Christ have to suffer *these things*? We believe that Christ died to save us from our sins, but how does dying in this way do that? Is the shedding of blood on the Cross like the shedding of blood in the animal sacrifices recounted and prescribed in the Bible? When God is brought into the picture, as he must be, the questions multiply. If God is all-powerful, can we say that any particular course of action is "necessary" for him? If God is all-good, then how could he have allowed his beloved Son to suffer so much? And so on.

Several things about this series of questions are noteworthy. For one thing, we see almost immediately that the initial question cannot be considered in isolation. In order even to think about it, we need to raise other questions as well. Quite significant is Christ's approach to answering the question as posed: from this we learn that the Bible is the first place to look in trying to get answers to questions like these. Fairly early in our inquiry we are likely to wonder what the Church, either in an official manner or within the broad context of her tradition, has thought and said about these questions. We find that the answers to some of our questions have already been formulated as doctrines of the Church. We recognize that our questions have been asked before by others, some of whom have had very interesting things to say about them. Eventually, we sense that questions in one area of our faith intersect with others. The question about why it was necessary for Christ to suffer is connected with questions about who Christ is, who God is, and who we are. Sometimes the questions that arise here lead to questions in other fields. We might wonder, for example, whether Christ's dying for our sake is in any way analogous to sacrificial death in other religious traditions.

Before proceeding further, we should take note of the possibility, despite the implicit scriptural warrant, of a principled objection to posing questions of this type. Someone might protest that the mysteries of Christian faith invite devotion and worship, not scrutiny. Although most Christians have taken to heart the cautionary nature of this objection, they have nonetheless been convinced that intellectual probing can itself be regarded as a form of worshipful response to the mysteries of faith. Because not only our hearts are called to adoration, but also our minds, scrutiny can be a form of worship. Because it has God and his mysteries as its object, theology can appropriately be done "on one's knees" (Balthasar, 1965).

The series of questions we have been considering shows *fides quaerens intellectum* in action. The phrase *fides quaerens intellectum* – "faith seeking understanding" – was coined by St Anselm of Canterbury (1033–1109), who was himself reframing some ideas of St Augustine (354–430). It has ever since been widely regarded as an apt description for the sorts of inquiries that are practiced in theology (Evans, 2000; 2004). Naturally, the phrase does not mean that raising questions of the type we have been considering automatically constitutes an inquiry as theological. The point is rather that faith by its very nature gives rise to a desire for deepened understanding, one that can, however, be pursued at a variety of levels of intensity and rigor. Built into faith is an intellectual restlessness (Cessario, 1996) and sense of wonder (Nichols, 1991) that drives inquiry.

Theology as such emerges, it seems clear, with the recognition that large bodies of questions can be related to one another and can usefully be ordered and addressed consecutively. By applying some systematic principles and careful reasoning, this kind of inquiry can provide an overall deepened understanding of the faith either for oneself or to form others in thinking about the Christian faith. Theology in the Catholic sense of the word can best be understood as an umbrella term for inquiries that pursue this deepened understanding of faith through the application of properly systematic and disciplined intellectual procedures such as are found in philosophy, in the physical and social sciences, and in history and the humanities (Congar, 1968).

Theology in Accord with Revelation

It has been precisely in connection with sorting out the similarities and differences between theology and other scholarly inquiries that its status as a distinctive field of study has come to be clarified and secured.

Although it is true that the types of interpretation and reasoning through which theology approaches its characteristic questions are like those found in other disciplines, the very fact that it presupposes faith seems to render it quite unlike other disciplines. To be sure, all fields of inquiry have to presuppose something or other in order to get started, even if nothing more than a given subject matter. But, unlike the given in other fields, theology seems to have to accept not only a particular given but what to think about this given as well. It is not only that certain materials – Scriptures, tradition, doctrines, etc. – are to be received in faith, but also that their fundamental meanings must be accepted in faith as in some sense already fixed. The very language we use betrays this: to say that we accept something "on faith" implies just the opposite of what we assume intellectual inquiries to be about – involving, as they do, an openness to finding out what is the case, rather than an acceptance a priori of some account of what is the case. Because theology seems to require as a starting point accepting beforehand an account of what is the case, it seems quite unlike other intellectual inquiries whose methodologies it apes. A more properly scientific approach to these materials and the questions they raise would be to expose them precisely to philosophical, historical, social, anthropological, and other types of inquiry – independently of the specifically religious commitments and expressions which these materials support in the life of those communities where they are taken on faith.

These issues have a modern ring to them and indeed they have been raised with particular force in modern times. But in fact, they arose well before modern times, serving to stimulate sustained reflection about the distinctive nature of theology in comparison with other scholarly pursuits. St Thomas Aquinas (1224–74) gave a great deal of thought to these issues, and his insights, at least in their essential drift, have been widely influential for all subsequent Catholic theology (Aquinas, 1964; 1986).

Presupposed to all the specific questions that reflection on the Bible and the Christian creeds elicits is a fundamental conviction about who God is and what he intends. This conviction is an essential feature of catholic Christian faith in almost all its varieties. It is the conviction that God is Father, Son, and Holy Spirit, a communion of life and love, and that he desires to share this communion of trinitarian life and love with persons whom he creates. Indeed, it would be true to say that no one has ever desired anything more than the triune God desires to share this communion with creaturely persons. God himself has disclosed to us (for how could we otherwise have known about it?) that this divine desire – more properly, intention and plan – lies at the basis of everything that God has done in creation, incarnation, redemption, grace, sanctification, and glory (Marshall, 2000).

To look at everything through the eyes of faith – to adopt, as it were, a "God's-eye view" – is to see everything in the light of this divine plan of salvation. To be able to do this is itself a divine gift involving the transformation of ordinary human capacities for knowing and thinking through what the Catholic tradition has called the infusion, at

Baptism, of the theological virtue of faith. When we look at things in faith – in the way God himself has taught us to do – we understand why we were created, why the Word became flesh, why Christ died and rose from the dead, how the Holy Spirit makes us holy, and why we will see God face to face. We were created so that God could share his life with us. God sent his only-begotten Son to save us from the sins that would have made it impossible for us to share in this life. Christ died for this, and, rising from the dead, gave us new life. To become holy is to be transformed, through the power of the Holy Spirit at work in the Church, into the image of the Son so that we may be adopted as sons and daughters of the Father. Glory is the consummation of our participation in the communion of the triune God – nothing less than seeing God face to face.

Faith, then, involves a kind of sharing in God's own knowledge of himself, and of things that he has done and is doing in creation and redemption. But it is, in a crucial sense, a *kind* of sharing. The triune God is one in being, action, *and* knowledge. He comprehends in a single act of knowledge the fullness of his Truth and Wisdom. Through the gift of faith, the believer is rendered able to participate in this divine vision, but always and only according to human ways of knowing. We know God truly, but not in the way in which he knows himself. Human understanding of the single mystery of divine truth is thus necessarily plural in structure. In this sense, we can speak both of the "mystery of faith" – referring to the single reality of the triune God who is one in being and action, and known by us through the gift of faith – *and* of the "mysteries of faith" – referring to our way of grasping the diverse elements of the single mystery of God's plan as we experience them in the life of the Church. All the mysteries of faith are facets of the single mystery of faith, which is nothing less than the triune God himself.

Catholic tradition uses the term "revelation" to describe the action and the content of this comprehensive divine disclosure. For the complex grace-enabled human response to this disclosure the specifically knowledge-related term is faith. The elaboration of this knowledge is called theology.

The existence of the body of knowledge to which revelation gives rise – sometimes called the deposit of faith – warrants the constitution of a field of study distinct from philosophy and the other cognate disciplines that typically investigate these areas of human experience (belief in God, religion, ritual, etc.). It also warrants the distinctiveness of the approach to the materials or sources in which this revelation is found, and establishes a vantage point from which to view all other fields of knowledge. The whole body of questions that can arise in theology are studied within the framework of a distinctive field of knowledge constituted by divine revelation.

According to this account, Aquinas was able to secure the scientific status of theology with reference to the model of scientific inquiry he found laid out in Aristotle's logical works (Chenu, 1959; Schillebeeckx, 1967). That theology derives its principles from a higher knowledge is not a factor peculiar only to theology. Aquinas noted that other so-called subalternated or subordinate disciplines do the same. Music, for example, depends on principles established not by itself but by arithmetic, and medicine on those established by chemistry and biology. Thus, we could say that music is subalternated to mathematics, since music depends on timing, intervals (of pitch), and other qualities which are measured by mathematics. This does not mean that doing calculus is more noble than playing the French horn, but only that musicians need arithmetic if they are to make headway in some of their own proper business, e.g., composing harmonies. Nor does it mean that one could reasonably demand that a musician answer questions about higher mathematics, nor that a mathematician must be able to play a musical instrument. It does mean, however, that one discipline depends on the other in such a way that the lower draws its principles from the higher.

According to Aquinas, the fact of such derivation or subalternation does not render the dependent science less scientific. While it is true that theology's principles are per se indemonstrable and thus not knowable in the way in which the arithmetical principles of music are, this does not rule out the scientific character of theology. Theology is like a derived or subordinate science with respect to the higher knowledge which is the *scientia dei* (God's own knowledge) as such.

For Aquinas, this permits in theology an inquiry of the highest possible degree of rigor – scientific in the sense described by Aristotle in his *Posterior Analytics*. But Aquinas' account is useful for describing the more broadly scientific or scholarly character of a whole range of practices and types of inquiry that fall under the broad umbrella of theology in its current forms. The level of conceptual precision that one is seeking in part determines the degree of rigor and the nature of the methodologies one employs in the study of the questions to which faith gives rise. Approaches that are more analogous to history, literary studies, and sociology than they are to philosophy can have a properly theological character if they are pursued within this framework of a principled acceptance, in faith, of the body of knowledge defined by revelation and thus constitutive for this field of study as such.

This account by no means excludes the possibility that the methods of philosophy, history, literary studies, sociology, or other disciplines could be applied to Christian materials independently of their status as vehicles of divine revelation. In other words, Christian materials can be considered under other descriptions – for example, as literary products or historical monuments – and can be studied with the formal interests associated with history or literary criticism. But in order for such studies to be properly theological, these materials must be viewed under a certain description – namely, as materials bearing revealed content – and with a specified formal interest – namely, as *fides quaerens intellectum*. Theology's distinctiveness as a science or independent discipline, as well as its scientific or scholarly character, are secured with reference to the body of knowledge created by revelation and in principle unknowable apart from it. While it is unlike other disciplines in taking this body of knowledge on faith, it is like many other disciplines whose principles are derived from other disciplines. In addition, it is like all other disciplines in possessing a formal interest in a particular body of knowledge and studying this body of knowledge with principles and methods appropriate to it.

Theology and Its Sources

In any scholarly discipline it is important to know where to look for the answers to our questions. Hence, in Catholic theology as in many other humanistic disciplines, the term "sources" is a handy one for designating the specific body of materials to be consulted and pondered in every theological inquiry.

If theology arises from faith in divine revelation, then it follows that its principal sources will be those in which this divine revelation is found and expressed. According to Catholic teaching, divine revelation is fully and definitively given in Christ who, as the incarnate Word, reveals God and his mystery to humankind. The Second Vatican Council states that "Christ . . . commissioned the Apostles to preach to all men the Gospel which is the source of all saving truth and moral teaching . . . This commission was faithfully fulfilled by the Apostles who, by their oral preaching, by example, and by observances handed on what they had received from the lips of Christ, from living with Him, and from what He did, or what they had learned through the prompting of the Holy Spirit. The commission was fulfilled, too, by those Apostles and apostolic men who under the inspiration of the same Holy Spirit committed the message of salvation to writing" (*Dei Verbum* §7).

The Sacred Scripture is "the message of salvation" as committed to writing and comprises, as earlier chapters of this *Companion* recount, the books of the Old and New Testaments. "Tradition" is a term used in an active sense to describe the handing down or transmission of the revelation received by the Apostles, and in a passive sense to describe everything that is transmitted in the creeds, institutions, liturgy, and other constituents of the Church's life.

In the Catholic view, Scripture and Tradition emerge from the same divine source and are inseparable. They are not two parts of a whole revelation, but rather are both faithful witnesses to the one revealed Word. The Apostles handed on "everything which contributes toward the holiness of life and increase in faith of the people of God; and so the Church, in her teaching, life, and worship, [by the help of the Holy Spirit] perpetuates and hands on to all generations all that she herself is, all that she believes" (*Dei Verbum* §8). But the Bible, relative to the continuing oral and practical tradition, is fixed in a way that the latter is not: the text of the Bible is inspired and authored by God (even though he uses human beings as instruments). Scripture is the *norma normans non normata* of Christian faith and practice, and thus the rule or measure for authentic Christianity. This does not mean, however, that the Bible is "self-interpreting" or revelatory on an entirely literal level. As the *Catechism of the Catholic Church* puts it, "the Christian faith is not a 'religion of the book.' Christianity is the religion of the 'Word' of God, a word which is 'not a written and mute word, but the Word which is incarnate and living.' If the Scriptures are not to remain a dead letter, Christ, the eternal Word of the living God, must, through the Holy Spirit, 'open [our] minds to understand the Scriptures'" (§108).

According to Catholic teaching, Scripture and Tradition make up one deposit of revelation, entrusted to the whole Church. The authentic interpretation of this deposit belongs to the Magisterium of the Church. In this context, the term "Magisterium" (derived from the Latin word *magister* or teacher) designates the official teaching authority of the Church, exercised by the Pope and bishops who are the successors of the Apostles and who determine that what is proposed for belief or practice accords with revelation in Scripture and Tradition. This authority is exercised in the name of Christ. The position of the Magisterium with respect to revelation is thus one of service. The Magisterium "listens devoutly," "scrupulously guards," and "faithfully explains" the Word of God, and "draws from this fountain of the living word everything that it proposes to the belief of the faithful as divinely revealed" (*Dei Verbum* §10). Scripture, Tradition, and the Magisterium "are so connected and associated that one of them cannot stand without the others" (*Dei Verbum* §10).

It is not hard to understand, then, why we can say that the primary sources of Catholic theology are Scripture and Tradition, as interpreted by the Magisterium. We will have more to say about Scripture and the Magisterium in the following sections of this essay. At this stage, some general comments about the sources of theology are in order.

Among the principal witnesses to tradition, Catholic theologians generally concur in listing the following sources: the Fathers of the Church; ecumenical and local councils; papal Magisterium; liturgy and Christian art; the leading doctors, theologians, and canonists of the Church past and present; and the sense of the faithful. Among the non-theological sources which can be consulted, it has been customary for Catholic theologians to include natural reason, the works of philosophers and jurists, and, more broadly, history and human tradition.

The breadth and comprehensiveness of this traditional list of "sources" suggest something of the wide-ranging character of the Catholic conception of theology. Revelation and everything else viewed in the light of revelation: these are the materials to be studied and pondered by *fides quaerens intellectum*. These sources do not of course each possess equal weight or authority in theological inquiry and argument. As the primary vehicles of divine revelation, Scripture, and Tradition, as interpreted by the Magisterium, are the privileged or primary sources of all theological inquiry.

The task of determining what the primary sources have to tell us about the particular set of questions we may be considering has, since the seventeenth century, been termed "positive theology" to distinguish it from the task of reflecting on these data in a systematic way in "scholastic" or "speculative" theology (Latourelle, 1979). While this terminology is no longer widely used, what might be called the "positive function" of theology remains a fundamental one. An essential phase of every theological inquiry is to establish what the primary sources have to say about the questions that are being addressed. The degree of comprehensiveness and precision that is being sought in the outcome of a particular inquiry to a certain extent determines how extensive this "positive" phase of a theological inquiry needs to be.

"Historical theology" or the "history of doctrine" are the terms normally used to designate the study of the witnesses of Tradition. This is a vast field, comprising many different historical periods and a wide variety of scholarly specialties. Earlier chapters of this *Companion* provide some indication of the range of materials in this phase of theological inquiry. The terms "biblical exegesis" or "hermeneutics" designate the positive phase of a theological inquiry which has Sacred Scripture as its object. Let us turn to that now.

Theology and Scripture

The Second Vatican Council described the relationship of theology and Scripture in words that every theologian would embrace: "The study of the sacred page [Sacred

Scripture] should be the very soul of theology." Theology is "powerfully strengthened and constantly rejuvenated" by the Scripture "as it searches out, under the light of faith, all the truth stored up in the mystery of Christ" (*Dei Verbum* 24). A central task in every theological inquiry is the determination of what the Scripture has to tell us about the particular question or set of questions which we happen to be addressing. Because our inquiry is a theological one, our reading and study of the Scripture proceeds "under the light of faith," assumes the revealed and inspired character of the passages under consideration, and views them within the perspective of a tradition of doctrinal formulation, theological interpretation, and liturgical usage.

The Catholic Church has generally understood the word "exegesis" to refer to scriptural reading and interpretation conducted within this perspective. The *Catechism of the Catholic Church* provides a handy summary of the Catholic understanding of the kind of interpretation of the Bible which serves properly theological inquiry. It involves using the best critical tools and methods available, and reading the Scripture within the context of the Catholic faith. According to the *Catechism*, the hermeneutical criteria proposed by Vatican II for genuinely Catholic theology are as follows:

1 *Be especially attentive "to the content and unity of the whole Scripture."* Different as the books which comprise it may be, Scripture is a unity by reason of the unity of God's plan, of which Christ Jesus is the center and heart, open since his Passover (§112).
2 *Read the Scripture "within the living tradition of the whole Church."* According to the sayings of the Fathers, Sacred Scripture is written principally in the Church's heart rather than in documents and records, for the Church carries in her Tradition the living memorial of God's Word, and it is the Holy Spirit who gives her the spiritual interpretation of the Scripture ("according to the spiritual meaning which the Spirit grants to the Church") (§113).
3 *Be attentive to the analogy of faith.* By "analogy of faith" we mean the coherence of the truths of faith among themselves and within the whole plan of revelation (§114).

In summary, then, the theological interpretation of the Bible must take account of its unity, divine authorship, or constant reference to Christ.

This ecclesial kind of reading has been rendered more difficult and complex by the emergence in roughly the seventeenth century of a style of historical-critical interpretation that has come to be seen with hindsight as an alternative way of reading the Bible (Kelsey, 1975). As we have understood the matter so far, the theological way of reading the Bible can be described as an endeavor to read it precisely as *Scripture* – as God's word heard and read in a community of faith. Historical-critical forms of exegesis, on the other hand, are best described as part of an endeavor to read the Bible as *text* – as a literary product, considered independently of its status as the Church's Scripture, whose historical sources and diverse meanings are susceptible of study and interpretation according to the same scholarly methods as are applicable to other ancient texts.

A properly theological exegesis needs to be distinguished from two other kinds of inquiries identified by the term "exegesis" – historical and literary exegesis. Historical exegesis is essentially reconstructive. Adopting critical methods applicable to texts of all kinds – not just the Bible – the aim is to identify the events and sources *behind* the text under examination. The main emphasis of this kind of criticism is historical, and its practitioners are concerned with establishing, by the standards common among modern historians, what realities *probably* gave rise to the text being studied. Literary exegesis, on the other hand, aims to establish what the text means *as written by its author.* This includes establishing what its author may have *meant* to convey to his contemporaries to whom he wrote.

Together these types of exegesis yield literary and historical judgments about the biblical texts *without* reference to the status of Bible as Scripture, understood as inspired by God and containing the revelation he intends to be received by the Church. Ordinarily, literary and historical exegesis enhance one another and influence the third type of exegesis, which is properly theological and which considers the text at hand not simply *as text* but precisely *as Scripture.* Theological exegesis takes cognizance of the text as identified by its place, not only within the whole scriptural corpus, but within and according to patterns of interpretation which logically and imaginatively *precede* commentary on that text *as normative for the community.* Thus, theological exegesis examines texts inasmuch as they relate to faith, doctrine, theology, and liturgy (Fowl, 1997).

This is not to say that theological interpretation is properly separable from historical or literary study. On the contrary, historical and literary exegesis serve to ground and limit theology's historical and literary assertions about a given text and influence the theological interpreter's rational and imaginative construal of revelation as a whole. Yet whatever impact literary or historical studies may have on theological exegesis as such, it is not the case that they supply a hermeneutical context sufficient for the task of theology. The use of Scripture as a rule or authority requires (absolutely speaking) an interpretive horizon or principles by which the reader can sift and make sense of the texts at hand. All Christian communities share a conviction that the theological exegesis must take as authoritative the trinitarian, Christological, and soteriological patterns discernible in the Scripture and, at least in part, formulated as doctrinal rules by the great ecumenical councils.

A book composed under the influence of the Holy Spirit is still a book, with a language, genre, historical setting, and other dimensions which cannot all be entirely accidental to the meaning of the text. It is plain that a knowledge of the "humanity" of Scripture – everything from its vocabulary and grammar to its poetic devices and the circumstances of its composition – can be helpful for understanding the biblical texts *as Scripture.* At the same time, historical and literary inquiries have an integrity and purposes of their own and exegetical studies of the Bible as *text* have a legitimacy independent of the theological uses to which their results may be put. But this implies that theological exegesis possesses its own integrity as an intellectual inquiry (or, as medieval theologians would have said, a science), with a distinctive set of principles which must guide its appropriation of the results of historical and literary studies.

Theology and the Church

With Scripture and Tradition, the Magisterium of the Church is among the primary sources for theology. The dependence of theology upon the Magisterium needs to be located within the broad context of the life of the Church. For the Church is the locus of a truth which she did not generate but which she received as a gift whose center is the truth of Jesus Christ. The function of the Magisterium is to guard and teach in its entirety this truth which the Church received as a gift and is bound to hand on. Both the Magisterium and theology are servants of a prior truth, received in the Church as a gift.

The gift of truth received in the Church thus establishes the framework for the actual practice of the discipline of theology. This ecclesially received truth, as articulated in the deposit of faith and handed on by the Magisterium, constitutes not an *extrinsic* authority that poses odious limits on an inquiry that would otherwise be free but an *intrinsic* source and measure that gives theology its identity and finality as an intellectual activity. "Is theology for which the Church is no longer meaningful really a theology in the proper sense of the word?" (Ratzinger, 1987: 323). Examined independently of the assent of faith and the mediation of the ecclesial community, the texts, institutions, rites, and beliefs of the Catholic Church can be the focus of the humanistic, philosophical, and social scientific inquiries that together constitute the field of religious studies. But Catholic theology is a different kind of inquiry. Its precise scope is to seek the intelligibility of a truth received in faith by the theologian who is himself a member of the ecclesial community that is "the place of truth" (Kasper, 1989).

A theological inquiry is thus free to seek the truth within limits imposed, not by an intrusive external authority, but by the nature of his discipline as such. "Freedom of research, which the academic community holds most precious, means an openness to accepting the truth that emerges at the end of an investigation in which no element has intruded that is foreign to the methodology corresponding to the object under study" (*Donum Veritatis* §12). The acceptance of the authority of Scripture and doctrines in theology is "not a limitation but rather the charter of its existence and freedom to be itself" (Dulles, 1992: 168). The freedom of inquiry proper to theology, is the "hallmark of a rational discipline whose object is given by Revelation, handed on and interpreted in the Church under the authority of the Magisterium, and received by faith. These givens have the force of principles. To eliminate them would mean to cease doing theology" (*Donum Veritatis* §12). The principles of theology are derived from revelation, as we have seen, and constitute the discipline as such. In accepting them, the theologian is simply being true to the nature of his subject, and to his vocation as a scholar in this field.

The Catholic understanding of theology and its relation to the Magisterium is contested wherever what has been called the "individualistic foundational rationalism" of modernity holds sway (Lindbeck, 2002: 7). But, as we have seen, the Church has a solid, well-substantiated, and historically warranted rationale for its account of the nature of theology as an intellectual discipline of a particular sort, and of the inner connection between this discipline and magisterial teaching. It is central to the convictions of the Catholic Church, and indeed of the Christian tradition as such, to give priority to a theonomous rationality – one that is exercised within the liberating order of divine truth – rather than to an autonomous rationality whose only measure is human reason. While it is true that the basis for this understanding is itself a properly theological one that is rooted in fundamental Christian convictions about the gift of truth and its reception in the ecclesial community, in the light of certain recent intellectual trends, the Church's claims for the community- and tradition-dependent character of theology are more readily intelligible (Lindbeck, 1984). Whatever other challenges it may pose, the post-liberal intellectual climate is, to a certain extent, more favorable to the defense of the principle of theonomous rationality that is crucial for the Catholic understanding of theology.

It would be a mistake to exaggerate the singularity of the dependence of Catholic theology on the authority of the Magisterium. Authoritative criteria and professional bodies exist in almost all intellectual disciplines. Authorities function to maintain the quality and standards of many of these disciplines. "The acceptance of a certain degree of authority – which those subject to it regard as more or less legitimate, which they accept more or less easily, and which they challenge only exceptionally – is the normal state of affairs" (DeGeorge, 1985: 1). In this sense, the Catholic understanding of the relationship of theology to the Magisterium has formal parallels to other academic disciplines in which authorities serve to foster rather than undermine intellectual and scholarly integrity.

Theology and Its Sub-fields

The tendency for related questions to be considered together has been a factor over the centuries in the emergence of sub-fields and specializations in Catholic theology. The many questions concerning the Blessed Trinity, for instance, or Creation, or Jesus Christ, or the Church have been grouped and considered together (as the titles of the following chapters of this section of the *Companion* indicate). So it has happened that one set of theological sub-fields is topical, comprising the areas of Christology, anthropology, ecclesiology, canon law, and so on.

Another set is more functional, concerned with determining what the sources have to say about the main questions of theology (Lonergan, 1972). Thus, the exegetical and historical functions of theology have given rise to a number of sub-fields, such as Old Testament and New Testament exegesis, biblical theology, patristic theology, history of doctrines and historical theology, and liturgical theology. In appropriating the results of inquiries in these sub-fields, the challenge to maintain a properly theological perspective is a continual one.

It is common now for individual theologians to concentrate their work on the questions that arise in one or another of the particular sub-fields that have become stable features in the organization of theological studies, teaching, and research. With this degree of specialization, there is always the threat of the fragmentation of theology. But the unity of theology will be sustained wherever its various sub-fields are viewed not as distinct disciplines but as integral parts of a single discipline with the same principles and the same dependence on revelation and the Church. While theologians specialize in certain groups of questions, there is a widespread recognition of the need to acknowledge and maintain the fundamental unity of the discipline.

The broadest division of labor is mapped out under the rubrics of fundamental theology, dogmatic theology, moral theology, spiritual theology, and pastoral theology. With roots in earlier periods of theological history, this division emerges clearly in the seventeenth century and reflects a natural grouping of the characteristic questions raised in theology. Some observations on this division of labor are in order.

For the most part, divine revelation in Scripture and Tradition, and thus the Church's teaching, are directed to leading us to salvation and holiness – to the present and future enjoyment of ultimate communion with the Blessed Trinity and with other persons in lives of ever-deepening charity. Through her teaching activities, the Church seeks to cultivate the intellectual and moral dispositions necessary for this enjoyment, to enhance understanding of its profound meaning, and to commend it to others. The whole ensemble of Catholic doctrine – the deposit of faith – embraces all the teachings that together serve to shape and direct our lives toward holiness. As the *Catechism of the Catholic Church* demonstrates, such doctrines answer questions about what must be believed, which courses of action should be pursued and which shunned, which interior dispositions must be cultivated and which avoided, and so on, in order to enjoy the life of ultimate communion to the full. Dogmatic theology concentrates mainly on questions about what Christians believe (the Creed), while moral theology and spiritual theology concentrate on questions about Christian life.

The work of *dogmatic theology* (also known as systematic theology) is chiefly to elaborate a penetrating knowledge of faith by identifying the mutual connections among the mysteries of the faith. There is a conviction at work here, as we have seen, that the entire ensemble of the mysteries and doctrines of the Catholic faith possesses an internal intelligibility which reflects the divine truth itself and which can be exhibited through contemplative prayer and theological inquiry. It is this intelligibility that dogmatic theology seeks above all else.

The task of *moral theology* and *spiritual theology* is a related one, except that it concentrates on those doctrines that concern the conduct of Christian life (holiness, the commandments, virtues, beatitudes, gifts of the Holy Spirit, and so on) and connects them with the all-embracing mysteries of trinitarian communion, incarnation, redemption, grace, and ecclesiology, as well as theological anthropology.

Much of the present chapter has been concerned with the sub-fields of *fundamental theology* and theological methodology. Typically, the questions that get attention in fundamental theology are those concerned not with *primary doctrines* (what must be believed and undertaken in order to grow in the life of grace and charity), but with *governing doctrines* (how it can be known reliably that such things should be believed and undertaken) (Christian, 1987). Governing doctrines concern such questions as the following: Is this really a doctrine of our community? What procedures do we have for deciding? Is this doctrine more important than other doctrines? Is it consistent with them? Is it appropriate to develop understandings that seem implicit in our doctrines? Should these also be considered as doctrines? Who in the community is authorized to decide?

The history of the Catholic Church has afforded many occasions for developing and invoking governing doctrines. But in recent times the sub-field of fundamental theology, along with its close relatives, apologetics, and foundational theology, has been of increasingly prominent interest to theologians (Rahner, 1978; O'Collins, 1981). One reason for this development is that questions of the authenticity of the primary Catholic doctrines have been pressed upon the Church almost without interruption for the past 200 years. Thus, for example, more explicit attention has been devoted to the doctrine of revelation during this period than in all the previous centuries taken together. Throughout this period, the Church has gradually formulated a range of previously implicit governing doctrines to affirm that her primary doctrines authentically express what is contained in Scripture and Tradition, that Scripture and Tradition themselves constitute the single source of revelation, that revelation involves a real divine communication mediated by Christ, the prophets and apostles, that the scriptural record of this revelation is divinely inspired, that the liturgical and doctrinal tradition embodies communally authorized readings of the Scripture, and that the Church under the Successor of Peter is divinely guided in its formulation of primary doctrines of faith and morals. In addition, the increasingly explicit formulations of the doctrine of the Magisterium over the past two centuries is part of the evolution that represented a response to the growing need for a clear articulation of the governing doctrines of the Catholic faith. In circumstances in which the authenticity of Catholic doctrines was a matter of persistent and unrelenting controversy, it was natural that doctrinal developments addressing this issue should take place along several fronts at once: the nature of revelation, the interpretation of Scripture, the authority of tradition, and the scope of the Church's teaching office.

Pastoral theology is the systematic reflection on questions concerning the activity of the Church in building up the Body of Christ in society, and is thus closely related to other sub-fields like missionary theology, ecumenical theology, theology of religions, and political theology. In this connection, it should be noted that new cultural and social situations, new theories, and new scientific discoveries are among the factors that can give rise to new questions for the Church and for theologians. Late twentieth-century theology saw the emergence of many new types of theological inquiry keyed to a range of social, cultural, philosophical, and scientific contexts (Kerr, 2006). A crucial challenge for theologians who reflect on these questions in a formal way is to maintain a properly theological perspective – one that gives priority to the truth of revelation as the Church understands and confesses it (Frei, 1992).

References and Further Reading

Aquinas, St Thomas (1964) *Summa Theologiae* Ia, 1, in *Christian Theology, Summa Theologiae*, vol. 1, trans. Thomas Gilby, OP. New York: McGraw-Hill and London: Eyre and Spottiswood.

Aquinas, St Thomas (1986) *In Boethius de Trinitate*, q. 6, a. 3, in *Saint Thomas Aquinas: Division and Methods of the Sciences. Questions V and VI of his Commentary on the De Trinitate of Boethius*, 4th edition, trans. Armand Mauer. Toronto: Pontifical Institute of Medieval Studies.

Balthasar, Hans Urs von (1965) *Word and Redemption*, trans. A.V. Littledale. New York: Herder and Herder.

Cessario, Romanus, OP (1996) *Christian Faith and the Theological Life*. Washington, DC: Catholic University of America Press.

Chenu, Marie-Dominique, OP (1959) *Is Theology a Science?* trans. A.H.N. Green-Armytage. New York: Hawthorne Books

Christian, William A. (1987) *Doctrines of Religious Communities.* New Haven, CT: Yale University Press.

Congar, Yves, OP (1968) *A History of Theology,* trans. Harvey Guthrie, SJ. Garden City, NY: Doubleday.

DeGeorge, Richard T. (1985) *The Nature and Limits of Authority.* Lawrence: University Press of Kansas.

Dulles, Avery, SJ (1992) *The Craft of Theology: From Symbol to System.* New York: Crossroad.

Evans, G.R. (ed.) (2000) *The Medieval Theologians.* Oxford: Blackwell.

Evans, G.R. (ed.) (2004) *The First Christian Theologians.* Oxford: Blackwell.

Fowl, Stephen (ed.) (1997) *The Theological Interpretation of Scripture.* Oxford: Blackwell.

Frei, Hans (1992) *Types of Christian Theology.* New Haven, CT: Yale University Press.

Kasper, Walter (1989) *Theology and Church,* trans. Margaret Kohl. New York: Crossroad.

Kelsey, David H. (1975) *The Uses of Scripture in Current Theology.* Philadelphia, PA: Fortress Press.

Kerr, Fergus, OP (2006) *Twentieth-Century Catholic Theologians: From Neoscholasticism to Nuptial Mysticism.* Oxford: Blackwell.

Latourelle, René, SJ (1979) *Theology: Science of Salvation,* trans. Sr. Mary Dominic. Staten Island, NY: Alba House.

Lindbeck, George A. (1984) *The Nature of Doctrine.* Philadelphia, PA: Westminster Press.

Lindbeck, George A. (2002) *The Church in a Postliberal Age.* Grand Rapids, MI: W.B. Eerdmans.

Lonergan, Bernard J.F., SJ (1972) *Method in Theology.* New York: Herder and Herder.

Marshall, Bruce D. (2000) *Trinity and Truth.* Cambridge: Cambridge University Press

Nichols, Aidan, OP (1991) *The Shape of Catholic Theology.* Collegeville, MN: The Liturgical Press.

O'Collins, Gerald, SJ (1981) *Fundamental Theology.* New York: Paulist Press.

Rahner, Karl, SJ (1978) *Foundations of Christian Faith,* trans. William V. Dych. New York: Seabury Press.

Ratzinger, Joseph (1987) *Principles of Catholic Theology,* trans. Sr. M. Frances McCarthy. San Francisco, CA: Ignatius Press.

Ratzinger, Joseph (1995) *The Nature and Mission of Theology,* trans. Adrian Walker. San Francisco, CA: Ignatius Press.

Schillebeeckx, Edward, OP (1967) *Revelation and Theology,* vol. I, trans. N.D. Smith. New York: Sheed and Ward.

Church Documents

Catechism of the Catholic Church, 2nd edition. Vatican City: Libreria Editrice Vaticana, 1994 and 1997.

Dei Verbum. Vatican Council II, Constitution on Divine Revelation, in *Vatican Council II: Constitutions, Decrees, Declarations,* edited by Austin Flannery, OP. Northport, NY: Costello Publishing Company (1996).

Donum Veritatis. Congregation for the Doctrine of the Faith, *Instruction on the Ecclesial Role of the Theologian.* Origins 20 (1990), 117–26.

CHAPTER 17

The Development of Doctrine

John E. Thiel

The idea of the development of doctrine or, in Catholic parlance, the development of dogma, has appeared relatively recently in the history of Christian thought. Only in the past 200 years have theologians conceived the development of doctrine as an idea that corresponds to a historical reality and that is theologically important. Ideas, of course, are constructions of human experience that surface in particular times and places for reasons that are more or less explainable. New ideas may cause the invention of things that previously did not exist, like constitutional democracies or automobiles. Or their appearance may be explained as the conceptual discovery of phenomena that previously existed but which had eluded recognition, like the heliocentric solar system. Whether explained from inside or outside the circle of faith, the idea of the development of doctrine is an example of the second kind of idea. It was understood as the discovery of previously existing, though unrecognized, phenomena. From outside the circle of faith, these phenomena are regarded only as the ebb and flow of religious beliefs in history, which, like all things historical, are simply subject to change. From within the circle of faith, these phenomena are regarded as the believing community's revisable account of its own sacred tradition, itself a record of the Holy Spirit's presence to time and culture. In order to appreciate what this new idea conceives, let us begin by considering some examples of the fact of historical change in doctrine that Christians more recently and in faith would explain as the development of doctrine.

The Historical Formation of Christian Doctrine

Christian doctrine or "teaching" is as old as the efforts of the earliest Christians to communicate their life-transforming experience of Jesus' resurrection from the dead. First in speech and behavior, and then gradually in writing, Christians began a tradition of *paradosis* or doctrine that conveyed to their communities and to the world at large their extraordinary claims about God's saving love manifested in the life, death, and resurrection of Jesus Christ. Some of that teaching was imbued with the authority of God's own revelation, as Paul's letters, the four Gospels, and other early Christian writings were accorded canonical status and normatively placed alongside the Hebrew Scriptures as the Christian Bible. Christian belief, worship, and practice became a matter of living out the story of God's redemption, in Nicholas Lash's compelling phrase, acts of "performing the scriptures" (Lash, 1986), and particularly the life of Jesus as presented in the four Gospels. And yet, even though early Christians demonstrated a remarkable commitment to living out this Gospel teaching, it is interesting to observe how often they struggled to clarify exactly what their true doctrine was.

The very mystery of the Christian claim that God had become a human being to save a fallen world, together with the diverse perspectives on this event in the various writings of the New Testament, offered a fertile field for interpretation. Whatever unity existed in the belief and practice of early Christian doctrine (and what besides such unity could explain the flourishing of the early, persecuted Christian churches scattered throughout the Mediterranean world?), it was a unity dwelling in a plurality of nuanced interpretations of even the most basic claims of faith. Historical scholarship continues to confirm Walter Bauer's famous thesis that orthodoxy was not an inherent quality of Christian doctrine, there from the beginning, but instead a normative judgment about a certain track in the doctrinal tradition that Christians reached slowly through the centuries, and typically through controversy with opposing views (Bauer, 1971). In principle, any enduring Christian belief or practice could illustrate this historical movement toward orthodoxy. Here, though, we will consider those beliefs that came to be expressed in the early Christian creeds.

The earliest creed of the tradition, known as the "rule of faith," was defined by the first Church fathers in their writings against the Gnostics. Gnosticism, like Christianity, was a fledgling religion in the Mediterranean world in the first centuries of the Common Era. Although the Gnostics professed belief in a savior named Jesus Christ, they held the dualistic belief that the material universe was evil, the work of a demonic being whom they believed to be the God of Jews and Christians. Christians began to define the doctrinal tradition against these Gnostic views, which were threatening precisely because they appealed to a certain reading of the Christian narrative for their justification, however distorted the Christian story was in Gnostic interpretation. First among the early patristic writers who opposed the Gnostics, Irenaeus of Lyons (c.130–200) proposed a creedal formula to regulate the right reading of the Christian story. Irenaeus' "rule of faith" professed the orthodoxy of Christian belief in the one creator God; in the redemption of the world through the life and death of Jesus Christ, Son of the Creator God, whose incarnation itself was testimony to the goodness of Creation; and in the resurrection of the body, an affirmation of the created goodness, and so salvational worthiness, of the entire human person (*Against Heresies*, Book I, chapter 22 in Roberts and Donaldson, 1977).

By providing a heuristic for the right interpretation of the Christian Scriptures, Irenaeus' short creed shaped Christian identity by clarifying the truth of Christian doctrine in the face of conflicting interpretations of the biblical story. In effect, Irenaeus' creed demonstrated the need for a supplement to the biblical text. This supplement could be recited or read as a short summary of the biblical plot. More crucially, though, in Christianity's formative period, the creedal supplement to the sacred Scriptures

functioned as a regulative principle, narrowing the scope of their authentic interpretation and thus the boundaries of the Church in which Christian teaching could
be authentically believed and practiced. The creedal summary of the biblical story
became a normative statement of the story's meaning that itself became an extension
of the story's inspired authority.

This tradition of doctrinal supplement reaches a higher level of detail in the creeds
sanctioned by the early ecumenical councils, particularly the councils of Nicea, Constantinople, and Chalcedon. The Council of Nicea (325) was called by the emperor
Constantine to settle an extensive division in the Church's belief about the divinity of the savior. On one side of the controversy stood Christians called "Arians," who
believed that the Son of God was an extraordinary creature who, like all things created, was brought into existence out of nothing by God the Father. On the other side
stood Christians who believed that the Son of God was eternal, and so fully and completely divine. It was this latter position that was sanctioned by the majority of bishops
in attendance at Nicea, even though the literary evidence shows that the former position, which regarded the being of the Son to be subordinate to the Father, had a longer
history in the belief of the Church. Nonetheless, increasingly by the late third century,
and preponderantly throughout the fourth and fifth centuries, Christians rejected this
Christological subordinationism, affirming as orthodox doctrine a belief in the full
divinity of Christ who, Nicea taught, is "begotten not made, consubstantial with the
Father" (Tanner, N., 1990). The Council of Constantinople (381) confirmed this teaching in its creedal statement known as the "Nicene Creed" and taught too that the Holy
Spirit shares in the eternal divinity of the Godhead, a belief that was contested in the
half-century that separated the councils.

Even though disputes continued into the sixth century between the Arian defenders of Christ's creatureliness and the Nicene defenders of Christ's eternal divinity, the
growing authority of the two fourth-century councils grounded a consensus on this
belief in Christ's complete divinity. By the middle of the fourth century, however, a
controversy erupted among those who shared this orthodox consensus. Some Nicene
Christians, who came to be labeled "monophysites," believed that the divine nature of
Christ was incarnated into the body of Jesus, which alone, as flesh, was the manner of
his appearance in history. The divine nature supplied all of the functions of Jesus' inner
life such as consciousness, knowledge, and will, and so completely that Jesus possessed
no human capacity for these powers. Expressed in the ancient categories, the incarnate
Jesus Christ possessed a divine nature but not a human soul, and so not a complete
human nature defined by the union of human soul and body. Two theologians from
the Cappadocia region of Asia Minor, Gregory of Nyssa (c. 330–95) and Gregory Nazianzus (330–89), were especially effective in arguing against the monophysite Christians.
Agreeing with the Nicene belief of their opponents regarding the eternal divinity of
the incarnate Christ, the Cappadocians yet insisted that this divine nature co-existed
in the incarnate Christ with a complete human nature that consisted both of bodily
existence and human inner life or soul. The Cappadocians claimed this "two natures"
doctrine as the orthodox faith of the Church, believing that the entire human person
could be saved through the incarnation only if, in the incarnation itself, human nature
in its entirety was joined to the graceful energy of Christ's divinity.

This controversy about the humanity of Christ lasted for nearly a century, as the religious sentiments of both sides – the monophysitic concern for the unadulterated source of saving power and the "two natures" concern for that power's personal target – vied for ascendancy, the one or the other achieving dominance in particular times and places. Finally, a settlement of sorts was reached at the Council of Chalcedon (451), where the voting bishops confirmed the orthodoxy of the Cappadocian "two-natures" Christology by professing in the Council's creed that the incarnate Christ is "consubstantial with the Father as regards his divinity, and the same consubstantial with us as regards his humanity," "acknowledged in two natures . . . [united] into a single person" (Tanner, N., 1990). Even though this doctrine became the faith of the Great Church, some monophysitic churches of the Christian East refused to accept its orthodoxy and continue that refusal to this very day. Moreover, the relatively unsettled character of the orthodox settlement can be observed throughout the next several centuries as the continued vying of monophysitic and "two-natures" sensibilities required both qualifications and reaffirmations of the Chalcedonian doctrine at the Councils of Constantinople II (553), Constantinople III (680–1), and Nicea II (787).

These Christological doctrines functioned in the same supplementary manner to Scripture as did the early patristic "rule of faith." The creeds of the early Councils provided parameters for the right reading and performance of the biblical story, both by articulating the truth of Christian belief and by explicitly rejecting particular beliefs that had flourished in Christian communities, even for long periods of time.

The historical phenomena that the idea of doctrinal development explains religiously could have been illustrated in our few examples in much finer detail or by appeal to any other belief or practice that has appeared in Christian history. The beliefs defined in the early creeds are especially apt illustrations not only because they are so basic to what Christians profess as their tradition but also because their history shows so clearly that things in history change, and that religious things are no exception. The principal reason that the idea of the development of doctrine is such a recent arrival in the history of thought is that early Christians, and indeed Christians who lived prior to the modern period, never conceived of the doctrinal tradition in the historical fashion presented above.

Premodern Doctrine

The earliest Christians confessed their faith in a sacred tradition of doctrine taught by Jesus himself to his apostles and handed on by them to their successors, the bishops of the proliferating Christian communities. They found this apostolic tradition expressed in the writings that would come to form the New Testament. By the early third century, these writings were identified as a sacred canon, their authority confirmed in the belief that they were inspired by God and the measure of Christian truth. As conflicts arose in the interpretation of the Bible, Christians began to regard their creeds, especially those defined in ecumenical councils, as the clearest expression of the apostolic tradition and so as norms for adjudicating disputes about the faith. As ecumenical councils were held with greater regularity after the fourth century, Christians extended a kind of canonicity to their doctrine by believing that their teachings too were inspired by the Holy Spirit and so were infallibly true.

This close connection between biblical text and conciliar doctrine led medieval Christians to conceive of the doctrinal tradition as a homogeneous whole within which the canonical authority of the Bible was highlighted but broadened to include the conciliar teachings. This homogeneous tradition included as well papal decretals and the writings of theologians whose authority was respected by later generations. Medieval Christians believed that there were any number of non-literary beliefs and practices that had been handed down by the apostles to later times. But the specific clarity of the holy texts, along with their non-inspired glosses, highlighted their authority to the degree that they were seen altogether as a single corpus of *sacra doctrina* (Thomas Aquinas, *Summa Theologiae*) or *scriptura sacra*, the normative expression of apostolic truth (Tavard, 1959; Congar, 1960).

The historical fact that Christian theology was married intellectually to the Hellenistic philosophical tradition encouraged Christians to conceive of doctrinal truth as transcending the vicissitudes of time and culture. Whether Platonic, Stoic, or Aristotelian epistemologies happened to be periodically ascendant in Christian history, all assumed that truth was apprehended by the mind's conformity to abstract ideas or universals that were the unchangeable principles of knowing. In Christian interpretation, these suprahistorical principles were regarded as God's own ideas, the same ideas that God had revealed in the inspired tradition of sacred doctrine. Doctrine, premodern Christians held, could no more change than God's own eternal nature and will, which the doctrinal tradition indirectly communicated. Premodern Christians did not regard the historicity of doctrine as productive. In their judgment, history at best was the sphere of faithful, hand-to-hand transmission of the apostolic faith. At worst, it was the sinful realm of doctrine's heretical corruption. The thoroughly historical sketch of gradual doctrinal formation recounted in the previous section would be unfathomable to pre-modern Christian assumptions. Christians *on both sides* of the Christological controversies, for example, understood their creeds as the reiteration of the apostolic faith that had been professed in the same way by all genuine believers since it was taught by Jesus himself.

These same premodern assumptions about the unchanging character of truthful doctrine held sway throughout the Reformation era, even though the authority of Christian doctrine was hotly contested in Catholic and Protestant debate. The mainline Reformers were quite willing to recognize the authority of the early ecumenical councils, but only because their teaching was faithful to the biblical text which was the sole means of God's revelation. While the Reformers acknowledged the unchanging truthfulness of the great councils, they judged that much in the Roman doctrinal tradition was human invention, an idolatrous corruption of Scripture's plain sense. Against the Reformers' denial of tradition as an inspired means of revelation, the Catholic Council of Trent (1545–63) taught that the apostolic "truth and rule are contained in written books and in unwritten traditions which were received by the apostles from the mouth of Christ himself, or else have come down to us, handed on as it were from the apostles themselves at the inspiration of the holy Spirit" (Decrees of the Ecumenical Councils). Trent affirmed the medieval homogeneity of *sacra doctrina*, but did so by differentiating two means of divine revelation within its truthful unity. In the heritage of Trent, up to and including the Second Vatican Council, this distinctively Catholic teaching has been expressed by appeal to the language of "Scripture and tradition," a rhetoric that rejects the distinctively Protestant doctrine of *sola scriptura*. The Catholic concern for the authority of tradition as revelation, coupled with the premodern assumptions that shaped this conception of tradition, has made the modern notion of the development of doctrine a more pressing and troubling issue for Catholic than for Protestant Christianity.

Nineteenth-Century Achievements

The modern age dawned in Western culture in the late eighteenth century through the stunning success of the Enlightenment, an intellectual and political movement committed to the overthrow of feudal authority. In the minds of many Enlightenment thinkers, the social system they inherited was thoroughly corrupt, both by the political authority of monarchical government and by the complicity of traditional Christianity in supporting the old regime. Enlightenment critics often attacked Christianity by demonstrating that its traditional claims to authority, grounded as they were in faith in God's saving miracles, could not meet a standard of truth set by universal reason. Enlightenment rationalists either rejected Christian belief entirely as fanatical superstition or attempted to recover some reasonable core at the heart of Christian faith that in turn reduced the narrative of miracles to dispensable metaphor. The rise of historical criticism at this same time supported the assault by highlighting inconsistencies in the biblical text and by exposing Christianity's history as scandal-ridden, evidence that undercut the purity that premodern assumptions ascribed to apostolic continuity in the orthodox tradition.

The development of doctrine appeared in Christian thought as a practical exercise in apologetics directed toward Enlightenment criticism. Its literary matrix was the new genre of theological encyclopedia, works on method that re-thought the theological task in light of the modern challenge. The idea of doctrinal development was first articulated by Friedrich Schleiermacher (1768–1834) in his 1811 work on theological method, *Brief Presentation of the Study of Theology*. Approaching the theological task from his own confessional commitments, Schleiermacher defined dogmatic theology as "the knowledge of doctrine now valid in the Evangelical Church" (Schleiermacher, 1910; 1973: 73, par. 195). Whereas premodern Christians would have conceived of orthodox doctrine as an expression of the unchanging truth of the past, Schleiermacher now proposed a thoroughly historical notion of doctrinal truthfulness in which validity and orthodoxy were no longer the same. For Schleiermacher, orthodoxy is but one quality of presently valid, developing doctrine that stands in dialectical, and positive, relation to doctrine's "heterodox" element. The orthodox dimension of the Church's present faith is its "true unity" (Schleiermacher, 1910; 1973: 78, par. 204) established over time and moored in the settled belief of the past. The heterodox dimension of the Church's present faith is "construed in the tendency of keeping doctrine mobile" by grasping novel, and yet authentic, manifestations of truth in the present moment (Schleiermacher, 1910; 1973: 77–8, par. 203). Valid doctrine, Schleiermacher maintains, appears in the coinherence of its orthodox and heterodox elements in every passing moment, the orthodox past informing and guiding the heterodox present and the heterodox present bringing vitality and relevance to the orthodox past. The validity of doctrine is, then, a changing truthfulness, ever redefined in history by this developing relationship between orthodoxy and heterodoxy.

Schleiermacher's idea entered Catholic theology in the work of Johann Sebastian Drey (1777–1853), who was a member of the Catholic theological faculty at the University of Tübingen. Drey's earliest lecture notes speak of the need to understand any historical event as "a development from a kernel and seed," itself the "seed of many other developments," and of the need to understand the Catholic history of doctrine as "enlivened by an inner spirit" (Drey, 1940). These sensibilities on historical development reached finer precision in Drey's own theological encyclopedia, *Brief Introduction to the Study of Theology* (1819), which directly appropriated Schleiermacher's account of the development of doctrine. With unmistakable reference to Schleiermacher's dipolar model, Drey acknowledges the historicity of doctrine by stating that "a complete system of [doctrinal] concepts that is thought of not as dead tradition from a time gone by but as the development of a living tradition necessarily bears within it a two-fold element: a *fixed* aspect and a *mobile* aspect" (Drey, 1819).

Drey was unwilling, however, to follow Schleiermacher in regarding doctrinal validity as an ever redefined confluence of relatively orthodox and relatively heterodox values. For the more traditionally-minded Drey, the fixed aspect of doctrine is "completed through previous development" (Drey, 1819). Doctrine that reaches this completeness achieves the status of dogma, and its completedness stands as the Church's "single, objectively . . . valid criterion of Christian *truth*" (Drey, 1819: 171 par. 258). And yet, Drey insists, ancient dogma alone cannot make for a living tradition. Doctrine also possesses a mobile aspect that "in the development [of history] . . . is yet conceiving [doctrinal truth]" (Drey, 1819: 170–1, par. 256). Drey calls this productive encounter between the fixed and mobile aspects of doctrine "orthodoxy," which he defines as the "striving to preserve the completed aspect in the doctrinal concept and to construct the mobile aspect in the sense of the completed aspect and in agreement with it" (Drey, 1819: 173, par. 260). Although Drey judges the settled development of the Christian past to be normative for the present development of doctrine, he is unwilling to embrace premodern Christian assumptions about the authority of the past. Indeed, he maintains that the fine balance of traditional orthodoxy can be falsely skewed by what he calls "hyperorthodoxy," the stance of "one who finally negates all mobility of the doctrinal concept" (Drey, 1819). As much as theological truth is conveyed through the completed dogma of the past, Drey insists that dogma only achieves its vital meaning for the Church through its developing relation to the present moment, which itself may offer a truth that will develop to the status of recognized dogma. "Human beings," Drey observes, "can distance themselves from the truth itself either by falling away from it or by lagging behind it"(Drey, 1819: 162, par. 240), a statement that constitutes a watershed in Catholic thought for its portrayal of doctrinal falsity either as apostasy or as a failure to keep pace with the historical development of truth.

Both Schleiermacher and Drey appealed to the insights of the burgeoning Romantic movement to conceive of history as a realm of developing truth and to explain doctrinal reconstruction as the work of the theologian's creative powers, lessons they learned especially from the early work of the philosopher Friedrich Schelling (1775–1854) (Thiel, 1997). The Romantic notion of historical progress proved an effective apologetics against the Enlightenment attack on Christianity, which had centered its assault on a classical understanding of divine revelation in Scripture and tradition. The idea of doctrinal development enabled Christians to argue that their Enlightenment critics had failed to appreciate the historicity of revelation by falsely identifying Christian truth with an ossified past at odds with the timeless truths of reason. To the contrary, the Romantic theologians argued that all things historical were thoroughly enmeshed in time, including divine revelation, and that it is faith's own imaginative sensibilities, not the powers of analytical reasoning, that truly fathom the unfolding of revelation in time.

The dialectical model of development advocated by Schleiermacher and Drey possessed a distinctly progressivist cast, particularly in its expectation for the revelatory character of the present moment (Thiel, 1991). This conceptualization enabled theologians to embrace the liberal spirit of the age while yet answering its hostility toward Christianity. Early conceptions of doctrinal development, however, could also be quite conservative in theological sensibility. Drey's talented student Johann Adam Möhler (1796–1838) made much of the organic analogy of growth, so prevalent in Romantic thought, to describe tradition as the developing manifestation of the Holy Spirit in the inner life of the Church. For Möhler, the Spirit's movement through history accommodates the present moment in ecclesial life to the authority of the past, itself the unity of the Church from which, he insisted, all growth proceeds. In this process, no special agency is ascribed to theological talent. Believers find the fullness of faith not in their own individuality, but in the totality of the entire community whose development in the faith is the graceful work of God (Möhler, 1957; Hinze, 1997). The Catholic "Roman School" of the mid-nineteenth century also offered a conservative version of doctrinal development by emphasizing the continuity of apostolic succession as the basis of the true, organic development of tradition, and, like Möhler, by regarding the historically new only as a coming to clarity of the historically old. This homogeneous perspective on doctrinal development was central to the work of the Roman theologians Carlo Passaglia (1812–87) and Clemens Schrader (1820–75), who prepared the 1854 bull of Pius IX that defined the dogma of the Immaculate Conception of Mary (Kasper, 1962).

Certainly the best-known account of doctrinal development in the nineteenth century is John Henry Newman's (1801–90) *An Essay on the Development of Christian Doctrine*, first published in 1845 and revised in 1878. Written while Newman was converting from Anglicanism to Roman Catholicism, the *Essay* is the fruit of his extensive historical studies of the early Church, especially the Arian controversy of the fourth century. Newman's reflections on the historical evidence of doctrinal development led him to propose a noetic analogy as a helpful way to think of the process toward settlement in the early ecclesial controversies. Truthful ideas, he argued, have "a nature to arrest and possess the mind" as they move through history, almost as though the ideas themselves possess an irrepressible life (Newman, 1989). This Romantic rhetoric of organic development served Newman well in conceptualizing the results of his historical investigations. Doctrines, he proposed, are like living ideas that make their way through history, momentarily causing conflict and confusion, but eventually, because they are the expression of truthful ideas, working their way into the very assumptions of the community that holds them dear. "This process," Newman claimed, "whether it be longer or shorter in point of time, by which the aspects of an idea are brought into consistency and form, I call its development, being the germination and maturation of some truth or apparent truth on a large mental field" (Newman, 1989: 38).

Just as the truthful idea gradually becomes clearer in the minds of those who embrace it, so too does the doctrinal idea achieve clarification through its historical development, which Newman attributed to God's providential guidance. Finally conservative in his theological sensibilities, Newman regards this process as "homogeneous, expanding and irreversible" (Lash, 1975). The present moment for him is not the meaningful point of productive encounter with the past that yields truthful novelties, as it was for Schleiermacher and, to some degree, Drey. For Newman, the present moment provides occasion for growth consistent with the orthodox past. The present moment also poses a temporal stance from which the believer can look back to the past for evidence of this continuous development. When this past evidence can be marshaled to show the consistency of development through time, it provides what Newman calls "antecedent probability" for contemporary judgments about authentic development (Newman, 1989: 55–121). Indeed, much of Newman's *Essay* is concerned with the issue of validation through the application of criteria for genuine development that he calls "notes" or "tests." Among Newman's criteria are a doctrine's "power of assimilation," its "logical sequence" from past to present, and its "chronic vigour." But all seven of Newman's notes assume that genuine development possesses a vitality that manifests itself over time in clarity, strength, and steadfast continuity (Newman, 1989: 169–205).

In spite of Newman's strong advocacy of papal infallibility in the *Essay*, as well as the decidedly institutional cast to his theory of development, the official Catholic theology of his day was reluctant to embrace his theory. The Roman Jesuits Giovanni Perrone (1794–1876) and his student Passaglia found Newman's acknowledgment of relative ambiguity in earlier stages of doctrinal development to be theologically problematic. Especially troubling to their mind was Newman's willingness to regard the communal sensibility of all the faithful as a powerful impetus to authentic development, a position he articulated more fully in an 1859 article entitled "On Consulting the Faithful in Matters of Doctrine" (Newman, 1961; Chadwick, 1957). Although Newman was elevated to the rank of Cardinal by Leo XIII in 1879, his name continued to be intertwined with a theological theory that, in the judgment of the Vatican, undermined both the newly-defined dogma of papal infallibility and a classical understanding of tradition.

Towards a Theological Axiom

The idea of the development of doctrine was embraced readily by the mainline Protestant confessions for a host of reasons. The Reformation attack on the authority of tradition, the new formulation of creeds by the Reformation churches throughout the sixteenth century, and the development of a sensibility of the Church as "always in need of reform" (*semper reformanda*), all made the idea of doctrinal development easier to accept on the part of the Protestant churches. These same reasons, polemically identified as Protestant beliefs, coupled with a premodern understanding of tradition increasingly justified by papal infallibility, all contributed to Roman Catholic resistance to the new idea as a threat to the integrity of the apostolic tradition.[1]

The clearest, and certainly most ironic, illustration of Catholic resistance to the idea of doctrinal development can be found in Rome's reaction to the theological debate between Adolf von Harnack (1851–1930) and Alfred Loisy (1857–1940) at the turn of the twentieth century. Harnack, who was deservedly regarded as the greatest Church historian of his day, published in 1900 a widely-read book entitled *The Essence of Christianity* (Harnack, 1957). In it, he presented a classically Protestant diatribe by arguing that Jesus' simple teachings in the Gospels had been corrupted in the early Catholic tradition by their mixture with the pagan beliefs of Hellenism. Loisy, a French priest and theologian, defended Catholicism against Harnack's attack in a 1902 book whose title, *The Gospel and the Church* (Loisy, 1976), tersely expresses his thesis. Loisy acknowledged Harnack's claim that the earliest Christian understanding of the Gospel had changed throughout early Catholic history. Rather than judging such change as the corruption of Jesus' original message, Loisy interpreted it as the productive development of Catholic tradition through which Jesus' message came to fuller and clearer consciousness in the Church. The Vatican's response to Loisy's Catholic defense by appeal to the principle of doctrinal development was his excommunication for the heresy of "Modernism." Indeed, it was Loisy's position that Pius X's encyclical *Pascendi Dominici Gregis* (1910) had in mind when it condemned this "pernicious doctrine [of the development of tradition] which would make of the laity the factor of progress in the Church" (Carlen, 1981).

The warming of the Catholic hierarchy to the idea of doctrinal development came as suddenly and unexpectedly as the spirit of *aggiornamento* that made the Second Vatican Council (1962–5) such a significant event in the life of the Church. In some respects, modern acceptance of the idea requires an appreciation for the historicity of the sacred, and so the recognition that historical-critical investigation of the sacred yields information that can be valuable to faith. Pius XII's (1876–1958) approval of historical-critical approaches to biblical study in his 1943 encyclical *Divino Afflante Spiritu* is an example of such appreciation, as were the historical studies of the *ressourcement* theologians of the 1940s and 1950s such as Henri de Lubac (1896–1991) and Yves Congar (1904–95) who understood their recovery of the early Church fathers for the present as a much-needed alternative to the ahistorical style of early twentieth-century Neo-scholastic theology. The infallible definition of the dogma of the Assumption by Pius XII in 1950 also encouraged theological reflection on how tradition develops.

Nothing, however, defines the need for a theory of development quite like the present fact of dramatic change before the eyes of the entire Church, and such was the effect of Vatican II. It is interesting to note that John XXIII (1881–1963) himself authorized such a theory in his 1962 address opening the Council:

But from the renewed, serene, and tranquil adherence to all the teaching of the Church in its entirety and preciseness . . . the Christian, Catholic, and apostolic spirit of the whole world expects a step forward toward a doctrinal penetration and a formation of consciousness in faithful and perfect conformity to the authentic doctrine, which, however, should be studied and expounded through the methods of research and through the literary forms of modern thought. The substance of the ancient doctrine of the deposit of faith is one thing, and the way in which it is presented is another. (Pope John XXIII, 1966)

The Council's teaching that all believers share in a sense of the faith capable of apprehending the infallible truth of the Holy Spirit sanctioned a theological premise at the heart of the notion of doctrinal development (Dogmatic Constitution on the Church). More explicitly, the Council's "Dogmatic Constitution on Divine Revelation" explicitly acknowledged the reality of doctrinal development by teaching that "[t]his tradition which comes from the apostles develops in the Church with the help of the Holy Spirit. For there is a growth in the understanding of the realities and the words which have been handed down" (Dogmatic Constitution on Divine Revelation).

On the eve of the Council and in its aftermath, Catholic theologians wrote explicitly on the theme of the development of dogma, or, relying on the work of others, began to assume that tradition could not be explained adequately without invoking some notion of development. Yves Congar's magisterial *Tradition and Traditions* (1960/63) provided compelling historical evidence to justify the growing acceptance of doctrinal development as a theological axiom (Congar, 1960; 1963; 1966). Theologians like Josef Rupert Geiselmann (1890–1970), Karl Rahner (1904–84), Edward Schillebeeckx (1914–), and Bernard Lonergan (1904–84) offered constructive explanations that placed the axiom among the most basic assumptions of the theological task (Rahner, 1961, 1966; Geiselmann, 1962; Schillebeeckx, 1968; Lonergan, 1972).

The commonly-accepted understanding of doctrinal development since Vatican II has been the reception model. This model locates the movement of tradition in the ongoing embrace of the authoritative past by the present generation of believers. Aptly labeled "re-reception" by Congar (Congar, 1972), this process accounts not only for how tradition develops in the present but also for how the ancient dogmas gained authority in their own present-day development, centuries ago. By according authority to a received past whose meaning is received anew in every passing moment, this explanation has been able to sacralize the otherwise profane power of historical change as tradition. The reception model acknowledges the continuity of the apostolic faith and yet portrays the event of "handing on" not as mere repetition but as the faithful accommodation of the orthodox past to the cultural setting in which the tradition is inevitably received. The reception model's attention to the variable circumstances of historicity and culture has encouraged the critique and reconstruction of tradition as indispensable dimensions of theological reflection, particularly as theology takes account of the traditionally marginalized perspectives of race, class, gender, and the histories of peoples in telling the truth of tradition well (Carr, 1988; Espín, 1997).

Often, the reception model has relied on a distinction between the "content" and the "form" of tradition to specify respectively what abides and what changes in the development of doctrine. The "content" of tradition is identified with the time-honored truth of revelation and tradition's "form" with the flexible contingencies of time and place. This distinction has been valued for its capacity to acknowledge the historicity of tradition while yet marking out a dimension of tradition that endures through the ages. It is this form–content theory of doctrinal development that particularly has become axiomatic in contemporary Catholic thought, accepted as a kind of theological commonsense by both theologians and the Magisterium (*Mysterium Ecclesiae*, 1973; *Origins 3*, 1973).

Post-modern Alternatives

The idea of doctrinal development is modern not only in its late arrival in Christian history but also in the intellectual cast of its assumptions. As we have seen, the earliest theories of development served as a defense of Christian tradition against the Enlightenment, drawing on the thought-world of Romanticism to reconcile revelation and history. Several critical voices have recently challenged the theological adequacy of the modern or Romantic assumptions at the heart of the axiomatic understanding of development. These theologians have proposed alternative models that claim to be better theoretical accounts of how doctrine develops in Christian history. We can call these alternative models "post-modern" if only because they share the judgment that the modern assumptions can no longer service a good theory. Considering several of these views will bring us into the current debate and to the end of our survey.

Certainly the most controversial alternative has been proposed by the Lutheran theologian George A. Lindbeck. In his influential book, *The Nature of Doctrine* (Lindbeck, 1984), he argues that Romantic understandings of religion have promoted an "experiential-expressivist" regard for Christian doctrine. In this conceptualization, the fullness of Christian truth flourishes in the inner depths of subjectivity and is only derivatively expressed in doctrine which, as expression, accommodates itself to the changing circumstances of time and culture. For Lindbeck, this Romantic version of the form–content theory encourages Christians to regard the most basic claims of faith as relative to culture, thus making non-Christian, societal standards normative for the expression of Christian truth. The consequence of this accommodation, Lindbeck laments, is that many modern Christians have lost the ability to speak, or even to recognize, the traditional language of faith, conflated as it is with modernity's secular parlance. To remedy this situation, Lindbeck proposes that Christians embrace a "cultural-linguistic" understanding of doctrine in which doctrine is understood in analogy to the cultural workings of language. This metaphor portrays doctrine as though it were a grammar of abiding rules for right Christian speech, practice, and belief. Doctrines, such as Nicea's teaching on the Father–Son relationship or Chalcedon's "two-natures" Christology, are not to be understood primarily as universally meaningful propositions about reality, but rather as parameters for meaningful belief and practice within the Christian community. As Lindbeck puts it, doctrines make "intra-systematic rather than ontological truth claims" (Lindbeck, 1984: 80).

The advantage that Lindbeck sees in the cultural-linguistic model is that it provides a way of preserving the continuity of tradition in an age in which that continuity is sorely threatened, if not largely lost. Lindbeck fully acknowledges the change that religious traditions undergo. Yet, that change (or in traditional language, "development") is better imaged as Christianity's variable vocabulary in particular times and places. Variability in development, he insists, should always be faithful to the consistency of tradition's grammatical rules. In effect, Lindbeck has proposed a "post-liberal" understanding of doctrinal development, one that judges that "liberal" or broadly-speaking "modern" versions of the new theological principle have actually encouraged the loss of Christian identity in their interpretive willingness to translate age-old Christian meaning into the foreign tongue of secular values.

Directly at odds with Lindbeck is Kathryn Tanner, who has argued for another kind of post-modern understanding of doctrinal development. Whereas Lindbeck faults modern theories of development for actually promoting the loss of traditional continuity, and with it Christian identity, Tanner problematizes the notion of traditional continuity itself. She draws on the insights of post-modern cultural theory to show that the modern principle of doctrinal development in the end fares no better than the premodern account of doctrine in explaining what abides in tradition. Both stumble and fall on the facts of history which demonstrate remarkable divergences in Christian belief and practice through the ages. Modern theories of doctrinal development self-consciously address the historical change that premodern sensibilities deny. But their efforts to preserve traditional continuity in the face of change cannot be squared with the historical evidence, which subverts the most basic assumption of Romantic theories: "that the [traditionally] later is already present in the earlier and the idea that the history of transmission of Christian materials is one of neatly ordered cumulative change by increments" (Tanner, K., 1997: 130). Finally, she argues, Romantic theories of development simply assert the existence of an ahistorical continuity that supposedly binds tradition together, as though traditional continuity were "a naturally preexisting reality" (Tanner, K., 1997: 132).

In Tanner's judgment, a naively hopeful metaphysics is no substitute for the empirical realism that cultural theory urges upon theology in explaining whatever commonalities can be found in Christian life. Tanner finds these commonalities not in traditional materials or in abiding agreement about basic beliefs but in the zeal that Christians bring to the task of discipleship, a zeal that manifests itself in ceaseless, heartfelt disagreements among Christians about the most authentic ways to live the Gospel faithfully. Premodern and developmental understandings of doctrine err in portraying continuity as a "what," when indeed the commonality of Christian identity remains the contested matter of "how" to practice the teachings of Jesus. Tanner is happy to admit all the data of the Christian past into the relentless debate in which the Christian community is continually engaged. What makes for the unity of tradition in her judgment, though, is ongoing concern among Christians about the values and direction of the Christian project. This concern becomes concrete in history not as a developing teleology but in a host of diverse beliefs and practices that are themselves the site of the unclosable discussion that Tanner judges the development of tradition to be. Even though Tanner's theory is not denominationally specific, it gives post-modern expression to the classical Protestant indictment of tradition as a seductive occasion for the sin of idolatry, the false god of tradition identified here with exclusivistic claims for the unity of tradition.

Whereas Lindbeck addresses the modern loss of traditional unity and Tanner highlights the failure of traditional theories to acknowledge the real ruptures to continuity in Christian belief and practice, Terrence W. Tilley and I have argued for pragmatic accounts of tradition that try to balance both concerns (Tilley, 2000; Thiel, 2000; Roman Catholic Theology of Tradition, 2002). Writing as Roman Catholic theologians, Tilley and I similarly describe tradition functionally, as the actual practices of believers in history. Tilley draws on the general outlines of Lindbeck's rule theory to show how historical change is shaped into the authority of tradition by believers acting in particular circumstances. Although tradition is ever revisable, Tilley argues, its abiding claims and repeated practice behave as a kind of grammar that yet allows for genuine diversity in the competent enactment of tradition by the faithful. I have proposed that Catholic theology would do well to seek the same interpretive flexibility for tradition that ancient Christians found in the four-fold interpretive senses of Scripture. I distinguish two "senses" of tradition that discern the traditional value of constancy: the literal sense (uncontroversial basic beliefs) and the sense of development-in-continuity (the developing consensus among the faithful about beliefs and practices affirmed as tradition). These senses, I argue, co-exist in the act of faith with two other "senses" that discern the traditional value of renewal: the sense of dramatic development (which judges the loss of a previously-affirmed claim for tradition) and the sense of incipient development (which claims that a novel belief or practice deserves recognition as the Church's tradition). The claims of the whole Church for the authority of tradition lie only in expressions of the first and second senses. And yet, I argue, the ongoing development of tradition entails the mutual influence of all four senses, and thus the continuous revision of what Catholic believers claim in faith as tradition. Like Tilley, I understand this process as a pragmatics of belief and practice.

I explain the workings of tradition by appeal to the metaphor of retrospection and criticize premodern and modern understandings of tradition for their prospective assumptions. Prospective accounts conceive tradition by picturing an observer situated in the apostolic age gazing into the future and clearly seeing the unbroken continuity of all truthful doctrines in every moment. Premodern prospectivity envisages this continuity as literal events in history, while modern prospectivity, a feature of theories of doctrinal development, imagines a continuous content manifesting itself in changing historical forms. The problem with the premodern understanding, I argue, is that it cannot be reconciled with the evidence of history, which clearly shows that many later Christian doctrines were not believed by Christians who lived in earlier times. The problem with the form–content theory of doctrinal development is that it is based on a faulty epistemology that makes doctrinal continuity into an invisible essence distinguishable from its historical appearance. The problem with both prospective conceptions is that they finally deny the real historical change that the apostolic heritage has undergone.

In my retrospective understanding of tradition, continuity is configured from present to past, as present and ever revisable acts of faith chart what the Church believes to be the Spirit's truthful movement through history. This retrospective conception of tradition is neither beholden to chronological time nor willing to regard any presently-affirmed path of continuity back to the apostolic age, in all its details, as the necessary, traditional heritage of some future time. In this model, continuity and development are not separable values, the former identified with abiding content and the latter with changing historical forms. Rather, what believers call "continuity" and "development" in tradition are actually the same. Tradition develops as believers together affirm, re-affirm, and, in re-affirming, revise their claims about what the pattern of traditional continuity is. The advantage that I find in this retrospective conception of tradition lies in its ability to explain not only the continuity of tradition but also its ruptures and its capacity to make room for new beliefs and practices that, in faith, are claimed as the age-old tradition of the Apostles (Guarino, 1996; Thiel, 2000).

This sampling of recent contributions to the theology of tradition evinces the extent to which theologians continue to address the central issue at stake in the idea of doctrinal development – how to speak well of the unity of Christian beliefs and practices through time while still acknowledging the remarkable changes that historical investigation shows these same beliefs and practices have undergone. As theologians strive to reconcile the evidence of faith and the evidence of history, they will continue this relatively recent practice of finding creative ways to describe the mystery of God's presence to time and place.

Note

1 The institutional understanding of development advocated by the nineteenth-century Roman School is one, qualified exception to this resistance, as is the recognition of the possibility of the "logical" development of doctrine in some neo-scholastic theologies of the early twentieth century. A logical theory of development infers derivative doctrines from more basic ones.

References and Further Reading

Aquinas, Thomas, *Summa Theologiae*, I, 1, any edition.

Bauer, W. (1971) *Orthodoxy and Heresy in Earliest Christianity*, ed. and trans. by R. Kraft and G. Krodel. Philadelphia, PA: Fortress Press.

Carlen, C. (ed.) (1981) *Pascendi Domenici Gregis*, in *The Papal Encyclicals 1903–1939*. Wilmington, NC: McGrath Publishing Company.

Carr, A.E. (1988) *Transforming Grace: Christian Tradition and Women's Experience*. San Francisco, CA: HarperSanFrancisco.

Chadwick, O. (1957) *From Bousset to Newman: The Idea of Doctrinal Development*. Cambridge: Cambridge University Press, 164–84.

Congar, Y., OP (1960) *La Tradition et les traditions*, vol. 1: *Essai historique*. Paris: Librairie Arthème Fayard, 124–7; vol. 2: *Essai théologique* (1963), Paris: Librairie Arthème Fayard; English translation: *Tradition and Traditions* (1966), London: Burns and Oates.

Congar, Y., OP (1972) "La 'réception' comme réalité ecclésiologique," *Revue des sciences philosophiques et théologiques*, 56, 369–403.

Decrees of the Ecumenical Councils, vol. 2, 663.

Dogmatic Constitution on the Church (*Lumen Gentium*), in *The Documents of Vatican II*.

Dogmatic Constitution on Divine Revelation (*Dei Verbum*), in *The Documents of Vatican II*.

Drey, J.S. (1819; reprint 1971) *Kurze Einleitung in das Studium der Theologie mit Rücksicht auf den wissenschaftlichen Standpunct und das katholische System*, edited by F. Schupp. Darmstadt: Wissenschaftliche Buchgesellschaft.

Drey, J.S. (1940) "Ideen zur Geschichte des katholischen Dogmensystems," in *Geist des Christentums und des Katholizismus*, edited by J.R. Geiselmann. Mainz: Matthias Grünewald.

Espín, O. (1997) "Tradition and Popular Religion: An Understanding of the *Sensus Fidelium*," in *The Faith of the People: Theological Reflections on Popular Catholicism*. Maryknoll, NY: Orbis, 63–90.

Geiselmann, J.R. (1962) *Die Heilige Schrift und die Tradition*. Freiburg: Herder.

Guarino, T. (1996) "Postmodernity and Five Fundamental Theological Issues," *Theological Studies*, 57, 654–89.

Harnack, A. (1957) *What Is Christianity?*, trans. T. Saunders. New York: Harper and Row.

Hinze, B.E. (1977) "The Holy Spirit and the Catholic Tradition: The Legacy of Johann Adam Möhler," in Dietrich, D. and Himes, M. (eds.) *The Legacy of the Tübingen School*. New York: Crossroad, 75–94.

Hinze, B.E. (1990) "Narrative Contexts, Doctrinal Reform," *Theological Studies*, 51: 417–33.

Lash, N. (1975) *Newman on Development: The Search for an Explanation in History*. Sheperdstown, WV: Patmos Press, 65.

Lash, N. (1986) "Performing the Scriptures," in *Theology on the Way to Emmaus*. London: SCM Press, 37–46.

Lindbeck, G.A. (1984) *The Nature of Doctrine: Religion and Theology in a Postliberal Age*. Philadelphia, PA: Westminster Press.

Loisy, A. (1976) *The Gospel and the Church*, trans. C. Home. Philadelphia: Fortress Press.

Lonergan, B., SJ, (1972) *Method in Theology*. New York: Herder and Herder.

Kasper, W. (1962) *Die Lehre von der Tradition in der Römischen Schule* Freiburg: Herder, 215–17.

Möhler, J.A. (1957) *Die Einheit in der Kirche oder das Prinzip des Katholizismus dargestellt im Geiste der Kirchenväter der drei ersten Jahrhunderte*, edited by J.R. Geiselmann. Darmstadt: Wissenschaftliche Buchgesellschaft.

Mysterium Ecclesiae (June 24, 1973), in *Origins* 3 (July 19, 1973), 110–11.

Newman, J.H. (1961) *On Consulting the Faithful in Matters of Doctrine*. New York: Sheed and Ward.

Newman, J.H. (1989) *An Essay on the Development of Christian Doctrine*. Notre Dame, IN: University of Notre Dame Press.

Pelikan, J. (1969) *Development of Christian Doctrine: Some Historical Prolegomena*. New Haven, CT: Yale University Press.

Pope John XXIII (1966) Opening Address to the Council, in *The Documents of Vatican II*, edited by W. Abbott, SJ. New York: America Press, 715.

Rahner, K., SJ (1961) "The Development of Dogma," in *Theological Investigations*, vol. 1, trans. C. Ernst. London: Darton Longman and Todd, 39–77.

Rahner, K., SJ (1966) "Considerations on the Development of Dogma," in *Theological Investigations*, vol. 4, trans. K. Smyth. Baltimore. MD: Helicon Press, 3–35.

Roberts, A. and Donaldson, J. (eds.) (1977) "Irenaeus of Lyons, *Against Heresies*," in *The Ante-Nicene Fathers*, vol. 1. Grand Rapids. MI: W.B. Eerdmans, 347.

Roman Catholic Theology of Tradition (2002) *Horizons*, 29: 299–325.

Schillebeeckx, E., OP (1968) *Revelation and Theology*, 2 vols., trans. N.D. Smith. New York: Sheed and Ward.

Schleiermacher, F. (1910; reprint 1973) *Kurze Darstellung des theologischen Studiums zum Behuf einleitender Vorlesungen*, edited by H. Scholz. Darmstadt: Wissenschaftliche Buchgesellschaft.

Tanner, K. (1997) *Theories of Culture: A New Agenda for Theology*. Minneapolis, MN: Fortress Press.

Tanner, N., SJ (ed.) (1990) *Decrees of the Ecumenical Councils*, vol. 1. Washington, DC: Georgetown University Press.

Tavard, G.H. (1959) *Holy Writ or Holy Church: The Crisis of the Protestant Reformation*. New York: Harper and Brothers.

Thiel, J.E. (1991) *Imagination and Authority: Theological Authorship in the Modern Tradition*. Minneapolis, MN: Fortress Press, 33–94.

Thiel, J.E. (1997) "The Universal in the Particular: Johann Sebastian Drey on the Hermeneutics of Tradition," in Dietrich, D. and Himes, M. (eds.) *The Legacy of the Tübingen School*. New York: Crossroad, 56–74.

Thiel, J.E. (2000) *Senses of Tradition: Continuity and Development in Catholic Faith*. New York: Oxford University Press, 76–95, 125–8.

Tilley, T.W. (2000) *Inventing Catholic Tradition*. Maryknoll, NY: Orbis.

Walgrave, J.H. (1972) *Unfolding Revelation: The Nature of Doctrinal Development*. Philadelphia, PA: Westminster Press.

Wiedenhofer, S. and Schoppelreich, B. (eds.) (1998) *Zur Logik religiöser Traditionen*. Frankfurt am Main: IKO Verlag.

CHAPTER 18

God

Robert Barron

There is a story told of the very young Thomas Aquinas. At the conclusion of an elementary catechetical instruction, the six-year-old Thomas raised his hand and asked his teacher, "but Master, what *is* God?" This was not the more familiar question – which the adult Aquinas would famously ask – concerning the "whether" of God's existence; this query was getting at something more elemental: what exactly was his Christian teacher talking about when he used the word "God"? It assumes that the meaning of this term is by no means self-evident, that it carries, perhaps, a surprising implication. It is sometimes presumed that, in inter-religious conversations, one can find unambiguous common ground in reference to the idea of God, that this belief somehow will link traditions otherwise sharply divided over doctrine and morals. It will be a central concern of this chapter to show that this presumption is false, that there is, in fact, an irreducible distinctiveness about the Christian conception of God, and that, therefore the question posed by the youthful Aquinas is both legitimate and illuminating. The Catholic Christian tradition argues that, most properly speaking, God is the strange and personal power revealed in the total event of Jesus Christ: his Incarnation, life, teaching, death, rising from the dead, and sending forth of the Holy Spirit. To be sure, one can find any number of family resemblances between this notion and understandings of God in other religious traditions, and upon that basis one can undertake fruitful inter-religious conversation. Nevertheless, the Christian conception of the divine remains unique, one-off, uplifting, precisely in the measure that it is unsettling. For the Christian notion is that God – ultimate reality – is nothing other than love.

The Incarnational Starting-Point

One could argue that all of Christian dogmatics flows from the assertion that, in Jesus Christ, God became a creature. This fundamental claim first unnerves us and then orients us, illuminating both the nature of the world and the nature of God. Christian anthropology, cosmology, ethics, and aesthetics follow from that first illumination and the Christian doctrine of God from the second. What is that divine power capable of *becoming* a creature without ceasing to be divine and without compromising the integrity of the creature that it becomes? In the New Testament period itself and then throughout the first several centuries of the Church's life, reflective Christians wrestled mightily with that question. Tentative resolutions emerged in the earliest creedal statements, in the speculations of the first systematic theologians such as Irenaeus, Tertullian, and Origen, and in the formularies of the councils of Nicea, Constantinople, and Ephesus. Much of this energetic intellectual work was summed up in a pithy statement at the Council of Chalcedon in 451. Attempting to walk a middle ground between monophysitism and Nestorianism, the fathers of Chalcedon said that Jesus Christ is the hypostatic union of two natures – human and divine – in one divine person. The *Logos* instantiates two modes of existence – created and uncreated – which come together in the closest possible unity, yet without "mixing, mingling, or confusion." This tells us that God cannot be, himself, a worldly reality, something qualitatively similar to a human nature. Worldly things, finite natures, exist in a kind of mutual exclusivity and over-againstness. Part of what it means to be a tree is *not* to be any other finite thing. Thus the only way for a creaturely nature to become another is to be absorbed by it or to devolve into it, as the antelope becomes the lion only by being devoured or the house becomes ashes only by being burned. Yet, in Jesus, a divine nature enters into a personal union with a non-divine nature in such a way that neither is compromised in its integrity. Therefore, the God revealed in Christ's incarnation cannot be a being in the world, one thing among others, a supreme reality in, above, or alongside the rest of the universe. This God is other than the world, but if I can borrow Kathryn Tanner's term, he must be "otherly other," that is to say, not distinctive in a conventional sense, but rather non-contrastively other. Robert Sokolowski has observed that there is a distinction between God and the world that is utterly unlike the ordinary distinctions that obtain among and between creatures: differences of size, position, color, quality, or ontological density (Sokolowski, 1995: 35–6). The Renaissance-era theologian Nicholaus of Cusa caught this paradox when he commented that God, while remaining absolutely distinct from the world, must nevertheless be named the *non Aliud*, the non-other. The God disclosed in the hypostatic union is not so much somewhere else (that would make him only a distant finite thing) but *somehow* else, and this peculiar mode of his transcendence is made plain precisely in the act by which he becomes non-interruptively close to the world.

In order to grasp the radicalness of the idea of God implied in the Incarnation it is particularly instructive to contrast this Chalcedonian theology with the competitive notion of God assumed by the great atheists of the modern period. For Ludwig Feuerbach, the "no" to God is tantamount to the "yes" for humanity; for Karl Marx, the sloughing off of the skin of religious belief is the condition for the possibility of human flourishing; and for Jean-Paul Sartre, the sheer fact of human freedom positively disproves the existence of an all-powerful God. In all three cases, the unquestioned assumption is that God is competitive to human nature, that divinity and humanity are locked, necessarily, in a zero-sum game of ontological rivalry. But none of this is congruent with the doctrine of God implicit in the Chalcedonian teaching of the non-contrastive divine transcendence. The true God can personally ground a human nature in such as way that that nature remains utterly uncompromised; this incarnational notion – alien to the modern atheists – stands behind St Irenaeus' dictum *gloria Dei homo vivens* (the glory of God is a human being fully alive).

God as *Ipsum Esse*

This non-competitive transcendence of God compelled the Christian tradition to speak of the divine in surprising and distinctive ways. Its greatest adepts tended to name God, not as *a* being, even the highest being, but rather as Being Itself. One of the clearest witnesses to this uniquely Christian conception of God is the medieval theologian Anselm of Canterbury. In his *Proslogium*, Anselm describes God as *id quo maius cogitari nequit* (that than which no greater can be thought), a characterization that, at first glance, seems obvious enough, but that in fact represents a radical departure from the pre-Christian and non-Christian manner of naming ultimate reality (Anselm, 1962: 7). However great the Greek gods were imagined to be, they were still realities within the general structure of nature; however magnificent the Platonic demiurge or Form of the Good are, they remain supreme beings alongside other realities; however ontologically impressive the Aristotelian prime mover, it is still one being among many. And then there is Anselm's "that than which no greater can be thought." Whatever this reality may be, it cannot be something in, above, or alongside the world, for if it were, it plus the rest of the world would be greater than it alone, thus rendering it not that than which no greater can be conceived. If Anselm's description is correct, then the world in its entirety does not add to or subtract from God's being. We could say that, after Creation, there are more beings, but no more perfection of being. "That than which no greater can be thought" cannot be ingredient in the finite realm in any ordinary sense; it cannot be the supreme being or, as David Burrell memorably observed, "the biggest thing around." Here we see the essential congruity between the Chalcedonian and Anselmian formulas: both signal the God who is otherly other and non-constrastively transcendent to the universe.

Anselm is certainly best known for the demonstration of God's existence which flows from this peculiar name and which Kant awkwardly designated "the ontological argument." In point of fact, it is not really an argument at all, but a showing forth of the implications of the name – which becomes clear when we attend to the introductory moves of the *Proslogium*. We find that Anselm is responding to the promptings of his monastic brothers, who were seeking one single elegant proof of God's existence. He tells us that he sought assiduously for that argument and finally despaired of ever successfully formulating it. Only when he surrendered did the sacred name force itself upon him. This little narrative is extremely illuminating, for it demonstrates the impossibility of capturing the true God in the nets of the mind or through an aggressive act of the will. That which is not ingredient in the world as one being among many could come to us only as a gift, through the grace of its own self-disclosure. What follows in the "argument" is a further elaboration of this basic insight.

Anselm tells us that "that than which no greater can be thought" cannot be simply an idea in the mind, since existing both inside and outside the mind is greater than existing within subjective consciousness alone. If, therefore, like the fool in the psalm, one were to say that there is no God, one would be falling into a strict logical contradiction. Within the brief compass of this chapter, I cannot even begin to enter into the roiled and complex history of the interpretation of this demonstration, but I will maintain that both its advocates and critics tend largely to miss the heart of the matter. As a believing monk writing for his brothers in religion, Anselm is hardly in doubt as to the existence of God and thus is by no means trying to argue the case on neutrally rational grounds. Rather, he is showing *how* "that than which no greater can be thought" must exist. This strange reality can be isolated on neither side of the subjective/objective divide, for such a sequestering would be incompatible with the very structure of its existence. "That than which no greater can be thought" transcends this standard division because it precedes it and grounds it. Once more, were God a being of any kind, he could be caught in the web of the subject/object dichotomy and be known precisely by way of conventional contrast. The same peculiar otherness implied by the Chalcedonian formula is insinuated by the Anselmian demonstration.

Another Christian witness to the strangeness of the divine being is Thomas Aquinas. Throughout his career, Thomas tends to avoid the designation *ens summum* (highest being) for God, consistently preferring *ipsum esse subsistens* (the sheer act of to-be itself) (*Summa Theologiae*, Ia, q. 3, art. 7). This sacred name implies the same transcendence of subjectivity and objectivity that we saw in Anselm's treatment, for *ipsum esse* must be, simultaneously, what is closest to any thing and what is utterly beyond the metaphysical confines of being a thing. It must be, to borrow Augustine's lyrical language, what is both *intimior intimo meo et superior summo meo* (closer to me than I am to myself and higher than anything I could imagine). Aquinas specifies this distinctiveness as the *simplicitas* (simpleness) of God, or the coincidence in God of essence and existence. In any creature – from quarks to archangels – there can be found an ontological complexity of *esse* (the act of to-be) and *quidditas* (whatness), the former as it were poured into the recepticle of the latter, so as to give rise to a particular existent. But in *ipsum esse*, there is no such play; the to-be of God is not received or delimited by any principle of *quidditas*, so that to be God is not to be this or that type of thing, but simply to be to-be. An immediate implication of the divine simpleness is the divine unknowability. Thomas comments at the beginning of his discussion of the divine attributes in the *Summa Theologiae* that he will not tell us what God is, only what God is not. Since our senses and minds are so naturally oriented to the universe of things in a nexus of contingent relationality, we cannot really know what *ipsum esse* is, except in a negative way, by removing from the idea of God any qualities that belong to creatures as creatures. Hence, we can say that God is not material, not finite, not temporal, not mobile, etc., but what precisely this infinite, eternal, immaterial, and unmoving reality is, we do not clearly know. The very negativity of Aquinas' theological method witnesses to the non-constrastive otherness of God that we have been insisting upon, for were God a being among others, he could be known through comparison with other things. Thomas sums up this insight by insisting that God can never be defined and hence that God is essentially and not simply provisionally incomprehensible.

God the Creator

Implicit in all that we have been arguing to this point in regard to God is that the universe, as such, has no necessity. Though the ancient Greeks and Romans certainly recognized contingency within the world of nature, they never imagined that nature itself could be contingent. Nature or matter co-exist as ultimate principles alongside the gods or, in a more philosophical framework of discourse, the prime mover or the Form of the Good. But this understanding of the world has to give way once we begin speaking of "that than which no greater can be thought" or of *ipsum esse*. Since the universe adds nothing to the greatness or perfection of the true God, the universe as such need not exist. God would be fully himself without it. But this introduces a dimension of contingency that the pre-Christian world never imagined, namely the radical dependency of the whole of finitude. To say that the universe in its entirety exists but need not exist is to say that it is created. As Christian theologians and philosophers explored the implications of this doctrine, they began to speak of *creatio ex nihilo*, creation from nothing. They saw that the non-constrastively transcendent God had to bring the whole of what is not God into being and that, therefore, there could be no pre-existing substrate upon which or with which the Creator acts. This is why Aquinas, for instance, could say that Creation is not, strictly speaking, a change or a making. A number of contemporary theologians have begun to point out that *creatio ex nihilo* – an ordering without presupposition or substrate – is necessarily a non-violent act (Milbank, 1990: 391). In the mythological and philosophical accounts that preceded and surrounded early Christianity, God or the gods establish order through some act of primeval manipulation, intervention, violence, or aggressive overcoming. Thus, one god or set of gods puts to death and dismembers the body of a rival deity, making the heavens and earth out of the parts of the conquered victim. Or, the most powerful metaphysical principle moves, guides, invasively orders some more pliable element (prime matter, nature, etc.) and thereby establishes the world in its present structure. But none of this obtains when we speak of creation from nothing, since there is, quite literally, nothing for God to move, change, order, or dominate when he brings the whole of finite existence into being. Rather, this coming-to-be occurs through a sheerly generous and non-violent act of love. In the alternative accounts of worldly ordering, being-over-and-against is primary, but on the Christian telling, being-for-and-with-the-other is ontologically basic. The non-competitiveness between the divine and human natures, which we see on display in the Incarnation, finds a more general parallel in the non-invasiveness of the Creator God in his Creation.

From this teaching concerning *creatio ex nihilo* flows the doctrine of metaphysical participation. Since the entire cosmos is made by God from nothing, it cannot have an extrinsicist relation to God, standing as it were apart from its Creator and relating to him in a mediated manner. Instead, everything in the world *is* a relation to God. In the disputed question *De potentia Dei*, Thomas Aquinas can make the Zen-like remark that that which receives creation from God is itself being created, breaking thereby the Aristotelian language concerning relationship as an accident mediating between two substances (*De Potentia*, qu. 3, art. 3). More to it, since it is so ontologically basic, Creation is not an act that can be relegated to the "beginning" of time; rather, it is the on-going, here and now dynamic by which finite things are, from moment to moment, constituted. Were God to withdraw his creative energy, things would fall immediately into nothingness. And this is why Aquinas designates Creation as *quaedam relatio ad Creatorem cum novitate essendi* (a kind of relationship to the Creator, with newness of being). Though it can be construed easily enough in a pantheist or panentheist direction, the only language that is even relatively adequate to this relationship is "participation:" the universe shares, in a derivative way, in the intensity of the divine to-be. In the light of this idea of participation, the Thomistic tradition speaks of the *analogia entis*, the analogy of being. "Being" is not a neutral word which can be applied to varying degrees of God and creatures; instead, *esse*, in the proper sense of the term, can be ascribed to God alone and only in an analogical manner of those things that participate in God's to-be. Another implication of the doctrine of creation *ex nihilo* is the radical interconnectedness of all things in and through God. Since all created realities are coming forth, here and now, from the ground of the divine creativity, they are, perforce, united to one another at the deepest level of their being, co-inherent with each another through God. Participation in God implies a mitigated but real participation in other creatures.

A final implication of this incarnation-based doctrine of Creation is the unique mode of the divine causality and providence. In Jesus, as we have seen, divine and human natures come together non-competitively, and this means that the human intellect and will of Christ are utterly uncompromised by the proximity to them of the divine intellect and will. This was confirmed, incidentally, in the resolution of the monothelite controversy in the eighth century, when the Church emphatically taught that there are two wills in Jesus, operating in a perfectly coordinated manner. Extrapolating from this incarnational state of affairs, Christian theologians saw that God can direct all things – including the free wills of his rational creatures – in a non-invasive way, allowing the ordinary causal processes of nature – physical and psychological – to unfold in coordination with his own providential direction of the whole of Creation. Because God's being is modally other than the world, his manner of causality is modally other than that of any agent in the nexus of interdependent causes. One can therefore say, for instance, that the downfall of the Soviet Union was the result of a complex congeries of economic, political, social, and religious factors *and* that it was ingredient in God's providential governance of the universe, the meta-cause in no way negating or interfering with the complex of particular causes.

Giving Names to God

It could be argued that the central task of theology is assigning names to God. We have been considering God under the rubric of one of his highest names, Being Itself, the roots of which are, to some degree, in the event of the Incarnation. But the earliest explicitly biblical warrant for speaking of God as "the one who is" is in the third chapter of the book of Exodus. When Moses, responding to the divine manifestation in the burning bush, asks God his name, he hears the voice say, "*ehyeh asher ehyeh*," "I am who I am" (Exod 3:14). During the 1960s there was a heated debate between Etienne

Gilson, who maintained that this divine self-description provided a legitimately biblical justification for the long tradition of naming God in metaphysical terms as being itself, and his critics, who claimed that the spiritually evocative and multivalent language of this Exodus story was seriously compromised by an abstractly ontological interpretation. Within the confines of this brief article, I cannot even begin to explore adequately the nuances of that debate. However, I would like at least to nod to both sides of the issue, maintaining that, in point of fact, the highest kind of metaphysical naming of God carries with it implicitly a powerful spiritual implication.

Genesis tells us that, in response to the suggestion of the serpent that God is a threat to their full-flourishing, Adam and Eve first grasp at the tree of the knowledge of good and evil, attempting to seize for themselves a properly divine prerogative. When this proves futile, they seek to hide from God, concealing themselves in the underbrush of Eden, where, of course, they are immediately found out (Gen 3). What are on display in this vividly symbolic narrative are the two principal paths of the sinner – grasping at God, and hiding from God – and also the very manner of God's existence which renders hopeless all such attempts. The moves of the first sinners are repeated by Moses in the Exodus scene under consideration. When he spies the vision of the bush on fire but not being consumed (a wonderful image, by the way, of the non-competitiveness of the divine presence in Creation), he rather aggressively seeks to understand: "I must turn aside and look at this great sight and see why the bush is not burned up" (Exod 3:3). But God frustrates any such attempt: "Come no closer! Remove the sandals from your feet, for the place on which you are standing is holy ground" (Exod 3:5). This God cannot be seized. On the other hand, this God cannot be avoided. He speaks Moses' name and then reveals himself as the God of Abraham, Isaac, and Jacob – and of their people who are suffering in bondage in Egypt. The one speaking from the burning bush is as intimate and immanent as any of the local divinities with whom Moses was acquainted. Inspired by this closeness and forgetting, perhaps, that he is on holy ground, Moses seeks once more to grasp, and this time in the boldest way possible, through the seizing of a name: "If I come to the Israelites and say to them, 'The God of your ancestors has sent me to you,' and they ask me, 'What is his name?' what shall I say to them" (Exod 3:13)? It is to this question that God gives his famous answer: "*Ehyeh asher ehyeh.*" Precisely in its strangeness, open-endedness, and indefinition, this answer/non-answer signals the unique mode of the divine existence as that which can be neither grasped nor hidden from, neither controlled nor avoided. "I am" must be utterly unlike any thing or combination of things in the world (in the measure that they exist as specified instances of being); and "I am" must be present, in the most intimate manner, to any thing or combination of things in the world (in the measure that they exist at all). Whether we render the Hebrew as "I am who I am" or, as some have suggested, "I will be who I will be," the name accomplishes the same undoing of the dysfunctional moves of Eden. Here we see that the description of God as *ipsum esse* is in line with both the dynamics of the Incarnation and the mysticism of Genesis and Exodus.

The more specific naming of God that occurs in the great tradition – the assigning of divine attributes – takes place under this rubric of immanence and transcendence. Certain names of God, which emphasize the divine otherness, are designed to keep the grasping tendency at bay, and others, which stress the divine closeness, are meant to frustrate the impulse to hide. Thus this ascribing of properties to God has the dual purpose of naming God more truthfully and luring us into the right relationship to God, that of friendship (Barron, 1998: 105). Among the chief anti-grasping names are infinity and unity. For the ancient philosophers, infinity is an imperfection, since it implies incompleteness, and hence it was, for them, not ascribable to ultimate reality. Parmenides, for instance, appreciated Being as a finite and perfect whole. For biblically formed thinkers, however, infinity must be ascribed to God, since it signals his pure and limitless actuality, God's possession of the fullness of ontological perfection. Thomas Aquinas sees the divine infinity as a function of the identity in God of essence and existence: since the divine being is totally unreceived, it must be without limit. God's reality is therefore inexhaustible, and thus inexhaustibly fascinating for the mind. Commenting on Aquinas' eschatology, Karl Rahner said that it is only in heaven that the blessed see for the first time just how incomprehensible God is – hinting thereby that the *via negativa* practiced in the *Summa Theologiae* is a sort of distant preparation for the mode of knowing that will obtain in heaven (Rahner, 1978). The assertion of the divine infinity is thus a salutary frustration to the mind's tendency to seize and define God. A name that flows rather directly from infinity is unity. If we speak of a multiplicity of gods, then we would be obliged to say that one god is not any of the others, and this distinction would imply demarcation and delimitation. There cannot be, in a word, two ontological infinities. Both the *Shema* of the book of Deuteronomy, "Hear O Israel, the Lord your God, the Lord is one" (Deut 6:4) and the opening words of the *Credo*, "I believe in one God," are affirmations that God escapes the nexus of finite things that stand contrastively over and against one another. And since the human mind knows precisely through the making of distinctions and the setting up of contrasts, this supreme unity of God holds off the temptation to grasp.

Still under the rubric of the divine transcendence, the tradition affirms that God is self-sufficient in his being, that he has, to use the medieval coinage, "aseity," by-himself-ness. As simple, one, and infinite, God must exist through himself and necessarily stands in need of nothing outside of himself. As we saw, Creation adds nothing to the divine perfection, and God requires nothing in the created realm in order to realize potentialities within himself. This divine aseity is correlated to the fact of creation from nothing, for how could God be ontologically beholden to anything that he has brought into being in its entirety? Once we appreciate the absoluteness of God's self-sufficiency, we are disabused of the illusion that we could, through our efforts and exertions, manipulate God or draw him into our sphere of influence. Relatedly, the tradion consistently speaks of God as free and sovereign. In creating, judging, making covenants, and redeeming, God acts freely, compelled by no agent outside of himself. Again, this claim is tightly linked to the affirmation of Creation, for nothing that God has completely made through his will could finally coerce the divine will. Since God acts consistently out of the integrity of his own being, it is pointless to seek to control, dominate, or coerce him.

Remaining under the rubric of the anti-grasping names, we can speak of the Lordliness of God. One of the most frequently-used terms for God in the Old Testament – as a sort of stand-in for the unpronounceable tetragrammaton – is *Adonai*, the Lord. Paul

Tillich has commented that this divine lordliness has both an aesthetic and a political sense (Tillich, 1986: 163). God's aesthetic lordliness is his sublimity and awesomeness, that overwhelming fullness of being in the presence of which the only proper response is bowing low. How often in the Psalms, the wisdom literature, and the prophets this divine sublimity is emphasized, along with the injunction to subject oneself to it in a spirit of humility. God's political lordliness is his capacity to command, to order and govern Creation, to reign supreme over all that he has made, to come unmistakably first. The only proper response to this modality of the divine being is obedience and trust. Whenever we are tempted to place ourselves in the prime position or to imagine that we are the commanders of our own lives, this divine attribute serves as the corrective.

Now these names protective of the divine transcendence (and there are obviously many others) are altogether appropriate and necessary for a proper description of God. But if they are exclusively emphasized, our idea of the divine becomes fatally distorted, God devolving into a distant object, or what Karl Barth termed "the deity of the God of the philosophers" (Barth, 1960: 45). As we have seen, what is remarkable about *Ipsum esse* is not transcendence in the ordinary sense, but rather strangeness, a non-constrastive otherness. Thus, alongside the anti-grasping names, the great tradition has listed an equally impressive number of anti-hiding names, attributes that describe the unavoidable closeness of Being Itself. Hence even as it affirms the infinity, simplicity, and unity of God, the tradition characterizes God as omnipotent or all-powerful as well. This symbol does not imply that God is the strongest and most influential being among beings or that God is capable of affecting anomolies (making two plus two equal to anything but four or declaring adultery morally praiseworthy). Such voluntarist fantasies are among the most glaring and dangerous distortions in the history of theology. Rather, the omnipotence of God signals that God, precisely as the ground of all existence, presses on the whole of finitude with an unconditioned authority. Similarly, God is described as omniscient, all-knowing. This does not mean that God is the most intelligent being among beings, knowing all things, as it were, from without. Instead, God knows all things in the measure that he knows them into being, his act of creation coinciding with his act of cognizing. It is not the case that God knows things because they exist; rather, things exist because God knows them. And omnipresence is ascribed to God as well, not to imply that he permeates all Creation like a force or energy, but that he, as Creator, grounds and gives rise to all space. Not restricted to any space, God is the Lord of all space and hence, if I can put it this way, geographically unavoidable. One could read Psalm 139 – "where can I run from your love?" – in this sense, as a sinner's lament, the cry of someone who wants to escape from God but can find no way to do so. And perhaps one could argue that the biblical stories of the Tower of Babel, David's murder of Uriah, and the attempted escape of the prophet Jonah were meant as narrative accounts of, respectively, the divine omnipotence, omniscience, and omnipresence.

Similarly, were God's self-sufficiency and freedom unilaterally stressed, God would become an overbearing and threatening supreme being. Hence the tradition has balanced these anti-grasping names with the anti-hiding attribute of the divine fidelity. The sheer act of to-be itself cannot fall into self-contradiction and therefore cannot undermine the structures of the created being which participates in him. God does not hover arbitrarily over affirmation and negation like a capricious tyrant, but rather remains faithful to himself and that which exists in and through his being. To be sure, God does not have to create, but once he creates, he is bound in love to what he has made. In the language of the Bible, this is God's rock-like reliability and covenant faithfulness, his parent-like devotion to his creatures: "could a mother forget her child? Even should she forget, I will never forget you" (Isa 49:15). It is in this context of the divine fidelity that I would affirm of God the much contested attribute of immutability. Though God's unchangeableness has been defended by the Magisterium and by practically every major theologian in the tradition, this attribution has been sharply criticized by many contemporary thinkers, especially those formed in the school of process theology. The difficulty is this: though immutability is clearly an attribute of the absolute being as conceived of by the philosophers, it hardly seems characteristic of the God described in the narratives and poetry of the Bible. The Lord spoken of by Isaiah, Jeremiah, and Ezekiel, the Yahweh who interacts with Abraham, Jacob, and Moses is passionate, deeply involved in history, responsive to the actions of his people. The key to the resolution of this difficulty is, once again, the fact of Creation. The God who continually brings the whole of finitude into being from nothing cannot, in an ordinary creaturely way, be changed by anything he has made. To say otherwise is to undermine the metaphysical structure of Creation and to turn God into a supreme being among many. But to say that God does not interact with his Creation according to the interdependent manner of finite things is by no means to imply that God is wanting in the passion and deep involvement to which the Bible witnesses, just the contrary. The God who knows all of created reality into being, who stands behind every thought, movement, development, action, and reaction of the world can only be described, in relation to that world, as connected and compassionate in the highest degree. Immutability and love for Creation are not, therefore mutually exclusive, but mutually implicative.

God's Highest Name

Guided by the doctrine of the Incarnation and by the divine self-definition in Exodus 3:14, we have been exploring the implications of God's name *Ipsum esse*. But there is, within the biblical revelation, a higher name than this, an unsurpassable name beyond any other. This is given in the first letter of John: "*ho theos agape estin*" (God is love). G.K. Chesterton remarked that the dogma of the Trinity is nothing but an explication of this claim, for if God *is* love, then there must be, within the structure of the divine to-be, a play of lover, beloved, and love. If love were simply an action that God performs, something extrinsic to his essence, he could exercise it adequately in relation to the world. But if God *is* love, an ordered relationality must obtain in him.

The ground for this extraordinary claim of the first Christians is the antecedent claim of Jesus himself to equality with the divine Father who sent him. By forgiving sins, asserting authority over the Torah, cleansing the temple in Jerusalem, saying of himself, "unless you love me more than your very life, you are not worthy of me," indeed by the very quality of the whole of his public life, Jesus proclaimed his divinity. He was a human being, to be sure, but he also knew and professed himself to be God, and he spoke to and of the divine Father as another. Now all of this could be seen as the ravings of a madman or the outrages of a blasphemer, and it was just such suspicions on the part of the ruling establishment of his time that brought Jesus to his death on the Cross. However, the resurrection of Jesus from the dead was read by the first believers as the ratification of the claims of Jesus on the part of the one he called Father. Thus it occurred to them that within the being of the one God of Israel there is indeed a play of duality, a conversation in love between the Father and the one he sent. Now this differentiated experience of God was further complicated by the sense that the very love which joins Father and Son, the love in which the Son was sent by the Father, had become a living presence within the community of the Church. This Holy Spirit, they intuited, was, like the Son and Father, divine, but other than the Son and Father in the measure that he had been sent by them. These insights – garnered gradually throughout the New Testament period – came to tentative expression in the Epistles of Paul and the Gospels, especially the Gospel of John, and found a paradigmatic formulation in the ecstatic phrase cited above: God *is* the love that joins Father, Son, and Holy Spirit. What was bequeathed to the Christian Church in the post-biblical period was the daunting theological task of thinking together the two great names of God that we have considered: being and love. That the accomplishment of this assignment was a tangled and conflict-ridden affair shouldn't surprise us; that it was achieved as convincingly as it was is the real surprise and remains one of the glories of Christian theology.

For the sake of brevity and clarity, I will consider the theology of the Trinity offered in the thirteenth century by Thomas Aquinas. A large part of the genius of Aquinas was his capacity to sum up and coordinate the wealth of material that the tradition had offered him, and his Trinitarian speculation is a particularly fine example of this synthetic power. Having in the first book of his *Summa Contra Gentiles* vigorously defended the unity and simplicity of God, Thomas sets out in the fourth book of that same work, to give an account of the Trinity (*Summa Contra Gentiles* IV, chapter 11). He begins with a sort of axiom: the higher the being, the more perfect and more interior its capacity for self-replication. The truth of this ipsedixistism can be verified in the hierarchy of existence apparent in nature. The lowest level of being – for Aquinas, an inanimate object such as a rock – has the power to produce an image of itself, but only in a most exterior and imperfect manner. It can, for instance, leave an impression of itself in the soft earth or it can be made to leave its mark on skin or sidewalk. As we move up the ladder of existence, we come to plants, those things enjoying vegetative life. These can reproduce themselves in the elemental mode of the rock, but they can also do so at a higher level of interiority and perfection, giving rise to a seed which, falling to the ground, creates in time a remarkably complete *imago* of the original. At the next level of ontological perfection, we find certain animals capable of generating within themselves – with, to be sure, outside influence – nearly perfect physical replicas.

Then, as we come to the human level, a quantum is crossed, for the human being – physical, vegetative, and animal – is able to reproduce himself in the ways already described, but he is also able, in his mind, to produce a self-image to a qualitatively more intense degree of interiority and perfection. This happens through the mind's capacity to form an interior word, a mirror of itself, what Augustine called *notitia sui*. All manner of autobiography, introspection, spiritual direction and psychotherapy depend upon this self-reflective power. Yet we have not come to the highest type of being, since even this intense self-imaging is less than perfect (otherwise, who would need the aid of a psychotherapist or spiritual director?) and less than utterly interior, since it, like all modes of human cognition, depends ultimately on the mediation of sense experience. So Aquinas speculates about a still higher type of creaturely being, namely the angels. Pure intelligences separated from matter, angels are capable of the formation of an interior word, a self-replication that is intuitive, immediate, and nearly perfectly interior. What prevents the angelic self-imaging from achieving complete interiority is the creatureliness of the angel. Though extremely high on the metaphysical scale, the angel is, nevertheless, a creature, which means that his being is received from outside, through the agency of God.

And this brings us to the highest degree of existence, to that reality in whom essence and existence coincide, to that which is the sheer act of to-be itself. And this means, in accord with Aquinas' dictum that we have arrived at that reality which is able to form a self *imago* that is utterly perfect and utterly interior. This is what happens when the Father (the primordial energy of the divine mind) knows itself through its interior word (the *Logos* or the Son). So perfect and selfsame is this *imago*, that one is compelled to say that it is one in being with the Father, that, in the words of John's Prologue, it *is* God. In the white-hot intensity of the generation of the Son from the Father, therefore, duality and unity coincide and coinhere. But there is one more step. The will, for Aquinas, is a modality of the intellect, since the good, understood as good, is immediately and *eo ipso* desired. Thus, when the Father knows the Son, he necessarily knows him as the supreme good, and by that very move, he loves him, he wills him. This divine love, proceeding from the Father and the Son, *is* the Holy Spirit, the sacred sigh of affection breathed back and forth between the Father and the Son. And since whatever God does *is* God (due to the coming together in God of essence and existence), we must say that this Holy Spirit *is* God. Guided by revelation and by the logic of the divine simplicity, we can see how the very unity of God *implies* the play of the Trinitarian persons. Because God is simple, he must be perfect; because he is perfect, he must have intelligence; because he has intelligence, he must know himself utterly; and because he knows himself utterly, he must love himself. Aquinas shows that Father, Son, and Holy Spirit *are* the divine simplicity, that the two great names of God – Being and Love – coincide, and in this he brings the Catholic Christian theological tradition to one of its highest points.

Now what more can we say about these "persons" that constitute the Trinity? In his *De Trinitate*, St Augustine famously commented that we call these realities *"personae"* only so that we might have something to say when people ask us what they are (*De Trinitate* VII, chapter 3)! And Anselm, many centuries later, called them simply *nescio quid* (I don't know what). The obvious danger sensed by both saints is that the use of the term "person" can give the impression that the Father, Son, and Holy Spirit are three separate beings – which would, of course, compromise the divine simplicity.

Nevertheless, there are certain positive clarifications that we can make. Following indications in Augustine's work, Thomas Aquinas argued that the Trinitarian persons are "subsistent relations," that is to say realities that have something in common with substances (since they do not come into and out of being) and something in common with relationships (since they are, necessarily, oriented to another). So God *is* a set of relationships. Just as unity and plurality co-exist in God, so substantiality and relationality come together seamlessly in the divine to-be; what display themselves as mutually exclusive in the realm of creatures, constitute a *complexio oppositorum* in God, the fullness of the divine perfection transcending and including these contrary perfections.

Aquinas further specifies that among the three persons in the Trinity there obtains a set of four immanent relations. The rapport of the Father to the Son is termed "active generation," and the relation of the Son to the Father is called "passive generation;" while the relation of the Father and Son to the Holy Spirit is termed "active spiration" (breathing out), and that of the Holy Spirit to the Father and Son is called "passive spiration." What this technical language signals is that there is, within the divine being, a kind of back-and-forth rhthym, a play of giving and receiving, something like the beating of a heart. Once again, if God *is* love, then the very to-be of God is a dynamism of loving and being loved, of looking and being looked at, or in the even more provocative language of Bernard of Clairvaux, of kissing and being kissed.

Conclusion

The English Catholic novelist Charles Williams once observed that the master idea of Christianity is co-inherence: that is to say, being in and with the other. He saw this dynamic in the Incarnation – the coming together without competition of divinity and humanity – as well as in Creation, the participation of all finite things in God and, through God, with one another. But the prime exemplar of co-inherence, he thought, was the *communio* of the Trinitarian persons, the existing-together of the Father, Son, and Holy Spirit in a bond so tight that it constituted the divine unity. In the course of this explication of the Christian doctrine of God, we have explored all of these modes of co-inherence. The radical communion of the Trinitarian persons, we saw, grounds the non-invasiveness of the act of creation and the non-competitiveness of the natures in Christ. What we hope to have shown thereby is that willing the good of the other as other is the dynamic that structures reality at all levels, that love, in a word, is the fullest and deepest meaning of existence.

To defend the uniqueness of the Catholic Christian doctrine of God is to defend the legitimacy of that claim.

References and Further Reading

Anselm (1962) "Proslogium," in *St Anselm: Basic Writings*. La Salle, IL: Open Court.
Aquinas, Thomas (1948) *Summa Theologiae*, trans. Fathers of the English Dominican Province. New York: Benziger Brothers.

Aquinas, Thomas (1965) *De Potentia* in *Quaestiones Disputatae Vol. II*. Turin: Marietti.

Aquinas, Thomas (1975) *Summa Contra Gentiles, Book Four: Salvation*, edited by Charles J. O'Neil. Notre Dame, IN: University of Notre Dame Press.

Augustine (1990) *The Trinity*, edited by Edmund Hill. Brooklyn, NY: New City Press.

Barron, Robert (1998) *And Now I See: A Theology of Transformation*. New York: Crossroad.

Barth, Karl (1960) *The Humanity of God*. Atlanta, GA: John Knox Press.

Milbank, John (1990) *Theology and Social Theory: Beyond Secular Reason*. Oxford: Blackwell.

Rahner, Karl (1978) "Thomas Aquinas on the Incomprehensibility of God," *Journal of Religion*, 58 Supplement, pp 107–25.

Sokolowski, Robert (1995) *The God of Faith and Reason*. Washington, DC: Catholic University of America Press.

Tillich, Paul (1986) *Dogmatik: Marburger Vorlesung von 1925*, edited by Werner Schussler. Dusseldorf: Patmos Verlag.

CHAPTER 19

Creation and Anthropology

Mary Aquin O'Neill

Belief in a Creator God undergirds all of Catholic life and practice. Through the weekly recitation of the Creed, the Catholic faithful profess faith in this God: *We believe in one God, the Father, the almighty, maker of heaven and earth, of all that is seen and unseen.* At the heart of each act of thanksgiving that Catholics call Eucharist is the confidence that this God comes to restore the Creation, broken and sullied by sin, in the person of Jesus Christ. The conviction that material things are created good and can be the medium for God's grace informs Catholic sacramental life and shapes the art found in Catholic churches. Catechesis at all levels seeks to form Catholic Christians who recognize their responsibilities as beings made in the image and likeness of God and redeemed by God incarnate. These responsibilities include caring for the earth, building up human societies of peace and justice, forming relationships between women and men that respect differences and create community, and shaping and sustaining loving human families.

The Story of Creation

The Creation story of Genesis is read annually at the Easter vigil, a special liturgy that prepares for the great Easter dawn. This reading keeps before the minds of Catholics revealed answers to the perennial questions about where the world came from, why it was created, what is its purpose – and ours. Belief in Creation is reinforced throughout the year by the recitation of psalms that hymn the work of God's hands, and the reading of the prophets, of Paul, and of Gospel accounts that make use of the new Creation theme.

In coming to understand that the Genesis Creation stories belong to primordial history and contain traces of mythic elements, Catholic believers are able to hold together the realm of faith with the realm of science. Contrary to the way the word is sometimes used, a myth is not a story that is untrue. Rather, the truth it yields is at the level of meaning rather than of fact. Myths are not scientific accounts and should not be compared with scientific answers. Narratives of origin, like those in Genesis, function symbolically. They reveal truths by embracing humankind as a whole in one ideal history, setting that history in a narration that includes movement from one stage to another, and getting at, through story, the enigma of human existence: that things are not as they ought to be (Ricoeur, 1967: 162–3). In this way the story of Creation helps the believer account, at the level of the imagination, for the way things are, the way things were meant to be, and the hoped for restoration, most often called salvation or redemption.

Properly understood, the Genesis account shapes a response to existence and can evoke, in a way that rational discourse rarely does, attitudes of worship and awe. The story of Creation introduces the faithful to a God whose goodness overflows in sharing life with all that is, whose intention is to give into the care of human beings stewardship of all Creation. Creation itself is depicted as a divine work. After work, comes rest – something the Creator makes time for on the seventh day. For the human creature, the story brings home the realization that human existence is contingent on the act of God. These insights inform the life of worship and praise that the Church community offers to God in thanksgiving. Catholics believe that in and through the Creation story, God has revealed aspects of reality that cannot be obtained by human reason alone.

The doctrine of Creation can be traced throughout the Old and the New Testaments. Of the Old Testament development, Anne M. Clifford writes, "There is good reason to conclude that each age of ancient Israel's faith reflection expressed its understanding of creation in a way intelligible to itself" (Clifford, 1991: 198). Recent scholarship maintains, in fact, that the Creation story of Genesis was written after many of the other texts that praise the God of Creation and marvel at what has come from God's hands (Batto, 1992). The prophets link the truth of Creation to their appeal for ethical action on the part of the people of God (e.g. Mal 2.10; Amos 4.2–13). The psalms express wonder and awe at the order and beauty of Creation (e.g. Ps 8; 19; 29; 89; 104), even as they praise the God who can crush alien powers in defense of a vulnerable and fragile creation (e.g. Ps 74.13–14; 89.10–11). The texts known as Wisdom literature (Proverbs, Job, Ecclesiastes [Qoheleth], Sirach [Ecclesiasticus], the Wisdom of Solomon, and some of the psalms) offer profound reflections on how to live in harmony with the created order, thus forging a close connection between Creation and the attainment of wisdom, which is "better than profit in silver" whose gain is "better than gold" (Prov 3.14). Wisdom, often in the figure of a woman, is seen as a co-principle of Creation in the sapiential books (e.g. Prov 8; Ecclus 24.3ff.; Wis 7.21f.).

The New Testament picks up on the theme of creation in a variety of ways. Elisabeth Schüssler Fiorenza has demonstrated that the early church interpreted Jesus by association with Wisdom, seeing in him the prophet of Sophia, or Wisdom personified as a woman (1995: 140–1; see Luke 7.35, 11.49). The creative power of Wisdom enables Jesus to perform the deeds that he does, deeds that make the reign of God a reality (Matt 11.19). This reign God has intended "from the foundation of the world" (Matt 25.34). Paul confesses belief in Christ's part in Creation in 1 Corinthians, where he writes:

yet for us there is one God, the Father, from whom all things are and for whom we exist,
and one Lord, Jesus Christ, through whom all things are and through whom we exist.
(8.6; see also Col 1.14–17)

The Letters of Paul take up the theme of the new creation (Rom 8.19–23; 2 Cor 5.15).
Such Wisdom theology culminates in the Gospel of John, where Jesus is understood to
be Wisdom incarnate and the Christian imagination drives backwards toward the pre-
existent *Logos* present "in the beginning" (John 1.1).

The Creation story is always interpreted by the Catholic tradition against this wide
backdrop. With that in mind, it is possible to discern the outlines of a doctrine of Creation that results from centuries of meditation on the revealed texts. Catholics share
with other Christians and with Jews the story of a God who creates by the power of the
Word. Unlike the gods of previous civilizations and cultures, this God does not resort to
violence to bring forth what is now known as the universe. The God of Genesis speaks
a great "let there be" and things come into being. And after each element familiar to
human consciousness comes into being – light, sky, earth, sun, moon, birds, fish, wild
beasts, cattle – God pronounces it good. When God has created human being in its
male and female form, the response of God is that the Creation is now very good.

The creation of human being is so important that it merits an extended and detailed
description in the second chapter of Genesis. This will be considered at length when
the attention of this study turns to anthropology. First, however, it will be important
to see what the Catholic faith tradition came to understand about the God who creates, the motivation for that creation, the dignity of what comes forth from the hands
of God, and the human capacity to know something about that God from the traces
of the divine in the created order. Then it will be possible to see the growing edge of
this faith tradition, by considering questions that are being posed in a new age to an
ancient tradition.

The Creator God

It was inevitable that, when stories that preserved God's revelation to the Jewish people
came into contact with the cosmology of the Greeks, questions would be raised that
required philosophical answers. One of them was of great concern. Was there anything "before" God? If so, God would be part of the created order and, like any human
maker, would have created from the materials at hand. If not, God was the beginning
of everything, not dependent on what was at hand, pure source of everything that
has being. The answer developed and believed to this day by Catholics is that God created *ex nihilo*, out of nothing. Yet this creation is not limited to the past, over and done
with; God sustains all that is by a *creatio continua*, a continuing act of creation. Human
beings are invited by the divine artist to take part in this continuing act as co-creators
through the works that repair and rebuild the created world and introduce the novelty
that stems from human imagination and ingenuity. Pope John Paul II expresses the
Catholic faith relative to this in *Sollicitudo Rei Socialis*:

Development and growth belong to humanity's vocation. The story of humankind in Sacred Scripture is one of constant achievements. In his turn Jesus asked us to use our talents and make them fruitful. All should work together for the full development of others: "development of the whole human being and of all people." (1987: 30)

Since there was nothing "before" God, and God is dependent on nothing for divine creative activity, creation is an act of supreme freedom. Another name for that freedom is love. The technical term for the love that sustains creation in being is Providence, belief in which allows Catholics to trust in the divine power at work in the world. Creation, in fact, is understood to be the beginning of God's saving works (Scheffczyk, 1970: 8). This salvific intention extends, not only to human beings, but to the entire universe. Thus efforts to care for the earth and to protect the resources divinely given by the creator God partake in the divine saving works.

In his World Day of Peace Message in 1990, Pope John Paul II addressed all in the Catholic Church to remind them of their serious obligation to care for all of Creation.

> The commitment of believers to a healthy environment for everyone stems directly from their belief in God the Creator, from their recognition of the effects of original and personal sin, and from the certainty of having been redeemed by Christ. Respect for life and for the dignity of the human person extends also to the rest of creation, which is called to join man in praising God (cf. *Ps* 148:96). (1990: §16)

It is the consistent Catholic teaching and belief that God created *all* things, material and spiritual. Since this God is pure goodness, all that comes from the divine hand is considered intrinsically good. Repeatedly in the history of Christianity there arose objections to this position. Whether in the form of Manichaeism or Gnosticism, distrust of matter and, particularly, of the human body led to positions that denied the goodness of material creation. The Catholic Church stands against this attitude toward the body, as well as against pantheism, the belief that God and matter are the same such that God is part of the world and the world a part of God.

The teaching regarding Creation can be found in the documents of the Fourth Lateran Council (1215), the Council of Florence *Decree for Jacobites* (1442), the First Vatican Council's *Dogmatic Constitution on the Catholic Faith* (1870), and the Second Vatican Council's *Pastoral Constitution on the Church in the Modern World* (1965). Richard McBrien points out that the last named document is especially important "because it underscores the autonomy of the created order and draws out the principal practical implication of such autonomy" (1970: 227). The implication of this is that methodical research carried out in a truly scientific manner cannot conflict with faith, because "earthly matters and the concerns of faith derive from the same God" (*Gaudium et Spes*, Second Vatican Council, 1965: §36).

It remains to ask whether anything can be learned about God from a study of Creation. Though the Creator is not to be identified with the world, Catholic faith holds that much can be learned about the Creator from a study of created reality, including the reality of human being. This belief was formally articulated by the First Vatican Council. There it is affirmed that human reason can yield true knowledge of God. This does not mean, however, that such knowledge is complete nor that reason need be understood as operating apart from faith. The position taken by Vatican I was based on an interpretation of Paul's Letter to the Romans (1.19–23), where the Apostle acknowledges that the Gentiles had a knowledge of God that was natural, that is, not part of the revelation by God to the Israelites (Coffey, 1970). According to Catholic thought, then, Creation itself discloses the reality of God (McBrien, 1970: 206).

The Image of God

The creation of human being is so important to the biblical account that it is referenced twice. In Genesis 1, the human couple is created together in the image and likeness of God. Again in Genesis 2–3, the story is told – this time being drawn out into a drama that begins in loneliness, passes through intimacy and communion, disintegrates in shared rebellion, and continues in the promise of a time of restoration. From the first Creation story the Catholic Church has drawn important lessons about what it means to be human. The human person, being made in the image and likeness of God, is unique in creation and unites in herself or himself the spiritual and material worlds (*Catechism*, 1994: §355). The human being is the only being capable of knowing and loving God, the only one God has willed for its own sake, and the only creature called to share in God's own life (*Catechism*, 1994: 357). As such, the human being possesses a dignity that is unsurpassed and is capable, like God, of the gift of self to others in freedom and in love.

Because it is the more anthropomorphic of the two accounts, that is, because God is imaged as a divine artisan working the soil and interacting with human beings as one like them, the second Creation story is often the more memorable. But, as Paul Ricoeur notes, if God is anthropomorphic, humankind is theomorphic (1995: 133). And that is part of the grandeur of the story of the creation of human being.

The drama of the second Creation story has two acts. The first act depicts the world as God intends it to be and takes place "before" the incursion of evil. The second act displays the event that introduces a rupture between the human couple and God, between the two human parties, and between them and the rest of Creation. In the movement from one act to the other there lies a mystery that has intrigued human beings as long as recorded history: the mystery of evil. After the Creation story comes a mystery that has sustained human beings despite the mystery of evil: the mystery of grace.

For the first act, the creation of the human couple is the highest and final deed. God personally creates *adam*, the earth creature, shaping and giving divine breath to this handiwork. To this creature, God gives dominion over all else created, parading before *adam* a display of animals. For all that, however, the creature is lonely. Nothing else that God has created is a match for *adam*. In a great act of mercy, God brings forth from the side of *adam* another creature, alike but different. Now there is sexual differentiation in humanity. The result calls forth a cry of pleasure from the one that can be now known as the man when he beholds the woman: "This one, at last, is bone of my bones and flesh of my flesh" (2.23).

Despite centuries in which this story of Creation was interpreted to mean that, in being created second, the woman was created subservient, meant to be at the disposal of the man not only in primordial time but in history, the Catholic Church has come to see what has been revealed in this text. Now church documents connect this great Creation story to the conduct and attitude toward women displayed by Jesus himself, and teach that God's intention for humanity is that male and female live in that mutuality and differentiated equality known as communion. Thus the official *Catechism of the Catholic Church* teaches:

> Man and woman have been *created*, which is to say, *willed* by God: on the one hand, in perfect equality as human persons; on the other, in their respective beings as man and woman (1994: §369).
> Man and woman were made "for each other" – not that God left them half-made and incomplete: he created them to be a communion of persons, in which each can be "helpmate" to the other, for they are equal as persons and complementary as masculine and feminine (1994: §372).

It is hard to overestimate what an advance this is in the history of Catholic thought.

There are other lessons to be drawn from this first act of the drama of Creation. By telling the story of a single human couple at the origin of the world, the Bible teaches that all human beings are from one "stock," related to each other in a shared humanity and equal to each other in dignity. The human race, in other words, constitutes a single "family." In the words of Joseph Ratzinger,

> There are not different kinds of "blood and soil," to use a Nazi slogan. There are not fundamentally different kinds of human beings ... We are all *one* humanity, formed from God's *one* earth. (1990: 58)

Moreover, the creation of human being is not just of the earth. God breathes on *adam*, thereby sharing divine life with this creature and, by extension, with all human creatures. Catholic theology interprets this to mean that every human person has a relationship to God that, known or unknown, places her or him under divine protection. That is the deep reason for the inviolability of human dignity.

The fact that God creates a companion for *adam* as a gift and a blessing teaches the further lesson that human being is social being. It is part of being human to long for another, to yearn to be in community. Together, the human couple is urged to "be fertile and multiply," to "bear fruit." They are also given "dominion" over all the other creatures of the earth (Gen 1.28). This last has caused great controversy in the age of ecological consciousness. Some have accused this Creation story of being responsible for the plundering of the earth, since it seems to teach that human beings, being highest in the created order, can do whatever they want with the rest of Creation. It is part of Catholic teaching that responsibility comes with any right. But to the extent that the faithful have missed that teaching or have misinterpreted the meaning of "having dominion," recent papal pronouncements serve to correct and reorient Catholic thought. In his first encyclical, Pope John Paul II, writing of the threats to the natural environment, said, "it was the Creator's will that we should communicate with nature as intelligent and noble guardians and not as exploiters and destroyers" (1979: 15).

The first act of the second Creation story, then, conveys the essential equality of male and female, the unity of the human race, the responsibility of human beings for the remainder of Creation, and the human being as a composite of body and soul – at once "of the earth" and participant in divine life. It also portrays an easy and familiar relationship between God and the human couple, such that they communicate without threat and without fear. This state of innocence, harmony, happiness, Catholic teaching refers to as "original justice" (*Catechism*, 1994: 376). It is the state that will be lost by sin.

There are many subtleties in the way the second Creation story tells of the transition from innocence to guilt, from original justice to original sin. The stumbling block, it seems, is the "interdict," the command that God gave Adam and Eve not to eat of the fruit of the tree of the knowledge of good and evil (Gen 2.16–17). This command, symbolic in so many ways of their finitude or creaturely status, becomes the entrée for a reinterpretation of God and of themselves. The serpent appears in the garden and insinuates to Eve that God is holding out on her and Adam, in order to keep from them the ultimate gift of being like God. Thus the serpent reinterprets the divine command from blessing (a reminder of their creaturely status and a reason to give thanks) to curse (a limitation on their powers and a reason to rebel). Eve eats of the fruit and gives it to Adam to eat. From that moment on, the ease and harmony of the garden are disrupted and the human couple knows shame before each other and before God (Gen 3.7). It is then that the punishments of God fall: on the man, on the woman, and on the serpent (Gen 3.14–19).

In the centuries' long interpretation of this part of the second Creation story, women have not fared well. Influenced perhaps by the Pandora myth, which blames the ills that afflict humanity on Pandora's curiosity, Christian thinkers taught that it was through a woman that evil came into the world (Børresen, 1995: 190). They became convinced that man's "lording it over her" was by divine right and that the sufferings of humankind could be blamed on her existence. There were times when being the image of God was denied her and theologians taught that she was only image of God when considered with the man and under his headship (Børresen, 1995: 191ff.). In a particularly unfortunate reduction of woman to body and, therefore, to the source of sexual pollution, Catholic practice came to exclude women from the sanctuary, from marriage to priests, and even from the sacraments at certain times of the month – on the assumption that she was defiled and defiling.

The real, if unacknowledged, influence of women scholars can be seen in the contemporary Catholic teaching on these issues. No longer is the woman seen as the source of original sin, or as a defiling element in the life of men. Pope John Paul II devoted four years of Wednesday audiences to the development of what he called "the theology of the body," in which he praised the human body – male and female – as the gift that makes communion possible (1997: 47–8). In an Apostolic Letter on women, he clearly teaches that women, as well as men, are "created in God's image" (1988b: §6). There is, in the words of the Pope, an "essential equality of man and woman from the point of view of their humanity" (1988b: §6). The "lording over" that women have experienced throughout history is, according to this document, a result of sin; women are right to oppose it (1988b: §10). There is no trace in the *Catechism* of the tradition that woman is responsible for original sin. Committed as the translators of that text were to the use of sex-exclusive language (e.g., "man" to represent human being), it is more likely that unsuspecting readers will think that man is responsible.

The best Catholic thinking today, then, considers the story of the primal couple's sin to reveal that woman and man are moral agents, co-equal in responsibility. Though Adam blames Eve and Eve blames the serpent in the wake of their rebellion against God (Gen 3.12–13), the punishment that God metes out is a sure sign that each is held responsible, along with the serpent, and each must bear the consequences of their decision to defy the commandment. The fact that each punishment is different respects the fact that they are not all the same in bodily experience.

The *Catechism of the Catholic Church* considers original sin an "essential truth of the faith" (1994: §388). It is intrinsically linked to the belief in a universal need for salvation – a salvation brought by the one who is not only "image of God," but God incarnate. Thus the theological tradition that understands Christ as the new Adam interprets his coming as the beginning of a new creation in and through which the human race is given a chance to realize a new humanity in the Church, believed to be the Body of Christ. Mary is the new Eve, reversing by her "yes" to God the reverberating "no" of Eve's rebellion (*Catechism*, 1994: §411). Mary, however, is in no way understood to be equal to Jesus the Christ and so the parallelism of the Genesis Creation story is not recognized in the story of the new creation.

Time and again, questions have been raised about the effects of original sin on human beings. Any suggestion that the effect is to render human persons incapable of doing any good, to make human nature totally corrupted, has been rejected by Catholic teaching. The Catholic position is that original sin left humanity wounded, weakened, inclined toward sin – but not so radically altered that it can be said that the human being is intrinsically disordered. The good Creation remains. Even the power to sin cannot undo the work of the Creator. The sacraments are the means by which the wounded human being is strengthened and restored, not to the state of original justice, but to the state of grace that enables her or him to live in union with Christ and thus as *imago Dei*. Since the outward signs of the sacraments are all natural things like oil, water, bread, and wine, material creation is taken up into the great work of salvation and becomes, through inspired human use, participant in the worship rendered to God.

One of the difficulties attached to the doctrine of original sin is that, since Augustine, it has been entangled with sexuality. That is, Augustine taught that original sin was passed down through sexual intercourse. This interpretation of original sin promoted a negative attitude toward sexuality that troubles Catholic life. The analysis of Paul Ricoeur captures the problem: original sin considered in the way that Augustine presents it unites "in an inconsistent notion a juridical category (voluntary punishable crime) and a biological category (the unity of the human species by generation)" (1974: 280). The Catholic Church teaching that original sin is "transmitted with human nature, 'by propagation, not by imitation'" requires careful exegesis, lest it perpetuate a negative attitude toward sexuality (*Catechism*, 1994: §419).

The lessons of the story of original sin are important. First, God is only responsible for good. Whatever is vain comes from human being. When the human being laments the suffering and death that come to all, he or she is not permitted, by this imaginative account, to blame the good God. Second, the beginning of Creation and the beginning of evil constitute two distinct and separate moments. They are not simultaneous. Evil, then, is a parasite on the good creation; it is not a co-equal power existing from the beginning. Third, concomitant with punishment, there is promise. The Catholic faith recognizes this promise in the mysterious words of God to the serpent: "I will put enmity between you and the woman, and between your offspring and hers; He will strike at your head, while you strike at his heel" (Gen 3.15). These words are interpreted as a prediction of the woman who will bear a child who will conquer evil and death.

The Easter liturgy recognizes, then, a certain ambiguity in original sin, calling it a "happy fault" because it "merited us such a redeemer." This redeemer "fully reveals man to man himself and makes his supreme calling clear"; he "restores the divine likeness which had been disfigured from the first sin onward" (*Gaudium et Spes*, Second Vatican Council, 1965: §22).

Growing Edges

The Catholic faithful receive instruction primarily through the liturgy. There, they hear the readings from the Bible, listen to sermons that break open the word and interpret the meaning of sacred Scripture, and participate in rituals that shape attitudes and imagination – in addition to the primary effect of offering opportunity for growth in grace through union with Christ. With the *Catechism of the Catholic Church*, an effort was made to organize and systematize Catholic teaching on the most important aspects of the faith. It constitutes a kind of "ready reference" for anyone who has questions about Catholicism. Thus the *Catechism* represents the solid center of Catholic faith. But it should be kept in mind that the Catholic faith admits of development. Development of dogma is one of the important realities in Catholic life and explains how the Church can teach at a later date aspects of the faith that were not apprehended at an earlier date. Paragraph 8 of *Dei Verbum* (*The Dogmatic Constitution on Divine Revelation*) captures this reality.

> The tradition that comes from the apostles makes progress in the church, with the help of the holy Spirit. There is a growth in insight into the realities and words that are being passed on. This comes about through the contemplation and study of believers who ponder these things in their hearts (see Luke 2.19 and 51). It comes from the intimate sense of spiritual realities which they experience. And it comes from the preaching of those who, on succeeding to the office of bishop, have received the sure charism of truth. Thus, as the centuries go by, the church is always advancing toward the plenitude of divine truth, until eventually the words of God are fulfilled in it. (1965)

One of the ways that development occurs is through the controversies or debates about interpretation that arise in Catholic life or in the larger Christian world, controversies that occasion a rethinking or a redefinition of the tradition. Some of the current controversies connect directly to the doctrine of Creation and to the Catholic understanding of what it means to be human.

With the resurgence of fundamentalism in Christianity, the approach to questions about creation known as "Creationism" has had a revival. "Creationism is in essence defined by resistance to modern scientific orthodoxy about the origin of life" (Major, 2005: 18). While there is a spectrum within Creationist thought, the proponents, in one way or another, insist that the Bible yields scientific information about the formation of the universe. They pit that information against what paleontologists, biologists, and other scientists have claimed to learn from the application of their methods of research. Darwin's theory of evolution is a particular target of the Creationists.

Since 1950, when Pope Pius XII wrote the encyclical, *Humani Generis*, Catholics have been instructed that "the teaching of the Church does not forbid . . . the doctrine of evolutionism, insofar as it inquires into the origin of the human body" (1950: §36). Pope John Paul II took this a step further in 1987, when he addressed a letter to the Director of the Vatican Observatory on the occasion of a conference called to explore current relations between science and theology. Pope John Paul II raised these questions: "Does an evolutionary perspective bring any light to bear upon theological anthropology, the meaning of the human person as *imago Dei*, the problem of Christology – and even upon the development of doctrine itself?" (1988a: M11). In 1996, the same pope told the Pontifical Academy of Science that "fresh knowledge leads to recognition of the theory of evolution as more than just a hypothesis" (cited in Major, 2005: 19). While letters and addresses do not have the same theological weight as a papal encyclical, they still give evidence of the direction of thought and of what is permissible in the development of Catholic teaching. Clearly, the teaching of Leo XIII in *Providentissimus Deus* – that the function of the Bible is not to inform on matters scientific – rules out "Creationism" as a Catholic position (1893: §18).

A recent refinement of Creationism goes under the name of "intelligent design," used as a term to mean that there are identifiable biological phenomena that require all scientists to posit an intelligent designer. A number of Catholic scientists have criticized the "intelligent design" variation of Creationism. George Coyne sj, director of the Vatican Observatory, for example, maintains that it diminishes God, making one who is essentially a lover into a mere designer (2005: 7).

Other questions about the Catholic interpretation of Genesis and, therefore, of the Catholic theological anthropology are being raised by the gay rights movement. The vision of the creation of human being in the Creation story is exclusively heterosexual and the bride and bridegroom language of the New Testament continues and reiterates that vision. Any trace of the Platonic myth, which included the creation of a being destined to couple with the same sex, is missing from the Genesis account (O'Neill, 1988: 12). As a result, Catholic teaching holds that it is the intention of God that human sexual desire be directed to the opposite sex and that this be the only context for human sexual activity. "Sexuality is ordered to the conjugal love of man and woman," declares the *Catechism* (1994: §2360). Homosexual acts are considered "intrinsically disordered" and "contrary to the natural law" (1994: §2357).

Several theologians working in the Catholic tradition have wrestled with that tradition's teaching on homosexuality: Margaret Farley, Mary Hunt, Mark Jordan, Patricia

Beattie Jung, James Alison. Alison's argument is particularly apposite because he bases his developing position largely on statements of the Council of Trent. The teaching that same-sex orientation is a fruit of original sin causes him concern because it seems to call for "drastic hatred of self in order to be good." In search of a different understanding, Alison undertakes a thorough study of original sin, guided by the insights of René Girard (1998: 2). He finds in canons 2, 3, 4, and 5 of the Council of Trent a Christological anthropology that teaches Christians to recognize something very important about original sin: it is a "death of the soul" that "does not admit of a cure . . . but only of a resurrection" (1998: 277).

Alison thinks that Trent threaded a fine line between extremes. This Council does not say that human beings can transform themselves from death to life, which would make the salvation brought by Christ unnecessary. Nor does Trent say that salvation makes no essential change in the worthlessness of human being, which would deny any transformation of being in salvation. To accept the teachings of the Council of Trent is to believe that all human beings stand in need of salvation. It is also to know that the salvation brought through the life, death, and resurrection of Christ initiates a real change, such that the human being is gradually transformed. For Alison, this transformation takes place in the reorientation of desire. All human desire bears the mark of original sin and stands in need of the reordering that comes with participation in the life of Christ. He believes and argues that homosexual desire is capable of such transformation. What is at stake in this interpretation of the Council's teaching is an understanding of the human being and of the creator as well. The way the Church justifies the prohibition against homosexual acts is problematic because it skews the image of God. Church arguments result in a God who says, "You are not. I didn't create you. I only create heterosexual people. You are a defective heterosexual. Agree to be a defect and I'll rescue you" (Alison, 2001: 202–3). The issues raised by Alison and others, then, challenge traditional understandings of the teachings about God and nature, the created body and Christian anthropology.

The movement that has arguably had the greatest impact on theological anthropology is the movement for the advancement of women (Graff, 1995). First, it brought hundreds of Catholic women into the various specialties of theology. Then, having learned the Catholic tradition, women gained the confidence to interpret it through our own experience, trying as we did so to right the imbalances brought about by an all-male tradition. While the official teachings of the Church now reflect an egalitarian anthropology – that is, the Church teaches that women and men are created equal in dignity – theologians differ on how that equality is to be conceptualized, given the differences between women and men. That conceptualization, in turn, affects Church practice with respect to what women and men can do.

The writings of Pope John Paul II and the *Catechism of the Catholic Church* espouse a position that considers women and men to be complementary to one another (1988b: §10; 1997: §45–8; *Catechism*, 1994: §2333). That is, men and women, while equal to each other in human dignity because equally created in the image of God, are different from one another in essential ways. These differences make them complementary to one another or, as Pope John Paul II prefers to say, destined for a *communio personarum*, a communion of persons (1997: 48). The governing model for this conceptualization is the nuptial relationship, in which the differently embodied beings are capable of a union that mirrors the very creativity of God, with its potential for creating new human life. The understanding of that nuptial relationship is then carried over into the life of the Church, such that Christ is the bridegroom and the Church the bride. The Pope makes this explicit in *Mulieris Dignitatem* (*On the Dignity and Vocation of Women*). There he works extensively with the imagery of bridegroom and bride. The Pope takes the position that, as members of the Church, "men too are included in the concept of 'bride'" (1988b: §25). Yet when it comes to the Eucharist, the Pope teaches that the redemptive act of Christ, the bridegroom, is only "clear and unambiguous" when the sacramental ministry of the Eucharist is "performed by a man" (1988b: §26).

This way of thinking has been soundly criticized by Catholic feminist theologians. Rosemary Radford Ruether analyzes it this way:

> Contrary to traditional Catholic teaching, recent Catholicism of this type affirms women's equality with men on the level of nature and secular society . . . But Eucharistic and priestly matters are removed to a second, supernatural sphere unconnected with gender equality in creation. (Ruether, 1995: 269)

This means that while "women are now said to 'image' God, we are still denied the capacity to 'image' Christ" (1995: 269). Such refusal on the part of the Church to see women "*in persona Christi*" at the altar puts Eucharistic theology in conflict with Baptismal theology, wherein women are believed to be baptized "into Christ," and to "put on Christ" in a way no different from men. The conflict between women as image of God and as image of Christ also raises questions about Catholic belief concerning the role of the male body in the incarnation of Christ and in the redemption of the bodies of women. Does it mean that women can be "*imago Dei*" because God does not have a body? Does the incarnation of Christ as a man prevent women from imaging him? And, if the incarnation itself is redemptive, can a male savior redeem women?

Elizabeth A. Johnson rejects the complementary model as a way of understanding the differences between women and men, finding that it nearly always leads to rigid role definitions that relegate women to a subordinate position. She proposes instead the vision of a single human nature in "an interdependence of multiple differences" (Johnson, 1991: 111). Johnson regards sexual differentiation as on a level with other differences, such as culture, race, geographical region, language, etc. The bodily differences that are so important in procreation are not necessarily indicative of anything with respect to the rest of human life. Basing her argument on the Nicene Creed, Johnson maintains that what is of importance to salvation is that Christ became human (*et homo factus est*), not that he is male. She argues, by way of Wisdom theology, that it is possible to retell the story of Jesus in an "egalitarian framework" and call the Church "to conversion, away from sexism and toward a community of the discipleship of equals" (Johnson, 1993a: 134). Still, there are unresolved tensions. Even Johnson's magisterial work, *She Who Is*, results in a theology of God developed through the use of female bodily images while attenuating the significance of the historical male body of Jesus, believed to be God incarnate (Johnson, 1997).

I have suggested an approach to theological anthropology that respects difference while honoring equality, and does so by recourse to the figures of Jesus and Mary. "Only the two figures together can reveal the radical saving truth about being male and female, virgin yet procreative, lover and life giver in the new age . . ." (O'Neill, 1993: 156). Accepting the complementarity revealed by the human body – male and female – I have argued that the significance of Mary and Jesus should be interpreted in that light, so that the real limitation and the real possibility of incarnation can be apprehended (O'Neill, 1993: 155). I have further argued that the symbol of the Immaculate Conception of Mary holds great promise for a redeemed understanding of the female body and of the life work of the laity in the Church (O'Neill, 2002: 48–50, 56–7). But such an approach runs headlong into the ecclesial backlash against Mariological excesses of the past and the feminist backlash against the use of the Marian symbol to domesticate women.

Feminist concern for the woman's body has been joined to Creation in another interesting way with the rise of ecofeminism. This strand of the women's movement identifies sexual dualism, with its consequent hierarchy of male over female, as the "taproot of the ecological crisis" (Johnson, 1993b: 17). Such dualism is also linked to an understanding of the creator God as "essentially separated from and over against the world" (Johnson, 1993b: 18). The effort to envision the world as sacred and care of that world as a sacred responsibility for human beings is deeply connected to a re-imagining of God. Catherine LaCugna accomplishes this move by linking Trinitarian theology once more to the doctrine of Creation and to theological anthropology (1993). God whose being is to-be-in-relation is connected to the world and to humankind in such a way that God can suffer with as well as rule over the created universe (LaCugna, 1991: 295–6). Ann Clifford finds in this understanding of God a basis for an ecofeminist theology of solidarity with God and the earth.

> Our solidarity with God as *imago Dei* does not set us apart from creation . . . Like the rest of creation, we are made of the same dirt – the same elements that are in the rocks of the hills, the birds of the air and the fish of the seas are in us. Our relationship to all the other creatures of Earth is, however, not one of simple sameness, but rather one of interdependent kinship with respect for diversity. (1995: 193)

The "same dirt" that, for Joseph Ratzinger means that all human beings are related, signifies, for the ecofeminist, a kinship among all things created.

The Doctrine of creation and the developing teaching about the meaning of human existence, male and female, can be, then, a source of that "deep amazement" that Pope John Paul II termed another name for gospel or good news (1979: §10). Amazement derives, not from the reiteration of insights codified into catechism, but from the discovery in each age of the revealed truth in the language and thought patterns of the day. Efforts to understand creation in light of new scientific discoveries and to understand human being in answer to newly perceived possibilities are critical to Catholic theology and to Catholic life.

References and Further Reading

Alison, J. (1998) *The Joy of Being Wrong, Original Sin through Easter Eyes*. New York: Crossroad.

Alison, J. (2001) *Faith beyond Resentment: Fragments Catholic and Gay*. New York: Crossroad.

Batto, B.F. (1992) "Creation Theology in Genesis," in Clifford, R.J. and Collins, J.J. (eds.) *Creation in the Biblical Traditions. The Catholic Biblical Quarterly* Monograph Series, 24: 16–38.

Børresen, K.E. (1995) "God's Image, Man's Image? Patristic Interpretation of Gen 1,27 and 1 Cor 11,7," in Børresen, K.E. (ed.) *The Image of God, Gender Models in Judaeo-Christian Tradition*. Minneapolis, MN: Fortress Press, 187–209.

Catechism of the Catholic Church (1994) Libreria Editrice Vaticana. Boston, MA: Pauline Press.

Clifford, A. (1991) "Creation," in Fiorenza, F.S. and Galvin, J.P. (eds.) *Systematic Theology*, vol. I, Minneapolis, MN: Fortress Press, 193–248.

Clifford, A. (1995) "When Being Human Becomes Truly Earthly," in Graff, A.O. (ed.) *In the Embrace of God, Feminist Approaches to Theological Anthropology*. Maryknoll, NY: Orbis Books, 181–97.

Coffey, D.M. (1970) "Natural Knowledge of God: Rom 1:18–32," *Theological Studies*, vol. 31, no. 4 (December), 674–91.

Coyne, G. (2005) "Infinite Wonder of the Divine," *The Tablet* (December 10), 6–7.

Dei Verbum [*Dogmatic Constitution on Divine Revelation*] (1965), in Abbott, W.M., SJ, (ed.) *The Documents of Vatican II*. New York: Guild Press, 111–28.

Fiorenza, E.S. (1995) *Jesus: Miriam's Child, Sophia's Prophet: Critical Issues in Feminist Christology*. New York: Continuum.

Graff, A.O. (1995) *In the Embrace of God, Feminist Approaches to Theological Anthropology*. Maryknoll, NY: Orbis Books.

John Paul II, Pope (1979) *Redemptor Hominis* (*Redeemer of Humankind*), in Donders, J.G. (ed.) *John Paul II, The Encyclicals in Everyday Language*. Maryknoll, NY: Orbis Books, 1–20.

John Paul II, Pope (1987) *Sollicitudo Rei Socialis* [*On Social Concern*], in Donders, J.G. (ed.) *John Paul II, The Encyclicals in Everyday Language*. Maryknoll, NY: Orbis Books, 126–42.

John Paul II, Pope (1988a) "Message of His Holiness," in Russell, R.J., Stoeger, W.R., SJ, and Coyne, G.V., SJ (eds.) (1990) *John Paul II on Science and Religion, Reflections on the New View from Rome*. Rome: Vatican Observatory Publications, M1–M14.

John Paul II, Pope (1988b) "*Mulieris Dignitatem*" [*On the Dignity and Vocation of Women*]. *Origins* (October 6), 262–83.

John Paul II, Pope (1990) "Peace with All Creation," *Origins* (December 14), 465–8.

John Paul II, Pope (1997) *The Theology of the Body, Human Love in the Divine Plan*. Boston, MA: Pauline Books and Media.

Johnson, E.A. (1991) "The Maleness of Christ," in Carr, A. and Fiorenza, E.S. (eds.) *The Special Nature of Women?* London: SCM Press, 108–16.

Johnson, E.A. (1993a) "Redeeming the Name of Christ," in LaCugna, C.M. (ed.) *Freeing Theology: The Essentials of Theology in Feminist Perspective*. San Francisco: HarperSanFrancisco, 115–38.

Johnson, E.A. (1993b) *Women, Earth, and Creator Spirit*. New York: Paulist Press.

Johnson, E.A. (1997) *She Who Is: The Mystery of God in Feminist Theological Discourse*. New York: Crossroad.

LaCugna, C.M. (1991) *God For Us: The Trinity and Christian Life*. San Francisco: HarperSanFrancisco.

LaCugna, C.M. (1993) "God in Communion with Us," in LaCugna, C.M. (ed.) *Freeing Theology: the Essentials of Theology in Feminist Perspective*. San Francisco: HarperSanFrancisco: 83–114.

Leo XIII, Pope (1893) *Providentissimus Deus.* <www.papalencyclicals.net/Leo13/l13provi.htm> as of June 1, 2005.

McBrien, R.P. (1970) *Catholicism.* San Francisco: Harper and Row.

Major, R. (2005) "The Bible's Battleground," *The Tablet* (30 April), 18–19.

New American Bible with Revised New Testament (1986) and the Revised Psalms of the New American Bible (1991). Washington, DC: Confraternity of Christian Doctrine.

O'Connor, D. (1969) "Introduction: The Human and the Divine," in O'Connor, D. and Oakley, F. (eds.) *Creation: The Impact of an Idea.* New York: Charles Scribner's Sons, 107–119.

O'Neill, M.A. (1988) "Imagine Being Human: An Anthropology of Mutuality," in *Miriam's Song II Patriarchy: A Feminist Critique.* West Hyattsville, MD: Priests for Equality, 11–14.

O'Neill, M.A. (1993) "The Mystery of Being Human Together," in LaCugna, C.M. (ed.) *Freeing Theology: The Essentials of Theology in Feminist Perspective.* San Francisco: HarperSanFrancisco: 139–160.

O'Neill, M.A. (2002) "Female Embodiment and the Incarnation," in Eigo, F.A., OSA (ed.) *Themes in Feminist Theology for the New Millennium.* Villanova: The Villanova University Press, 35–66.

Pius XII, Pope (1950) *Humani Generis.* <www.vatican.va/holy_father/pius_xii/encyclicals/documents/hf_p-xii_enc_12081950_humani-generis_en.html> as of June 1, 2005.

Ratzinger, J. (1990) *"In the Beginning . . . ,"* *A Catholic Understanding of the Story of Creation and the Fall*, trans. B. Ramsey, OP. Huntington: Our Sunday Visitor, Inc.

Ricoeur, P. (1967) *The Symbolism of Evil*, trans. E. Buchanan. Boston, MA: Beacon Press.

Ricoeur, P. (1974) "'Original Sin': A Study in Meaning," trans. P. McCormick, in Ihde, D. (ed.) *The Conflict of Interpretations: Essays in Hermeneutics.* Evanston: Northwestern University Press.

Ricoeur, P. (1995) "On the Exegesis of Genesis 1:1–2:4a," in Wallace, M.I. (ed.) *Figuring the Sacred: Religion, Narrative, and Imagination*, trans. D. Pellauer. Minneapolis, MN: Fortress Press.

Ruether, R.R. (1995), "*Imago Dei:* Christian Tradition and Feminist Hermeneutics," in Børresen, K.E. (ed.) *The Image of God, Gender Models in Judaeo-Christian Tradition.* Minneapolis, MN: Fortress Press.

Scheffczyk, L. (1970) *Creation and Providence*, trans. R. Strachan. New York: Herder and Herder.

Second Vatican Council (1965) *Gaudium et Spes* (*The Pastoral Constitution on the Church in the Modern World*), in Abbott, W.M., SJ (ed.) *The Documents of Vatican II.* New York: Guild Press, 199–308.

CHAPTER 20

Jesus Christ

Edward T. Oakes

"Christology," as the name indicates, means "the study of Christ," a word obviously built on the analogy with other "-ology" words, such as "biology" (the study of life), "psychology" (the study of the mind), and so forth. But the resemblances with these other "-ology" words can be deceptive. For most sciences regard themselves as *publicly accessible*, accessible precisely because their field of study is recognized by all.

But not with Jesus Christ. Here the "science" of Christ becomes accessible only to believers, that is, to people who confess that an itinerant rabbi in first-century Galilee was also "God from God, Light from Light, true God from true God." How can that be? How can one wave, foaming up for its brief allotted time and pathetically going back at death into the ground of being whence it came, claim to be the sea, the seabed, indeed the very world encompassing that meager little wave; and even more, how can it claim to be identified with the Creator of that world – indeed, of that very wave so outrageously making the claim? Such is the problem set before that branch of theology called "Christology." Even a cursory glance at the history of this branch of theology shows that the fundamental problem running through all Christological thought centers on this identification of the infinite with the finite, of "God from God" with a first-century Galilean. But as we have just seen, that problem has itself a problem of its own: the problem of the-infinite-becoming-finite in Jesus of Nazareth is recognized only by Christian believers. In fact, non-Christians stand outside the precincts of Christianity precisely because they deny that Jesus is the very enfleshment of God.

A further ambiguity plagues the word "Christology": the word "Christ" is actually a specific *title* applied to Jesus of Nazareth by his earliest followers and not, as some naïvely think, his last name. But "Christ" was but one of many titles applied to Jesus. Others include "Suffering Servant," "Son of Man," "Son of God," "*Logos*," and, perhaps most important of all, "Lord." Now the word "Christ" comes from the Greek word *christos*, a past participle meaning "anointed," which was a direct translation of the Hebrew word "messiah," which had a specifically *royal* meaning connoting "king," because in the ancient world (as well as in Great Britain today) kings were anointed with oil as part of the coronation rite.

But what makes the title "Christ" somewhat unique among the other titles applied to Jesus in the New Testament is that, in Greek, as opposed to Hebrew, it stopped sounding like a title and began to seem more like part of his name. This is partly because the institution of king had lost much of its significance in the Roman Empire. The Roman emperors might well have acted like kings, but they continued to maintain the fiction that they were ruling in continuity with the outmoded forms of the Roman Republic, which had no kings (the word "emperor" comes from the Latin word for military commander, *imperator*). But more crucially, "messiah" remained a true *title* for the Jews of first-century Palestine because, under Roman oppression, they looked forward to a restoration of the kingdom first established by King David. The title "messiah," in other words, was highly charged politically; indeed it was the title for which the Romans executed Jesus (which we know because the Roman governor of Judea at the time, Pontius Pilate, ordered the charge to be posted on the Cross justifying the Nazarene's execution: "Jesus Christ, King of the Jews").

With the death of Jesus, the matter would seem to have been settled. Pretenders to the throne can no longer claim their crown once they are dead; and when legitimate kings die, the heir takes over ("The king is dead, long live the king"). So the execution of Jesus seemed to be the end of the matter. But then something extraordinary happened: the followers of Jesus soon, very soon, began to report him alive. Not only was the tomb where he was laid empty, but he began to appear to them the very day they discovered the tomb empty. And so the title "Christ" was immediately revived: when Jesus appeared to them risen, the disciples realized that Jesus really *is* a liberating king, whose victory over death would surely lead to the expulsion of the Romans, or so the first Christians initially concluded (Acts 1:6). In fact, the earliest strata of the New Testament insist that it was by virtue of the resurrection that Jesus was *made* Christ. For example, St Peter, on the Jewish Feast of Pentecost (50 days after Passover), said "God has raised this Jesus to life, and we are all witnesses of this fact . . . Therefore lest all Israel be assured of this: God has *made* this Jesus, whom you crucified, both Lord and Christ" (Acts 2:32, 36). Similarly, St Paul in the opening of his Letter to the Romans said that Jesus "was *declared* with power to be the Son of God by his resurrection from the dead, Jesus Christ our Lord" (Rom 1:4).

In other words, the titles of Jesus were (with some exceptions, like "rabbi" and "prophet") *confessional* titles that the earliest Christians applied to Jesus by virtue of their belief in what God had done to Jesus in raising him from the dead. For the New Testament, the connection between the major titles applied to Jesus and his resurrection is indissoluble. For that reason, Christology cannot be regarded, at least without due caution, on the analogy with other sciences like biology and psychology, for it is a confessional "science" based on belief that God raised Jesus from the dead. Moreover, because the title "Christ" soon lost its specifically saving significance in the non-Jewish circles of the Roman Empire, other titles tended to move to the foreground to function as something specifically confessional, above all the titles "Savior" and "Lord," whereas the word "Christ" tended to become so fused to Jesus' "first" name that it more and more came just to identify Jesus of Nazareth from the many other Jews of the first century who also bore the Jesus-name (a quite common one at the time, which derived in Hebrew from the name "Joshua," meaning "God saves"). Thus, the word "Christology" now refers not to the study of this specific title "Christ" but to the entire identity of Jesus as God's agent of salvation in the world.

The history of the development of Christology has been marked from the beginning by complexity and controversy. This does not stem so much from the innate disputatiousness of Christians, as Edward Gibbon and David Hume claimed, as from the inherent complexities of its subject matter. There is first of all the initially puzzling equation of God with Jesus, which comes through especially in the title "Lord" given to Jesus. The Greek word for "lord" is *kyrios*, which in some contexts can mean nothing more than a title of respect, like the English "sir" (the German for "lord" is *Herr*, which is also the German for "Mr" or "sir"). But two developments prior to the growth of Christianity gave the title *kyrios* divine connotations. First, the proper name of God revealed to Moses was YHWH (perhaps pronounced "Yahweh," although that is a guess since the ancient Hebrew alphabet did not specify vowels); but pious practice after the Babylonian Exile forbade its explicit pronunciation except by the High Priest once a year in the Holy of Holies on the feast of Yom Kippur. Instead, the Hebrew *Adonai*, meaning "Lord," was substituted, so that when the Jews of Alexandria translated the Bible into Greek (roughly in the two or three centuries before the birth of Jesus), they always inserted the word *Kyrios* whenever the text read YHWH. Second, although the Roman emperors maintained republican fictions as the source of their authority in Rome, in the eastern parts of the Empire they grew more and more insistent that they be addressed in civic-religious rites as *kyrios*, Lord. These two developments led to a direct conflict of loyalties among the early Christians, whose confession of Jesus as Lord meant they had to refuse the same title to the emperors, prompting the Roman authorities to accuse the Christians of disloyalty and to persecute them accordingly.

The history of these persecutions is not directly relevant to Christology except as an indication of how seriously the early Christians took their confession of Jesus as Lord. More significant for this branch of theology is the seeming equation of Jesus with the sovereign God of the Old Testament, the Lord of history who created the world, chose Abraham and his children for his special people, and designated Jesus as "both Lord and Christ" by raising him from the dead. But if Jesus is "God" in some sense, in what sense is that? It would hardly do to equate Jesus with God outright, for otherwise to whom was he praying when he suffered in the Garden of Olives the night before he died; and why did he even refuse what to us seems the rather harmless moniker "good," insisting that only God could be regarded as good (Mark 10:18)? In other words, if Jesus himself regarded God as other than himself, how could he be called Lord?

Complicating the issue even further is the question of the Trinity, meaning the doctrine that God is somehow still the one God proclaimed over and over by the Old Testament (Deut 6:4; Isa 45:1–7) and yet somehow differentiated in his inmost being. This doctrine too, despite the claims of some historians of dogma, can be found in the earliest strata of the New Testament, indeed in the same speech of St Peter on Pentecost where he confesses Jesus as both Lord and Christ: "Exalted to the right hand of God, he [Jesus] has received from the Father the promised Holy Spirit and has poured out what you now see and hear" (Acts 2:33).

Given Peter's later apparent reluctance to admit Gentiles (non-Jews) into the Church without first undergoing circumcision (that is, without first becoming Jews), his proto-trinitarian language on Pentecost is most significant (Peter is hardly one who comes across as either a speculative theologian or as one seeking to undermine Jewish mono-theism). What his speech (or better, his sermon, the first one ever preached in the history of the Church) really signifies is that *the saving death of Jesus and his subsequent resurrection cannot be understood except in trinitarian terms*: Jesus could save us by his atoning death precisely because he was in some sense (not worked out of course by Peter himself) both God ("Lord") and man. (In this sermon Peter constantly stresses Jesus' humanity: "Jesus of Nazareth was a *man* accredited *by God* to you by the miracles, wonders, and signs that *God* worked among you *through* him . . . This man was handed over to you *by God* . . . But *God* raised him from the dead" [Acts 2:22–4]; note how Jesus is described entirely in passive terms as the "conduit," so to speak, through whom God does his saving work.)

But if Jesus is, somehow, both God and man, then that must mean that God is, some-how, not just "one" without further ado. In other words, if Jesus is in some sense God, then God too must somehow be differentiated, a realization that is so much a part of regarding Jesus' death as a saving death that even so devout a Jew as St Peter resorts to trinitarian language in his very first sermon.

It is this juxtaposition of seemingly contradictory terms – Jesus is both human and divine, and God is both one and three – that accounts for the subsequent complexity of later Christological doctrine. In other words, if to be human means to be finite, and if God is infinite, how can finitude be equated with infinity; and if God is one, how can He also be three? This way of putting the matter might sound overly philosophical, but its very starkness shows that in fact there was an important philosophical component to the debate, so much so that often the disputants were perhaps not sufficiently aware how much their own implicit philosophical presuppositions were governing the posi-tions they adopted in the controversies that make up the subject matter of Christology.

In an essay of this length, it will be impossible to survey the history of these many controversies in adequate detail, so that risks of overhasty schematization will prove unavoidable. With due regard for those risks, however, it might prove pedagogically, if not historically, useful to align the various positions taken in Christological debate along two sets of emphases: some theologians, when confronted with the paradox of God as both one and three, stressed the oneness of God while others stressed God's "threeness." Similarly, when confronted with the paradox of Jesus as both human and divine, some theologians stressed Jesus' humanity (as Peter, for example, did in his first sermon), while others stressed his divinity (as shines through, for example, in the Gospel of John). Generally speaking, a stress on the oneness of God fit better, logi-cally at least, with a stress on Jesus' humanity, whereas a stress on the divinity of Jesus often led to a stress on the threefold distinction of Persons in the Trinity.

This can be seen most especially in two early heresies, "adoptionism" and "modal-ism." Adoptionism is that heresy that takes the notion of the *titles* of Jesus literally: they are just that, merely titles. Jesus was granted the honorific title of Son of God by a kind of legal fiction, the way someone might be declared the legal son of someone who is not his biological father through the legal process known as adoption.

This view was quickly rejected for a reason that again goes back to St Peter's sermon at Pentecost: the reason Peter spoke of Jesus being made "Lord and Christ" and receiving from "the Father the Holy Spirit" was because the death of Jesus was a *saving* death: "But God raised him from the dead, freeing him from the agony of death, because it was impossible for death to keep its hold on him" (Acts 2:24). This clearly implies two important points about Jesus: (1) there was something about his inherent identity that made him *already* impervious to the ultimate victory of death over his own human life; and (2) that very inability of death to keep its grip on him meant that other humans too could somehow share in that victory, a point clearly implied in the question that greeted Peter when he completed his sermon, when the crowds asked what they must then do to be saved. The head of the apostles replies: "Repent and be baptized in the name of Jesus Christ for the forgiveness of yours sins" (Acts 2:38).

In other words, debates about the *identity* of Jesus (Christology, strictly defined) are intimately related to the question of the *salvation* of others (soteriology, strictly defined). For that reason, adoptionism had to be rejected, for a fictive sonship would imply a fictive salvation.

But if Jesus is truly God, what happens to the oneness of God? Another early heresy, centered, it would seem, mostly in Rome, claimed that when the New Testament speaks of God as Father, Son, and Spirit, it is speaking of three *modes* of God (hence the name "modalism" for this heresy), that is, of three ways God appears in salvation history: in the Old Testament God "comes across" as Father, in the New Testament he "comes across" as Son, and in the era of the Church he "comes across" as Spirit, but always remains one in his essence. This view (also called "Sabellianism," from one of its chief proponents, the Roman priest Sabellius) certainly preserves the unity of God, but at a heavy price. For it implies that during the life of Jesus the entirety of the Godhead was present in him. But this view is absurd, for to whom then is Jesus praying when he asks God on the night before he dies to take the chalice of suffering from him? (And who, by the way, is running the universe while the infant Jesus is in the crib in Bethlehem?)

The only way out of this obvious dilemma was to posit a greater distinction within the Godhead. But of course that move would again lead to the same danger of downplaying the unity of God. The way out seemed to be offered by another heresy known as "Arianism" (from the name of its chief proponent, the fourth-century priest from Alexandria, Arius, who died in the year 336). A more descriptive name for this heresy is "subordinationism," from the Arian insistence that the Son of God was a *subordinate* god in contradistinction to the one "true" God, the Father of all. The trouble with that terminology is that nearly all the theologians in the second and third centuries were subordinationist in some sense. Jesus after all says that "the Father is greater than the Son" (John 14:28), and St Paul calls the Son "the first-born of all *creation*" (Col 1:15). Even the terminology of "father" and "son" implies subordination (as does calling the preexistent Son "the Word," since a word demands a speaker who is obviously superordinate to the word he speaks).

For that reason it would be better to speak of Arius as someone who saw the latent difficulties in subordinationism and then "took them too far," so to speak, by drawing out their logic in such a way that their heretical implications soon became clear – at least to St Athanasius (296–373), who for most of his life had to fight the implications of presuppositions that most of his contemporaries shared, without perhaps realizing their heretical potential.

His argument was – again as with so many theologians whose arguments eventually won out – soteriological, that is, based on salvation. If the Son of God were really just a part of Creation, though the summit of all Creation, then that must mean there was a time when he was not ("There was when he was not" was a favorite slogan of the Arians). But that would mean in turn that the Son is *changeable*, which would put our salvation on the shaky ground of this ever-changing world of Becoming. For that reason, Athanasius insisted that the *Logos* or Son of God must be entirely God, different from the Father only in that he was *eternally* "begotten" (not born!) of the Father. And what the Father begot was *entirely* "God from God, Light from Light, true God from true God," to borrow the famous phrase from the Nicene Creed which definitively accepted Athanasius' theology as its own.

But if the Father stints nothing of his divinity in begetting the Son, this raises once more the question of how the divinity and humanity of Jesus are to be understood. If Jesus were somehow to be understood as a "lesser god," and a changeable one at that, it becomes possible to interpret certain puzzling passages in the New Testament that seem to ascribe ignorance to Jesus, such as the famous crux where Jesus says "No one knows that day or hour [of the end of the world], not even the angels in heaven, *nor the Son*, but only the Father" (Mark 13:32). If, however, the *Logos* or Son is fully divine, if the Father, that is, holds nothing back in begetting his Son, then how can that same Son confess ignorance about anything, how indeed can he be said to "grow in age, wisdom, and grace" (Luke 2:52)?

Several solutions were proffered, most of which proved unworkable. One solution, called Logos–Sarx (or Word–Flesh) Christology, claimed that when the Gospel of John said that "the Word became flesh and dwelt among us" (John 1:14), this meant that what would have been Jesus' rational soul had been *replaced* by the divine *Logos* (the word "*logos*" in Greek also means "reason" as well as "word"; hence our word "logic"). The problem is, this makes it impossible to interpret Jesus' confession of ignorance or his need to *grow* in wisdom. But more crucially for the opponents of Logos–Sarx Christology, our salvation would be threatened; for whatever part of our human nature that has not been touched by the incarnation would thereby not be saved. As the Cappadocian theologian of the third–fourth century, St Gregory of Nazianzus (240–332), famously said, "What has not been assumed [by the incarnation] has not been saved." And since human beings sin first and above all in their rational faculties, Jesus' soul must be fully human in *all* its aspects, which means that he too must learn, must find out things he had not previously known, must know the intellectual and cultural constraints of his time, and so forth.

The Letter to the Hebrews states that Jesus was like us in all things but sin (4:15), and since ignorance can hardly be called a sin (except perhaps when willful), the way seemed clear to a rejection of Logos–Sarx Christology. But a rejection of this school of Christological thought brought other problems in its wake, for it seemed to give the person of Jesus two centers of rationality, one divine, the other human. The fifth-century bishop of Constantinople Nestorius (died 451) was the theologian who had the least difficulty with this implication, for he realized that a rejection of Logos–Sarx Christology meant that Christians had to profess a faith in the full and adulterated presence of two natures in Jesus, one fully divine and the other fully human.

So far, so good. But as with Arius in his own day, Nestorius proved to be the one who took these newly won insights too far. This quickly emerged when, soon after assuming his duties as bishop of the capital of the eastern Roman Empire, he objected to the title of Mary as "Mother of God." If the two natures of Christ, human and divine, were to be kept as separate as Nestorius' Two-Natures Christology seemed to demand, then Mary could obviously only give birth to the human nature of Jesus; therefore, she should only be called the "Mother of Christ" (and anyway, how can the Creator of the world have a mother, a notion that struck Nestorius as a frank reversion to pagan mythology).

This not only aroused the ire of most devout Christians in Constantinople, more crucially it provoked the fierce opposition of Cyril (died 444), bishop of Alexandria, who quickly realized that Two-Natures Christology, when pushed too far, would lead to an ontologically schizophrenic Jesus. In fact theologians centered around the city of Antioch, most famously Theodore of Mopsuestia (350–428), openly said that when Jesus wept or slept, that was his human nature operating, and when he performed miracles, that was his divine nature at work. They even divided the sentences of Jesus accordingly. When he said "I am going away and I am coming back to you" (John 14:28), his human nature spoke the first clause and his divine nature the second.

These weird exegetical contortions clearly brought the implicitly schizophrenic presuppositions of this school of Christology to the fore, for the New Testament gives no indication whatever of a dual subjectivity in Jesus. So bringing his considerable polemical (and political) skills to bear, Cyril won around to his viewpoint the bishops assembled at Ephesus in the year 439, who declared in solemn council that Mary was indeed the Mother of God (the near unanimity of the decree was helped by the fact that the bishops from the Syrian area around Antioch were late in arriving in Ephesus due to a flood at the time, a delay that did not stop Cyril from calling the Council to order).

Once the dogma of Mary's divine motherhood was established, it then became imperative to make clear just *how* the human and divine natures of Jesus were to be united in a single subjectivity. Now Cyril died in 444, but his followers were not shy in pushing forth his views, perhaps even in pushing them too far (always a bad sign in this history). At all events, a council was called in 451 to meet in Chalcedon, a suburb of Constantinople. Again speaking generally, the bishops from the Syrian regions around Antioch were suspicious of any solution that would "dilute," so to speak, Jesus' humanity, lest the Church lapse once more into the absurdities of Logos–Sarx Christology, while the bishops of Egypt and Greece generally saw any excessive emphasis on Jesus' humanity as threatening the single subjectivity of Christ, which to them was crucial if our salvation were to be secured.

Up to this time in Church history, Rome had been relatively disengaged from these debates, although both Constantinople and Alexandria were eager to win the support of the bishop of Rome throughout the long years of this controversy. With the Council of Chalcedon this Roman disengagement came to end. The Pope at the time, Leo I, sent two deacons as delegates to represent him, and they read before the assembled fathers Leo's famous "Tome," which proposed a solution that was quickly adopted by the Council ("Peter speaks through Leo!" they acclaimed). In this sense, the Tome was successful, but later history would prove how hard it would be to win consensus outside the council chamber. For each side of the debate had its extremists who refused to assent to Chalcedon's decree, with the Nestorians going their own way and evangelizing the countries east of the Roman Empire, even to the western reaches of China, while the Alexandrians insisted that the single *divine* subjectivity of Christ had *absorbed* the humanity of Jesus, so much so that after the incarnation Christ had in effect just one nature, a view that gave them the name of "Monophysites" (meaning "one-nature-ists"). Indeed, Nestorian and Monophysite churches live on to this day, the Nestorians primarily in Armenia, Iraq, and (vestigially) in western China, and the Monophysites in Egypt (the Copts) – although both Churches reached doctrinal consensus with the Church of Rome in the 1990s, so that no Orthodox Church now regards Chalcedon as Church-dividing.

So what, then, was Chalcedon's solution? Basically, it took the legitimate insights of both the Antiochene Two-Natures Christology and of Cyril's more typically Alexandrian insistence on the single divine subjectivity of Christ. This unity of two natures in one person, however, must not be understood as a commingling of the two natures into some *tertium quid* (new third element), like a chemical mixture leading to a new substance. The natures had to remain what they always were (this was the part of Chalcedon rejected by the Monophysites); yet in remaining what they always were, these natures still had to be fully *united* in one person, one single source of subjectivity, one "I" who speaks as God's very Word (Nestorians feared that this would obliterate the human and psychological subjectivity of Christ, leading to a more subtle version of Logos–Sarx Christology).

Such was the dilemma facing the bishops at Chalcedon: the legitimate insights of both schools had to be preserved, while the heretical implications lurking in each school had to be rejected. Hence the famous four adverbs of Chalcedon's decree, usually translated in English as four prepositional phrases: the two natures of Christ were united in his one person, says the Council, "without confusion, without change, without division, without separation." The first two adverbs attack any notion that Jesus became some kind of intermediate being: humanity remains fully human, and divinity remains fully divine. In so far as Jesus is human (and he is fully human), he can be, and in fact was, ignorant and in need of learning, he needed to eat and sleep, and so forth; but insofar as he is divine (and he is fully divine), everything the Father has, the Son has, and he shares fully in the divine life of his Father.

This might seem to raise the ugly specter of two centers of subjectivity in Jesus all over again, which is where the second set of adverbs comes in: "without division, without separation" means that, while there is no *mixture* of the two natures in Jesus, there is full and total *unity* – for Chalcedon (and above all for Cyril and Leo) a very different concept. Keeping these two sets of adverbs together in one synoptic view is of course not easily done, for we are speaking here of a unity that brings together in one Person finite and infinite, the unchanging God who yet *becomes* flesh. But it was never the purpose of Chalcedon to provide a logical "explanation" for what must remain essentially a mystery of God's condescension to save humankind through the atoning death of his Son.

One further point must be made about Chalcedon: although it did in fact, as a matter of history, lead to the breaking away of certain Nestorian and Alexandrian churches, it proved – again as a matter of history – remarkably cohesive for the rest of the Church. For Chalcedon remained the touchstone of orthodoxy for all the rest of the Churches, Roman, Greek, and (later) the Russian Orthodox. Moreover, the Protestant Reformers – or at least the classical ones, Martin Luther and John Calvin – explicitly adhered to Chalcedonian Christology (later Protestant figures like John Milton and Isaac Newton drifted toward Arianism). Prior to the nineteenth century, the consensus held remarkably well, so that Christological reflection tended to concentrate on more technical issues pertaining to the consciousness of Jesus or, above all, on questions of the atonement, as in the famous theory of St Anselm (1033–1109) that only a being fully human and fully divine could atone for sins, because only such a being could pay the infinite debt owed to God by a sinful human race: being both a member of that same race and yet infinitely capable of paying that debt, the divine-human Jesus could offer "sacrifices for men" (Hebrews 2:17).

With the dawn of the historical sciences in the nineteenth century, however, the ground began to shift under the foundations laid by Chalcedon. Two factors especially led to a reopening of the Chalcedonian settlement: a minute analysis of the historical circumstances that led to New Testament Christology, and the growing awareness of other religions and civilizations as yet untouched by the Christian message.

Nineteenth-century biblical criticism was especially enamored of the notion, derived from the German philosopher G.W.F. Hegel (1770–1831), that human social consciousness grows through a historical process of "dialectic," meaning a clash of conflicting views ("thesis" and "antithesis") that eventually leads to a higher "synthesis" incorporating the best of both previous views that had at the time of their clash seemed irreconcilable. Applied to the New Testament, biblical critics like the German F.C. Baur (1792–1860) saw this same process at work in the clash between the earliest Jewish Christians, who insisted on circumcision as a prerequisite for joining the Jesus Movement, and the Gentile converts of St Paul, who demanded complete liberation from the Mosaic Law. According to Baur, these Jewish Christians were largely adoptionist in their Christology, while Paul was influenced by Hellenistic (and even Gnostic) speculations about a pre-existing *Logos* who came down from heaven to save humans from a world of darkness and woe. Out of that clash came the later synthesis of "early Catholicism," which fused into one synthesis a (quasi-Jewish) respect for law-and-works and a (quasi-Pauline) insistence on the saving efficacy of the sacraments of baptism and the Eucharist.

If this schema was correct, then it would mean that the earliest Christians in Palestine started off with a "low" Christology of adoptionism and strict Jewish monotheism and then, through the influence of Paul and the Gospel of John (universally assumed to be much later than Mark), the Gentile Christians adopted a "high" Christology more in keeping with what they already knew from other mystery religions that worshiped such pagan gods as Isis, Osiris, and Mithras. At a stroke this schema removed any notion that the New Testament spoke with one voice about the identity of Jesus. No longer could the Gospels of Mark and John be used equally, with one verse trumping another.

If that *internal* pluralism were not enough, nineteenth-century minds were also becoming increasingly aware of the pluralism of cultures. If Jesus was "the only name by which men can be saved" (Acts 4:12), then what was to become of all those who, through no fault of their own, had never heard of the Christian message? (This issue had already been mooted earlier, with the dawn of the Age of Exploration and the missionary efforts that came in its wake, but it received new impetus with the scientific study of the religious texts of India, China, and Islam in the nineteenth century.)

Out of this crisis, often called the "scandal of particularity" (meaning the supposed "scandal" of God choosing to express his love for the *whole* world by sending his Son to just one corner, and a very isolated and obscure one at that, of the world), came a whole new flood of Christological thought, first among Protestants and then later in the Catholic Church as well.

In a Blackwell *Companion* devoted to Catholicism, this essay can hardly discuss Protestant developments at any length; but since Protestants were the first to realize the problem, the first to propose solutions, and therefore the ones who would later influence Catholic thought as well, their basic positions must at least be mentioned. No doubt the most influential of these theologians was Friedrich Schleiermacher (1768–1834), who realized that, in order to meet the challenge of pluralism, a way had to be found to unify all religions under one overarching concept, which he claimed could be done by using the concept of "absolute dependence." Since humans are quintessentially biological beings who never lose their dependence on the environment and who sense equally that the entire universe is itself in some way contingent (that is, dependent on a higher being for its existence), the feeling grows within the human breast that we are all absolutely dependent on God, and this feeling gives birth to all the religions of the world without exception. And what the great founders of world religions do is to *teach* the reality of that dependence, not so much in specific doctrines (that is where the religions differ), but in the example of their lives.

But where, then, does Jesus fit in? For Schleiermacher, Jesus was the one who realized – and lived out – that absolute dependence most of all, as shown especially in his utmost clinging to the will of his Father in season and out, even unto death.

This approach had many advantages. First of all, it made theology once again academically respectable, for it placed religion in a sphere of discourse that could be scientifically investigated. But it soon ran into severe difficulties of its own. For one thing, biblical criticism kept advancing, one result of which was to show that, however early the Gospel of Mark might be in relation to John, it was still just as confessional and as purpose-driven (to win converts) as was the allegedly more "theological" Gospel of John. Precisely because Mark had no more interest in presenting a neutral biography of Jesus than did any of the other Gospels, it could not be mined for data about the alleged consciousness of Jesus and his supposed sense of absolute dependence. The early twentieth-century biblical scholar Rudolf Bultmann (1884–1976) was especially insistent that the New Testament provided no data whatever about the inner awareness of Jesus; for him all we knew about Jesus (from a strictly scientific and historical point of view) was that he existed and died on the Cross.

Worse still, the whole basis for this style of biblical criticism was that old Hegelian chestnut, his notion of progress, a dogma that came to a crashing refutation in the killing fields of World War I. Out of that immolation of European civilization, Karl Barth (1886–1968) shouted out his ringing No to liberal Protestantism. For him the human dimension of the Bible (which he never denied) was not the point: God still existed, God was still sovereign over the world (even atheism, for Barth, was but one episode in God's ongoing drama with the world), and God acted decisively in Christ in a way that rendered all religions void before God (including, paradoxically, even Christianity – in its human dimensions). Far from being signs of the universal sense of dependence on God, human religions were for Barth but one more effort by man to build the Tower of Babel, efforts that were sure to bring down the wrath of God once more, as World War I proved.

Finally, more careful study of the New Testament was undermining the old Hegelian framework that claimed "high" Christology as a later, Gentile development. C.H. Dodd (Dodd, 1936) showed that Peter's sermon on Pentecost reflected the earliest traditions of Palestinian Christianity (rather than being the unhistorical projection onto Peter of the personal theology of Luke, the author of Acts of the Apostles). Later Martin Hengel (Hengel, 1988) showed that the "high" Christology of Paul's Letter to the Philippians (which speaks of the pre-existence of Jesus, who emptied himself of his *prior* divinity to take on the form of a slave) was derived from an early Christian hymn. And since Philippians was one of Paul's earliest letters, and since he converted within three to six years of the resurrection of Jesus (the amount of time depends on when one dates the death of Jesus, which was probably in 33, but possibly 30), "high" Christology was part of the early Church's preaching from the outset. (It is for that reason that Hengel famously said that more happened in the development of Christology in the first 18 years than in the next seven centuries.)

All the trends, in other words, seemed to favor a return to Chalcedonian Christology. From the year 1919, when he published the first edition of his epochal commentary, *The Epistle to the Romans*, to the first decade after World War II, Barth had been the dominant figure of Protestant theology, giving new life to orthodox Christology (for which reason the movement he started has often been called "Neo-Orthodoxy"). Above all, he showed how his biblical view of world religions demanded a rigorously Alexandrian Christology; for only if Jesus was fully divine and fully human, could God act to save the world that had been, until the coming of Jesus, the object of divine wrath (for Barth Jesus, in his human nature, was just as much an object of God's wrath as all other human beings in the world, a view stressed by Martin Luther as well).

Since Barth's death in 1968, however, his influence has notably waned in Protestant divinity schools, largely because of the revived influence of a trend that now goes under the name of "post-modernism," a school of thought that resolutely refuses to privilege one culture over another and indeed sees any claim to universal truth (at least in the sphere of culture, if not of mathematics and the natural sciences) as but a power-driven need to impose one's views on the other. This view, which was first adumbrated by the late nineteenth-century philosopher Friedrich Nietzsche (1844–1900), has now become widespread, so much so that it might perhaps be described as its own kind of hegemonic discourse. Be that as it may, against these post-modern trends, Barth's influence has waned, which leads us now back to Catholic Christology.

While these developments were proceeding apace in the Protestant world, Catholics were holed up in a "fortress mentality" Church. This religious psychology of condemnation followed in the wake of the papal condemnations of a heresy called "Modernism," an all-encompassing term referring to the early efforts, mostly by French theologians, to take into account Protestant biblical criticism. Pope Pius X (1835–1914; reigned 1903–14) harshly condemned this early *rapprochement* with modern biblical criticism, and forbade any historical study of the Bible that would threaten the Mosaic authorship of the Pentateuch (the first five books of the Old Testament) or question the historical reliability of the Gospels. As a result of that clampdown, Christological thought in the Catholic Church was largely confined to technical discussion of the Messianic consciousness of Jesus, a discussion largely determined by deductions from the dogmatic principles derived from Chalcedon, with the New Testament brought in more as a fund of proof-texts than as a challenge to the received tradition, as it had been for Protestants in the wake of historical study of the sources.

With the Second Vatican Council (1963–5), however, all that changed. Pope John XXIII (1881–1963; reigned 1958–1963) called for *aggiornamento* (updating), and the Council itself called for dialog – an irenic, reconciling dialog – with Protestants, and indeed with "all men of good will" irrespective of their religious (or even irreligious) convictions. Suddenly Catholics found themselves studying Protestant theology and encountering firsthand the challenges of pluralism; and what had once been seen to be a specifically Protestant dilemma had now become the universal dilemma of all Christians facing a pluralistic world gradually becoming one "global village." Not surprisingly, Catholic proposals to the Christological dilemma followed lines largely hammered out by the Protestants first, Schleiermacher and Barth above all.

Again, the schematization required for an essay of this size prevents treating Catholic Christology with all of the due allowances needed to do justice to the subtleties of Catholic thinking about this most convoluted topic. Nonetheless, one cannot help but notice some formal similarities between Schleiermacher's Christology and that of the renowned Jesuit Karl Rahner (1904–84), who posited a universal outreach (*Vorgriff*) toward God implicit in every act of knowing, a reaching out that he called part of the "transcendental" equipment of the human knower. This transcendental outreach means that man is by nature open to the revelation of God, should it come; and once it does come (which of course Rahner never denied), we must speak of a *de facto* "categorial" revelation, a revelation which answers the question that the "transcendental" longing of man could only pose but never answer on its own. And Jesus is the perfect realization of the union between these two constituents of man, transcendental and categorial.

Against this version of theological idealism stands Rahner's contemporary, the Swiss theologian Hans Urs von Balthasar (1905–88), who feared that Rahner was dismembering God's self-manifestation into two aspects, a *more basic* transcendental versus a *merely confirmatory* categorial. For Balthasar, this runs the danger that Christian truth becomes, at best, a key to, and at worst, simply a confirmation (in mythological clothing, no less) of, what is any case already given to humanity in the universal God–world relationship.

Balthasar, as it happens, was a close friend and neighbor of Barth in Basel, and the influence of the latter on the former was deep and long-lasting (Balthasar's influence on Barth, however, was less notable). What the two had in common was an insistence that the Bible be taken on its own terms, even if both accepted as well the results of historical criticism (provided they were reliable). For both as well, accepting the Bible on its own terms meant that it would be impossible, *pace* Schleiermacher and Rahner, to subsume the figure of Jesus into some more overarching framework. In other words, Jesus' claim to be "the Way, the Truth, and the Life" (John 14:6) must be taken *on its own terms*, quite independent of the historical process by which that claim came to be embedded in the Fourth Gospel and not in the others. And if that claim is taken on its own terms, it shows that Jesus was not merely a teacher who pointed *to* the way but was, in himself, in his own person, *the* Way itself.

But to any world-view whatever, such a claim, no matter how mediated, must lead to outrage. For a claim to be *the* Way, *the* Truth, *the* Life means at core that one white-cap atop a wave claims to be not only the sea and the seabed but the generating matrix of the world as well ("Before Abraham was, I am"). Moreover, that claim is so preposterous that it can only be validated by God himself in the resurrection. Thus the three together – Claim, Death, and Resurrection – form a triadic pattern (*Gestalt*, one of Balthasar's favorite words) that is the indissoluble core of the Christian proclamation.

But how can that claim continue to resound for all the rest of history, down to the last syllable of recorded time, without provoking yet another objection, one that sees the positivity of the existence of the historical Jesus fade and fade into the recesses of ancient history? In the words of a Swabian proverb that Hegel liked to quote from time to time: "That's been true for so long it has finally stopped being true." (This, in effect, is the challenge of external pluralism.)

Altering his image of wave and sea slightly, Balthasar answers this objection by comparing the image of any one human being in history to the ripple effect of a stone dropped into the sea. But with all other human beings who emerge out of the components of the universe and merge back into them at death, their ripple effect eventually fades away. Thus the stone which is Jesus must differ in its radiating power if Hegel's objection is to be met.

For Balthasar that can only occur if this one stone, and no other, plunged all the way to the bottom of the sea on Holy Saturday, when Christ descended into hell, landing, so to speak, with a thud that continues to reverberate from the ocean floor. But *that* can only happen if the weight of that single, historically unique stone can serve as the counterweight (*Schwergewicht*, another key term in Balthasarian theology) outweighing all other truths and sufferings in the world, which is conceivable only in trinitarian terms. Only then does the center where the stone was dropped continue to reverberate and radiate outward. Nor can the effects of Christ's reverberation extend only along time's future-bound arrow (as with all other human beings in history, whose effects live on only subsequent to their finite, temporal existence). On the contrary, Christ's outward radiation moves concentrically in such a way as to influence previous history as well. This for Balthasar is the essential soteriological significance of the scriptural references to Christ's descent into hell, where according to the Petrine tradition he rescues the "spirits in prison who disobeyed God *long ago*" (1 Peter 3:19–20; see also 1 Peter 4:5–6 and 2 Peter 2: 4–10).

When these startling images of stone, wave, and sea are seen in their full implication, one arrives at what is perhaps the most startling innovation in Balthasar's theology: his quasi-Origenistic vision of the possible redemption of all these "disobedient spirits in prison." Origen's own theory was rejected as heretical several centuries after his death, no doubt because he posited an inevitable redemption of all souls, when God would be "all in all." (Perhaps Origen went astray here because of his habit of forcing revelation into the neo-Platonic schema of *exitus–reditus*: just as Creation seemed an inevitable "emanation" for the neo-Platonist, so too, perhaps, was the "return" of that creation to God's redemptive love inevitable for Origen.) But Balthasar grounds his hope of *apokatastasis* (to use the technical term for universal restoration of all lost souls) not in neo-Platonism but in the event of Holy Saturday. In his descent into hell Jesus experiences *all* that is hellish about the world in its difference, otherness, and divergence from God, which means that hell is, in Balthasar's famous description, "a Christological place" where sinners experience, by the very nature of their isolated partiality, only a portion of what Christ himself experienced in a pre-eminent way. And since any experience of Christ is by definition salvific, we may at least hope for – if not confidently expect – the salvation of all.

References and Further Reading

Dodd, C.H. (1936) *The Apostolic Preaching and its Developments*. London: Hodder and Stoughton. This famous work established the historical Palestinian basis of Peter's sermon on Pentecost, showing that all of the Church's later Christological and Trinitarian doctrines were contained *in nuce* in this crucial sermon.
Grillmeier, Alois (1975) *Christ in Christian Tradition*. Philadelphia, PA: John Knox Press. A full account of the Christological debates in the first seven centuries of the Church, although its polemics against St Cyril of Alexandria should be treated with caution.
Hengel, Martin (1988) *Between Jesus and Paul: Studies in the Earliest History of Christianity*. Minneapolis, MN: Fortress Press. A study of the presence of high Christology in the earliest years of Christianity.
Kereszty, Roch (2002) *Jesus Christ: Fundamentals of Christology*. New York: Alba House. All the basics of Christology, biblical, historical, and systematic, written from a Catholic perspective.
McIntosh, Mark (1996) *Christology from Within: Spirituality and the Incarnation in the Theology of Hans Urs von Balthasar*. South Bend, IN: University of Notre Dame Press. The best work in English on Balthasar's Christology and one which, as the title indicates, seeks to get beyond the jejune categories of "high" and "low" Christologies.
Robinson, John A.T. (1987) *The Priority of John*. San Francisco, CA: HarperCollins. One more attack on the Hegelian hammerlock that still to some extent grips New Testament scholarship. The author is willing to admit that John might be the last of the four Gospels to be *published* since, says Robinson, the last chapter was added by a redactor from the Community of the Beloved Disciple before it was sent out for general circulation in the last quarter of the first century. But except for that chapter, all the others go back to John of Zebedee, one of the Twelve Apostles. Moreover, it was written for a community composed almost entirely

of Jewish Christians in the north of Palestine and reflects a Christology that differs only in emphasis, and not in substance, from the Christology of the Synoptics (the first three Gospels). A *tour de force* of New Testament scholarship and essential reading for anyone seeking to ground Christology in the Bible.

Sanders, E.P. (1996) *The Historical Figure of Jesus*. London/New York: Penguin. A sober and balanced account, geared to the general reader, of the results of research in the historical Jesus. An appendix discusses the likely dates for the crucifixion of Jesus and opts, with due sobriety, for AD 33.

CHAPTER 21

Mary

Trent Pomplun

> No one can understand this Gospel, unless he has lain on Jesus' breast
> and received from Him Mary as his own mother.
>
> Origen of Alexandria

The fervor of devotion to the Virgin Mary in Roman Catholicism is arguably its single most distinctive trait. As a result, Mariology runs a close race with Ecclesiology as the theological discipline that most rankles non-Catholics. If the Blessed Virgin, more than any of the Church's other saints, is a sign of contradiction among believers, we might do well to consider the logic that underlies Roman Catholic doctrines of Mary. *In nuce,* this logic comprises three elements: the spiritual exegesis of the fathers, the aesthetic arguments of the schoolmen, and the spiritual theology of the early modern Church. The dogmatic theology of the Blessed Virgin thus mirrors the historical development of the Church's devotion to her; in this essay, we shall treat both in turn.

The Virgin Mary in Scripture and Tradition

It is often said – mistakenly – that Scripture tells us very little about the Virgin Mary. The New Testament actually tells us more about the Blessed Virgin than anyone except St Peter, St Paul, or Our Lord Himself. Matthew and Luke recount the virginal conception of Christ: Matthew as the culmination of the Messiah's genealogy (Matt 1:18–23); Luke, as an event of universal significance traced not merely to Abraham but to Adam himself (Luke 3:23–38). True to the catechesis of the primitive Church, as seen in Peter's sermon (Acts 10:36–43) or the Gospel of Mark generally (Mk 1:1–8), Luke begins his account with John the Baptist, but in such a way that the Baptist's miraculous birth as the last prophet of Israel (Luke 1:67–79) serves as the prelude to the Messiah's own (Luke 2:1–7). So, too, Luke devotes a great deal of attention to Mary's role in the history of salvation, lingering over the Annunciation (Luke 1:26–38), the Visitation (Luke 1:39–56), and Mary's presentation of Jesus in the Temple (Luke 2:22–35). Luke also presents the Virgin as one of the "lowly" (Luke 1:48), the "chosen portion" of Israel exalted by the Lord (Cf. Ps 138:6; Prov 3:34; 11:2; 16:9). This last point is important. When the woman lifted her voice in the crowd and exclaimed "Blessed is the womb that bore you, and the breast that you sucked" only to hear Jesus respond, "Blessed rather are those that hear the word of God and keep it" (Luke 11:27–8), Christ does not rebuke the woman for praising Mary (an interpretation sometimes held by Protestant provocateurs). The Gospel had presented Mary as the "hearer of the word" *par excellence* (Luke 1:38), who is "forever blessed" (Luke 1:48) on account of her faith. She is the one who kept Jesus' words in her heart and pondered them (Luke 2:19, 2:51). Clearly the Gospel denigrates neither Mary nor her maternity, but only the exaltation of either according to the flesh alone. Much the same can be said about the Synoptics' account of Jesus' "true" family (Matt 12:46–50; Mk 3:31–5; Luke 8:21).

Mary plays a similarly exalted, but similarly misunderstood, role in the Gospel of John. She frames Christ's public ministry from His first miracle at Cana (John 2:1–11) to the manifestation of His glory on Calvary (John 19:25–7). In John, her intimate connection to the mystery of Christ's "hour," the work by which Christ glorifies the Father and the Father glorifies Christ (John 17:1–5) culminates in Christ's famous words to John from the Cross, "Behold thy mother!" (John 19:27), an injunction that is all the more mysterious since the Apostle's own mother was also present at the foot of the Cross (Matt 27:56). The Acts of the Apostles presents Mary among the disciples at Jerusalem in the upper room (Acts 1:14). Catholic tradition, basing itself on the parallel between Acts 1:14 and Acts 2:1, also places her together with Peter and the other disciples at Pentecost itself, so that the Blessed Virgin is overshadowed by the Holy Spirit at the beginning of the parallel narrative arcs in both Luke and Acts. Mary even finds a place in the proto-creedal statement of the fourth chapter of Galatians: "When the fullness of time had come, God sent forth his Son, born of a woman, born under the Law, to redeem those who were under the Law, so that we might receive adoption as sons" (Gal 4:4–5). It is important not to overlook this text too hastily: it contains the germ of the Church's later teaching on the divine maternity. For our purposes, however, it is noteworthy that St Paul mentions the Blessed Virgin in tandem with the Law. He thus singles her out as a daughter of Israel, to whom "belong the sonship, the glory, the covenants, the giving of the Law, the worship, and the promises" as well as patriarchs and Christ Himself (Rom 9:4–5).

A discussion of the Blessed Virgin in the New Testament cannot ignore the battle between the serpent and the "woman clothed with the Sun" in the Apocalypse (Rev 12:1–17). Like the young woman of Isaiah's prophecy, this woman is a "portent" (Rev 12:1. Cf. Is 7:14). Moreover, the disciples are counted as her offspring (Rev 12:17), echoing the primordial conflict between Eve and the serpent in the Protevangelium (Gen 3:15). Her anguish and birth pangs (Rev 12:2) are not the throes of physical childbirth – since such interpretation is ruled out by the Church's teaching on Mary's *virginitas in partu* – but the spiritual pangs of the new creation itself (Rom 8:22), not the nativity in Bethlehem, but the birth of the Church from Christ's side (John 19:34). Such a spiritual reading of the text is supported by the parallel of the place where the woman finds refuge (Rev 12:6) with the place that Christ prepared for his disciples (John 14:3), as well as by the presence of the immolated Lamb in the sky earlier in the Apocalypse (Rev 5:6).

The early Church did not seek such parallels; they came as a natural consequence of her practice of reading Scripture. In seeing Mary prefigured in the Old Testament, the Fathers of the Church only repeated the example of the New Testament authors. A modern reader might reject canonical parallels, but Matthew and Luke make it crystal clear that the early Church saw Mary as the typological fulfillment of earlier prophecies. Matthew saw in Mary the virgin prophesied by Isaiah (Is 7:14; 11:2), and Luke typologically related her to Sara (Gen 18:14), Hannah (1 Sam 2:1–10), and, to a lesser extent, Miriam (Exod 15:20–1). The archangel's salutation that commences the Annunciation likewise echoes Nathan's oracle to David (2 Sam 7:12–16), Zechariah's praise of the prince of peace (Zech 9:9), Joel's assurances to the "sons of Zion" (Joel 2:21–7), and Zephaniah's song of the restoration of Israel (Zeph 3:14–17). By the same token, Mary's "overshadowing" recalls the cloud that covered the Tabernacle of Moses (Exod 40:36) and filled the Temple of Solomon (1 Kings 8:10–13).

Marian reflection in the early Church thus followed a path already set forth by the New Testament itself. Her first theologians were most impressed by the typological reflection of the Blessed Virgin as the "New Eve." In the writings of St Justin Martyr (c.100–65) and St Irenaeus (c.130–200), Mary became the "mother of all living" (Gen 3:20) spiritually. Just as sin entered the world through Eve's disobedience, so Redemption entered by the Virgin's *fiat*. Other Old Testament texts that were favored in the Marian reflection of the early Church were "There is a river whose streams make glad the city of God, the holy habitation of the Most High. God is in the midst of her, she shall not be moved" (Ps 46:4–5) and "Many daughters have gathered riches, but you have surpassed them all" (Prov 31:29). The Song of Solomon was a particularly fertile field for Marian cultivation. "A garden enclosed is my sister, my bride, a spring shut, and a fountain sealed" (Cant 4:12) was read as a prophecy of Mary's virginity. "You are fair. My love; there is no flaw in you" (Cant 4:7) was read as a prophetic anticipation of Mary's holiness. The application of "I am black, but comely" (Cant 1:5) to the Virgin gave rise to the iconography of the Black Madonna in Europe, most famously at Montserrat, Spain.

Mary's divine maternity became the symbol of orthodoxy during the time leading up to the Third Ecumenical Council, which convened under the leadership of St Cyril of Alexandria (c.375–444) at Ephesus in 431. While the title *theotokos* was used in Alexandria in the fourth century (and earlier as a title for the goddess Diana), St Cyril wished to define the title dogmatically in order to combat the heresy of Nestorius, who had argued that Mary had given birth to Jesus, but not to God. One might, Nestorius maintained, refer to the Virgin as *christotokos*, insofar as the Christ was a man, but to call her *theotokos* violated the divinity of the deity. St Cyril acknowledged that the New Testament did not employ the term, referring to Mary rather as the "mother of Jesus" (John 2:1) or "the mother of the Lord" (Luke 1:43), but felt it in perfect consonance with the previous tradition. More importantly, the term prevented one from making the drastic Christological mistake of assuming that Christ was two persons in addition to having two natures. Thus the Council proclaimed, "If anyone does not profess that Emmanuel is truly God, and that consequently the Holy Virgin is the Mother of God insofar as she gave birth in the flesh to the Word of God made flesh, according to what was written 'The Word was made flesh' – let him be anathema."

Mary's virginity was subject of no small amount of theological wrangling during the age of the fathers. Tertullian (c.155–230), for example, taught that Mary did not remain a virgin after the birth of Christ, assuming that the "brothers" of Christ mentioned by scripture (Matt 13:55 and elsewhere) implied that Mary assumed normal conjugal relations with St Joseph after the Messiah was born. Later theologians usually rejected this reasoning, pointing to other instances where "brethren" clearly meant kin, including uncles and cousins. St Epiphanius (c.310–403) felt that Christ's brothers were children of St Joseph by a previous marriage, although this position, too, was generally rejected from the time of St Jerome (c.340–420) onwards. St Gregory of Nyssa (c.330–95), St Ambrose (c.340–97), and St Augustine (354–430) thought nothing of arguing that the Blessed Virgin had vowed perpetual virginity. If the fathers agreed that Mary remained a virgin after giving birth to Christ, several expressed doubts about her virginal integrity *during* birth – St Jerome most notably – fearing that a seemingly miraculous birth implied that Jesus was not like other men and women in all things "except sin" (Heb 4:15). Nor did the Docetists' fondness for Mary's *virginitas in partu* help matters. The tradition generally developed that Jesus' kinship to humanity was secured as long as He was conceived in the womb and born as all other children, even if Mary's integrity was ensured by a miracle of divine providence. As a result of these various difficulties, the Church proclaimed the dogma of Mary's perpetual virginity at the second and third Councils of Constantinople, that is, the fifth and sixth Ecumenical Councils in 553 and 680. The latter council says simply, "The virginity of Mary remained before, during, and after parturition."

Theological reflection on Mary's holiness also grew during the Patristic era. The Eastern Churches held rather strong notions of Mary's fullness of grace and early sanctification – although not in the same sense as later Catholic teaching – but they did not as a rule uphold Mary's personal sinlessness. St John Chrysostom (c.347–407), for example, taught that feminine vanity moved Mary to address her Son at Cana. St Basil the Great (c.329–79) and St Cyril of Alexandria interpreted Simeon's prophecy to refer to a supposed doubt that the Mother of God had concerning the Crucifixion. The degree to which these views reflect a deficient understanding of women's full capacities and privileges as images of God is open to debate, although it is worth pointing out that the fathers, like St Jerome, who defended Mary's personal sinlessness generally felt that women's souls were naturally equal to men's (Brown, 1988: 367–73). Although Latin theologians generally championed Mary's personal sinlessness, they did so with some hesitancy, especially in light of the Pelagian heresy. St Augustine, unable to reconcile Mary's sinlessness with the gratuity of grace, famously side-stepped the problem (*De Natura et Gratia* 36, 42). Such paradoxes that arose with the emerging consensus on Augustinian accounts of grace and free will would only be solved by the theologians of the Middle Ages.

Carolingian theologians such as St Radbertus (786–c.860) devoted some effort to Mary's mediation, but the most important trends in Marian devotion belong to the period after the Gregorian Reform. In 1060, the Church began to celebrate the Feast of the Conception of the Virgin, first in England, then in Normandy and France. St Bernard of Clairvaux (1090–1153) was the feast's most famous opponent, even as he contributed to the development of Mariology by popularizing the title *mediatrix*. Theological reflection on the Assumption also became more common in the late medieval world, largely due to the influence of the twelfth-century *de Assumptione* by Pseudo-Augustine. The Angelus and the Rosary date to this period, championed by the Franciscans and the Dominicans, respectively. As theologians became increasingly systematic in their practice, they began to pay greater attention to certain problems that would later come to dominate Catholic theological reflection on Mary. Peter Lombard (*c.*1100–64) included a series of questions about the sanctification of Mary in his four books of "sentences" (*Quatuor libri sententiarum*). The first Mariological synthesis, the *Mariale super missus est*, long attributed to St Albert the Great (*c.*1206–80), was composed in this spirit. Although many would find its systematic artifice off-putting, the *Mariale* explained Mary's fullness of grace as the inclusion of all graces, a position – and logic – that would influence Catholic theology considerably. Not surprisingly, St Thomas Aquinas (1225–74) also made significant contributions to Mariology, devoting four questions of his *Summa Theologiae* to the Virgin. Although Aquinas denied that the Virgin was sanctified before her soul animated her body (*Summa Theologiae* IIIa, q. 27, a. 2) – a position that occasioned some impressive theological contortions among later Thomists – it is to the Angelic Doctor that we owe the first sustained theological application of the arguments *ex convenientia* that served as the foundation for St Anselm's earlier reflections on the Blessed Virgin. The Angelic Doctor argued, for example, that it was becoming that the Mother of God remain a Virgin on account of the unique character of the God-man, the honor accorded to the Holy Spirit, the dignity and holiness of Mary's devotion to her Son, and the honor of St Joseph himself (*Summa Theologiae* IIIa, q. 28, a. 3). The importance of this theological aesthetic must be stressed; while the fathers recognized that Mary enjoyed certain prerogatives as a result of her dignity as the Mother of God, the schoolmen discerned and expressed the principle that served as the foundation for the fathers' spiritual reading of the Old Testament.

At the risk of sounding too partisan – our collection has a strong Dominican flavor after all – it is the glory of Blessed John Duns Scotus (*c.*1266–1308) to have given this aesthetic logic lasting expression. While his intuition of the supreme fittingness of the Blessed Virgin's Immaculate Conception is sufficient to secure the medieval Franciscan's lasting place among the greatest theologians, his true contribution is to have laid the foundations for the Church's subsequent Marian dogmas. Indeed, Scotus' argument for the Immaculate Conception is arguably the most famous argument *ex convenientia* in the history of theology. The most perfect Mediator, he reasoned, must have a most perfect act of mediation; since the most perfect Mediator had no more exalted relationship than that to His own mother, it is fitting that He merited for her a most perfect redemption. Preservation from sin is more perfect than redemption from sin. *Potuit*; *decuit*; *ergo fecit*. It is possible; it is fitting; it is done (*In Sent.* III, d. 3, q. 1).

The theologians of the Tridentine Church perfected this line of reasoning. With the invention of the printing press and the subsequent publication of Patristic and medieval authors, Tomasso de Vio (Cajetan) OP (1469–1534), Peter Canisius SJ (1521–97), Francisco Suárez SJ (1548–1617), and Denis Petau (Dionysius Petavius) SJ (1587–1652) produced the first truly systematic accounts of the Blessed Virgin. These last two theologians are also important for Catholic speculation on the development of doctrine. Suárez applies it to Mariology explicitly (*De Mysteriis Vitae Christi*, d. 3, sect. 6). New devotions to Mary also flourished during this time, given impetus by the Catholic Reformation, and the Virgin took pride of place in its ascetical and mystical theology. The iconography of the baroque Church aided the growth of Marian doctrine – Murillo's painting of the Immaculate Conception immediately comes to mind – providing the Church with the visual means to establish Mary's role as the dispenser of all grace or, more figuratively, the heart of the mystical body. Such conceptions were not unknown in the Middle Ages, but they proliferated after the Reformation in the writings of Sts John Eudes (1601–80), Louis-Marie Grignion de Montfort (1673–1716), and Alphonsus Liguori (1696–1787).

Although earlier Tridentine visionaries, such as Maria de Agreda (1602–65), displayed an almost morose delectation for the Virgin, even detailing seemingly unknowable aspects of her private life, the nineteenth century was the golden age of Marian apparitions. The first of such, to St Catherine Labouré (1806–76) in 1830, entrusted the Miraculous Medal to the Church. Engraved with the words, "O Mary, conceived without sin, pray for us who have recourse to thee," the Miraculous Medal gave the modern Church one of her most popular Marian prayers. It also furthered the devotion to Mary's immaculate heart that had been promoted by the French School generally. The appearance of the Virgin to St Bernadette Soubirous (1844–79) at Lourdes in 1858 led to the foundation of one of the most famous Catholic pilgrimage sites of the past 200 years. It also confirmed Pius IX's dogmatic definition of the Immaculate Conception four years earlier: after a series of increasingly familiar visions, St Bernadette asked the Virgin her name and received the response, "I am the Immaculate Conception." These two apparitions are only the most famous among the manifold visions of the early modern Church. Two aspects of these Marian apparitions are striking – apart from their frequent espousal of Marian doctrines. They have a particularly international character. Important apparitions include Juan Diego's vision of the Virgin of Guadalupe (1531); the apparition of Our Lady of Good Health in Vailankanni, Tamil Nadu, India (1600); and the appearance of Our Lady of La Vang during the intense persecutions of the Church in Vietnam (1798). Even more striking, perhaps, is their persistence. Apparitions of the twentieth century, at Fatima, Portugal (1917), Garabandal, Spain (1961), and Medjugorje, Bosnia (1981) still excite followers with apocalyptic messages, often amid great controversy. Devotion to the Virgin of Guadalupe, arguably the national icon of Mexico, shows no sign of abating (Poole, 1996; Brading, 2002). My own archdiocese has investigated alleged apparitions of the Virgin in nearby Emmitsburg, Maryland, since 1993.

Mariology itself underwent significant development in the nineteenth century. Most importantly, Pius IX promulgated the dogma of the Immaculate Conception in 1854. Although *Ineffabilis Deus* is rather minimal in character, remarking merely that the Virgin "in the first instance of her conception, by a singular privilege and grace granted by God in view of the merits of Jesus Christ, the Savior of the human race, was preserved from all stain of original sin," Mariology fairly exploded after its promulgation. The bull's author, Carlo Passaglia SJ (1812–87), initiated Matthias Scheeben (1835–88) into the study of Mary. Scheeben coined the term "Mariology" and gave the Church one of the most comprehensive (and creative) treatments of Mary in her history (Scheeben, 1946–7). It is to Scheeben that we owe the later Mariological treatises of Jean-Baptiste Terrien SJ (1832–1903) and Réginald Garrigou-Lagrange OP (1877–1964), among others. The famous letter of John Henry Newman (1801–90) to Edward Pusey of November 28, 1865 also deserves mention, if only because it put Newman's theology of doctrinal development to the supreme test. In it, the new convert to Catholicism tried to explain some of the Marian extravagances of St Louis-Marie Grignion de Montfort to his less-than-sympathetic Anglican friend.

The popes of the late nineteenth and twentieth centuries also advanced a theology of the Blessed Virgin's cooperation in the redemption of mankind through a series of encyclicals, apostolic exhortations, and sermons. Leo XIII articulated this doctrine in both *Iucunda Semper* (1884) and *Adiutricem Populi* (1895); Pius XII reserved a special place for Mary in *Mystici Corporis* (1943), recognizing the Virgin as the most Spirit-filled of all the saints and her special connection to the Eucharistic sacrifice. This same Pope's *Ad Caeli Reginam* (1954) proclaimed Mary Queen of Heaven and instituted the feast of Mary the Queen. From Paul VI we have the Apostolic Exhortations *Signum Magnum* (1967) and *Marialis Cultus* (1974), and John Paul II followed suit with the encyclical *Redemptoris Mater* (1987) and the Apostolic Exhortation *Rosarium Virginis Mariae* (2002). The single most important Mariological event of the twentieth century, however, was the promulgation of the dogma of Mary's Assumption by Pius XII in *Munificentissimus Deus* (1950). As with the definition of the Immaculate Conception, the dogma defined is rather spare, but its underlying theological principle married a strong spiritual exegesis with a distinctly late medieval argument *ex convenientia*. In fact, the Pope justified the logic of the dogma's definition with a quotation from Suárez: "Keeping in mind the standards of propriety," he wrote "and when there is no contradiction or repugnance on the part of Scripture, the mysteries of grace which God has wrought in the Virgin must be measured, not by ordinary laws, but by the divine omnipotence" (*De Mysteriis Vitae Christi*. q. 27, a. 2, d. 3, sect. 5).

This Mariological march forward hit a rare snag in the late twentieth century when John Paul II controversially asked an International Theological Commission of the Pontifical International Marian Academy to judge the suitability of defining the dogma of Mary's Mediation and Coredemption. On June 4, 1997, he received a negative judgment. Apart from this minor setback, John Paul II promoted traditional Marian devotion with great vigor, especially in his beatification of John Duns Scotus and canonization of Juan Diego. At the same time, the Pope underlined the active, historical, and existential aspects of the Marian mystery that had been developed in the twentieth century. Joseph Cardinal Ratzinger (now Pope Benedict XVI) said the "new approach" of *Redemptoris Mater* did not "display before our wondering eyes any static, self-contained mysteries" but invited us "to enter into the dynamic quality of salvation that reaches out to us as a gift and a challenge and that assigns to us our place in history." Mary, he continued, "dwells not just in the past or in the lofty spheres of heaven under God's immediate disposition; she is and remains present and real in this historical moment; she is a person acting here and now . . . She offers a key to interpret our present existence, not in theoretical discourse, but in action" (John Paul II 1987: 20–1). Various forms of feminist and liberation theology ironically shared this existential interpretation of Mary's mediation. It would be churlish to deny that these theologies, insofar as they violate none of the Marian dogmas already established by the Church, should be welcomed as authentic – and much needed – developments in Mariology. It is largely through them and the various movements associated with them that Christ's grace has been felt where it is most needed, in the poor, the oppressed, and those at the margins of globalization (Johnson, 2003).

The Virgin Mary in Systematic Perspective

The systematic presentation of Marian reflection largely follows its historical development; starting from scripture, Mariology begins with the divine maternity and ends in Mary's distribution of Christ's grace. Although Francisco Suárez is generally believed to be the first author to write a genuinely systematic Mariology, similar treatments of the Blessed Virgin are to be found in most of the sustained Christological reflections in the Middle Ages. And rightly so: Mariology is a natural outgrowth of Christology and soteriology, and is thus situated between these two treatises in later expressions of dogmatic theology. The Virgin Mary is the "Mother of God" because Jesus of Nazareth is truly God and man, and insofar as Jesus is the Christ and our Redeemer, His mother plays a unique role in the history of redemption. This unique role is summarized by the Blessed Virgin's title *theotokos*. Mary's divine motherhood is the source of all of her supernatural gifts, which theologians generally refer to as her "fullness of grace" (*plenitudo gratiae*). As a result of this fullness of grace, Catholic theologians recognize five special prerogatives unique to the Virgin among all created persons: her Immaculate Conception, her sinlessness, her perpetual virginity, her heavenly assumption, and her secondary mediatorship. Any interesting – and indeed any responsible – Mariology will address each of these topics. After discussing the dogma of Mary's divine maternity, we will as well.

The dogma of Mary's divine motherhood, which was affirmed by the Council of Ephesus in 431, contains two truths. Mary is truly a mother, but truly the Mother of *God*. Scripture clearly attests to the first of these two truths: Mary conceives, she bears her Son during a normal nine-month gestation, and she gives birth to him in an ordinary manner (Matt 1:18; Luke 1:31, 2:7). In sum, Mary contributes everything to the formation of Christ's human nature that every other mother contributes to the formation of her children. Secondly, the dogma asserts that Mary conceived and gave birth to the Second Person of the Holy Trinity, not according to His divine nature, but according to the human nature He truly assumed. Asserting that Mary's motherhood is a true motherhood in every respect establishes and deepens our understanding of the mystery of the Incarnation of Christ Himself, who was like all men and woman in every respect, except sin (Heb 4:15). Because the Word is eternally begotten of the Father, God from God, light from light, true God from true God, Jesus is the true and consubstantial Son of God; because the Incarnate Word is temporally born of the Virgin Mary, Jesus is truly her son. Being but one divine Person, the Son of God who is eternally begotten is thus absolutely identical with the Virgin's child, and Mary is truly the Mother of God.

As *theotokos*, the Blessed Virgin thus enjoys a unique relationship to each person of the Most Holy Trinity. With the Father, Mary alone can claim one and the same Son, a relationship that theologians often refer to as her "daughterhood," a prerogative that differs formally from the adoptive sonship that we all enjoy in Christ. Since the Apostles' Creed teaches that Christ "was conceived by the Holy Spirit," Mary also has a special relationship with the third person of the Trinity. Mary, then, is unique among all men and women in that she is daughter of the Father, mother of the Son, and bride of the Spirit. Since this unique relationship is implied by the primordial decree of the Incarnation itself, it is legitimate to say that God conceived the Virgin in the divine plan before all other creatures, save the sacred humanity of Christ. To put the argument another way: The divine maternity is a real relation to the person of the Incarnate Word; since the terminus of this relation is Christ Himself, this relation belongs to the hypostatic order and transcends the order of grace. The Blessed Virgin was thus predestined to be the Mother of God before she was predestined to the fullness of grace and glory. This argument need not assume Scotist or Suárezian accounts of the motive of the Incarnation – although it bears a certain consonance with them – the great Dominican Mariologist Réginald Garrigou-Lagrange articulated it in the context of a strict Cajetanian Thomism (Garrigou-Lagrange, 1949: 20–5).

Since God's decree of the Incarnation includes the decree to redeem men and women from sin, Mary's "fullness of grace" depends upon Christ's merits and not the hypostatic union itself. Theologically speaking, this *plenitudo gratiae* is formally contained in the angelic greeting, "Hail Mary, full of grace, the Lord is with thee" (Luke 1:28). Here, too, St Thomas Aquinas has a particularly useful explanation: "The more closely one approaches a principle, the more one participates in the effect which flows from it. Now Christ is the principle of grace; as God He is its author, as man He is its instrument. But the Virgin Mary was nearest to Christ in His humanity, because He assumed human nature from her. Thus she must have received from Him a greater fullness of grace than anyone else" (*Summa Theologiae* IIIa, q. 27, a. 5). Later scholastic theologians conceived Mary's *plenitudo gratiae* by analogy to the hypostatic union. If the hypostatic union substantially sanctified Christ's humanity in direct proportion to His infinite dignity as the Son of God, they reasoned, Christ must have enjoyed the fullest perfection of human being, even the beatific vision itself, since the lack of any positive perfection would be repugnant to the dignity of the hypostatic union. In an analogous way, such theologians felt that Mary must have enjoyed exceptional purity and holiness in direct proportion to her dignity as the Mother of God. Even if one reduces the angelic greeting to "favored one" for historical-critical reasons, one still must hold that the favors bestowed upon Mary were consonant with her dignity as Mother of God.

Mary's *plenitudo gratiae* thus stands midway between the holiness of her Son and the "fullness of grace," attributed by scripture to the Apostles and St Stephen (Acts 2:4, 6:8). Differences of opinion are the rule when Catholic theologians compare Mary's holiness to the holiness of the angels and the saints. Suárez, for example, argued that the Virgin's holiness exceeded the combined holiness of all the angels and saints (*De Mysteriis Vitae Christi*, d. 18, sect. 4). A few theologians have been guilty of exaggerations in this regard, variously attributing to Mary such things as the beatific vision or an infused knowledge of all natural truths. Unfortunately quite a few non-Catholic theologians, both Protestant and Orthodox, often take these aberrations to be Catholic dogma. In light of such misunderstandings, I should stress that Mary's fullness of grace does not entail that God blessed her with all supernatural prerogatives. That Mary did not have the beatific vision, for example, is proved by "Blessed art thou who has believed" (Luke 1:45). At best, a Roman Catholic theologian might, with Suárez, hold that Mary had a brief, but obscure, intuition of the Holy Trinity at the moment when she conceived, and later when she gave birth to Christ. Beyond these mystical graces, one might also suppose that the Virgin possessed many, if not all, of the gifts given to the ancient Church at Pentecost, such as healing, teaching, and tongues. Thomas Aquinas certainly felt that Mary possessed a special gift of contemplation, whereby she increased in grace and holiness until her death (*Summa Theologiae* IIIa, q. 27, a. 5).

Mary's negative prerogatives consist in the absence or removal of anything that is not consonant with her dignity as Mother of God. Traditionally, Catholic theologians have identified four such prerogatives: (1) her preservation from original sin, (2) her immunity from personal sin, (3) her freedom from "bodily defilement,"[1] and (4) her freedom from the dominion of death. These four negative prerogatives are expressed in four Marian dogmas: the Blessed Virgin's Immaculate Conception, her sinlessness, her perpetual virginity, and her bodily Assumption into heaven. Mary's positive prerogatives are particular privileges that God bestowed upon the Virgin according to her unique role as Mother of God, including her secondary mediatorship and her special place in Catholic devotion.

The dogma of the Immaculate Conception maintains that Mary's soul was preserved from the stain of original sin from the first moment of her existence. The Immaculate Conception does not refer to the procreative act of Sts Anne and Joachim – which may or may not have been undertaken with inordinate concupiscence – but rather to the creative act by which God infused her immaculate soul into her material body. Nor does the dogma teach that Mary was exempt from the universal necessity of the debt incurred by original sin (*debitum peccati originalis*). Catholic theologians also distinguish between proximate and remote debts. The *debitum remotum* is the universal debt of all who are born of Eve. At its most basic, such a debt signifies membership in the human race and the consequent need for redemption. The *debitum proximum*, on the other hand, is incurred by Adam's willful rejection of grace. While a few Scotist theologians argued that Mary incurred neither the *debitum remotum* nor the *debitum proximum*, most Catholic theologians argue that Mary's freedom from the *debitum proximum* is sufficient to guarantee the dogma. Most Catholic theologians, following Suárez, even think that Mary was subject to both debts logically speaking, even if she was miraculously preserved from both at the actual moment of her conception (*De Mysteriis Vitae Christi*, d. 3, sect. 2). Scotus remarks that Mary was a daughter of Adam in the order of nature (*ordo naturae*), but that her sanctification was simultaneous with her creation in the order of time (*ordo temporis*) (*In Sent. III*, d. 3, q. 1). Mary thus owes her *praeredemptio* or *redemptio anticipata* to the redemptive merits of Jesus Christ, whether or not one thinks that she incurred either debt.

The dogma of Mary's sinlessness develops largely from the dogma of the Immaculate

Conception and her consequent fullness of grace. Although the Council of Trent affirms that Mary, by a special divine privilege, was free from sin during her life (Session 6, can. 23), there is no small amount of debate about what the dogma actually entails. If one believes that concupiscence is a penalty of sin, then it goes without saying that the slightest *fomes peccati* cannot be found in the Virgin. If one believes, however, that concupiscence logically precedes sin, it remains licit to maintain that Mary's soul did possess the *fomes peccati*, even if she was preserved from any inordinate motions that might result because of it. Most Roman Catholic theologians, truth be told, would find this position perilous. Much the same can be said about the disputed question about whether the Virgin's sinlessness is analogous to the state of Adam and Eve's original justice. If one takes the *iustitia originalis* to refer to the entirety of those praeternatural and supernatural prerogatives that our first parents enjoyed in Eden, no analogy obtains. Unlike Adam and Eve, Mary was in need of a Redeemer, without whom she was subject to suffering and death. If original justice refers simply to perfect sanctity and holiness providentially appropriate to one's state in history, one might licitly assert not merely that Mary's sinlessless is analogous to the original justice of Adam and Eve, but even that it surpasses it. A final disputed question concerns whether Mary's freedom from sin (*impeccantia*) is the result of an inability to sin (*impeccabilitas*). Even if a Catholic theologian believes that the one entails the other, it still must be noted that the impeccability so gained is not the impeccability that belongs to God alone, nor the impeccability that the soul of Christ possesses by virtue of the hypostatic union, nor even the impeccability of the angels and the saints who enjoy the beatific vision. A perfect perseverance against mortal sin (even with an absolute confirmation against venial sin) would not preserve Mary from the defects that came into the world as a result of sin, insofar as these ordinary defects imply no moral imperfection. She felt pain when pricked.

The dogma of Mary's personal sinlessness presumes a perfect interior chastity on the part of the Virgin, a virginity of both the mind and senses. The dogma of Mary's perpetual virginity asserts that Mary also maintained perfect virginity not merely before the birth of Christ, but also during and after it. In this regard, Christ's virginal birth often presents greater difficulties to the believer than His virginal conception, since giving birth seems to entail parturition. The objection that Mary would not have had to be purified had not Christ opened her womb notwithstanding (Luke 2:23) – all that is required to account for this passage is that every first-born child be consecrated to God, not the *apertio vulvae et purgatio sanguinis* – Mary's *virginitas in partu* and *virginitas post partum* are dogmas distinct from the *virginitas in conceptione*. While the latter is established by the angelic greeting itself (Luke 1:30–1), the former two are established by a spiritual reading of Ezekiel: "And the Lord said; This gate shall be shut, it shall not be opened, and no man shall pass through it, because the Lord God of Israel has entered by it" (Ez 44:2). The dogma of Mary's perpetual virginity merely asserts the fact thereof, without determining how its finer details might be physiologically explained. Of course, the fathers and the schoolmen conceived the continuance of Mary's physical virginity as a miraculous birth in which her hymen remained intact. Modern theologians generally feel that Mary's perpetual virginity need not rest upon such miraculous preservation (Rahner, 1964b).

The dogma of Mary's Bodily Assumption teaches that through Christ's grace, the Virgin attained total victory over sin and its consequences, remained unharmed by the corruption of the tomb after her death, and was taken up to heaven body and soul to be united with her Son. While there is no explicit scriptural testimony to this doctrine – and the first 500 years of tradition are silent about the Virgin's death – Pius XII defined the dogma as an implication of the Protevangelium. His definition assumes that the Scotist notion of a most perfect redemption can be applied to St Paul's words, "When corruption has put on incorruption, then shall come to pass the saying that is written: Death is swallowed up in victory" (1 Cor 15:54). Perfect redemption, in other words, must entail perfect triumph. The bishops who supported the definition of the dogma at the First Vatican Council argued from other Pauline texts (Rom 5:8; 1 Cor 15:24–6; Heb 2:14–15). The opening of the graves of the saints at Christ's resurrection (Matt 27:52–3) certainly supports the possibility, although many, if not most, theologians would reject such an exotic reading of Matthew's Gospel. More commonly, theologians justified the dogma with an appeal to the Psalms, particularly "Thou wilt not give thy holy one to see corruption" (Ps 15:10 [Vulgate]), which was applied to Mary in a secondary sense because she was of one flesh with her divine Son. "Arise, O Lord, into thy resting place: thou and the ark, which thou hast sanctified" (Ps 131:8 [Vulgate]) and "Who is this that cometh up from the desert, flowing with delights, leaning upon her beloved?" (Cant 8:5) were read similarly. The dogma's chief theological argument was that it is unfitting that Mary, conceived immaculately and remaining pure, would be subject to the dominion of death and decay.

The Church has not defined Mary's last prerogative, her secondary mediation in the work of redemption, as dogma, causing some Catholics to clamor for the definition of a "fifth Marian dogma." (Presumably this method of counting assumes that Mary's sinlessness is included in either her Immaculate Conception or her perpetual virginity.) Before addressing the Virgin's role as an intermediary between Christ and other men and women, we should note that any such mediation depends entirely upon her divine motherhood. Her mediation, then, can only be a secondary and participated mediatorship (*meditatio participata sive secundaria*), whose graces derive solely from Christ's. For those who are counting Marian dogmas, the Second Vatican Council's Dogmatic Constitution on the Church defines Mary's cooperation in the work of redemption (*Lumen Gentium* nn. 58, 61); it is the dogmatic definition of the titles associated with such cooperation that is controversial, particularly *Mediatrix* and *Coredemptrix*. While these titles raise Protestant hackles, strictly speaking they entail no more than that Mary cooperated with God's grace in a unique way. A minimalist rendering of the doctrine, then, asserts only that Mary's voluntary concession made the Incarnation possible. More luxurious interpretations hold that Mary cooperated in the atonement, confected the divine victim in her womb, prepared Him as an oblation to be poured out upon Calvary, and/or offered Him for the salvation of mankind on the Cross. Such interpretations thereby liken Mary to a priest and her spiritual crucifixion to the trials of martyrdom. A fully maximalist reading, such as one finds in Sts Bernard of Siena (1380–1444) or Alphonsus Liguori ascribes to Mary a special mediation, such that she is the *dispensatrix omnium gratiarum* or *gratiarum aquaeductus*.

In any case, that Mary obtains graces for Christians and circulates them among the members of the mystical body has been the common teaching of the popes from Leo XIII to John Paul II. Leo XIII's encyclical on the Rosary says, "As no one can go to the Father except through the Son, so generally no one can draw near to Christ except through Mary" (*Octobri Mense*, n. 4). Here, too, an argument *ex convenientia* prevails. If the humanity of Christ is the instrumental cause of all grace (*Summa Theologiae* IIIa, q. 43, a. 2; q. 48, a. 6; q. 62, a. 5), it is fitting to think that Mary's sanctified flesh is a secondary instrumental cause by which all grace is distributed, as an immaculate heart circulates blood among the various members of the mystical body. Sometimes such maximalist renderings of the doctrine presume that Mary is also present in some undefined sense in the Eucharistic meal itself. The Virgin, it is said, cannot be a stranger to the mysterious vitality that we receive in the Eucharist, since her own body and blood became the body and blood of which we partake in Holy Communion.

Such are the outlines of the Church's teaching on the Blessed Virgin. Whether one's theological tastes incline to minimalism or maximalism, Roman Catholics have always seen in the Blessed Virgin a sign of the Church. Assumed bodily into heaven, Mary is the eschatological icon of our redemption, the face through which the light of Christ shines most fully, the Queen of Heaven and the Mother of all Christians. She is a model for all, religious or lay, priest or prophet, male or female. If we praise Mary to the heavens, it is because she is the one who drank most deeply of Christ's words, "Learn from me, for I am meek and lowly in heart" (Matt 11:29).

Note

1   Although "bodily defilement" is the traditional designation, it should in no way imply that conjugal relations are themselves defiling. The catchphrase rather assumes the absence of several phenomena that are incongruous with the Mother of God's dignity, including ritual defilement (Lk 2:22–4. Cf. Lev 12:2–8; Exod 13:2, 12) and pain in childbirth (cf. Gen 3:16).

References and Further Reading

Balthasar, Hans Urs von (1993) *Theo-Drama III: Theological Dramatic Theory: The Dramatis Personae*, trans. Graham Harrison. San Francisco, CA: Ignatius Press.

Brading, D.A. (2002) *Mexican Phoenix: Our Lady of Guadalupe: Image and Tradition Across Five Centuries*, 2nd edition. Cambridge: Cambridge University Press.

Brown, Peter (1988) *The Body and Society: Men, Women, and Sexual Renunciation in Early Christianity*. New York: Columbia University Press.

Cantalamessa, Raniero (1992) *Mary: Mirror of the Church*, trans. Frances Lonergan Villa. Collegeville, MN: Liturgical Press.

Carol, Juniper (ed.) (1955) *Mariology*, 3 vols. Milwaukee, WI: Bruce Publishing.

Daley, Brian E. (trans.) (1998) *On the Dormition of Mary: Early Patristic Homilies*, Crestwood, NY: St Vladimir's Seminary Press.

Gambero, Luigi (1999) *Mary and the Fathers of the Church*, trans. Thomas Buffer. San Francisco, CA: Ignatius Press.

Gambero, Luigi (2005) *Mary in the Middle Ages*, trans. Thomas Buffer. San Francisco, CA: Ignatius Press.

Garrigou-Lagrange, Réginald, OP (1949) *The Mother of the Saviour and Our Interior Life*, trans. Bernard J. Kelly. St Louis, MO: Herder.

John Paul II (1987) *Mary: God's Yes to Man*. San Francisco, CA: Ignatius Press.

Johnson, Elizabeth A. (2003) *Truly Our Sister: A Theology of Mary in the Communion of Saints*. New York: Continuum International Publishing Group.

Pelikan, Jaroslav (1996) *Mary through the Centuries: Her Place in the History of Culture*. New Haven, CT: Yale University Press.

Poole, Stafford (1996) *Our Lady of Guadalupe: The Origin and Sources of a Mexican National Symbol 1531–1797*. Tucson: University of Arizona Press.

Rahner, Karl (1964a) "Visions and Prophecies," in *Inquiries*, trans. Charles Henkey and Richard Strachan. New York: Herder and Herder, 88–188.

Rahner, Karl (1964b) "Virginitas in Partu," in *Theological Investigations*, vol. 4. Baltimore, MD: Helicon Press, 134–64.

Scheeben, Matthias J. (1946–7) *Mariology*, 2 vols., trans. T.L.M.J. Geukers. St Louis, MO: Herder.

CHAPTER 22
Church

Avery Cardinal Dulles

Foundations and Development

The Christian Church from the beginning understood herself as emerging from ancient Israel and as being the New Israel, that is to say, the people of God of the New Covenant. Catholics recognize Jesus Christ as the founder of the Church, not simply as the person upon whom the Church was founded. Jesus did not establish the Church all at once but, as it were, piece by piece. He did so by proclaiming the Kingdom of God, by gathering disciples, then by selecting an inner group of 12 Apostles to whom he gave special instruction in the mysteries of the Kingdom. He organized them under Peter as the chief Apostle, to whom he entrusted the "power of the keys." The New Testament records his institution of the great sacraments of baptism and the Eucharist, to be celebrated after his departure. Some of the Fathers saw the flowing of blood and water from the side of the crucified Christ as the true birth of the Church, analogous to the birth of Eve from the side of the sleeping Adam. In his risen life, Jesus gave the Apostles the mandate to spread the Gospel to all nations of the earth. But the Church did not function as a living and life-giving organism until Pentecost, when the Spirit descended in the form of fiery tongues upon the 120 disciples, including the Apostles, the holy women, and other close disciples.

The Church, even though she began to exist at Pentecost or even earlier, was still in a state of infancy throughout the first generation, as we can gather from the New Testament. Her Scriptures, creeds, sacraments, and ministerial structures were still gradually taking form with the help of the Holy Spirit. Only by stages did the Church become a social body fully distinct from Judaism and the Synagogue. The apostolic council of Jerusalem, recounted in the fifteenth chapter of Acts, was a crucial turning point in this process.

The New Testament, composed for the most part in the second half of the first century, does not contain a thematic ecclesiology, but the Church figures in every writing. The various books express a common faith together with different perspectives on the Church. The Gospel of Matthew emphasizes the status of Jesus as the new Moses legislating for the new People of God and giving a share of his authority to Peter and the Twelve. Luke and Acts portray the missionary expansion of the Church under the dynamic leading of the Holy Spirit. The Johannine writings insist on the mystical union among the believers and between them and the divine persons. Paul dwells by preference on the image of the Body of Christ and on the various vocations by which the faithful build up the Body in unity. The post-Pauline Pastoral Letters show the transition to the sub-apostolic age, when the Church became responsible for preserving the apostolic deposit of faith, sacraments, and ministry. The Letter to the Hebrews depicts the Church as the People of the New Covenant, a pilgrim people undergoing persecution but confident of final victory. The First Letter of Peter portrays all the baptized as citizens of a new priestly Kingdom. And finally, the Book of Revelation holds forth the vision of the New Jerusalem, the glorious Church decked out as a Bride to meet her heavenly Spouse.

In the first few centuries the Church acquired a certain maturity. She became a network of local and regional churches that maintained communion with one another, recognizing each others' professions of faith, pastors, sacraments, and members. All the particular churches had their own bishops, who were subject to the metropolitan bishops and patriarchs of their respective regions. The center of communion for the entire body of churches (the Church Catholic) was the see of Rome, the city where the chief Apostles had shed their blood for the faith and where Peter had for some years exercised his ministry as universal pastor.

As soon as the imperial persecutions came to an end, the bishops were free to hold universal councils to deal with problems confronting the Church as a whole. Beginning with Nicea (325) the early ecumenical councils settled a number of debated points of faith and Church order. They gave permanent shape to the Church's trinitarian and Christological faith. Under the supervision of the bishops and local councils of the East and West, the Church drew up an agreed canon of Holy Scripture. Thanks to the decisions of councils and letters of prominent bishops, many important points about sacraments and ministry, including papal primacy, were also clarified. By about the fifth century the Catholic Church had taken on the salient features that have characterized her ever since. Ecclesiology in the patristic era developed in great part in response to heresies of the day. In the second century Irenaeus emphasized the apostolicity of the Church in opposition to the innovations of the Gnostics. In the third century Cyprian accented the unitive role of the pope and the bishops in opposition to rigorist Novatian schismatics in North Africa. In the fourth and fifth centuries the great Fathers of the Eastern Church (Cyril of Jerusalem, Gregory of Nyssa, Cyril of Alexandria, and others) found in the Church a mystical union of Christians with the Lord mediated by the sacraments. In the same period Western Fathers such as Hilary, Ambrose, and Augustine likewise reflected on the Church as Christ's mystical Body, but did so with greater attention to her social structures. In controversy with the Donatists, Augustine insists on the catholicity or worldwide unity of the Church. In his great work *De Civitate Dei* he seems to identify the Church with the City of God, while admitting that the Church on earth is a mixed community, not all of whose members are predestined to eternal glory. Augustine remained the great master for medieval Western theologians and even for Luther and Calvin in the sixteenth century (Jay, 1980: 84–92).

In the Middle Ages the political rivalries between the Eastern and Western Empires, together with the domination of large parts of the Mediterranean by the Turks, made it very difficult to maintain unity between Greece and Rome. After a series of misunderstandings and interruptions of communion, Catholics and Orthodox became separated in 1054 by a breach that has never yet been healed.

The doctrine of the Church continued to develop in the West through the activity of popes and councils, canon lawyers and theologians. Monastic theologians cultivated a mystical and contemplative ecclesiology on the basis of biblical metaphors, but cared little for systematic rigor. Thomas Aquinas, the leading representative of university theology, discusses the Church rather briefly in his *Summa Theologiae* under the topic of Christology. Christ, he says, has a "grace of headship" that flows down into men and angels, making them members of his Mystical Body (*Summa Theologiae*, III. 8. 1–4). Thomas treats other aspects of the Church here and there throughout his works.

In the High and Late Middle Ages ecclesiology underwent further elaboration. The permanence of apostolic authority and the necessity of sacramental mediation were emphasized in reaction to the Albigensian and Waldensian heresies and the millenarist enthusiasm of Joachim of Fiore and the Franciscan Spirituals. Papal lawyers and theologians magnified papal authority in their refutations of the parliamentary leanings of the Conciliarist party.

The earliest treatises on the Church, in the Late Middle Ages, dealt chiefly with the tensions between the temporal and spiritual powers – in other words, between the Emperor and the Pope. Under pressure of this controversy, Catholic theologians tended to define the Church rather legalistically in terms of her jurisdictional powers.

In response to Wycliffe, Hus, and the Protestant Reformers, some of whom depicted the Church as an invisible communion of souls who were predestined to the life of glory, Catholic controversialists such as Robert Bellarmine insisted on the Church's visibility as an organized international society under the supreme authority of the Pope as Vicar of Christ. In the seventeenth and eighteenth centuries, the Gallicans in France, and their counterparts in Austria and Germany, known respectively as Josephinists and Febronians, sought to subject papal determinations to the approval or veto of national hierarchies. These decentralizing tendencies were opposed by "Ultramontane" Catholics, who upheld the primatial authority of the Holy See.

At the First Vatican Council (1869–70) the Ultramontane party was successful in obtaining the definition of papal primacy of jurisdiction and papal infallibility. The definitions were moderately worded so as to take account of the concerns of thoughtful bishops who insisted that the Pope is under the Gospel and is bound to uphold the divinely given structures of the Church.

Over and above its pronouncements on the papacy, Vatican I planned to enact a comprehensive ecclesiology. A "Dogmatic Constitution on the Church" was prepared, but the draft never came to the floor because the Council had to be abruptly prorogued upon the outbreak of the Franco-Prussian war. The various drafts of that schema continued to be studied after the Council and furnished material for the ecclesiological encyclicals of Leo XIII and especially the great encyclical of Pius XII, *Mystici Corporis Christi* (1943).

The Second Vatican Council (1962–5), taking up where Vatican I had left off, decided to focus its agenda primarily on the Church: what the Church is and does, and how it is related to other realities in the world. Nearly all the documents of Vatican II dealt in one way or another with the Church. Its principal document was the Dogmatic Constitution *Lumen Gentium*, which constitutes a relatively complete treatise on the Church as officially understood in contemporary Catholicism. In its third chapter, *Lumen Gentium* made several dogmatically important statements about the episcopate. This contribution will be considered in the systematic section of this chapter, which will follow the main lines of *Lumen Gentium*.

Nature of the Church

Pius XII in *Mystici Corporis* had taught quite simply that the Church is the Mystical Body of Christ (MC 13; Carlen, 1981: 39). Catholics continue to recognize this identity, but Vatican II made it clear that the Body of Christ is only one of a number of biblical images. The Church may also be described by other analogies such as the new People of God, the flock of Christ, the Bride, and the Temple of the Holy Spirit. The idea of the Body expresses the profound unity between the members and Christ. Taken alone, it could give the impression that all the actions of the Church have Christ as their subject. But other images, such as People of God and Bride, bring out relative autonomy and potential opposition between the community and her divine Lord. As a free covenant partner, the Church may on occasion be less than faithful. Since the Church as a mystery eludes clear definition or description, a plurality of images serves better than any single one to express her nature (Dulles, 2002).

According to Vatican II the Church is a complex reality made up of visible and invisible elements. She is both a visible assembly and a spiritual communion (LG 8). The society equipped with hierarchical agencies is subordinate to the mystical communion of grace, somewhat as the humanity of Christ serves the person of the Word, as his living instrument. The two aspects of the Church do not perfectly coincide, but they are not two Churches, as some have imagined. There is no merely visible or merely invisible Church. The one Church has visible and invisible facets.

Some theologians have portrayed the Church as a continuation of the Incarnation. The analogy of the Incarnation is useful inasmuch as it brings out a real resemblance, but the kind of union between the Body and the Head is different in the two cases. Although Christ is always truly present in her, the Church is not hypostatically united to the person of the Son as was the human nature of Christ. In *Mystici Corporis* Pius XII warned against the exaggerations of those who fail to distinguish between the physical and the social Body of Christ and who depict the divine Redeemer and the members of the Church as coalescing into one person (MC 86; Carlen, 1981: 54). The union is not physical but, precisely, mystical.

Other theologians like to think of the Church as a kind of incarnation of the Holy Spirit. This pneumatological analogy, like the Christological one just examined, is useful up to a point. The Spirit may be called by analogy the Church's "soul," but the analogy should not be pressed too far. The Spirit of Christ dwells in the Church, guides and directs her, but the Spirit does not become incarnate. It is the nature of the Spirit to be present in other persons; to be, as Heribert Mühlen puts it, "one person in many persons." The Church is a multitude of persons, who together constitute what Thomas Aquinas called "one mystical person" (*Summa Theologiae* III.48.2 ad 1; Mühlen, 1968: 40–4).

Exploiting what is probably the most fruitful analogy, Vatican II spoke of the Church as "sacrament." No fewer than ten times it asserts that the Church is, in Christ, a kind of sacrament: a universal sacrament of communion and salvation (LG 1, 9, 48, 59; SC 5, 28; GS 42, 45; AG 1, 5). This theme, which had become popular in several countries, was greatly favored by German authors in the years leading up to Vatican II. They promoted it most vigorously at the Council (Semmelroth, 1953; Boff, 1972; Wassilowsky, 2001).

The term "sacrament" is a technical one, taken over from sacramental theology, in which it refers to certain specific rites of the Church. In a more general sense, a sacrament is a divinely instituted visible sign and bearer of invisible grace. Jesus Christ himself is the great sacrament of God. The Church is a sign and instrument of the living Christ. In her sign-aspect, the Church represents God's saving plan for humanity. In her capacity as an instrument, she is used by him as a means of salvation. The Church is a sign, a means, and a fruit of grace. Christ is really and mysteriously present in her through the Holy Spirit.

Vatican II nowhere directly states that the Church is a communion (Saier, 1973). But the Extraordinary Assembly of the Synod of Bishops of 1985, after describing the Church as a sacrament, asserted: "The ecclesiology of communion is the central and fundamental idea of the Council's documents" (II C 1; Synod, 1985: 448). To speak of the Church as a communion is not to deny that she is a sacrament. Since the sacrament is a sign and instrument of communion, the Church cannot exist in the absence of communion. Communion arises because the members are united to one another and to God by a multiplicity of bonds, especially the interior bonds of grace and charity. The notion of communion expresses one facet of the Church but does not fully convey her nature. As sacrament the Church is a sign and instrument of communion. As a sign she expresses the communion that already exists in her, and as an instrument she strives to intensify and extend communion. Christ gave her a mission to reach out to the whole world, so that as many people as possible may be part of this sacred fellowship.

One of the major problems confronting the Second Vatican Council was to clarify the relationship between the Church of Christ and the Roman Catholic communion. Pius XII had taught that the two were identical in *Mystici Corporis* (MC 13; Carlen, 1981: 39) and even more emphatically in his 1950 encyclical *Humani Generis* (HG 27; Carlen, 1981: 179). But Pius XII's treatment of the problem failed to give an adequate account of the ecclesial status of other Christian bodies and their members. Are non-Catholic Christians in any sense incorporated into Christ's Church? Do they enjoy a status distinct from that of non-Christians? Or can they, like pagans, be united to her only by some positive relationship? Pius XII seemed to suggest that non-Catholic Christians did not belong to the Church except by virtue of a desire (or *votum*) – one that might be merely implicit and unconscious (MC 103; Carlen, 1981: 58).

Since the third century the Catholic Church has formally recognized that sacraments such as baptism can validly be administered in churches separated from Rome.

With a quotation from St Paul (Col 2:12), Vatican II affirmed that every valid baptism truly incorporates the recipient into the crucified and glorified Christ (UR 22). Because the Church is the Body of Christ, all baptized Christians should be seen as having at least an inchoate membership in her. Baptism is the first step in a process that leads to full incorporation. To be fully incorporated one must accept the entire system of Catholic teaching and polity (LG 14).

Sacramental ecclesiology enables communities separated from Rome to be seen as being in their own measure ecclesial. The Church is made up of a number of elements or endowments, including both interior gifts such as sanctifying grace, charity, and the gifts and fruits of the Holy Spirit and external gifts such as sacraments, Scriptures, doctrines, ministries, and forms of worship. Thanks to their ecclesial endowments, non-Roman Catholic Churches and ecclesial communities have a true salvific significance and can serve as channels of grace for their members (UR 3 and 4). The Council set no limits on what the Holy Spirit can achieve in these ecclesial communities by way of sanctification. Some of their members have been faithful to Christ even to the shedding of their blood (LG 15).

Vatican II thus found a way of acknowledging the ecclesial status of other Christians while continuing to affirm that the Church of Christ is present in her completeness in the Catholic Church. The Church of Christ, it declared, "subsists in" (*subsistit in*) the community governed by the bishops in union with the successor of Peter (LG 8). The meaning of the term "subsists" has been debated. Some interpret it as meaning simply "is present." But recent research shows that the term was adopted to replace "is present" ("*adest*"), which seemed too weak, in an earlier draft. According to the clear intention of those who proposed the term, it means to continue to exist in its substantial completeness (Teuffenbach, 2002: 380–8).

The final wording was chosen to exclude the idea that the unity of the Church had been shattered and that the true Church no longer existed anywhere on earth. Nor did the Council admit that the true Church is just an aggregation of elements found in a variety of denominations. On the contrary, it reaffirmed the teaching of *Mystici Corporis* that the totality of the Church of Christ continues to be present within her and nowhere else, while at the same time granting that other communities may possess elements of the true Church and enjoy a measure of communion with her. The more they have of authentic Christianity, the more closely are they bound to the Catholic Church.

Properties of the Church

Catholic theology takes from the Nicene-Constantinopolitan Creed the belief that the Church is by her very nature one, holy, catholic, and apostolic.

The Church is and must be *one* because all the members are in communion with one another and with Christ their Head. To the extent that they are united to the true Church they share the same faith, the same Scriptures, and the same sacramental rites. United under the same set of pastors, they constitute a single social body that extends all over the world. They look upon one another as brothers and sisters in Christ.

The Church is *holy* because she is united to Christ her Head and to the Holy Spirit. Her doctrines, sacraments, and ministries are objectively holy (or "sacred") because they are supernatural gifts coming from God and conveying the grace of God. All who receive the sacraments with the right dispositions, and who sincerely profess, and faithfully abide by the teachings of Christ and the Church, are sanctified by the Holy Spirit and are personally holy (or "saintly").

The Church is *catholic* because she has from the Lord a commission to proclaim the Gospel to all nations, to baptize them, and to bring them into the family of God. The tendency to expand and take in people of every race and class is not sheer obedience to an external command. Catholicity is an inner dimension of the Church's own life. Like other living organisms, she strives to become in manifest actuality what she already is by nature and intent: the universal sacrament of salvation.

The Church is *apostolic* because she passes on to all generations and regions of the earth the gifts that the first Apostles received from Christ. She perseveres in their teaching, shares their faith, and perpetuates their ministry. The bishops who govern her are the successors of the Apostles. The Pope, as universal primate, succeeds to the office of Peter.

These four attributes belong to the Church of Christ, and therefore "subsist" in the Catholic Church as gifts she can never lose. But the Church can realize them more or less perfectly in her historical actuality. When the members fully share her faith and are spiritually united to pastors who are orthodox and holy, the Church has greater unity and holiness than when this is not the case. The actual catholicity of the Church is imperfect to the extent that there are whole nations and sociocultural regions that do not accept her faith and ministrations. Her apostolicity is strengthened to the extent that her leaders and members adhere to the teaching, sacramental life, ministries, and mission of the Apostles.

Structures of the Church

According to the Catholic understanding, all the members of the Church are equal in their dignity as sons and daughters of God. They share the same baptismal grace and the same vocation to holiness and eternal life. But there are diversities of calling within the one body. Jesus in his public ministry called only Twelve to be Apostles, and within the college of the Twelve he gave Peter the first place and the power of the keys. He also promised that the Church would never perish and that he would remain with her apostolic leaders throughout all ages. As the Apostles died off and as the Church expanded, it became necessary to provide official leaders who would carry on the tasks of Peter and the Twelve. The Apostles took care of this need by ordaining suitable members of the community to collaborate with them and eventually take their place. The initial stages of this process are recorded in the New Testament, particularly in the Acts of the Apostles and in the Pastoral Epistles (1 and 2 Timothy; Titus).

In current Catholic teaching bishops are understood as priests who through ordination have received the fullness of the sacrament of orders (LG 21; cf. John Paul II, 2003: nos. 6 and 8). The bishop of Rome, as the successor of Peter, exercises primacy in teaching and government over the whole Church, and hence also over the other bishops. Bishops who are in full communion with him and with one another constitute the episcopal college, which enjoys, together with the Pope and never without him, the plenitude of authority to teach and govern. The college of bishops is not an association of strict equals but one in which the head has primacy over the other members. The college cannot act except with and under its head, the bishop of Rome. He must call the whole body of bishops into collegiate action or at least approve of their collective acts. Acts of the college have no force unless the Pope, as the principal member of the college, approves of them. This point, already made in *Lumen Gentium*, 22, was further clarified in the "Prefactory Note of Explanation" appended to the third chapter of *Lumen Gentium* (Tagle, 2004: 227–67).

Although the other members of the episcopal college have no powers apart from the Pope or in opposition to him, their cooperation with him is meaningful. At an ecumenical council, for example, the acts proceed not from the Pope alone but from the whole body, all of whom act as responsible pastors in hierarchical communion with one another. Acting as they do in concert, each benefits from the input of the others into their conjoint action. The resulting acts have a solemnity and a practical impact exceeding that which normally accrues to the acts of a pope alone.

The collegial relationship among the bishops is expressed not only in formally collegiate actions involving the entire college but also in collective actions of groups of bishops who are in hierarchical communion with one another and with the Holy See. The Synod of Bishops, established by Pope Paul VI during the Second Vatican Council, provides an example of this "collegial spirit" or "affective collegiality" (La Tour, 2004). The Synod normally meets about every third year in Rome. Its assemblies include the Pope, a representation of bishops from the Roman Curia, elected representatives from bishops' conferences in the various nations, and a few bishops appointed by the Holy See. Since the Synod involves only a relatively small proportion of the world's bishops it cannot speak for the college as a whole. It serves as a forum for an exchange of views, for advising the Holy See, and for issuing documents registering a consensus. Rather frequently, assemblies of the Synod of Bishops have been followed by Apostolic Exhortations signed by the Pope. In these post-synodal exhortations the Pope gives his own synthesis of the conclusions reached by the assembly and approved by him.

The papacy, as the universal governing authority, has ultimate responsibility for the selection and appointment of bishops. By ordination and hierarchical communion, bishops become members of the universal college, and by a process known as "canonical mission" they receive a special assignment from the supreme government of the Church. Some are assigned to particular churches as diocesan bishops, coadjutor bishops, or auxiliary bishops. Bishops who are not placed in charge of dioceses are as a matter of convention assigned to titular sees (ancient sees that are today extinct).

The Church is made up not only of individual persons but also of particular churches, each governed by its diocesan bishop. The diocesan church is not a mere administrative district of the universal Church. According to the insight of Vatican II, each particular church reproduces in itself the features of the Church as a whole. The most vivid actualization of the Church occurs when the people of a diocese are gathered at a Eucharistic celebration together with their bishop, who presides with the assistance of his clergy (priests and deacons). Vatican II reiterated this point in several important texts (SC 41–2; LG 26; CD 11).

In the day-to-day life of the faithful, the parish church is the normal place where the Church is most keenly experienced. It is there that they normally hear the proclamation of the word of God and receive the sacraments. Pastors of parishes are priests appointed by the diocesan bishop.

In the course of time the Church has developed certain supradiocesan agencies, which exist by ecclesiastical law. In the ancient Church the apostolic sees (those that could trace their genealogy to Apostles) enjoyed particular authority, as did the patriarchates of Rome, Alexandria, Antioch, Jerusalem, and (later) Constantinople. The only apostolic and patriarchal Church in the West is that of Rome. The other four ancient patriarchates fell into disunion with Rome and are today located in predominantly Muslim regions. For Catholics, therefore, Rome counts as the Apostolic See *par excellence*.

The major urban sees have archbishops or metropolitan bishops, who enjoy a certain degree of authority over the other sees of their province, which are known as suffragan sees. From time to time supradiocesan synods or councils are held, in which a number of bishops, together with representatives of other clergy and laity, legislate and make pastoral provisions for the churches in the region. The bishops of an entire nation sometimes hold national councils, such as the three Plenary Councils of Baltimore in the nineteenth century.

Since Vatican II, episcopal conferences have been set up all over the world and have practically taken the place of particular councils (Reese, 1989). Every bishop is a member of one such conference, which normally includes all the bishops of a given nation or group of nations. In the United States, for example, all bishops are members of the United States Conference of Catholic Bishops. The episcopal conference is primarily an organ for pastoral consultation among the bishops of a region, but it can issue binding decrees under certain circumstances specified by law.

The Church is not by any means complete with the clergy. Bishops, priests, and deacons are ordained for the service of the entire People of God. The Church as a whole, including every one of its members, shares in the threefold office of Christ as prophet, priest, and king. All together constitute "a chosen race, a royal priesthood, a holy nation, God's own people," called out of darkness into God's marvelous light (cf. 1 Peter 2:9). As members of that priestly people, the laity participate in official worship of the Church, including the offering of holy Mass. Lay persons are entitled to receive the word of God and the sacraments, and have a responsibility to disseminate the light of Christ in the world by word and by example. The ecclesial status of the laity, treated in chapter 4 of *Lumen Gentium*, was set forth at greater length by Vatican II in its Decree on the Apostolate of the Laity, *Apostolicam Actuositatem*, and by John Paul II in his Apostolic Exhortation *Christifideles Laici* (Miller, 1998: 331–462).

In its teaching on the laity, Vatican Council II emphasized that, while they laudably perform certain ministries within the Church, their vocation has a certain "secular" quality (LG 31). Their primary and distinctive responsibility is to bring the light and strength of the Gospel to bear upon the world by their activities in the home, the neighborhood, the workplace, and the public square. They can bring the influence of Christ into areas where the clergy cannot easily penetrate, and by so doing serve the salvific mission of Christ and the Church.

The division of the Catholic faithful into clergy and laity is adequate, in the sense that every Catholic is either the one or the other and can never be both. But the Church accords a special status to members of religious institutes and institutes of the consecrated life, whether their members are canonically clerical or lay. Some such institutes are primarily contemplative, in that they emphasize prayer and worship; others are primarily active, in their dedication to the apostolate; still others pursue a combination of the contemplative and the active, seeking to hand on to others the fruits of their contemplation. Distinctive to the consecrated life is the profession of the three vows (or counsels) of chastity, poverty, and obedience for the sake of a more intimate union with Christ. Pope John Paul II, in his Apostolic Exhortation on the Consecrated Life, pointed out that this state is "an integral part of the Church's life and a much needed incentive toward ever greater fidelity to the Gospel" (VC 3). Whether they are canonically in the lay or the clerical state, consecrated persons are set apart by their commitment to a particular way of life. Jesus Christ himself observed the evangelical counsels and recommended them as a way of life to his close disciples.

Functions of the Church

In contemporary Catholic theology it is customary to expound the functions of the Church in relation to the threefold office of Christ as prophet, priest, and king. These offices, as understood in Scripture and in the theological tradition, are not fully separable from one another; they interpenetrate. The royalty of Christ is priestly, as is his prophetic calling. As prophet, he reveals the Father, overthrows the power of Satan, and undergoes a sacrificial death on the Cross, which is eminently priestly.

The Church exists in order to perpetuate the saving ministry of Christ in all three of its aspects. First of all, she stands in the world as a prophet, called to proclaim the message that Christ has entrusted to her. The whole Church is called to remind the world of its need for redemption and to herald the good news that redemption is available through Jesus Christ. The more exact verbal articulation of the Christian message takes the form of doctrine. To formulate the public or official doctrine of the Church is the special task of the hierarchy: that is to say, the Pope and the bishops. When controversies arise within the Church, the Pope and the bishops have the responsibility to render judgment, clarifying what must, may, or may not be held within the Church. Their "Magisterium" is their power to preach and teach in the name of Christ the Lord. Without a Magisterium the Church would have no way of publicly articulating her faith and dissociating herself from heterodox opinions. She would degenerate into a loosely knit private association of individual believers and would be unable to maintain a definite stand based on revelation as distinct from the spirit of the age.

The second function of the Church is the priestly. She offers worship to God in and through Christ, the great High Priest. The official worship of the Church (her liturgy) is centered in the sacraments. The two major sacraments are those of baptism, by which the Church acquires new members, and the Eucharist, by which she offers the supreme sacrifice of Christ and nourishes the faithful with his Body and Blood in Holy Communion.

All Christians by reason of their baptism enjoy a share in the royal priesthood of Christ. But for certain official acts of worship, such as the Eucharist, it is necessary to have a minister who stands over against the community, speaking and acting in the person of Christ. Priestly ordination by a bishop in the apostolic succession confers this power. The Second Vatican Council clearly teaches that the ordained priesthood differs from the common priesthood of the baptized not merely in degree but in nature or "essence" (LG 10). The ordained ministry does not make its recipient a superior person but renders him capable of performing certain types of service for the benefit of the People of God. The priest is ordained to lead the people in prayer and worship and to minister to them by word and sacrament.

The ministerial priesthood should not be understood as though it were a personal prerogative of the ordained. Diocesan priests are ordained to assist their bishop in his spiritual service toward the diocese. They are in hierarchical communion with him and with their fellow priests. Each diocese has a presbyteral college, which is related to the diocesan bishop analogously in the way that the college of bishops is related to the Pope. The analogy limps, however, because the priests have a lower degree of the sacrament of orders than their bishop, whereas the Pope and the bishops have the same degree of the sacrament of orders.

The third principal function of the Church is that of ruling in the name of Christ. In a sense the whole Church shares in the royal office, because baptism brings its recipients into Christ's Kingdom and makes them fellow laborers in service of the Kingdom. The Pope and the bishops, as hierarchical leaders, have the responsibility of ruling in the name of Christ. The Pope is Christ's vicar for the universal Church, and the bishops are Christ's vicars for their particular churches (LG 27). They have authority from Christ to issue commands to the faithful that are binding in conscience. Other members of the clergy and, on occasion, lay persons may receive governing powers by delegation from the hierarchy.

The whole Church, clergy and lay faithful together, has a responsibility to extend the Kingdom of Christ. Although the Church has no jurisdiction over states and nations, she uses her influence to promote a social order marked by freedom, peace, justice, and charity. In this task the contribution of the lay faithful is indispensable.

Finality of the Church

The Church as sacrament is a sign and instrument of that which God intends to signify and effect through her. The Second Vatican Council uses a variety of terms to designate this reality. It speaks, for example, of communion with God and among the members themselves, of the realization of the Kingdom, and of salvation or sanctification. These are not three distinct goals, but three ways of describing one and the same goal under different aspects.

Communion, as that term is used in contemporary Catholic theology, refers especially to a mysterious interior union among persons who participate in the supernatural

life brought into the world by Christ. All who share in the grace of Christ enjoy a wonderful solidarity with one another and with the Lord. This solidarity, hidden from
human sight, is discerned by the eyes of faith and gives rise to mutual charity. Jesus
speaks of the loving union of his disciples at some length in his discourse at the Last
Supper: "The glory that thou hast given to me I have given to them, that they may be
one even as we are one, I in them and thou in me, that they may become perfectly one,
so that the world may know that thou hast loved them even as thou hast loved me"
(John 17:22–3).

The Kingdom of God is a term often used by Jesus in his public ministry. The Kingdom became present on earth in Christ's very person; it extends beyond him to include
the whole new order that results from his saving presence. According to Vatican II the
Church is "the Kingdom now present in mystery" (LG 3). Already here on earth she is
the initial budding forth of the Kingdom (LG 5), but the Kingdom will not be complete
until the Church enters into glory at the end of history, when Christ returns to transform all things.

Although the Kingdom is present in the Church, it is also at work beyond her visible
borders, wherever Christ's grace is operative. The Church seeks to serve the Kingdom
and to contribute to its full realization, and in so doing she disseminates the grace of
Christ in the world. She "prays and labors in order that the entire world may become
the People of God, the Body of the Lord, and the Temple of the Holy Spirit" (LG 17).

Salvation in Holy Scripture signifies the fullness of life for which human beings are
made. Salvation is to be achieved not by unaided human effort but by actively receiving God's gifts through his Son. Faith, as an attitude of receptivity and responsiveness
to the word of God, is the foundation of all salvation. In this life we can receive the first
fruits of salvation, but for the plenitude we must await the life beyond death.

In the documents of Vatican II, the Church is several times described as the "universal sacrament of salvation" (LG 48; AG 1; GS 45). As a sacrament the Church is an
efficacious sign – a sign that is also an instrument. The Church, as an instrument used
by Christ for the redemption of all (LG 9), is necessary for salvation (LG 14; AG 7). She
is an essential link in God's saving plan.

The gift of God's grace produces in all who receive it an "ordination" to the Church.
Those who are not already members of the Church will be oriented toward her if they
are faithful to this inner inclination. If and when her teaching is credibly proclaimed
to them, they will wish to join her. Those who never have the opportunity to join may
be saved if they cooperate with the graces given to them. They can be saved through
their "ordination" toward the Church, even though they are not conscious of it. If they
are baptized, they are already in the Church, at least initially, and on the way to full
incorporation. Thus there is no salvation strictly outside the Church. In that sense the
ancient axiom "extra Ecclesiam nulla salus" still holds true.

Here on earth, the Church seeks to bring her own members to salvation and to
overcome in them anything that could be an impediment to God's saving grace. The
Church makes her own the saying of Paul: "This is the will of God, your sanctification" (1 Thess 4:3). Regarding nothing more important than holiness, the Church
ceaselessly reminds them of the saying of Jesus: "You, therefore, must be perfect as
your heavenly Father is perfect" (Matt 5:48). All the structures and ministrations of

the Church are intended to serve and facilitate the salvation and sanctification of the world. To emphasize this point Vatican II's Constitution on the Church devoted its entire fifth chapter to "The Universal Call to Holiness in the Church."

Salvation and sanctification should not be understood in a purely individualistic way. It its seventh chapter the Constitution on the Church taught that the Church still awaits the time of the restoration of all things, when she herself will enter into the glory of heaven. Only then will the true but imperfect holiness of the Church on earth yield to the desired goal. Fully purified, the Church will be what Christ willed her to be: "without spot or wrinkle or any such thing" (Eph 5:27). This transformation will not be the dissolution of the Church but her completion and fulfillment: she will become in fact what on earth she is only in hope and in promise.

In the most comprehensive sense the Church exists in three phases. Here on earth she is the pilgrim Church, the Church militant, "proceeding on its pilgrim way amidst the persecutions of the world and the consolations of God" (LG 8). In the hereafter those who are still undergoing purification on the passage to blessedness compose the Church suffering. And those who are already with the Lord belong to the glorious or triumphant Church. The three are not three Churches but three states of the same Church, intrinsically linked with one another.

In her liturgy the Church on earth sings the praises of God in union with all the saints and angels. We below ask for their intercession, and they intercede for us with our heavenly Advocate, the risen Lord. Most of all in the Eucharistic sacrifice we are united to the worshiping Church in heaven, with which we join in venerating the memory of the ever-Virgin Mary and the blessed saints and martyrs (cf. LG 50). The separation among the three states of the Church is to some degree overcome. We who are still pilgrims experience an anticipation and a first installment of the glory that is to be.

Abbreviations

AG   Vatican II, Decree *Ad Gentes*
CD   Vatican II, Decree *Christus Dominus*
GS   Vatican II, Pastoral Constitution *Gaudium et Spes*
HG   Encyclical of Pius XII, *Humani Generis*, 1950
LG   Vatican II, Dogmatic Constitution *Lumen Gentium*
MC   Encyclical of Pius XII, *Mystici Corporis Christi*, 1943
SC   Vatican II, Constitution *Sacrosanctum Concilium*
UR   Vatican II, Decree *Unitatis Redintegratio*
VC   Apostolic Exhortation of John Paul II, *Vita Consecrata*, 1996

References and Further Reading

Abbott, Walter M. (ed.) (1966) *The Documents of Vatican II*. New York: America Press.
Aquinas, Thomas, *Summa Theologiae*. Any edition.

Boff, Leonardo (1972) *Die Kirche als Sakrament im Horizont der Welterfahrung*. Paderborn: Bonifacius.

Carlen, Claudia (ed.) (1981) *The Papal Encyclicals 1939–1958*. Wilmington, NC: Consortium.

Dulles, Avery, Cardinal (2002) *Models of the Church*. Expanded edition. New York: Doubleday.

John Paul II, Pope (2003) Post-Synodal Apostolic Exhortation *Pastores Gregis*. Vatican City: Libreria Editrice Vaticana.

Jay, Eric G. (1980) *The Church: Its Changing Image through Twenty Centuries*. Atlanta, GA: John Knox.

La Tour, François Dupré (2004) *Le Synode des évêques et la collégialité*. Malesherbes: Parole et Silence.

Miller, J. Michael (ed.) (1998) *The Post-Synodal Apostolic Exhortations of John Paul II*. Huntington, CA: Our Sunday Visitor.

Mühlen, Heribert (1968) *Una Mystica Persona: Eine Person in Vielen Personen*, 3rd edition. Munich: Schöningh.

Reese, Thomas J. (ed.) (1989) *Episcopal Conferences: Historical, Canonical and Theological Studies*. Washington, DC: Georgetown University Press.

Saier, Oskar (1973) *"Communio" in der Lehre des Zweiten Vatikanischen Konzils*. Münchener theologische Studien, kanonistische Abteilung, Bd. 32. Munich: Max Huebner.

Semmelroth, Otto (1953) *Die Kirche als Ursakrament*. Frankfurt am Main: Knecht.

Synod of Bishops, Extraordinary Assembly of 1985 (1985) "Final Report," *Origins* 15 (December 19), 444–50.

Tagle, Luis Antonio (2004) *Episcopal Collegiality and Vatican II: The Influence of Paul VI*. Manila: Loyola School of Theology.

Teuffenbach, Alexandra von (2002) *Die Bedeutung des Subsistit in (LG 8): Zum Selbstverständnis der katholischen Kirche*. Rome: Pontificia Universitas Gregoriana.

Wassilowsky, Günther (2001) *Universales Heilssakrament Kirche: Karl Rahners Beitrag zur Ekklesiologie des II. Vatikanums*. Innsbruck: Tyrolia.

CHAPTER 23
The Liturgy and Sacraments

Susan K. Wood

Catholicism is deeply sacramental. This is to say that it is characterized by a sacramental world-view in which the created, finite, material reality is revelatory of the divine and communicates God's presence and activity on our behalf. According to the principle of sacramentality: "God is present in the visible, the tangible, the finite, and the historical" (McBrien, 1994: 10). The corollary of the sacramental principle is the principle of mediation by which "God works through the visible, the tangible, the finite, and the historical." Catholicism is not sacramental simply because it celebrates seven sacraments, but because it views the world through the lens of sacramentality. In this view creation becomes diaphanous of the divine. In the words of the poet Gerard Manley Hopkins:

> The world is charged with the grandeur of God.
> It will flame out, like shining from shook foil; ("God's Grandeur")

Invisible realities are known in and through visible realities. Thus Augustine defined a sacrament as "a visible sign of invisible grace," and Pope Paul VI in his opening address before the second session of the Second Vatican Council in 1963 defined it as "a reality imbued with the hidden presence of God."

Thomas Aquinas articulated the principle, "that which is received is received according to the mode of the receiver" (*Summa Theologiae* I, q. 84, art. 1). The principle of sacramentality respects the way of being human in the world. We receive all our knowledge through our senses, including the most spiritual. Here a theology of creation meets the theology of incarnation, the mystery of God become flesh. The fittingness of the incarnation is that we encounter the divinity of Christ through his humanity. Just as human communication and our presence to one another occurs only in and through our bodiliness, so too, God's communication and presence to us occurs in and through visible realities – Creation, sacraments, and, most of all, the humanity of Jesus. Human beings cannot receive the revelation of God unless they are "wired" to receive it, much like an AM radio cannot receive FM frequencies. God adapts his revelation and self-gift to the structures of our humanity.

Jesus, Sacrament of the Father/Church, Sacrament of Christ

Jesus' life illustrates the sacramental principle. He utilized outward signs to signify inward realities in his ministry. Physical healing was a sign of inner healing, the forgiveness of sin (Luke. 5:23–4). Most important, however, he himself embodied the sacramental principle as "the image of the invisible God, the first born of all creation" (Col 1:15; 2 Cor 4:4) so that anyone who saw him saw the Father (John. 14:9). Jesus was the manifestation, the epiphany of the hidden essence of God (Heb 1:1–2; 1 John 1:1). Later theologians such as Karl Rahner and Edward Schillebeeckx would identify Jesus as sacrament of the Father. There is one God and one mediator between God and humankind, the man Jesus Christ (1 Tim 2:5). Jesus "as the personal visible realization of the divine grace of redemption, is the sacrament, the primordial sacrament, because this man, the Son of God himself, is intended by the Father to be in his humanity the only way to the actuality of redemption" (Schillebeeckx, 1963: 15). When we encounter Jesus, we encounter the living God. Similarly, sacraments are first of all encounters before they are things (Schillebeeckx, 1963: 3).

This identification of Jesus as sacrament rests on the New Testament theology of the *mysterion* (Vorgrimler, 1992: 31). Both the Letter to the Ephesians and the Letter to the Colossians (Eph 1:9–10; 2:11–3:13; Col 1:20, 26–7; 2:2), speak of the mystery of God's will, which is none other than the incarnation of his Son for the reconciliation of humanity to himself in Christ. *Mysterion* was translated into Latin as *sacramentum*. Jesus was the outward sign and realization of this divine intention. Thus Jesus Christ is the *sacramentum Dei*, and sacramentality is intrinsically associated with salvation.

This salvation is definitive only in the eschaton, the end time. In sacraments we celebrate in symbol, under the aegis of sign, what is incomplete in the temporalities of human history, but whose completion we anticipate. Sacraments really make present under the modality of "real symbol" what will be achieved definitively when all is fulfilled in Christ, namely the communion with the Triune God through incorporation by the power of the Spirit into the body of Christ and his self-gift to the Father.

The Church as efficacious sign of this communion is also a sacrament. The Second Vatican Council identifies the Church as sacrament in three different articles in *Lumen Gentium*, variously describing the Church as a sacrament of intimate union with God and of the unity of all humankind (LG 1), as a sacrament of saving unity (LG 9) and as a universal sacrament of salvation (LG 48). In addition, three instances of identification of the Church as sign occur in the Constitution on the Sacred Liturgy, articles 2 and 26, stressing the Church as a sacrament or sign of unity, and article 5, associating the Church with the blood and water issuing from the side of Jesus, these also symbolizing baptism and Eucharist.

The idea of the Church as sacrament is closely related to the image of the body of Christ. In the concept of sacrament, there is unity and difference, unity between the sign of the sacrament and what is signified, difference, because what is signified is not absolutely identical with the sign which makes it present. Historical presence and sacramental presence are two different modalities. The Church as the body of Christ is the sacramental presence of Christ in the world in an analogous way in which Christ is the sacrament of the Father. Christ is the image of and self-expression of the Father. The one who sees the Son sees the Father (John 14:9). He shares the same divine nature as the Father (unity) and yet is distinct from the Father as the Father's object of self-knowledge (difference). The identity between Father and Son lies in the identity of their divine nature, and their difference lies in their relationship. The Father generates the Son and the Son is begotten of the Father. The Son does not generate and the Father is not begotten.

In a similar way there is both a unity and a difference between the Church, under the aspect of the biblical image of the body of Christ, and Christ. The guiding principle is that you can have as high an ecclesiology as you want as long as your Christology is higher. Strictly speaking, the Church is not a prolongation of the Incarnation, but is that which enables Christ to act sacramentally in the world. This distinction allows the Church's members to be frail human beings liable to sin. In the case of the Church, the visible sign includes the institutional and social aspect of the Church, that is, all that is manifest in history and located in space and time. The referent of the sign is the resurrected Christ. As with the incarnation, in the Church there is the union of the divine and the human, the human being the manifestation and revelation of the divine (LG 8).

Even though the concept of the Church as the sacrament of Christ is closely related to the image of the Church as the mystical body of Christ, it avoids a major weakness of this image of being too close an identification between Christ and the Church. The concept of sacrament is able to express the unity between the sign and the referent of that sign at the same time that it maintains the distinction between sign and referent. This unity and distinction is analogous to the relationship between the divine and human natures in Christ: "as with Christ the distinction between his Godhead and his humanity remains without confusion though they are inseparable signs and reality, manifest historical form and Holy Spirit are not the same in the Church, but as in Christ, are not separable any more either" (Rahner, 1964: 201).

The seven sacraments (baptism, Eucharist, confirmation, reconciliation, anointing of the sick, marriage, and holy orders) are both acts of Christ and acts of the Church. They express the nature and mission of the Church and bring the Church to visibility, for in celebrating its sacraments, the Church manifests itself most intensively. The Church as sign of salvation expresses itself through sacraments of salvation. Moreover, the sacraments manifest and effect a relationship with the Church. For example, the sacraments of initiation (baptism, confirmation, Eucharist) incorporate us into the Church. Penance reconciles us not only with Christ, but also with the Church. The retrieval of the ecclesial meaning of the sacraments represents one of the most significant developments in sacramental theology of the twentieth century.

The sacramentality of the Church enables Catholics to explain their belief that Christ "instituted" the seven sacraments even though a direct and explicit institution by Christ cannot be supported through biblical exegesis. We cannot find "proof texts" for all seven sacraments in the Scriptures. Jesus instituted the sacraments analogously to how he founded the Church. Just as he did not found an institutional Church with a blueprint of the structures and ministries that would evolve after his death, so he did not dictate the seven sacraments. The Church has its origin in Jesus, in his proclamation of the kingdom of God, in his mandate to make disciples, and in his request at the Last Supper to "Do this in remembrance of me." The seven sacraments have their origin in Jesus because they derive from the sacramentality of the Church and the ministry of Jesus. Karl Rahner argued that "the institution of a sacrament can ... follow simply from the fact that Christ founded the Church with its sacramental nature" (Rahner, 1963: 41).

The Liturgy

The liturgy, the proper context for a consideration of the seven sacraments, in turn finds its own place within the sacramentality of Christ and the Church. Liturgy is the priestly prayer of Christ publicly and officially enacted by his body which is the Church (Vatican II, 1996: SC 7). In fact it is "extremely effective in enabling the faithful to express in their lives and portray to others the mystery of Christ and the real nature of the true Church" (SC 2). Vatican II's "The Constitution on the Sacred Liturgy" identifies it as "the summit toward which the activity of the Church is directed; it is also the source from which all its power flows" (SC 10). The liturgy participates in the symbolic world of signs and ritual activity described in the sacramental world-view since our sanctification "is given expression in symbols perceptible by the senses and is carried out in ways appropriate to each of them. In it, complete and definitive public workshop is performed by the mystical body of Jesus Christ, that is, by the Head and his members" (SC 7). The liturgy is the place where an ecclesial community preserves its traditions, symbols, and texts and expresses its self-identity. These traditions, symbols, and texts are also operative extra-liturgically, but they derive their primary meaning from their liturgical context.

Liturgy is both an act of God and an act of the Church. Thus there is both a descending movement, comprised of God's saving action directed toward us, and an ascending movement, of our praise and thanksgiving, directed toward God (Verheul, 1968: 18). Thus liturgy is dialogic, comprised of a divine word and human answer, an encounter with God through the mediatorship of Christ in the power of the Spirit. The purpose of liturgy is thus twofold: the sanctification of women and men and worship of God. The dynamic of liturgical prayer is doxological and Trinitarian. We give thanks and praise to the Father, we remember the Son, and we invoke the Holy Spirit. This dynamic movement is most evident in the celebration of the Eucharist, which commemorates the great *exitus-reditus* wherein we recognize the Father as the Creator and giver of gifts which are transformed in the power of the Holy Spirit into the body of Christ and returned in offering to the Father. The sacrament is given for the glorification of God through Christ's self-gift to the Father and through our transformation into Christ and incorporation in that same self-gift.

The movement of God's saving action and our response is related to two essential liturgical elements, *anamnesis*, and *epiclesis*. *Anamnesis*, translated as "memorial," "commemoration," or "remembrance," actually has the much stronger meaning of making present an event or person from the past. *Anamnesis* asks God to remember his saving work in Jesus Christ in order that the benefits of Christ's sacrifice may be made present to the faithful here and now. The Eucharist, for example, remembers the paschal mystery of Jesus Christ in his life, death, resurrection, and exaltation. This paschal mystery of salvation is not only Christological, it is Trinitarian for the Father sends the Son who lives, dies, rises, and sends the Spirit that we, too, may ascend to the Father through Christ in the power of the Holy Spirit. These deeds are actually made present in the liturgy in the *anamnesis*, not as a repetition of his saving deeds or a mere recollection of them, but an actualization of them within the modality of sacramental sign. Participants in the liturgy actually participate in Jesus' paschal mystery and his present glory through the mediation of the Eucharist. The *epiclesis* calls on God the Father to send the Holy Spirit to transform the gifts into the body and blood of Jesus and to effect the unity of the Church, forgiveness of sin, life, and salvation.

Within the ritual time of the liturgy, the past and the future are gathered into the present moment through memorial, presence, and anticipation. A past historical event is transposed into the present life of the community in its remembrance and becomes a promise of future fulfillment and completion. This is true both of the material symbols of the liturgy and the word of God proclaimed liturgically. For example, the Eucharistic symbol of the meal commemorates a past meal and sacrifice which becomes present now, and a liturgical reading of the Scriptures proclaims a past event which becomes the autobiography of the present faith community. Both have an eschatological meaning of future completion: the future eschatological meal of the heavenly banquet and the future realization of unity within the human family and with God proclaimed under the symbol of the kingdom of God. The fullness we celebrate symbolically in ritual time awaits its completion in our everyday lives in historical time.

The liturgical assembly experiences the tension between the "already" and the "not yet" of a pilgrim people within a posture of waiting and anticipation until the final reconciliation of all with the Father in Christ by the power of the Spirit. This relationship between the past, present, and future is possible on account of the risen Christ, for as Thomas J. Talley explains: "By virtue of the resurrection, Christ is now transhistorical and is available to every moment. We may never speak of the Risen Christ in the historical past. The event of his passion is historical, but the Christ who is risen does not exist back there, but here, and as we live on this moving division line between memory and hope, between the memory of his passion and the hope of his coming again, we stand always in the presence of Christ, who is always present to everyone. This is where the real substance of our *anamnesis* lies" (cited by Taft, 1992: 200).

Sacramental presence concealing yet revealing the presence of Christ with us under sign refers us back to our everyday lives, to the "here" of faith. This can be none other than the historical, social, economic, and cultural specificity and particularity where the love of Christ and the bond of charity can be made manifest. Sacraments drive us to the ethical enactment of that which we acclaim and celebrate in faith, for it is only within the ethical that sacramental modality can be translated into social, economic, and cultural activity.

Liturgical worship, because it belongs to the incarnational order, cannot be privatized or spiritualized, but has an ethical dimension. The materiality of sign and symbol inherent to the liturgy belongs to the incarnational order. Eucharistic liturgy points to the fulfillment of the incarnation in the redemption of the material world. Eucharistic bread is "the symbol of all bread shared." The common life centered on the breaking of bread has social consequences. The bread has often been seen as the symbol of human labor and human struggle, placed upon the altar so it can be sanctified. According to the prayer at the Preparation of the Gifts, it is bread "which earth has given and human hands have made." Similarly the wine has been seen as symbolizing human fellowship. Liturgy becomes the microcosm of the work that God is doing in the world. This is theme of Romans, chapter 8, which speak of all creation being set free from its bondage to decay, obtaining the freedom of the glory of the children of God, groaning in labor pains as we wait for adoption and redemption, the reconciliation of all things in Christ. Thus worship and respect for the material order are inseparable.

Sacramental Principles

According to "The Constitution on the Liturgy," "the purpose of the sacraments is to sanctify people, to build up the body of Christ, and, finally, to worship God" (SC 59). Thus there is both an individual and a communal dimension to the sacraments, establishing those who participate in them in a relationship of communion with God and communion in faith with one another. Each of the seven sacraments is embedded in the liturgy. As public prayers of the Church they express worship of God before they are objects received. As worship "they not only presuppose faith, but by words and objects they also nourish, strengthen, and express it. That is why they are called sacraments of faith" (SC 59). As signs of faith they have the power to evoke and increase faith even as they express it, analogously to how signs of love reinforce love as they express it.

Faith is really the personal active response of the participant to God's offer of grace through Christ in the Spirit as is fitting within the paradigm of sacraments as encounters. Such a personalistic approach corrects a more mechanistic, juridical, and objectified approach which spoke of sacraments as objects "administered" and "received." In this neo-scholastic approach, all that was necessary for a fruitful reception of a sacrament was to have the intention to receive the sacrament and to have the required disposition for the particular sacrament. Grace was imaged as a quantifiable "thing" that increased or decreased rather than as a relationship of communion that is more intimate or more distant, strengthened or broken. In short, grace was commodified and sacraments were instrumentalized (Chauvet, 1995: chapter one). As "instruments of grace" they became pipelines through which God channeled grace.

The Council of Trent taught that "celebrated worthily in faith, the sacraments confer the grace that they signify" (Council of Trent (1547) DS 1605, DS 1606). Thomas Aquinas had taught that sacraments cause grace precisely insofar as they signify it, and the grace conferred is directly related to the sign of the sacrament. There is a certain visibility to sacramental grace. The grace received is related to the sign of the sacrament. For example, we are spiritually nourished through a sacred meal. Baptismal immersion signifies dying and rising with Christ. Thus a principle of the liturgical renewal mandated by Vatican II is that "both text and rites should be so drawn up that they express more clearly the holy things that they signify and so that the Christian people, as far as possible, are able to understand them with ease and to take part in the rites fully, actively, and as benefits a community" (SC 21). In other words, the quality of symbols matters: bread needs to look like bread and oil and water need to be used more abundantly in order to represent more fully what they signify.

Two sacramental principles reflect both the fact that sacraments are God's gracious action on our behalf and that we are active rather than passive participants in the sacramental action. On the one hand, sacraments effect grace *ex opere operato*, literally translated as "by the work worked." That is, they do not depend on the worthiness of the minister or the personal merit of the recipient, with the qualification that the recipient must not place an obstacle in the way. Negatively, obstacles may be serious sin for those sacraments requiring that the recipient be in a state of grace. More positively, this means that the sacraments must be received in faith. *Ex opere operato* means that when sacraments are carried out with the correct matter and form with the appropriate intention by an ecclesially authorized minister, the sacramental action has the power to effect what it signifies through the agency of the risen Christ and his Spirit. The term does not mean that sacraments cause the grace they signify magically or automatically. The term does mean they cause grace "by the power of Christ and God" (Schillebeeckx, 1963: 85). Christ is the principal minister of the sacrament, and sacraments are efficacious because he is faithful to his promises.

On the other hand, sacraments also effect grace *ex opere operantis*, translated as "from the work of the person working." This refers to the right disposition of the person participating in the sacrament enabling a "fruitful" reception of the sacrament. This means that we cannot receive a sacrament with personal benefit without being actively engaged in the sacramental event through faith and interior conversion.

Sacraments are signs effecting a present reality and signifying the grace and eschatological completion of what is made present within the sacramental symbol. The scholastics referred to these three elements of a sacrament as the *sacramentum tantum* (the sign), the *res et sacramentum* (the enduring present reality), and the *res tantum* (the graced effect of the sacrament). For example, the *sacramentum tantum* of the Eucharist is the bread and wine, the *res et sacramentum* is the body and blood of Christ, and the *res tantum* is the unity of the mystical body. Theology since Matthias Scheeben's (d. 1888) *The Mysteries of Christianity* recognizes that the *res et sacramentum* includes an ecclesial as well as Christological reality. Thus the Eucharist is not just the risen Christ, but also the whole Christ, members of Christ in union with their head, the Church. The baptismal character conforms us to Christ and also imparts a relationship with the Church.

The *res et sacramentum* is also identified with the sacramental "character" of baptism, confirmation, and holy order. This is a permanent effect of the sacrament such that these sacraments are not administered to the same person more than once during his or her lifetime. Within an ecclesial understanding of the *res et sacramentum*, the sacramental character establishes a permanent ecclesial relationship. Thus baptism and confirmation initiate a person into the ecclesial priesthood of the faithful. Baptism invests a person with the priesthood of the Church, commissioning that person to live visibly as a member of the Church and deputing that person for the public worship of the Church in its liturgy. Confirmation empowers a person to witness to the Church's

prophetic mission of proclaiming the kingdom of God. The sacrament of order constitutes an ecclesial repositioning so that the recipient is empowered to represent both
Christ the head of the Church, acting *in persona Christi capitis*, and the Church, acting
in persona ecclesiae. The sacramental character is an enduring Christological and ecclesial relationship whose permanence testifies to God's fidelity regardless of whether a
person renounces his or her membership in the Church or is "laicized" when leaving
the ordained ministry. In a sense, a person can leave the Church, but the Church does
not leave a person. The theology behind this is that God is faithful to God's promise
despite human infidelity.

The subject of liturgical action is the whole Church, Christ, and the people of God,
even though ordained ministers have a unique role in the liturgy. The presiding priest
acts together with the people rather than simply for them (*Eucharisticum Mysterium*,
12). The Eucharistic prayer is prayed in the first person plural apart from the words of
consecration: "Blessed are you . . . we have these gifts to offer." Liturgical prayer is not
the individual prayer of those present. As "The Constitution on the Sacred Liturgy"
expresses it, "liturgical services are not private functions but are celebrations of the
Church which is 'the sacrament of unity,' namely, 'the holy people united and organized under their bishops'" (SC 26). Liturgy is thus essentially a communal activity,
the prayer of the Church, even when it seems to be most private as in the reconciliation
of an individual penitent or a single priest reciting the Liturgy of the Hours in his room
at the end of the day. In the liturgical renewal promoted by Vatican II, the "full and
active participation by all the people is the paramount concern, for it is the primary,
indeed the indispensable source from which the faithful are to derive the true Christian spirit" (SC 14). Private devotions "should be so drawn up that they harmonize
with the liturgical seasons, accord with the sacred liturgy, are in some way derived
from it, and lead the people to it, since in fact the liturgy by its very nature is far superior to any of them" (SC 13).

Sacraments of Initiation

Baptism, confirmation, and Eucharist are sacraments of initiation. The norm or standard for interpreting the theology of Christian initiation is *The Rite of Christian Initiation
of Adults* (RCIA) even though the Church may actually baptize more infants than adults.
This means that all other rites are to be understood in the light of the full rite of adult initiation. Christian initiation is a process beginning with a period of evangelization and
precatechumenate during which the inquirer attains a basic grounding in Christian
teaching and experiences the beginnings of faith and conversion of life. The catechumenate, a period of formation lasting from one to several years, engages the catechumen
in the life of the community, the Church's worship, and its mission. The third stage, the
periods of purification and enlightenment, usually coincides with Lent and is a time of
proximate spiritual preparation accompanied by a number of rites: the rite of election,
the scrutinies and exorcisms on the third, fourth, and fifth Sundays and presentations
of the Creed and the Lord's Prayer. The sacraments themselves – baptism, confirmation,
and Eucharist – are normally received during the Easter vigil. After renouncing evil and

making a profession of faith, the elect are baptized, the minister pouring water over their foreheads or immersing them, saying "I baptize you in the name of the Father, the Son, and the Holy Spirit." "Explanatory" rites follow: the anointing of the head with chrism signifying incorporation into the priestly, prophetic, and kingly body of Christ (done only in the rare situation where confirmation is deferred), clothing in a white robe as a sign of the new creation, and presentation with a lighted candle as sign of the light of Christ.

Normally, confirmation follows immediately, administered by a presbyter in the absence of the bishop. The confirmation prayer asks for the sevenfold gifts of the Spirit and the prayer accompanying the anointing speaks of being sealed with the Holy Spirit. After these rites, the liturgy of the Eucharist continues, and the initiates receive the Eucharist with the rest of the assembly. The final stage is the period of post-baptismal catechesis or *mystagogia*, which minimally extends throughout the Easter season, but may be extended further. This stage seeks to explain to the newly baptized the spiritual and theological significance of the signs, symbols, and gestures of the initiation rite.

A unified rite of initiation makes the trajectory from baptism to Eucharist very clear. One is really baptized into the Eucharist since baptism initiates a person into the priesthood of the faithful, deputing that person for public worship in the Eucharist. Both baptism and Eucharist celebrate the same mystery, the death and resurrection of Jesus Christ. Traditionally, catechumens were dismissed after the liturgy of the word before the liturgy of the Eucharist since they had not yet received that deputation.

In the West, the Scripture text dominating baptismal theology is Rom 6:3–4: "Do you now know that all of us who have been baptized into Christ Jesus were baptized into his death Therefore we have been buried with him by baptism into death, so that, just as Christ was raised from the dead by the glory of the Father, so we too might walk in newness of life." Immersion in the baptismal waters signifies death to sin and the "old man," and emerging from the waters signifies new life in Christ. Baptism confers not only membership in the Church, but incorporation in Christ as we identify with his life, death, and resurrection.

In the East the dominant baptismal texts are Jesus' baptism in the Jordan (Mk 1:9–11). The primary image is not death and resurrection, but the manifestation of the Trinity and deification through the gift of the Spirit. Baptismal grace is the presence of the Holy Spirit. Thus it is erroneous to assume that we are incorporated into Christ at baptism, but only receive the Holy Spirit with confirmation even though the symbols of baptism are primarily Christological and the symbols of Confirmation emphasize the reception of the Holy Spirit.

Faith is both required for baptism and is an effect of baptism. The primary difference between those ecclesial traditions who baptize infants and those who practice believer baptism is not whether faith is present or not, but where faith is located. Baptists and groups issuing from the Anabaptist arm of the Reformation require a personal profession of faith on the part of the person who is baptized. In the Roman Catholic tradition, as in many other Christian traditions, faith is expressed by proxy by the godparents and the parents. In the baptism of infants, the faith of the Church precedes the initiation of the child, signifying that all are welcomed into a faith community through baptism, that proclamation and evangelization on the part of a faith community must precede any individual confession of faith, and that faith is God's work in us and not our own work.

We are baptized only once, but in the Eucharist our communion in the body of the Lord, both in the Christ dead and risen and in his ecclesial body, achieves a repeatable visibility. Our participation in the Eucharist is as profoundly baptismal as our baptism is profoundly oriented to the Eucharist. In baptism we become the priestly people of God, and in the Eucharist we exercise that priesthood.

Almost every aspect of the origins, history, rite, and theology of confirmation has been disputed. Key questions concern its relation to baptism and whether it constitutes a second gift of the Spirit distinct from the gift conferred in baptism. Confirmation was separated from baptism in the West because the postbaptismal rites were reserved to the bishop who was unable to be present for the baptism due to the practice of baptizing infants, the large number of candidates in general, the growth of the Church in rural areas, and the tendency to enroll male infants in the catechumenate, but to delay their initiation. In contrast, the East views baptism and chrismation as essentially the same sacrament, retains the unity of the three sacraments of initiation, and regards the presbyter as their legitimate minister.

When confirmation is celebrated separately from the baptism rite, the liturgy of confirmation begins with the renewal of baptismal promises and the profession of faith. The bishop extends his hands over the whole group of the confirmands and invokes the outpouring of the Spirit in a prayer recalling the sevenfold gift of the Spirit in Isaiah 61:2. The essential rite of the sacrament follows. The Latin rite consists in "the anointing with chrism on the forehead, which is done by the laying on of the hand and through the words: 'Be sealed with the Gift of the Holy Spirit'" (Paul VI, Apostolic Constitution, *Divinae consortium naturae*, cited in *The Rites of the Catholic Church* 1990: 663).

As the age at which a person is confirmed migrated from childhood to adolescence and the order in which the sacraments of initiation are received changed, so did the theology of confirmation, sometimes adopting incorrect explanations. Erroneous theologies of confirmation include: (1) Confirmation confers the Spirit for the first time; (2) Confirmation is the sacrament by which a Catholic personally ratifies the baptismal promises made in one's infancy by one's godparents; (3) Confirmation is the sacrament marking an adolescent's passage to adulthood. A more adequate theology of confirmation situates confirmation within a unified rite of initiation so that confirmation is "the pneumatic conclusion to baptism, a modest rite which is part of the great sacrament of baptism and which leads to the climactic sacrament of the eucharist" (Quinn, 1990: 285).

The Eucharist completes Christian initiation and thus more profoundly incorporates the baptized into Christ and the Church. It is "the source and summit of the Christian life" (SC 11), "the sum and summary of our faith" (*Catechism*, 1327), the primary act by which Christians worship God, and the primary locus of Christ's sacramental presence in the Church. "The Constitution on the Liturgy" summarizes the meaning of the Eucharist: "At the Last Supper, on the night when he was betrayed, our Savior instituted the eucharistic sacrifice of his body and blood. He did this in order to perpetuate the sacrifice of the Cross throughout the centuries until he should come again, and so to entrust to this beloved spouse, the Church, a memorial of his death and resurrection: a sacrament of love, a sign of unity, a bond of charity, a paschal banquet in which Christ is eaten, the mind is filled with grace, and a pledge of future glory is given to us" (SC 47).

The Eucharist calls to mind Jesus' actions in his paschal mystery, an enactment of a new covenant, and effectively makes them present now in accordance with Jesus' command (1 Cor 11:24–5). This *anamnesis* is not a mere memorial on the part of the community. Within a Hebraic theology of covenant, a sign of the covenant is presented to God "so that God will remember and act once again according to the covenant" (Fink, 1990: 438). This enables the present assembly to share in the body and blood of Christ, himself the very sign of the covenant. This participation in the covenant is a communion (*koinonia*) not only with the risen Christ, but also with all who are members of Christ (1 Cor 10:16–17). This sacramental communion anticipates an eschatological future (Luke 22:16; 1 Cor 11:26). Thus within the sacramental symbol the Christian community encompasses the past, recalling what God has done in Christ, the present, participating in the covenant through communion in Christ, and the future, expecting God to act again to complete that which is celebrated as fullness under the aegis of sign in the present time.

The entire Eucharistic liturgy is constructed around two hinges, the Liturgy of the Word and the Liturgy of the Eucharist. The Liturgy of the Word consists of readings from the Old and New Testaments which become the interpretative lens for the Christian community's life experience seen through the eyes of faith. In proclaiming the Scriptures we "remember" God's plan for salvation. In the Liturgy of the Eucharist, the community takes the gifts of creation and the results of human labor, the bread and wine, and offers them to God in obedient surrender. In offering the gifts, the people of God offer themselves as Christ offers himself and the Church offers Christ. They invoke the Holy Spirit (the *epiclesis*) to transform these gifts into the body and blood of Christ, effecting two transformations – the bread and wine into the body and blood of the risen Christ, and the assembly into the ecclesial body of Christ, his mystical body. This transformation takes the gifts of creation making of them a new creation. Traditionally, the Church has called this transformation the "consecration" of the elements. Then, in the communion rite, the assembly communes with the risen Christ, and in Christ, with one another. Communion is really an action of uniting oneself with another before it is an object received.

Communion commissions us to live lives for others, to live out ethically what we have celebrated sacramentally. In John's Gospel, the washing of the feet of the disciples replaces the institution narrative. Both narratives ask the disciples to do as Jesus did. The institution narratives end with "Do this in remembrance of me." The footwashing narrative ends with: "So if I, your Lord and Teacher, have washed your feet, you also ought to wash one another's feet. For I have set you an example, that you also should do as I have done to you" (John 13:14–15). In the liturgy of the Eucharist and in the liturgy of their ethical lives for one another, the people thus join with Christ in his priestly action by which God is perfectly glorified and we are sanctified (SC 7).

The Eucharist as the real presence of Christ is the sacramental pledge of the transformation of all creation in Christ (Rom 8:18–25). Thus sacramental theology integrates a theology of creation and redemption. The Council of Trent taught that the change of the whole substance of bread and wine into the substance of the body of Christ is fittingly called transubstantiation. Transubstantiation means that the substance of bread and wine are changed into the body and blood of Christ even though the accidents, that is, the appearances, of bread and wine remain. Vatican II taught that Christ is really present in the Word, in the presider, and in the assembly in addition to his special presence in the Eucharist (SC 7). Christ is present sacramentally so that the unity of all in Christ may be achieved. This is our reconciliation with God and our salvation.

Sacraments of Healing

The sacraments of initiation establish our relationship to Christ and his Church. The other four sacraments in the Roman Catholic system exist for the healing and building up of those relationships. Tertullian called the sacrament of reconciliation, also known as penance, the "second plank" thrown to a drowning man after the first plank of baptism, the paradigmatic sacrament of reconciliation. The sacrament's purpose is to "obtain pardon through God's mercy" and to be "reconciled with the Church which they [sinners] have wounded by their sins and which by charity, by example, and by prayer, labors for their conversion" (LG 11). The current rite stresses the ecclesial and communal nature of the sacrament since the sacrament reconciles us not only with God, but also with the Church. The three ritual forms are the rite of reconciliation of individual penitents, the rite of reconciliation of several penitents with individual confession and absolution, and the rite of reconciliation of several penitents with general confession and absolution. The Church is both a reconciling community continuing Christ's ministry of forgiveness of sin and a reconciled community seeking the mercy of God.

The sacrament of the sick, formerly called extreme unction (last anointing), offers to those seriously impaired by sickness or old age the prayer and support of the Church community at a time when they are weakened and isolated because of illness. The scriptural foundation of the sacrament is found in James 5:14: "Are any among you sick? They should call for the elders of the Church and have them pray over them, anointing them with oil in the name of the Lord." The sacrament forgives sin, heals the effects of sin, gives comfort and spiritual strength, arouses confidence in God's mercy, and reminds the sick person that illness is a participation in Christ's redemptive suffering. At times it even bestows health of body. The sacrament of the sick is not the sacrament of the dying, the "last rites," which is properly the Eucharist received as *viaticum*, food for passage through death to eternal life.

Sacraments of Vocation

The sacraments of matrimony and holy order both represent the Church and build up and serve the Church. Marriage is a covenant sealed by irrevocable personal consent which establishes an "intimate partnership of life and love" (Vatican II, 1996: GS 48). The love and union of the spouses symbolizes the community of life and love between Christ with his Church (Eph 5:22–32, GS 48). Marriage as a microcosm of the Church in covenant with Christ is called a "domestic church" (LG 11). Marriage builds up the

Church by helping the spouses to attain to holiness in their married life and through the rearing and education of their children, fostering new citizens of human society and perpetuating the people of God (LG 11).

The sacrament of order confers on candidates one of the offices of bishop, priest, or deacon. Ordained ministry builds up the Church in imitation of Christ who was priest, prophet, and king through the ministry of sanctification, through the administration of the sacraments, the preaching of the Gospel, and pastoral leadership and governance. Priests and bishops are charged with maintaining the Church in communion – with the apostolic faith of the primitive Church, within the local church, and in the communion of local churches with one another. Bishops, who are members of the Episcopal college through ordination to the Episcopate and through hierarchical communion with the Bishop of Rome, represent their local church in the communion of Churches within the universal Church. Presbyters are co-workers with bishops. Presbyters and bishops represent the Church and Christ in their priestly liturgical role as they preside over the sacraments in the name of Christ and present the prayer of the Church to the Father. Deacons share in the office of ministry to the word, are able to preside at funerals and solemn baptism and witness marriages. Traditionally they have assisted the bishop in Church administration, but they are not ordained to the priesthood (LG 29).

The Liturgy of the Hours, including psalms, canticles, and Scripture readings, is another liturgical prayer of the whole Church which is not just for monastic communities or clerics. However, not all Roman Catholic prayer is liturgical or sacramental, nor should the liturgy be asked to bear the full weight of Roman Catholic spirituality. Contemplation, meditation on the word of God in Scripture, the rosary, and popular devotions enrich the spiritual lives of Roman Catholics and enable them to participate more fully in the liturgical life of the Church.

References and Further Reading

Aquinas. Thomas, *Summa Theologiae* (ST)
Catholic Church (1994) *Catechism of the Catholic Church.* www.vatican.va/archive/ccc/index. htm. Accessed 7/21/05.
Chauvet, L.-M. (1995) *Symbol and Sacrament: A Sacramental Reinterpretation of Christian Existence.* Collegeville, MN: The Liturgical Press.
Fink, Peter E. (1990) "Theology of Eucharist," in *The New Dictionary of Sacramental Worship,* edited by Peter E. Fink. Collegeville, MN: The Liturgical Press.
Hopkins, Gerard Manley (1963) *Poems and Prose of Gerard Manley Hopkins,* edited with an introduction and notes by W.H. Gardner. New York: Penguin Books.
International Commission on English in the Liturgy (1990) *The Rites of the Catholic Church,* vol. 1. New York: Pueblo Publishing Company.
McBrien, R. (1994) *Catholicism,* new edition. New York: HarperSanFrancisco.
Paul VI, Apostolic Constitution, *Divinae Consortium Naturae,* cited in International Commission on English in the Liturgy (1990) *The Rites of the Catholic Church,* vol. 1. New York: Pueblo Publishing Company, p. 663.

Quinn OP, Frank C. (1990) "Theology of Confirmation," *The New Dictionary of Sacramental Worship*, edited by Peter E. Fink, SJ. Collegeville, MN: The Liturgical Press.

Rahner, K. (1963) *The Church and the Sacraments*. New York: Herder and Herder.

Rahner, K. (1964) *Studies in Modern Theology*. London: Burns and Oates.

Sacred Congregation of Rites (1967) *Eucharisticum Mysterium* [*Instruction on Eucharistic Worship*] May 25.

Schillebeeckx, E. (1963) *Christ the Sacrament of the Encounter with God*. Kansas City, KA: Sheed Andrews and McMeel.

Taft, Robert (1992) "What Does Liturgy Do? Toward a Soteriology of Liturgical Celebration: Some Theses," *Worship* 66 (3, May). 200. See also Robert Taft (1984) "Toward a Theology of the Christian Feast," in *Beyond East and West: Problems in Liturgical Understanding*. Washington, DC: The Pastoral Press, 1–13.

Vatican II (1996) *The Documents of Vatican II*. Austin Flannery OP, General Editor. New York: Costello.

Vatican II (1996) "The Dogmatic Constitution on the Church," *Lumen Gentium* (LG).

Vatican II (1996) "The Pastoral Constitution on the Church in the Modern World," *Gaudium et Spes* (GS).

Vatican II (1996) "The Constitution on the Sacred Liturgy," *Sacrosanctum Concilium* (SC).

Verheul A. (1968) *Introduction to the Liturgy*. Collegeville, MN: The Liturgical Press.

Vorgrimler, H. (1992) *Sacramental Theology*. Collegeville, MN: The Liturgical Press.

CHAPTER 24
Moral Theology

David Matzko McCarthy

Introduction

A report on a recent Gallup survey begins with an intriguing statement: "American Catholics as a whole tend to express views similar to those of non-Catholics on many moral issues" (Newport, 2005). As a leading story line, the statement intends to grab the reader. The potentially captivating point is that the Catholic Church's public stance against abortion, the death penalty, physician-assisted suicide, homosexual acts, divorce, and embryonic stem cell research is not convincing, even within its own flock. People tend to believe whatever they want. For this reason, the report might cause consternation for moral theologians (as well as bishops of course). If the task of moral theology is to convey morality from a theological point of view, shouldn't theology make a difference? Shouldn't Catholics share a point of view?

The leading line of the report suggests that the connection between moral rules of the Church and its individual members is tenuous but, as it turns out, the intriguing first line is just a rhetorical teaser. The rest of the report shows that a person's stance on the list of issues cited above (abortion, death penalty, and so on) corresponds to attendance at Mass. Most Catholics who attend Mass weekly hold what are identifiably "Catholic" moral views. Catholics who seldom worship tend to reject these views. Those who attend Mass, but not regularly, fall somewhere in between. The consistency is clear. Although not an exciting draw, the lead line of the article could have read, "Gathering for worship corresponds to moral unity among the faithful." A follow-up Gallup report confirms this far less provocative summary. Complementary surveys of Protestants indicate that practicing Protestants hold traditional moral positions associated with the Catholic Church, either at the same level or to a higher degree than even practicing Catholics (Jones, 2005). Again, the lead line could have been, "Worship works," or at least, "Religious practices correspond to unity of moral perspective."

The connection between moral views and gathering for worship deflates the troublesome implications of the survey for practicing Catholics, but not for moral theologians. The surveys indicate that pronouncements (and perhaps arguments) about morality do not seem able to establish a unity of convictions; or more accurately, statements and explanations about morality seem unable to transcend dividing lines of religious practice. These facts raise basic questions for moral theory. Shouldn't morality overcome different habits of prayer and Mass attendance? Shouldn't a system of moral norms stand on its own?

The first section of the chapter outlines a context for investigating these questions by attending to the origins and history of moral theology. For the sake of argument, let us assume that the discipline of ethics arises in order to bridge moral differences – to establish unity on a rational basis. If this is the case, it seems to undermine the whole enterprise to admit that the discipline does little to actually overcome those differences. What is moral theology good for? What is its purview?

The historical outline offered in the first section of the chapter is extended in the second. In the first section, we will see that the end of the sixteenth century witnesses the beginning of moral theology as a distinct "science" (Mahoney, 1987). The budding discipline takes root on the eve of the modern era, and moral theology is, in effect, an ongoing engagement with modern (and typically narrower) conceptions of human nature, human community, and moral reasoning from a much more comprehensive point of view. On the matter of moral reasoning, it is fair to say that the leading line of the Gallup report succeeds as a rhetorical "grabber" because it reflects modern assumptions about how morality is supposed to work. The survey shows that worship makes a difference in what people believe, but the report on the survey seems to assume that religious practices ought not to make a *moral* difference.

The assumption is that official Church teaching ought to convince Catholics regardless of their ways of life, otherwise we fall into moral relativism. According to a common view, an objective (rather than subjective and relativist) morality ought to be separate from religious practices and convictions. According to a common view, morality ought to convey a disinterested point of view, that "to study morality, we must first divorce ourselves from any vestige of our own morality" (Lysaught and McCarthy, 2007). A similar theory of "detachment" (although more sophisticated than this popular view) is assumed to be a sign of moral maturity in well established political theories and studies of moral psychology (Rawls, 1971; Kohlberg, 1981). This issue of moral reasoning and detachment will be the topic of the second part of the chapter. How we approach the issues of rationality and objectivity in ethics depends upon our account of what we are made for, how we come to know, and what will fulfill us as human beings.

The final section of the chapter will begin where the first section concludes: with recent development in Catholic moral theology. The first section ends with two unanswered questions – how can moral theology become more theological, and what will be its system and method? The second section offers a critique of modern conceptions, systems, and methods. It is a lengthy section, and the reader might worry about wandering too far from the particulars of moral theology. Take heart. The second section is necessary to move us toward the conclusion that *moral* systems and exacting theories about decision-making fade the more moral theology becomes theological – the more that it is at home in the life of the Church. In effect, we will return to the theme of the Gallup poll (it is worship that works). Moral theology has its source in and points us back to a way of life, and it is the way of life (not the discipline of moral thought per se) that is the context for moral thinking.

Moral Theology in Historical Outline

In Catholic moral theology, a span of 400 years anchors how the history is told – roughly from the end of the Council of Trent (1563) to the end of Vatican II (1965). The beginning of this period is the beginning of moral theology as a distinct field of study. The period as a whole is characterized by the use of similar kinds of textbooks in moral theology. It is the era of the manuals. These handbooks, written in Latin, are used to prepare priests for their role in hearing confession and otherwise communicating the requirements of the moral life. Certainly, the textbooks do not rise instantly in 1563. They emerge along with reforms in the education and training of priests that is initiated by the Council of Trent. They fit as well with the Council's concerns about the sacrament of penance (in response to Protestant criticisms). Although the textbooks develop over time, there is a consistency among them, both in their framework of moral law and in the fact that they were written for priests (who would sit in the confessional booth).

Consistency is good, but these manuals in moral theology are criticized by almost everyone on our side of Vatican II. However, we should be careful not to create a caricature of "wicked" books as if they had no good purpose. John Mahoney, in his *Making of Moral Theology*, notes the "help, warmth, and meaning" as well as grace and healing that is found in the confessional by people during the age of the textbooks (1987: 28). It should be noted also that the manuals of moral theology form only a part of the education of priests who receive spiritual formation and are trained as pastors. The textbooks are set within a rich tradition; they are learned amid the struggles and aspirations of living a good and holy life. At close inspection, the textbooks reveal subtleties which show deep concerns for the welfare of people and the care of souls. To this degree, criticisms of the textbooks do not necessarily apply to their application. They do not impose a dark ages of the moral life.

Given these caveats, we can consider the basic criticisms, not of the moral life during the period, but of the narrow conception of morality that is conveyed by the manuals. They present morality as a set of requirements that can be cut off from theology as a whole. Early on Thomas Aquinas' *Summa Theologiae* – usually an explanation of Thomas' thought and not his actual text – is used in the education of priests. But the part of the *Summa* that attends to moral acts and law is separated from the parts on God's relationship to Creation and our return to God in Christ (Gallagher, 1990: 29–47). As a result, the textbooks are structured by the obligations of the moral law. They tend to focus on sin, that is, on what to avoid rather than the kind of people we should aspire to become, and they hardly inspire the reader.

Because the textbooks assume the context of confession, they draw attention, almost exclusively, to discrete acts rather than a course of life; morality is reduced to understanding an act in relationship to the moral law and issues of conscience. In other words, morality is studied as a set of commands and problem cases. The moral law (typically summarized by the Ten Commandments) presses upon the individual as a set of constraints. Moral deliberation does not attend to our fulfillment in what is good and beautiful, but is understood as charting out room to maneuver within moral constraints (Pinckaers, 1995).

If the manuals give an uninspiring and unattractive picture of the moral life, why would they be used for centuries? The most plausible explanation is that these textbooks and the very field of moral theology are conceived during the sixteenth century as a compress to stop the equivalent of spiritual and social hemorrhaging (Sherwin, 2003). Before the era of the manuals, moral theology does not exist as a distinct discipline. The age-old practices of teaching about and studying the moral life are considered part of preaching, worship, biblical study, and the understanding of doctrine and discipleship, in other words, part of theology in general. Bishops and theologians write treatises and give homilies on specific topics like marriage or the use of property, but these efforts are not considered separate from inquiry about Scripture, redemption in Christ, and the call of the Church to be a holy people. As a "compress," the approach of the manuals offers the means to simplify, separate out, and isolate moral issues. They narrow the context of moral deliberation by attending to the practices of penance. Handbooks on penance or "Penitentials" had been in use since the sixth century. By taking the model of the Penitentials, the manuals set moral deliberation in a manageable context and free priests and lay people from having to grapple with arcane and sometimes controversial theological questions.

The era that gives rise to the manuals comes on the heels of the Protestant reformation and amid corruption and controversial movements for reform within the Roman Catholic Church. During the age of the manuals, new forms of piety and theological ideas are emerging. Colonial empires and capitalism are expanding and presenting new problems. Traditional forms of community and religious practices are being dismantled (Bossy, 1987). New scientific methods and theories will emerge that will challenge the way both God and human beings are understood to act in Creation. As early as the fourteenth century, some theologians are leveling arguments against the Church's authority in worldly matters, and monarchs are beginning to claim absolute authority in temporal and ecclesiastical affairs. According to Gerald McCool, the theology at the beginning of the period is "problem conscious and controversial in its approach," and is "restricted by the immediate needs of an embattled Church" (2000: 80).

The analogy of a compress implies that the manuals and moral theology as a discipline emerge as a means to give clarity and direction amid the torrents of ecclesiological controversy, spiritual upheaval, and social change.

> Many of the faithful were spilling out into strange doctrines and practices with regard to them. One way to contain this spillage was separating the study of these "troubled" subjects from the study of morals. The clergy could safely teach the faithful the principles of the moral life, now regarded primarily as rules to follow. They could then later teach the more gifted and discerning among the faithful about grace, beatitude, and life in the Spirit. In other words, moral theology as the domain of rules becomes something clerics teach to all the faithful, while dogmatic theology, ascetical theology, and mystical theology become the reserve of a chosen few. (Sherwin, 2003: 18)

The reader is likely to respond that this two-tiered framework (of moral law for most people and higher spiritual pursuits for a few) sounds too hierarchical and paternalistic, too "medieval" for the modern world. Indeed, the analogy of the compress suggests that the remedy itself (the manuals themselves), if applied too long, will inhibit healing and may cause sepsis. The compress will be the source of the problem. Likewise, decades before the era of the manuals comes to an end, the textbooks are seen as barriers to understanding the moral life. For instance, in the decade before Vatican II, Bernard Häring's *Law of Christ* attempts to push aside the law-governed framework of the manuals for the sake of God's grace and covenant as well as the call of discipleship.

When those gathered for Vatican II take time to consider the state of moral theology, they do so through the document *Optatam Totius*, the Council's "Decree on Priestly Training" (Paul VI, 1975). This "location" for treating the topic makes sense: from its inception, moral theology is understood as a discipline developed in the formation of priests. The decree calls for a renewal of the discipline

> through a more living contact with the mystery of Christ and the history of salvation . . . Its scientific exposition, nourished more on the teaching of the Bible, should shed light on the loftiness of the calling of the faithful in Christ and the obligation that is theirs of bearing fruit in charity for the life of the world. (no. 16)

This call for renewal fits with the other documents of the Council, even though they do not attend directly to moral theology – documents on Scripture, the Church, and the mission of the Church in the modern world.

The "location" and manner of dealing with moral theology make sense, but the Council's directives do not chart an obvious course. If moral theology has been developed as a discipline distinct from an exposition of "the loftiness of the calling of the faithful in Christ," it is not clear how it will be maintained as a discipline while also departing from its narrow but manageable focus on basic obligations and prohibitions of moral law. What changes will occur when the moral theology moves beyond the confessional and the training of priests? How will texts in moral theology look when written directly to the whole Church? Writing 20 years after Vatican II, John Mahoney describes an entirely new set of problems. We are far beyond the narrow focus of the manuals into a sea of foci and contexts.

> No decades in the history of moral theology have been so productive of literature on the subject as the past two . . . Nor have any decades witnessed to such an extent, in the five centuries since the formal identification of moral theology as a theological science, the lack of an agreed systemization and the exploration, specification, experimentation, and altercation to be found today in the literature of moral theology, not only relating to the many new and urgent questions facing society and individuals, but equally in the examination of the every foundations and methodology of the subject. (1987: xii)

We will consider these matters of systemization, foundations, and method in the final section of the chapter – the section that lies between deals with the difficulties of heeding Vatican II's call to make moral theology more scriptural and theological. During the era of the manuals, modern philosophy and moral theory are fighting their own battles in attempting to understand the purposes of human life and how God acts in the world. The next section will discuss challenges in accounting for how humans reason about life in the world, and the subsequent section takes up where the current section has ended, with questions of method and of making theology more theological.

Life in the World and Practical Reason

According to evolutionary psychologist Paul Bloom, religious convictions and human intuitions about the meaning and purpose of life are inherent in us. "They are part of human nature" (2005: 112). However, he also argues that our inclinations to see order and purpose in life are biological adaptations that take a random and useless turn; they are "accidental by-products of our mental systems." In other words, purposes other than genetic survival have no real purpose. This point encourages some evolutionary scientists to conclude that genes rather than people are the real agents in life (Dawkins 1989). According to this interpretation of the data, there is a disjunction between what humans are naturally inclined to think about the world and how the world really is – a disconnection between seeing meaning and purpose *in* our lives and the fact that there is no meaning *for us* other than what we contrive.

Our concern in this section of the chapter is not to debate with Bloom and other evolutionary biologists about the meaning of human life, but to understand the problems created by the disconnection between our moral agency and the meaning *in* life. According to Bloom's evaluation, we human beings are naturally inclined to an irrational understanding of life. This section will ask, "how can practical (moral) reasoning be rational, particularly reasoning from a theological context?" While the last section begins with the sixteenth century and looks forward to issues subsequent to 1965, this section will start with Bloom's current-day proposal and look back to how moral reasoning develops in modernity. Bloom's proposal gives a good example of the modern crisis of moral reason: our crisis in having a meaningful place in the world.

From the perspective of Catholic theology, there is no essential conflict between faith and science, even evolutionary biology (John Paul II, 1996). Bloom's essay, "Is God an Accident?" (Bloom, 2005), is interesting, not because of the scientific data that he presents, but because of its philosophy – its metaphysical assumptions about what makes up the human being. Bloom accepts only biological/physiological explanations. There is a difference between the scientific data of evolution and a philosophical view (Bloom's materialism) that "all objectively meaningful questions can be reduced to scientific ones, and only natural explanations are rational" (Barr 2006). For example, Bloom believes that he can explain a person's concern for the poor in a distant country or her enjoyment of art by proposing a random mix of adaptive traits (2005: 107). But his explanations, because they are philosophically limited to the story of our genes, require that these human behaviors have no real purpose. Human beings cannot be *meant* to care for others or to enjoy beauty. These activities do not really get us anywhere; there is no place for these kinds of human activities and intentions to go. They are biological adaptations gone awry

In relationship to religion and morality, Bloom states a typical modern attitude that religious faith is tolerable "as long as that faith grounds moral positions one already accepts" (2005: 105). It seems that morality must have an independent rational ground but, as philosophical materialist, Bloom offers little help as to how that "rational ground" might be conceived. The moral foundation, insofar as it gives purpose and meaning to life, would have to be disconnected from the way things really are. Indeed, Bloom notes that altruism can be disastrous and suicidal "from the perspective of one's genes" (2005: 107). More will be said later on this "disconnection" between moral agency and our place in the world. For now, we turn to what Bloom affirms, as a scientist, on empirical grounds.

The evidence for Bloom's arguments comes from the techniques of cognitive science used, primarily, in studies of infants and children. For instance, evidence suggests that infants are able to fit inanimate objects into narrative relationships when an ordered sequence of events is provided by the researcher. When one object seems to be chasing another, infants appear to form expectations that events *should* conclude in the one catching the other. Bloom's conclusion is that the identification of agents, roles, and intentions in these sequences seems hardwired. After citing a study of autistic children, Bloom proposes that we all have two cognitive systems, one for real physical objects and another for social relationships. In the human brain, it is hard to keep them apart. We attribute human intentions to pets and anthropomorphize such things as bicycles; we see patterns among random objects, and we ascribe meaning to accidental events. Moreover, studies have shown that children have an innate conviction that life continues after death (we naturally look beyond physical reality). It seems that the social and meaning-giving system of the brain transcends our system of understanding physical objects.

These studies are hardly earth shattering; they confirm common sense. A sense of purpose and our capacity to see meaning in life have a strong footing and, from this conclusion, we have reason to argue that our convictions about life's order and purpose are rationally defensible. They are deeply connected to being human. Indeed, Bloom points out the vast majority of people in the world, including a high percentage of scientists, hold strongly to non-scientific beliefs about the meaning of life and God's relationship to the world. These convictions accord with how people live and aspire to live: human beings have been made to enjoy beauty, to be moved by the suffering of others, and to see a connection between these activities and the way the world really is.

Bloom comes to a very different conclusion. He presupposes (but does not argue) that the only explanations that are reasonable to accept are those that attain the certainty of natural science. He is convinced that humans see meaning in life, but the kind of meaning and purpose that humans are inclined to see cannot be explained by scientific materialism. Such meaning and purpose cannot, by definition, meet the requirements of rational certainty. (Evidence that you are loved by your parents does not count as evidence. What you can be sure of is that they are driven to want their genetic pool to survive though you.) In effect, Bloom assumes that what makes human beings distinctively human is disconnected from what the world really is. This is the modern problem of moral theory: disconnected from how the world *is*, we have to contrive what we ought to be. On this point, we will turn back to the beginnings of moral theory in the modern world.

Bloom's assumptions about purposelessness of life are relatively recent and would not be found among seventeenth- and eighteenth-century scientists. Isaac Newton (1642–1727), for instance, looked for God within his natural explanations. The disconnection between the natural world and knowing "what life is about" is usually marked toward the end of the eighteenth century with Immanuel Kant (Buckley, 1987). Kant, however, was confident in the self-sufficiency of reason, so that references to human fulfillment and purposes were not only unnecessary but a hindrance. Although there are clear changes and differences in the modern age, there is a consistent conception of reasons and explanations that is usually traced as far back as the philosopher, physicist, and mathematician René Descartes (1596–1650). Modern reason is expected to stand on its own, apart from received wisdom and authorities passed on by generations before. Historically, modernity is characterized by a political and intellectual struggle to be free of the old order, including the authority of Scripture, Christian doctrine, and the Church.

In terms of philosophy and science, modern reason is understood to be unified in such a way that the same rational standards are required of both scientific and practical reason (McCool 2000: 83–6). One can find a foundation of all reason which will stand on its own apart from wisdom and the qualities of the knower. In this regard, there begins to be a divide between subjective knowing and objective knowledge, between moral inclinations like compassion and the cold calculation of reason. On one hand, physics and mathematics set standards of rational certainty; on the other, modern philosophers try to make space for free moral action, sometimes against the constraints of our nature and sometimes apart from the constraints of rationality.

In the modern world, moral theory is fragmented by this disconnection between "detached" reason and our "embedded" moral agency (Taylor, 1989). The following are a few historical reference points. In one proposal, David Hume (1711–76) argues that what we desire and decide to do must come from a source other than what we *reason* about the world – other than from our rational ideas or principles about how things are. He holds that our moral action, drawn from natural sentiments, is not moved or determined by rational argument (Hume, 1966). Sentiments, for Hume, are beyond rational judgment (MacIntyre, 1998: 175). In contrast to this disjunction between reason and morality, Kant (1724–1804) sustains an account of practical reason by setting the rational will over against the directives of experience, colored as it is by our natural self-interest and desires for pleasure (Kant, 1959). We act morally through the power of the will to rationally transcend, not only the givens of our nature but also givens of ordinary life – in our particular commitments to friends and family and our desires for a good life. John Stuart Mill (1806–73) combines both Kant's and Mill's disjunctions (Mill, 1931). On one hand, his Utilitarianism requires a rational calculation to transcend and manage non-rational pleasure (Kant) and, on the other hand, a pre-rational motivation (a feeling) is needed to move us to act (Hume). Typically, Utilitarianism is criticized, on one hand, because its cold calculation undermines basic moral intuitions (like fidelity to our own children) but, on the other hand, because its account of pleasure defies rational calculation (how is one non-rational pleasure measured against another?).

In each case, reason is understood to be instrumental, a means to impose our

362   DAVID MATZKO McCARTHY

will or emotive preferences on the mechanisms of the world. Here is the connection to Bloom: no longer is it possible to have a role *in* the world or play one's part in the meaning of life. Likewise, each theory looks for a foundation outside an account of the purposes, roles, and relationships of everyday life. Kant looks, instead, to the rational consistency of an act in itself. Hume looks to sentiments that cannot be adulterated or reformed by a reasoned account of "what life is about."

Consider a counter proposal. Rational consistency and the direction of our sentiments depend upon a wider context of social relations that are connected to what life is about. To cite a quick example, parents make judgments about how they think and feel about their children, and what to do about discipline within a community, sharing the activities of parenting and education, and drawing on a tradition of practical wisdom that comes through exemplary parents and the "evidence" embodied in their children. They see raising children in the relationship to how the world works. The ordinary practice has wider implications. Raising children refers us to the meaning of life, and our wisdom about the meaning of life is enhanced through raising children. Certain sources of wisdom will be recognized as authorities. One might also consult social scientific studies on childhood development, parenting books, and the like; but the usefulness of the science or what one looks for from the experts is judged according to how one conceives of the purposes of life. We ask, what kind of person is it good for anyone, especially my child, to become? What is life about? Do we correct self-centered behavior, and if so, how much? Do we scold boys when they cry? After a disagreement, do we insist that siblings say, "I'm sorry"? These practical judgments are made reasonably within a web of convictions about what life is about, reasoning through what is consistent, evidence of what works, gut feelings, and efforts to adjust our gut feelings about how to give our best to our children.

Now we return to how Bloom represents the modern problem of purposes. He puts the questions of the good life and the purpose of life in the realm of irrationality but, apart from these questions of "ends," practical reason falls apart. He presupposes that the kind of knowledge, evidence, arguments, and explanations that are found amid social endeavors gives us no access to how the world and human beings really work. Likewise, characteristically modern moral theories put forward conceptions of reason and human nature that circumvent both a conception of the purpose of human life and the context where purposes are operative. As the parenting example suggests, the purpose *in* life is hopelessly abstract apart from the practices of day-to-day life, an ongoing tradition of thought and action, a shared life with diverse roles and interlocking obligations, and wisdom identified with a recognized authority (MacIntyre, 1984).

The point that we are headed toward is this: reasoning, especially moral reasoning, is shaped within the context of what we do and how we live. The role of "doing" – the realm of the practical – does not contaminate our reasoning. Rather, reasoning, especially moral reasoning, develops coherently only in a context that offers practical coherence. Without its location in a tradition of thought and action, our reasoning loses its reference point to "how the world is." The big picture is worked out locally. Even Bloom, in his attempt to give us a purely biological account of human life, gives us an explanation of human reason and human life. He clearly thinks that we will be better off when we do not take our purposes too seriously (and don't kill anyone over them), because they do not correspond to anything real. In the process, however, he undermines his own purposes. Even though he is arguing that the human construction of purpose is disconnected from how the world really is, he is attempting to make that connection. Has Bloom made this contradiction inevitable for himself?

In relationship to similar questions, a fundamental re-evaluation of reason starts to gain momentum in the second half of the twentieth century. Some take modern conceptions of reason to the inevitable conclusion of relativism. They claim that there is no access to what is real. How human beings reason is always contaminated by our social and meaning-giving systems. Bloom's own scientific view will not escape this criticism. Is not his own account of science adulterated by his own account of the purposes of life? Many scientists do not agree with his interpretation of the evidence (Brockman 1995). So, it seems, relativism is everywhere. On this point the theory heads into trouble. Isn't relativism an account of how things really are? If so it contradicts itself by making a non-relativist claim. Although a challenge to modern confidence in reason, relativism follows the modern logic of "disconnected" but universal claims. It accepts a modernist view of reason "detached," and then claims that such reasoning does not work.

In contrast to relativism, another line of inquiry has developed that holds that the problem lies not in human reason but in the modern conception of it. In the philosophy of science, for instance, there is a recognition that knowledge from empirical evidence is not free of beliefs about what one expects to see, presupposed models and paradigms that shape an understanding of evidence, and the history and culture of scientific inquiry (Murphy, 1990). That is not to say that science is partly irrational. On the contrary, beliefs are always operative, but they can be evaluated and revised, judged to be accurate or inaccurate, warranted or not. Beliefs are analyzed rationally, not in the way we evaluate molecules, but in a way appropriate to convictions: in their explanatory power, coherence, and consistency in relationship to empirical evidence, and their competence in directing us to what is significant and true. In fact, Bloom's essay, although written in the twenty-first century, is surprisingly outdated in its philosophical assumptions (and therefore a good example of the typical "modernist" perspective). A purpose-giving evaluation of life does not fit with his view of natural science, but it is operative in how scientists reason; it is a rational activity and can be evaluated as such. The problem with Bloom, let's say, is not his evidence, but the fact that he attempts to disengage the evidence from the meaning of the ordinary things that we do, including studying the world as an evolutionary biologist. Bloom does not test his convictions for their adequacy in giving an account of his own practices within the scientific community.

This account of "beliefs" in science complements (but does not correspond to) the time-honored understanding of faith within the Catholic tradition. Faith is "a habit of mind" (Newman, 1998). Faith is not the conclusion of a rational proof, but it does present and ground both convictions and knowledge from which practical and theological reasoning proceed. We do not reason our way to belief, although reasons do contribute to our movement toward faith. We can give reasons for what we believe. We do not accept matters of faith on the certainty of evidence, but through faith, we are able to see evidence of what we believe. Hope and love come into play as well. Faith is knowledge akin to knowing and loving a person; we receive the self-giving of God in Jesus Christ (Pieper, 1997: 55–66). We hope in God's love. Hope is a persistent movement of faith toward our fulfillment in the love of God (Pieper, 1997: 99–112). Like presumptions which operate in science, faith is evaluated within an ongoing tradition and amid a community that puts the convictions to use. Faith is put to use in understanding how to live, explaining matters of everyday life, and getting to the bottom of what it means to be human. For Christians, two basic practices that form the contexts for the "convictions-in-use" are worship and discipleship (thanksgiving and following). Within this context we make rational judgments about our beliefs and their application.

Knowledge in science and convictions of faith are very different in kind, but they are both practices of the same human beings. They both are embodied in communities of thought and action, located in ways of life, and directed to purposes and standards of judgment. Like the philosophy of science, moral philosophy and theology are re-evaluating modern conceptions of reason and are giving a more complete and convincing picture of how human beings reason about how to live well and act on what is good. A main reference point in moral philosophy is the work of Alasdair MacIntyre (2006). A realistic understanding of the moral life does not emerge from the transcendence of the rational will over the habits of everyday life, from a formula or calculus of action, or from a non-rational core of sentiments. Moral thinking is at home in a web of social roles and duties, shared convictions about the good life, common practices like raising children, pursuing good work, settling differences, and the like. Our access, as human beings, to what life is all about is through the pursuit of our purpose in life and the embodiment of life well lived.

The key shift is from thinking of moral reason as transcending traditions and cultures to being embedded and embodied in them. This is not a relativist point of view. Certainly moral disagreements and cultural differences exist but, from a theological point of view, they are not believed to be the final word. We are united as creatures in the image of God and in our ultimate destiny of shared life with God. If an answer to moral differences can be achieved, it will be possible through attention to our ongoing habits of thought and action. On this point, the specific purposes of the Christian life come into play. A practical understanding of moral reason recognizes that action shapes thought as much as thought shapes action. Christians call this conversion and becoming a new creation (1 Cor 5), just like principles or statements, actions, and activities can be true or false, and the Church is called to a way of life that is a sign (a sacrament) that points toward what is true. In practical reasoning, what we do and how we live constitute the context for thinking well about life and how things really are.

The reference to truth will sound to some like either an imposition of theocracy or a withdrawal into a Christian enclave. On the contrary, it simply recognizes that moral thinking cannot be detached from a way of life, and that Christians engage in matters of the world by living in such a way that tells us about being created and redeemed by God. It would not make sense, in these terms, to force a way of thinking upon others. It makes sense, however, to walk with others and invite them to share a way of life. The Church has a role in the world: to be open to God's hospitality (in thought and practice) and, in doing so, be an invitation in the world, a sacrament of God's love and reconciliation. Recall the parenting example: immersion in certain responsibilities and shared practices opens us to an understanding of what life is about. Worship and discipleship are the local practices that open us to knowing what human beings are for (and will lead us to see depth of parenting as well). And with this point, we return to the leading line of the Gallup report (that indicates disparity in "Catholic" views). It reveals an instrumental conception of reason, which presupposes that moral pronouncements should be able to overcome the fact that some Catholics worship and others do not. The actual study, however, underlines the fact (that "worship works") that moral reasoning needs a practical home.

Methodology and Foundations

The previous section sets the coherence of moral reason in a context of shared practices and, in the final paragraphs, it specifies worship and discipleship as basic practices of the Church. The closing reference to worship helps us to pick up the history of moral theology where we left it, at the close of Vatican II. Recall that the Council's "Decree on Priestly Training" calls for a renewal of moral theology through its "living contact" with Christ as well as by drawing on Scripture and the call to disciples to live out God's love for the world. Recall also John Mahoney's description of the decades that follow Vatican II. The discipline witnesses a proliferation of proposals and lines of inquiry, along with a lack of common ground on the method and system in moral theology. This section, first, will look at debates about methods and systematic approaches for determining moral goods and making judgments about moral and immoral acts. Second, it will consider attempts to set moral theology within theology as a whole.

As Mahoney notes, the literature after Vatican II is broad in scope. Central themes and trends can be noted, but they will look more orderly than how the conversation and debates actually proceed. A chapter on like this one, on "Catholic moral theology," leaves out too much. With this caveat, we will chart debates about moral judgment with three reference points, the end of manual tradition, Pope Paul VI's encyclical on contraception, *Humanae Vitae* (1968), and *Veritatis Splendor* (1993) – John Paul II's encyclical on moral theology. In the 1970s and 1980s, the (sometimes explicit, but usually implied) context of debate on methods of moral decision-making is the rejection of artificial means of contraception in *Humanae Vitae*. Contraception becomes the lightning-rod issue, not only for debates on method, but also for disagreements on the Church's place within modern culture, the authority of the teaching office of the Church, and an understanding of conscience. Our focus will be narrow: on the modern elements of moral theory and the shift toward a more comprehensive setting for moral deliberation.

We will begin the discussion of method just before *Humanae Vitae*, with an article by Peter Knauer on "the determination of the good and moral evil by the principle of double effect" (1965), later re-worked as "The Hermeneutical Function of the Principle of Double Effect" (1967). Knauer self-consciously works within and intends to move beyond the manual tradition. Drawing from the manual tradition's focus on law, Knauer sets out to develop an analysis of the moral act in-itself within a similar, but much improved modern frame. He is looking for a "fundamental principle of all morality," and he finds it in the principle of double effect, which is marginal in the manuals (1967: 132).

Double effect takes its paradigmatic expression in Thomas Aquinas' discussion of self-defense, where one would intend a good act of preserving life, but foresee the possibility of the unintended effect of killing another. When the case of self-defense becomes a set of principles, double effect requires that an act be good and directed toward a good end, and allows an evil but unintended effect if the good (as in self-defense) is proportionate to the evil. In his effort to develop a single principle of morality, Knauer collapses the various criteria of double effect into an expanded account of the idea that the good must be proportionate to the evil – to how we determine that the good done is in greater proportion to the evil effects.

With Knauer, we see a clear move beyond the manuals and toward modern conceptions of morality: With his revised principle of double effect, the structure of law (typically based in the Ten Commandments) is supplanted by a single principle, through which immoral acts can be seen as irrational and self-contradictory (1967: 143). In a review of Knauer's proposal (in 1965), Richard McCormick criticizes it for lacking an adequate context for reasoning about acts. Knauer allows the intentions of the agent to be the sole determinant of the morality of an act (McCormick, 1981: 11). His theory might go where he would not want it to go, like justifying killing an innocent person in order to save other people. McCormick is careful not to accuse Knauer of the ulitilitarian view that "the consequences define the means" or that "acts in themselves are meaningless," but Knauer and those who develop the theory of proportionate reason (also called the revisionists) will have to defend themselves against this accusation time and time again (Curran, 1977). Critics worry that the theory can be used consistently and rationalize just about anything (Grisez, 1983: 151–4).

By the early 1970s, McCormick is defending a more sophisticated version of Knauer's proportionalism. What causes the change? It is hard to say exactly, but it is clear that revisionism gains momentum after the promulgation of *Humanae Vitae* in 1968. Many believe that the encyclical puts an unwarranted burden on married couples by rejecting artificial means of contraception and allowing only the rhythm method for spacing births. Bernard Häring argues that the unitive good of marital sexuality (the relational good) is undermined by the encyclical insofar as it limits the good of sexuality to its physical structure (Häring, 1969). Proportionalism is a complex theory, but suffice it to say that (1) it seeks to allow more latitude of action than permitted by traditional Catholic morality and the official teaching of the Church, and (2) the teaching on contraception is the paradigm case. Proportionate reason provides a way to sustain the Church's teaching on "openness to procreation" as a general principle, but in the circumstances (burdens and benefits) of a particular case, show that couples are able to make a judgment to use contraception.

As the theory develops, revisionists continue to field criticisms like those levied by McCormick in 1965. For instance, they indicate that they are not undermining basic conceptions of good and evil acts, but showing that the description of an act is complete only in the particular context of the act, which includes circumstances and consequences. In the end, it is fair to say that the revisionists are not consequentialists or utilitarian, but what keeps them from falling into such problems are accounts of goods and descriptions of acts that their own theory cannot provide. Jean Porter argues that proportionalism confronts and perpetuates problems in defining acts that can be resolved only by "a more comprehensive theory that sets basic goods into a wider context of significance . . . a context that can provide substantive moral guidance . . ." (1989: 132).

John Paul II's encyclical, *Veritatis Splendor* (1993), is our next reference point because it deals directly with the decades of debate about decision-making and proportionate reason and it looks to a more comprehensive location for understanding morality. On the matter of proportionate reason, the encyclical makes arguments similar to McCormick's critique in 1965, that the theory allows intentions to run free from the character of the act that is chosen and willed (no. 78). (An example is given of making the choice to steal with the intention of giving to the poor.) Because of its challenge to the revisionists, the encyclical's defenders and detractors often mistakenly associate its arguments with the work of Germain Grisez and others who are proponents of a theory called the new natural law. In doing so, they separate the arguments in the second chapter (on issues of moral law and intrinsic evils) from the whole of the document (from chapters one and three).

Through the decades following *Humanae Vitae*, proponents of the new natural law carry on a debate with revisionists and provide an alternative and much more comprehensive account of practical reason (Grisez 1983, 1993). However, Grisez and his collaborators attempt to counter proportionalism with a similar kind of focus on the application of principles to acts (again we see the legacy of the manuals and modern moral theory). Unlike Knauer (and Kant), the new natural lawyers set moral reason in reference to goods that fulfill human beings, but like Kant, they attempt to ensure the reasonableness of norms through epistemology – through an account of what practical reason in-itself requires. In an effort to resist shallow appeals to experience and happiness, their reference to the human good is conceptual: it is a test of rational consistency. Like Knauer, they are looking to define moral evil as a rational contradiction.

John Paul II sets his account of practical reason in a different context. In the first part of the encyclical, he uses the biblical story of the rich young man who asks Jesus, "What good must I do to have eternal life?" (Matt 19:16–21). This question, according to John Paul II, is not an attempt to calculate an entry fee into heaven, but a sign that the young man is drawn to the wonder and beauty of Jesus' proclamation (Mark 1:15), "The time is fulfilled, and the kingdom of God is at hand; repent and believe in the Gospel" (1993: no. 8). The encyclical presents the moral life "as the response due to the many gratuitous initiatives taken by God out of love for man" (1993: no. 10). It pushes beyond morality as mere adherence to precepts to fulfillment in the love of God. Within the frame of Catholic social thought, human beings are *meant* for love – for being fulfilled in the goods of life (the work, relationships, beauty, and pleasures), for seeking the good for others and the good that we share in common.

After the second chapter on moral theory (proportionalism and such), the encyclical concludes with discussions of freedom, faith, and the moral life as a witness for the world. In effect, moral theory is framed by a more comprehensive vision of the character and purpose of living a Christian life – of following Jesus. The basic (and very local) moral question is: what are we Christians called to do in the world? This question (recall the analogy of parenting) puts moral theology in the context of theology as a whole, and it a context where the Christian life connects us to an understanding of what it means to be human – of what life is all about. This is our concluding point: the basic questions of discipleship draw together the introduction on "worship works," what we need to do when the "compress" of a narrow understanding of ethics is lifted, how we make sense of everyday life in relationship to the big picture, and where moral theology becomes more theological.

Let a few examples serve as a conclusion. Shortly after Vatican II, when moral theology attempts to find its place in theology as a whole, two issues that arise are how to use Scripture and if the Christian life presents a distinctive ethics (McNamara 1985). Within the modern framework, these questions must be answered in the abstract in relationship to a free-standing account of practical reason. On the nature of Scripture, we would ask how revelation and revealed morality square with what a Kantian or Humean might determine as rational duty or natural sentiments. The question is, not what are Christians called to do, but what is required of anyone and everyone apart from the specific call of discipleship? Predictably, the question of the distinctiveness of Christian ethics becomes central, and the conclusion (within the typical modern frame) is that Christians have no particular ethics, but religion does give a particular motivation to be moral (Gustafson 1975). Ironically, the first attempts at a Scriptural ethics lead to restating the approach of the manuals by isolating ethics in a separate sphere.

What is the role of a Christian in the world? This chapter, particularly the second section, argues that this kind of question offers a more consistent and reasonable approach to moral inquiry. It puts the particulars of the Christian life (worship and discipleship) in terms of what life is about for human beings and, at the same time, sets moral theology more deeply in the context of Scripture and theology as a whole. The Christian profession of faith that God is with us in Jesus Christ guides how Christians think about life. Scripture, in this frame, is not primarily a book of principles that should be made to correspond to a disinterested point of view or popular ideas of happiness and pleasure. Nor is it a how-to manual where we mechanically repeat Jesus' actions. The biblical narrative gives us purpose and direction, and in doing so, provides a context to think practically and imaginatively about how to live. Entering into the Christian life offers a practical connection to a comprehensive picture of human life.

The biblical story of redemption in Christ "enables us to recognize *which* features of experience are significant, guides *how* we act, and forms *who* we are in the community of faith" (Spohn, 2000: 2). Christians learn to see life through entering into a life of prayer, common worship (especially the celebration of Eucharist), and following Jesus' way of love and works of mercy. We Christians often go wrong in our call and must learn to be truthful about our sins: to see the difference grace makes to our failures. This way of life forms our vision and imagination insofar as we are open to God's loving presence in the world. This distinctive (but not exclusive) way is a role in the world. In this regard, a dismissal of the particularity of being Christian seems to assume a posture of openness, but, in fact, it cuts Christians (as Christians) off from playing a part in social and political life. By taking a deep look into the logic of worship and discipleship, we better engage matters in the world (Cavanaugh, 2003). Worship opens us to God's offer of friendship, which brings us into a life of forgiveness and calls us to see the good

(God's good) in our neighbors (including enemies) and to an everyday life of seeking their good. In other words, we are called to a life of love and justice (Wadell, 2002).

References and Further Reading

Barr, S.M. (2006) "The Miracle of Evolution," *First Things*, 160, 30–3.

Bloom, P. (2005) "Is God an Accident?' *The Atlantic Monthly*, 296: 5, 105–12.

Bossy, J. (1987) *Christianity in the West 1400–1700*. Oxford: Oxford University Press.

Brockman, J. (1995) "The Emerging Third Culture," in Brockman (ed.) *The Third Culture: Beyond the Scientific Revolution*. New York: Simon and Schuster, 17–37.

Buckley, J., SJ (1987) *At the Origins of Modern Atheism*. New Haven, CT: Yale University Press.

Cavanaugh, W. T. (2003) *Theopolitical Imagination: Discovering the Liturgy as a Political Act in an Age of Global Consumerism*. New York: T. and T. Clark.

Curran, C. E., SJ (1977) "Utilitarianism and Contemporary Moral Theology: Situating the Debates," *Louvain Studies*, 6: 239–55.

Dawkins, R. (1989) *The Selfish Gene*, 2nd edition. Oxford: Oxford University Press.

Gallagher, J.A. (1990) *Time Past, Time Future: An Historical Study of Catholic Moral Theology*. Mahwah, NJ: Paulist Press.

Grisez, G. (1983) *The Way of the Lord Jesus*, vol. 1: *Christian Moral Principles*. Chicago, IL: Franciscan Herald Press.

Grisez, G. (1993) *The Way of the Lord Jesus*, vol. 2: *Living a Christian Life*. Quincy, IL: Franciscan Press.

Gustafson, J. M. (1975) *Can Ethics Be Christian?* Chicago, IL: University of Chicago Press.

Häring, B., CSsR (1961) *Law of Christ*, trans. E.G. Kaiser, Westminster, MD: Newman Press.

Häring, B., CSsR (1969) "The Inseparability of the Unitive-Procreative Functions of the Marital Act," in Curran, C.E. (ed.) *Contraception: Authority and Dissent*. New York: Herder and Herder, 187–92.

Hume, D. (1966) *Enquiries Concerning the Human Understanding and Concerning the Principles of Morals*, ed. L.A. Selby-Bigge, Oxford: Clarendon Press.

John Paul II (1993) *Veritatis Splendor*. Boston, MA: St Paul Books.

John Paul II (1996) "Truth Cannot Contradict Truth: Address of Pope John Paul II to the Pontifical Academy of Sciences," *L'Osservatore Romano*. October 22.

Jones, J. M. (2005) "Preaching to Another Church's Choir?" *Gallup Poll New Service*, Princeton, NJ (April 26).

Kant, I. (1959) *Foundations of the Metaphysics of Morals*, trans. L. W. Beck. New York: Liberal Arts Press.

Knauer, P., SJ (1967) "The Hermeneutic Function of the Principle of Double Effect." *Natural Law Forum* 12: 132–62.

Kohlberg, L. (1981) *The Philosophy of Moral Development*. San Francisco, CA: Harper and Row.

Lysaught, M. T. and McCarthy, D. M. (2007) "Introduction: The Course of Moral Thinking," in Lysaught and McCarthy (eds.) *Gathered for the Journey: Moral Theology in Catholic Perspective*. Grand Rapids, MI: W.B. Eerdmans.

Mahoney, J., SJ (1987) *The Making of Moral Theology: A Study of the Roman Catholic Tradition*. Oxford: Clarendon Press.

McCool, G., SJ (2000) "The Christian Wisdom Tradition and Enlightenment Reason," in Cernera, A.J. and Morgan, O.J, (eds.) *Examining the Catholic Intellectual Tradition*, vol. 1. Fairfield, CT: Sacred Heart Press, 75–102.

McCormick, R.A., SJ (1981) *Notes on Moral Theology 1965 through 1980*. Washington, DC: University Press of America.

MacIntyre, A. (1984) *After Virtue.* 2nd edition. Notre Dame, IN: University of Notre Dame.

MacIntyre, A. (1998) *A Short History of Ethics.* 2nd edition. Notre Dame, IN: University of Notre Dame.

MacIntyre, A. (2006) *The Tasks of Philosophy: Selected Essays.* Cambridge: Cambridge University Press.

McNamara, V. (1985) *Faith and Ethics: Recent Roman Catholicism.* Dublin: Gill and Macmillan.

Mill, J. S. (1931) *Utilitarianism, Liberty, and Representative Government*, ed. A.D. Lindsay, New York: E.P. Dutton and Co.

Murphy, N. (1990) *Theology in the Age of Scientific Reasoning.* Ithaca, NY: Cornell University Press.

Newman, J.H. (1998) "Faith and Reason Contrasted as Habits of Mind," in *Fifteen Sermons Preached before the University of Oxford between A.D. 1826 and 1843.* Notre Dame, IN: University of Notre Dame Press, 176–201.

Newport, F. (2005) "U.S. Catholics Vary Widely on Moral Issues." *Gallup Poll News Service*, Princeton, NJ (April 8).

Paul VI (1975) *Decree on Priestly Training, Optatam Totius*, in Flannery, A. (ed.) *The Conciliar and Post-Conciliar Documents, Vatican Council II.* Dublin: Dominican Publications.

Pieper, J. (1997) *Faith, Hope, Love.* San Francisco, CA: Ignatius Press.

Porter, J. (1989) "Moral Rules and Moral Actions: A Comparison of Aquinas and Modern Moral Theory," *Journal of Religious Ethics* 17: 123–49.

Prümmer, D. M., OP (1931) *Manuale Theologiae Moralis.* Freiburg: Herder.

Rawls, J. (1971) *A Theory of Justice.* Cambridge, MA: Belknap Press.

Sherwin, M., OP (2003) "Four Challenges for Moral Theology in the New Century." *Logos* 6: 1, 13–26.

Spohn, W. C. (2000) *Go and Do Likewise: Jesus and Ethics.* New York: Continuum.

Taylor, C. (1989) *Sources of the Self: The Making of the Modern Identity.* Cambridge, MA: Harvard University Press.

Wadell, P. J. (2002) *Becoming Friends: Worship, Justice, and the Practice of Christian Friendship.* Grand Rapids, MI: Brazos Press.

CHAPTER 25
The End

James J. Buckley

Natural and Supernatural Promises and Hopes

For what do we hope? The future holds numerous joys and griefs in store for us: a next meal or a new friend, wars or peace, a slow or quick death, a cosmos that will wear itself out or eternally recur. For what, then, shall we hope, and how? I begin with the assumption that "hoping" is not simply expecting but also desiring – and that our hopes are dispositions enacted in sundry practices in which we engage. More importantly, for persons of Catholic faith, our hopes are intertwined with God's hopes or, better, God's promises – ignoring them, resisting them, responding to them in thanks and petition and trust. The triune God, we shall see, holds out the promise of the judgment of the living and the dead as well as resurrection and eternal life. But what does this future have to do with our hopes as individual persons situated in communities across cosmic time?

The goal here is to sketch an answer to this question – or, as it turns out, three inseparable questions: What does God promise for us? How do we hope in response? How will God's promises and our hopes be fulfilled? I use monuments from Scripture to focus the first question, some highlights of Catholic tradition to focus the second question, and some contemporary disputed questions to focus the third question. But the goal of the essay here is not to survey Scripture, Tradition, and contemporary signs of the times in some encyclopedic fashion. Instead, using signposts from these traditional sources of Catholic living and thinking, the goal is to describe and re-describe Catholic hopes in the light of God's promises for us. We could call this a Catholic "eschatology": the language and logic (*logos*) of last or ultimate things (*eschata*). But, for reasons we shall see, academics use "eschatology" and "eschatological" in diverse and competing ways today. I will usually use more ordinary language.

God's Promise and Human Hopes

God's Word of promise

The Bible begins with God creating the world and ends with a vision of Jesus' coming again – with much in between about God's saving activity and human response. Thus, the Word of God calls Catholics to think and feel and act not only in the light of our beginnings as God's creatures and our current lives as disciples of Jesus but also in light of our future. How so?

Why does God create the world? In Genesis 1, God creates a good world, a world of light and darkness, sky and water, land and plants, day and night, birds and wild animals. This physical world is good, and God has a future for it as well as for the male and female whom God creates in God's image and likeness. What are these plans? The God of Genesis does not create us to go out of existence, or to be reincarnated. But the Genesis saga of our origins also does not explicitly tell a story of God raising us from the dead. Instead, when God finishes (completes, perfects) the multitude of Creation, God rests. Thus, in Genesis 1, God creates the world for Sabbath rest. That is, God creates the world for Israel and for that climactic day of worship when all Creation will join the Jewish people "resting" with the Lord. In still other words, God creates the world for communion with God. The end God has in store for the world does not just arrive in the future. This end (communion with God) is built into this beginning (God creates us). A Catholic eschatology, we shall see, concerns itself with innumerable hopes and fears about the end-time. But Catholics need to constantly ask what these diverse events have to do with the singular event God intends from the beginning (communion with God and each other).

There are many puzzling features of this story of God's promises and human hopes – mysteries probed throughout the Old and New Testaments, the Christian (as well as Jewish) traditions, and today. For one example, are we created (body and soul) mortal or immortal? On one reading of Genesis, God created us immortal, not only as spirits or souls but also as embodied dust of the earth. Adam and Eve's disobedience includes a loss of that immortality – and God's promises are a promise to restore that immortality. But if Adam and Eve were created immortal, how is their loss of immortality different from a loss of their identity as God's good creatures? Perhaps the promised eternal Sabbath rest with God is not natural but a "superadded" (as Catholics with Augustine have sometimes said) gift to them *for* which rather than *in* which they were created. What, then, is the relationship between our identity as created (finite, mortal) beings and the promised immortality? Genesis is seemingly redefining death to include not only the perishing of individuals and groups (biological and social death) but also the possibility of eternal exile from the very communion with God Genesis promises – a possibility against which God works by clothing Adam and Eve (in the Torah, Jews might say – in Christ's baptismal garments, Christians would say) (Anderson, 2001).

But such unresolved issues in the Genesis saga are part of the reason there are so many diverse practices, stories, and beliefs about death in the Old Testament. For example, Psalm 88 is the lament of an innocent sufferer as his life "draws near to Sheol" (the time and space of the dead), charging God with terrorizing him by putting him in the Pit where "the shades" can hardly declare God's steadfast love. The Psalmist is skeptical that God can work wonders for the dead. Perhaps most famously, Job not only laments that those who go down to Sheol do not return (e.g., Job 7: 9–10) but also prefers death to his life of suffering. We are mortal, and there are fates worse than death. What we might call psychological or political death is as serious a problem as biological and physical death: the darkness visible of depression and the ravages of poverty and hunger as serious as our personal death or that of the cosmos.

On another hand, the book of Wisdom – a deuterocanonical book written during Israel's exile – echoes some of the arguments for the immortality of the soul in the *Phaedo* of Plato (d. 347 BC). In the face of his own death, Plato's Socrates argued that the souls of our bodies are immortal, reincarnated until we reach full participation in the immortal forms of beauty and goodness. These forms, Socrates also argued, were the unchanging foundation of our changing world. But Wisdom argues not that an eternally reincarnating soul attains unchanging immortality in union with the forms but that religious martyrs are made immortal by virtue of being created in the image of God's own eternity (Wisdom 2:24). On a third hand, the book of Daniel concludes, after Daniel's visions of the wars and anguish of "the time of the end," by offering hope that the dead shall arise for their reward at the end of days, after death's "rest" (Daniel 12:13). This is the apocalyptic promise of the resurrection of the dead so influential on later Jews like the Pharisees who (unlike the Sadducees) hoped for the resurrection of the dead in the time of Jesus.

Gospels

The New Testament drama is enacted on Israel's stage – the Israel in exile, remembering the lamentations of the innocent, continuing the debate with their Greek Gentile world on immortality, yearning for the resurrection of the dead that would become a central conviction of rabbinic Judaism. But New Testament thinking about the dead is shaped not only by engagement with death in all its naturalness and unnaturalness in the Gentile world, nor only by the lamentations and apocalyptic convictions of Israel. It is most specifically shaped by the narratives of the life and teaching, the death and resurrection of Jesus Christ. In the Synoptic Gospels (Matthew, Mark, and Luke), Jesus comes on the public scene preaching that "the kingdom" is at hand – whether the kingdom of God (Mark and Luke) or the kingdom of heaven (Matthew). "Heaven" here is not an abstract space in which people should hope. Catholics hope for more than the heaven and the earth that are God's good creation (Gen 1:1). The kingdom of heaven is God near to earth – or, perhaps for Christian philosophers, God's space created by God. Jesus' words and deeds announce that God's promises to Israel and therefore to all the families of the earth are being fulfilled. Jesus' parables of joy and festivity, of the apocalyptic judgment of the mighty and the raising up of the powerless (Mark 13 and parallels) are stories of a new time within our midst – just as his wondrous deeds (miracles) are enactments of the promised coming of God's promised communion (Schnackenberg, 1963).

But it has been rightly said that "the Gospels were written backwards" in the sense that all the Gospel writers – indeed, all the books of the New Testament – begin with the conviction that the Jesus whose life and death they narrate is the risen One both in their midst and still coming again. Jesus' words and deeds announcing that the promises to Israel and therefore to the nations are being fulfilled (the kingdom is at hand!) must be responded to in the context of his death and resurrection. The end of the world is happening.

But what is this resurrection, and how does it bear on the resurrection of others? The brief (sometimes very brief) stories of Jesus' resurrection are peculiar – and not simply because there are many differences in their details. Unlike the story of Jesus' raising of Lazarus, we have no story of Jesus rising and walking out of the tomb. The stories of the risen Jesus are also not mere stories of the rise of faith. Jesus invites the early disciples to touch him and then eats with them, suggesting that his risen identity is physical and spiritual (Luke 24:39–42). In John, Jesus offers his body to the doubting Thomas to see and touch – yet also praises those who have not yet seen but still believe (John 20:27–8).

In sum, the Gospels portray Jesus' resurrection as unique to him: it is not resuscitation like we might imagine Lazarus', or a fiction, or merely spiritual – and yet the risen Jesus is real, physical as well as spiritual. The modern versions of these efforts to see and touch the risen Jesus are efforts to "(dis)prove" historically that Jesus rose from the dead, and they need to be treated with similar narrative nuance: Jesus is risen "historically" if at all – but his resurrection is at the same time the fulfillment of all history and therefore unlike other merely "historical events" (Peters, Russell, and Welker, 2002). No wonder that, in John's Gospel, Jesus does not simply rise from the dead but says "*I am* the resurrection and the life" (John 11:25), even before his resurrection. Resurrection is not simply something that happens to Jesus or that Jesus does. Resurrection is who Jesus Christ is. God's hopes for Jews and Gentiles are thus focused on Jesus' life and death and resurrection – resurrection in the light of the final judgment of his crucifixion, crucifixion in the light of Israel as God's suffering servant, judgment in the light of God's intended communion (Ratzinger, 1988; Wright, 2003).

Paul

Thus, Jesus is the kingdom come – and yet Jesus has his disciples continue to pray for the coming kingdom as they pray the Lord's Prayer. We can see some of the perplexity this causes among early Christians in Paul's letters – for example, in the Letters to the Thessalonians (commonly thought to be the earliest writings in the New Testament). Paul and at least some members of the Thessalonian community expect the end (the completion of God's plans) soon, before they die. What is happening to those who have already died? How can the community grieve for them with hope rather than without hope? (1 Thess 4:13). Note that Paul's faith in resurrection does not lead him to teach that mourning is itself unhopeful, any more than Jesus' tears at Lazarus' tomb are unfitting. Paul says that "through Jesus God will bring with him those who have died" and that at the end-time "the dead in Christ will rise first." Those like himself who are living "will be caught up [in Latin, *rapiemur*] in the clouds together with them to meet the Lord in the air." Paul is imagining a resurrection (a rising) of those who have not died, the metaphor of being passively "caught up" emphasizing that it is God who will raise them (and not they who raise themselves) (compare Matt 24:37–41). Hence, Paul implies, we can encourage each other to be hopeful in our grief. Blessed are they who mourn. Paul develops his theology of the resurrected body further in 1 Corinthians 15. In Romans he places our hopes in the context of a cosmos that groans with labor pains for the end (Rom 8:23), convinced that God's promises to Israel are irrevocable but in sorrow and anguish over how this can be so (Rom 9–11).

Apocalypse

The Book of Apocalypse (Revelation) – visions and auditions of "what must soon take place" from the God who is and was and is to come in the midst of persecution (1:1, 4) – has been the most controversial book in the New Testament. On the one hand, it is a narrative that begins with Jesus Christ who is Alpha and Omega (1:8) presiding over a Church of martyrs and the lukewarm. It concludes with the arrival of the new heaven and new earth, a new Jerusalem descending amid Gentile politics, a wedding feast during which "mourning and crying and pain will be no more" (Revelation 21). Catholics have traditionally read these visions and used them in the Eucharistic liturgy, presuming the Gospel narratives (including Jesus' own apocalyptic teachings [Mark 13:2–27 with parallels in Mark, Luke, and John]) and Paul's letters (including Paul's apocalyptic teachings in 2 Thessalonians and elsewhere), distinguishing what is to be taken literally and metaphorically in the light of these other sections of the New Testament.

But this is not always easy to do because (on the other hand) the Book of Revelation presents detailed scenarios of the events of the end-time that most Catholics have been reluctant to make communal teaching, except in a metaphorical sense. The most famous instance of such detail is the vision of beheaded martyrs reigning with Christ for a millennium, after which there will be a battle between Satan and the saints, at the end of which "Death and Hades were thrown into the lake of fire" in a "second death" (Rev 20). The Book of Revelation raises the important question of how detailed a vision of the object of their eschatological hopes Catholics are permitted and required to have.

Traditions of Catholic Hopes

What are the key traditional monuments of Catholic hopes in response to God's promises? Here is one selection, focused on Christian councils and creeds, but with more popular dispositions and practices in the background as the traditions were changed and maintained in life and thought.

Worldly and otherworldly

"Gnosticism" continues to be the dominant name for a style of living and thinking that influenced ancient Jewish, Christian, and pagan communities. Gnostics held that the end of the world would mean the destruction of the material world, leaving enlightened elites to enjoy their largely secret but somehow saving truth (Daly, 1991: 28). Early Christians rejected Gnostic depreciation of God's material creation, the flesh

God's Word became, and the promised resurrection of the fleshly body. The Catholic alternative to Gnostic beliefs emerges clearly in the early creeds, with their clear affirmations of God's creation of all things visible and invisible, Jesus Christ's incarnate life and death and resurrection and promised return in glory, and the resurrection of the dead and the eternal life of the age to come (creed of Constantinople, 381 AD in Neuner and Dupuis, 2001: paragraph 10). But a Gnostic style of thinking persistently emerges inside as well as outside the Catholic tradition. For example, it was against medieval Cathars (at least some of whom were nourished by Gnostic literature) that the Fourth Lateran Council (1215 AD) taught that "all rise again with their own bodies which they now bear . . ." (Neuner and Dupuis, 2001: paragraph 20). And some argue that there is now a "gnostic return in modernity" (O'Regan, 2001).

Sometimes the same Gnostics tempted to radically other-worldly hopes could also take the Apocalypse's promise of Christ's this-worldly thousand-year reign literally (John 20:1–21:5). But variants of such "millenarianism" (mille being Latin for one thousand) were also positions in some orthodox Christian communities, articulated by theologians like Justin (d. c.165) and Tertullian (d. c.220) as well as by saints like Irenaeus (d. c.200). The Greek theologian Origen (d. c.254) was scornful of millenarians for taking passages like Apocalypse 21 to imply an earthly beatitude (On First Principles 2.11.2). Latin theologians took the promised millennium more seriously, but Augustine (d. 604) would come to interpret the millennium allegorically as the era of the Church (City of God 20.7). Like Gnosticism, millenarianism also persistently emerges in the later tradition. Joachim of Fiore (d. 1202), a Cistercian abbot out to reform the Church, offered one particularly influential version of the medieval pursuit of the millennium (Cohn, 1970). He divided world-history into three ages (Christ to Constantine, Constantine to his present, and the coming more spiritual Church), paralleling the Trinitarian revelation of Father, Son, and Spirit. In 1215 the Fourth Lateran Council condemned his Trinitarian theology for underplaying the unity of the triune God – and overplaying the unity between creator and creature (Neuner and Dupuis, 2001: paragraphs 317–20). But he influenced later movements from the Spiritual Franciscans in the thirteenth and fourteenth centuries to the great nineteenth-century Romantics in their quest for a God and a world other than those that currently exist. To this day (see below on Dispensationalism) arguments over whether to take the millennium of Revelation 21 literally are one instance of a larger set of issues about the importance and the limits of the material and the political in Christian hopes.

Apokatastasis and predestination

In the background of the disputes over the worldly and otherworldly aspects of God's promises and human hopes are controversies over the end and beginning of God's promises and Catholic hopes. Followers of Origin were deeply involved in debates with followers of Plato about the laws governing the destiny of the cosmos. Such Originists taught that there would be a complete restoration (apokatastasis) of all things at the end of time, saying or implying that "the punishment of the demons and of impious human beings is temporary." The central creeds are entirely focused on God's promises rather than any threats of punishment. But the first Council of Constantinople condemned the doctrine of *apokatastasis* in 543 AD (Neuner and Dupuis: 2001, paragraph 2,301). The Catholic, Latin West would be shaped less by debate with Origen's followers than by St Augustine's deep understanding of the persistence of human sin. Augustine came to teach that God predestines some to punishment and some to salvation (*Enchiridion* 26.100). Human history is the theater in which the two cities battle, under the grace of God. The Council of Orange (529 AD) vindicated Augustine's doctrine of grace, while condemning those who believe that God predestines some to evil (Neuner and Dupuis, 2001: paragraph 1,922). As we shall see, this struggle between the confession that Jesus will come to judge (saving some, condemning others?) and the confession that the Sprit brings resurrection and eternal life (for all?) shapes Catholic practice and belief to this very day.

Immortal souls and resurrected bodies

The Catholic tradition of eschatology also developed practices and teachings for responding to questions about Catholic hopes for individuals in the wake of Paul's teaching on "spiritual bodies" (1 Cor 15). While some Catholics were tempted to hope for a purely spiritual end (Plato's immortal soul in a world of spirits, or forms), the more frequent temptation was materialist – imagining that our risen bodies will be our present bodies simply reconstituted (Tugwell, 1990; Bynum, 1995). But, particularly after Thomas Aquinas (d. 1274), Catholics came to think of human beings not as two things (body and soul) but as body "formed" by soul. For example, the Council of Vienne (1312) rejected any teaching "which rashly doubts that the substance of the rational soul is truly and essentially the form of the human body" (Neuner and Dupuis 2001: paragraph 405). Not even in the tomb does God abandon the body. Bodily relics on this view are not simply remains of the dead but, indwelt by the Spirit, anticipations of bodily resurrection.

In the fourteenth century popes could dispute whether the vision of God would occur only at the final judgment or (as most of the tradition held and holds) immediately after death, leaving open the question of whether there might be an increase in intensity in beatific vision between personal death and final judgment (Neuner Dupuis: paragraph 2,305). The dispute was seemingly trivial. However, it occurred not long after what is in many ways the climax of the traditional Catholic visions of the end: the *Divine Comedy* of Dante Alighieri (1265–1321) – an imagined journey through hell, purgatory, and paradise. Even more divisive disputes were to come.

Purgatory

What happens in between death and resurrection? Catholics have appealed to Jewish apochryphal literature, some of the sayings of Jesus (Matt 12:31; Luke 16:19–26) and Paul (1 Cor 3:11–15), and popular accounts of after-death journeys in other worlds to answer this question. But such intermediate states do not form a central topic in canonical Scriptures, or early creeds. It was as the practice of prayers for the dead (particularly as part of the Eucharist) became important that the logic of purgatory developed (Le Goff, 1984). Prayers for the dead along with prayers to the saints (particularly the martyrs) were part of the communion between the living and the dead brought about by Jesus Christ's death and resurrection.

The first large-scale controversy over the doctrine of purgatory occurred as part of a larger argument between Greek and Latin Christians. Greeks worried that the doctrine of purgatory and its allied practices (especially praying for the dead) could sound too much like a promise of the *apokatastasis* of all things condemned at the Council of Constantinople (above). At the Council of Florence (1439 AD) both sides could agree that the souls of the penitent are "cleansed after death by purgatorial penalties" and the prayers of the faithful (Neuner and Dupuis, 2001: paragraph 2,308). But the Council failed to affect the unity professed.

The sixteenth-century Catholic and Protestant Reformations were centrally arguments over justification by faith as well as an argument over the sources of the faith justified (Scripture and/or Tradition). But prayers for the dead in purgatory were tightly tied to both issues. Evangelical Lutherans confessed that purgatory "is contrary to the fundamental article that Christ alone, and not the work of man, can help souls. Besides, nothing has been commanded or enjoined upon us with reference to the dead. All this may consequently be discarded, apart entirely from the fact that it is error and idolatry" (Smalkald Articles [1537], Part II, Article II in Tappert, 1959: 295). Reformed and other Protestant Christians would have, by and large, agreed. Practices bearing on purgatory (praying for the dead, venerating relics of saints) were at least not required by Scripture and at most idolatrous. In response, the Council of Trent (1563) reaffirmed the traditional teaching of the Councils of Lyon and Florence about purgatory and prayers for the dead, while calling for the elimination from sermons of "difficult and subtle questions which do not make for edification" and extirpation of anything generated by "curiosity or superstition, or smack of dishonorable gain" (Neuner and Dupuis, 2001: paragraph 2,310). Divisions between Catholics and Protestants came to eclipse their common hope in the triune God's promises of judgment, resurrection, and eternal life, until more recent times.

Mary's assumption, and a new heaven and a new earth

One locus of Catholic eschatology in modernity was the question of whether Mary has already been raised, or assumed. Mary is not always an important character in the New Testament (e.g., in Paul). When she is important in the Gospels, the stories are episodes in the larger story of Jesus. Early councils taught that Mary was "mother of God" (*theotokos*), but such teachings about Mary were part of larger debates about the triune God, incarnate in Jesus Christ. Nonetheless, popular piety and Church worship extended these snapshots of Mary into a more comprehensive story, from her beginning to her end. Mary is, like us, human. Mary is, unlike us, mother of God. Therefore, Mary was among the first to participate in Christ's resurrection. In 1950, Pius XII sol-

emnly taught that Mary, "preserved from the corruption of the tomb," has already
been "taken up body and soul into the glory of heaven" (Pius XII, *Munificentissimus
Deus* [1950]; Neuner and Dupuis, 2001: paragraphs 713–15).

Even as Catholics came to agree on the dogma of Mary's assumption before Vatican II, there was a wider debate among Catholics in France and Germany during
and after World War II between Incarnationalists (Henri de Lubac, Pierre Teilhard de
Chardin, G. Thils, A. Dondeyne) and Eschatologists (L. Bouyer, J. Danielou, R. Guardini, and Josef Pieper) (Hayes, 1989). The former emphasized how God's incarnation
called for Christians to be deeply involved with the modern world in all its materiality;
the latter emphasized how God's promised coming called for Christians to focus on the
coming God's apocalyptic transformation of the world. The debate was distinct from
yet informed by the dramatic debates rethinking eschatology among liberal and neo-
orthodox Protestant theologies and historians in the nineteenth and early twentieth
centuries. It was also symptom of much larger changes to come.

The Catholic reformation that surfaced at the Second Vatican Council (1962–5) was
informed by a renewed view of the nature and mission of the Church in the modern
world. As the *Constitution on the Church* puts it, the Church's mystery is not itself but the
triune God who calls the Church to be a sacrament for the world. The Church, a people
of God and hierarchy, is a pilgrim Church whose holiness is "true though imperfect."
The saints in heaven are more intimately united to Christ than we are, and therefore "bring greater consolation to the holiness of the whole Church" (Neuner and
Dupuis, 2001: paragraphs 2,311–22). Further, the *Pastoral Constitution on the Church
in the Modern World* describes a Church that exists pastorally in solidarity with the
world, particularly the world of the poor and afflicted. This solidarity (including communion with the living and the dead) sets the context for human activity throughout
the cosmos. One of the climaxes of the Council is the teaching that the hope for a new
heaven and new earth should energize our transformation of this world rather than
evacuate it, for God is now "preparing a new habitation and a new earth in which justice resides, and whose happiness will fulfill and surpass all the longings for peace
which arise in human hearts" (Neuner and Dupuis, 2001: paragraph 2,316). This solidarity with the poor and oppressed was in particular articulated in the "liberation
theologies" (including feminist theologies) that dominated Latin America and other
countries after Vatican II (Gutierrez, 1988; Johnson, 1998).

A central challenge for a post-Vatican II Church is how to embody the *Pastoral Constitution on the Church in the Modern World*'s claim that "the expectation of a new earth
should not weaken but rather stimulate the resolve to cultivate this earth" throughout
its life, while adhering to the claim of the *Dogmatic Constitution on the Church* that our
hope is focused not on us and our world but on Christ and the saints.

Disputed Questions

God promises the world communion with God and each other, mediated through Jesus
Christ and the Spirit's community of Jew and Greek, male and female, slave and free.
Catholic hopes are centered on this promised life with God – on Jesus' return to judge

the living and the dead, Mary's and their own resurrection, a communion of the living and the dead enacted in prayers to the saints and for the dead, aiming to avoid both Gnostic spiritualizing of their hopes and also millenarian confusions of this age and the next. Will these promises and hopes be fulfilled? Here I focus on three disputes.

Dispensationalism and Catholic ecumenism

Christians have long thought of history as a series of "dispensations." The Old and New testaments are "dispensations." Augustine's *City of God* divided history into seven dispensations or eras, modeled on the seven days of creation and rest. Joachim of Fiore, as we saw, proposed three dispensations. But it was not until modernity that entire theological systems were constructed around the notion that there are set dispensations, headed toward a literal reading of the apocalpytic scenarios we saw in the Book of Revelation. In these circles, vigorous arguments take place about whether Christ will come before or after (or neither) this millennial pause. Dispensationalism is often vigorously anti-Catholic, sometimes arguing that Catholics will surely be among those left behind at "the rapture" (that event or those events to which Paul is alluding in 1 Thessalonians) (Olsen, 2003).

The Dispensationalist challenge to Catholic eschatology is multi-dimensional since Dispensationalist assumptions about God and Scripture and the Church are so different from Catholic assumptions. On the one hand, Catholics can respect Dispensationalist eschatological realism in the face of the variety of non-Jesus-centered hopes that inspire the world. Catholics also cannot object to the possibility that they will be "left behind," given Vatican II's reminder that Catholics will be judged more severely than others at the last judgment (*Dogmatic Constitution on the Church*, paragraph 14 in Tanner, 1990, volume II, 860).

On the other hand, Dispensationalism is too easily distracted from the last things that matter most – God's overcoming of sin and suffering and death in Christ and the Spirit's work fulfilling the communion for which God created us and the world. A series of often inscrutably ordered end-time events takes the place of that singular end-time event that is central to Catholic eschatology: God's bringing of our physical, social, historical, and personal world, purged of its self-incurred sin and suffering, into communion with God. Finally, when the story of the end-time eclipses the story of Jesus and the Church, such Dispensationalists sound like those Gnostics whom Catholics have vigorously opposed: Christians become the elite rescued from this corrupt world for another one – yet another species of "the Gnostic return in modernity" (O'Regan, 2001).

It is important that Catholics not confuse such Dispensationalism with "Protestant theology." Dispensationalism is hardly representative of Lutheran and Reformed and more radical reformation traditions that constitute the diverse and competing communities that arose in the sixteenth century. Indeed, thanks to prior ecumenical initiatives in Protestant communities, ecumenical discussions among Christians since Vatican II have discovered much common ground in their shared eschatological convictions prior to the sixteenth-century reformations – and, even more, in their common hope for the Scriptural new heaven and new earth, when God will be all in all. This eschatological common ground has helped Catholics and Orthodox and Protestants relocate their traditional disputes in a larger Trinitarian and Christological context than was traditional (Anderson et al., 1992). For example, the debate over purgatory and prayer for the dead has becomes a debate over the sort of communion between the living and the dead brought about by Christ's death and resurrection. Protestant theology and practice have looked and sounded to Catholics as if they denied or were agnostic about this communion central to all other communions in Christ; Catholic theology and practice have looked and sounded to Protestants as if they affirmed or at least permitted a veritably pagan trafficking between the living and the dead. But for Vatican II Catholics, our praying to the saints and for the dead is embedded in Christ's communion with the living and the dead. In the Catholic liturgical practice of "the litany of the saints," Catholics pray to God (not the saints) for mercy and salvation. In the repeated litany "pray for us" at the Easter vigil, Catholics pray to the saints not as we pray to the Head of the Body but as members of Christ's body, knowing the saints (unlike us) pray as those already in full communion with Christ. Similarly, theologians argue that locating disputes about Mary's assumption (not part of the original sixteenth-century disputes) in this larger Trinitarian, Christological, and ecclesiological context might help Evangelical Protestants see the dogma as at least permissible (Blancy et al., 2002), while showing Catholics its correct location amidst what Vatican II calls "the hierarchy of truths" (Decree on Ecumenism, paragraph 11, in Neuner and Dupuis 2001, paragraph 381).

Pluralism and the culture of death

Catholics profess faith in and place their hope in the God who creates and redeems us and the world for communion with God and each other. Some Jews and most Muslims profess a similar faith, including resurrection of the body. But Catholics and other Christians disagree with Muslims and (most tragically) Jews about the role of Jesus and the Church in God's plans in comparison to the Torah and synagogue, the Qur'an and *ummah*. And there are a variety of what most people today call "religions" that have still other ultimate goals for our lives – perhaps reincarnation and Nirvana, the "scientific" creation of immortal bodies or cybernetic minds, or (less commonly nowadays) the immortality of Plato's world of forms. There are also diverse non-religious views we might call "mortalist" (Callahan, 2003) – popular psychology manuals and neighborhood mortuaries that ask us to "cope" with death (like the ancient Stoics), existentialist endorsement of anxiety and despair in the face of death, terrorist advocates of death as political instrument. Some of these are ingredients of what John Paul II called "the culture of death" in contrast to "the Gospel of life" (Neuner and Dupuis, 2001: paragraph 2,253). We live in a world populated by sundry and conflicting practices and teachings bearing on "last things." No wonder that theologians and others use notions like "last things" or "eschatology" in such diverse and competing ways today.

These diverse and competing eschatologies challenge Catholics hopes, even as Catholic hopes must challenge them. In the face of such plurality, Catholics have been satisfied with neither a facile relativism that leaves our hopes isolated from each other, nor a facile rationalism that posits a hope we all share as the rational foundation for the distinctive hope of disciples of Christ. Among the responses to such eschatological pluralism, two are particularly important. First, in the confidence that only God has a God's-eye view of humanity's diverse and competing hopes, such hopes must be considered one by one, not expecting that a conversation with the Jewish people will be exactly like the dialog and debates with Muslims or Buddhists, with Platonists who hold out for union with immortal forms, or existentialists who hold death to be the end of it all, or more reasonable mortalists. We need to engage in what some Catholic and Protestant theologians have called "ad hoc apologetics" (Werpehowski, 1986) – proceeding in very occasion-specific fashion with Jew first, and then Greeks.

Another way to proceed in the face of this plurality of promises and hopes is by developing a more occasion-comprehensive understanding of hope, death, and the ends of the world using the best of the current physics and biology, the sociology and psychology, the poetry and philosophy of human hopes in the face of death, the dying, and the dead (e.g., Küng, 1984; Ellis, 2002; Peters et al., 2002). For example, I began with the modestly pragmatic assumption that "hoping" is not simply expecting but also desiring – and that our hopes are dispositions enacted in sundry practices in which we engage. Our universal, natural hopes are embedded as much or more in our attitudes toward and practices for the dying and the dead as they are in our myriad beliefs about death and dying. No Catholic theology can ignore this common ground across cultures, even as the Gospel will fulfill and surpass all that culture's longings (e.g., Rahner, 1965; Marcel, [1962] 1978).

But the issue of how Catholics should live and think in a world of diverse and competing promises and hopes is merely tactical unless it addresses a final question: In a world of plural, conflicting promises and hopes, what has happened to God's intent to save everyone?

Heaven, hell, and universalism

God promises and Catholics hope for a new heaven and new earth, when God will be all in all. This communion with God is personal (particular to each individual), social (we are saved together, not alone), and physical (we are saved in our materiality, not only spiritually).

But the world of violence and conflict (in which Catholics too participate) threatens to block God's promises and frustrate Catholic hopes. What then?

It is sometimes said that the key question here is whether non-Catholics (or non-Christians) can be or will be saved. This question is too provincial. Many non-Catholics do not care about the Catholic answer to that question, just as not many Catholics think the question whether everyone (not just Buddhists) will attain Nirvana or whether mortality renders life insignificant are of crucial importance. The key question for Catholics has less to do with whether you or I or our neighbors are saved than with what God intends, and whether God's intent – the goal on which God has set God's hopes – will come about. What God intends is communion with God, not another time and space.

How will God emerge victorious in his communion-project with a world that is violently against or utterly indifferent to that peace project? The Bible's drama, we have seen, frames the question. God creates a world for communion with God and elects the Jewish people to be a blessing unto the nations. The Word became Jewish flesh and dwelt among us, suffering and dying and being buried, raised again on the third day. The Spirit speaks through the prophets, creates the holy Catholic Church with baptism for the forgiveness of sins – all for resurrection and eternal life. Catholics who dare to hope "that all be saved" (1 Tim 2:4) base their hope on God's enacted promise to save us from our sin and death (Balthasar, 1988). God's solidarity with the living and dead extends to death itself, and whatever might be worse than death. Jesus' death resurrects us and the world, saving us from the illusion that our mortuary practices and cemeteries and memorials are more than distant images (which can become idols) of God's present and coming victory to redeem what worldly wisdom would call the irredeemable, including perhaps ourselves. Jesus' parable of the separating of the sheep and the goats (Matt 25) remains a terrifying warning for those who do not practice the corporal works of mercy the parable commends and commands. But the Parabler goes on to become the thirsty, naked prisoner who suffers and dies and is buried for us. Our central fear should not be that we or our neighbors will be among the goats but that we will not be willing to participate in this descent – perhaps to join in Paul's willingness to endure condemnation for the sake of Israel (Rom 9:3) or "the dark night of the soul" of Carmelite contemplatives such as John of the Cross or Thérèse of Lisieux, perhaps and more likely to participate in more ordinary and mundane activity on behalf of those subject to the pseudo-condemnations of the world.

Is this what we earlier called *apokatastasis*, the claim that there will be a universal restoration of all things? We speak here of hope, not knowledge of the outcome of the engagement of divine and human freedoms. *Apokatastasis* (universal restoration) continues to be mistaken, for it constrains divine and/or human freedom. But the claim to know that some are eternally damned is also mistaken insofar as it too constrains the God who has become flesh, died, and descended into hell for us and our salvation. The truth in double predestination is that human history offers many examples of damnable events and deeds and people – and that God's promised communion excludes such things from the beginning. But the truth in *apokatastasis* is that God does indeed intend the salvation of the world God has created. Catholic hope for the end is that God will continue to do a new thing, raising the dead for communion with God.

References and Further Reading

Anderson, Gary A. (2001) *The Genesis of Perfection. Adam and Eve in Jewish and Christian Imagination*. Louisville, KY: Westminster John Knox Press.

Anderson, George H., Stafford, Francis J., and Burgess, Joseph A. (eds.) (1992), *The One Mediator, the Saints, and Mary. Lutherans and Catholics in Dialogue VIII*. Minneapolis, MN: Augsburg.

Augustine (1998) *The City of God against the Pagans*, ed. and trans. R.W. Dyson. Cambridge: Cambridge University Press.

Augustine (1961) *The Enchiridion on Faith, Hope, and Love*, trans. J.F. Shaw. South Bend, IN: Gateway Editions.

Balthasar, Hans Urs von (1988) *Dare We Hope "That all Men be Saved"? With a Short Discourse on Hell*, trans. David Kipp and Lothar Krauth. San Francisco, CA: Ignatius Press.

Blancy, Alain, Jourjon, Maurice, and the Dombes Group (2002) *Mary in the Plan of God and in the Communion of Saints. Toward a Common Christian Understanding*, trans. Matthew J. O'Connell. New York/Mahwah, NJ: Paulist Press.

Buckley, James J. (2004) "On the Invocation of Saints: A Theological Interpretation," *Pro Ecclesia*, 13, 389–92.

Bynum, Caroline Walker (1995) *The Resurrection of the Body in Western Christianity, 200–1336*. New York: Columbia University Press.

Callahan, Daniel (2003) "The Desire for Eternal Life: Scientific Versus Religious Visions," *Harvard Divinity Bulletin*, 31, 13–17.

Cohn, Norman (1970) *The Pursuit of the Millennium. Revolutionary Millenarians and Mystical Anarchists of the Middle Ages*, revised and expanded edition. New York: Oxford University Press.

Daly, Brian E., SJ (1991) *The Hope of the Early Church. A Handbook of Patristic Eschatology*. Cambridge: Cambridge University Press.

Dante Alighieri (1977) *The Divine Comedy*, trans. John Ciardi. New York: Norton.

Ellis, George F.R. (ed.) (2002) *The Far-Future Universe. Eschatology from a Cosmic Perspective*. Published in Association with the Pontifical Academy of Sciences and the Vatican Observatory. Philadelphia, PA and London: Templeton Foundation Press.

Gutierrez, Gustavo (1988) *A Theology of Liberation. History, Politics, and Salvation*, revised edition with a new introduction, translated and edited by Sister Caridad Inda and John Eagleson. Maryknoll, NY: Orbis.

Hayes, Zachary, OFM (1989) *Visions of a Future. A Study of Christian Eschatology*. Wilmington, DE: Michael Glazier.

Johnson, Elizabeth A. (1998) *Friends of God and Prophets. A Feminist Theological Reading of the Communion of Saints*. New York: Continuum.

Küng, Hans (1984) *Eternal Life. Life after Death as a Medical, Philosophical, and Theological Problem*, trans. Edward Quinn. New York: Doubleday.

Le Goff, Jacques (1984) *The Birth of Purgatory*, trans. A. Goldhammer. Chicago, IL: University of Chicago Press.

Marcel, Gabriel ([1962] 1978) *Homo Viator. Introduction to a Metaphysic of Hope*, trans. E. Crauford. New York: Harper and Row.

Neuner, J., SJ and Dupuis, J., SJ (2001) *The Christian Faith in the Doctrinal Documents of the Catholic Church*, 7th edition. New York: Alba House.

Olsen, Carl E. (2003) *Will Catholics be "Left Behind"? A Catholic Critique of the Rapture and Today's Prophecy Preachers*. San Francisco, CA: Ignatius Press.

O'Regan, Cyril (2001) *Gnostic Return in Modernity*. New York: State University of New York Press.

Origen (1966) *On First Principles*, trans. G.W. Butterworth. New York: Harper and Row.

Peters, Ted, Russell, Robert John, and Welker, Michael (eds.) (2002) *Resurrection. Theological and Scientific Assessments*. Grand Rapids, MI and Cambridge: W.B. Eerdmans.

Plato (1914) *Euthyphro, Apology, Crito, Phaedo, Phaedrus*, trans. Harold North Fowler. London: Heinemann and Cambridge, MA: Harvard University Press.

Rahner, Karl (1965) *The Theology of Death*, trans. C.H. Henkey. New York: Herder and Herder.

Ratzinger, Joseph (1988) *Eschatology. Death and Eternal Life*, trans. Michael Waldstein, edited by Aidan Nichols, OP. Washington, DC: The Catholic University of America Press.

Schnackenberg, Rudolph (1963) *God's Rule and Kingdom*, trans. John Murray. New York: Herder and Herder.

Tanner, Norman (1990) *Decrees of the Ecumenical Councils*. 2 vols. London: Sheed and Ward and Washington, DC: Georgetown University Press.

Tappert, Theodore G. (1959) *The Book of Concord. The Confessions of the Evangelical Lutheran Church*. Philadelphia, PA: Fortress Press.

Tugwell, Simon, OP (1990) *Human Immortality and the Redemption of Death*. London: Darton, Longman, and Todd.

Werpehowski, William (1986) "Ad Hoc Apologetics," *The Journal of Religion*, 66, 282–301.

Wright, N.T. (2003) *The Resurrection of the Son of God. Christian Origins and the Question of God*, vol. 3. Minneapolis, MN: Fortress Press.

PART IV
Catholic Practices

CHAPTER 26

Spirituality

Wendy M. Wright

While there are various ways to understand the terms "spirituality" or "the spiritual life," in a traditional Roman Catholic context the latter term generally refers to a life opened to and transformed by the Spirit of God. There are numerous practices, both exterior and interior, that can dispose a person to become responsive to the Spirit. The varied ways in which Roman Catholics at present practice and in the past have practiced the Christian spiritual life are shaped by the Church's long history and its geographical and cultural diversity. This essay will explore both the general character-istics of Roman Catholic spirituality, and some of its historical and cultural diversity, and focus on several exemplary Catholic spiritual practices.

The Pattern of the Christian Spiritual Life

Implied in all Christian spiritual practice is the pattern of transformed life discov-ered in the life, death, and resurrection of Jesus the Christ. The dynamic of dying in order to be raised, of emptying self in order to be given new life, is fundamental. This basic kenotic and resurrected pattern has taken a variety of forms over the centuries. In addition, the forms, while changing according to historical and cultural circum-stance, build on one another. There is then a distinct history of Catholic Christian spirituality that develops over the centuries. It is as if the melody of dying and being raised plays over and over again in different keys with varied harmonies, contrapuntal elements, descants, and rhythms throughout the years.

Implied as well in all Catholic spiritual practice is the understanding, rooted in Scripture, that human beings were originally created in the image and likeness of God and destined to love and serve God. That image, however, is dimmed or wounded through sin. Yet God's redemptive love, incarnated in Jesus the Christ and manifest in the continuing activity of the Spirit, has made a radical restoration possible. It is through the action of God's Spirit that the original image can be cleansed or healed. Thus sanctification, becoming holy and sharing in the holiness of Christ, is the true destiny of each human being. Human beings, prompted by divine grace, cooperate in the process of sanctification through the manner in which they live. In so doing they also participate in the ongoing sanctification of others and of all creation. The spiritual practices of all sorts in which they engage are directed to this larger, God-directed end. Put another way, having been loved into being and loved enough to be sought out and redeemed, human beings complete the circle of love and become what they were intended to be, their "true selves," by loving in return. The pattern for this love is mapped out in the mysteries of the Christ event. Catholics understand this pattern not only as one from which they individually and communally benefit but as one in which they *participate*. The life, death, and resurrection of Jesus, while historical events, are not merely past but events whose dynamic power continues to operate in the world. This dynamism, as it were, enfolds one as he or she opens the self to the power of the transforming Spirit. This, the tradition understands, is as God would have it.

Thus the basic pattern of death and resurrection and the vision of the human person as created by and for God and participating in God's longing for the world through the ongoing action of the Spirit is implied in all Catholic spiritual practice – those varied ways in which Catholics open themselves to and respond to the influence of the Spirit.

In this essay a sharp distinction will not be made between devotional practices associated with laity and other practices long associated with monastic, religious, or clerical status. Rather, the underlying themes that join devotional and elite practices will be explored. Further, as Catholicism is an ongoing and dynamic *tradition* that sees itself as explicitly unfolding under the influence of the Spirit, the historical and geographical extension of the practices discussed will be emphasized. Correspondingly, because Catholic sensibility favors the idea of a cumulative tradition, the continuities rather than the discontinuities between the pre- and post-Reformation and the pre- and post-Vatican II Church and its practices will be underscored. Finally, the approach taken in the essay is descriptive rather than evaluative and the suitability or efficacy or theological interpretation of any given practice will not be attempted. What Catholics have done and continue to do to open to and respond to the breath of the living Spirit is the essay's focus. It remains to listen to the many harmonies, descants, and rhythmic variations of the basic Christocentric melodic line.

Asceticism

Many Catholic spiritual practices have their origins in the experience of the early desert ascetics of Egypt, Palestine, and Syria. The individuals and communities that were part of the "flight to the desert" in the third to sixth centuries took seriously the idea that the Christian life was one of radical transformation by the Spirit. They inherited a tradition in which martyrdom, literal dying, made one a "second Christ." Desert ascetics in their turn died, not to physical life, but "to themselves." They perceived that the untransformed self, shaped by the values of an unredeemed culture, were antithetical to the Christ-life. Greed, luxury, self-aggrandizement, lust, and power-mongering were the values of "the world" while humility, charity, purity of heart, and constant prayer were the qualities of a self transformed by God's Spirit. To empty themselves of the "world" the ascetics sought an environment and cultivated practices that allowed them to die to their former selves and to be receptive to the new, "true" self responsive to the Spirit.

Some of the primary ascetic means to self-emptying were the cultivation of silence and solitude, fasting, celibacy, and voluntary poverty. These exterior practices de-habituated the former self: they allowed the ascetic to listen anew, not to the voices of "the world" but to the voice of God heard in the silence of an emptied heart. They weaned the ascetic from attachment to material goods so that he or she could cleave to God alone. They disciplined the passions so that the ascetic was free to allow the Spirit of God alone to rule the mind and heart. It gradually became understood that the virtues, the gifts of the Spirit, would be given as the self was made spacious enough for the Spirit's entry. Exterior practices were paralleled by interior practices dedicated to the same dynamic of dying to self for the values of the world held sway not only in the "world" the ascetics had left: they held sway as well in the human heart. For example, pride was evidenced not only in the flaunting of society's honors and pedigree but in subtle spiritual one-upmanship, one ascetic lording it over another because of his austere exploits.

In this context the practices of spiritual guidance and the discernment of spirits developed. The desert path to spiritual transformation, it was revealed, was best accompanied by another who had successfully traversed the treacherous byways of the ascetic path. Manifestly holy men, and a few holy women, became recognized as the fathers and mothers of the spiritual life. To these *abbas* and *ammas* neophytes came. Chief among the gifts that the masters offered was the gift of discernment of spirits: the ability to discern the texture, quality, and sound of the Spirit of God from the many other movements occurring in the human mind and heart. Spiritual guidance and the discernment of spirits thus emerged in the tradition as central components of the Spirit-transformed life.

Common Prayer

Alongside the de-habituating and purifying asceticism and the arts of discernment and spiritual guidance, the desert tradition took seriously the biblical injunction to "pray always." Prayer, of course, was from the beginning central to the Christian life as it emerged from its Jewish origins. Distinctly interior forms of prayer were cultivated but the desert tradition had a place for common prayer, especially the repetition of the Psalms. Desert spiritual practice took institutionalized form in monasticism which became the chief carrier of spiritual practice within the Church for over one thousand years. The life of Spirit-led transformation, pursued in common under the guidance of a Rule, became the norm and ideal of the Western Church by the early Middle Ages. The Benedictine tradition is exemplary of Western Christian monasticism and is the type of monastic life that has most influenced Roman Catholicism and thus shaped spiritual practice for vowed religious, clerics, and laity to the present day. Benedict of Nursia (480–543) provided a Rule for Monte Cassino, his men's monastery, and for the cognate female community presided over by his sister Scholastica. The genius of

Benedict's Rule is in the wisdom and balance that it gives to the monastic, and thus the spiritual, life. It incorporates in moderate ways the essential elements of the desert tradition – an asceticism consisting of poverty, chastity, obedience, silence, stability, regulated fasting, and a routine of work alternating with common and individual prayer, all practiced within the context of a community vowed to mutual sanctification under the guidance of a Rule administered by an abbot or abbess assisted by gifted spiritual elders. The dynamics of the kenotic and resurrected life thus became encoded in the practices of the monastery itself.

Perhaps most characteristic of Benedictine life was and is the corporate practice of prayer – the Divine Office – keyed to the rhythm of the Church year. The biblical injunction to "pray always" became the communal responsibility of the monastery, a responsibility enacted in the Divine Office, the seven times daily common prayer drawn from Scripture, especially the Psalms. Through the liturgical cycle the great mysteries of the faith – incarnation, the Pascal mystery, the Triune God – were not merely remembered, but were woven into the fabric of a transformed consciousness. Sacred time was the warp upon which the woof of created time was threaded, the interpretive lens through which human events and identity were viewed, the temporal practice through which the Christocentric pattern of the true self was realized. The Divine Office created, as it were, a lattice-work in time: a series of moments in which created time intersected with and opened out onto eternity. In these moments the monks, prepared by silence and asceticism, listened to God speak through the scriptural prayer and responded with words hallowed by sacred tradition. Time for private prayer was also encoded in the Rule.

Out of this matrix a distinctive method of praying with Scripture developed. *Lectio divina* (divine reading) is a practice that allows for the Word of God to become the transforming food that nurtures the Spirit-filled life. The words of Scripture are metaphorically "eaten": broken open, chewed, savored, and ingested so that they become the substance on which one is fed. The dynamic movements of *lectio* are four, although they need not all be practiced nor need they be done sequentially. *Lectio* (reading a passage aloud, often more than once), *meditatio* (considering or reflecting on the passage, phrases or words from the passage), *oratio* (prayer; responding to the Word heard spoken to you), *contemplatio* (resting lovingly in the divine presence experienced) make up the movements. Through this practice a person is formed by and into the Word of God. The monk Guerric of Igny (born c.1067), a Cistercian (a reformed branch of the Benedictines) in a sermon written for the feast of the Annunciation (celebrating the announcement by the Angel Gabriel to the Virgin Mary that she will bear a child conceived by the Holy Spirit), gives evidence of his deep internalization of Benedictine spiritual prayer practices. "She who conceived God by faith promises you the same if you have faith; if you will faithfully receive the word of God from the mouth of the heavenly messenger you too may conceive the God whom the whole world cannot contain, conceive him, however, in your heart, not in your body . . . Thanks be to you Spirit, who breathe where you will. By your gift I see not one but countless souls pregnant with that noble offspring."

The practice of common prayer emphasizing the Psalms and aligned with the liturgical calendar was to influence the way in which generations of Catholics prayed. The

Breviary is a book of prayer for the clergy, giving directions for all of the various services of the Divine Office throughout the year. Whether the Office is recited publicly in choir or privately by an individual, it is not a private prayer, but the daily service of public praise, rendered to God, as prescribed by the Church. Those who recite the Divine Office do so in the name of all the faithful and for the benefit of all the members of the mystical body of Christ.

Contemplative Prayer

Of course, common prayer was not the only type of prayer associated with monasticism over the centuries. Within the enclosure of the monastery women and men pursued a life of transformation. Presumed was the common life of ascetic discipline. But a more intimate union with God was also sought. Early Greek Church fathers like Origen had written of the mystical ascent of the soul in its return to its creator and, in varying ways, Western monastics continued to cultivate this contemplative process. Often the language of the Song of Songs was the vehicle through which the ineffable transforming union was described: the story of contemplative union was the love story of a lover and a beloved, a tale of seeking and being sought, desiring, unrequited love, and consummation. Classic descriptions of the practice of the contemplative life abound. Several that have special importance today are *The Cloud of Unknowing* written by an anonymous fourteenth-century English contemplative, *The Ascent of Mount Carmel* and *The Dark Night of the Soul* by sixteenth-century Carmelite John of the Cross, and *The Interior Castle* by his Carmelite contemporary Teresa of Avila.

The *Cloud* describes a quiet non-discursive practice of interior prayer that involves placing a "cloud of forgetting" between self and creatures and a "cloud of unknowing" between one's self and God, and relies on a simple phrase expressing the love felt toward the divine to carry the longing of the heart God-ward. This practice is ascetic in its assumption that even the myriad images and thoughts that connote God must be pruned away for authentic union with the mystery of the divine to be effected. *Centering Prayer* is a modern-day popularization of the wisdom of the *Cloud* that from the mid-twentieth century has been taught and promoted for Christians in all walks of life by the Cistercian monastic order.

The great sixteenth-century Carmelites bequeathed to the Catholic world detailed descriptions of the way in which the process of contemplative union may take place. Teresa's classic imagery of the bride-soul spiraling metaphorically through the rooms of a castle toward the center where the bridegroom waits for the consummation of their love, and John of the Cross' austere yet passionate analysis of the process of sensory and spiritual stripping that must occur for union with the divine to occur, have definitively shaped the way the Catholic tradition has come to view the contemplative life. Up through the mid-twentieth century Catholic theorists of spiritual theology considered these Carmelite descriptions of the interior landscape as normative and today, while it is acknowledged that there are other treasured anatomies of the contemplative life that stand alongside these sixteenth-century luminaries, Teresa and John are yet regarded as unparalleled teachers of contemplation.

For centuries monastic life was the yardstick against which any spiritual practice was measured. Even as non-monastic movements such as the Mendicants (Franciscans and Dominicans) emerged in the High Middle Ages, even as laity began to feel that the Spirit-filled life could be cultivated outside cloister walls, the ethos of monastic spirituality dominated. Whether one lived in a vowed community or inside monastery confines or not, asceticism was seen as the prerequisite for genuine spiritual transformation. Medieval holy women who were not members of monastic communities, such as Catherine of Siena (1347–80), Angela of Foligno (1248–1309), and Catherine of Genoa (1447–1510), had their teachings authenticated and witness valued in part because of their asceticism. In addition, with the notable exception of the Jesuits discussed later, when one joined an early modern Catholic religious community that was dedicated to active service such as teaching, hospital work, or missionary outreach, the recitation of the daily Office was seen as a constituent part of spiritual practice for religious. The imprint of the ascetic-monastic model continues well into the present. Echoes of the link between clerical life and asceticism are heard in the continuing Catholic mandate for priestly celibacy. And even while the twentieth-century documents of the Second Vatican Council (*Lumen Gentium*, chapter 5) affirm the universal call to holiness for persons in all walks of life, the evangelical counsels (poverty, chastity, and obedience) are described as constituting a more perfect way of practicing the spiritual life. Finally, the vestiges of ascetic practice have been observed by the rank and file of Catholics for centuries through the obligatory Lenten fasts and Friday abstinence and the practice of fasting before communion that was universally observed up until the mid-twentieth century. These practices have survived in attenuated form to the present day.

There are other ways in which the monastic legacy is still vigorously felt. In the past half century the practice of *lectio divina* has emerged out of the cloister and been promoted as a spiritual practice in which all Christians might profitably engage. Spiritual retreats incorporating silence and solitude, long seen as a practice reserved for religious or priests, now are offered regularly for all at Catholic retreat houses and monasteries. The ancient practice of coming away from the de-formative influences of the larger society to an environment in which intentional spiritual formation can take place is no longer reserved for the few. In addition, spiritual direction is in many places now offered to any in the Church community who wish to deepen their spiritual lives. Nor is the role of spiritual director seen as necessarily linked to monastic, religious, or clerical status. Presently, men and women, lay and religious alike, are actively engaged as spiritual guides while training programs for this ministry flourish.

Embodied Participation

In the West other distinctive non-monastic lifestyles developed that would give rise to new spiritual emphases and practices. The human experience of Jesus captured the imagination of the late medieval Church. The spiritual practices and sensibility of Francis of Assisi (1181/2–1226) may serve as an example. When Francis approached the Gospel stories he perceived not simply an invitation to die to self, and certainly not an invitation to flee the world, he felt rather the call literally to live and die as Jesus of Nazareth had and to preach that to others through his life. Intense identification with the One who was born naked and vulnerable and who died bereft and abandoned led Francis to adopt a life of radical material and spiritual poverty. He wore no shoes, carried no money, held no titles, owned no property, and called no man father. In imitation of the cross-hung God-man who had no place to lay his head, he founded a mendicant (begging) community, the friars minor: the littlest brothers. Radical Franciscan poverty was not expressed in the communal sharing of goods, as it was in the monastic life. It was expressed as a sharing in the absolute poverty of Jesus. Clare of Assisi (1194–1253) who founded the second, female order of the Franciscan movement, managed to gain for her enclosed community of women the unprecedented privilege of poverty without endowment or outside means of support. Radical identification with Jesus meant as well sharing in his suffering and this Francis did to the degree that toward the end of his life his body was marked with the *stigmata*, the wounds that Jesus bore on the Cross. For the poor man of Assisi, "pure joy" was to experience utter rejection and deprivation as did Jesus. To experience this was to enter into the mystery of God.

Variations on this radical, embodied participation in the experience of the suffering Jesus, manifest in the Franciscan movement, were to mark Catholic spirituality for centuries. Affective and methodical meditation on Jesus' life and passion became a widespread practice in religious life and among laity from the thirteenth century. Manuals of prayer from the fourteenth century European *Devotio Moderna* movement encouraged the devout to daily emotive entry into the mysteries of salvation. On Monday one might meditate on the Creation, the incarnation, the Last Supper, and the Eucharist. On Thursday one might meditate on the three Magi and the revelation of Christ's universal majesty and the wounding of Jesus as he was scourged and crowned with thorns. On Friday the crucifixion was the focus of meditation.

Devotion to the crucified and his sufferings was promoted by the Franciscan, Dominican, Carthusian, Benedictine, and Jesuit orders. Popular piety replicated the devotion in pictorial form. It became popular to meditate on visual images of the five wounds, the implements of the passion, and the pierced heart of Jesus that revealed the immensity of divine love. Visionary accounts appeared saturated with the imagery of the sufferings of the Cross and the mystery of divine love revealed there. One stunning example of this is found in the *Showings* of Dame Julian of Norwich, a fourteenth-century English anchoress whose visions of the bloodied Savior were occasioned by her prayer that she have a truer recollection of Christ's passion, receive the gift of a bodily sickness so as to be more closely knit to his sufferings, and receive the three "wounds" of contrition, compassion, and longing for God. Julian was granted her wishes as well as a series of graphic visions of the blood-soaked Savior that communicated to her the secrets of divine love.

It was precisely through this impulse to be identified with the mystery of suffering and dying embodied in the cross-hung Jesus that one participated in the very mystery of redemptive love itself. To sear this knowing on the body was to sear it on the soul and to make this mystery manifest in the world. For Julian the participation took the form of an illness and the visions whose wisdom she then interpreted and shared with others.

But the impulse to radical identification took other forms as well. Passion plays involved whole communities in reenacting the Passion narrative as it was found in Scripture and as tradition had enriched it with details. Today the famous German Passion play at Oberammergau and popular Latin American Passion processions are evidence of the sensibility that embodied participation in Jesus' suffering journey to Calvary has more than pedagogical power. They have deep spiritual significance for individuals and the community. At El Santuario in Chimayo, New Mexico, United States, an area whose resident population is Spanish speaking and which is culturally linked to Latin America, Holy Week is a time of intense spiritual practice. Thousands of people make their way – many on foot, some carrying heavy crosses – to the remote chapel in the hills. They make the pilgrimage for many reasons – thanksgiving, healing, expiation, devotion – but overwhelmingly they experience themselves as participating in the suffering and redemptive power of Jesus. The journey itself involves sacrifice and suffering and the pain of those on pilgrimage is aligned with that of the suffering savior. They are changed – transformed – in the process. The Holy Week practices are not unique to Chimayo but are echoed all over the Latin American Catholic world.

Spiritual practice as participation in the suffering of Jesus has taken other forms and given rise to a number of devotional practices. In the late seventeenth century Margaret Mary Alacoque (1647–90), a nun of the order of the Visitation of Holy Mary, received a series of visions promoting liturgical devotion to the Sacred Heart of Jesus. While devotion to the divine heart was not new, Margaret Mary's form of liturgical devotion was. Eventually, the practice of observing First Fridays as days of special adoration of the Sacred Heart in order to make reparation for sins against God, the practice of a Thursday hour of adoration, and the observance of a yearly feast were sanctioned by ecclesial authority. At the center of devotion to the Sacred Heart, a Catholic devotion universally popular until the mid-twentieth century, was the sense that through consecration of oneself, one's family, or one's locale to the Sacred Heart, the redemptive energy entering the world in Jesus' death and resurrection would continue. One might be protected by the power of the Sacred Heart but one also could make reparation for the sins of others and even console Jesus himself for the rejection and pain he suffered not only in his crucifixion but as he was neglected and desecrated in the sacrament of the altar.

Another variation of this embodied cruciform spirituality, most evident in the nineteenth and early twentieth centuries, was the tradition of the "victim soul," a tradition made well known through the popular early twentieth-century spiritual autobiography of Carmelite Thérèse of Lisieux (1873–97), *Story of a Soul*. Thérèse's practice of what has been called the "little way" has many sources: a sense that intimacy with God can be practiced in ordinary circumstances (echoes of Carmelite Brother Lawrence's *Practice of the Presence of God*), the significance of little, loving relational gestures and words (echoes of Francis de Sales' teachings), the austerity of the purifying dark night of the soul (echoes of Carmelite John of the Cross). But deep in Thérèse's spirituality is the idea of the victim soul, a chosen one whose suffering is mysteriously aligned with the redemptive suffering of Christ and can be offered up for the redemption of others. The once common practice of "offering it up" when suffering occurs, is a derivative of the "victim soul" spirituality.

Perhaps the most familiar form that this embodied cruciform practice takes today is the devotional practice of the Stations of the Cross. Most Fridays in Lent Catholic churches all over the world offer the Stations. Growing out of the long-lived practice of meditation on the Passion, the Stations have been incorporated into parish liturgical life. Most Catholic churches provide visual evidence of the devotion: pictorial or sculptural images show the 14 traditional moments of Jesus' sorrowful journey to his death. Bare crosses may mark the stations, but either way, the arrangement of the stations around the perimeter of a church suggests the embodied participation of the faithful. One follows in his footsteps, is condemned, scourged, falls, is comforted, falls again with Jesus. The *Stations* may recall past events but they are also designed to engage the present participant affectively. Sung responses and affecting readings accompany the devotees on their journey with the crucified one. The Stations of the Cross may also be translated in a contemporary idiom: the present-day crucifixion can be discovered in the suffering of those living under oppression or unjust conditions. Today one can make a contemporary Stations of the Cross in Haiti, retracing the steps of those martyred in the Haitian people's struggle against a violent, totalitarian government or one can prayerfully peregrinate with other Catholics through the shelters for the homeless, refuges for battered women, and prisons of an inner-city American landscape, seeing in the disfigured faces of the forgotten and impoverished the face of the crucified today.

Imaginative Meditation

Early modern Catholicism bequeathed to the Church a variant way of praying, connected but not identical to the above described tradition, that has become influential over the centuries. Ignatius of Loyola (1491–1556), founder of the Society of Jesus (Jesuits), inherited the medieval tradition of meditation on the Passion but elaborated upon it. The impulse toward radical incorporation in the Christ-event was central to his methods of prayer. Loyola's *Spiritual Exercises*, which contain many discrete practices, were originally the fruit of his own prayer. The Basque desired to draw up a manual for the conversion of the whole person and to create a process which could capture the intellect, memory, and will (considered the core elements of the person) for the love, service, and greater glory of God. Ignatius' motivations were apostolic. The revitalization of a Catholic Christendom torn apart by confessional conflict was his goal. To this end he desired to form "contemplatives in action."

In their classic form the *Exercises* are a month-long retreat process in which a directee, under the guidance of a spiritual director skilled in giving the *Exercises*, prays each day with a set pattern of meditations. The dynamics of the process invite the participant to grasp the profundity of God's goodness and the reality of human sin, to experience the beauty of the Kingdom that Jesus proclaims and to commit to love and service of that Kingdom and Jesus, its Lord. In the course of the *Exercises* the imagination is used freely: a distinctive feature of Ignatian meditation is the "composition of place." All the senses and affections are engaged to create in the mind and heart a picture of a scene in the life of Jesus. The directee senses, sees, smells, feels, and responds to the scene as it imaginatively unfolds. This imaginative method of prayer weaves the story and meaning of the life of Jesus personally into the consciousness of the directee, providing motivation for the commitment that is to issue. Another distinctive Jesuit practice is the Examination of Conscience or, as it is known contemporarily, the Examination of Consciousness. This practice involves taking time at the end of each day to review the day, to note where one has or has not lived intentionally in the presence of God, and to commit to the amendment of life. This simple practice allows one to cultivate consciousness of God's ongoing activity and presence in the midst of everyday life.

The *Spiritual Exercises* were originally designed as a practice for men considering entry into the Society but over time were adapted, took different forms, and were used for the spiritual formation of people in all walks of life. Presently, the *Spiritual Exercises*, in their many forms, are widely practiced. In the twentieth century the Jesuits made a world-wide commitment to sponsor and promote spiritual formation in an Ignatian key. Through their various apostolates the Jesuits have formed large numbers of lay people who have then gone on to engage in Ignatian spiritual practices. Some of these Jesuit-trained laity now provide spiritual direction for others.

Presence to God and One Another

Perhaps one of the most characteristic features of Catholic spirituality is the abiding sense of the intimate proximity of the divine presence and the intimate connection between those who are members of the Church. This takes many forms and gives rise to a plethora of practices. From earliest times, the Church has been perceived as the Body of Christ. This has meant for Catholics that the redemptive work of Jesus Christ continues to be operative through the Church – its sacraments, its teachings, its liturgical life, and its members both living and dead. Most explicitly, the Real Presence of Christ is believed to be intimately available in the Eucharist. The Catholic reception of communion is not simply a symbolic ritual or a remembrance, but is understood to be a real encounter, an incorporation of the divine life into ordinary life. Spiritual practices that heighten this sensibility have grown up around the Eucharist. The popular liturgical service of Benediction of the Blessed Sacrament, during which the sacrament is exposed in a monstrance upon the altar and the priest makes the sign of the cross (benediction or blessing) over the congregation kneeling before the Eucharist, is a case in point. Hours of Adoration or Perpetual Adoration of the Eucharist provide opportunities for Catholics to experience the Eucharistic mystery of the Real Presence. Separate Eucharistic chapels in parishes or retreat houses provide sacred space where the Real Presence may be honored and intimately encountered. Catholics bring their joys, sorrows, hopes, and fears to these hallowed spaces, seeking the divine presence and finding it there.

Sacred Presence is not only felt in the Eucharist, however. It can be said that Catholics inhabit a "sacramental universe." If one defines a sacrament as a visible expression of an invisible reality, one discovers that Catholics live in a world saturated with sacred presence. There are the official seven sacraments of the Church – baptism, confirmation, the Eucharist, reconciliation or confession, anointing of the sick or extreme unction, holy orders, and marriage – through which Catholics understand God's grace most especially to flow. But the Catholic spiritual universe is more porous than that. That universe is, first and foremost, a corporate one. An individual is intimately connected to all other members of the Church, the Body of Christ. Those who are part of the Mystical Body are part of divinity's life and are part of each others' lives in a profound and inseparable manner. This unity is expressed in the shared liturgical life in which Catholics participate. Common patterns and gestures of communal worship knit the worldwide communion together as does the rhythm of the liturgical year. Catholics move together through the seasons of the Church year – Advent, Christmastide, Lent, Holy Week, the Easter season, and Ordinary Time – and enter festively together into the great mysteries of faith. As a communal spiritual practice, liturgical prayer forms Catholics and opens them to the Living Spirit in countless ways.

"I am the vine, you are the branches," the Jesus of John's Gospel proclaims. This organic metaphor has many analogs, none more striking than the doctrine of the Communion of Saints: the spiritual solidarity and interconnection which binds together the faithful on earth, those in purgatory, and the saints in heaven. The veneration of the saints with its corresponding sense of being accompanied in life is a deeply embedded Catholic practice. It might be argued that the veneration of the saints has only a distant relation to the traditions of spiritual practice exemplified by Teresa of Avila, Ignatius of Loyola, or Benedictine monasticism. Dying to self in order to be opened to the breath of the Spirit may seem a far cry from lighting a candle or visiting a shrine. It is true that saints, those recognized as holy ones, especially those who have gone before, have functioned for Catholics in different ways over the centuries: they have been wonder-workers, patrons, intercessors, advocates, companions, and models for those who look to them. At times saints function as supernatural conduits of holy power rather than as inspiration for a transformed life. Sometimes they have been presented as super-human and inimitable, but always the abiding love that Catholics have had for the saints speaks to the sensibility that the Spirit works not only in individual lives but in and through the community. No spiritual practice is pursued solely for personal gain or achievement. The gifts of the Spirit are given for the whole Body, to be shared with and to enrich the entire Church and the world. Thus, divine presence, accessible in the sacraments, is also approached more obliquely through the saints, those persons whose manifest transparency to the Living Spirit gives sanctity a human face.

A weekday tour of the thousands of Catholic parishes in the urban sprawl of the archdiocese of Los Angeles, California, the most ethnically and culturally diverse city and thus Catholic archdiocese in the world, will reveal a repeated scene: men and women, young and old, kneeling or standing or sitting, alone or together, praying quietly in one of dozens of languages before the shrines of the saints. Much of the prayer that rises from these petitioners is spontaneous. But there are Catholic forms of common prayer that make the intimate presence of the saints explicit. Litanies are a responsive form of petition used both in public and in personal prayer. The Litany of All Saints, of the Holy Name, of the Sacred Heart, of Loreto, and of Saint Joseph are officially used in common recitation. The litany attests to the sense that the saints are available to and responsive to the prayers of the living. The Novena, a nine days' private or public devotion to obtain special graces, is another distinctive Catholic practice often associated with one of the saints. Finally, the stories of the saints are collectively recalled throughout the Church year: the Sanctoral Cycle, the cycle of saints' memorials, is interwoven into the fabric of the Church year.

The recitation of the Rosary is another practice that holds pride of place in Catholic hearts and which attests to the same sacramental sensibility. A repetitive form of prayer performed with the fingered use of prayer beads to "count" the prayers, the Rosary is said to have its origins in the thirteenth century under Dominican sponsorship. The Rosary became one of the defining Catholic practices during the Catholic reform of the early modern period and continues to be such today. Until recently the Rosary consisted of 15 "decades" or tens of *Hail Mary* prayers with an *Our Father* prayed between each ten. Pope John Paul II added five more mysteries of "Light" to accompany the traditional Joyful, Sorrowful, and Glorious mysteries. At each of these decades one considers one of these mysteries of redemption. Recitation of the Rosary brings the divine presence into the community and the community into the presence of the divine and aligns the ones who pray with the object of their prayer.

The Rosary is, of course, a quintessentially Marian prayer and it is Mary, Queen of Saints, Virgin, and Mother of God who has captured the hearts of generations of Catholics and whose sensed accompanying presence attests to the power of the Catholic sacramental universe. Mary's titles and functions are legion. In the Gospels she is a simple young woman approached by an angelic messenger and told that she is to bear a child and call him Jesus. For the contemplative tradition she has been the archetypal image of the human person opening itself to the inflowing, generative Spirit. She is patroness of religious orders, dioceses, cities, nations, and continents. She is the one who gifts devotees with signs of favor: the scapular of Our Lady of Mount Carmel, the Miraculous Medal, the protection of Our Lady of Czestochowa. She is the one whose appearances have promised healing and peace and who has been reported to warn against impending trials: she is Our Lady of Fatima, Knock, Lourdes, Medjugorje, La Salette, Beauraing, and Pontmain. In Argentina she is Our Lady of Lujan, in South Korea Our Lady of Degu, in England Our Lady of Walsingham, in Lithuania Our Lady of Šiluva, in Algeria Our Lady of Africa, in the Dominican Republic Altagracia, in New Zealand Our Lady of Otaki, in Sri Lanka Our Lady of Madhu. Mary has inspired the most beautiful of religious poetry and prayers. Her many-faceted image, painted, sculpted, drawn, carved, frescoed, engraved, and etched in glass, graces the worldwide Catholic landscape.

The extraordinary enthusiasm which *Nuestra Señora de Guadalupe*, patroness of Mexico and of the Americas, evokes is exemplary of the dense cultural and theological matrix of Marian devotion. The origin of the devotion, as with many Marian images, is located in an appearance: a sixteenth-century encounter between a baptized Aztec, Juan Diego, and a female figure announced by *flores et cantos* and calling herself (according to the legend) Holy Mary, Mother of God. The shrine that marks the site of the encounter is the most visited pilgrimage site in the Western hemisphere. A miracle is associated with it. To convince the Bishop of Mexico to build a shrine for her veneration, Guadalupe led Juan Diego to roses in wintry December. When the Aztec brought the flowers to the skeptical bishop and opened the cloak in which he carried them, a vivid photographic impression of the Lady was revealed. The venerable image now hangs in the basilica and a conveyor belt yearly carries over ten million devotees along to view the image. The story of the encounter has been recalled in countless variations and given birth to poetry, art, music, and distinctive devotional practices. It has also supported the conflicting theological, political, and cultural claims of indigenous peoples, Spanish colonial authorities, and advocates of Mexican independence, and has provided religious and cultural identity for migrant workers from Mexico all over the hemisphere. Guadalupe is both a devotional figure and a popular secular image. Of the dozens of devotional practices that honor her, the festivities that take place on the eve or morning of her December 12 feast day are some of the most notable. In Latin America extravagant musical performances, fireworks, and special Masses are offered. Generally, *Las Mañanitas* is observed. After midnight or at dawn people gather to vigil and "wake the dark Virgin" on her festive day. Mariachis play and the devout sing tenderly and lovingly to the beautiful one, the rose.

Works of Mercy and Social Justice

It is not through prayer, asceticism, and devotional practices alone that Catholics both past and present have been opened to the transforming power of the Spirit. As the Catholic universe is a communal one, to love and serve others is part of spiritual practice. Traditionally such care for the world and the people that God created has been referred to as the practice of the works of mercy. Instructing, advising, consoling, and comforting others are spiritual works of mercy, as are forgiving and bearing wrongs patiently. The corporal works of mercy consist of feeding the hungry, sheltering the homeless, clothing the naked, visiting the sick and imprisoned, and burying the dead. Generations of Catholics understood the practice of the works of mercy as enjoined by divine mandate: "Do unto others as you would have them do unto you." The practice of seeing and loving Christ in the outcast and poor has a long Catholic pedigree. In the nineteenth century a Belgian priest known as Damian of Molokai (1840–89), was sent as a missionary to Hawaii. He discovered on the outlying island of Molokai a community of misery: exiled lepers shunned by the government and Church alike because of their horrifying communicable disease. Fr Damian saw in the lepers the face of the crucified and took up residence with them, improving the conditions in which they lived and providing spiritual succor. He shared their life and died their death. For him, ministry to the least of the least was spiritual practice. It was identification with the One who died for humankind. It was the way the Spirit led and taught him.

In the contemporary Catholic world, fueled by a growing recognition of the human causes of much misery and violence, contemporary reflection on the love and service due to neighbor has frequently moved beyond the language of the works of mercy to the biblical language of social justice. While it is good to feed the hungry, one must also apply oneself to discovering and eliminating the causes of hunger. While it is considered worthy to have compassion for the poor and marginalized, it is more essential to be in solidarity with them, to make a radical "option for the poor." Catholic advocacy for justice, especially on behalf of the most vulnerable in society, is expressed in myriad ways on local, national, and international levels. Perhaps the story of the much-admired Oscar Romero (d. 1980), martyred Archbishop of El Salvador, can serve as an example of the work of justice as spiritual practice. When he was appointed to his ecclesial position, Romero was known as a non-controversial, bookwormish cleric. His country was in the midst of a brutal civil war; government and elite forces were aligned against a peasantry that agitated for more humane conditions. When one of his priests was murdered for his support of the people, Romero experienced a conversion: he came to feel that solidarity with the poor and the quest for justice was the Gospel path and that it was the Living Spirit that animated him. In 1980, the year of his death, the Salvadoran civil war claimed the lives of 3,000 per month, with cadavers clogging the streams, and tortured bodies thrown in garbage dumps and the streets of the capital weekly. Few of his fellow ecclesiastics supported him but Romero spoke out against the atrocities, pleaded for international intervention, and promised the people, "I do not believe in death without resurrection. If they kill me, I will be resurrected in the Salvadoran people." Romero was assassinated while saying Mass. His life continues to inspire and encourage Catholics who struggle for justice for the oppressed. Pressing beyond the works of mercy, Romero witnessed to the conviction that the struggle for social justice can be a spiritual practice, that solidarity with the marginalized can dispose a person to become responsive to the Spirit and that the quest for justice is a constituent part of the Spirit-filled Catholic life.

CHAPTER 27

Institutions

John A. Coleman

Not for nothing has the Roman Catholic Church been persistently dubbed *the* institutional Church. Seeing the Church as a visible, hierarchically structured, institution captures one of the characteristic, if potentially one-sided, Catholic models of the Church. The institution, however, is called to be, simultaneously, a communion, the people of God, a herald of salvation, a sacramental unity, a community of disciples, and a leaven for the world. Each of these models of the Church complements and corrects possibly one-sided over-emphases on word, sacrament, peoplehood, organizational visibility, etc. (Dulles, 1991). The Catholic Church, moreover, also comprises the institutional Church in a more sociological sense: it continuously generates a host of institutions, organizations, networks.

It should hardly be surprising that a Church which, in 2000, encompassed 1,045,055,100 people in every continent and region of the world engages in institution building (Froehle and Gautier, 2003: 5). Institutions entail organizational embodiments of a mission, a pastoral vision, and a clarified chain of command for authoritative decision structure and redress. Institutions enshrine ideals and reach specialized niches, populations, sectors of Church and society. If an ideal or vision is worth promulgating, it needs, eventually, to become institutionalized. Purely charismatic authority, devoid of institutionalization, as Max Weber famously argued, remains ephemeral and dies with the demise of the originating charismatic figure (Weber, 1993: 46–59). The Church is never simply some ephemeral "event" without institutional continuities and undergirding. Nor are institutions ever merely weightless carriers of ideals. They conserve values, enshrine traditions and ideals, enable agents, serve as storehouses of resources, and channel and constrain behaviors.

Purely Ecclesial Institutions

Some Catholic institutions are, in the narrow sense, purely ecclesial. While I will not be focusing, primarily, on such purely ecclesial institutions in this essay, a word about them seems in order. Roman Catholicism is divided into 2,846 dioceses or ecclesiastical territories worldwide. It embraces 218,196 parishes. A diocese denotes a demarcated portion of the people of God established by the Holy See and entrusted to the pastoral care of a bishop with the cooperation of his *presbyterium* (i.e., body of priests). A diocese constitutes what is called "a particular church" or "a local church." A diocese is both an administrative subdivision of the world-wide Church as well as, theologically, a fully constituted Church in its own right, a particular Church, in communion with all other particular Churches in the world. Dioceses ordinarily cohere around geographically delimited territorial units. Exceptions to this territorial rule are found in military ordinariates (i.e., a complex of bishops and priests entrusted with the pastoral care of the military) and in Eastern rite Catholic Churches (whose territory may overlap and span several Western rite dioceses). Each diocese is divided, in its turn, into parishes.

Dioceses across the world Church differ dramatically in size of Catholic population, geographic extent, and number of priests. Thus, for example, the average size of dioceses (in square kms) for Africa is 62,226; in the Americas, 37,985; in Asia, 70,100; in Europe, 13,644 and in Oceania, 109,089. The average number of Catholics per diocese also varies widely: in the Americas, 550,202; in Europe, 414,416; the average population of a diocese in Oceania is 113,919. Similarly, while in Europe a typical parish embraces 2,162 people, in the Americas the average parish includes 9,498 and in Africa, 11,796 (Froehle and Gautier, 2003: 22). Such disparities reveal a skewing of Catholic institutional resources. "In 2000, Europe contained 60 percent of all parishes but only 27 percent of the world's Catholics. The Americas have 25 percent of the world's parishes but 50 percent of all Catholics" (Froehle and Gautier, 23). Africa, on the other hand, shows weak institutional capacity. It contains only 5 percent of all parishes worldwide, although its Catholic population represents 12 percent of global Catholics. A similar unequal balance shows up in the distribution of diocesan priests worldwide: 55 percent are in Europe; 28 percent in the Americas; 10 and 1 percent, respectively (about the just proportion to their Catholic population) in Asia and Oceania. Africa with 12 percent of the world's Catholic population (and growing) has only 6 percent of diocesan priests (Froehle and Gautier, 2003: 38).

Parishes, like dioceses, ordinarily, are territorially based. In mission areas, some territorial units are mission stations which do not have the status of a parish. Thus, "In Africa, the number of such mission stations is roughly six times the number of parishes . . . In Africa, only 218 of 69,074 mission stations have a resident priest" (Froehle and Gautier, 2003: 17). They are typically staffed by lay catechists.

A parish, in its turn, represents a defined, stable community of the Christian faithful established within a geographical section of a diocese and ordinarily entrusted by the bishop of the diocese to the pastoral care of a priest as its pastor. Diocesan bishops have the power to establish, suppress, or alter parishes.

Individual bishops who are responsible for the pastoral care of their own territories are also co-responsible, under the Pope, for the unity of the Church across dioceses. Thus, organizationally, dioceses have been grouped together into Ecclesiastical Provinces which cluster a number of dioceses under the supervision of a metropolitan archbishop. Within nations or regions, dioceses may also be organized around an episcopal conference (e.g., for the United States, Australia, Belgium). At every level – episcopal conference, ecclesiastical province, diocese, parish – a ramified set of institutions or organizations or functioning bureaucracies may address issues of clergy support and education; catechesis; evangelization of non-Catholics; liturgy; ministry to youth; fundraising; support for immigrants and refugees; mission-outreach, social justice advocacy; provision of social services; ecumenical relations, etc.

Specialized Catholic Institutions with Pluralist Clientele and Staff

The Church, typically, alongside its primarily territorial pastoral institutions of dioceses, parishes, episcopal conferences, has spawned a host of specialized institutions – hospitals; orphanages; schools, at every level of education, primary, secondary, university-level; communications media; social service agencies. The remit of this essay focuses on such specialized institutions. Any inspection of a diocesan or national Church directory will uncover a wide swathe of specialized Church institutions which may address refugee resettlement; include journals of opinion and magazines, such as, for example, *The Tablet* in Great Britain, *Commonweal* in the United States, and *Mensaje* in Chile; Catholic sponsored radio or television networks; the provision of insurance for Church employees, etc. Some of these specialized Church institutions fall directly under the aegis of dioceses but others are sponsored by religious orders and congregations or lay groups. Some of these non-diocesan ecclesial institutions are local in character; some, national; some involve a global networking across continents and nations.

Because of their ubiquity over time across the world Church and their intrinsic importance, three sets of institutions stand out in world Catholicism: health care institutions; educational institutions; institutions which provide social service and care for the needy or distressed. These three (health care; education; social services) exhibit institutional peculiarities since, even when sponsored by a diocese or parish, they tend to serve and be staffed by a significant proportion of non-Catholics. Their clientele and "mission" do not restrict them to exclusively Catholic stakeholders. Much more than a diocese or a parish, such institutions also tend, frequently, to fall under the sway, regulation, and mandate of secular (including the State) professional organizations and norms. Even when ecclesiastically sponsored, such institutions are never merely or purely ecclesial. They have a wider societal function. A number of Church health care, educational, and social service organizations around the world receive substantial state funding. Moreover, many such institutions do not fit directly into diocesan structures. They achieve separate incorporation from the juridical reality of the diocese under state law. Nor are their missions and scope totally subject to internal ecclesial control. Outside professional accrediting organizations and state regulatory boards deeply shape their ultimate institutional contours and direction. I want to turn now to a brief description of the extent and scope of hospital, social services, and educational units in the worldwide Church. After providing a brief survey of the location and extent of these three institutions world-wide, I will then address three other issues. First, how do these institutions see themselves as, legitimately, an integral part of the mission of the Church yet, simultaneously, justify a large proportion of their service to a non-Catholic clientele? I will, then, focus on how outside secular agencies tend to help shape the final face and contours of these Catholic institutions of education, health, and social service, through what sociologists refer to as "institutional isomorphism" (DiMaggio and Powell, 1982). Finally, I will raise the increasingly salient question of how one should try to guarantee or maximize "the Catholic nature" of such institutions, without turning them into sectarian ghettos or losing their secular impact.

Extent and Scope of Education, Health Care, and Social Services Worldwide

There were, in 2000, 125,016 Catholic schools across the globe: 89,457 of them primary schools and 35,559 secondary schools. Except for Europe (where the number of Catholic schools declined by about 18 percent in the period 1975–2000), elsewhere in the world the number of Catholic schools increased in that same time frame, outpacing the increase in parishes (Froehle and Gautier, 2003: 18). Catholic universities, university colleges, and specialized tertiary instruction institutions number 1,046 – although they range widely from truly comprehensive universities, including graduate studies and professional degrees in law, medicine, and engineering, to undergraduate colleges, to what are mainly seminaries for the formation of priests. Some of these universities are, strictly speaking, ecclesiastical universities. A pontifical university falls, officially, under the auspices of the Holy See. There are 19 pontifical universities in Europe and some 30 pontifical universities outside Europe (most of them in the Americas). The United States stands out in its number of comprehensive universities (221). Most countries have, at most, only one or two such universities. Generally, universities which are not pontifical fall under the sponsorship of a religious order but some (for example The University of Notre Dame in Fremantle, Western Australia) are incorporated under a lay aegis.

Worldwide, there are 5,853 Catholic hospitals, but this number does not include a large number of specialized homes for the elderly and handicapped run under Church auspices. Nor does it include smaller clinics and dispensaries. Thus, to get some comparative vantage, we can contrast Australia (65 Catholic hospitals and 312 specialized homes for long-term care of the elderly/handicapped); Belgium (126 hospitals; 374 specialized health facilities); Germany (573 hospitals; 2,304 specialized health units); the United States (585 Catholic hospitals, 1,134 other specialized health units); and Canada (67 Catholic hospitals; 117 specialized care units). Australia which has less than half the Catholic population of Canada has almost the same number of Catholic hospitals. All told, some 103,437 different charitable organizations connected to the Church can be found across the globe. These range from smallish, single service organizations, such as local soup kitchens or St Vincent de Paul societies to larger concentrations such as Catholic Charities USA or the Catholic Centacare network in Australia, both of which receive substantial governmental funds and represent, in their respective countries, the largest non-governmental welfare agencies. Various Caritas organizations in Europe have a similar status, size, and scope of services to Catholic Charities USA.

In some settings, the Church's secular and institutional impact on society is considerably enhanced by its network of schools, hospitals, and charitable institutions. The case of Chad is illustrative. Catholics in Chad (a predominantly Muslim country of almost eight million people) constitute 623,000 or 8 percent of the population. But there are 64 Catholic primary and secondary schools, nine hospitals, 102 parishes, and 237 priests. All told, this institutional capacity allows Catholic leaders in Chad, despite their modest numbers, to play a very significant role in shaping public debates about the impact of globalization on Chad and the way the increasing oil revenues of the country should be used to foster economic development (Froele and Gautier, 2003: 132). Again, Catholics represent about 10 percent of the population of Zimbabwe yet of the 124 hospitals in the country, 47, or more than one-third, are under Catholic auspices. Often, Catholic facilities become crucial because they reach out to rural and other areas that are hard for the government to service (www.zebc.co.zw). In a similar vein, Catholics represent a mere 3 percent of the population of Bombay (now called Mumbai) in India but supply 20 percent of primary schools, 10 percent of literacy programs and 30 percent of social and medical welfare provisions in the area. Clearly, this Catholic institutional outreach in Bombay and Zimbabwe extends far beyond the Catholic population.

Precisely because of the emphasis on schools, Catholics in developing countries have frequently contributed a cadre of elites in government and business beyond their comparable numbers. Catholic schools, typically, also include an emphasis on education for women and, thus, contribute to women's rise in status in many countries. The percentage of Catholics, themselves, who attend Catholic schools varies greatly by country. In the United States, for example, Catholic schools represent a little less than about 10 percent of all schools and educate roughly two in 10 Catholics. In Australia, Catholic schooling represents closer to a quarter of the school population and educates more than 60 percent of all Catholics. In some countries, government funding is provided to help subsidize Catholic schools, charitable institutions, and hospitals. Some countries leave all funding of Catholic institutions to non-government sources. In still others, the Church is prevented entirely by the host governments from undertaking such service. In still other countries, new economic and other pressures have forced a number of previously existing Catholic institutions to merge or close altogether.

Moreover, there is a possible anomaly in basing religious outreach primarily through schools. In many countries (e.g., Belgium, Australia) Catholic parents still, primarily, opt for the Catholic school system for their children, since it is subsidized to the same extent as state schools. Australia, thus, has 664,517 Catholic students in Catholic schools, 368,796 in primary schools, and 295,748 in secondary schools. Belgium, similarly, has 2,304 primary schools and 1,148 secondary schools to service a Catholic population of about 8 million. The United States, lacking state subsidies for the Catholic school children, has three times the number of primary schools as Belgium (6,793) but almost the same number of secondary schools (1,297) to serve a Catholic population eight times the size of Belgium's. Frequently, however, in a country such as Australia where attendance at Mass is relatively low (about 12–15 percent weekly attendance for adults and somewhere around 3–4 percent for those aged 17–30), the emphasis on schools as a prime vehicle of Catholic identity, absent a more vibrant parish life, may be somewhat self-defeating. The best evidence about Catholic schools is that they bolster and reinforce (as a significant added value variable) already given Catholic identities from practicing families and parishes. Absent parental practice, however, the Catholic school's contribution to Catholic identity is more minimal (Greeley, 1976). Catholic parents still may choose the Catholic school system because it provides better discipline or better concern for the education of the whole child. Non-practicing parents do not seem to value the schools as a special vehicle for religious formation and catechesis (National Catholic Education Commission Report, Australia, 2003).

When Catholic institutions represent a significant sector of the health, education, and charitable sectors in a society, they provide a ready resource of expertise and credibility for the Church's public teaching and pronouncements on health care issues, education, and welfare. The Church's moral teaching embraces a host of life and death issues (euthanasia, abortion, sterilization, *in vitro* fertilization, bioethics) and social welfare issues (immigration policies, penal policies, unemployment, foreign aid, a social safety net for the needy). Without its institutional immersion in health, education, and welfare institutions, the Church's moral voice would seem a bit airy, lacking experience and abstract or merely moralistic. These institutions give the Church some clout to take part in larger public policy debates. In a number of countries (e.g., Australia, the United States, Belgium), Catholic institutions represent the largest single non-governmental providers of social services, health care, or education.

Yet more is involved than Church clout and voice on public policy issues. Each of these institutional sectors claims to represent historic and indispensable ministries which continue the Gospel ministries of Jesus as teacher, healer, and provider of compassionate care for the poor and marginalized. We turn now to Catholic rationales for building and maintaining institutions concerned with social welfare, health care, and education, and why such Catholic institutions, in principle, must reach beyond the Catholic population to others in need.

Catholic Rationales for Education, Health Care, and Social Services

Documents (both more learned and practical-pastoral) abound, expounding why and how the Church gets involved in health care, education, and social services. Institutions run by the Church for health care, education, and social services are found almost everywhere across the world Church, although the density of such institutions varies by country and region. Indeed, historically, after the fall of the Roman Empire up to the period of early modernity, the Church held a virtual monopoly in providing for all three of these ministries. Wherever the Church is denied the right to build or maintain institutions of health care, welfare, and education (as it was in the period 1948–89 in much of the Communist world and is also today in some countries), it protests that its religious freedom and integrity have been compromised. These three sets of institutions are not seen as some adventitious, merely desirable set of ministries –

the way, for example, having a Catholic television network might be. They go to the very heart of the Catholic self-understanding of ministry.

Ultimately, the commitment to health care institutions involves an attempt to continue Jesus' healing ministry, where Jesus healed not only physical ailments but also mental and spiritual ills. The suffering (physical and mental) of the sick is seen as a possible meaningful participation in Christ's passion. Death gets viewed as a portal to eternal life. One heals or dies with dignity and care and unto the Lord. Catholic Health Australia, the national umbrella organization for the 58 hospitals, 485 aged care facilities, seven teaching hospitals, and multiple day centers and rural clinics across Australia, represents the single largest non-governmental health provider in the country, capturing 13 percent of the health care market and employing 30,000 doctors, nurses, and staff. Its vision statement reads: (A) "To ensure the healing ministry flourishes as an integral part of the mission of the Catholic Church" [note the insistence that this ministry is absolutely integral to the Catholic mission]; (B) "To promote a just system that has at its heart an imperative for those who are poor and marginalized." Catholic Health Australia builds on eight foundational principles: (1) the dignity of the human person; (2) caring service to those in pain or need; (3) the common good; (4) a preference for the poor and under-served; (5) wise stewardship of resources; (6) subsidiarity (a principle from Catholic social teaching which argues that decisions and responsibilities should, by preference, be taken at the lowest appropriate level and, at the least, that the voice and integrity of local units should always be honored); (7) human equality; (8) human association as a fundamental right (www.catholichealthcare.au).

Catholic Health Australia commits itself not only to strengthening all those in health care ministry in its facilities in understanding, articulating, and acting on a Catholic identity but, because it serves non-Catholics and articulates with wider public sectors, also promises to maintain a watchdog brief on legislative reforms and to engage in advocacy. In some of its advocacy, it argues for better coverage for the poor by government schemes and opposes "a commodification of health."

Catholic health care units commit to a pastoral as well as a medical provision, envisioning compassionate caring. Similar kinds of vision statements and principles to those of Catholic Health Australia can be found on the web pages and documents of the Catholic Health Care Association of America or parallel links for health care institutions in Canada, Belgium, and Germany. Episcopal conferences (and the Vatican) provide specific guidelines for the ethical and religious scope of health care (DeBlois, 1996; Cochran, 1999; Keane, 2001).

Catholic educational systems, for their part, look toward an ideal of integration of faith and knowledge, a care for the spiritual well-being and character formation of students, a broad education for justice and service to the community. Vatican II's "Declaration on Christian Education" (*Gravissimum Educationis*) directs Catholic schools to integrate the Christian faith into the whole pattern of human life in all its aspects. It counsels Catholic educators to strive "to relate all human culture eventually to the news of salvation, so that the life of faith will illumine the knowledge which students gradually gain of the world, of life and of humankind" (Abbott and Gallagher, 1989: 646). More than is usual in secular state schools (especially in pluralistic societies),

Catholic schools emphasize character formation and moral training for virtue and service. Ultimately, as the American bishops once put it, in the title of a pastoral letter they wrote, the desire is that, in Catholic schools, educators will "teach as Jesus did" (American Catholic bishops, 1976). This stress on formation and the enablement of a kind of virtuous person can be found in most of the characteristic Catholic treatments of education (Boys, 1989; Groome, 1999, "The Catholic School"; www.ncea.org).

In a similar way, Catholic commitments to social welfare are rooted in a sense of social service as a ministry which continues Jesus' compassion and outreach to the poor and needy. Once again, this generic mission of Jesus receives a kind of specification. Thus, one group of Catholic Charities directors of the 13 agencies for dioceses of California which I studied, were asked in a survey to specify their answers to the following two questions: "(1) How do you operationalize Catholic identity for your agency? Please describe, using examples, for the following groups: clients, employees, management and staff, board members, the Catholic community, the broader community (e.g., funders, public, media)." Although responses varied, many included elements of prayer at meetings or some orientation for staff around Catholic social teaching. Many pointed to specific Christian symbols (crucifixes, religious pictures) in their buildings. One agency even engaged in faith-sharing among staff. Most had boards appointed by or approved by their bishops and most of the board members were Catholic. Few, however, mentioned explicit hiring restrictions toward Catholics in preference to non-Catholics. All stressed an inclusive outreach in service. Most chose what are best described as *distinctive* (i.e. characteristic of Catholicism, even if also found in other Christian, religious or even non-religious groups) rather than *unique* (i.e. found only in Catholicism) traits to conceptualize their Catholic identity: e.g., a welcoming and hospitable atmosphere; a sense of empowerment and dignity of clients; values of compassion, service, and justice. At a board meeting of the California Catholic Charities Directors, the board adopted a statement of Catholic identity (clearly distinctive rather than unique to Catholics) around the values of justice, service to those in need, being champions of the poor and vulnerable, respect for human dignity and human difference, empowerment of clients, accountability, collaboration.

Two things need to be lifted up about typical Catholic rationales for health, education, and welfare. Catholic social teaching, with its emphasis on human dignity and the common good, reaches out, beyond confessional differences, to a broader sense of human rights and empowerment. Thus, rationales for Catholic health stress the human right to adequate health care and compassionate medical service; rationales for education stress a holistic education but also the right of all to a good education; rationales for social service stress the right of those in need to have a minimal level of sustenance as to housing, jobs, food, access to health care, etc. So, Catholic rationales for health, education, and welfare, although ultimately rooted in the ministry of Jesus, include more secularly grounded principles which non-Catholics can and do also accept and foster. Secondly, since Catholic health and social welfare organizations (in principle) and, to a lesser but still real extent Catholic education (which often educates a sizable minority of non-Catholics) have multiple staff, clients, and, sometimes, sources of revenue which are not Catholic, they must look for rationales which are not merely confessional. Indeed, in some Catholic health or social service units around the world, the majority of staff and clientele may be non-Catholic. Hence, a distinctively but not uniquely Catholic yet inclusive rationale (based on values and principles non-Catholics could endorse) becomes necessary in defining the Catholic identity of the institution.

Specialized Catholic Institutions and Institutional Isomorphism

A number of social scientists and sociologists of religion have suggested that it is much more difficult to maintain even a religious, let alone a distinctively Catholic, identity in hospitals, universities, and social service agencies than in parishes or purely ecclesial organizations. The religious authority structure in these specialized organizations only in places meshes with and, in places, is in conflict with the functional agency structure. Such specialized institutions widely overlap with their secular counterparts in providing education, health care, and social services.

Many specialized Catholic institutions such as education (more saliently for universities), hospitals, and social service agencies, for legitimate reasons, are separately incorporated, under state law, from the juridical reality of a parish or diocese. They do not fall, unmistakably, under the oversight and competency of the episcopacy. Many are subject to a large set of governmental mandates (especially if they receive governmental funds) which regulate their operations and sway (for example, commanding that hiring practices reflect a nation's ethnic, gender, or even religious diversity). Most such specialized Catholic institutions include – in administration, staffing, funding sources, clients – significant numbers of non-Catholics. Many of these institutions, at least in the advanced industrial countries, face new inner pressures due to competition from other non-profit agencies in their institutional fields or from market forces (e.g., for-profit education or provision of social services has been expanding). In pluralist societies, even Catholics do not, necessarily, patronize their own Catholic schools, hospitals, and social service agencies.

Sociologist Mark Chaves argues that a kind of "inner secularization" of religious specialized agencies can occur more easily than in the firmly rooted authority structures in parishes or denominational, specifically religious, structures (Chaves, 1998). Paul DiMaggio and Walter Powell have probed the process of "institutional isomorphism" (the term refers to the ways all institutions within a societal sector seem, over time, to resemble each other closely as to norms, procedures, and standards in societal institutional sectors). The process of institutional isomorphism yields a general similarity (and consequent interchangeability) in role definitions, sectoral standards, programs, and processes of evaluation across all agencies within a given institutional sector (DiMaggio and Powell, 1991).

Governmental regulations tend to span the whole sector (religious and secular) of health, education, welfare. Professional norms for doctors, nurses, teachers, social workers pervade whole sectors as well. Such professional norms, standards, and procedures are rarely specifically religious. They often put such a large stamp of secular professional identity on an institutional sector that any alternative ethos seems merely a kind of rhetorical "window dressing" on the real identities. Again, one of the emerging themes concerning leadership and management in the non-profit sector stresses new pressures, from within and without, to achieve (at least in pluralist societies) greater racial and ethnic diversity on boards and staffs; to involve clients and constituencies more substantially in the governance of the agency; and to work more closely with cognate organizations in new forms of cooperation (Young, 1995: 9). Agencies within each major sector tend to imitate and emulate the leading and successful models within their respective institutional sectors. Catholic universities, for example, seek the kinds of excellence in research and teaching found in secular universities. A Catholic hospital emulates the best professional health care in its nation.

Institutional isomorphism tends, then, to eclipse any specialized organizational ethos, including religious ones. Even, for example, in Catholic primary and secondary schools which tend to be more closely linked to diocesan and parish authority structures, teachers – even practicing Catholic ones – may be recruited from non-Catholic schools, lacking any vibrant sense for the texture and content of a Catholic ethos. Textbooks, in topics such as civics, history, literature, may simply mirror the texts used in state schools (which could make the integration of faith and human learning more difficult). Often such textbooks are not religiously neutral (or, at least, not religiously sensitive) and their secularized world-views may eclipse and marginalize a Catholic or religious vision.

Because of their inner pluralism and their intersection with secular or public agencies, it is palpably more complex and difficult (but by no means impossible) to maintain a distinctively Catholic ethos in specialized Catholic institutions of health, welfare, and education than in inner ecclesial agencies. Yet it would be a mistake to address this difficulty by misunderstanding the nature of such institutions. They are not parishes. They are not catechetical centers. They are not merely inner ecclesial units. They perform civic and ecumenical tasks. Nor should one rush too quickly to an appeal to external ecclesial authority to closely monitor and interfere with governance or day-to-day operations. Parish priests and bishops, per se, are not experts on (or, often, even really conversant with) health, education, and welfare. Their direct interference and control over such institutions could undermine the internal excellences, competence, and credibility of these institutions. Thus, it is important to conceptualize rightly what kinds of institutions specialized agencies for health, education, and welfare are.

Studying religious specialized organizations, such as Catholic Charities or a hospital, is not at all like studying a parish but more like studying a self-consciously Catholic ecumenical citizen who draws on internal religious identity resources to engage more broadly in action in public and for the common good. These institutions manifest a distinct face of the Church, the face of the Church as a public citizen, a leaven in society. As religious citizens, Catholic specialized institutions serve the common good, cater to all in need and cooperate with all men and women of good will around shared institutional interests and goals. In the end, the inclusive, distinctive, but not confessionally unique set of values used to champion Catholic identity – justice, respect for human dignity and difference, service to need, commitment to human community and excellence, empowerment, collaboration, preference for the poor, compassion – can each find grounding in theology, Catholic social teaching, and a religious vision. But these values also serve to include, rather than exclude, to allow for their being subscribed by those who are not Catholic. The values may have secular resonance but they are also distinctively Catholic and apt for institutions especially marked by the interaction and encounter of the Church with the world.

The Catholic Nature of Specialized Catholic Institutions Serving a Pluralist Clientele

Clearly, because of institutional isomorphism, the mixed ecclesial yet also civic character of specialized Catholic institutions, and the fact that they exhibit an internal pluralism as to staffing, clientele, and funding sources, special attention needs to be given to retaining and nurturing their Catholic nature but in ways appropriate to their partially secular overlapping mandates. Luckily, a number of social scientists have paid some attention to the criteria for adjudicating how religious a specialized agency is or can be. Thomas Jeavons, an organizational sociologist, presents an ideal-typical characterization of religious, as opposed to purely secular, non-profits. His ideal types can serve as a kind of inventory or heuristic device (Jeavons, 1998; 2000). Religious groups, in actual fact, fall differently across the items in Jeavons' inventory which looks at the following six prime variables to gauge the extent and kind of religiousness of specialized institutions:

1 *Self-identification as religious.* Religious groups often explicitly self-identify as religious organizations. One sees it in their name, e.g., Catholic Charities; St Vincent's Hospital. On the other hand, some religious organizations seem to hide their religious provenance under secular sounding or innocuous names. I was surprised, for example, to discover that, in Australia, the Catholic social service organizations are simply called Centacare. The name in no way reveals their religious auspices. In a similar way, religious groups often display their religious identities in quite visible ways – in displaying religious statues, icons, crucifixes, in having a chapel on the premises. No one should walk into the offices of a Catholic agency without seeing somehow displayed or enacted its religious origins and commitments. Most importantly, some explicit reference to the specifically Catholic-Christian nature of the organization should be found in the mission statement of the organization. In increasingly competitive markets among non-profits, these agencies more and more turn to what has been called " branding" – finding a key pithy slogan and logo to capture their unique mission and niche. Some reference to the Catholic and religious character of the institution should always appear in such slogans and *logos*, even if marketing experts might suggest otherwise.

2 *Participants are significantly Catholic or religious.* Jeavons notes that participants (i.e., paid staff, administrators, volunteers, funders, clients) in religious groups tend to be religiously committed individuals, either because of specific organizational requirements or because the culture of the organization appeals to those who share religious ideals. One study, comparing secular with religious organizations working to combat homelessness in the Houston, Texas area, discovered that religious organizations, even when they did not, by preference, hire only fellow members of their denomination, did prefer hiring religious people who would find resonance with the organization's religious agendas

and grounding (Ebaugh et al., 2003). At some point, an organization which calls itself Catholic does have to bite the bullet and raise the issue of explicit attention to hiring for mission. This need not entail only hiring practicing Catholics, since experience shows that other Christian or religious staff, even some non-believers, often buy into the mission as much as Catholics do. For many Catholic institutions, no fixed formula exists for just how many of the administrators and staff must be practicing Catholics, although a Vatican document on Catholic universities does foresee that "the number of non-Catholic teachers should not be allowed to constitute a majority within the institution which is and must remain Catholic" (*Ex Corde Ecclesiae*, article 4, #4). Note the ambiguity, however, of the authoritative weight of "should not" meant as an ideal as opposed to "must not" which expresses a clearer prohibition. Absent a significant core of committed Catholics who work on the Catholic-religious character of the institution, a kind of inner secularization becomes, however, more likely. Probably the director of the work should, by preference, ordinarily be a practicing and informed Catholic. Many Catholic organizations have also found it necessary to appoint another officer whose terrain is the oversight, formation, and inculcation of the mission. He or she is in charge of "forming" and socializing into the Catholic roots of the mission.

3 *Material resources provided by Catholic sources.* He or she who pays the piper, calls the tune. So, attention must be paid to the reality and extent of material resources such as money, in-kind donations, volunteers, buildings provided by Catholic sources. The comparative study of religious versus secular providers of services to the homeless in Houston found that religious organizations were more likely than secular ones to receive funds (and draw on a pool of volunteers) from religious groups. This variable was not totally a zero-sum proposition, since secular organizations also received money and volunteers from religious groups but to a significantly lesser extent than the religious groups. Nor is this criterion a stricture against accepting money from governments or secular foundations. Religious groups in the Houston study took money from government and secular foundations. So long as money received from these sources is focused on the legitimate religio-civic goals and mission of the Catholic organization, non-religious sources of money cause no special problems for the religious nature of the organization. I have found, however, in a comparative study of agencies of Catholic Charities USA that I have been conducting, that agencies which receive no monies at all from their diocese are less likely to be able to carry out specific programs geared toward parish outreach and education about social service. Their connection to the wider Catholic community becomes more tenuous.

4 *Organizational goals and services are religious.* In religious non-profits, Jeavons argues, organizational goals, products, and services provided by religious groups are of a religious nature. He contends that an organization's religious culture and core values are expressed in rituals and routines, such as starting a meeting with a prayer (even if, in pluralistic religious settings, the prayer may be led by a Buddhist or Muslim or Jew), engaging in faith-values sharing and, on suitable occasions, in a formal Eucharist. Catholic organizations which hire for mission must also periodically engage with the already hired staff in exercises of on-going formation in mission. My home university, Loyola Marymount University in Los Angeles, for example, holds a yearly week-long seminar for about 20 faculty (both Catholic and non-Catholic) focusing

on the Catholicity of the university. One cannot stress enough the need for a continuous, regular, and on-going formation in the mission of the Catholic institution with all constituents: administrators, staff, board members, clientele, outside public, funding sources. Such on-going formation in mission is especially important in larger institutions which experience a relatively large periodic turnover of staff (Bergner, 1998). Generally, the mission of a school, social service agency, or hospital will be grounded in reflection on how each of these institutions constitutes a ministry and not just a secular purpose; how roles within the institution are "a calling," not just "a career." The mission will stress how the work is a continuation of a specific ministry of Jesus. Catholic social teaching serves as another crucial resource for rooting the Catholic identity of the institution. Increasingly, one finds in mission statements of health care, social service, and educational institutions specific evocations of the values of human dignity, the common good, a preferential option for the poor, subsidiarity, solidarity – the core concepts of Catholic social teaching. But somewhere in the mission statement or its elaboration (which will include many secular sounding goals such as service, empowerment, excellence in teaching and research) should be some indication of a religious justification for inter-religious/ecumenical cooperation and/or service to non-religious clients. The concept of "a servant Church" provides one such rationale, as does Jesus' outreach to those who were not believers.

5 *Development, distribution and use of power within the organization.* Decision structures and processes of interaction within a Catholic organization should embody and reflect Catholic principles of respect for human dignity and the common good. They will ordinarily commit the organization to a just wage, an acceptance of the right to unions, and justice as participation. Frequently, religious institutions require that leadership be active in the life of the Church and/or have some theological education in their background. Often, too, boards contain by-laws which state that only Catholics may serve, although that may seem too stringent, even counter-productive, for some pluralistic specialized organizations. Just as clearly, a significant portion of the board should be Catholic. Frequently, the ecclesial nature of the organization gets expressed by having a bishop serve as a member (if not the chair) of the board. Minimally, umbrella national Catholic organizations for health, social service, and education will maintain close ties with the episcopacy.

6 *Ecumenical preferences.* Religious organizations (as a point of empirical fact) tend to interact more with other religious organizations. Care must be paid, however, not to fall into religious ghettos . Thus, for example, Catholic Charities may, often, link up with Jewish and Lutheran social service organizations or the Salvation Army. Interaction with cognate religious institutions reinforces the religious character of the organizations. However, because Catholic specialized institutions for health, education, and social service also serve a civic function, they will also frequently collaborate with specifically secular organizations to pursue the common good. At times secular agencies (e.g., concerning immigration policies, education for the handicapped, new medical technologies) contain resources and knowledge not found in religious agencies.

Jeavons' checklist or inventory can be helpful to reinforce the Catholic nature of specialized Catholic institutions. Yet no one formula will guarantee a Catholic ethos and sensibility once and for all. It needs to be continuously and imaginatively worked at, but in ways which do not compromise the mixed ecclesial-civic/humane nature of the Catholic institutions of Catholic health care, education, and social services. By the nature of the case, all three are involved in outreach and influence to the secular and wider society. They are the face of a "public Church" – the Church in the world – and their Catholic nature should reflect this unique mission and competency.

References and Further Reading

Abbott, Walter and Gallagher, Joseph (eds.) (1989) "Declaration on Christian Education," in *Documents of Vatican II*. New York: Crossroad.

Bergner, David (1998) *Toward a Leadership Style for the Twenty-First Century*, Richmond, VA: Catholic Charities of Richmond.

Boys, Mary (1989) *Educating in Faith: Maps and Visions*, San Francisco, CA: Harper.

The Catholic School, Rome (1977) *Congregation for Catholic Education*. Sydney: St Paul Publications.

Chaves, Mark (1998) "Denominations as Dual Structures," in Demerath, N.J., III, Hall, P., Schmidt, T., and Williams, R. (eds.) *Sacred Companies: Organizational Aspects of Religion and Religious Aspects of Organizations*. New York: Oxford University Press, 175–94.

Cochran, Clarke (1999) "Sacrament and Solidarity: Catholic Social Thought and Health Care Policy Reform," *Journal of Church and State*, vol. 4, no. 3 (June), 475–90.

De Blois, Jean (1996) *The Revised Ethical and Religious Directives for Catholic Health Care Services: Seeking Understanding in a Changing Environment*, St Louis, MO: Catholic Health Association of the United States.

DiMaggio, Paul and Powell, Walter (1982) "The Iron Cage Revisited: Conformity and Diversity in Organizational Fields," *PONPO Working Paper*. New Haven, CT: Yale University Institution for Social and Policy Studies.

DiMaggio, Paul and Powell, Walter (eds.) (1991) *The New Institutionalism in Organizational Analysis*. Chicago, IL: University of Chicago Press.

Dulles, Avery (1991) *Models of the Church*. New York: Doubleday Image.

Ebaugh, Helen Rose, Pipes, Paula F., Chafetz, Janet Saltzman, and Daniels, Martha (2003) "Where's the Religion? Distinguishing Faith-Based from Secular Social Service Agencies," *Journal for the Scientific Study of Religion*, vol. 42, no. 2 (September), 411–26.

Ex Corde Ecclesiae (1990) available on www:vatican.va/apostolic constitutions.

Froehle, Bryan and Gautier, Mary (2003) *Global Catholicism: Portrait of a World Church*. Maryknoll, NY: Orbis Press.

Greeley, Andrew (1976) *Catholic Schools in a Declining Church*. Kansas City, KS: Sheed and Ward.

Groome, Thomas (1999) *Christian Religious Education: Sharing Our Story and Vision*. San Francisco, CA: Jossey-Bass.

Jeavons, Thomas (1998) "Identifying Characteristics of 'Religious' Organizations," in Demarath, N.J., III, Hall, P., Schmidt, T., and Williams, R. (eds.) *Sacred Companies: Organizational Aspects of Religion and Religious Aspects of Organizations*. New York: Oxford University Press, 185–99.

Jeavons, Thomas (2000) *Growing Givers' Hearts: Treating Fundraising as a Ministry*. San Francisco, CA: Jossey-Bass.

Keane, Philip (2001) *Catholicism and Health-Care Justice: Problems, Potential and Solutions*. Mahwah, NJ: Paulist Press.

"National Catholic Education Commission Report," Australia, 2003 – available from the Conference of Australian Bishops, Canberra, Australia.

"To Teach as Jesus Did" (1976) Washington, DC: United States Catholic Conference.

www.catholichealthcare.au – website of the Catholic Health Care umbrella organization, Australia.

www.ncea.org – website of the National Catholic Education Association of the United States.

www.zebc.co.zw – website of the Bishops' Conference of Zimbabwe.

Weber, Max (1993) *The Sociology of Religion*, trans. Ephraim Fischoff. Boston, MA: Beacon Press – see especially 46–59, "The Prophet"

Young, Denis R., Hollister, Robert M., and Hodgkinson, Virginia A., & Associates (eds.) (1995) *Governing, Leading and Managing Non-Profit Organizations.* San Francisco, CA: Jossey-Bass.

CHAPTER 28
The Holy See

Francis A. Sullivan

The Holy See

"Holy See" and "Apostolic See" are names for the supreme governing authority in the
Catholic Church, which is held by the Pope and administered with the assistance of the
Roman Curia. The term "See" is derived from the Latin word *sedes*, meaning "seat" or
"chair." Just as "throne" signifies royal authority, so also "chair" can signify episcopal
authority. A bishop's church is called a cathedral because that is where one finds his
cathedra (Greek for "chair") that symbolizes his role as chief pastor in his local church.
The Pope holds the supreme authority in the Catholic Church because, as Bishop of
Rome, he is the successor of St Peter. In the mid-third century, St Cyprian, bishop of
Carthage in North Africa, wrote to St Cornelius, bishop of Rome, warning him about
some rebellious subjects who had "the audacity to sail off carrying letters from schismatics and outcasts from religion even to the chair of Peter."[1] The Catholic belief that
the Bishop of Rome has "the chair of Peter" and inherits the "Petrine ministry" explains
the term "Apostolic See" and the papal authority it signifies. The Code of Canon
Law states that the Holy See "has the nature of a moral person by divine law itself"
(Can. 113). This means that it is an abiding subject of rights and obligations which
receives its existence and authority from God, rather than from any human social contract. At the same time, the Holy See is not merely an idea, but is a concrete reality;
the same Code says that the term "Apostolic See" or "Holy See" applies not only to the
Roman Pontiff but also to the institutions of the Roman Curia (Can. 361). As the central
government of the worldwide Catholic Church, the Holy See maintains diplomatic relations with 174 nations, which recognize it as the juridical equal of a sovereign state. It
is true that such diplomatic activity began when the Pope was ruler of the Papal States,
which for many centuries had included much of central Italy. However, after the loss
of the Papal States in 1870, many of the nations that already had diplomatic relations
with the Papal States continued to maintain them with the Holy See. Since then many
other nations, including the United States of America, have begun to exchange diplo-
mats with the Holy See, which is also recognized by many international treaties and
organizations, such as the United Nations. All of these nations and organizations realize that it is the Holy See, and not Vatican City State, with which they are dealing.

The Vatican

Vaticanus was the name the Romans gave to a hill on the west side of the Tiber River, which was near the circus of Nero, and was the site of a public cemetery. There are good reasons to believe that St Peter was martyred in the circus of Nero and was buried in the nearby cemetery on Vatican Hill. Excavations under St Peter's basilica have proven that when Constantine built the original basilica in honor of St Peter on this hill, he took great pains to have the main altar right over a place that from the second century had been venerated as a memorial to St Peter. The location of the basilica in honor of St Peter in that place naturally led to its becoming a goal of pilgrimage for Christians. But it was only after the return of the papal court from Avignon to Rome in 1377 that the popes began to live near St Peter's at the Vatican. This led gradually to the construction of the complex of palaces, galleries, and museums that have become a mecca for pilgrims and tourists from the whole world.

One can distinguish three meanings of the term "the Vatican." First, it means a place: the walled enclave consisting of 108 acres, located on the Vatican Hill but within the modern city of Rome, in which are the Basilica of St Peter, the papal palace, galleries and museums, and a private garden. It was this walled enclave that Pope Pius IX had in mind when, after the loss of the Papal States, he described himself as "prisoner of the Vatican." It was, of course, his own choice to remain within those walls, and never again set foot in the city of Rome, as a protest at the fact that its temporal sovereignty had been taken from him by force. His successors followed his example, until 1929, when Pope Pius XI and Mussolini signed the Lateran Treaty.

"The Vatican" can also mean the State of Vatican City, which was created by the Lateran Treaty. Most of this state lies within the enclave at the Vatican, but there are some other properties that belong to it by that same treaty. Vatican City State is the last absolute monarchy in Europe. The Pope holds all authority in it, which he entrusts to the Pontifical Commission for Vatican City State, whose Cardinal President delegates some of it to the lay man who has its day-to-day management. Vatican City State is recognized under international law as a sovereign state, but it does not have diplomatic relations with other states. For the protection of the Pope, it maintains the Swiss Guard, made up of 100 Catholic, German-speaking men whom the Swiss government allows to volunteer for this service. It also has a modern police force, and a penal system to deal with crimes committed within its territory, most of which are thefts committed against tourists, three million of whom visit the Vatican museums each year. However, several years ago it had to deal with a case of murder and suicide within the Swiss Guard. Vatican City State issues its own passports, has a post office and issues its own stamps, has a bank, a publishing house, and a short railway that connects it to the Italian system. The total number of employees of Vatican City State is about 1,500, most of whom are Italian lay people. (They are not the same as employees of the Holy See.)

The term "the Vatican" most often really means "the Holy See." Just as people might say "Washington" when they mean the central government of the United States of America, they say "the Vatican" when they mean the central government of the Roman Catholic Church. Fr Thomas Reese, former editor of *America* magazine, has published a very informative book with the title *Inside the Vatican*. In his book he has a few pages about Vatican City State, but his book is about the Holy See. This is evident from the sub-title he chose for it: "The Politics and Organization of the Catholic Church."

As we have seen above, the Code of Canon Law describes the Holy See as a "moral person," but it also says that this term refers to the Roman Pontiff and the Roman Curia, as indicating the physical persons and structures by which the Catholic Church is actually governed. I shall begin with the persons: first the Roman Pontiff, and then the cardinals, who are the most important members of the Roman Curia.

The Roman Pontiff

The word "pontiff" is derived from the Latin word *pontifex*, which in pre-Christian Rome was the name given to the priests who performed the ceremonies of the state religion. The word *pontifex* literally means "bridge-builder," but it is not known why the pagan priests of Rome were given that name. Strangely enough, the same word came to be used of the Christian bishops. Originally it was used of any bishop, but in modern times it has come to be used almost exclusively of the Bishop of Rome. In any case, the term "Roman Pontiff" means "Roman Bishop," and it is indeed essential that the Pope be the Bishop of Rome, since it is in that capacity that he has the "chair of Peter," and inherits the Petrine ministry. Given his weighty responsibility for the universal Catholic Church, he delegates authority for the normal pastoral care of Rome to one of the cardinals as his Vicar. The cathedral of the diocese of Rome is not the Basilica of St Peter, but that of St John Lateran, which was built by Constantine, the first Christian emperor, and got its name from the Laterani family, previous owners of the adjacent palace, which Constantine gave to the Bishop of Rome for his residence. The popes continued to use the Lateran Palace as their ordinary residence until the return from Avignon in 1377, when they took up residence at the Vatican.

The first official recognition by a great body of Christian bishops that the authority of the Bishop of Rome extended beyond the limits of Rome itself was given by the first of the ecumenical councils, that of Nicea, in 325, when it spoke of such extended authority being held by the bishops of Alexandria, Antioch, and Rome. However, it was only with regard to the Bishop of Alexandria that it specified the extent of his authority. It is of the nature of authority that it effectively extends to the limits of the area in which people recognize their obligation to submit to it. The history of papal authority can be summed up as the interplay between the claims made by the Bishops of Rome to this authority and the acceptance of those claims by the rest of the bishops. It was during the second half of the fourth century and the first half of the fifth that the Bishops of Rome fully developed their understanding of the source and extent of papal authority, and began to exercise it on the basis of that understanding. They understood Christ himself to be the source of papal authority, in the role that he gave to Peter, as Prince of the Apostles. As the rock on which the Church was built, holder of the keys of the Kingdom of Heaven, and shepherd of the whole flock of Christ, Peter had received supreme authority over the universal Church. The Bishop of Rome, as the holder of Peter's chair, inherited the fullness of the authority that Christ gave to Peter. As Pope Leo I put it,

Saint Peter himself continued to live on and govern the Church in the person of his successor.

However, there was a gap between the popes' understanding of this authority and their effective exercise of it. First of all, there was a great difference between the Eastern and the Western halves of the Roman Empire, as far as papal authority was concerned. The Church in the East was dominated by the Christian emperors, and led by the patriarchs of Constantinople, Alexandria, Antioch, and later, Jerusalem. While these bishops recognized Rome as the see of Peter and its bishop as the first among the bishops, and at the Council of Chalcedon had acclaimed the letter that Pope Leo I had sent to it, declaring, "Peter had spoken through Leo," they never granted to the popes the kind of authority that Pope Leo I claimed for them. Even in the West, where the Bishop of Rome was the only patriarch, the powerful archbishops who ruled the ecclesiastical provinces into which Charlemagne divided his empire, possessed a great deal of autonomy from Rome. To counteract their authority, a large number of documents were forged, probably in northern France, giving to bishops the right to appeal to Rome against their archbishops, and enhancing the authority of Rome in other ways as well. These documents, known as the "False Decretals," were accepted in Rome as genuine, and were used by subsequent popes to bolster their authority. But in the tenth century the power and prestige of the papacy was seriously damaged by its falling under the domination of powerful Roman families, who installed many popes who were unworthy of their office.

The eleventh century saw the separation between the Eastern and Western patriarchates that brought an end to any recognition of papal authority in the East, but it also saw the beginning of the development of a truly monarchical papacy in the West. A series of strong reforming popes, beginning with Leo IX in 1049 and ending with Gregory VII (1073–85), played a crucial role in the strengthening of papal authority in the West. The watchword of this reform was "freedom of the Church," a primary element of which was the freedom of the Church to choose and install its own bishops – something that secular rulers in much of Europe had come to see as their prerogative. By using the powerful weapon of excommunication against the Emperor Henry IV, Gregory VII succeeded in his campaign against this abuse, with the result that during the eleventh and twelfth centuries, most bishops were elected by cathedral chapters, the group of senior priests of a diocese. However, during the thirteenth century cathedral chapters, often composed of priests belonging to the nobility, tended to be so divided by political loyalties that they could not reach the majority required for election, and appeal had to be made to Rome to resolve the issue. As a result the appointment of bishops became a papal prerogative, more by default than by usurpation, but it was one factor in the apogee of papal power reached during the reign of Innocent III (1198–1216).

The notion that the Pope is "the vicar of Christ" and his sole representative on earth is characteristic of the papal theory developed by Pope Innocent III. As Christ is the head of his body the Church, so the Pope, as his vicar, is the head of the Church on earth, and all power and authority in the Church comes from him, and flows to the lesser authorities, even including the patriarchs. The medieval popes, as the recognized heads of Christian Europe, summoned bishops, abbots, and secular rulers to councils, whose decrees were issued with the fullness of papal authority. Inevitably, claims to absolute papal monarchy led to conflict with the secular powers, such as that between Pope Boniface VIII (1298–1303) and Philip the Fair, King of France. The eventual defeat of Boniface VIII by Philip IV marked the end of the supremacy of the medieval popes, as it was followed by the 60 years of the Avignon papacy, followed by the 40 years during which there were two, and then three, claimants to the papal throne. The resulting schism could be resolved only by the application of the theory that a general council would have the authority to judge and depose a Pope who was found guilty of heresy or schism. The Council of Constance (1414–18) invoked this theory, and settled the schism by getting the Roman claimant to resign, deposing the other two, and electing a legitimate pope. The papacy emerged from its ordeal much weakened, but it regained strength through the success of the following council, that of Florence. In the sixteenth century the area of effective papal authority in Europe was gravely reduced by the Protestant Reformation. However, it was vastly extended in the rest of the world through the missionary effort that followed the great discoveries of that period. The strong decrees enacted by the Council of Trent for the needed reform of the Catholic Church, and the effective role played by several reform-minded popes in seeing to the implementation of these decrees, contributed to the strengthening of papal authority in the post-Tridentine period.

The nineteenth century saw a remarkable swing of Catholic opinion in favor of a strong papacy, in the movement called Ultramontanism. The triumph of Ultramontanism among Catholic clergy and laity during the period from 1820 to 1870 undoubtedly played a role in the fact that the Catholic bishops gathered at Vatican I chose to focus their attention on the papacy, and defined as dogmas of faith the Pope's full and supreme power of jurisdiction over the whole Catholic Church, his supreme teaching authority, and his infallibility when he exercises this authority to its highest degree by defining a dogma. The dogmas defined by Vatican I are the doctrinal foundation of the authority with which the popes govern the universal Catholic Church.

The Papacy and Christian Unity

When Pope John XXIII announced his intention to convene the Second Vatican Council, he spoke of his hope that it would foster unity. During the following year he established the Secretariat for Promoting Christian Unity and appointed Cardinal Bea as its President. He had the Secretariat arrange for the presence at the council of observers delegated by the "world confessional bodies," and gave it the responsibility of drafting the Decree on Ecumenism.

After presiding at the second period of the council, Pope Paul VI had a historic meeting in Jerusalem with Patriarch Athenagoras, the fruit of which was the solemn consigning to oblivion of the mutual excommunications that had been symbols of the schism between the Churches of the East and the West since 1054. Paul VI also signed declarations of common faith with the Patriarchs of the Coptic and the Syrian Churches which had been separated from Rome since the fifth century. In 1969 he visited the headquarters of the World Council of Churches, and thereafter fostered the establishing of ecumenical dialogs with the confessional bodies separated from Rome since the Reformation.

During his first year as Pope, John Paul II had a meeting with Patriarch Dimitrios, the successor to Athenagoras, during which they agreed to inaugurate a theological dialog between their Churches. John Paul II also signed a common Christological declaration with the Assyrian Patriarch of the East. In *Ut Unum Sint*, he said, "A significant part of my Pastoral Visits is regularly devoted to fostering Christian unity." After speaking of his visits to Germany, the United Kingdom, Switzerland, Finland, Sweden, Norway, Denmark, and Iceland, he said: ""In an atmosphere of joy, mutual respect, Christian solidarity and prayer I met so very many brothers and sisters, all making a committed effort to be faithful to the Gospel." In that encyclical he took what is no doubt his most memorable initiative for the promotion of Christian unity when he said: "Whatever relates to the unity of all Christian communities clearly forms part of the concerns of the primacy . . . I am convinced that I have a particular responsibility in this regard, above all in acknowledging the ecumenical aspirations of the majority of the Christian Communities and in heeding the request made of me to find a way of exercising the primacy which, while in no way renouncing what is essential to its mission, is nevertheless open to a new situation . . . I insistently pray the Holy Spirit to shine his light upon us, enlightening all the Pastors and theologians of our Churches, that we may seek – together, of course – the forms in which this ministry may accomplish a service of love recognized by all concerned."

Almost a quarter of a century before he became Pope Benedict XVI, Joseph Ratzinger published a book in which he discussed the conditions that would have to be met for the restoration of full communion between the Catholic Church and the Orthodox Churches. There he said: "As far as the doctrine of papal primacy is concerned, Rome should not require more of the East than was formulated and lived during the first millennium . . . Reunion could take place on this basis: that for its part the East should renounce attacking the western development of the second millennium as heretical and should accept the Catholic Church as legitimate and orthodox in the form which it has found through this development, while for its part, the West should acknowledge the Church of the East as orthodox in the form which it has maintained."[2] It remains to be seen whether this opinion will become the official position of Rome during the current pontificate.

The Cardinals

The word "cardinal" is derived from the Latin word meaning "hinge." Various explanations have been offered for the association of that image with the role played by the parish priests and deacons of Rome and the bishops of the suburban dioceses, who in the course of the first millennium came to be called "cardinals." The popes increasingly looked to the cardinals for advice, and their importance in the affairs of the Church was greatly enhanced in 1179 when Pope Alexander III gave the college of cardinals the exclusive right to elect the Pope. During the twelfth century the popes began to add bishops of other sees to the college of cardinals, which was seen as the

Pope's "senate" with the role not only of advising him, but of sharing in his authority. Meetings of the whole college of cardinals, called "consistories," were held more and more frequently, until in the fourteenth century they came to be held three times a week. This meant that the cardinals had to reside where the Pope did, even though many of them held the title and obtained the revenue of some distant diocese. The Council of Trent put a stop to this abuse by decreeing that all diocesan bishops had to reside in their sees, thus reducing the number of cardinals able to take part in frequent consistories. To meet the need of regular assistance in governing the universal Church, Pope Sixtus V in 1588 distributed the cardinals residing in Rome into 15 groups called "congregations," assigning to each of these a special area of competence. By doing this, he effectively established the Roman Curia.

Until the time of Pope Pius XII, the great majority of the cardinals were Italian. Since then the college has become much more international, the majority of them being archbishops of major sees throughout the world. John XXIII was the first Pope to exceed the limit of 70 cardinals set by Sixtus V. At present there is no limit to the number a pope can "create," but the number who can elect a pope is limited to 120, and those over 80 years of age may not take part in the election. According to present law, one must have been ordained a priest to be named a cardinal, and those who are not bishops must then be ordained to the episcopate. However, elderly priests, in most cases honored with the cardinalate because they have served the Church well as theologians, are granted a dispensation from this obligation if they request it.

A year after his election, Pope John Paul II gave to the college of cardinals an important role it had not had for many centuries, by summoning the whole college to a consistory for the purpose of consulting them on problems facing the Holy See. For a long time, consistories had been held only to add a certain solemnity to such occasions as the canonization of saints and the naming of new cardinals. John Paul II made it clear that it was his intention to consult the whole body of cardinals when he wanted their advice on more serious matters affecting the universal Church, and he introduced these "extraordinary" consistories as an institution into the Code of Canon Law. Between 1979 and 2001, he summoned all the cardinals to six of these consistories. It remains to be seen whether his successors will follow his example. In any case, the cardinals play their most important roles in the government of the universal Catholic Church as electors of the Pope, and as members of the Roman Curia. Prior to the Second Vatican Council only cardinals were members of the curial congregations. The Council recommended that diocesan bishops who were not cardinals should be members as well, and Pope Paul VI began the practice of appointing such diocesan bishops to them. However, cardinals still outnumber the bishops in most of them. The moderators of all the congregations are cardinals, and many of them are members of several other congregations as well. It is the cardinals who play the major role in the Roman Curia.

The Roman Curia

Vatican I described the Pope's jurisdiction, or power of governance, as "episcopal." The word "episcopal" is derived from the Greek word *episkopé*, which means "oversight."

As a bishop relies on his parish priests to pastor the local congregations, but exercises oversight over the whole diocese, so the Pope relies on the bishops to pastor the particular churches, but exercises oversight over the whole Church. It is obvious that for the exercise of oversight over the worldwide Catholic Church, the Pope needs a great deal of help. Most of this help is provided by the Roman Curia, which brings to him the affairs of the whole Church that need his attention. Inevitably, the Pope's ordinary, every-day exercise of authority over the whole Church will consist in his examining the proposals and reports that he receives from the Curia, and making decisions about them.

The Roman Curia is the complex of dicasteries and institutes which help the Roman Pontiff in the exercise of his supreme pastoral office. (The name "dicastery" is based on the Greek word for the body of judges in ancient Athens.) The four kinds of dicasteries that are the principal structures of the Curia are the Secretariat of State, the Congregations, the Pontifical Councils, and the Tribunals. The members of a Congregation are the prefect and a body of cardinals and diocesan bishops. A Council's members are the president along with cardinals, bishops, clergy, and lay persons. Each dicastery will also have a secretary, sub-secretary, consultors, senior administrators, and officials. All the above, except the officials, are appointed by the Pope for a five-year renewable term. Cardinal prefects must submit their resignation to the Pope when they have reached the age of 75. Presidents and secretaries cease to hold office at 75; members lose their membership at 80.

Matters of greater moment are dealt with in plenary sessions, held once a year, to which all members must be invited. For ordinary sessions it is sufficient to convoke the members who reside in Rome. Consultors are expected to make a diligent study of the matter to be treated, and to present their considered opinion, usually in writing. Matters touching the competence of more than one dicastery are to be examined together by the dicasteries concerned. Decisions of major importance are to be submitted to the approval of the Supreme Pontiff. The dicasteries cannot issue laws or general decrees having the force of law without the specific approval of the Supreme Pontiff. Nothing grave or extraordinary can be transacted unless the Supreme Pontiff is previously informed by the moderator.

Reforms of the Curia

The bishops at Vatican II expressed the desire that the Roman Curia be reformed so as to be adapted to the needs of the times. Pope Paul VI complied with this wish by promulgating his Apostolic Constitution *Regimini Ecclesiae Universae* in 1967. A key provision of his constitution was the establishment of a number of councils and secretariats to supplement the work of the traditional congregations. After two decades of experience with the Curia as restructured by Paul VI, John Paul II reorganized it further, with his Apostolic Constitution *Pastor Bonus* of 1988. However, questions are still being raised whether the proposals made by the bishops at Vatican II for the reform of the Roman Curia have been fully realized. John R. Quinn, the retired archbishop of San Francisco, raised such questions in his book *The Reform of the Papacy*, where he recalled that in its decree on the Bishops' Pastoral Office in the Church, Vatican II had called for a reorganization of the Curia more in accord with the needs of the times and the diversity of places and rites in the Church. Quinn explained, "In other words, a reformed Curia should more manifestly take into account the great diversity in the Church, geographical, cultural, and historical, not only in its composition but more importantly in its policies and procedures. Specifically, Vatican II called for three things: (1) internationalization, (2) better communication and coordination among the departments of the Curia, (3) participation by diocesan bishops and by lay persons."[3] Quinn noted that since the council there has been a significant internationalization of the Curia, but saw a problem in the fact that those appointed to the Curia often lose real contact with their countries and with the pastoral realities of the local churches from which they come. He recalled recent events that showed that there is still need of better communication and coordination among the dicasteries. He observed that while there is now greater participation of diocesan bishops in the Curia, lay persons are not members of any Congregation, and half the Pontifical Councils still have no lay members. He concluded by offering four suggestions for the further reform of the Curia.

1 Giving more responsibilities in the Curia to lay men and women.
2 Limiting continued service in the Curia to two five-year terms, with a period of pastoral service in one's own local church before any re-appointment to Rome.
3 Providing for greater participation of the local church in the selection of persons to be appointed to the Curia.
4 Establishing a commission to advise the Pope on further reform of the Curia.

Congregations

There are nine congregations, each of which is under the direction of a Cardinal Prefect, with an Archbishop as secretary, assisted by a sub-secretary. Only cardinals and diocesan bishops are members of a congregation. At present the number of cardinals in a congregation varies from 10 to 40. Most congregations have more cardinals than diocesan bishops as members. The cardinals who reside in Rome, who are usually members of several congregations, are able to attend their ordinary as well as their plenary sessions. A cardinal who does not reside in Rome will usually be the bishop of one of the most important archdioceses of the Catholic Church, and will necessarily be selective in his attendance at ordinary sessions of the Roman congregation (or congregations) to which he belongs. Each congregation has its own area of competence, with authority received from the Pope to deal with matters in that area.

The Congregation for the Doctrine of the Faith was founded by Pope Paul III in 1542 with the title "Holy Roman and Universal Inquisition." Its original function was to act as a tribunal to investigate and judge cases of heresy and schism. The Latin word *inquisitio* means "investigation," so in name, at least, it was like the Federal Bureau of Investigation. In 1588 Pope Sixtus V broadened its scope to include all matters of faith and morals. Pius X, in 1908, changed its name to Sacred Congregation of the Holy Office. One still hears it referred to as the Holy Office; in fact, its offices are in a building called the Palace of the Holy Office. However, Paul VI changed its name to Sacred Congregation for the Doctrine of the Faith, giving it also the positive function of promoting sound doctrine about the faith. In *Pastor Bonus* John Paul II dropped "Sacred" from the name of all the congregations, and described the function of this congregation as to promote and safeguard the doctrine on faith and morals in the whole Catholic world, with competence in things that touch this matter in any way. One competence that has been given to this congregation is to judge cases of the sexual abuse of minors by members of the clergy.

To fulfill its duty of promoting sound doctrine, the Congregation fosters studies so that the understanding of the faith may grow and a response in the light of faith may be given to new questions arising from the progress of the sciences or human culture. From time to time it publishes the fruit of such studies in documents that are approved by the Pope either in "ordinary form" or in "specific form." Those approved in ordinary form are published as statements of the Congregation, with the teaching authority that is delegated to it by the Pope. Those approved in specific form have the authority that is attached to documents issued by the Pope himself, but they do not share papal infallibility.

The congregation has the responsibility to examine writings that seem dangerous to the faith. If, after examination, that is judged to be the case, the author is given the opportunity to justify what he or she has written, first in a written response, and then, if further clarification is needed, in a colloquium with some theologians appointed by the prefect. The results of this process are then discussed in a regular meeting of the members, who decide what action, if any, to take. There are several actions the congregation may take, all needing papal approval. It may publish a "notification" warning the Catholic public against errors it has found in the author's work, or ambiguities that might lead readers to draw erroneous conclusions from it. In more serious cases it may declare that the author is not to be considered a Catholic theologian, and that any canonical mission or mandate he or she has received to teach theology should be withdrawn.

The congregation also makes use of work done on its behalf by the Pontifical Biblical Commission and the International Theological Commission, both of which are attached to this congregation and are presided over by its prefect. Scripture scholars and theologians are chosen by the prefect and appointed to these commissions for five-year terms. They study matters suggested to them by the prefect, and the conclusions they reach need the approval of the Holy See in order to be published. However, they do not have the authority that is attached to documents published by the Congregation.

The Congregation for the Oriental Churches deals with matters that concern the Eastern Catholic Churches. Eastern Catholic Churches are particular churches that are in communion with Rome, but follow one of the Eastern rites. A rite is a distinctive heritage of liturgy, theology, spirituality, and canonical discipline. The competence of this Congregation extends to all matters proper to the Eastern Catholic Churches that are to be referred to the Holy See. In 1990 Pope John Paul II promulgated a special Code of Canons for these churches.

The Congregation for Divine Worship and the Discipline of the Sacraments does whatever pertains to the Holy See concerning the regulation and promotion of the sacred liturgy, primarily of the sacraments. It sees to the drawing up and revision of liturgical texts. It examines and decides whether to approve translations of liturgical books that have been prepared by conferences of bishops.

The Congregation for the Causes of Saints deals with everything which, according to the established procedure, leads to the canonization of saints.

The Congregation for Bishops deals with everything that pertains to the exercise of the episcopal office in the Latin Church. It has a particularly important role in the process by which bishops are chosen, as it examines the qualifications of the candidates who are proposed by the nuncio who represents the Holy See in the nation where a bishop is to be appointed, and it presents its recommendation to the Pope, who usually follows it in making the appointment.

The Congregation for the Evangelization of Peoples was originally founded by Clement VIII in 1599, and re-founded by Gregory XVI in 1622, at a time of great missionary expansion. Its task is to direct and coordinate the work of the Catholic Church in spreading the Gospel throughout the world. It has special competence and authority in what are considered by the Holy See as mission territories. At present these are Africa, the Far East, and Oceania, with the exception of Australia and the Philippines. Most of its members are chosen from among the cardinals and other bishops who preside over local churches in mission territories. It provides for the education of their clergy, for which purpose it maintains the Pontifical Urban University in Rome, founded by Pope Urban VIII in 1627.

The Congregation for the Clergy deals with matters regarding priests and deacons of the diocesan clergy with regard to their persons and pastoral ministry, and the resources available to them for the exercise of this ministry. It is competent concerning the life, conduct, rights, and obligation of clergy, and fosters their ongoing education.

The Congregation for Institutes of Consecrated Life and for Societies of Apostolic Life is popularly referred to as the Congregation for Religious. It promotes and supervises the practice of the evangelical counsels as they are lived in approved forms of consecrated life and societies of apostolic life. It erects and approves such institutes, or passes judgment on the suitability of their erection by a diocesan bishop. It deals with everything that belongs to the Holy See concerning their life and work, such as the approval of their constitutions, the recruitment, training, rights, and obligations of members, their dispensation from vows, and their dismissal. Many of its members are also superiors of religious orders.

The Congregation of Seminaries and Educational Institutions gives practical expression to the concern of the Holy See for the training of those called to Holy Orders, and for the promotion and organization of Catholic education. It sees to it that the way of life and government of the seminaries be in full harmony with the program of priestly education and formation for sacred ministry. It sets the norms by which Catholic schools are governed. It erects or approves ecclesiastical universities, ratifies their statutes, and exercises supervision over them. With regard to other Catholic universities it deals with matters that are within the competence of the Holy See.

Pontifical Councils

Pontifical Councils were first introduced into the Roman Curia by Pope Paul VI in 1967. There are now 11 of them. They differ from the Congregations in several respects.

Rather than a cardinal prefect, their moderator is a president, who does not have to be a cardinal, although at present seven of them are cardinals. The other presidents are titular archbishops. Besides cardinals and diocesan bishops, most Pontifical Councils also have priests and lay persons as members, and some also have members of religious communities.

The Pontifical Council for the Laity is unique in that the number of its members who are lay people is presently greater than that of the members who are cardinals and bishops combined. It is competent in matters pertaining to the Holy See regarding the promotion and coordination of the apostolate of the laity, and, generally, in matters respecting the Christian life of lay people as such. It deals with matters regarding Catholic lay associations, erects such associations of an international character, and approves their statutes.

The Pontifical Council for Promoting Christian Unity engages in ecumenical work, seeking to restore unity among Christians. It deals with the correct interpretation of the principles of ecumenism as set forth by the Second Vatican Council, and publishes the Directory for Ecumenism. It maintains relations with Christians of churches and ecclesial communities that do not have full communion with the Catholic Church and organizes dialog and other meetings with them. In this Council and presided over by its president there is the Commission for Religious Relations with Jews, which deals with matters of a religious nature concerning Jews.

The Pontifical Council for the Family promotes the pastoral care of families and protects their rights and dignity in the Church and in civil society. It works for a deeper understanding of the Church's teaching on the family, and encourages studies on the spirituality of marriage and the family. Among the members of this council there are 17 married couples.

The Pontifical Council for Justice and Peace promotes justice and peace in the world in accordance with the Gospel and the social teaching of the Church. It studies the social teaching of the Church and ensures that it is widely known and put into practice. It cultivates relationships with international organizations that strive to advance peace and justice in the world.

The Pontifical Council Cor Unum expresses the solicitude of the Catholic Church for the needy, and its effort to foster human fraternity and make manifest Christ's charity. Its function is to foster and coordinate the initiatives of Catholic organizations that work to help peoples in need, especially those that go to the rescue in urgent crises and disasters.

The Pontifical Council for Pastoral Assistance to Health Care Workers provides help to those who serve the sick and suffering, so that their apostolate of mercy may ever more effectively respond to people's needs. It spreads the Church's teaching on the spiritual and moral aspects of illness, as well as the meaning of human suffering. It follows new health care developments so that these may be duly taken into account in the pastoral work of the Church.

The Pontifical Council for the Interpretation of Legislative Texts is competent to give authoritative interpretations of the laws of the Church. It determines whether laws and general decrees issued by legislative authorities below the level of the supreme authority are in agreement with the universal laws of the Church.

The Pontifical Council for Inter-Religious Dialogue fosters and supervises relations with members of non-Christians religions, promoting dialog and other kinds of relations with them. It has a commission, under the direction of the president of the council, for fostering relations with Muslims from a religious perspective.

The Pontifical Council for Culture fosters relations between the Holy See and the realm of human culture, especially by promoting communication with various contemporary institutions of learning, so that secular culture and those who cultivate it may be more open to the Gospel. As appropriate, it participates in important organizations in the field of culture.

The Pontifical Council for Social Communications deals with questions regarding the means of social communication. Its chief task is to encourage and support the action of the Church and its members in the many forms of communication.

The Secretariat of State

The Secretariat of State provides close assistance to the Pope in the exercise of his office. It is presided over by the Cardinal Secretary of State. It is composed of two sections: the first is the section for general affairs, under the direction of an archbishop whose title is "Substitute for general affairs." The second section is for relations with states, under the direction of its own secretary, who is also an archbishop.

It is the task of the first section to coordinate the work of the other dicasteries of the Holy See, and to deal with matters that are outside their ordinary competence. It supervises the office and work of the legates of the Holy See, especially as concerns the particular Catholic churches, and deals with everything concerning the ambassadors of states to the Holy See. It takes care of matters concerning the presence and activity of the Holy See in international organizations. It draws up and dispatches documents entrusted to it by the Pope, and prepares them for publication in *Acta Apostolicae Sedis*. It is in charge of the Press Office, through which it publishes official announcements of acts of the Pope or of the Holy See. It oversees *L'Osservatore Romano*, the Vatican Radio Station, and the Vatican Television Office.

The Section for Relations with States has the special task of dealing with the heads of government. It fosters relations, especially those of a diplomatic nature, with states and other subjects of public international law. It represents the Holy See in international organizations and meetings concerning questions of a public nature. Within the scope of its competence, it deals with what a papal legate, called a nuncio, does in his role as ambassador to one of the 174 nations with which the Holy See maintains diplomatic relations.

Tribunals

The three tribunals are the judicial component of the Roman Curia. The Apostolic Penitentiary is a unique tribunal which deals with matters of personal conscience to be handled in the "internal forum." In this forum it is competent to grant absolutions, dispensations, and the like.

The Tribunal of the Roman Rota is a court of higher instance, usually at the appellate stage, with the purpose of safeguarding rights within the Church. It consists of a college of judges selected by the Supreme Pontiff from various parts of the world. It adjudicates cases that have been decided by ordinary tribunals of the first instance and are being referred to the Holy See by legitimate appeal. It also judges cases concerning bishops and other ecclesiastical persons who have no superior below the Supreme Pontiff.

The Supreme Tribunal of the Apostolic Signatura could be described as the Supreme Court of the Catholic Church. It is competent to adjudicate all cases that could not be settled by an inferior ecclesiastical court, or that are appealed to it. It exercises vigilance over the correct administration of justice in the whole Catholic Church.

Notes

1   G.W. Clarke, *The Letters of St Cyprian of Carthage*, Ancient Christian Writers, 46. New York: The Newman Press, 1986, vol. 3, 82.
2   *Theologische Prinzipienlehre: Bausteine zur Fundamentaltheologie*, Munich, 1982, 209 (my translation).
3   *The Reform of the Papacy: The Costly Call to Christian Unity*. New York: Crossroad, 1999, 162.

References and Further Reading

Allen, John L. Jr. (2004) *All the Pope's Men. The Inside Story of How the Vatican Really Thinks*. New York: Doubleday.
Reese, Thomas J. (1996) *Inside the Vatican. The Politics and Organization of the Catholic Church*. Cambridge, MA: Harvard University Press.
Schatz, Klaus (1996) *Papal Primacy from its Origin to the Present*. Collegeville, MN: Liturgical Press.
Tillard, J.M.R., OP (1983) *The Bishop of Rome*, trans. John de Satgé. Wilmington, DE: Michael Glazier, Inc.

CHAPTER 29
Ecumenism[1]

Michael Root

"Ecumenism" is a word without a long Catholic history. Its Greek root, *oikumene*, refers to "the whole inhabited world." When Luke's Gospel begins its account of the birth of Jesus with the decree of Caesar Augustus that "the world" should be registered (Luke 2:1), the term for "world" is *oikumene*. Thus, one meaning of "ecumenical" is "applying to the whole world." An ecumenical council of the church, such as the Second Vatican Council, is thus a council of the worldwide church, not just a national or regional council.

In the late nineteenth century, however, the word "ecumenical" came to take on a different meaning in Protestant missionary and student circles. These groups were particularly sensitive to the problems created by the divisions of the churches. Potential converts in missionary lands could be baffled by the diversity of Christian communities; students were often impatient with denominational barriers to fellowship. The term "ecumenical" came to refer to efforts to overcome these divisions among Christians (for the history of "ecumenical," see Visser 't Hooft, 1953). In the first half of the twentieth century, isolated efforts toward cooperation and fellowship gained momentum and flowed together into a more comprehensive ecumenical movement. Representatives of the Orthodox Churches became involved following World War I and the most important ecumenical institutions came together in 1948 to form the World Council of Churches (WCC).

On its surface, the Catholic Church's engagement with ecumenism is marked by a drastic reversal during the Second Vatican Council. Initial Catholic reactions to the ecumenical movement were predominantly negative. There was only one solution to the divisions among Christians and it was simple: non-Catholics should return to the Catholic Church. Ecumenical efforts by Catholics that did not communicate that message were misleading. Vatican II, however, declared that the ecumenical movement was a work of the Holy Spirit, a Vatican office was created for "promoting Christian unity," and dialog with "the separated brethren" became the order of the day. This reversal was affirmed by John Paul II in the last decade of the century, when he said in a solemn encyclical that the Catholic Church's ecumenical commitment is "irrevocable" (John Paul II, 1995: paragraph 3).[2]

Catholic ecumenical engagement is fundamentally misunderstood, however, if this narrative of rupture fully determines how one reads Catholic ecumenical history. Within the very real discontinuity, certain fundamental and traditional convictions were at work, both motivating the change and shaping it according to Catholic principles. Without the perception of these continuities, contemporary Catholic ecumenism can appear baffling. Traditionalists do not see how ecumenical conviction flows from Catholic commitment; ecumenists cannot grasp the internal consistency of ecumenism with the other deeds and thoughts of John Paul II and Benedict XVI. The inner coherence of Catholic ecumenism requires a more balanced historical reading.

Three texts will provide the focus for this presentation: Yves Congar's *Divided Christendom* of 1937 (with an English translation in 1939); Vatican II's Decree on Ecumenism *Unitatis Reditegratio* of 1965; and John Paul II's encyclical on the church's commitment to ecumenism, *Ut Unum Sint* of 1995.

Yves Congar's *Divided Christendom* (1937)

Yves Congar (1904–95), a French Dominican, was the most important Catholic ecumenical theologian of the twentieth century. In an autobiographical sketch written in 1963, he explained the early roots of his ecumenical vocation: the importance of the Protestant church in his home town offering its chapel for the use of the Catholic parish after their church was destroyed in World War I and his meditation on John 17, Jesus' prayer that "they may all be one," just prior to his ordination in 1930 (Congar, 1966: 2–5).

Mortalium Animos (1928)

Congar's work illumines the theological deep structure of Catholic ecumenical commitment. Christian division had not been ignored by the Catholic Church of the nineteenth century. Johann Adam Möhler, a professor at the Catholic faculties of Tübingen and Munich in Germany, laid the foundations for Catholic ecumenical theology early in the century (Möhler, 1997). Pius IX had invited Orthodox bishops to attend the First Vatican Council in 1870 (though in a highly clumsy and self-defeating fashion; Butler, 1930: 93–5). Leo XIII in 1897 dedicated the week prior to Pentecost to prayer for "the consummation of Christian unity" (Leo XIII, 1928), which later became the Week of Prayer for Christian Unity in January. From 1921 to 1926, the Archbishop of Malines (Belgium) sponsored a series of ecumenical conversations with leading Anglicans, the first of the ecumenical dialogs of the twentieth century (Denaux, 1997).

Nevertheless, all such efforts took the form of an "ecumenism of return;" they sought "to bring back to the fold . . . sheep that have strayed" (Leo XIII, 1896: paragraph 1). As the ecumenical movement gathered momentum following World War I, with large international conferences, encompassing official representatives from a wide range of Protestant and Orthodox churches, official Catholic attitudes seemed to harden. The

Vatican insisted that Catholics must not attend these conferences. In 1928, a papal encyclical, *Mortalium Animos* (hereafter, MA; Pius XI, 1930), stated that participation in such meetings would be support for a "false Christianity quite alien to the one Church of Christ" (paragraph 8).

Three objections were decisive, each reflecting a Catholic doctrinal commitment. First, the ecumenical movement was seen as pursuing the unity of the Church as if it were a "mere ideal," as something which does not now exist and must be brought into existence by human efforts (paragraph 7). In response came the insistence that, as Congar stated, "because the unity of the church is from above, from God, it cannot be broken by the secession of this or that member of it" (Congar, 1939: 59). The church *is* one, holy, catholic, and apostolic; unity is thus an essential characteristic of the church. If Christ is true to his promise that the gates of hell shall not prevail against his church (Matt 16:18), then the church must continue to exist as one.

Second, this unity is not a hidden or secret matter. The church is "visibly the one body of the faithful, agreeing in one and the same doctrine under one teaching and governing authority" (paragraph 6). This unity of the church has been preserved in the church in communion with the Bishop of Rome, the Catholic Church.

Third, the ecumenical movement was seen as pursuing a unity that did not rest upon an agreed understanding of the faith, a common grasp of Christian doctrine. The Stockholm conference on Life and Work of 1925, the first of the great post-World War I ecumenical conferences, included both Unitarians and non-sacramental groups such as the Quakers. MA insisted: "It is chiefly by the bond of one faith that the disciples of Christ are to be united. A federation of Christians, then, is inconceivable in which each member retains his own opinions and private judgment in matters of faith, even though they differ from the opinions of all the rest" (paragraph 9).

MA's judgment about the ecumenical movement is simply negative. "Such efforts can meet with no kind of approval among Catholics" (paragraph 2).

Congar's affirmation of ecumenism

Writing in 1937, Congar in *Divided Christendom* affirmed the convictions and specific criticisms of MA, but was able to develop a far more open ecumenical perspective, on the basis of other convictions equally Catholic. As noted, he affirmed that unity is a characteristic that the church cannot lose and that the unity of the church is preserved in the Catholic Church (Congar, 1939: 142, 237). He insisted on the necessity of doctrinal agreement for true church unity (Congar, 1939: 107ff.). He was critical of the attitudes toward unity and doctrine present among the first generation of ecumenical leaders (but also noted a different outlook in the group coming to leadership in the 1930s; Congar, 1939: 134–9). The way in which Congar worked within the doctrinal affirmations of MA while producing a quite different ecumenical theology proved prophetic for later Catholic ecumenism.

Congar frames his discussion of ecumenism with an ecclesiology less juridical, more open and dynamic than that implicit in MA. Congar understands the church as a participation in the life of the Trinity. Through Christ and the Spirit, the church as a body is taken into the divine communion of love. "The Church is the community of souls living the very life which is the life of the Blessed Trinity because the object of their lives is the same as that of the life of God Himself" (Congar, 1939: 57f.). The unity of the church is thus a function of the unity of the Trinity. "The oneness of the Church is a communication and extension of the oneness of God Himself" (Congar, 1939: 48). Church structure and formal doctrine are important because, but only because, they serve this interior life of communion with God.

Are non-Catholic Christians utterly cut off from this life in God, a life inseparable from the church? In answering, Congar does not first appeal to his experience of non-Catholic Christians (although his later remarks indicate the importance of such experience), but to the classic Catholic affirmation that a baptism correctly performed even out-side the church is a valid baptism. If so, then baptized non-Catholics, especially those born into non-Catholic churches or communities and who thus have never themselves broken with the Catholic Church, are not simply outside that life which is the heart of the church, for "valid baptism *ipso facto* incorporates the recipient into the true Church" (Congar, 1939: 229). Their relation to the one church is imperfect, but not non-existent.

Baptism is not just significant for individuals; it is one element that constitutes the church as the church. If the church were to cease to baptize, it would cease to be the church. But if a Lutheran or Presbyterian baptism is a valid baptism, then such bodies, even if not churches in the full theological sense of the word, contain in their lives constitutive elements of the church. And far more must be said about the Ortho-dox. While doctrinal differences played some role in the separation of East and West, Congar agrees with many Western observers in seeing the primacy of the Pope as the "only real point at issue" between Catholic and Orthodox (Congar, 1939: 199). Congar agrees with most of Catholic tradition in seeing the Orthodox churches as gen-uine churches, as having "a true though incomplete ecclesiastical reality" (Congar, 1939: 245). Thus, not only are there Christians outside the communion of the unified church, there are bodies which must be called churches outside that communion.

Even if the Catholic Church preserves all the essential qualities of the church despite these divisions, division still wounds and deforms the church. The most important non-Catholic movements "appear to represent one-sided and therefore false devel-opments of originally true spiritual intuitions" (Congar, 1939: 43). In reacting, the Catholic Church tended to emphasize what its opponents neglected, becoming itself less than balanced. Congar notes this tendency especially in Catholic reactions to overly spiritual understandings of the church among the Protestant Reformers:

> Controversial theologians have more frequently dealt with the organization of the visi-ble Church than with the organism of the Mystical Body, and . . . the edifice constructed by them, being undertaken and carried on in a state of siege by builders who wielded the sword as well as the trowel, like the Jews in the time of Nehemiah, has turned out to be as much like a fortress as a temple. (Congar, 1939: 32f.)

Thus, Catholic unity is not destroyed by such division, but it is made poorer. Reconcil-iation with other Christian bodies is then not just for the good of the non-Catholic; the Catholic Church will itself gain.

What is true in, for instance, the Lutheran or the Wesleyan experience is, in its Lutheran or Wesleyan setting, a loss to the Catholic church of today, and calls by its very nature for reintegration in it . . . Dissidence does not destroy the unity of the Church; . . . yet while it does not make the Church less One, there is a sense in which we may truly assert that it does make it less *actually* Catholic. (Congar, 1939: 256)

Precisely as *Catholic*, the church will gain from the reconciliation of such traditions.

Divided Christendom demonstrated that the fundamental convictions that under-girded MA – the necessity of doctrinal agreement for true unity, the existence of the unity of the church as a reality and not just an ideal, and the preservation of that unity in the Catholic Church – were compatible with an attitude different from that encyclical's thoroughgoing suspicion of ecumenism. For Congar, while the *church* is not essentially divided, *Christians* are and "the disunion of Christians is verily a rending of Christ and a continuance of His passion" (Congar, 1939: 223). What it also demonstrates is that the roots of Catholic ecumenism do not lie in an easygoing tolerance or doubts about Catholic claims, but in traditional Catholic affirmations about the nature of baptism and the inclusive nature of the church's catholicity.

Congar's outlook in *Divided Christendom* pointed to the future. Congar would be one of the most influential figures at Vatican II and, just before his death, he would be appointed a cardinal by John Paul II. In the short run, however, his outlook was not greeted by Catholic officialdom. In his encyclical of 1943, *Mystici Corporis Christi* (*On the Mystical Body of Christ*), Pius XII threw cold water on any notion that non-Catholics might be members of the church (Pius XII, 1943: paragraph 22). Congar himself states that "from the beginning of 1947 to the end of 1956 I knew nothing from that quarter [Rome] but an uninterrupted series of denunciations, warnings, restrictive or discriminatory measures and mistrustful interventions" (Congar, 1966: 34).

Vatican II and *Unitatis Redintegratio* (1965)

Catholic attitudes to ecumenism were already changing during the decade following World War II. When the World Council of Churches was constituted at an Assembly in Amsterdam in 1948, the bishops of the Netherlands, while voicing standard Catholic concerns, also greeted the new development: the assembly "has been born out of a great and sincere desire for the unity willed by Christ on the part of many who are prepared to accept him as their God and their Savior" (Archbishop and Bishops of the Netherlands, 1958: 19). The following year, the Vatican cautiously loosened its prohibition of Catholic participation in ecumenical conferences (Sacred Congregation of the Holy Office, 1958). Nevertheless, such small steps did not hint at the profound shift in attitude that would occur with the Second Vatican Council.

In his first speech announcing his intention to call a council (delivered, probably not accidentally, on January 25, the last day of the Week of Prayer for Christian Unity), John XXIII stated his hope that the Council would further the cause of the reconciliation of Christians (Alberigo and Komonchak, 1995: 15). His ecumenical intent was embodied in his invitation to Protestant and Orthodox churches to send observers to the Council. The office created to look after these observers became the Secretariat (now Pontifical Council) for Promoting Christian Unity, the ecumenical office of the Vatican (Alberigo et al., 1995: 318–27). The head of the Secretariat, Augustin Bea, would become a major figure of the Council, shaping texts well beyond the limited field of ecumenism.

The Catholic Church and the one church of Christ

Unitatis redintegratio (The Restoration of Unity, hereafter UR), the Council's Decree on Ecumenism, is the most important and authoritative text of modern Catholic ecumenism.[3] Its three chapters describe "Catholic Principles of Ecumenism" and "The Practice of Ecumenism," followed by a detailed consideration of Catholic relations with both the Orthodox and Protestant churches. Along with the 1993 *Directory for the Application of Principles and Norms on Ecumenism* and the encyclical *Ut Unum Sint* (1995), it forms the normative and practical framework for Catholic ecumenical engagement.

    UR cannot be read in isolation, however, from the other works of the Council. As the text itself states (UR: 1), its relation is especially close to *Lumen Gentium* (LG), the Dogmatic Constitution on the Church. UR can be read as the extension into the ecumenical area of the understanding of the church outlined in LG. Section 8 of LG was decisive in expanding the breathing room for ecumenism in Catholic theology. It describes the church as instituted by Christ, uniting divine and human elements, and then continues:

> This is the one church of Christ which in the Creed we profess as one, holy, catholic and apostolic . . . This church constituted and organized in this world as a society, subsists in the Catholic Church . . . although outside of its visible structure many elements of sanctification and of truth are found, which, as gifts belonging to the church of Christ, impel toward catholic unity.

This much discussed and much disputed assertion needs careful interpretation. In one of the decisive theological moves of the Council, the verb in the second sentence was changed from "is" ("This church of Christ *is* the Catholic Church") to "subsists." Precisely what it means to say that the church of Christ subsists in the Catholic Church has been the subject of vehement debate. What is clear, however, is that the text denies any simple identity between the one church of Christ and the Catholic Church, even while maintaining that the one church of Christ is to be found in the Catholic Church. A conceptual space is opened up between the Catholic Church and the one church of Christ. Part of what might occupy this space is clarified in the rest of the sentence: "elements of sanctification and truth," elements which are integral to the church's life, are to be found outside the structures of the Catholic Church. (The Council's Doctrinal Commission pointed to these gifts outside the Catholic Church as a reason for changing "is" to "subsists"; Alberigo and Komonchak, 2003: 42). Since the natural home, so to speak, of these gifts is in the Catholic Church, however, they create a pull toward "catholic unity." The ecumenical drive toward greater unity is rooted in the inherently unifying character of the elements shared by the divided churches.

The Decree on Ecumenism expands on this paragraph. Important elements of life in Christ can be found in non-Catholic communities. "Some and even very many of the significant elements and endowments which together go to build up and give life to the church itself, can exist outside the visible boundaries of the Catholic Church: the written word of God; the life of grace; faith, hope and charity, with the other interior gifts of the Holy Spirit, as well as visible elements" (UR: 3). These elements are not without effect in the lives of members of these communities. "These most certainly can truly engender a life of grace in ways that vary according to the condition of each church or community. These liturgical actions must be regarded as capable of giving access to the community of salvation" (UR: 3) Within the lives of non-Catholic bodies, grace is communicated and received. If grace is inseparable from Christ and the Spirit and if the reception of Christ and the Spirit has an inherently social (and thus churchly) dimension, then persons are brought into the community of salvation (i.e., the church) within these communities. As with Congar, baptism is again decisive. "Those who believe in Christ and have been truly baptized are in some, even though imperfect, communion with the Catholic Church . . . All who have been justified by faith in Baptism are incorporated into Christ, and have a right to be called Christians, and so are correctly accepted as brothers and sisters by the children of the Catholic Church" (UR: 3; cf. 22). (An important accompanying affirmation in the same section is that such persons born and raised in the Christian faith within non-Catholic churches "cannot be charged with the sin of separation" and thus cannot be said to have rejected baptismal grace by a decision to leave the Catholic Church.)

The status of non-Catholic churches

If non-Catholic communities can bring their members into the community of salvation and a "real, but imperfect communion with the Catholic Church," what does this imply about the status of those communities? While the Council views them all as "defective" in varying degrees, it also affirmed that they "have by no means been deprived of significance and importance in the mystery of salvation. For the Spirit of Christ has not refrained from using them as means of salvation which derive their efficacy from the very fullness of grace and truth entrusted to the Catholic Church" (UR: 3). As in the past, the traditional affirmation is made that the fullness of the means of salvation is to be encountered in the Catholic Church. Nevertheless, a far more positive view is here offered of the place of non-Catholic churches in the economy of salvation. Catholic theology has never denied that non-Catholics could be redeemed, but the sense was often that they were redeemed *despite* their membership in non-Catholic churches. The Council now makes clear that they are redeemed precisely *through* such membership.

This more positive view of other Christian communities is nuanced; all non-Catholic communities are not viewed as equal. UR's discussion of other churches has two large sections: "The Special Position of the Eastern Churches" and "The Separated Churches and Ecclesial Communities in the West." These titles are significant. The Eastern churches are *churches*, genuine realizations of the one church. They "possess true sacraments and above all, by apostolic succession, the priesthood and the Eucharist, whereby they are linked with us in closest intimacy" (UR: 15). The distinctive character of Christian life within the Orthodox Churches is celebrated. "Far from being an obstacle to the church's unity, such diversity of customs and observances only adds to her splendor, and is of great help in carrying out her mission" (UR: 16). The Western "separated churches and ecclesial communities," including both Old Catholic and Protestant communities, are described more circumspectly, partly because of the great variety among them. The phrase "ecclesial community" was introduced to describe those communities which have a genuinely ecclesial or churchly character because they realize various elements that constitute the church (e.g., a valid baptism, a reverence for Scripture, a confession of the Trinity), but which nevertheless, because they lack certain other essential features, cannot be said to be genuine churches, as the Orthodox are said to be (on the phrase "ecclesial community," see especially Hamer, 1972). In the one passage that seems to state what such communities lack, the Council said that such communities "have not preserved the genuine and integral substance of the Eucharistic mystery, especially because of the lack or defect [*defectum*] of the sacrament of order" (UR: 22). Because such communities suffer from a *defectus* in their ordinations and thus, since a validly ordained priest is needed for a valid celebration of the Eucharist, lack something integral to the Eucharist, they cannot be said to be churches, but only "ecclesial communities."

This passage has been a bone of ecumenical contention, in more than one sense. While the text never states which bodies are churches and which only "ecclesial communities," the clear implication of Catholic practice has been that all communities that stem from the Reformation (including Anglicans, since Leo XIII declared Anglican ordinations invalid in 1896, see Hill and Yarnold, 1997) are to be referred to only as "ecclesial communities," a designation they naturally find problematic. When in the Lutheran–Catholic *Joint Declaration on the Doctrine of Justification* (noted below) the Lutheran churches insisted on referring to themselves as churches, the Vatican in turn insisted on a footnote, stating that such language did not imply that Rome was recognizing them as such (Gros, Meyer, and Rusch, 2000: 582, n. 9).

The interpretation of this passage in UR has also been contested. Does *defectus* imply absence or lack, or merely defect? To say that such communities lack true ordinations is one thing; to say that their ordinations have some defect is quite another. Walter Kasper, head of the Pontifical Council for Promoting Christian Unity, has himself argued for the latter interpretation (Kasper, 1990: 345).

The need for a balanced reading

This real but limited recognition of the ecclesial status of the Reformation churches points to the need for a balanced reading of the ecumenism endorsed by Vatican II. The Council did not simply reject the affirmations that shaped MA. The underlying dogmatic principles of the earlier text are, for the most part, implicitly affirmed. In a way quite similar to Congar's *Divided Christendom*, these earlier affirmations are not rejected but joined with affirmations with an equal claim to Catholic authenticity, but the implications of which had not been earlier spelled out (most notably, the validity of baptism even outside the church and the power of such baptism to join persons to the church). This mixture of continuity and change is particularly visible in the way the Council treats the unity of the church. As in pre-conciliar teaching, the unity Christ wills for his church is not treated as an ideal to be achieved; "We believe that this unity subsists in the Catholic Church as something she can never lose" (UR: 4). As with Congar in 1937, however, this affirmation is paired with a recognition that, even if the *church* is not divided, *Christians* are. The first paragraph of UR states that the present division among Christians "openly contradicts the will of Christ, scandalizes the world, and damages the holy cause of preaching the Gospel to every creature" (UR: 1). As with Congar, this division of Christians is seen as harming the church's catholicity. "The divisions among Christians prevent the Church from attaining the fullness of catholicity proper to her, in those of her children who, though attached to her by Baptism, are yet separated from full communion with her. Furthermore, the Church herself finds it more difficult to express in actual life her full catholicity in all respects" (UR: 4). The church cannot fully express its catholicity, the universality of its message, and the comprehensive scope of its life, when large strands of the Christian tradition exist outside its communion. UR thus combines striking affirmations of the "scandal of division" with traditional statements of the preservation of unity within the Catholic Church.

This combination of continuity and innovation is widespread in the way the Council handled various issues of ecumenical significance. On the whole, Catholic doctrine was expounded at Vatican II in a way that non-Catholics, both Protestant and Orthodox, find far more understandable and attractive than the scholastic and juridical emphases of previous centuries. The affirmation of religious freedom in the Declaration on Religious Liberty was a true and, for non-Catholics, welcome innovation in Catholic teaching and political practice. The inclusion of the discussion of Mary within the Constitution on the Church (chapter 8 of LG) placed Mary in a theological context which Protestants could at least comprehend, even if not accept. Nevertheless, on many of the issues that present significant ecumenical difficulties, the Council reaffirmed traditional teaching. The emphasis on the collegiality of the bishops placed Vatican I's teaching on papal primacy in a new interpretive context, but papal primacy itself is clearly enunciated (LG: paragraphs 22–3, 25).

Ecumenical engagement

The Council did not lay out the details of a program of ecumenical action, but in its chapter on "The Practice of Ecumenism" it did point to crucial aspects of such practice. Most strikingly, it emphasized the spiritual side of ecumenical effort. "There can be no ecumenism worthy of the name without interior conversion. For it is from the renewal of our minds, from self-denial and an unstinted love that desires for unity arise and develop" (UR: 7). Prayer and humility are particularly stressed (UR: 8). While the Catholic Church is understood to lack nothing essential to the faith, it still can learn from other traditions. "Anything wrought by the grace of Holy Spirit among our separated brothers and sisters can contribute to our own edification" (UR: 4). Most of all, the "primary duty" of Catholics in the ecumenical area "is to make a careful and honest appraisal of whatever needs to be done or renewed in the Catholic household itself, in order that its life may bear witness more clearly and faithfully to the teachings and institutions which have come to it from Christ through the Apostles" (UR: 4).

UR foresees that "'dialogue' among competent experts" (UR: 4) will be an important aspect of the pursuit of greater unity. The text makes two important conceptual contributions to understanding the nature of such dialog. First, the concept of the "hierarchy of truths" is introduced. Doctrines "vary in their relation to the foundation of the Christian faith" (UR: 11). This hierarchy does not imply that some teachings are dispensable or less true than others (Congregation for the Doctrine of the Faith, 1982: 433). It does imply, however, that teachings further from the core of the faith are to be interpreted in relation to that core. A teaching such as the bodily assumption of Mary should not float free, but be interpreted in its relation to God's eschatological intention to raise all in Christ. Progress in ecumenical understanding often hinges on making these relations clear.

In relation to doctrine, UR also echoes the opening speech of the Council by John XXIII (Abbott, 1966: 715), distinguishing "the deposit of faith" from "the way church teaching has been formulated" (UR: 6). Similar convictions can sometimes be expressed in quite different language. At least some ecumenical differences are rooted in a failure to see the valid theological intent behind unfamiliar forms of speech.

Continuity and change

In ecumenism as in so much else, Vatican II was a great turning point in Catholic life. The significance of this turning point should not blind us, however, to the continuities that connect the Council to pre-conciliar convictions. Ecumenical *attitudes* and *practice* were profoundly altered at Vatican II, but the underlying *doctrines* of the nature of the church, while re-shaped in significant ways, were not truly altered. In the post-conciliar period, these changes and continuities would become more evident.

After the Council and *Ut Unum Sint* (1995)

The period following the Council saw an explosion of ecumenical activity and enthusiasm. (A comprehensive overview of post-conciliar Catholic ecumenical work can be found in Cassidy, 2005: 20–103.) The Secretariat for Promoting Christian Unity became a permanent office of the Vatican. In 1967, the first part of an Ecumenical Directory to guide Catholic ecumenical work was published by the Secretariat (revised in 1993; Pontifical Council for Promoting Christian Unity, 1993). Ecumenical dialogs were begun at various levels with a wide range of churches. Liturgical reform and the celebration of the Mass in the vernacular brought the worship of the Catholic Church closer to that of other traditions. The wide range of ecumenical activity cannot be surveyed here; the focus will remain on doctrinal issues that form the context for the Catholic Church's ecumenical work.

A warning that the ecumenical euphoria that immediately followed the Council might be exaggerated came in discussions with the World Council of Churches. In 1965, a Joint Working Group was created between the Catholic Church and the WCC "to work out the principles to be used in further collaboration" (Rusch and Gros, 1998: 482). An immediate question was whether the Catholic Church should join the WCC. Complications became evident as the matter was explored (Joint Working Group between the Roman Catholic Church and the World Council of Churches, 1972). Some problems were procedural. The membership of the Catholic Church is greater than that of all the member churches of the WCC combined; what would be a fair role for the Catholic Church within the decision-making of the WCC? Theological questions were also prominent. What implications would membership in the WCC have for the Catholic Church's self-understanding that it has preserved within itself the essential unity of the church? In 1972, the Vatican decided not to seek WCC membership, but to cooperate extensively in WCC activities. Catholic theologians are full members of the WCC's Faith and Order Commission and Catholics are involved in varying capacities in a wide range of WCC projects.

Bilateral relations and the pursuit of reconciliation

International Catholic ecumenism since Vatican II has focused less on organizations of churches such as the WCC than on relations with individual Christian traditions, such as the Orthodox, Anglicans, or Lutherans. Where doctrinal issues have divided such bodies from the Catholic Church, these differences must be addressed. The preferred instrument for addressing such doctrinal disputes has been formal dialogs between theologians representing the two traditions. The Catholic Church is engaged in a wider range of international dialogs than any other Christian tradition. They include dialogs with the Eastern Orthodox, Oriental Orthodox, Anglicans, Lutherans, Reformed, Methodists, Baptists, Disciples of Christ, Mennonites, Pentecostals, and Conservative Evangelicals. With some traditions, the goal of dialog is only greater understanding; with others, the hope is that dialog can make a significant contribution to the re-establishment of communion. (The reports from the international dialogs through 1998 are collected in Meyer and Vischer, 1984 and Gros et al., 2000.)

The greatest success of this dialog process came in 1999 with the signing of the *Joint Declaration on the Doctrine of Justification* by representatives from the Vatican and the churches of the Lutheran World Federation (Gros et al., 2000: 566–73). Differences over justification, i.e., how the Christian stands justified before the righteous judgment of God, were central to Luther's protest against Rome. The *Declaration* clearly states that not all differences between Lutherans and Catholics on justification have been eliminated, but the differences that do remain "are no longer the occasion for doctrinal condemnations" (paragraph 5). They are differences theologians might argue over, but which need not stand in the way of communion. The *Declaration* embodies a central ecumenical principle: agreement needs to be reached on essentials, on genuine matters of doctrine, but need not be reached on every detail of theological interest.

The other major success of doctrinal reconciliation since Vatican II came out of a mixture of formal dialogs and more informal contacts. The longest lasting division in Christendom has been that between the majority of the church which affirmed the decision of the Council of Chalcedon in 451 that Jesus is one integral person who must be described as two distinct, yet inseparable natures, human and divine, and those Eastern churches which rejected Chalcedon's language. These churches are often referred to as Oriental Orthodox and include the Coptic churches in Egypt and Ethiopia, the Armenian and Syrian churches, and others centered in the Middle East and South Asia. In a series of agreements, the first reached already in 1973, Catholic and Oriental Orthodox leaders were able to affirm a common faith in Christ that lies behind their varying attitudes toward the doctrinal language of the fifth century. In 1984, John Paul II and the Patriarch of the Syrian Orthodox Church affirmed that their differences were only "differences in terminology and culture and in the various formulae adopted by different theological schools to express the same matter" (Gros et al., 2000: 691). A second central ecumenical principle is embodied here: differences in language may not constitute differences in faith. Especially when churches have differing theological terminology and concepts, rooted in traditions which have developed independently over long periods, careful historical and theological examination is required to determine the significance of differences in language.

This kind of "dialog of experts" works best when addressing relatively traditional doctrinal issues: justification, Christology, the Eucharist. Its methods have proved less effective when the topics relate more immediately to church practice: ministry, authority, infallibility, papacy. The international dialog with the Anglican communion has addressed these issues most directly and with significant creativity, emphasizing the role that the reception by the whole church plays as a sign (but not condition) of the right exercise of authority at all levels (see the dialog reports on Authority in the Church in Meyer et al., 1984: 88–118 and Anglican–Roman Catholic International Commission, 1999). These proposals, however, received only a qualified affirmation from the Anglican Communion and a decidedly negative response from the Vatican (Hill and Yarnold, 1994: 153–66). The Anglican dialogs and their evaluation confirm that questions of authority in the church now lie at the center of what divides Catholics and Protestants.

The greatest disappointment in bilateral relations has been the failure to make significant progress in reconciliation with the Orthodox. The differences here are more focused and less abstract, centering on the doctrine, practice, and history of papal primacy. A new initiative toward reconciliation between Catholic and Orthodox began even before Vatican II concluded. At the last public session of the Council on December 7, 1965, a joint statement by Pope Paul VI and Athenagoras, Ecumenical Patriarch of Constantinople, was read, in which they "regret and remove from memory" the mutual excommunications between Pope and Patriarch of 1054. Together they "condemn these to oblivion" (Stormon, 1987: 127). Similar gestures followed.

Ecumenism is not, however, isolated from the world around it. At the moment when the international Catholic–Orthodox dialog was about to take up the decisive issue of the papacy, the fall of Communism not only faced many of the Orthodox churches with a radically altered situation, but also revived bitter, centuries-old disputes about the place of the Eastern Catholic Churches, i.e., churches with a liturgy and canon law in the Orthodox tradition, but in communion with Rome. Disputes between Orthodox churches and the Eastern Catholics, now free to reassert themselves after repression under Soviet rule, at times led to physical violence. Although attempts have been made by the dialog and church officials to resolve the dispute (Borelli and Erickson, 1996: 159–90), the process of Catholic–Orthodox reconciliation ground to a standstill.

The dialog process has produced striking theological results; the reports are monuments to scholarship and to creative theological fidelity. Nevertheless, no church has moved into significantly closer communion with Rome because of them. (The one exception might be relations with the Oriental Orthodox, but even in this case, the shift in relations seems small compared to the significance of the theological breakthrough.) The dialogs have been compared to airplanes in a perpetual holding pattern, never receiving permission to land (Nilson, 1995: 5).

Ut Unum Sint (1995)

John Paul II's encyclical *Ut Unum Sint* (*That All May Be One: On Commitment to Ecumenism*, hereafter UUS; John Paul II, 1995) is all the more significant against the background of the mixed result of ecumenical efforts to date. It stands as a culmination of the ecumenical development of twentieth-century Catholicism.

UUS is unambiguous in its affirmation of the Catholic Church's "irrevocable" commitment to "the path of the ecumenical venture" (paragraph 3). Ecumenism "*is not just some sort of 'appendix'* which is added to the Church's traditional activity. Rather, ecumenism is an organic part of her life and work, and consequently must pervade all that she is and does" (paragraph 20; emphasis in original). The theology of ecumenism the text elaborates is very close to that of Congar and UR. The unity of the church is a participation in the communion of the Trinity: "the communion of Christians is none other than the manifestation in them of the grace by which God makes them sharers in his own communion, which is his eternal life" (paragraph 9). A shared baptism is the most important bond of communion with other Christian communities: "How is it possible to remain divided, if we have been 'buried' through baptism in the Lord's death, in the very act by which God, through the death of his Son, has broken down the walls of division?" (paragraph 6).

While the text for the most part restates and affirms the ecumenical teaching of Vatican II, it does affirm more clearly than before the positive implications of the phrase "ecclesial communities." "To the extent that these elements [of sanctification and truth] are found in other Christian Communities, the one Church of Christ is effectively present in them" (paragraph 11).

Striking in UUS is John Paul's affirmation that the responsibility of the Bishop of Rome to care for the universal church and to be a focus of unity requires that the Pope take up the ecumenical task as "a specific duty" (paragraph 4). UUS repeats in brief the full doctrine of papal primacy (paragraph 94), but that doctrine, itself a major ecumenical obstacle, is treated as also a prime ecumenical spur. If Christ's command to Peter is to "feed my sheep" (John 21:15–17), then the successor of Peter must be concerned for the unity of all the sheep, even those who belong to another fold (John 10:16). Just because of the ecumenical importance of the papacy, John Paul invites other churches to engage in "a patient and fraternal dialogue" on the papacy (paragraph 96). Catholicism cannot imagine a re-united church in which the Bishop of Rome does not play a decisive unifying role (and in that sense, even UUS represents what a certain sort of non-Catholic will denounce as an "ecumenism of return"), but the papacy has taken quite different shapes in the course of its 2000-year history and Catholics and others should explore how that shape might change again to foster the papacy's unifying role.

As with Vatican II, UUS must be read in a balanced way. The doctrinal affirmations that shape MA noted above are still present. The unity Christ wills for his church is realized in the Catholic Church, "with all the means with which God wishes to endow his Church" (paragraph 11). The need for complete agreement in doctrine is affirmed with vigor: "The unity willed by God can be attained only by the adherence of all to the content of revealed faith in its entirety" (paragraph 18). What places UUS in a different ecumenical universe than that of MA is the attitude and commitment that pervade it. Where the earlier text is defensive, suspicious, and convinced of the self-sufficiency of Catholicism in relation to others, UUS reaches out with an obvious passion rooted in the sense of the scandal of division and of the urgency of the call to be a more fully and truly catholic church. Without expressing any doubt about traditional Catholic teaching, in fact on the basis of such teaching, ecumenical dialog is presented as a "dialog of conversion" conducted in the presence of God.

> This vertical aspect of dialog lies in our acknowledgment, jointly and to each other, that we are men and women who have sinned. It is precisely this acknowledgment which creates in brothers and sisters living in Communities not in full communion with one another that interior space where Christ, the source of the Church's unity, can effectively act, with all the power of his Spirit, the Paraclete. (paragraph 35)

It is this interior aspect, already enunciated in UR but expressed more powerfully in UUS, that sets UUS apart from such pre-conciliar texts as MA.

Ecumenism in the twenty-first century

Congar's pioneering work in the 1930s, the Second Vatican Council, and John Paul II's encyclical constitute an ecumenical trajectory covering almost the entire twentieth century. Where is movement along that trajectory headed in the twenty-first century?

Optimism is difficult to find. In a recent collection of essays on ecumenism, Walter Kasper, the head of the Vatican ecumenical office, speaks of a "spirit of resignation," "a phase of hibernation," "a critical moment," and that is only on the first page of the book (Kasper, 2004: 1)! That progress has been slow is undeniable. The ecclesiological problems that stand at the center of division have proven intractable. Creative suggestions, as those of the Anglican dialog on reception, have received little encouragement. In addition, new potential causes of division have arisen since Vatican II, most notably in relation to the significance of gender differences. Can only men or men and also women be ordained? What is the church's attitude toward homosexual relations? The Catholic Church and some Protestant churches are moving in different directions on these questions.

As UR noted (paragraph 4), ecumenical progress is inseparable from internal renewal. Internal renewal, however, is often controversial. What is renewal to one is betrayal to another. To discuss the nature of ecclesial authority in an open and creative way with representatives of another church is complicated when authority is a controversial matter within one's own church. Ecumenical questions are inevitably intertwined with internal questions; church authorities may take some action or make some statement with an internal audience in mind without cognizance of its ecumenical effect. The challenge is how to make this interweaving of the ecumenical and the internal fruitful for both.

This interweaving will not become fruitful until an ecumenical mindset comes to "pervade all" that the church "is and does" (UUS, paragraph 20). In all churches, ecumenism has tended to become the province of experts. The explosion of dialogs and other ecumenical activities has made experts necessary and certainly not every Christian, priest, or even theologian needs to know the ecumenical sphere in detail. The question is how throughout the church to think about the mission of one's particular community within the context of the mission of the one church and the unity of all Christians in Christ and the Spirit.

Reflecting on the period in the 1950s when he and ecumenism were out of favor, Congar said that he learned to be "patient in an active way."

> This is something quite different from merely marking time. It is a quality of mind, or better of the heart, which is rooted in the profound, existential conviction, firstly that God is in charge and accomplishes his gracious design through us, and secondly that, in all great things, delay is necessary for their maturation. (Congar, 1966: 44)

Ecumenism in the coming century will probably continue to be a school for active patience.

Notes

1   I received helpful comments on an earlier draft of this essay from Susan Wood.
2   Publication data is given for official Catholic ecumenical documents. Almost all documents cited, however, including papal encyclicals, Vatican II texts, and dialog reports, can be found on the Vatican website (www.vatican.va), which is a documentary gold mine.
3   Texts of Vatican II are cited according to section number. Translations are my own and are often more literal than most published translations. The original Latin and an English translation of all the texts of Vatican II can be found in Tanner, 1990. A significant problem is that Latin lacks the definite and indefinite articles and does not capitalize proper nouns. Thus, *ecclesia catholica* can be translated either "catholic church" or "the Catholic Church," a not inconsiderable difference. Here, the phrase will generally be translated as "the Catholic Church."

References and Further Reading

Abbott, W.M. (gen. ed.) (1966) *The Documents of Vatican II*. London: Geoffrey Chapman.

Alberigo, G. and Komonchak, J.A. (eds.) (1995) *History of Vatican II: Vol. 1, Announcing and Preparing Vatican Council II: Toward a New Era in Catholicism*. Maryknoll, NY: Orbis.

Alberigo, G. and Komonchak, J.A. (eds.) (2003) *History of Vatican II: Vol. 4, Church as Communion, Third Period and Intersession, September 1964–September 1965*. Maryknoll, NY: Orbis.

Anglican–Roman Catholic International Commission (1999) *The Gift of Authority: Authority in the Church III*. London; Toronto; New York: Catholic Truth Society; Anglican Book Centre; Church Publishing Inc.

Archbishop and Bishops of the Netherlands (1958) "Pastoral Letter on the Occasion of the First Assembly of the World Council of Churches," in Bell, G.K.A. (ed.) *Documents on Christian Unity: Fourth Series 1948–1957*. London: Oxford University Press, 17–21.

Borelli, J. and Erickson, J.H. (eds.) (1996) *The Quest for Unity: Orthodox and Catholics in Dialogue. Documents of the Joint International Commission and Official Dialogues in the United States 1965–1995*. Crestwood, NY: St Vladimir's Seminary Press.

Butler, C. (1930) *The Vatican Council*. London: Longmans, Green.

Cassidy, E.I. (2005) *Ecumenism and Interreligious Dialogue:* Unitatis Redintegratio, Nostra Aetate. Rediscovering Vatican II. New York: Paulist Press.

Congar, Y. (1939) *Divided Christendom: A Catholic Study of the Problem of Reunion*. London: Geoffrey Bles.

Congar, Y. (1966) *Dialogue between Christians: Catholic Contributions to Ecumenism*, trans. P. Loretz. London: Geoffrey Chapman.

Congregation for the Doctrine of the Faith (1982) "*Mysterium Ecclesiae:* Declaration in Defense of the Catholic Doctrine on the Church against Some Present-Day Errors," in Flannery, A. (ed.) *Vatican Council II: More Postconciliar Documents*. Northport, NY: Costello, 428–37.

Denaux, A. (ed.) (1997) *From Malines to ARCIC: The Malines Conversations Commemorated*, in collaboration with J. Dick, *Bibliotheca Ephemeridum Theologicarum Lovaniensium*, vol. 130. Leuven: Leuven University Press.

Gros, J., Meyer, H., and Rusch, W.G. (eds.) (2000) *Growth in Agreement II: Reports and Agreed Statements of Ecumenical Conversations on a World Level, 1982–1998*. Geneva: WCC Publications.

Hamer, J. (1972) "Die ekklesiologische Terminologie des Vatikanum II und die protestantischen Ämter," *Catholica*, 26, 146–53.

Hill, C. and Yarnold, E. (eds.) (1994) *Anglicans and Roman Catholics: The Search for Unity*. London: SPCK.

Hill, C. and Yarnold, E. (eds.) (1997) *Anglican Orders: The Documents in the Debate*. Norwich: Canterbury Press.

John Paul II (1995) Ut Unum Sint: *On Commitment to Ecumenism*. Vatican City: Libreria Editrice Vaticana.

Joint Working Group between the Roman Catholic Church and the World Council of Churches (1972) "Patterns of Relationships between the Roman Catholic Church and the World Council of Churches," *Ecumenical Review*, 24, 243–88.

Kasper, W. (1990) "Die apostolische Sukzession als ökumenisches Problem," in Pannenberg, W. (ed.) *Lehrverurteilungen – kirchentrennend?: III Materialien zur Lehre von den Sakramenten und vom kirchlichen Amt*. Freiberg im Breisgau: Herder, 329–49.

Kasper, W. (2004) *That They May All Be One: The Call to Unity*. London: Burns and Oates.

Leo XIII (1896) Satis Cognitum: *On the Unity of the Church*. www.papalencyclicals.net/Leo13/l13satis.htm.

Leo XIII (1928) "*Divinum Illud Munus*: On the Holy Spirit" (1897), in Calvet, J. (ed.), *Rome and Reunion*. Milwaukee, WI: Morehouse, 154–61. www.papalencyclicals.net/Leo13/l13divin.htm.

Meyer, H. and Vischer, L. (eds.) (1984) *Growth in Agreement: Reports and Agreed Statements of Ecumenical Conversations on a World Level*. New York: Paulist Press.

Möhler, J.A. (1997) *Symbolism: Exposition of the Doctrinal Differences between Catholics and Protestants as Evidenced by Their Symbolical Writings*. trans. J.B. Robertson. New York: Crossroad.

Nilson, J. (1995) *Nothing Beyond the Necessary: Roman Catholicism and the Ecumenical Future*. New York: Paulist Press.

Pius XI (1930) "*Mortalium Animos*," in Bell, G.K.A. (ed.) *Documents on Christian Unity. Second Series*. London: Oxford University Press, 50–63.

Pius XII (1943) Mystici Corporis Christi: *On the Mystical Body of Christ*. Washington, DC: National Catholic Welfare Conference.

Pontifical Council for Promoting Christian Unity (1993) *Directory for the Application of Principles and Norms on Ecumenism*. Rome: Vatican Press.

Rusch, W.G. and Gros, J. (eds.) (1998) *Deepening Communion: International Ecumenical Documents with Roman Catholic Participation*. Washington, DC: United States Catholic Conference.

Sacred Congregation of the Holy Office (1958) "*Ecclesia Catholica*: Instruction to Local Ordinaries on the Ecumenical Movement (1949)," in Bell, G.K.A. (ed.) *Documents on Christian Unity: Fourth Series 1948–57*. London: Oxford University Press, 22–7.

Stormon, E.J. (ed.) (1987) *Towards the Healing of Schism: The Sees of Rome and Constantinople. Public Statements and Correspondence between the Holy See and the Ecumenical Patriarchate 1958–1984*. Ecumenical Documents. New York: Paulist Press.

Sullivan, F.A. (1989) "The Significance of the Vatican II Declaration that the Church of Christ 'Subsists in' the Roman Catholic Church," in Latourelle, R. (ed.) *Vatican II: Assessment and Perspectives. Twenty-five Years After (1962–1987)*. Vol. II. New York: Paulist Press, 272–87.

Tanner, N.P. (ed.) (1990) *Decrees of the Ecumenical Councils*. London: Sheed and Ward.

Visser 't Hooft, W.A. (1953) *The Meaning of Ecumenical*. London: SCM Press.

CHAPTER 30

Inter-Religious Dialog

Gavin D'Costa

Introduction

Christianity was born into an inter-religious world. In some respects today's situation is no different, and in other ways it is quite novel. In this essay I shall trace the outlines of the official Church's attitude to other religions, focusing especially on the twentieth century. I will also examine the theological debate since Vatican II, showing the internal tensions within Catholic theology on a whole range of issues. The vigor of the debate testifies to the vital importance of this subject for the future of the Church. The Church on the one hand is faced by secularization in western Europe, and by relatively small Christian communities in Asia and Southeast Asia, home to the great Eastern religions. On the other hand it is growing in Africa (home of Islam) and Latin America. I shall also look at some different types of inter-religious dialog in practice, showing that actual cooperation and engagement with other religions is possible from a wide variety of theological approaches to these religions.

Two qualifications are in order before proceeding. My interpretation and selection is partial and would be contested by a number of Catholic theologians. I shall try and indicate alternatives to the reader so that they can work their way through the tangles. I take it for granted that the Magisterium provides a basic framework within which theologians can fruitfully explore issues.

Official Attitudes Leading to the Modern Period

The New Testament Church emerged in a Jewish world, in the presence of numerous Greek cults and mystery religions. Two features are important in this initial period. First, the relationship to Judaism was very complex, for many early followers saw themselves as Jews following Christ, rather than "Christianity" being a separate religion. As the two religions separated and established very different identities, Judaism would always bear a special *sui generis* relationship to Christianity, for as St Paul noted, it was out of Judaism that the wild shoot was grafted (Rom 9–11). The second feature was the missionary drive of the early Church to evangelize first the Jews, then subsequently the pagans to the ends of the earth. Central to this mission was the conviction that in Jesus Christ, God had made himself known fully as Father, Son, and Spirit, and faith in Christ marked by baptism into the Church was required for salvation (Acts 4:12, John 3:5, Mark 16:15–16, Acts 2:37–41). Christians were martyred for refusing to renounce their faith, starting with Stephen and continuing to the present day. Here we see the emergence of the famous axiom that dominates Catholic history: *extra ecclesiam nulla salus* (no salvation outside the Church, subsequently *extra ecclesiam*). This axiom was central to the way in which other religions were perceived.

Some of the early Fathers had a high regard for Greek philosophy and later, Roman law, and both these traditions along with Jewish religious thought and practice marked the development of Christianity – in response to the triune God. At the same time, there was a concerted criticism of all religions other than Christianity, even if Justin, Irenaeus, Clement of Alexandria, and others developed theologies to account for the wisdom found outside Israel and Christianity mainly in the reference to Greek philosophy, not religion. They never affirmed non-Christian religious structures (Hacker, 1980: chapter 2; for a more optimistic reading see Dupuis, 1997: 53–109), but saw elements within non-Christian cultures as a form of *preparatio evangelica* (a preparation for the Gospel), and Christianity as a fulfillment of all that was good and true in these cultures. *Extra ecclesiam* was initially formulated by Origen (*c*.185–254), followed by Cyprian (*c*.206–58) who gave it considerable attention, from whom Augustine (*c*.354–430) took it. The phrase occurs in the Fourth Lateran Council (1215), and in two papal documents, and most famously at the Council of Florence (1438–45), citing Fulgentius of Ruspa (*c*.467–553), Augustine's disciple, to affirm that the Catholic Church believes:

> that those not living within the Catholic Church, not only pagans, but also Jews and heretics and schismatics cannot become participants in eternal life, but will depart "into everlasting fire which was prepared for the devil and his angels" (Matt 25:41), unless before the end of life they are joined to the Church. (Denzinger, 1955: 715)

It is not possible to fully trace the complex history which properly contextualizes this statement, except to note seven important factors (see Dupuis, 1977: 84–109; D'Costa, 1990a; Sullivan, 1992). First, Cyprian's use of *extra ecclesiam* bore reference to schismatics, not to adherents of the world religions. Second, Jews, heretics, pagans, and schismatics belonged to the same category: they knew the truth and willfully perverted and rejected it (Islam was also later assimilated within this category). This was an assumption shared widely until the discovery of the New World at the end of the fifteenth century. Third, whether these four groups are actually guilty of this willful rejection is an open question. Most historians today would hesitate to make this move, but we must not be anachronistic in judging the tradition or we will fail to see the real import of the *extra ecclesiam* teaching, even if we can question cases of its historical applicability. Fourth, in so much as truth was rejected and charity and grace spurned so as to follow the devil, the subsequent destiny of such people was inevitable. Fifth, the positive significance of the *extra ecclesiam* teaching (constantly reiterated) is to affirm the intrinsic connection between Christ, the mediator of salvation, and his visible body, the Church. (A Protestant rendering of this axiom would be "outside Christ, no salvation.") Sixth, while this axiom actually affirmed a positive truth, it was sometimes used in a rigorist and politically manipulative manner, the former being formally condemned when in 1949 the Jesuit Leonard Feeney applied *extra ecclesiam* to Protestants and Hindus. Tragically and sadly, his refusal to retract led to his excommunication. Seventh, it has been a constant teaching since the Middle Ages, although variably applied, that those who die without actually rejecting the Gospel and who follow the natural law in their hearts and actions are not condemned to perdition. This category chronologically first related to the great philosophers of antiquity, the holy pagans of the Old Testament, then to the holy men and women of Israel, and eventually, after the discovery of the New World, to people of different faiths – who could, in some circumstances, be understood analogically to the holy pagans of the Old Testament.

Putting these seven considerations together we can conclude that the official Catholic attitude to other religions for most of Christian history is understandably negative, in so much as these religions were understood to have heard and rejected the Gospel. Positively, it stemmed from a proper affirmation of Jesus Christ as the source of all salvation, mediated through his Church.

The discovery of the New World also led to some other important factors that helped shape the modern period. Politically, the most significant is the imperial expansion of Europe, initially with Catholic Spain and Portugal, and eventually the Protestant factor through the Dutch, English, and French. By World War I European colonial powers "owned" most of the earth. Closely and complexly related to imperial expansion was Catholic mission. The issue is this. Did Catholicism come to be a world religion through its being an imperial religion, and did it reach the ends of the earth through denigration of indigenous religions? The answer is as diverse as the countries, religious orders, infrastructures, and political powers that make up this complicated drama. To take one example, Rivera-Pagán (2003) shows how the fifteenth-century Spanish *Reconquista* under the command of Hernán Cortés would legitimate slavery and land acquisition on the basis of the conflict being perceived as a holy war for Christian truth. On the other hand, in the sixteenth century, Bartolomé de las Casas, with some Dominicans and Jesuits launched a scathing prophetic attack against the behavior of the European powers and even Church officials against the local people. The King of Spain's angry intervention, as well as that of the Dominican prior of Spain, were unable to convince las Casas otherwise.

The discovery of the New World slowly instigated a shift in consciousness: the superiority of Christian culture came into question from within, the value of non-Christian cultures came to light, as well as the recognition that entire continents and religions had never heard the Gospel.

Another factor was the Enlightenment and its concomitant secularization (see Buckley, 1987). The Catholic view of other religions faced serious challenges. Kant's great leap-frog over contesting exclusivist historical religious traditions to a universal transcendental ethic and religiosity was seen by many as a way of bypassing warring and corrupt religious institutions. Further, a critique developed from the mainly

German romanticization of ancient cultures and traditions, especially Greek and Eastern (Hinduism and Buddhism), in contrast to a denigration of Christianity. This meant that Christianity was forced to articulate its relationship more sharply with Western culture as well as other religious cultures. In the modern period, Vatican II represents a major step in this process.

The Modern Period: Vatican II

Vatican II has often been characterized as drawing the Catholic Church into the "modern world," although the exact legacy of the Council is strongly contested. (Different assessments of the Council documents on this question are to be found in Knitter, 1992; Ruokanen, 1992; Dupuis, 1997: 158–79; D'Costa, 2000: 101–17; all citations of Council documents from Abbott, 1966). Certainly the *Declaration on the Relationship of the Church to Non-Christian Religions* (1965), subsequently *Nostra Aetate*, its Latin name, contains the first formal statement of a Council on other religions (understood in their own terms, and theologically evaluated). It is worth noting that this Council was primarily pastoral, not dogmatic. We find in it dogmatic teachings that are in continuity with the *extra ecclesiam* tradition as well as a new positive pastoral and historical appreciation of the major world religions as containing elements of truth, beauty, and goodness. Let us briefly take the latter positive pastoral appreciation first, noting both its contents and context.

Nostra Aetate relates the world religions to Catholicism historically and theologically in "concentric circles of closeness. It is concerned to emphasize what 'human beings have in common'"(1). Closest to the Church is Judaism, sharing the covenant, Scriptures, and many spiritual traditions. It is the only tradition of which the word "revelation" is used and *Revelationem* refers solely to the Old Testament. Mutual understanding and respect are called for, as well as dialogs focusing especially on theological and biblical studies (4). "Anti-Semitism" is deplored "at any time and from any source" (4). Then comes Islam, with its devotional theism, strong ethics, Abrahamic roots, and reverence for Mary. All these are held in high "esteem" (4). The past of "quarrels and hostilities" must give way to "mutual understanding" and cooperation on "common cause" in "fostering social justice, moral values, peace and freedom" (4). As with Judaism, it is important to note that many forms of cooperation, both practical and theological, are encouraged without any doctrinal change in the *extra ecclesiam* teaching. Then followed Hinduism and Buddhism, rather thinly characterized, but nevertheless very positively, in terms of their meditation techniques, lofty philosophies, devotional and ascetic elements (3). Finally, "other religions to be found everywhere" are also acknowledged, referring to African primal religions. Hence the overall positive appreciation of non-Christian religions is geared toward "dialog and collaboration" toward the common good in "society and culture" (2). Inter-religious dialog on the practical level has been given strong endorsement in so much as it serves the aim of the "common good" and enshrines respect for the dignity of each person.

Alongside this positive appreciation and its practical context, it must be noted that nowhere in the Council documents is there an affirmation of other religions *per se* as vehicles of salvation. Indeed, in *Nostra Aetate* it is expressly said at the outset that the Church is called to "ever proclaim Christ, 'the way, the truth, and the life' (John 14:6), in whom men find the fullness of religious life, and in whom God has reconciled all things to Himself (cf. 2 Cor 5:18–19)" (2). This contains the basic *extra ecclesiam* teaching: the necessity of Christ for salvation and baptism as a mark of this acceptance. This is expressly stated in the *Dogmatic Constitution on the Church*, 1964, subsequently *Lumen Gentium*, 14: "that the Church, now so journeying on earth as an exile, is necessary for salvation." This must be kept in mind through all of the positive evaluations of the religions. So must the fact that *Nostra Aetate* is a pastoral document, not a dogmatic constitution, and explicitly focuses on what men and women "have in common and what tends to promote fellowship among them" (1). It is not concerned to draw attention to the differences that must also be faced in mature dialog, nor those differences that might amount to error, falsity, or even evil. This dynamic is underlined in *Lumen Gentium*, 16 where it is stated that "very often, deceived by the Evil One, men have become vain in their reasoning, have exchanged the truth of God for a lie." Rightly, no one is identified in this statement. In *Lumen Gentium*, 16, the Council is unequivocal with the tradition that salvation can be attained by anyone, be they religious or non-religious, on three conditions. First, that they do not know the Gospel through no fault of their own. Second, the inculpably ignorant who have "not yet arrived at an explicit knowledge of God, but who strive to live a good life, thanks to His grace" are not lost. Third, the good life can be lived through following the dictates of conscience and the natural law within the created order. How this relates to the visible Church is left to the theologians to explicate. Finally in *Ad Gentes* it is said that missionary activity to the nations takes what is good and true and "frees" it "from all taint of evil and restores to Christ its maker, who overthrows the devil's domain and wards off the manifold malice of vice" (9).

It is important to understand this subtle dialectic within the Council documents, for their authoritative parameters should inform subsequent theological reflection. However, Paul Knitter observes that: "The majority of Catholic thinkers interpret the Conciliar statements to affirm, implicitly but clearly, that the religions are ways of salvation" (Knitter, 1984: 50). I have been arguing that this is an inaccurate exegesis. This reading actually leads to indifferentism (viewing religions as equal paths to salvation), which has always been condemned. It was perhaps the reverse side of this misreading, an equal misreading, that had led various schismatic Catholic groups, such as those led by Archbishop Lefebvre, to argue that the Council was heretical in formally teaching indifferentism (Lefebvre, 1986).

After Vatican II: the Theological Debate

Strictly speaking many of these debates had started before the Council. However, in the period following Vatican II there was much theological discussion regarding other religions. Before looking at some of these debates, four contextual statements are in order. First, the positive appreciation of other religions and the need for dialog was deeply embraced by some creative Asian and European missionary theologians who lived as minorities among the great Eastern traditions. The majority of Catholics also embraced this positive appreciation. However, the former group were rightly concerned to disassociate colonialism from the enterprise of mission, and mission came to be viewed increasingly in terms of dialog. These theologians were also keen to work together with their non-Christian sisters and brothers for the "common good," the relief of the poor and oppressed, a common praxis that had been inhibited by what appeared to some non-Christians as Christian superiority. This embrace of rightful positive elements within the Council was sometimes unduly stressed with either a neglect or distortion of dogmatic issues. Second, these same positive themes were also taken up and rigorously developed by European theologians keen to overcome Christianity's bad press (sometimes rightfully bad!) regarding its colonial ties. Certain types of liberation and feminist theologians saw the Church finally opening the door to acknowledging God's activities outside the visible bounds of the Catholic Church and drew various dogmatic conclusions from this, regarding Christ, the Church, mission, and dialog. Again, the sincere motivation and genuine concerns of these theologians are not to be questioned, although their occasional adoption of certain ideologies to develop their theologies is. Third, in reaction to various "liberal" excesses, there also inevitably occurred two severe counter-thrusts, one genuinely Catholic, the other less so. The issues revolved along two points: one material, one formal. The material issues related to the *extra ecclesiam* tradition and the calling into question of the uniqueness of Christ, the necessity of the Church for salvation, and the necessity of mission. The formal issue related to theological method: whether the adoption of certain methods in theology was actually inimical to the nature of theology. The less genuinely Catholic response to these "liberal" trends, characterized by Archbishop Lefebvre, was to exclusively stress the dogmatic elements of the *extra ecclesiam* tradition, condemn all developments since Vatican II on this front, and totally downplay the positive appreciation of other religions so fully affirmed in the Council. The "conservative" response, remembering the inadequacies of these labels, was to reiterate the dogmatic material contents of the *extra ecclesiam* tradition, call into question the formal methodological elements within these "liberal" trends, both Asian and European, but affirm and support many forms of inter-religious dialog and cooperation. Fourth and finally, somewhere in between these positions, the vast majority of Catholic theologians are still engaged constructively in exploring a whole range of formal and material issues related to other religions. In a survey such as this, I can only allude to the tip of a rich Catholic iceberg, inevitably losing the complex nuance involved in the many slopes, pinnacles, and crevices, most of which remain well within the obvious parameters of legitimate discussion and practice set out by the Magisterium.

Let us begin with the debate between two of the giants of twentieth-century Catholic theology, Karl Rahner (1904–84) and Hans Urs von Balthasar (1905–84) over Rahner's notion of the "anonymous Christian." We will see in this debate many of the formal and material issues clearly set out and the European construal of the question. We will also see that the labels "liberal" and "conservative" become hopelessly inadequate.

Karl Rahner's theory of the anonymous Christian is based on two possible types of argument. The first (Rahner, 1969: 390–8), stems from Rahner's philosophy of the "supernatural existential" in which he argues that all people have an implicit revelation of God which is adequate for salvation, even though it is only fulfilled in the historically particular revelation of Jesus Christ, and partially thematized and expressed in other religious texts and practices. This meant that while Christianity was the absolute truth and Christ the source of all salvation, other religions could act as provisional mediators of this saving grace because of the "supernatural existential." This position kept intact the *extra ecclesiam* tradition (salvation only through Christ, and only through the Church – although both now take on an implicit dimension). Further, Rahner went on to argue for both the notion of the "anonymous Christian" (Christ's grace working implicitly) and "anonymous Christianity" (through the provisional saving structures called "religion"). This is the outworking of Rahner's first major work, *Spirit in the World*, and here his argument is philosophically derived. The second type of argument is theologically founded (Rahner, 1966: 115–34), and Rahner here argues that since God desires the salvation of all people, and all people do not know the Gospel, and that God is loving and good, there must be a means of salvation offered to all such people. Using the analogy of Israel, valid until confronted by the truth of Christ, Rahner suggests that other religions may be deemed, analogically to Israel, as provisionally "lawful religions." It is through acts of faith, hope, and unconditional love that those in other religions say "yes" to God. Here again, the terms "anonymous Christian" and "anonymous Christianity" are employed.

Rahner's "anonymous Christianity" was bitterly attacked by Balthasar on two counts in his book *The Moment of Christian Witness* (1967). The first, against Rahner's first type of argument, was that Rahner's *Spirit in the World* was dependent on German Idealism, and in so much as his theology was shaped by philosophy (rather than critically engaging with it) Rahner exemplified theology's capitulation to modernity. Here we see a formal problem affecting the material outcome of theology. Hence, for Balthasar there was very little difference between the anonymous and explicit Christian. The good Hindu, Buddhist, and atheist were already living Christ-filled lives and nothing particularly was added to their becoming Christians. The explicit form of the Church was minimized. Second, Balthasar claimed Rahner's theology had no place for martyrdom, for the scandal of the Cross, whereby the entire world was turned upside down and called into question by Jesus Christ. This was a material difference and would endure even if Balthasar's first criticism failed. The world for Rahner according to Balthasar was full of well-meaning people, hardly touched by the depths of sin, well able to survive within their human-made systems of religiosity. Mission was undervalued, even dissolved, for Rahner failed to understand the radical novelty of the Christian phenomenon. In this Balthasar was supported by Henri de Lubac (1969). In a word, Rahner had sold the Christian tradition into the hands of modernity. In the second edition of *The Moment of Christian Witness* Balthasar concedes some ground, agreeing with de Lubac that an "anonymous Christian" was possible (although the term was not felicitous) in so much as Christ's grace is operative outside the visible Church, a position held clearly by the Tradition and Vatican II. But there could be no such thing as "anonymous Christianity" for this actually affirmed other religions as salvific structures, even if only provisionally.

In my opinion, Balthasar's first criticism is decisive against Rahner's first form of the argument (from philosophy), but not against his second (from theology). This exchange alerts us to the questions of methodology in theology. Do we begin theology from the crucified Christ and then understand and practice "liberation," or do we begin from the philosophies or ideologies of the modern world? The latter may be German Idealism (Rahner), or Marxism with its problematic notion of praxis preceding theory (Pieris, 1988; Wilfred, 1991; Knitter, 1996), or some forms of feminism that defines what liberation is prior to the Gospel (Ruether, 1987). I am not saying all forms of Marxist, feminist, post-modern, and other ideological influence are negative (indeed, the opposite is true), but only the manner in which some theologians use them. However, formally speaking, Balthasar's first criticism does not affect Rahner's second type of argument, and here I am making the contentious assumption that the second type is independent of the first (supported by Kilby, 2004: 70–99, 115–26). Nevertheless, Balthasar's second criticism does affect Rahner's second type of argument. Balthasar surely rightly criticizes the possibility of "anonymous Christianity," for it fails to adequately signal the distortions, sinfulness, and even evil *also* present along with the good, truthful, and beautiful elements in other religions. Both were identified in Vatican II. It is not that Balthasar is unaware of the riches and depths present in the world religions, nor that he is against all types of practical cooperation between Christianity and others, but he simply sees that the *extra ecclesiam* tradition is better articulated and practiced in terms of the explicit historical form and shape that Christ generates through his Church.

In many respects, there are moments when the difference between these two are slim, for Balthasar strongly argues for universalism, that all people will be saved regardless of whether they are Christian or not (Balthasar, 1988), and so does Rahner, although ironically he is more cautious (Rahner, 1961). This is why labels like "liberal" and "conservative" begin to dissolve. But these similarities should not mask profound differences, materially and formally.

Rahner's influence in Asia, directly or indirectly, has been enormous. Immensely rich and stimulating works following in his trajectory are those of Rayumando Panikkar, who actually fleshes out the anonymous Christ within Hindu scripture and philosophy in his classic *The Unknown Christ of Hinduism* (1964, revised edition, 1981). In *The Trinity and the Religious Experience of Man* (1973) Panikkar further argues that the three aspects of the Trinity provide a useful framework for understanding religious plurality, showing how other religions relate to one or more of these triune dynamics. Monastically, the Benedictines Bede Griffiths and his precursor Swami Abhishiktananda (the Belgian, Henri le Saux) develop these themes with special reference to spiritual theology (see Mattam, 1975 for an extensive survey of Christian attitudes to Hinduism in this period). A very positive dialog also developed with Buddhism and of course Judaism (especially due to the *Shoah*) and is only now gathering pace with Islam. Soon, the torch would pass to indigenous rather than European missionary theologians – see below.

Joseph Cardinal Ratzinger's criticisms of newer forms of Catholic theology of religions often echo Balthasar's points in his debate with Rahner (Ratzinger, 1997), and some see Rahner's theology of nature and grace leading directly to secularizing liberation and feminist theologies (Milbank, 1990: 206–58). This is not to say that theologies concerned with these themes are secularizing *per se*. This debate is not yet resolved.

I shall now heuristically treat together the North American liberationist/eclectic theologian and ex-missionary priest, Paul F. Knitter, the Sri Lankan Indoligist and liberationist Jesuit, Aloysius Pieris, the liberationist secular Indian priest, Felix Wilfred, and the North American feminist lay theologian, Rosemary Ruether. (Knitter's background is made evident in his publications, and I mention it solely because of earlier comments regarding contextualizing concerns that drive various positions.) This procedure of treating them together hides important nuances and differences, but the reader must decide whether such a conflation actually does violence to the subject matter or is justified in bringing out a new thematic, both formal and material, in the inter-religious debate. (I have dealt with them in detail in D'Costa, 2000a (Knitter), 2000b (Pieris and Wilfred), 1990b (Ruether).) For the sake of conceptual clarity I shall collectively call them liberatory pluralists. After treating them, I will outline various objections to their general position.

There are three steps to liberatory pluralism. The first argues that theology comes from praxis, especially those emancipatory practices liberating the poor and the oppressed. Both categories include many women. This liberation is the coming of the "kingdom of God." Helping usher in the kingdom is the vital task facing Christians, in both the so-called "developed" and "developing" nations. Second, in so much as these emancipatory practices are found in all religions, and equally, since all religions are guilty of oppressive practices in the forms of patriarchy and capitalism, Christians cannot claim any moral or spiritual high-ground. Of course, Christians must claim the liberating power of Christ, which is the source of these liberation and feminist theologies, but they must also recognize this power of service and social transformation to be present within the world religions, often in greater measure than Christianity. Third, this learning from praxis calls into question doctrinal formulations, cast as they were during an expansionist, imperialist, and patriarchal age. Hence, what get called into question through this hermeneutic of suspicion are the *extra ecclesiam* doctrines regarding Christ, the Trinity, the Church, and the nature of mission. Christ is one source of liberation, alongside the Buddha, alongside Hindu women acting together against violence. The Spirit acts outside the Church and therefore independently from the historical Jesus and his mission. The Church is clearly not the exclusive ark of salvation, as the "kingdom of God" is found outside its visible boundaries. The Church's mission must be to transform structures of oppression, within and without, listening and learning from the religious Other.

In many respects, there is much that is attractive and open-handed in these positions: the recognition of various forms of oppression within Christian history; the affirmation of the vitality and goodness found within other religions; and the necessity of the Church's involvement in promoting the kingdom of God. In this sense, the pastoral and pragmatic concerns of liberatory pluralism are vital. However it is worth focusing on the dogmatic content implied in some of the three steps.

Regarding the first step, while it is true that theology comes out of practice, especially those practices that inaugurate the "kingdom," I would argue that this claim must also be located within a wider set of considerations to sustain its theological coherence. Let me develop two specific objections to this first step, the first found in the Encyclical Letter, *Redemptoris Missio* (*The Mission of Redemption*) (1990). First, the Kingdom is to be found in Gospel values such as care for the sick and poor, promoting the full dignity of each person, opposing the exploitation and sexism against women, questioning unjust social structures, and so on, to which other religions unquestionably contribute. These actions testify to the presence of the action of the Holy Spirit. However, the Kingdom is not fully defined in these values without reference to the person of Christ and the triune God. In this sense salvation is first and finally a personal relationship with Christ, not a political program, however close such programs might be to the actions of Christ's disciples. Hence, in *Redemptoris Missio* 20, precisely this issue is addressed:

> It is true that the inchoate reality of the Kingdom can also be found beyond the confines of the Church among peoples everywhere, to the extent that they live "Gospel values" and are open to the working of the Spirit who breathes when and where he wills (cf. John 3:8). But it must immediately be added that this temporal dimension of the Kingdom remains incomplete unless it is related to the Kingdom of Christ in the Church and straining toward eschatological fullness.

Hence, it cannot be deduced from the following: (a) because Gospel values and therefore the Holy Spirit are to be found outside the visible boundaries of the Church and further, (b) because the Church has failed to live by its own Gospel in various instances, that therefore (c) other religions should be viewed as salvific structures or that the action of the Spirit is independent and separate from the incarnation of Christ. By refusing this equation "a + b = c," one need not idealize the Church for "not c" is independent of the Church's merits as such, but relies on the nature of God's revelation as trinitarian and as forming an ecclesia. Hence, regarding the tendency to develop theologies of the Kingdom or the action of the Spirit without their full relationship to the Church and the Son and Father, *Redemptoris Missio* 29 continues the argument that the Spirit is

> not an alternative to Christ, nor does he fill a sort of void which is sometimes suggested as existing between Christ and the *Logos*. Whatever the Spirit brings about in human hearts and in the history of peoples, in cultures and religions, serves as a preparation for the Gospel and can only be understood in reference to Christ.

In sum, while the presence of the kingdom and the Holy Spirit outside the Church is uncontested, the dogmatic implications regarding Christ, his Spirit, the Kingdom of God, the nature of the Church, and mission drawn by liberatory pluralists is. The subsequent Declaration from the Congregation of the Doctrine of the Faith, *On the Unicity and Salvific Universality of Jesus Christ and the Church, Dominus Iesus* (1998), pithily reiterates *Redemptoris Missio* and previous documents, upholding the *extra ecclesiam* tradition.

Clearly, there are many questions left open, requiring extensive theological exploration. Precisely how is the Spirit in non-Christian religions related to Christ and the Church? How is the kingdom of God outside the visible boundaries of the Church related to the person of Christ? What, if any, is the providential role of non-Christian religions? Is inter-religious prayer possible? How can dogmatic, ethical, and liturgical practices and formulations be enriched in engagement with other religions, without either syncretism or indifferentism, an issue that has repercussions for mission, dialog, and inculturation? These are just some of the many questions facing the Church in the twenty-first century.

If the first issue to liberatory pluralists concerned material dogmatic items, the second concerns formal question regarding theological method. Herein lies a very profound problem that faces the Church in the twenty-first century, with major growth in Africa and South America. Both are non-European countries, but profoundly affected by European culture and not only in terms of economic imperialism. Some Asian theologians like Wilfred and Pieris argue that they are of course subject to the Bible, but since so much of the tradition is culturally European, to be subject to tradition is to perpetuate the Europeanization of Christianity. Surely the Asian Churches must forge and develop their own traditions in unity with the Catholic Church and under the authority of the Magisterium, but not in conformity to the long European history of theology. This is not to say that either theologian simply dismisses the tradition. A similar methodological objection to tradition is made by Ruether regarding a "man-made" tradition. Were these critiques to touch on the Bible (that it too must come under a new hermeneutical authority, be it Asian experience or women's experience, or whatever) then clearly this would amount to a post-Christian theology. None of our theologians champions such a position.

Two points can be made about this complex issue. First, the male European production of theology has led to certain kinds of blindness in concerns and sensitivities. Elsewhere, I have called into question various aspects of the male-centered tradition (D'Costa, 2000b). Second, the Church's own history shows that "tradition" is a complex cluster, neither unitary nor irreformable (Congar, 1966). To illustrate, regarding tradition, married priests are permissible within the Greek Orthodox Church which is in full communion with the Roman Catholic Church. Slavery has been now officially rejected when once it was widely accepted. Even the most recent Catechism underwent amendments, especially regarding the position on capital punishment. However, to call into question the tradition because it has developed in Europe might amount to calling into question the providential design of God. Indeed, this is argued in *Faith and Reason, Fides et Ratio* (1988: 72), regarding the great wisdom of India and its inculturation: "the Church cannot abandon what she has gained from her inculturation in the world of Greco-Latin thought. To reject this heritage would be to deny the providential plan of God who guides his Church down the paths of time and history." It is important not to read this statement as the Magisterium's European self-defensiveness, for paragraph 72 also makes clear the sense in which the future Church will look back on the heritage provided by the inculturation of the Indian Church with similar respect and reverence. Testing this statement will require time.

By focusing on these areas of contention, the picture is necessarily skewed but nevertheless useful for the student. I have sought to indicate various formal and material issues that have been contentious, but one should not forget the wealth of rich and insightful Catholic writings both on theology of religions in general and also on specific engagements with particular religions. (See the journal *Pro Dialogo* issued by the Pontifical Council for Interreligious Dialogue for further references, and Dupuis, 1997 for a good overview.)

Practical Dialog

I would like to finish by indicating the many levels of inter-religious dialog that have been generated within the Catholic Church since Vatican II. I have already noted that very differing theological positions can generate fruitful dialog and that dialog will always be related to specific contexts such as the nature of the state, the socio-economic positions of the different partners, the history of the meetings between two traditions (or whatever number), the history of the country within which dialog is taking place, and so on. Perhaps the most contentious recent question, as we have seen, is the relation of mission to dialog. For the moment, I want to suggest four artificial categories to indicate some of the avenues along which dialog proceeds. These categories necessarily overlap and interpenetrate: the dialogs of friendship, social, and political cooperation, spirituality, and intellectual understanding. In what follows I will briefly define and illustrate each type, without in any way attempting to be exhaustive.

The dialog of friendship defines the major context of inter-religious dialog, although it is the least covered in the literature. It is not institutionally managed and springs from the homes and families of millions of Catholics who live in pluralist societies who seek to serve the "common good," desiring peace and harmony with their neighbors. Here the simple virtues of truthfulness, honesty, respect, charity, and justice are especially required to build up communities for the future of the church and society. There is abundant failure in these areas as well as successes. Recalling my own childhood experience, in the Asian community in East Africa during the 1950s to 1960s, Asians would often celebrate each other's festivals with cards, sweets, and common events – bringing together Muslims, Hindus, Sikhs, and Catholics. It was through these small events that children and adults might learn mutual respect and understanding. Here the teaching of Vatican II on the dignity of the human person is particularly helpful (*Declaration on Religious Liberty, Dignitatis Humanae*, 1965: 1), requiring that whoever our neighbor may be, their holistic welfare and intrinsic dignity is central to Catholic practice.

Out of this dialog of friendship arises a raft of social and political forms of dialog. A very high profile case worth citing is the Vatican's cooperation with Muslims regarding the United Nations International Conference on Population and Development in Cairo (1994). The lay Harvard Professor, Mary Ann Glendon, headed the Vatican delegation that worked hard with Muslim groups to advance shared values and beliefs regarding women and abortion against a highly instrumentalist UN agenda. In India we can find Catholic communities joining with Muslims, Sikhs, and Hindus calling for religious calm and peace at times of inter-communal strife and violence, and opposing the unjust treatment of Hindu outcastes. My own experience of interfaith cooperation was unintendedly through my involvement with the Campaign for Nuclear Disarmament during the 1970s, when many Hindus and Buddhists joined with Pax Christi (and others) in street demonstrations and other political actions in the UK. Vatican II was very encouraging toward all forms of dialog in this arena. It is also clear that the Church's social teachings will be clarified and developed through this engagement, as will various questions on the relation of faith to politics.

The third form of dialog I have called spiritual dialog. It is beautifully exemplified in John Paul II's invitation to leaders of world religions to take part in the Day of Prayer for Peace in Assisi in 1986. This event was technically not inter-religious prayer, but witnessing to each other's prayer tradition in the common drive to peace. Despite some opposition to this event within the Church, the Pope justified it in these terms:

> every authentic prayer is called forth by the Holy Spirit, who is mysteriously present in the heart of every person. This too was seen at Assisi: the unity that comes from the fact that every man and woman is capable of praying, that is, of submitting oneself totally to God and of recognizing oneself to be poor in front of him. (John Paul II, 1987: 60)

Long-term sustained monastic dialog with Buddhism has been a task for the Benedictine order, and Trappist monks had been involved in a remarkable Christian–Muslim prayer group in Tibhirine, Algeria, that ended with the brutal murder of seven monks by radical Muslims opposed to such dialog. On a more ordinary level, the inculturation of the liturgy in Asian countries also testifies to this spiritual dialog. (See further discussion on these matters in D'Costa, 2000a: 143–71.) As with all these levels of dialog, misunderstandings and mistakes are always possible. The Pope's Assisi day was subject to many misgivings, as to some it implicitly supported syncretism. This is the same charge aimed at various forms of liturgical inculturation. The murdered monks of Tibhirine are also a painful reminder of the cost of dialog in some countries. However, if there is a sense in which God's Spirit is present in the world religions, then the spiritualities of these religions are a proper arena for respectful learning and reverence, with appropriate critical discernment.

Finally, the dialog of learning takes place at all levels, from the simple faithful to the highly learned. This process requires the support of high levels of learning in engagement with scholars from other religions, as well as learning from the actual communities of faith in day-to-day activities. It is a process that has no boundaries.

Catholic theology of religions is still struggling with important issues and the dialog with specific religions is sure to further illuminate and complicate these contentious areas. Catholic interfaith practices are vital to the future of the Church and society and the general track record in the modern period is a cause for some hope.

References and Further Reading

Abbott, W. (ed.) (1966) *The Documents of Vatican II*. New York: Guild Press.

Balthasar, Hans Urs von (1988) *Dare We Hope "That all Men be Saved"? With a Short Discourse on Hell*, trans. David Kipp and Lothar Krauth. San Francisco, CA: Ignatius Press.

Balthasar, Hans Urs von (1994 [1967]) *The Moment of Christian Witness*, trans. R. Beckley. San Francisco, CA: Ignatius Press.

Buckley, M. (1987) *At the Origins of Modern Atheism*. New Haven, CT: Yale University Press.

Cavanaugh, W. (1995) "'A Fire Strong Enough to Consume the House': the Wars of Religion and the Rise of the State," *Modern Theology*, October, 397–420.

Congar, Y. (1966 [1960]) *Tradition and Traditions*, trans. M. Naseby and T. Rainborough. London: Burns and Oates.

D'Costa, G. (1990a) "*Extra ecclesiam nulla salus* Revisited," in Hamnett, I. (ed.) *Religious Pluralism and Unbelief*. London: Routledge, 130–47.

D'Costa, G. (1990b) "One Covenant or Many Covenants: Towards a Jewish–Christian Theology," *Journal of Ecumenical Studies*, vol. 27, no. 3, 441–52.

D'Costa, G. (2000a) *The Meeting of Religions and the Trinity*. Maryknoll, NY: Orbis.

D'Costa, G. (2000b) *Sexing the Trinity*, London: SCM Press.

D'Costa, G. (2002) "*Nostra Aetate* – Telling God's Story in Asia: Problems and Pitfalls," in Lamberigts, M. and Kenis, L. (eds.) *Vatican II and Its Legacy*. Leuven: Peeters Press, 229–350.

de Lubac, H. (1969) *The Church: Paradox and Mystery*, trans. James R. Dunne. Shannon: Ecclesia Press.

Denzinger, H. (1955) *The Sources of Catholic Dogma*, trans. Roy J. Defarrari. 13th edition. Fitzwilliam, NH: Loreto Publications.

Dupuis, J. (1997) *Towards a Christian Theology of Religious Pluralism*. Maryknoll, NY: Orbis.

Hacker, P. (1980) *Theological Foundations of Evangelisation*. St Augustin: Franz Steiner Verlag.

John Paul II (1987) "Address to the Roman Curia," December 22, 1986. *Bulletin*, 64, 58–62.

Kilby, K. (2004) *Karl Rahner. Theology and Philosophy*. London and New York: Routledge.

Knitter, P. (1984) "Roman Catholic Approaches to Other Religions: Developments and Tensions," *International Bulletin of Missionary Research*, 44–51.

Knitter, P. (1992) "Interpreting Silence: A Response to Mikka Ruokanen" and "Author's Reply" from *International Bulletin of Missionary Research*, 1990; reproduced in Ruokanen (1992), 133–56.

Knitter, P. (1996) *Jesus and the Other Names*. New York: Orbis.

Lefebvre, M. (1986) *An Open Letter to Confused Catholics*. Leominster: Fowler Wright.

Mattam, J. (1975) *Land of the Trinity: A Study of Modern Christian Approaches to Hinduism*. Bangalore: Theological Publications of India.

Milbank, J. (1990) *Theology and Social Theory*. Oxford: Blackwell.

Pannikar, R. (1973) *The Trinity and the Religious Experience of Man*. Maryknoll, NY: Orbis.

Pannikar, R. (1981 [1964]) *The Unknown Christ of Hinduism*, 2nd edition. London: Darton, Longman and Todd.

Pieris, A. (1988) *An Asian Theology of Liberation*. Maryknoll, NY: Orbis.

Rahner, K. (1961) *On the Theology of Death*, trans. Charles H. Henkey. Freiburg: Herder.

Rahner, K. (1966/1969) *Theological Investigations*, vol. 5, 1966; vol. 6, 1969. London: Darton, Longman and Todd.

Rahner, K. (1968 [1957]) *Spirit in the World*, trans. William V. Dych. New York: Herder and Herder.

Ratzinger, J. (1997) "Central Problem for Faith," *Briefing*, vol. 27, no. 1, 36–42.

Rivera-Pagán, L. (2003) "Violence of the *Conquistadores* and Prophetic Indignation," in Chase, K. R. and Jacobs, A. (eds.) *Must Christianity Be Violent? Reflections on History, Practice, and Theology*. Grand Rapids, MI: Brazos Press, 37–49.

Ruether, R. (1987) "Feminism and Jewish-Christian Dialogue," in Hick, J. and Knitter, P. (eds.) *The Myth of Christian Uniqueness. Towards a Pluralist Theology of Religions*. Maryknoll, NY: Orbis, 137-48.

Ruokanen, M. (1992) *The Catholic Doctrine of Non-Christian Religions According to the Second Vatican Council*. Leiden: E.J. Brill.

Sullivan, F. (1992) *Salvation Outside the Church? Tracing the History of the Catholic Response*. London: Geoffrey Chapman.

Wilfred, F. (1991) *Sunset in the East? Asian Challenges and Christian Involvement*, Madras: University of Madras Press.

CHAPTER 31

Art and Literature

Patrick Sherry

Imagine that a non-Catholic friend asked us to recommend a program of reading, in order to come to a deeper understanding of Catholicism. We would probably think first of listing some books of theology. But it might be equally illuminating for the person concerned to read, say, Dante's *Divine Comedy*, Newman's *Apologia pro Vita Sua*, or Graham Greene's *The Power and the Glory*. Moreover, to take this approach further and move from literature to the arts, we might also suggest a visit to Chartres Cathedral, a viewing of Fra Angelico's paintings in San Marco, Florence, or Michelangelo's in the Sistine Chapel, and a listening to a Palestrina Mass or Berlioz's *Te Deum*, to mention only a few examples. The suggestions that I have just made point to the fact that, historically, there has been a close connection between Catholicism and the arts and literature. In this article I shall show something of the nature of this relationship, taking most (though not all) of my examples from the visual arts, and then seek to explain it, appealing to the sacramental principle, understood widely, that is that the invisible can be known through the visible, the internal and spiritual can be expressed through the perceptible, so that God can be glimpsed in the world through the signs and likenesses that He has created. I have found that many people who are put off by the Catholic Church's apparently authoritarian and hierarchical structure are attracted by its sacramental sense, narrowly or widely construed.

Catholic Art

It is sometimes claimed that Catholicism is a religion of the image and Protestantism one of the word. Obviously, this oversimplifies matters, for it fails to do justice to Protestant religious painters like Rembrandt and theorists of art like Ruskin, and ignores too the fact that there are certain distinctively Catholic exemplifications of the word, especially the "Catholic Novel," i.e. the tradition of the novel that emerged in the late nineteenth century and flourished in the twentieth century in the works of Georges Bernanos, François Mauriac, Graham Greene, Evelyn Waugh, Flannery

O'Connor, Heinrich Böll, Shisaku Endo, and many others. They are novels of grace and redemption, but ones which often emphasize the roles of priests, sacraments, and saintly figures. They are usually realistic in their descriptions of the world, which is however seen as an arena of grace, hence raising the questions of what is the "real" world, and how God acts in it. I prefer, therefore, to work rather with the distinction between word and sacrament. Nevertheless, there is some truth in the first claim, in that Catholicism has favored the use of painting, both in murals and in altarpieces, in churches, as well as mosaics, sculptures, and statues, and that the Protestant Reformers in the sixteenth century reacted against this practice. Sometimes such religious art illustrates specifically Catholic beliefs like the Immaculate Conception and Assumption of the Virgin Mary, or the Real Presence in the Eucharist (as conveyed in e.g. Ugolino's frescoes of the Miracle of Bolsena in Orvieto Cathedral). Sometimes, too, it depicts particular saints: thus the frescoes in the Church of S. Francesco in Assisi, some of them by Giotto, narrate the story of St Francis' life, following St Bonaventure's biography. More commonly, however, it illustrates central Christian beliefs: the Incarnation, shown through the birth of Christ, his salvific role (of which the Good Shepherd was a common representation in the early Church), the Crucifixion, the Resurrection, and Pentecost. The earliest known such works are in the Roman catacombs and in the third-century house-church at Dura-Europos.

Such a use of paintings, mosaics, etc. should be considered in connection with the later use of stained glass in churches, especially when the development of the Gothic style increased the amount of wall-space available for windows. The description "Bible of the poor" has been used of these windows; and if one looks at the large numbers of them in Chartres Cathedral (174) or York Minster (128), one can see its appropriateness: with such a space available to them artists could depict the main events of the Gospels and many from the Hebrew Bible, as well as a range of saints (abstract designs, common in modern stained glass, were favored in Cistercian churches). Such sequences tended to displace earlier ones in sculpture on the portals, not to mention the mosaics of the first Christian centuries, e.g. in Ravenna. They would serve both to instruct the illiterate and to foster the devotion of all Christians.

It must be emphasized that most religious paintings, like mosaics and stained-glass windows, were originally features of churches: when one sees a lot of religious paintings in a modern art gallery, one tends to forget that many of them were once altarpieces, and that they have now been torn from their contexts of worship. Since, too, their original homes, churches, are "spaces for worship," they also must not be judged simply as examples of architecture: religiously, their interiors are more significant than their exteriors. There are also more particular liturgical constraints on church architects. The liturgical changes consequent on the Council of Trent (1545–63) and the Second Vatican Council (1962–5) both resulted in changes in church architecture. In the latter case, for instance, circular churches (not unknown in earlier centuries) were encouraged, e.g. Liverpool Metropolitan Cathedral, in which the priest at the altar faces the congregation, thus symbolizing the belief that the whole assembly shares in the offering of the Mass. Sometimes, too, there are more indirect links between architecture and religious belief and practice. E.I. Watkin says that the early Jesuits, in the period after the Council of Trent, were "determined to conquer humanism for Christ," and so found the Baroque style, with its free use of splendid display and forms of beauty, congenial (Watkin, 1942: 117). He also mentions the Jesuits' use of drama, as part of their educational curriculum, because of its value in fostering the imagination.

Liturgical constraints played an important part in music too. The earliest church music was probably derived from Jewish psalmody, extended to the rest of the liturgy, especially the Mass, the monastic offices, and hymns. Organs had begun to be used in churches by 400, though it was not for several centuries that solo organ music was used. The earliest known form of sung liturgy was plainsong, where there is a single line of music, sung by everyone; and the best-known version of this is Gregorian chant, so called because St Gregory I (Pope 590–604) set about collecting and systematizing such music – though we do not know how much of what we have goes back to his time, since our earliest written examples date from the ninth century. Polyphony was introduced in church music in that century, and by 1600 it had developed into the elaborate settings of the Mass by Byrd, Lassus, Palestrina, Victoria, and others. Later, with the development of the orchestra, we get the Masses of Bach, Haydn, Mozart, Beethoven, and subsequent composers. Sometimes these are operatic in character, with virtuoso solo parts, so that one might confuse, for example, an aria from a Mozart Mass with one from *The Marriage of Figaro*. Some famous Masses are too long and elaborate for liturgical use, most notably Bach's B Minor Mass (an example which also shows that one need not be a Catholic in order to compose Catholic liturgical music).

Not surprisingly, Church authorities sought from time to time to encourage simpler styles of music in churches. The Council of Trent taught that church music should be sufficiently simple for the words of the liturgy to be heard clearly, a principle which Palestrina (1525–94) especially managed to observe in his polyphonic Masses. Trent's implicit criticism of much church music was echoed by St Pius X (Pope 1903–14) and by the Second Vatican Council, which sought to encourage greater participation by the congregation; they both recommended a return to plainsong, no doubt in reaction to the operatic character of some eighteenth- and nineteenth-century church music (though a few composers, e.g. Anton Bruckner (1824–96), embraced a simpler and purer style).

Trent's reforms also extended to paintings in churches, which were to be confined to orthodox religious subjects, treated in a reverent manner. The most famous example of the Church's seeking to regulate the work of artists occurred in connection with Veronese's *Last Supper*, a large picture of finely dressed people at a banquet in an elaborate architectural setting. The Inquisition in Venice in 1573 enquired why the artist had introduced "buffoons, German soldiers, and similar scurrilities." He was told to alter the painting; but as far as we know Veronese simply changed the title of the painting to *Feast in the House of Levi* (now in the Accademia, Venice). A few decades earlier, the nudity of some of Michelangelo's figures in his work in the Sistine Chapel had been criticized as inappropriate to paintings in a church; and early in the next century the "indecorum" and "low realism" of Caravaggio were attacked by some.

Trent was meeting in the wake of the Protestant Reformation, which had imposed much more severe restrictions on artists and musicians. Luther criticized only some images and still praised the educational value of religious art (though preferring works based on scriptural themes). Calvin, however, sought the removal of paintings and sculptures from churches, so much so that many of them were destroyed, especially in the Low Countries and Britain during the Reformation, and in the latter case also under Cromwell. This was no mere philistinism, for Calvin saw painting and sculpture, like music, as gifts of God; but he also thought that Exod 20:4 showed that it was wrong to attempt a visible representation of God, so that, to avoid the risk of idolatry, painting, and sculpture should depict only visible bodies and events.

The Reformation did not prevent the production of *religious* art as such: Rembrandt, for example, produced many such works. But most of them are drawings and etchings, and so of a more private nature, often seeming like meditations on the Gospels. It is worth contrasting the intimate character of much of his religious art with the large-scale and sometimes flamboyant works of his Catholic contemporary, Rubens. More obviously, one can contrast too the subject-matter of Protestant and Catholic religious works. Neil MacGregor, for instance, contrasts Rogier van der Weyden's *The Seven Sacraments* (in Antwerp) with the Weimar Altarpiece by Lucas Cranach the Younger: the former depicts the Crucifixion as taking place in a cathedral, in which priests and bishops are administering the sacraments, thus expressing the Catholic belief that the sacraments are channels of grace and continue Christ's redemptive work; the latter, on the other hand, expresses a Lutheran "salvation by faith alone" doctrine and a preference for word over sacrament, for it depicts a thin stream of blood squirting from Christ's side onto the head of the painter's father, who is standing by the Cross, together with St John the Baptist and Martin Luther, holding his Bible open at certain texts regarded as supporting his doctrine (MacGregor, 2000: 198–204). Many Counter-Reformation artists responded to the Protestant Reformers by choosing sacramental themes, or by depicting saints and so encouraging their veneration (criticized by many Protestants).

Calvin's attack on church art was anticipated to some extent in earlier centuries. St Bernard (*c.*1090–1153) criticized what he saw as the excessive opulence of many churches, especially at St Denis and Cluny. Most famously, the Iconoclastic disputes of the eighth and ninth centuries anticipated both later debates about the nature of religious art and the destructions of the Reformers and of Cromwell. Again, those who attacked the use of paintings in churches (the Iconoclasts) were not philistines, for their central position was that images in places of worship led to idolatry, and should be removed. Their opponents agreed with them that it is indeed wrong to try to depict God, but they defended the use of icons by appealing to the fact of the Incarnation. For in Jesus Christ we have one Person, the image of God (2 Cor 3:17), but with two natures, divine and human. He may, therefore, be represented as a man (some also claimed that his human nature is the image of his divine one). Thus St John of Damascus (*c.*675–749) justified the making of images of God Incarnate: "I do not draw an image of the immortal Godhead, but I paint the image of God who became visible in the flesh" (*On the Divine Images*, 1:4). He emphasized, too, the materiality of the Incarnation (ibid., 1:16, 2:14). Likewise, the Patriarch of Constantinople, St Germanus (*c.*634–733) argued that the making of such artworks is entailed by the Incarnation, for Christ's humanity was a form of God's self-expression (Nichols, 1980: 83).

A further stage was to defend the use of pictures of saints in churches, because all of us were originally created in the image and likeness of God, and saints are those who have been sanctified and have recovered something of what was lost through the Fall. They are, however, to be "venerated," but not worshipped.

Although the Seventh Ecumenical Council of 787 at Nicea, which sanctioned the use of art-works in churches, is recognized by both the Catholic and Orthodox Churches, the art and music of the two Churches has tended to go in divergent directions since they split off from each other in 1054. In Orthodox churches, choirs are unaccompanied by organs or other musical instruments (though modern Orthodox composers like Arvo Pärt and John Tavener compose religious music – which is not the same as liturgical music – using instruments). Sculpture is not favored, and icons and murals are supposed to follow traditional patterns, representative but not realistic (for instance, perspective is ignored). The style of early Italian painters like Giotto and Duccio is not so far from their Byzantine contemporaries, but thereafter, East and West diverge, so that modern Orthodox writers criticize Western Renaissance painting for making religious art either didactic or decorative, as contrasted with icons, which are regarded as specifically liturgical forms of art and intended to lead to the worship of God. Thus, Paul Evdokimov criticizes developments in art in the West since the thirteenth century, as having made it less drawn to conveying the transcendent or integrated with the mystery of the liturgy, so that it becomes more and more autonomous and subjective, and by the middle of the sixteenth century has artists treating Christian themes with a total lack of religious sense. Even Fra Angelico, an artist who has much in common with Eastern icon-painters and who seems to have avoided whatever excesses appeared in later religious art, is rapped over the knuckles by Evdokimov for being strongly gripped by "Dominican intellectualism" (Evdokimov, 1970: 67–8). Orthodox writers also criticize the Western "cult of the artist," which they think led to the later emphasis on self-expression, contrasting it with the customary anonymity of icon-painters.

Despite their polemical edge, a Catholic could agree with a lot of such criticisms of later Renaissance religious art, and also with the theology of beauty developed by Evdokimov and other Orthodox writers, which is not limited to the beauty of icons. The stances of St Bernard, the Council of Trent, and Pius X, already mentioned, show that there has sometimes been an internal critique of religious painting and music in the Catholic Church. But I would be inclined to trace the inadequacies of poor religious art to a lack of a sense of the sacramentality of art, and of beauty too, rather than to its distance from liturgy as such.

This lack of a sense of sacramentality appears also, I think, in Calvin's view of religious art. He recognizes, as we have seen, that artistic talent is a gift of God, but fails to consider whether the works created by those so gifted might not reflect the Giver in some way. But this is part of a wider lack of a sacramental sense, which emerges, I think, in Calvin's treatment of marriage. He allows that it is a "good and holy ordinance of God"; but then, he says, so also are farming, building, shoemaking, and barbering, but they are not sacraments. He denies therefore that it is a sacrament in the sense understood by the Catholic Church, and questions its reading of Ephesians 5:21–33, which sees the relationship between husband and wife as a sign of Christ's love for his Church, and was, therefore used as a "proof-text" of matrimony's being a sacrament; and he says instead that St Paul is simply using a similitude (*Inst.* IV.xix.34–6).

Calvin goes on immediately to attack the Catholic Church for its inconsistency in proclaiming that marriage is a sacrament and yet at the same time depreciating sexuality. There is some truth in this: it was not until the twentieth century that theologians began to elaborate a true theology of marriage which sees that human love (including sexual love) may become both a sign of divine love and an effective channel of it. Yet Calvin's own position rules out such a development.

This sacramental theology should be related to some other fundamental beliefs: to the doctrine of the Incarnation, according to which the Son of God condescended to enter the world of matter, as mentioned already; to the fact that we are embodied persons in this world, and so our senses respond to colors, sounds, tastes, and so on; and to a wider sense of sacramentality, which sees earthly beauty as a sign of God's presence. Such a wider sense of sacramentality is possessed by many who are not Catholics. For instance, Michael Mayne (an Anglican) writes, "Not only does God like it [matter] but he clothes himself in it. It is one of his languages." Hence, the starting-point of spirituality for a Christian is not, he says, a striving for another world, but "a deepening awareness of the true nature of this world and our place within it," so that we come to realize that the whole world is sacramental. He goes on to quote the visionary painter Samuel Palmer (1805–81) who wrote during his time at Shoreham, "I must paint the hills so as to give us promise that the country behind them is paradise" (Mayne, 1995: 65–70, 152).

Mayne argues that such a view of the world, which issues in wonder and gratitude, requires first our attentiveness so that we learn to truly see it (ibid.: 10–11). Many people, however, who share his standpoint might be unfamiliar or unhappy with his use of the term "sacramental," or at any rate with its use in aesthetics. So to see what is at stake here, I think that we need to go a little deeper in our explanation of the concept.

Art and Sacrament

There are two important ways relevant to our inquiry in which what is now unknown can be related to what is known, first causally, and second through signs and likenesses. The first includes examples in ordinary life like an undiagnosed medical condition causing pain, as well as more abstruse cases in science, such as some undetected factor setting off a chemical reaction. The second likewise includes examples from ordinary life like orphans resembling their now unknown parents, and more difficult cases such as the relationship between a language like Linear B or a code and what it denotes.

What I have said so far covers only the *existence* of a relationship, which may well remain unknown. Whether the unknown can be *known* from the known is another matter, to some extent the subject of the present discussion. Obviously one may infer the force of a tornado from its effects; and scientists constantly hypothesize theoretical explanations of natural phenomena. But whether God's existence or creativity can be known from the world is more disputable and the subject of natural theology. In the case of signs and likenesses I may come to know something of your dead parents through coming to know you, but only if you tell me in what respects you resemble them. Similarly, religious believers who think that they may come to know something of God's nature from what he has made already believe in his Creation and in his having made some beings in his own image and likeness. But others may not recognize these relations. Thomas Traherne wrote "The World is a Mirror of infinit Beauty, yet no Man sees it" (*Centuries* i.31). I will return to this question later.

Both these kinds of relation between the known and the unknown are combined in the notion of a sacrament, which has been defined traditionally as an "effective sign": St Thomas Aquinas, for example, notes that the sacraments confer grace not only because they are liturgically instructive (like a catechism) but because they "cause as well as signify" grace (*On Truth* xxviii.4). I shall argue that the combination of a sign and a cause extends far beyond the context of sacramental theology, if the latter is confined to the seven defined sacraments. I shall follow the Welsh poet-painter David Jones (1895–1974), author of *In Parenthesis* and *The Anathemata* and a Catholic convert, in extending the sacramental principle to the arts and to natural beauty. But it is worth noting now that the principle has already been extended even within religion: both Catholicism and Orthodoxy refer to certain things, like making the sign of the cross or, in the latter case, icons, as "sacramentals." Often too saints are described in the language of signs and likenesses: in Old Slavonic the word for saint is "like" (*sc.* God), and the Abbé Huvelin described saints as "living images painted by Christ Himself for His Church that he might recall some of His own features to her mind and console her in her widowhood" (Huvelin, 1927: lxxvi).

Jones maintained that any understanding of the sacraments depends on a wider sense of sacramentality, which he thought had been lost to a great extent in the modern world: "People speak of sacraments with a capital 'S' without seeming to notice that sign and sacrament with a small 's' are everywhere eroded and in some contexts non-existent." For they tend to take things at their face-value. Fortunately, he notes, one cannot really stay at this level all the time. Hence the creative artist's task is to "make radiant 'particular facts' so that they become intimations of immortality, or . . . of some otherness of some sort" (Jones, 1973: 13, 16).

Jones is detaching the concept of sacrament from the connotations of ritualism, because this is to restrict its applicability. This comes out in his seminal essay "Art and Sacrament," where he sees artistic activity as a universal human function, and one which is "form-making" and "sign-making" (unlike the works of animals, which can nevertheless be beautiful, e.g. honeycombs). He defines human beings, unlike both beasts and angels, as sign-making and therefore as sacramental animals. Now since signs must be significant of something, hence of some "reality," Jones goes on to claim that they must be of something good, and so of something that is sacred, hence "the notion of sign implies the sacred" (ibid.: 157).

Here, Jones is going upwards, as it were, from human making to God, and his line of argument depends on certain Thomistic positions. But we can also proceed downwards: in the order of being, we go from God to the world, e.g. in Creation; and this is what is believed to happen in the sacraments too. Jones also moves in this way, for toward the end of his essay he quotes Maurice de la Taille as saying of Christ on Maundy Thursday that "He placed Himself in the order of signs" (ibid.: 179).

Jones does not here analyze the variety of signs and the ways in which they signify. One obvious distinction to be made is between linguistic signs and signs where a relation of *likeness* is claimed. The picture of Lord Nelson on an inn-sign may resemble its original, but the words "Public Footpath" do not resemble a footpath, for the relationship between language and reality is not one of resemblance (except in the case of onomatopoeia). Here then, we have a fundamental distinction, between resemblance and linguistic and other forms of symbolic representation. Likenesses are not necessarily signs, for one penny is very like another, but it is not a sign of it. However, when one thing is created in the likeness of another, it may serve as a source of knowledge of it; and indeed if the archetype no longer exists or is not available to us, the likeness may serve as a source of information about it. Thus, Rembrandt's self-portraits, if good likenesses, give us information about him, though in a different way from linguistic signs like contemporary descriptions of him or biographies.

Clearly the arts and literature involve signs of the two kinds that I have mentioned. But so too, do the sacraments with a big "S." Baptism, for instance, trades on a resemblance between its use of water and our ordinary use of it in washing; and it also uses language and another form of symbolic action, anointing. This is not surprising, for in the Hebrew Bible the notion of a sign from God is closely related to the idea of his speaking, and the former serves as a way of *identifying* claimed instances of the latter. Thus, Gideon prays to God, "Give me a sign that it is you who speak to me" (Judges 6:17) after an angel has appeared to him with a message from God, and then sees the food that he has left on a rock suddenly consumed with fire. Similarly, Hezekiah is promised that the extraordinary movement of the sun will be a sign that God will fulfill his promises (Isa 38:4–8). In the New Testament, likewise, there is a close connection between God's words and signs, in that Jesus' "signs" are linked to his authority and to his claims on people's belief. The Jews ask him "What sign will you give us to show that we should believe in you?" (John 6:30), and Peter later preaches that "Jesus . . . was a man commended to you by God by the miracles and portents and signs that God worked through him when he was among you" (Acts 2:22).

To see what is at stake here we need, I think, to move into a wider theological context. If God is believed to act through signs, then this belief goes with a wider belief in his creative actions in nature and history. The American philosopher C.S. Peirce (1839–1914), who did much to classify and explain the different types of sign, described the universe as "a vast representamen, a great symbol of God's purpose, working out its conclusions in living realities" (*Collected Papers* V, sec. 119). But Christians and Jews at least would make some more specific connections: Aidan Nichols notes that it was Israel's abhorrence of its neighbors' idolatrous worship and its desire to protect God's transcendence that led it to ban all images of God; yet at the same time Judaism taught that we are all created in the image and likeness of God (Gen 1:26–8; 9:6). The latter is a daring claim, for, as Nichols remarks, it gives to human beings the power of divine disclosure which, in pagan cultures, was attached to the image of the God (Nichols, 1980: 19). It also, one might add, raises the question, very pertinent for us now, of whether there is such a thing as a purely "secular" portrait.

We move further down the path indicated by Nichols when we recollect that Christ is described both as the Word (John 1:14) and the image or likeness of God (2 Cor 4:4; Col 1:15), "the radiant light of God's glory and the perfect copy of his nature" (Heb 1:3), texts which are very important for our discussion of iconoclasm in the light of the Incarnation, and also for the claim of later generations of theologians that Christ is *the* sign or sacrament of God. The latter claim is, I think, as important for our understanding of sacramental theology as any particular Gospel texts about Christ's words and actions. Thus Edward Schillebeeckx, for example, first describes Christ as *the* primordial sacrament, and then goes on to present the seven sacraments as his actions continuing through the Church (Schillebeeckx, 1963, especially chapters 1–2); the Second Vatican Council likewise describes the Church as "a kind of sacrament of intimate union with God, and of the unity of all mankind" (*Lumen Gentium*, 1).

The biblical texts that I have quoted should discourage us from divorcing word and image, or word and sacrament (as tended to happen at the Reformation), for each pair embraces two complementary notions. As we have seen, sacraments involve words as well as signs like pouring water or anointing with oil; and the Mass has two parts: the Liturgy of the Word, which includes readings from Scripture and preaching; and the Liturgy of the Eucharist.

An Enchanted World

Now if the world we live in is indeed a sacramental one, then we might well expect this fact to influence the way we see it and how we judge what is "realistic." A recent book begins with the striking claim that, because of their sense of sacramentality, "Catholics live in an enchanted world . . ." (Greeley, 2000: 1). The writer does not mention David Jones, but emulates him in enlarging the concept of sacrament; he is more optimistic, however, about the survival of a sacramental sense, at least among Catholics. If these two writers are right, this helps to explain a widely noted fact, that Catholicism often seems "worldly" (which may be regarded with approval or not!).

Worldliness covers a lot of things. In the realms of literature and the arts it would include the use of classical Greek and Roman art-forms by Renaissance artists, and the use of secular knowledge and activities in the service of religion by Jesuits and many others, which we have discussed already. A particular example of such a use, very important historically, is Catholicism's favorable attitude toward philosophy, styled as "the handmaid of theology" in the Middle Ages. I think that this attitude is based on an optimistic view of the intelligibility of the world and of human powers of reason, a view that would lead one to reject the attitude of those who, like Tertullian, wish to dissociate Athens and Jerusalem, i.e. secular wisdom and religious learning. A specific philosophical thesis, worth singling out now as relevant to our present concerns, is that God usually works in the world through what Aquinas calls "secondary causes" (e.g. in his *Summa Theologiae* 1a.105.5); that is, although He can act directly in the world in Creation, miracles, and within human souls, for the most part God works through the ordinary course of events and natural laws. He thus achieves his purposes more through the working of regular laws than through special interventions.

Behind such particular issues there is often the benign assumption that the world which God created and "saw that it was good" (Gen 1:10) is still good, despite the ravages caused by sin, an optimistic attitude that can be contrasted with the Calvinist emphasis on human depravity. As far as art is concerned, E.I. Watkin saw such a philosophy as anticipated in St Clement of Alexandria's statement that "It is meet to glorify the Creator by the enjoyment of the sight of beautiful objects" (*Paedagogus* I.ii.8), and realized especially in the Christian humanism of the Renaissance. Among artists Watkin singles out Michelangelo, whose nudes, he thinks, "are pure in their reference to God, temples of the Holy Ghost built divinely in the flesh." He mentions particularly the artist's depiction of the creation of Adam, on the ceiling of the Sistine Chapel, which he regards as the greatest of all religious pictures: "Here Hellenism in the naked Adam confronts Hebraism in the Divine Creator. Humanism is reconciled with theism. Man fulfils himself by seeking God" (Watkin, 1942: 89–90).

Such a reconciliation involves an appreciation of bodily beauty, and indeed a reverence for the world of bodies and matter, and it goes against a common tendency in some strands of Christianity, including Catholicism at times, to despise these realities, resulting in a failure to develop theologies of the world and of the body. This tendency probably derives from certain aspects of Plato's philosophy, as interpreted by early theologians like Origen, and it may well have contributed to iconoclasm. In his disputes with the Iconoclasts St John of Damascus, as we have seen, stressed that in the Incarnation God deigned to dwell in matter and through it to effect our salvation. One might adapt de la Taille here and say that if on Maundy Thursday Christ placed himself in the order of signs, on Christmas Day he placed himself in the world of matter. Recent theologians influenced by the ecological movement have stressed that in virtue of the doctrine of Creation, we are stewards of the world, and in virtue of the Incarnation the whole cosmos, and not just human beings, is to be redeemed and sanctified. Here, they are drawing out a line of thought already present in St Paul: he saw the whole of Creation as awaiting redemption (Rom 8:20–2), and as being reconciled through the risen Christ (Col 1:20).

For early Christian writers, such an ultimate redemption of the cosmos would be seen in terms of "glorification"; and some modern writers point to the connotations of beauty in the concept of glory, and see the beauty of the natural world and of art as an anticipation of the redeemed and transfigured world that is to come. This conclusion presupposes, however, that we have an adequate appreciation of the beauty that is before us, and that we have begun to reflect on its religious and theological significance. Gerard Manley Hopkins begins his poem "God's Grandeur,"

> The world is charged with the grandeur of God,
> It will flame out, like shining from shook foil;

Here, he was expressing a traditional theme: that God's glory is shown in the beauty of the created world. Behind this theme lies the doctrine of Creation, according to which God not only made the world but communicated something of his own perfections to it, and continues to manifest himself in it. St Augustine wrote, "God works the sensible and visible things which he wills, in order to signify and manifest Himself in them . . ." (*On the Trinity* III.iv.10). Here too we have an exemplification of the sacramental principle.

A theology of beauty will need to proceed in stages. First of all there is the claim that God is beautiful – some would say he is beauty itself. This claim is found in several early Christian writers, and is influenced by both Greek and Hebrew sources, especially Plato's *Symposium* and the biblical ascription of glory to God. There are also a few biblical passages, mostly in the Psalms, which ascribe something akin to beauty to God or to places and things associated with him (most importantly, Ps 27:4, 46:6, 50:2, 71:8, 145:5). Second, there is the belief that God communicated some of his own qualities to the world, hence the latter bears some likeness to him, even if only an analogical likeness. Here again, there are both Greek and Hebrew influences: Plato's belief that particulars resemble or "participate in" forms like beauty, and biblical passages like "The heavens declare the glory of the Lord" (Ps 19:1), and Genesis 1:26–7, already mentioned.

The likeness of the world to God has been described in various ways, many of them appealing to light, as in Hopkins' poem or in the description of beauty as "the radiance of God's goodness" in the commentary on Plato's *Symposium* by the Renaissance humanist Marsilio Ficino, who influenced the painter Botticelli. Often the metaphor of a mirror has been used, as in Traherne's *Centuries*, a metaphor commonly used by medieval writers to describe God's diffusion of his wisdom and other perfections in the world.

This second stage of a theology of beauty has, as presented so far, however, been deficient in that it appeals only to the natural world, and fails to take into account beauty found in the arts and literature. To remedy this deficiency we need, I believe, to enlarge the concept of God's creativity to include inspiration. If the latter is God's bringing about the production of something by working through the mental capacities of a human author, then it would seem to be a particular case of God's working through secondary causes. Here, God is using the natural powers of human creators, though greatly enhanced, in such a way that he is letting them, through his Spirit, share in his creativity. Of course, God may also use other parts of nature as secondary causes in creating beauty, as in the creation of coral through coral-insects.

Having established these ontological claims about divine and worldly beauty and the relations between them, a theology of beauty may go in different directions. It may treat our perception of beauty as a particular kind of what is sometimes called "extrovertive" mysticism, found in those who see the same world that we all behold, but come to see it in a new way. The Cornish poet Jack Clemo wrote,

> I was a spirit and sense mystic, and the artist in me demanded realism – landscapes, people, events. I had an inner vision that gave transcendent meaning to the external world, not an inner vision that was independent of the external world. (Clemo, 1980: 107)

One may also emphasize the practical. Eric Gill, with whom David Jones worked for a time, wrote, "The beauty and loveliness of the natural world bears its witness to God's love; it is necessary that man's works should bear witness to his love of God" (Gill, 1940: 206). He exemplified this principle in his own work as an artist and craftsman, and also criticized the tendency of modern industrial manufacture to produce shoddy and ugly work – a criticism made by Ruskin and others in the nineteenth century, accompanying their denunciations of the inhuman squalor of the industrial towns and cities of the time.

Finally, one may move to a much more ambitious theology of beauty in terms of the Persons of the Trinity, both in their relations among themselves and in their creative actions together in the world. The most outstanding example of such a theology in our time is Hans Urs von Balthasar's *The Glory of the Lord*, the subtitle of which is *A Theological Aesthetics*. The author understands the term "aesthetics" far more widely than it has been understood since the mid-eighteenth century when it came to denote a distinct area of philosophy. He regards modern aesthetics as a fragment broken off from a true aesthetics. Balthasar starts from the literal sense of the Greek *aesthesis* as perception, but his particular concern is with the manifestation of God's glory in Jesus Christ, in the Incarnation, Cross, and Resurrection. There is, however, a similarity between his concern and aesthetics in the more limited and conventional sense, in that he draws an analogy between carefully attending to a work of art and contemplating the Christian mystery: in both cases we behold what is presented to us, and then reflect on it.

Balthasar follows a long tradition in Western Christianity of associating beauty particularly with the Son, a tradition going back to St Augustine. In his *On the Trinity* Augustine mentions St Hilary's characterization of the three Persons as Father, Image, and Gift, and then associates beauty with the Son, who is the "exact image of the Father and the perfect Word, and, so to speak, art of the almighty and wise God." Although he goes on immediately to treat of the Holy Spirit's outpouring of his gifts on creatures, he does not mention beauty among these gifts (VI.x.11). Balthasar largely follows Augustine here: he describes Christ as the form (*Gestalt*) of God, and therefore as the aesthetic model of all beauty, and he sees the Holy Spirit's function in the world as being to witness to the Son (as the Son witnesses to the Father) by creating within us the ability to perceive God by apprehending the form of the Son (von Balthasar, 1982: 465, 609–10). His work may be contrasted with Evdokimov's *L'Art de l'icône*, which also has a developed Trinitarian theology of beauty, but one giving a fuller treatment of the role of the Holy Spirit in this connection.

We have, it seems, traveled a long way from our concern in the earlier part of this essay with particular works of art, particularly paintings. There are, however, connections to be made. Balthasar's analogy between attending to a work of art and beholding the glory of God on the face of Christ again points to the sacramental principle, widely understood. But, more importantly, he has given us a developed theology of beauty, one which is keyed into a doctrine of the Trinity; he realizes, too, that beauty is what may draw many people to Christ. Moreover, in starting from *perception* he has given the lie to a common tendency in the West, especially since the Enlightenment, to assume that in approaching non-believers we start from *argument*, e.g. by attempting to demonstrate the existence of God philosophically. That is why I suggested earlier that an enquirer might start by reading Dante, Newman, and Graham Greene. While the beauty of art and literature is not the only exemplification of beauty (there is also the moral and spiritual beauty of the saints), it is of inestimable importance because of its sacramental nature. It is one of the glories of the Catholic tradition that it has realized this, even if only implicitly sometimes. Perhaps its main weakness today is caused by its failure to convey its vision to the world.

Conclusion

I have chosen to dwell in this essay on examples of art that might be regarded as beautiful, because they best exemplify the claim that art may be sacramental. But a lot of art and literature does not claim to be beautiful, or it has what W.B. Yeats called in his poem *Easter 1916* "a terrible beauty"; and a lot too does not even merit this description or other popular ones like "satisfying" or "life-enhancing." There are ugly or dissonant works of art and literature, or ones which may disturb us, like Grünewald's *Crucifixion* (in his Isenheim Altarpiece) or Shakespeare's *King Lear*.

Such works may be of great religious significance, as much as beautiful ones: they may be profound and moving, and express directly religious feelings or beliefs. Thereby they may be, in themselves, vehicles of religious understanding. Grünewald's painting, which needs to be viewed in conjunction with other parts of the altarpiece, especially the *Resurrection*, conveys, as few works do, the agony of Christ's Passion; moreover, the lamb and the chalice at the foot of the Cross convey symbolically its atoning significance and its connection with the Eucharist. Dante's *Purgatorio* is not simply illustrating a pre-existent doctrine of Purgatory, for he is getting away from the prevalent medieval understanding of it as a place of punishment, and (e.g. by representing it as a mountain) moving toward seeing it as a state of purification and development. Beethoven (not a particularly devout Catholic) wrote at the top of the score of his *Missa Solemnis* "From the heart; may it return to the heart," and in its margin he wrote, of the words *"Dona nobis pacem"* in the *"Agnus Dei,"* "a prayer for inner and outer peace." The music, I think, is not merely an adjunct to the words, but expresses Beethoven's own prayer. Likewise, the words *"non confundar in aeternum"* in Berlioz's *Te Deum* seem to me to express a heartfelt prayer of hope and confidence in God's mercy.

The capacity to express feelings and beliefs directly is not, of course, confined to religious art and literature. A love poem is a direct expression of the poet's love, and may convey to the reader some understanding of love; and a novel like Tolstoy's *Anna Karenina* may tell us more about the joys and sorrows of marriage than works of any other kind. But the expressive possibilities of religious art and literature, and their consequent ability to serve as channels of understanding, have been unduly neglected by theologians.

When such expressive qualities are combined with beauty, the works that embody them may seem especially profound and moving; and if they stand the test of time they may attain a classic status. Moreover, in the case of religious works they may also, I have argued, have a role analogous to a sacrament, for they may be signs and likenesses of the divine.

References and Further Reading

Balthasar, Hans Urs von (1982) *The Glory of the Lord: A Theological Aesthetics.* vol. 1: *Seeing the Form*, trans. E. Leiva-Merikakis. Edinburgh: T. and T. Clark.

Clemo, Jack (1980) *The Marriage of a Rebel.* London: Gollancz.

Evdokimov, Paul (1970) *L'Art de l'icône: theologie de la Beauté.* Paris: Desclée de Brouwer.

Gill, Eric (1940) *Autobiography.* London: Jonathan Cape.

Greeley, Andrew (2000) *The Catholic Imagination.* Berkeley, CA: University of California Press.

Huvelin, Henri (1927) *Some Spiritual Guides of the Seventeenth Century.* London: Burns Oates and Washbourne.

Jones, David (1973) *Epoch and Artist.* London: Faber and Faber.

Koch, Guntram (1996) *Early Christian Art: An Introduction*, trans. J. Bowden. London: SCM Press.

MacGregor, Neil, with E. Langmuir (2000) *Seeing Salvation: Images of Christ in Art.* London: BBC.

Maritain, Jacques (1930) *Art and Scholasticism*, trans. J. Scanlan. London: Sheed and Ward.

Mayne, Michael (1995) *This Sunrise of Wonder: Letters for the Journey.* London: Fount.

Murray, Peter and Linda (1996) *Oxford Companion to Christian Art and Architecture.* Oxford: Oxford University Press.

Nichols, Aidan (1980) *The Art of God Incarnate: Theology and Image in Christian Tradition.* London: Darton, Longman and Todd.

Schillebeeckx, Edward (1963) *Christ the Sacrament of Encounter with God.* London: Sheed and Ward.

Watkin, E.I. (1942) *Catholic Art and Culture.* London: Burns and Oates.

CHAPTER 32

Science and Theology

Michael Heller

Introduction: the Original Tension

Christianity started as a sect within the Jewish religion, but embraced the ancient world in the course of a few generations, largely because it furthered the erosion of mythical religions that Greek thinkers had begun several generations before. The widespread demythologization in the ancient world might be regarded as the first conflict between faith and reason. As a result, gods or deities sometimes appeared in these philosophical systems, not as subjects of worship, but as means to give the system "conceptual closure." Thus gods like Plato's demiurge or Aristotle's First Mover were philosophical ideas "to whom no altar was ever erected" (Pedersen, 1992: 13). Of the many confrontations between Greek thought and Christian doctrine, perhaps none is as important as the hermeneutic conflict that ensued when early Christians read their Bible in light of the philosophical wisdom of the Greeks. Such Christians could reject pagan philosophy or strive for a synthesis of Greek wisdom and Christian doctrine. In fact, early Christian writers adopted both attitudes, but the synthetic position, whose most famous proponents were Origen and St Augustine, soon marginalized the rejection of pagan philosophy found in Lactantius, Tatian, and Tertullian. As a result, Christian theology as we know it was born.

The Christian synthesis of faith and reason was born of the necessities of preaching the Gospel. When St Paul Apostle was in Athens among educated Greeks, he spoke of God who "made the world and all things therein," and for whom "we live, and move, and have our being" (Acts 17, 24–8). The Areopagites listened to him with interest, but dismissed him when he started speaking of the resurrection of the dead. This episode reveals the tension, so typical for Christianity, between its claim of God's entry into human history and a pursuit of a rational vision of the world. Today, after unquestionable achievements of analytical and hermeneutic philosophy, we better understand how much the content depends on the language in which it is expressed. Greek wisdom passed to Christianity its conceptual framework, and in this way philosophy entered into the very core of the Christian message. And that is how it remained. All particular conflicts between "faith and reason" or between "science and theology" that occur are but derivatives of the "lack of proportion" between the finite and the infinite. In whatever language, through whatever conceptual systems one might wish to express the transcendent in history, an abyss will always stand between the thing to be expressed and our expression of it.

The main goal of this essay is to understand the present relationship between Catholic theology and the sciences, but this relationship is so heavily marked with history that this cannot be achieved without looking to the past (Lindberg and Numbers, 1986; Brooke, 1991). To this end, we will discuss two of the central episodes in this history, the Galileo affair and the case of Charles Darwin, which even today cast their shadows onto the relationship between the Church and science. By and large, the modern theological reaction to these two crises was elaborated in terms of Neo-Thomism. Although this philosophical school is no longer dominant in the Catholic Church, its solution to the problem of faith and reason, or theology and science, is still significantly present in the official statements of the Church and in academic theological studies. Even so, there are signs that a new dialog between theology and science is slowly emerging, but still a great deal of work remains to be done that such new approaches might come to light.

Physicotheology

The roots of the modern empirical sciences can be found in both Greek philosophy and medieval scholasticism (Funkenstein, 1986). The creators of the modern empirical sciences, Kepler, Galileo, Newton, Huygens, Hooke, Boyle, and others, pioneered what historians call "physicotheology," which represented an unprecedented rapprochement between the natural sciences and theology. Although these men shared deep religious convictions, physicotheology was the invention of neither theologians nor philosophers, but was born within the sciences under a great pressure of new discoveries. One of the most influential centers of physicotheology was the Royal Society in London, whose members styled themselves *virtuosi*, and were strongly influenced by Puritan theology. John Ray's *The Wisdom of God Manifested in the Work of Creation* (1691) was typical for this popular new genre. Even earlier, Robert Hooke's *Micrographia* (1665) not only established the role of the microscope as a scientific instrument, but also wondered at the skillful design manifest in the smallest things of creation, such as a mere gnat's eye. In *A Disquisition about the Final Causes of Natural Things* (1688), Robert Boyle, among the most prominent of the *virtuosi*, claimed that this way of reasoning was "one of the best and most successful arguments to convince that there is God." Even Isaac Newton himself, especially in his four letters to Richard Bentley, expressed his strong inclination toward this way of thinking.

Physicotheology lasted but a brief period of time and produced effects contrary to the best intentions of its protagonists. Their "proofs," as we see them today, were based on gaps in their knowledge and understanding of the world. As science progressed, the gaps were gradually filled in, and the "hypothesis of God" seemed less and less necessary. As a result, the first authentically atheistic literature, such as La Mattrie's *L'Homme et machine* (1748) or von Holbach's *Système de la Nature* (1770), began to appear, and the split between science and religion, and between the world of science and the Church, became more pronounced. Quite opposed to the religious convictions of its founders, physicotheology is one of the main reasons (although certainly not the only reason) of modern atheism and materialism. In contrast to the Middle Ages, when Christian thinkers and Church authorities created an imposing pedagogical edifice of theological doctrine and secular teaching that consolidated methods of collecting and communicating knowledge, the new sciences that resulted from physicotheology created an "independent territory" that was no longer controlled by Church authorities.

This split into two worlds, the world of theology and the world of science, had enormous consequences for the future relationships between the Catholic Church and academic culture. As the sciences conquered new fields of knowledge and study, intellectuals in the Church often found themselves on the defensive, and often responded by isolating themselves further. The inertia of the institutionalized Church structures for collecting and transmitting knowledge and the growing specialization of the new sciences favored this isolation. The increasing specialization of the sciences led to the exclusion of philosophers and theologians from the scientific world, namely because the correct understanding of scientific theories required more protracted training than ever before, and thus became increasingly inaccessible to "learned outsiders." So, too, the protracted study required for scientific competence left scientists woefully unprepared for the metaphysical subtleties of philosophy and theology. Both fields progressed independently of one another, and when they rarely interacted, conflict was the norm.

The Galileo Affair

In the seventeenth century the medieval image of the world collapsed. Since this world constituted the backdrop of the previous synthesis of reason and faith, this collapse marked a deep crisis within the Christian world. Galileo alone was not responsible for this crisis; he was but a link in a long chain of events whose culmination was inevitable. Galileo probably discovered the Copernican system as early as 1590. He was deeply impressed by Copernicus' work, and from then on he started looking for physical proofs for the Earth's motion. Seven years later, in 1597, Galileo boasted in a letter to Kepler that he "had written down many proofs" for the Copernican system and "had undone the contrary arguments," but had not presented them. Astronomers of that time, including Copernicus himself, were well aware that such proof could be supplied by the discovery of the parallax of a fixed star (i.e., the annual displacement of a star caused by the motion of the earthly observer around the Sun), but parallax was not measured until 1837, by Friedrich Bessel.

Galileo's troubles begun in March 1610 when he published his *Sidereus Nuncius* (*Starry Messenger*). In this little book of about 60 pages, Galileo described the new discoveries he made with the help of the telescope, an instrument that had been invented earlier, probably in Italy or in England, but which had never been used for astronomical observations. His discoveries were indeed fascinating. He discovered an enormous number of stars invisible to the naked eye, and demonstrated that the Milky Way consisted of yet greater numbers of them. But from the Copernican point of view, more important were his two further findings, namely the mountainous surface of the Moon and the four satellites circling Jupiter. (Galileo called them "planets.") The first of these discoveries falsified the traditional Aristotelian doctrine of immutability of astronomical objects and negated the difference between "earthly physics" and "heavenly physics." The second discovery clearly demonstrated that not all celestial bodies moved around the Earth. The publication of the *Sidereus Nuncius* was too much for Galileo's adversaries. Forming an association called "Liga" ("The League"), his adversaries took action. The Dominican Friar Tommaso Caccini denounced the teaching on the earth's motion as "approaching heresy" in a sermon preached in Florence on December 21, 1614. Although it did not mention Galileo by name, Caccini's sermon briskly criticized Galileo's ideas and clearly alluded to him by beginning *Viri Galilaei, quid statis adspicientes in coelum?* ("Men of Galilee, what are you looking for in the sky?") (Acts 1:11). Soon after his sermon, Caccini informed the Holy Office of Galileo's teaching and the investigation was initiated.

Galileo was never summoned before the Holy Office, but he did prepare a defense in the event that he was. In 1613 Galileo wrote a letter to his friend, the Benedictine monk Benedetto Castelli, a professor of mathematics in Pisa, in which he discussed possible biblical objections to the Copernican system. The expanded version of this letter assumed the form of the *Letter to Madama Christina* (the Great Duchess of Florence). In this letter he accused his enemies of composing "some writings full of vain discourses and, that which was even more serious, littered with testimonies from Sacred Scripture taken from passages not well understood by them and used in a way that had nothing to do with the case" (Fantoli, 1996: 189). Then he recalled an interpretative rule that the biblical passages speaking about the motion of the Sun should be understood "in such a way as to accommodate the capacities of the very unrefined and undisciplined masses." Otherwise "one would have to attribute to God feet, hands, eyes and bodily sensations, as well as human feelings like anger, contrition, and hatred . . ." Galileo felt that "this doctrine is so commonplace and so definite among all theologians that it would be superfluous to present any testimony for it" (Fantoli, 1996: 191). Nevertheless he amply quoted St Augustine to support his view.

On February 19, 1616 the Holy Office asked the experts (*qualificatores*) to prepare a judgment on the two following statements: (1) "The Sun is the center of the world and hence immovable of local motion. (2) The Earth is not the center of the world, nor immovable, but moves according to the whole of itself also with a diurnal motion" (Fantoli, 1996: 215). The formulation of these statements allows us to guess that the Holy Office was not totally against Galileo's interpretation of biblical texts, but made use of another interpretative rule, also going back to St Augustine, that one should not deviate from the literal sense of a given biblical passage unless it contradicts "a well scientifically established truth." Therefore, the first thing to do is to establish whether the doctrine of the motion of the Sun and the immovability of the Earth were well scientifically established. The great error of the Holy Office was to commit purely astronomical judgments to theologians who were not astronomers themselves, which caused them to misapply the very principle that could have reconciled Galileo's findings with the faith of the Church.

Their answer came in less than four days. The judgment concerning the first statement was "this proposition is foolish and absurd in philosophy, and formally heretical since it explicitly contradicts in many places the sense of Holy Scripture ..." (Fantoli, 1996: 20). As we can see, the exegetical rule was used "upside down": it was a literal understanding of the biblical text that had decided whether the statement was scientific or not, rather than the other way around. As a result, the judgment concerning the second statement confirmed the first: "this proposition receives the same censure in philosophy and that in regard to theological truth it is at least erroneous in faith" (ibid.). On February 24 the Holy Office approved both "qualifications" and on March 5 issued a decree condemning the Copernican system and putting Copernicus' *De revolutionibus orbium coelestium* on the Index *donec corrigatur* ("until it is corrected"). Galileo was not summoned before the Holy Office, nor was he mentioned in the final decree, but he was officially informed by Cardinal Robert Bellarmine about the outcome of the process and warned that Copernicanism could not be taught as an established truth and that he himself was not allowed to teach or defend it as such. Galileo obtained from the Cardinal a written attestation that he was not involved in the process and no penance was imposed on him.

Olaf Pedersen remarks that the process of 1616 was theologically of a poor quality. Even the sensitivity of the post-Tridentine period Church authorities to innovations cannot justify the enormous speed with which the *qualificatores* formulated their judgments, which present a striking contrast to the generally ponderous manner of such procedures. For instance, when Spanish *conquistadores* tried to justify their bad treatment of Indians by claiming that the Indians are not humans, the case was extensively discussed in both courts and universities before a decision was made in favor of the common nature of all human beings (Pedersen, 1988). But the "Galileo case" was not yet closed. Its second act began in 1632 when Galileo, encouraged that his friend Maffeo Barberini became Pope Urban VIII, published his *Dialogo sopra i due massimi sistemi del mondo*. In this book, written in elegant Italian, Galileo defended the Ptolemaic system, but in such a way that it was obvious that he really denied its validity. Galileo was personally accused of having violated the decree of 1616, was forced to abjure his Copernican views, and was sentenced to life imprisonment. (This sentence was immediately changed into house arrest in his own villa in Florence.) Olaf Pedersen compares the two processes in the following way: "[In 1616] the confrontation was a meeting between a particular astronomical theory and a particular theological opinion masquerading as faith; and in 1633 the target was not a theory at all, but an individual person" (Pedersen, 1988: 6, 22.) Pedersen is largely correct, although it is somewhat misleading to suggest that the Church was not attacking the heliocentric theory. In fact, Galileo's name was so closely connected with the new physics and with the defense of Copernicanism that both processes have enormously contributed to the image of the Church as an "enemy" of science. In the thirteenth century, people like Albert the Great and Thomas Aquinas were able not only to stop the crisis caused by the recovery of Aristotelian physics and philosophy through Arabic learning, but also to show the rich theological perspectives latent in these new doctrines. In the seventeenth century, such theologians were sorely lacking. Perhaps the crisis between faith and reason was deeper in the seventeenth century. Foundational Christian events, such as the Incarnation, Cross, and Resurrection seemed to make the Earth special among other celestial bodies. To make the distinction between the astronomically distinguished position of the Earth and its theologically distinguished position required much more courage and ingenuity than the *qualificatores* had. In the 1757 edition of the *Index* the mention of the decree of 1616, "which prohibits all books which teach the immovability of the sun and the mobility of the earth," was omitted (Fantoli, 1996: 497), although the book of Copernicus was not removed from the Index until 1835. Only then could the "Galileo affair" be considered closed but, as the matter of fact, such a painful lesson will remain open for quite some time. In the discourse delivered to the Pontifical Academy of Sciences, on October 31, 1992, Pope John Paul II said: "From the Galileo case we can learn a lesson which remains valid in relation to similar situations which occur today and which may occur in the future" (*Pontifical Addresses*, 2003: 341).

The Case of Charles Darwin

After physicotheology the new sciences became aggressive as a result of their great successes and manifested a tendency toward totalitarianism in their extreme interpretations of scientific method and its results. Church thinkers often isolated themselves and, in the long run, their isolation had greater consequences than open conflict. One might even judge such conflict to be a good thing, inasmuch as it unveiled the utopian dimension of isolation. The example of Charles Darwin is a case in point.

Darwin's theory of evolution scandalized both theologians and men of science in the nineteenth century, not merely because it was novel, but because biology in the seventeenth and eighteenth centuries, unlike physics, was still greatly influenced by traditional philosophy. Two irreconcilable philosophical doctrines formed the biological paradigm in those times, one from Plato, the other from Aristotle. In the former case, Plato taught "that true reality is not the mundane world of varied and varying sense experience, but rather the transcendent world of pure and immutable forms" (Durant, 1987: 16). Among many interpretations of this Platonic doctrine, theologians generally identified Plato's forms with ideas existing in God's mind. It seemed quite natural to relate the concept of biological species to the philosophical notion of form. This in turn gave strong support to the doctrine of species immutability. Aristotle modified Plato's idea of form by situating forms in things, particularly by emphasizing their functionality, rather than in any transcendental domain. In this doctrine, "an essential part of explaining anything consisted in giving an account of the end or purpose for which that thing exists (its 'final cause')" (16). These two traditional foundations of seventeenth- and eighteenth-century biology were augmented by taxonomy, or the classification of living organisms. The new classification done by Linnaeus well fitted into the Aristotelian passion of looking for "natural kinds" of beings and later doctrine on the scale of nature (*scala naturae*) (Lovejoy, 1960).

John Durant asserts that these three elements (the doctrine of forms, teleology, and taxonomy) were neatly combined with Christian theology to form an "idealistic synthesis, according to which each species (or other chosen natural kind) of plant or animal is the embodiment of a transcendent idea in the mind of the creator" (Durant, 1987: 17). This synthesis could be compared to the previous synthesis of the Middle Ages, when the commonly accepted model of the cosmos formed a backdrop for theological speculations. When both these syntheses had to be rejected, it seemed that the core of Christian doctrine was in jeopardy. The principle of natural selection, discovered by Darwin, abolished the concept of species as a reflection of an immutable idea in the mind of God, and replaced it with the concept of species as a product of a historical process of struggle for survival and adaptation. From the very beginning it was "implicitly evident" that the traditional doctrine could not compete with Darwin's conception, which accounted for the observed variety of organic forms and their manifold structures in one stroke. But the significance of Darwin's idea went far beyond the field of biology. It destroyed the long alliance of the natural sciences, philosophy, and theology. Darwin's work finally discredited physicotheology as a scientific explanation of the world. Anti-religious interpretations of Darwin's achievement were inevitable. Ernst Haeckel preached Darwinism as a sort of secular philosophy with the idea of evolution extended to contain the progressive development of matter into mind. Thomas Huxley saw in the theory of evolution the final liberation of humankind from the slavery of theology. Karl Marx adopted Darwin's theory as the scientific basis of his dialectical materialism. There were, to be sure, also religious interpretations of Darwinism (More, 1889; Newman, 1976), but their influence, as compared with anti-religious ones, was almost negligible. John Durant interestingly remarks that the very fact that Darwin's theory was "capable of sustaining an indefinitely large number of different philosophical and religious interpretations" had a "profoundly secularizing effect" (Durant, 1987: 22).

As time passed, the idea of evolution through natural selection gradually changed its status from a radical hypothesis to the well-founded biological paradigm. Opinions of theologians slowly changed as well (if we put aside views of extreme fundamentalists). A good example is the evolution of the attitude of Church authorities and Catholic theologians to the French Jesuit and paleontologist, Pierre Teilhard de Chardin, who argued for an evolutionary vision of the universe, starting with the "Primeval Atom" (an antecedent of the present Big Bang idea) and ending at the "Omega Point," which the Jesuit interpreted as a kind of synthesis of humanity, maximally advanced in its evolutionary process, with the "Cosmic Christ." Teilhard's work initially met with official reservation or even hostility. Teilhard himself was ordered by his Jesuit superiors to postpone his theological study and confine himself to purely scientific work. His main work, *The Phenomenon of Man*, was never granted permission from Rome to be published during its author's life. (Teilhard died in 1955.) These circumstances did not prevent Teilhard de Chardin's writings from exercising great influence on its readers, both Catholics and non-Catholics.

After the Second Vatican Council, Teilhard de Chardin's ideas became popular among Catholic theologians. There were many attempts to incorporate the theory of evolution into a larger theological scheme and to build theology onto an evolutionary cosmology. Indeed, for many theologians, even today, to build upon the theory of evolution means to build upon the ideas of Teilhard de Chardin. Theologians often seem not to be aware of the fact that Teilhard's vision is by no means a scientific theory but rather its far-reaching extrapolation. Even so, the official Church's attitude also became more favorable toward the theory of evolution, albeit in a much slower and more cautious way. In 1950 Pius XII opened the door in his Encyclical Letter *Humani Generis*, in which he dealt with many threats coming from various modern intellectual trends, for Catholics to endorse evolution "as far as it inquires into the origin of the human body as coming from pre-existent matter – for the Catholic faith obliges us to hold that souls are immediately created by God" (*Humani Generis* 36). It is interesting to note that Pius XII's general hermeneutic strategy was not unlike the Galileo case. The Pope did not hesitate to add: "However, this must be done in such a way that the reasons for both opinions, that is those favorable and those unfavorable to evolution, be weighted and judged with the necessary seriousness, moderation, and measure . . ." (36). In other words, the theory of evolution should be treated as such.

Almost a half-century later Pope John Paul II delivered an address to the Pontifical Academy of the Sciences on the occasion of its Plenary Session devoted to "The Origins and Early Evolution of Life." Although the atmosphere of this document is different (it does not take the form of a warning, but rather the form of a discussion of an important problem), it is balanced and still cautious. The distinction of evolution with respect to the body and with respect to the soul was now replaced by "an ontological leap" that occurs when changing from animal to man, and which has to be interpreted accordingly (*Pontifical Addresses*, 2003: 370–4). At the same time the theory of evolution was freely discussed ("with the Pope's blessing") both as a scientific theory and as a worldview having far-reaching theological consequences during the series of conferences organized by the Vatican Observatory. Of course, discussions will go on, but one could say that this stage of the "affair" has been settled for Catholic theologians (putting aside some fundamentalists whom even papal documents regard as "too progressive"), but the future is pregnant with potential conflicts. Neuroscience and cognitive sciences are ready to say something important about the "ontological leap" alluded to by John Paul II. Will theologians learn the lesson from the past?

The Neo-Thomist Response

We can risk a statement that the Church was never, before or after, in such a critical situation, as far as its relations with science were concerned, as in the second half of the nineteenth century. Positivistic philosophy was at its peak and exercised more and more profound influence on educated circles of society. Positivistic claims led to materialism, and scholastic philosophy was unable to face the challenges of the crisis positivism engendered. It was evident that some radical means should be undertaken. In 1879, Pope Leo XIII, in his Encyclical Letter *Aeterni Patris* called upon Catholic philosophers and theologians to renew the study of the scholastics, especially the thought of St Thomas Aquinas. This encyclical initiated a powerful stream of works and ideas, collectively called neo-Thomism or neoscholasticism, the latter term being used when stress is laid upon the method rather than upon the content. The neoscholastic movement was a great success. The level of philosophy taught in seminaries and Church universities rose; studies of medieval philosophy developed quickly; and interest in the sciences increased, especially in the Louvain version of neo-Thomism. This certainly constituted progress, but only within the stream of the theology and philosophy in the Church. Neo-Thomism had a negligible influence on secular science. A Neo-Thomist philosophy of nature developed quite quickly, but it consisted mainly in applying principles of neo-Thomist philosophy to specific scientific theories, and this approach held no interest for scientists themselves.

In the meantime, the world of science underwent profound changes. Classical physics was giving place to new physical theories. Einstein's theories of relativity (both special and general) revolutionized the existing views on space, time, and gravity; quantum mechanics opened new vistas on the world of atoms and elementary particles. The revolution at the foundation of mathematics (epitomized by Gödel's famous theorem) was slightly less spectacular, but had equally far-reaching consequences, which even today are not fully understood. The first philosophical reaction provoked by these changes was conventionalism (mainly in France) – a set of ideas aiming at mitigating radically new scientific statements by stressing their conventional character. Quite unexpectedly, the conventional movement soon gave way to logical positivism, or neopositivism, which tried to understand the revolutionary changes in physics by reducing the content of physical theories to narrowly understood empirical data. According to neopositivist criteria, the only meaningful task for philosophy was a critical reflection on the sciences and their methods. And – one has to admit – neopositivist philosophers fulfilled this task very well. With only a small exaggeration we can say that logical positivists created modern philosophy of science.

This situation was a challenge to neo-Thomist philosophers. Their reactions were manifold, but the most influential was that of Jacques Maritain, who created what can be termed the "neo-Thomist philosophy of science." His first source was the Aristotelian view of science, which drew its inspiration mainly from his metaphysics, such that the classification of the sciences reflected the ontology of the world. In this regard, the three "levels of being" corresponded to the three degrees of abstraction, which in turn define three, fundamentally different, types of sciences: the science of nature (first degree of abstraction), mathematics (second degree of abstraction), and metaphysics (third degree of abstraction). According to Maritain, mixing these degrees of abstraction leads to contradictions and paradoxes. The second source of the neo-Thomistic methodology was, as it should be expected, contemporary philosophy of science, which was unfortunately contaminated by positivism. Strangely enough, this turned out to be an opportunity of sorts. According to neopositivistic philosophy, science deals only with phenomena, i.e., measurable effects, and the essences of things are mere fictions. Neo-Thomists were eager to admit the first part of this statement. The second part, in their view, demanded a modification: the essences of things are fictions only when looked at with the help of empirical methods, but they are accessible to metaphysical analysis. This doctrine, combined with the Aristotelian teaching on the three degrees of abstraction, created a safe space for philosophy and theology. Any conflicts between their statements and those of the sciences can only be the result of going beyond one's own methodological competence and the logically illicit mixing of distinct levels of cognition. Such an approach to the sciences (in many variations and modifications) became common among neo-Thomists. As a result, Catholic thinkers generally viewed, and will continue to view, the standard philosophy of science with suspicion, by virtue of its stigma of positivism.

New Developments

The Second Vatican Council marked the great change in the life of the Catholic Church. It opened new avenues for pastoral development, doctrinal interpretation, inter-religious dialog, and engagement with the contemporary world. Strangely enough, it had little to say about the Church's relationship with the sciences. In fact, the only relevant passage that can be found in the Council documents is the Pastoral Constitution *Gaudium et Spes* which deals with the "autonomy of earthly affairs." We read there: "by the very circumstance of their having been created, all things are endowed with their own stability, truth, goodness, proper laws and order. Man must respect these as he isolates them by the appropriate methods of the individual sciences and arts" (GS 36). There is nothing new in this statement. However, we should remember that such a statement, being uttered by the Council, acquires a special weight. And indeed, it did – together with the whole of the Council – open theological doors to the human sciences and other modern philosophical currents. But there were no substantial changes in the post-Council era as far as the sciences were concerned. More friendly declarations abounded, but the general attitude continued to be that elaborated by neo-Thomist thinkers, even as Thomism lost its privileged position in the Church.

But positivism began to lose its influence as well at this time. Two major factors were responsible for this process: first, progress in physics broke many rules set by neo-positivistic methodology; second, self-awareness began to grow among positivists and their successors that their philosophy was flawed in many respects. An important role in this process was played by historical studies, which revealed that the sciences never followed positivistic rules. The decline of positivistic ideology was not rapid, but it was irreversible, and it clearly implied the gradual opening of the world of science to areas of rationality extending beyond the domain of strict empiricism. A growing number of scientists, liberated from the burden of positivism, openly turned to metaphysics. Some of them cherished the conviction that physics would soon provide a final explanation of the world. The so-called Theory of Everything has found its way to the media and became an often discussed subject. Recent physical and cosmological theories reveal how much of the world's structure and its history can be deciphered from the laws of physics, especially when assisted by the sophisticated experiments made possible by rapid technological progress. Scientists even began to question the origin of natural laws themselves. These and similar questions, generated also by enormous progress in biology, neuroscience, and other rapidly developing disciplines, have created a vast field touching upon the territory traditionally reserved for metaphysics.

Owing to these developments, the debate between science and theology entered a new phase in the 1980s. International conferences and symposia on science and religion were organized. Several major societies devoted to this goal (both in Europe and in America) consolidated their activities. Many books of various levels of quality appeared on the market. It is worthwhile to emphasize that not only philosophers and theologians but also many scientists took part in these activities. Two decades earlier, a group of thinkers in America, mainly Protestants, had initiated research in the field of science and religion, using modern methodological tools. An inspiring role in this movement was played by Ian G. Barbour whose book *Myths, Models, and Paradigms* (Barbour, 1974) became a reference point for many later studies. In 1987, at the request of John Paul II, an International Symposium was organized in Castel Gandolfo to celebrate the 300th anniversary of Isaac Newton's *Philosophiae Naturalis Principia Mathematica*. The topic of the symposium was "Our Knowledge of God and of Nature: Physics, Philosophy, and Theology." The Symposium gathered about 20 experts in physics, the history of science, philosophy, and theology with the clear intention of creating a new movement within interdisciplinary research. As a result of the meeting, a book was published (Russell et al., 1988) containing a letter to the Reverend George V. Coyne SJ, the director of the Vatican Observatory. The letter was welcomed – not only by Catholic scientists (Russell et al., 1990) – as a new attitude of the Church toward science. In the subsequent years 1991–2000, five more symposia followed. Under the common heading "Scientific Perspectives on Divine Action," the following topics were studied: quantum cosmology and the laws of nature, chaos and complexity, evolutionary and molecular biology, neuroscience and the person, and quantum mechanics. After each meeting a volume was published containing the papers delivered during each symposium. Although these volumes are far from unified in their approaches and claims – some of which remain disputable – they are often regarded as constituting the most important contribution to the science–theology dialog at the turn of the millennium.

In the beginning of his letter to the Reverend George V. Coyne, Pope John Paul II, after the usual courtesies, emphasized that the Church and the academy engage one another as two very different institutions that powerfully influence the ideas and values of humanity. Science gives us an understanding of the universe as a whole and its rich variety of processes and structures, which contributes to a better understanding of ourselves and of our role in Creation. The unity we perceive in Creation and the unity for which humanity strives is reflected and reinforced in recent scientific achievements. For example, physicists search for the unification of the four fundamental forces: gravitation, electro-magnetism, and the strong and weak nuclear forces. Similarly, in biology it has been discovered that the same underlying genes and proteins serve in the make-up of all living organisms on earth. These developments are heartening. The Church and the sciences should not only continue a dialog with each other, but must also strive for mutual understanding and gradual uncovering of common concerns. Are we ready for this endeavor? A simple neutrality is no longer possible, but the unity we should seek is not a mere identity. As the Pope remarks, "We are asked to become one. We are not asked to become each other."

When we seek to understand the multiplicities around us, we must integrate many factors into a common vision and much data into an overwhelming structure. This is certainly a challenge for theology. It must enter into an exchange with science as it once had with philosophy and other forms of knowledge. Indeed, theology's mission for humanity depends, in a profound way, on its ability to incorporate scientific findings, especially as far as they concern the concept of human person and the intelligibility of nature and history. Theologians might ask themselves whether they have accomplished this difficult task with respect to science as well as their medieval predecessors did with respect to philosophy. Could contemporary cosmology offer something to illuminate our reflections on creation? Is an evolutionary perspective able to shed any light on theological anthropology, the meaning of the human person, the problem of Christology, or even on the development of doctrine itself? To pursue these questions fruitfully some theologians should be trained in the sciences, in order to prevent theologians "from making uncritical and overhasty use for apologetic purposes of such recent theories as that of 'Big Bang.'"

For the Pope, this is an urgent matter: "Science," he says, "can purify religion from error and superstition; religion can purify science from idolatry and false absolutes." Both communities, the Church and the world of science, will inevitably interact. The only question is whether they will do this in a critical and responsible way or not. The Pope's question, "Are we ready for this crucial endeavor [dialog between theology and science]?," is as important now as it was 20 years ago. In these two decades the world has radically changed, and the question of the mutual relation between theology and science, on the one hand, and the Church and the world of science, on the other, has changed accordingly, less because of its intrinsic evolution but rather because of the different social, economic, and political environments of each. In the past two decades, one can observe signs of a systematic lowering of cultural standards in the richest countries. Technocratic optimists like to believe that we are witnessing the beginning of a cultural revolution, largely triggered by the increase in information technology, out of which something radically new will emerge. In this view, only we – the people of an ending epoch – experience these changes as a deep crisis. Pessimists prefer to speak simply about a declining culture. In any case, there are reasons to believe that these processes, however they are interpreted, are of a lasting character. One of their results is a splitting of the society into great masses of "consumers" and a rather narrow group of "creators." The consequences of this split for the science–theology dialog are clear. A successful dialog can only be carried out when both scientists and theologians are intent upon being responsible creators of human culture, and thus avoid furthering or constructing ideologies of hostile indifference to one another. It almost goes without saying that such hostility prevents responsible dialog and can only deepen already existing misunderstandings between science and theology. On the other hand, a better understanding of these processes can greatly contribute to the fruitfulness of the dialog between science and theology, since the rise of modern irrationality and its assorted fundamentalisms is of great danger to both science and theology, both of which have common roots in Greek philosophy and both of which share the goal of the betterment of mankind.

References and Further Reading

Barbour, I.G. (1974) *Myths, Models, and Paradigms.* Hagerstown, NY: Harper and Row.
Brooke, J.H. (1991) *Science and Religion: Some Historical Perspectives.* Cambridge: Cambridge University Press.

Durant J. (1987) "A Critical-Historical Perspective on the Argument about Evolution and Cre-
    ation," in Andersen, S. and Peacocke, A. (eds.) *Evolution and Creation.* Aarhus: Aarhus University
    Press.
Fantoli, A. (1996) *Galileo for Copernicanism and for the Church*, 2nd edition. Vatican City State: Vati-
    can Observatory Publications.
Funkenstein, A. (1986) *Theology and the Scientific Imagination from the Middle Ages to the Seventeenth
    Century.* Princeton, NJ: Princeton University Press.
Lindberg, D.C. and Numbers, R.L. (eds.) (1986) *God and Nature: Historical Essays on the Encounter
    between Christianity and Science.* Berkeley, CA: University of California Press.
Lovejoy, A.O. (1960) *The Great Chain of Being.* New York: Harper.
More, A.L. (1889) *Science and Faith: Essays on Apologetic Subjects.* London: Kegan Paul.
Newman, J.H. (1976) *The Letters and Diaries of John Henry Newman*, vol. 28. Oxford: Birmingham
    Oratory.
Pedersen, O. (1988) "Interactions between Science and Theology," manuscript (lectures delivered
    at Cambridge, book in preparation).
Pedersen, O. (1992) *The Book of Nature.* Vatican City State: Vatican Observatory Publications.
Pius XII (1950) *Humani Generis.* New York: Pauline Books and Media.
*Pontifical Addresses to the Pontifical Academy of Sciences 1917–2002 and to the Pontifical Academy
    of Social Sciences 1994–2002* (2003) Vatican City State: The Pontifical Academy of Sciences,
    Scripta Varia, vol. 100.
Russell, R.J, Stoeger, W.R., and Coyne, G.V. (eds.) (1988) *Physics, Philosophy and Theology: A
    Common Quest for Understanding.* Vatican City State: Vatican Observatory Publications.
Russell, R.J, Stoeger, W.R., and Coyne, G.V. (eds.) (1990) *John Paul II on Science and Religion – Reflec-
    tions on the New View from Rome.* Vatican City State: Vatican Observatory Publications.

CHAPTER 33
Justice and Peace

Kelly Johnson

Catholicism, thick with ritual, overlaid with art and tradition, music, incense, and pomp – this is the classic image of "the opiate of the people." Catholic laity fingering rosaries and emerging from confessional booths have long been a favored stereotype of social passivity. Yet Catholics through the ages and across the globe have understood their faith to forbid passivity in the face of injustice. In the famous opening words of *Gaudium et Spes*,

> The joys and hopes, griefs and anxieties of people of this age, especially those who are poor or in any way afflicted, these too are the joys and hopes, the griefs and anxieties of the followers of Christ. Indeed, nothing genuinely human fails to raise an echo in their hearts. For theirs is a community composed of humans. United in Christ, they are led by the Holy Spirit in their journey to the kingdom of their Father and they have welcomed the news of salvation, which is meant for every human.

The coincidence of the practical and political with the liturgical and supernatural is the hallmark of Catholicism, and it is nowhere in greater evidence than in Catholic work for justice and peace. To say that Catholicism is practical and political is not to say that it is intent on establishing theocracy or that it authorizes itself to use force. Indeed, Benedict XVI has reasserted recently that "Catholic social doctrine . . . has no intention of giving the Church power over the State." Nevertheless the Church does have a responsibility "to help purify reason and to contribute, here and now, to the acknowledgment and attainment of what is just" (*Deus Caritas Est*, n. 28). To this end, the Magisterium offers teaching regarding social justice and Catholic laity act directly in their societies, animated by Christian charity (ibid., n. 29).

But the whole Church, clergy and all the baptized united in Christ's Spirit, do form a peculiar kind of society of their own around the Eucharist, a community of historical, embodied persons from and in all nations and cultures, for whom, "Faith, worship and *ethos* are interwoven as a single reality which takes shape in our encounter with God's *agape"* (*Deus Caritas Est*, n. 14). This *diakonia* of the Church is organized and public, and in this sense we can say the Church is itself a politics – an embodied witness to the love given and shared in Eucharistic community. Understood in this way, being political is inevitably part of the Church's mission, which is to be caught up in and to carry on Jesus' mission: "Bring good news to the poor . . . to proclaim release to the captives and recovery of sight to the blind; to let the oppressed go free, to proclaim a year of the Lord's favor" (Luke 4:18f).

Christ's early followers, according to Acts, were filled with his Spirit and immediately began to call together God's scattered people, from all nations and languages. They became a community of prayer and material sharing, and they organized their sharing of property under appointed public leaders who had charge of the material common good. From its origins in Judaism and the work of Jesus to fulfill their covenant with God, Christian faith has produced the organization of communities for mutual welfare, as persons are made to love one another and to grow together in love of God. Christian faith is concerned with the personal and with the eternal, but the faith of the Church does not see the human heart or the work of grace as distinct from the life of the community, which includes practices for distributing and using power.

This political content of Catholicism has, however, looked quite different in different eras. Addressing kings and republics, presidents and soviets and khans, Catholics have had to be political in different ways. Martyrs stood firm in the Roman Empire, testifying to their membership in a community that worships only the God of Abraham, Isaac, and Jacob. Christians of this era were notorious for their charity, attracting the poor into their company and in some cases drawing soldiers out of their military offices. But where possible in conscience, Christians strove to be obedient even to pagan authorities, and in all circumstances, they prayed for civic leaders' welfare (1 Tim 2:4–6). Their rejection of paganism did not make them less engaged in political action; it meant that they acted politically as Jesus did, sometimes by confronting, sometimes by building alliances, always formed by the ideal of charity without guile or violence.

In the centuries following Constantine, the Church's own financial power and the extent of its authority grew, and its practices regarding the common good evolved to meet new circumstances. For the sake of correcting injustice and defending the innocent, Christians began to develop a tradition of casuistry, based in classical thought and in the command of Christ that his followers love their enemies, about when and how one might engage in warfare. Christians were authorized to take up the sword to protect their neighbors from invading pagans, and eventually they took up the sword against one another. Such recourse to military solutions was limited by the Church's penitential disciplines, the liturgical cycle, reverence for holy places as sites of peace, and by the witness of the saints, whose lives overwhelmingly testified that the following of Christ is more clearly seen in suffering injury than in inflicting it, even in a just cause. While war was allowed as a tragic concession to human sin, priests were expected not to engage in it out of respect for the ministry of the altar, and even lay Christians who fought in just wars were expected to do penance for spilling blood before they could be fully returned to the Church's communion. Thus the Church both accepted certain acts of warfare as defense of justice and simultaneously maintained places, times, and persons in whom the teaching "turn the other cheek" (Matt 5:39; Luke 6:29) was upheld as the closer following of Christ.

In the twentieth century, by contrast, the Church no longer stood simply as either partner or rival to temporal authorities. Having accepted liberal states as temporal powers that could and should be oriented toward protecting the common good, the Church had to develop a new way to speak of its role. As *Gaudium et Spes* notes, "The role and competence of the Church being what it is, she must in no way be confused with the political community, nor bound to any political system. For she is at once a sign and a safeguard of the transcendence of the human person" (76). Nevertheless, Church teaching continues to address economic, political, and military issues, insofar as these are moral matters. What then is the Church's role? It can appear to be simultaneously a grouping of individuals within a state and a sort of international advisory body. Whereas in earlier centuries in Europe, political work was carried on within the life of the Church as princes and investors submitted their work more or less willingly to the discipline of the Church, now the Church speaks to states and corporations that do not submit to its discipline and to individuals who are concerned, but remain materially subject to other powers, the State and market. It is under this arrangement that the present-day construct of "social justice" as a particular category of Church life appears. As always, Catholics as individuals and the Church as a whole are involved in the organization of resources and power, but to specify that this is not the intrusion of the ecclesial into the secular world of state power, this is referred to under the heading "social justice" or "Catholic social teaching."

The 1891 encyclical *Rerum Novarum* is generally cited as the "beginning of Catholic social teaching." While Catholic teaching on matters political and economic certainly did not begin in 1891, *Rerum Novarum* drew on new Catholic engagement with the modern and industrial organization of society to offer, along with the oft-repeated call to return to the faith, specific arguments condemning both Communism and unbridled capitalism. *Rerum Novarum* did not spring full-grown from the mind of Leo XIII, but emerged from several different conversations dating back to the middle of the nineteenth century regarding the "worker-question." Indeed, a share in the credit for the teaching of *Rerum Novarum* must go to those thousands of unnamed Catholics who forged a way out of necessity, learning how to be members both of a union and of the Church. But this intervention on behalf of workers and acceptance of associations that could offer them some power against the abuses of owners, Leo XIII was eager to point out, was not a form of class warfare. Rather, it was an attempt to defend the common good and recall for workers and owners alike their mutuality in an attempt to correct the grossly unequal distribution of power.

This organic relation between the activism of individual Catholics, organizations of Catholics, and the Magisterium is characteristic of Catholic work for justice and peace. John Paul II made rich use of Leo XIII's ideas under the concept "solidarity," a term employed with profound resonance in the encyclical *Sollicitudo Rei Socialis*, as it was also the name of the Polish labor union that had been suppressed by the Communist government in 1982. With the election of John Paul II, Poles sensed that the Church as the public forum of opposition to the government was now unquestionably international. In his person, they saw the solidarity of the Church international with them, and their resistance took on new life.

Another well-known principle of Catholic social teaching, subsidiarity, holds that power should be devolved to the lowest level at which the corresponding issues can be addressed. Thus parents have control over a child's upbringing; cities over their trash collection; national governments over relations to other countries. This principle, far from being concerned with limiting federal taxation, emerged as a way to protect the participation of all members of society against excessive centralization of power, whether motivated by the political left or the right. It indicates not an interest to allow individuals to go their own way but a concern that all persons contribute as befits them to the common good. This same letter applied this principle to Catholic activism itself: the letter itself was addressed not only to clergy but also to laity, and it urged the laity to take the teachings of Catholicism into their workplaces and use their expertise to apply them there. "Catholic Action" referred to groups of such lay people at work in the world, under the moral guidance of clergy but claiming their own expertise and responsibility toward the good of all. Much work for justice and peace among Catholics is led by lay people, such as Chiara Lubich who founded Focolare in Italy during World War II. Focolare, an Italian lay association that now has communities in dozens of countries, has cultivated a different response to globalization called "the economy of communion." Its communities are set up like villages, and its members work together in industries that invest one-third of their profit into their own growth, one-third into the works of mercy, and one-third into the development of other businesses through their community. They thus build up a network of companies committed to the wellbeing of the community and to its business partners. While the impact of the economy of communion is financially miniscule, its experimentation has attracted international attention, and it raises new questions and new possibilities in the field of Catholic social action.

The Church's teaching on private property likewise aims to encourage full, active, conscious participation of all parties in the economy, and it was developed substantially during medieval years of famine, when the question of the extent of property rights was played out in confessionals as well as on the streets. Catholic teaching defends a right to private property, which, according to *Rerum Novarum*, allows its owner to provide for a family and to plan for the future. It protects individual workers from domination by those who would turn them into mere cogs in a machine. But this right has limits: it has to contribute to the common good, for example. In fact, in the Patristic and medieval teaching cited by *Gaudium et Spes*, property that is not ordered to the common good is theft and the failure to give to one in need, if it costs him his life, is murder. Thus in Catholic theology, the political order depends upon the right understanding of property and exchange. This teaching is behind Catholic support for the Sem Terra (Landless) movement in Brazil, which began as a local struggle, supported by the local priest, to have land-reform laws put to use. It has become an independent popular movement claiming a million members, who draw on Brazilian law and Catholic moral teaching to bring about land reform. Though not always welcomed by fellow Catholics, these landless peasants are supported in their nonviolent direct action and in their legal struggles by religious orders and by the Church's Pastoral Commission on Lands, and they have succeeded in organizing 1.5 million members and winning titles to land for more than 250,000 families by peacefully occupying fallow land. At this writing, some 200,000 more families are encamped on land not under cultivation, making a case for its redistribution to them.

Catholic teaching and Catholic activism challenge and enrich each other, and while exchanges between Magisterium and activists can be conflictual and for long periods unresolved, they can and often do bear fruit as the whole Church grows in its comprehension and commitment. It might be, in fact, more precise to say that Catholic teaching is an element of Catholic activism, as it too aims to bring about change. The work of promoting justice and peace is carried on in various ways by dioceses, religious orders, conferences or synods of bishops, organizations explicitly identified as Catholic, organizations allied in some respects with the Church, as well as by parishes, families, and individual Catholics, and these layers of activism are continually interacting with each other. The local work of the diocese of Chiapas, Mexico, to defend the rights of peasants, for example, arose from its bishop's learning about the need to accompany, rather than to dominate, in evangelization; but his openness to consider this problem has contributed to international understanding of cultural difference, as well as to the formation of local groups officially connected to the Church, like the Fray Bartolomé de las Casas Center for Human Rights, and to popular organizations like Las Abejas, or the Civil Society of the Bees, who, committed to nonviolence and prayer, maintain their own dignity and solidarity as they work against injustice. Such movements in Chiapas have demonstrated the power, and difficulties, in the taking up of the much-discussed "option for the poor" advocated by liberationists, Latin American bishops, and eventually the Vatican.

This same organic connection between teaching and activism, the local and the international, can be seen in the story of a few high school students in Rome in 1968 who, inspired by Church teaching, started what they called "peace schools" in poor urban areas. The result was the Community of Sant'Egidio, a now-international movement of prayer, education, solidarity, and peacemaking, credited with a significant role in negotiating peace in the civil war in Mozambique. The members of this lay movement claim prayer as their primary practice and anchor their hope in God's work to bring all humanity to salvation, and as participants in that work, they count ecumenism as another of their central commitments. And that international community has partnered with Maryknoll, the USCCB Office for International Justice and Peace, the Center for International Social Development at the Catholic University of America under the leadership of Catholic Relief Services, and the Kroc Institute for International Peace Studies at the University of Notre Dame to establish the Catholic Peacebuilding Network, connecting local peacemakers around the world in a network of solidarity, mutual learning, and development of a fuller theology of peace.

Catholic activism for justice has also been a key site for the practice of ecumenical and interfaith relationships. Those committed to social justice work within four overlapping networks: in international organizations, to resolve conflicts among nations and to advocate for globally sensitive economic practices; in the national forum, to encourage awareness and social action; locally, in thousands of small ventures to empower families and neighborhoods; and ecclesially, to educate and form their own members in faithfulness to the tradition. The first three frequently involve the Church and Catholic organizations in speaking to and partnering people who are not Catholic or with organizations whose charters do not include Catholic faith. Encyclical letters have paralleled this kind of effort, addressing since *Pacem in Terris* (1963) not only the faithful, but also "all people of goodwill." The letters therefore speak in several idioms, at times drawing on the Catholic tradition of natural law to discuss human rights while at others emphasizing the witness of the saints and practice of prayer. Neither idiom is foreign to the Church, which is after all a very large body with a long history, but commentators tend to gravitate to one or the other, most commonly to the natural law arguments, which can more readily be adapted to standard political and economic conversations.

Catholic activism around the Jubilee year, for example, drew not only on the intrinsically international character of Catholicism, but on the openness of Catholic teaching to engagement with all people of goodwill, as the Church joined in a worldwide movement to advocate for debt relief to the world's poorest nations. Catholic tradition marks every fiftieth year as a jubilee, a year of forgiveness and renewed devotion. Drawing on the teaching in Leviticus that debt should be forgiven and land redistributed every fiftieth year, the Jubilee 2000 movement argued that the moment was right for forgiving the debt of the world's most impoverished countries, debt that could not be paid in full but was being serviced on the backs of the most vulnerable members of those societies. These two Jubilees joined force, as in November 1998, Rome hosted the first international conference for the Jubilee 2000 movement, which brought people of all faiths and none together, to work for global debt release. The movement was an opportunity to explore how Catholics could – and needed to – make common cause with non-Catholics. While the Jubilee year did not, as John Paul II had hoped, mark the reunion of Christians in one communion, it did at least demonstrate the capability to work together in a movement of the Spirit. Examples of such cooperation stymie the stereotype of Catholic insularity: Catholic Relief Services director Ken Hackett in early 2005 praised the energetic work of five new program officers in Banda Aceh, all of whom were Muslim women.

But Catholic activism is not all camaraderie and mutual aid. The most pressing issue in sub-Saharan Africa, the AIDS pandemic, has created a controversy yet to be resolved among many people committed in good faith to the work of justice. Catholic hospitals, clinics, and social services provide crucial care in areas where AIDS is destroying the adult population. Catholics are known for efforts to increase the availability of ARV drugs for the HIV positive, as in a venture in Mozambique organized by the Community of Sant'Egidio. Catholic teaching has also been clear that people with AIDS are to be respected, not to be seen as under a curse. When it comes to prevention, Catholic organizations provide counseling, education, and empowerment of women, to encourage chastity before marriage and faithfulness within marriage. But should Catholic organizations distribute condoms for the purpose of preventing the spread of the disease? Catholic teaching forbids the use of artificial birth control, and while there has been no specific official pronouncement on whether the use of condoms to prevent the spread of AIDS from an infected spouse to a non-infected one falls under that prohibition, some leaders have opposed the distribution of condoms on those grounds. Other Catholics argue that when condoms are used to prevent communication of a disease, birth control is a foreseen but unintended side effect that should not determine the moral status of the act. For many, the scandal of a mixed message is the real problem. At this writing, the debate is heated and ongoing.

This listing of an array of tactics and issues is merely the tip of the Catholic iceberg. Many other groups are at work, and in fact, parishes and homes are sites of more ventures and more approaches than anyone but God can number. Catholics work in these organizations, in others that are not explicitly connected to Catholicism, in their parishes, schools, neighborhoods, and homes. And this multiplicity of ventures is not altogether univocal in what it means to be a Catholic engaged in such work. Courageous and energetic Catholics often disagree with each other about how Catholics should address issues, or what issues should take priority. Some Catholics argue that women's ordination is a fundamental justice issue, or that contraception should play some role in the Church's response to poverty. Some argue that liberation theology's sympathy for socialism is destructive of individual dignity. Some argue that the just war tradition should be laid to rest, given the present realities of war. Others claim that pacifism is contrary to the Catholic spirit of practical engagement with temporal authorities. The arguments, like the work, are multiple and many-sided.

But this diversity does not mean that "Catholic" is an empty term. While it is a large and complex category, Catholic work for justice and peace does have distinctive qualities. First, it is rooted in the tradition outlined above, a tradition of teachings, but also of rituals, institutions, personalities, networks. Second, it is characterized by concern for the good in each situation and each person, rather than with a specific political or economic system. The ability of persons to grow in the love of God and to fulfill their duties is the basis of Catholic concern for justice and peace, and there may be many ways to fulfill that vision. Third, it includes elements that some of its allies find peculiar if not contradictory: along with a commitment to human dignity and freedom, Catholics also hold to a hierarchical structure and the virtue of obedience; with the demand for just wages and improvements in welfare, an honoring of holy poverty; with an all-male clergy, continued energetic and intelligent leadership of women; with deep western European roots, a commitment that where Mass is celebrated, there the whole Church is, regardless of continent or language; with a profound international consistency, an ability to adapt to diverse cultures.

All of these characteristics and characteristic tensions are present in the Catholic Worker movement. Though this is not a "representative" example of Catholic activism – nor could there be such a thing given the scope and complexity of the category – in its own life, the Catholic Worker mirrors the tensions implicit in contemporary Catholic activism. Because it works locally and emphasizes the personal, many observers think that it fails to engage political problems. Because the Worker in its writing and action remains close to the Gospel, observers worry that it cannot participate in pluralist conversations, where the Sermon on the Mount is not accepted as God's word. Because it is pacifist and committed to voluntary poverty, some observers see it as incapable of engaging in the real struggles to transform society. While the Worker is certainly not the only group that could provide a window into the varied practices and difficulties faced by Catholic justice work, it has this advantage: it illuminates the whole scene by casting light on its most controversial elements.

In fact, its history is a tale of activism inspired by teaching and teaching responding to activism. Decades before the view was legitimated by bishops, the founders of the
Catholic Worker movement claimed that Jesus' teaching meant Christians should not
go to war; they advocated voluntary poverty as an element of personal commitment to
activism with the poor decades before the language "preferential option for the poor"
became popular; they were enthusiastic members of the liturgical movement decades
before Vatican II; they were led by a single mother long before lay women's leadership
became even an issue in the Church; they advocated an end to racism and anti-Semitism
in the 1930s; they fostered conversations among Catholics, Protestants, Jews, and atheists from the beginning of their work and have continued to challenge the split of US
Catholics along conservative/liberal lines, claiming a Catholic position that does not fit
simply into US national politics but which is, nevertheless, coherent and substantial.

The Catholic Worker movement combined theory and practice, sanctity and prag-
matism from the start, originating in the plan for a newspaper about Catholic teaching
on justice founded by a journalist-activist and a scholar-mendicant. The elder of this
odd couple was Peter Maurin, a Frenchman trained as a Salesian to educate the lower
classes. After his novitiate and some involvement in movements for social reform,
he emigrated to Canada to avoid military service and supported himself first as a
homesteader and later as a French teacher, manual laborer, and beggar. But Catholic thought on economic and political life had gotten a hold on him early and it never
let go. He grew up in a large peasant family, and this childhood marked him with a
deep sense of the common good, of the social as a sphere of cooperation and mutual aid
rather than of competition – cooperation centered around sharing in the Eucharist. As
a young adult, Maurin eagerly engaged in attempts by Catholics to challenge the existing order, but did so as a devout Catholic, not as a social reformer. *Rerum Novarum's*
simultaneous call for the modern world to return to the faith and for the modern world
to respect the natural law rights of workers did not seem to him incongruous. On the
contrary addressing poverty was for him a theological mandate, as it was for Leo XIII.
But the mandate was not simply to achieve this result by any means – instead, the goal
and method were one and the same, a growth in mutual charity as revealed in Jesus
and poured out in his Spirit.

Maurin read voraciously. Over years of study and life as a worker, he developed an
account of what was wrong, how it had come to be wrong, and what work could be
done to fix it. He agreed with Leo XIII that a truly sound social order had to be rooted,
finally, in a return to the Church, because the separation of Church and state only
meant, as Maurin saw it, a removal of faith from political and economic life. Separation of Church and state and business meant, to him, that society would be organized
by the profit motive rather than by morality. Such "organization" could only produce disorder, and the Industrial Revolution was evidence of this thesis. In an effort to
promote efficiency, the Industrial Revolution sacrificed human creativity and responsibility to the techniques of mass production. Meanwhile, workers themselves fell in
line with this new disorder, selling themselves to the highest bidder or combining into
unions to increase their bargaining power as they sold their labor. Haggling over the
price of labor distracted attention, Maurin thought, from the more fundamental issue:
the nature of human work, the dignity of personal creativity, the beauty of the well

made object, the love of a farmer for his own land. A great deal of work was producing a great deal of material, but workers were not respected for their work, did not flourish in it, and produced inferior products. Although more and more was produced, jealousy and alienation were no less common. A system that undermined workers' creativity and destroyed their power to hold sufficient property in which to exercise that creativity could never be good, regardless of how many cheap products it churned out.

Nor, Maurin thought, could an economy founded on interest. No gentleman would profit from another person's labor, much less from another person's need. The practice of taking interest seemed to Maurin a way to avoid two great and difficult goods: working hard to earn a living and sharing with others in need. Further, it was based in the absurd idea that time is a commodity, that "time is money." Time is the continuing gift of God and the medium in which work is done, in which fields ripen to harvest, in which people work out their salvations. In an age, however, in which efficiency is the yardstick of virtue, time becomes a factor of production, rather than the measure of maturity toward eternity. As such, it is to be hoarded, scrimped on, traded: and the stuff of human life which should unfold in this given medium is sacrificed to the medium itself. Such is the social sickness of an economy based on interest.

Maurin's analyses are not creative. On the contrary, he was fond of pointing out how many of his ideas were very old – "so old they look like new." The taking of interest had been condemned in Scripture and in Church teaching; the medieval guild system offered a model for competition that valued skilled labor more than the ability merely to cut corners; manual labor, in association with prayer, was a component of the highest form of Christian life, the monastic. Maurin was frankly utopian and his utopia was frankly medieval, for he saw there a social structure centered around Christian charity, around concern for one's fellow Christians. The root – and Maurin liked to call himself a radical because his thought went down to the roots – of the disorder of the early twentieth century lay in the isolation of the economic, political, legislative, social from Christian charity, from the Eucharistic table. As the center was lost, the facets of a good society and a good life came unhinged.

This analysis led Maurin not to a desire for Catholics to seize political and economic power so as to dominate others. His program, as he expounded it in the 1930s and 1940s, called for a rebuilding of society from the bottom up, from cells of good living and networks within the Church. Specifically, he advocated three measures: houses of hospitality (under the direction of the bishop, preferably) to meet immediate needs in the crisis of the depression; agronomic universities, where workers and scholars could work and study together, particularly reclaiming the importance and dignity of agricultural work; and roundtable discussions for the clarification of thought, in which people of all backgrounds and faiths would listen to each other and learn to avoid the double-speak of modernity, to re-integrate faith, economics, politics, and culture. Maurin often spoke of his program as "cult, culture, cultivation": worship of God stands at the center of human society, which is rooted in work on the land. With the English distributists Chesterton and Belloc and with Leo XIII, Maurin saw the goal to be "widespread ownership of private property" (*Rerum Novarum*) so that persons could work responsibly and profitably in a society of mutual aid, a society where people could love one another in their work as in their works of mercy.

Maurin appeared to most who met him to be a crank, albeit a well-read one. He had adopted voluntary poverty and with it the look of a bum. But George Schuster at Commonweal listened to him enough to advise Maurin that he should be talking to Dorothy Day. Day, a reporter who had converted to Catholicism after giving her twenties to radical causes and a bohemian leftist intellectual set, became a Catholic when, after suspecting that an abortion had left her infertile, she bore a child. She was moved by beauty and joy and gratitude to pray, and in spite of the fact that the Church seemed in some respects to be the enemy personified, she had her daughter baptized. Eventually, when she lost hope that her common law husband would agree to marry her in the Church, she locked him out and became a Catholic herself. She did not regret it, but the cost was high: her old set of friends and employers saw her conversion as a betrayal of the cause of justice. She herself was frustrated at her inability, as a Catholic, to act on behalf of workers. At the Shrine of the Immaculate Conception in Washington, DC, after reporting on a workers' march, Day offered a tearful prayer that some way would be shown to her to love Christ in the poor, the workers. When she got home to New York, Peter Maurin was waiting for her at her apartment, and her education in Catholic social teaching began.

They started a newspaper, Maurin assuring Day that they should imitate the saints, who always simply prayed, did the work at hand, and trusted that necessary funds would arrive. A small circle of friends hawked the paper on the street. As word of Maurin's program spread, people began to turn up looking for these houses of hospitality. Maurin's emphasis on personal responsibility and the works of mercy meant that they took people in and shared what little they had with whoever came to them in need. Critics sometimes claim that Maurin's thought leaps from mountain peak to peak, leaving the details of implementation to be discovered. But this was precisely his intent: in each locale, with each person, prudence must fill in the details in ways appropriate to the case, acting creatively and prayerfully, as he and Day did. The first paper was published for May Day 1933 and by 1936 they had a circulation of 160,000. Maurin was not always happy with the paper, which he had expected to be a sheet of his writings, but Day knew how to move her readers, and her articles on workers' causes as seen through Catholic teaching attracted supporters across the US and abroad.

The newspaper started a movement. Houses of hospitality sprang up all over the US, as did a few attempts at agronomic universities. The Worker community in New York, which lived in not very genteel poverty in the Bowery, played host to theologians and intellectuals of many stripes. Virgil Michel of the liturgical movement was a friend; Jacques Maritain visited and was impressed with their work; W.H. Auden turned up to give Day enough money to cover a fine she had to pay in court. When Catholic leadership was sometimes uneasy with articles from the paper, Day gladly accepted the recommendation that her confessor act as advisor to the paper, checking that it did not teach anything dangerous to the faith. This informal *censor fidei* post, held by a sympathizer of Day's choosing, did not seem to her an infringement on her rights, nor was her acceptance of it an act of servile acquiescence. She wanted the paper, after all, to be faithful to Catholic teaching. But she and Maurin also wanted to reveal the dynamite contained in that teaching.

In the 1940s, the movement came to a moment of crisis. As the US decided to enter World War II, Day laid down the law. Hitherto, anyone fool enough to want to claim to be a Catholic Worker had been welcome to the name. It was, as Maurin said, an organism, not an organization, existing always as a matter of personal, local initiative. But as war fever gripped the nation, Day announced that as the Worker movement had always been pacifist, so it still was. Anyone unwilling to maintain that position should resign the name. Houses around the country closed as the young men staffing them shipped out. Subscription cancellations poured in. But the work continued, and as the Christians of the world slaughtered each other again in obedience to their political leaders, as Dresden and Frankfurt burned, as Hiroshima and Nagasaki vaporized, Day carried on her work of comforting the poor and writing to afflict the comfortable. To those who called her a coward, who claimed that she taught people to take the easy way out, she issued an invitation: come do the works of peace with us, living among Christ's poor, enduring the smells of poverty, the noise and disorder, the heartbreak, the bedbugs. The way of peace is not for the lazy or for cowards.

While Day's pacifism at this point certainly was unusual among Catholic thinkers, her horror at the brutality of the war and particularly at the bombing of Hiroshima and Nagasaki was not. In the aftermath of this war, Catholic leadership began to speak differently of war. The days of confidence in just war theory waned; total warfare and its technologies were redefining the terrain, and when *Gaudium et Spes* was promulgated including its statement of support for conscientious objectors, Day saw it as an answer to her prayer and fasting outside the Council in Rome. Meanwhile, the movement had continued quietly welcoming those in need without aiming to turn them into something else, without bureaucracy. Communities of Catholic Workers across the US had developed their own ways of working and their own charisms. Some focused on welcoming homeless men, some on working with women or with families or with refugees, some engaged more in nonviolent resistance to militarism in its many forms, others shifted toward developmental or therapeutic models for addressing the ills of poverty.

Among the many movements that emerged out of Maurin and Day's unfunded and unofficial initiative, a few stand out. During the 1950s, Catholic Workers refused to participate in air raid drills that simultaneously fed paranoia and the unrealistic hope that New York could survive a nuclear attack, and their leadership was instrumental in ending those drills. The Catholic Peace Fellowship was founded by two Catholic Workers, Tom Cornell and Jim Forest, to support Catholic conscientious objectors to military service in Vietnam. Michael Harrington, author of *The Other America*, the book credited with creating the energy behind the "War on Poverty," was an editor of the *Catholic Worker* in the early 1950s, although he left the Worker movement and the Church eventually. Other workers became involved in what would become the Plowshares movement. The Berrigan brothers, Phil and Dan, led the movement of prophetic actions, infiltrating military sites to hammer on nuclear warheads in reference to Isaiah: they shall hammer their swords into plowshares. Day herself participated in and inspired others to participate in the civil rights movement and the United Farm Workers' actions. Catholic Worker formation is in the background of Kathy Kelly, who took part in founding the School of the Americas Watch and later founded the organization

Voices in the Wilderness. SOA Watch has campaigned for the closure of the US military training school for Latin American soldiers at Fort Benning, Georgia, where the assassins of many Latin American Christians were trained. Voices in the Wilderness campaigned through the 1990s for an end to sanctions in Iraq, which disproportionately hurt the poorest, youngest, and oldest members of that society. The US bishops, in fact, shared in the campaign to end the sanctions that had that effect. Within the US and far beyond, the penny-a-copy New York paper has inspired many Catholics to consider anew their own ability to act courageously, in the company of the saints.

This introduction to the Worker movement allows us now to see in what ways it deals with the characteristics of Catholic activism. The Worker's approach is based in magisterial teaching, Scripture, and the lives of the saints, and all of that is put into direct action in local communities, with great faith in the power of personal action. Pacifism was not adopted as a social strategy, but as a matter of obedience to Christ's command to put away the sword, to love the enemy, and to turn the other cheek, but it required of those who adopted it profound engagement with the deepest struggles of the day. While the poverty that reduced people's health, mental wellbeing, family relationships, and faith is a scandal, Workers adopt poverty themselves in imitation of the saints and of Christ himself, who lived poor among the poor, and in Maurin's thought, that voluntary poverty has a beneficial impact on economic life. In the spirit of *Rerum Novarum*, the Worker defended workers' rights, but even while supporting strikes and taking part in boycotts, Day described them as a work of mercy – admonishing the sinner – rather than an engagement in class warfare. As papal encyclicals included both admonitions about workers' rights and government obligations, they also urged prayer, participation in the sacraments, attending to the example of the saints, and personal self-sacrifice; at the Worker, these two sides were not lived as a tension, for to defend workers and to create a world in which human work could be the occasion for creative acts of charity that it was intended to be, self-sacrifice was necessary. Dying to self and living as Christ meant learning to share space and time with people in need – smelly, cantankerous, mentally unstable people. The path to a world of human dignity is the narrow path of discipleship.

While the Worker's answers are distinctive, the questions it faces are common among Catholics committed to work for peace. The problem considered above, the spiritual and effective, is one aspect of the classical Catholic problem of nature and grace: no one would deny the real importance of food and housing, the necessity of working out systems of distribution of power, but Catholic circles argue about the way in which grace, the supernatural, is necessary to that good. Similarly, Catholics often argue about the relationship of the "institution" of the Church and the Church as the mystical body of Christ. One, it appears, is a fallible and sometimes scandalous human bureaucracy; the other is the union made possible by Christ's redemption and through which Christ's work continues among us. Day, in keeping with Catholic tradition, makes no strong distinction between these two. She was not naïve about the sinfulness of Church leaders. She simply held that, those failures notwithstanding, Jesus was faithful to the Church and therefore her calling was to be faithful to him in it. But this question has plagued later Catholic Worker communities, particularly when specific conflicts with their local ordinary have threatened their work.

The form of Catholic conversation with Protestants, Jews, Muslims, and others who do not share the Catholic faith is another hot topic in Catholic life. The Worker movement was deeply grounded in Catholic faith, and it is no exception to that faith that it also was from its inception engaged in conversations with non-Catholics. Maurin read everything he could find and talked to more people than would actually listen to him. The paper, sold at a penny a copy on street corners, offered their insights to all, and people of many faiths responded and participated in Maurin's roundtable discussions. To say that the Worker movement is tolerant is too little. It is pacifist, so that even enemies can come in and find rest; it is personalist, built on Maurin's faith in each person's ability to contribute to and recognize in others the truth. And as it is Catholic, it holds that real peace and freedom are built on truth, not on leaving each person to think whatever he or she likes. The tradition of roundtables for the clarification of thought continues in many Catholic Worker houses, formally and informally, as vigorous and courteous discussion of pressing topics. Still, some communities have become uneasy, particularly after Day's death in 1980, with their identity as Catholic. In fact, from house to house the understanding of their relationship to the Church and the Catholic roots of the movement cannot be taken for granted. While no Catholic Worker community ever forced guests or volunteers to become Catholic, for some houses, even claiming Catholicism as the root of the work and the basis of discussion dishonors the participation of non-Catholics.

In spite of all these tensions and the ordinary stresses of work for justice and peace in a world of injustice and war, the Worker movement and Catholic activism generally remain remarkably resilient. It may be that, long before John Paul II said it, Catholics have known that "the human being is the primary route that the Church must travel in fulfilling her mission: he is the primary and fundamental way for the Church, the way traced out by Christ himself, the way that leads invariably through the mystery of the Incarnation and the Redemption" (*Redemptor Hominis*, 14). The Church is a living body, meeting Christ alive in billions of faces, in new political and economic and ecological situations, always pilgrim but always already encountering Christ. The very complexity of the Church across history and geography gives a flavor of patience to Catholic action: patience to endure over the long haul and patience to attend to each person.

And as grim as death to self and participation in the struggle for justice in a world where so many live in misery can be, Catholic Workers often speak of the joys of the life, its absurdities and consolations, and the confidence that God is not mocked. Hope in grace, in God's continued presence and undeniable triumph feed into a tender and determined humor. Day called it "the duty of delight" – it would be a sin to forget to rejoice in creation and salvation. Day herself, not generally remembered as a particularly jovial person, was fond of the quotation, "All the way to heaven is heaven, for Jesus said I am the way." As the goal of activism is the same as the means – charity – so the joy here and hereafter are fundamentally the same – friendship with God. And if, in these acts of love, patience, personal responsibility, the power to achieve great effects seemed far off, Day taught her community to look to St Thérèse of Lisieux, the nineteenth-century contemplative who wrote of her "little way." Thérèse saw herself called to be a great saint, but her situation and health left her with a tiny circle of acquaintances and no communication with the great events of the world. But she committed herself to great love and forgiveness within the small circle of her life, and trusted that her little, childlike acts could be used by God for purposes beyond her imagining. Day claimed that Thérèse was the saint most needed for activists of her day, faced with overwhelming problems. No one need despair that their actions are too small. In courage and faith, we do the small act of love and trust that the results are in God's hands, who makes of a mustard seed a tree large enough for birds to nest in. Keeping the feast of hope is an essential element of work for justice and peace.

 Catholic action for justice and peace is a noisy business, energetic and argumentative, layered and complex. But there lies at its heart a stillness that drives the whole business, prevents its degeneration into despair and outrage, and suffuses it with beauty even in the face of horror. It is the same stillness Evelyn Waugh's Charles Rider discovered in the end of *Brideshead Revisited*: "a small red flame – a beaten-copper lamp of deplorable design, relit before the beaten-copper doors of a tabernacle . . . Burning anew among the old stones."

References and Further Reading

Benedict XVI (2005) *Deus Caritas Est* (*God Is Love*). Available from www.vatican.va/holy_father/benedict_xvi/encyclicals/documents/hf_ben-xvi_enc_20051225_deus-caritas-est_en.html. Accessed June 15, 2006.

Coleman, John A., Ryan, W.F., and Ryan, Bill (eds.) (2005) *Globalization and Catholic Social Thought: Present Crisis, Future Hope*. Maryknoll, NY: Orbis Books.

Day, Dorothy (1992) *Selected Writings: By Little and By Little*, ed. Robert Ellsberg. Maryknoll, NY: Orbis Books.

Ellis, Marc H. (1981) *Peter Maurin: Prophet in the Twentieth Century*. New York: Paulist Press.

Hackett, Ken (2005) "Ken Hackett's Travel Blog." Available from www.crs.org/our_work/where_we_work/overseas/asia/tsunami/ken_blog.cfm. Accessed June 15, 2006.

Himes, Kenneth R., OFM (ed.) (2005) *Modern Catholic Social Teaching: Commentaries and Interpretations*. Washington, DC: Georgetown University Press.

John Paul II (1979) *Redemptor Hominis* (*The Redeemer of Man*). Available from www.vatican.va/holy_father/john_paul_ii/encyclicals/documents/hf_jp-ii_enc_04031979_redemptor-hominis_en.html. Accessed June 15, 2006.

John Paul II (1987) *Sollicitudo Rei Socialis* (*On Social Concern*). Available from www.vatican.va/holy_father/john_paul_ii/encyclicals/documents/hf_jp-ii_enc_30121987_sollicitudo-rei-socialis_en.html. Accessed June 15, 2006.

Kovic, Christine (2005) *Mayan Voices for Human Rights: Displaced Catholics in Highland Chiapas*. Austin: University of Texas Press.

Leo XIII (1891) *Rerum Novarum* (*On the Condition of Labour*). Available from www.vatican.va/holy_father/leo_xiii/encyclicals/documents/hf_l-xiii_enc_15051891_rerum-novarum_en.html. Accessed June 15, 2006.

Maurin, Peter (1984) *Easy Essays*. Chicago, IL: Franciscan Herald Press.

Pontifical Council for Justice and Peace (2004) *Compendium of the Social Doctrine of the Church*. Vatican City: Libreria Editrice Vaticana (distributed by United States Conference of Catholic Bishops, Washington, DC).

Second Vatican Council (1965) *Gaudium et Spes* (*Pastoral Constitution on the Church in the Modern*

World). Available from www.vatican.va/archive/hist_councils/ii_vatican_council/documents/ vat-ii_cons_19651207_gaudium-et-spes_en.html. Accessed June 15, 2006.

Troester, Rosalie R. (ed.) (1993) *Voices from the Catholic Worker*. Philadelphia, PA: Temple University Press.

Wright, Angus and Wolford, Wendy (2003) *To Inherit the Earth: The Landless Movement and the Struggle for a New Brazil*. Oakland, CA: Food First Books.

Index